W9-CCW-351

Curriculum and Instructional Methods for the Elementary School

Johanna Kasin Lemlech

UNIVERSITY OF SOUTHERN CALIFORNIA

Macmillan Publishing Company
NEW YORK

Collier Macmillan Publishers
LONDON

Printed in the United States of America.

Macmillan Publishing Company
866 Third Avenue, New York, New York 10022

Collier Macmillan Canada, Inc.

Library of Congress Cataloging in Publication Data

Lemlech, Johanna Kasin.
Curriculum and instructional methods for the elementary school.

Includes bibliographies and index.
1. Elementary school teaching—Handbooks, manuals, etc. 2. Classroom management—Handbooks, manuals, etc. 3. Education, Elementary—Curricula—Handbooks, manuals, etc. I. Title.
LB1570.L453 1984 372.11′2 83-9432
ISBN 0-02-369730-X

Printing: 1 2 3 4 5 6 7 8 Year: 4 5 6 7 8 9 0 1 2

ISBN 0-02-369730-X

PREFACE

Contemporary teachers differ from their historical colleagues in their professional preparation for teaching. There was a long period in American history when the teacher "drifted" into the educator's role, but today teachers choose their profession and have appropriate skills and resources to respond to the needs of a multicultural society. Teachers of the 1980s and 1990s will be more secure than their forebears because of their awareness of contemporary problems and their knowledge of the curriculum, the principles of learning, and the techniques of teaching.

Although this text is directed primarily to students beginning their professional careers, experienced teachers may also find the descriptive and practical information useful as a reference for updating knowledge. The teaching episodes in the book are based upon actual classroom experiences that the author, a former classroom teacher, either personally experienced or observed.

The text is organized in four parts. In Part One, challenges that are the consequence of social change are discussed as factors affecting curriculum and professional practice (Chapter 1). Choices and the teacher's daily professional responsibilities for planning and managing the instructional program to meet students' diverse interests, needs, and abilities are featured in Chapters 2, 3, and 4. Research citations in these chapters emphasize the social context of learning, grouping, direct instruction, and classroom management.

Part Two presents the content of the curriculum as well as teaching approaches for each subject, goals, objectives, resources, and methods of evaluation. To provide a basic structure for understanding the scope and sequence of curriculum, California State Framework examples are given for most subject fields. These may be used as a springboard for discussion of local school district and state guidelines for curriculum fields. Actual teaching examples pertinent to the subject field are included in each chapter. Throughout the text the author emphasizes the importance of a balanced curriculum, and the unit teaching models presented in Chapter 14 and the Appendix exemplify the integration of subject fields.

In Part Three the focus is instructional processes. This text emphasizes that most teaching strategies require planning and practice. Teaching skills are developmental and the beginning teacher should not expect everything to be perfect the first—or even the second—time that an instructional technique is tried.

Chapters 12 and 13 are devoted to the generic teaching strategies of exposition, guided discussion, and inquiry/problem solving. Direct instruction for teaching skills and questioning techniques are discussed in Chapter 12. Chapter 14 is devoted to the unit planning process and to research techniques for gathering, organizing, and analyzing information.

Chapter 16 discusses the importance of learning materials, their evaluation, and their use during instruction. Chapter 17 completes the instructional component by focusing on both formal and informal means to evaluate learning progress. Suggestions for parent-teacher conferences are provided in this chapter.

Part Four (Chapter 18) discusses professional growth through school improvement strategies, team teaching, and working with other adults in professional associations. The chapter emphasizes personal responsibility for continuing education and recommends self-evaluation, the development of significant interaction with others, and involvement in socio-civic affairs.

Certain aspects of teaching are of particular importance to new teachers. Classroom management, mainstreaming, and the integration of subject fields represent ongoing concerns. As a consequence, these elements are discussed throughout the text so that pertinent ideas and teaching hints are related both to specific subjects and to general instructional strategies.

The author is indebted to editor Lloyd Chilton, for his confidence and encouragement, and to many individuals at the university and in the public schools who contributed both substantively to the manuscript and to morale during the long period of conception.

To my colleagues in the Department of Curriculum and Instruction, thank you for your good-natured understanding and for the acceptance of the extra professional burden caused by my periodic absence.

For outstanding photographic coordination I am indebted to Michael Stieger, and for additional photographic assistance to Donna Stieger, John Wood, and Hillary Foliart.

To Molly Parsons and her faculty at the Denker Elementary School, Los Angeles Unified School District, and to Shirley Levine and her faculty at the Heschel Day School, I am grateful for the opportunities provided me to observe, record, gather materials, and photograph activities.

To Sue Wood, for exercise demonstrations, modeling, critical review of Chapter 10, and for insightful encouragement, I owe a special thank you.

To Fara Wexler, Los Angeles Unified School District, and Dwaine Greer, Southwest Regional Laboratory, thank you for assistance with Chapter 11.

To Barbara Kornblau, for the contribution of time and thought in reviewing the manuscript, thank you.

To my "exercise buddies," thank you for the frequent therapy sessions!

To Helen Jones, I am most appreciative for the candid editorial comments and the final preparation of the manuscript.

And to my family—particularly husband Bernie—for assistance, consideration, and thoughtfulness throughout the writing period, I send a *very* special thank you.

J.K.L.

CONTENTS

PART **ONE**

CHALLENGE, CHOICE, AND RESPONSIBILITY OF ELEMENTARY SCHOOL TEACHERS

Teaching in the elementary school requires knowledge of the past, present, and future. The elementary teacher influences the lives of students and the quality of future life. Curriculum decisions are based on an understanding of children and learning, our society, our history, and possibilities for the future.

Chapter I

Issues of the 1980s Affecting Elementary Teachers

To the Reader:

Each chapter in *Curriculum and Instructional Methods for Elementary Teachers* is prefaced with learning objectives. These objectives identify the important ideas or concepts of the chapter. The behavioral objectives are arranged to conform to the sequence of the chapter; therefore, they may be used to structure your reading and study of the chapter, and serve as a means to self-evaluate your understanding after you have completed the study of the chapters.

After you have completed the study of Chapter I, you should be able to accomplish the following:

1. **Contrast the elementary school of the future with the elementary school that you knew as a child and the elementary school of the present.**
2. **Speculate about education in the future and write a list of probable educational practices in the elementary school of the future.**
3. **Identify ways in which the challenges of the future could affect the content of elementary education.**
4. **Write a list of goals for the elementary school; sequence your list; share and compare with others.**
5. **Explain why some individuals believe there should be alternatives to the public elementary and secondary schools.**
6. **Discuss your beliefs about teacher accountability.**
7. **Identify the link between competency tests for secondary students and elementary teachers' professional responsibility.**
8. **Discuss the inferred relationship between competency testing of teachers and the competency testing of students.**
9. **Identify the issues related to bilingual education that affect elementary teaching.**
10. **Cite the reasons why Congress specified that handicapped students must be educated in the "least restrictive environment."**
11. **Distinguish between "good" stress and "bad" stress; explain why teachers are subject to burnout and suggest ways to relieve tension.**
12. **Identify additional issues that will affect elementary teachers during the eighties.**

Humanity faces a quantum leap forward. It faces the deepest social upheaval and creative restructuring of all time. Without clearly recognizing it, we are engaged in building a remarkable new civilization from the ground up (Toffler, *The Third Wave*, p. 4).

It is September 18, 1998. Mary Hogan teaches heterogeneously grouped children ages ten to twelve. The children have been purposefully grouped together because of their diversity. The school where Hogan teaches is part of a large educational park complex. When Mary Hogan arrives at school in the morning her first task is to begin an attendance check to verify the day's educational plans for each student.

Some of the children will be working in peer groups with the older children teaching the younger ones. She notes that she will have to observe their progress.

Another group of children has selected to work in the music center of the complex. Today, they will be working with a group of retired musicians. The musicians will demonstrate jazz improvisation techniques. The children, using instruments provided in the center, will learn to accept clues from each other and begin to experiment on their own. Mary Hogan will not have to visit this center to verify progress; but in time the children will demonstrate what they have learned and in that way performance will be evaluated.

A third group of children will be working in their homes using individual video systems. These children will be studying topics of their own choosing. They will "call in" to their teacher, using a special terminal that connects each child's home system with the school. In this way Mary Hogan will provide individual feedback to each child.

A few students will work in the resource center of the educational complex conducting individual research. They will receive help from the adults in the library resource center.

Later in the afternoon all the children will gather in the large television viewing center, where they will observe a congressional hearing. They will discuss the hearing and then simulate it. They will write their own questions to ask "witnesses" and they will respond to the ideas and questions of others—striving to find out "What would happen if . . . ?"

The children in Mary Hogan's class learn to make personal decisions about their education. They also learn that they must be accountable for their choices. They learn to work with others of all ages. There is a great deal of talking and thinking, construction of projects, and writing about what they have learned.

Mary Hogan began her professional career in 1982 teaching in a school that was not too different from the one she attended as a child. The impact of the eighties changed society and the concept of the school as Mary Hogan once knew it. Since Hogan believed in lifelong learning, she continued her own professional education. As a result she learned to manage an enormous communicating system built to accommodate education in the twenty-first century. She learned to depend on other adults to assist in the education of her students, and she learned to trust her students to make intelligent choices and to share in their own education.

Challenge of the Future

Teachers whose professional life will flow into the third millenium will need to know more than what is available now in current curricula and methods of instruction. For instance, classroom management procedures will be expanded to include management of communication systems, of adult learning, of home and community education. Teachers may need to lead a team of uncertificated adult volunteers who will participate by modeling particular skills. It is not the intent of this text to provide the skills and competencies necessary for the twenty-first century; however, an awareness of the future can be gained by taking note of current and anticipated trouble spots or problems and by engaging in the process of consequential thinking. Teachers of the 1980s and 1990s will be utilizing these known and anticipated problems for the development of curriculum because education cannot be considered apart from the social setting in which it occurs. Methods of instruction will also reflect future needs as teachers utilize processes to involve students in thinking about the future.

If the modes of communication in the future facilitate individual programming, how will Mary Hogan develop individuals who can work together and participate in the life of the community?

How can teachers of today assist students in making value choices in a change-oriented society?

Global Problems

We have been aware for some time now of certain environmental problems resulting from pollution and the depletion of natural resources. Social studies and science teachers have attempted to avert the collision course resulting from what Harold Shane (1981) calls the "frontier" ethic versus the "spaceship" ethic. As Americans moved West during the expansion period of American history, carelessness prevailed. Soil, stream, and forest depletion were commonplace. In contrast to the "frontier" ethic, the "spaceship" ethic has to do with the recycling process and the renewal of our resources. Much has been written about these problems, and they are certainly appropriate areas for student study. Overpopulation in some areas of the world and our current over-infatuation with complex technology are additional problems which need to have insightful teaching.

Shane, an educator who has studied the impact on curriculum of anticipated events in the social sciences, describes several worldwide problems that are less recognized but which could have an impelling effect on educational content (Shane, 1979, 1981). These problems are: (1) worldwide economic competition, (2) worldwide unemployment, and (3) the impact of "experience compression."

Worldwide Economic Competition. A recent headline in the *Los Angeles Times* (July 7, 1981) stated: "Cash-Laden Foreign Interests Make U.S. Energy Firms Takeover Targets." This article dealt with the pursuit of Canadian firms to gain control of U.S. resource companies. The building industry faces a similar challenge from Japanese, French, British, and Canadian firms. Lower interest rates abroad favor foreign builders (*Wall Street Journal*, July 9, 1981). U.S. builders fear that Japan will match in the area of housing its already successful penetration of the U.S. automobile and electronics industries. The decline in U.S. productivity is best illustrated by the fact that in 1950 with 6 per cent of the world's population, the U.S. produced 50 per cent of the world's goods, but in 1981 with 5 per cent of the world population, the U.S. produced only 35 per cent of the world's goods.

Shane provides some interesting examples of the decline in productivity in industrialized nations. On a visit to Scotland he discovered garments of tweed material that had been sent to Hong Kong to be tailored by French designers and then sent back to Scotland to compete with other fashions made of the same materials in Scotland.

Other examples of worldwide competition are the car radio for the Mercedes Benz automobile, once made in Germany—now made in Mexico and shipped to Germany for installation, the German 35 mm Rollei camera—made by Rollei in Singapore, and its zippered case—produced in Taiwan (Shane, 1979).

Worldwide Unemployment. The influence of science and technology is apparent in the 1980s. Social scientists predict the possibility of jobless growth as a consequence of the computer age. While the workers in Latin America and Asia have profited from worldwide economic competition, the industrialized nations are hurting because of inflation and technology.

In the United States unemployment benefits, welfare, and food stamps have decreased workers' motivation to work. The cost of inflation as well as the benefits of technology contribute to induce women to join the labor force. Two-career families have become typical, but the consequence of this development is that the two jobs that once supported two families support only one family today. Also, women frequently hold jobs that once supported less qualified males and older teenagers. By 1977, 41 per cent of mothers with children under six years of age had joined the labor force in the United States. By 1990 it is estimated that nearly 10.5 million children under six will have working mothers (Hofferth, 1979; Long, 1981). Senior citizens in the United States, who in prior years would have enjoyed retirement, cannot afford to retire; they are finding it necessary to continue their jobs.

As a consequence younger adults are unemployed or misemployed (Salerno, 1981).

As underdeveloped countries attempt to modernize, they too utilize sophisticated technology which actually penalizes their people because the capital invested in technology can no longer be used to assist small employers, farmers, and unskilled workers.

Experience Compression. The third problem identified by Shane (1979) has two elements: (1) the conceptual mode in which individuals perceive an artificial and technological environment and (2) a set of techniques by which individuals participate in decision making. Experience compression occurs when the balanced relationship among our senses, our reasoning, and our beliefs and values is upset or threatened. Toffler (1970) defined this experience similarly as "future shock."

The bombardment of our senses occurs primarily as a consequence of the sophistication of our communication systems. For instance, as we watch television we may learn about a terroristic attack in Italy and an earthquake in some far off corner of the globe, yet we may be watching a soap opera when these news spots are flashed across the screen. The confusion of these simultaneous and mismatched experiences results in a feeling of temporal incongruity.

The media can also affect our sense of geography. As we observe an Australian "walkabout," a revolution in Iran, and the Easter parade on Fifth Avenue in New York, we suffer from a loss of geographic coherence. These unrelated events have been linked through television as if they were not occurring thousands of miles apart. Rational analyses of visual and aural observations become difficult as our beliefs and values are challenged by the compression of experiences.

Another problem caused by the compression of experiences is information overload. We frequently hear someone say, "That speaker told us more than we really wanted to know." Information overload relates to the amassing of so much knowledge that it is impossible to deal with all the information. Teachers experience this condition when they attempt to read all of their professional journals; doctors and accountants relate similarly as they attempt to keep abreast of the latest in their fields.

Television contributes to yet another aspect of experience compression by causing sensory overstimulation. Shows like "That's Incredible" compel the viewer to observe a man drowning himself as his heartbeat is monitored, and then observe another person barely avoiding a snakebite. Such programs become addictive, and the viewer's sensory system is so confused that considered thought becomes impossible; but less exciting shows cannot compete.

All three of these developments interrelate with one another: worldwide competition due to the influence of science and technological improvements; unemployment, a consequence of competition, technology and inflation; and experience compression due to rapid change in our communication systems. These problems can be expected to have an effect on the content of education.

Other interrelated problems and sources for curriculum content during the 1980s include the danger of sophisticated weaponry, the disposal of nuclear wastes, accidents in nuclear plants, crime, and terrorism.

Trends in the Social Sciences

Today, more people are educated than ever before in history; we are able to travel to far-off places and to communicate with and learn from almost all cultures. Yet, despite these lofty achievements, the challenges confronting us have never been greater (Toffler, 1980). Let us consider career planning and alternative futures. The evidence indicates that in the next twenty or thirty years the individual will not prepare for one career, but instead several complementary careers may be anticipated. Provision for lifelong learning from childhood to old age will be a necessity.

Sociologists indicate that a variety of family forms may dominate our society during the 1980s and 1990s. The nuclear family (mother, father, and children without extended relatives) will still exist, but there will also be families of sister and brother, mother and aunt, mother and children, couples. During the 1970s there was a large increase in single-parent families. This trend is expected to continue; approximately one in seven children grows up in a single-parent home, and in urban areas the percentage may be one in four.

New family-life structures and advancement in technology contribute to change in the ways people enjoy their leisure time. In industrialized nations, where there are fewer children in the home, life becomes more adult oriented. Also, with a greater number of adults living in singles' communities, there are different recreational needs. The proliferation of health clubs that offer such services as laundry, lounge (rest) facilities, dining, special interest classes, as well as the anticipated recreational and exercise opportunities, attest to new trends in adult living.

Toffler (1980) stated that the structure of family life will be dependent upon societal change in technology and work. Just as the factory system of industrialized nations influenced the formation of the nuclear family, so, too, will any shift away from the factory system influence the form of family life. Toffler predicted that there will be a shift in workplace from office and factory back to the home. If this change does occur, family members will consequently spend much more time with each other. Obviously relationships and home-job sharing will thereby be affected. Life in the electronic cottage may motivate seeking a mate who provides complementary skills along with sexual and psychological gratification.

Political scientists point out that in the future we can expect decreased personal freedom. Aspects of this prophecy are already with us: speed limit restraints; odd-even gasoline buying days; limits on food items to be purchased on "special" at the supermarket; thermostat controls to save energy; gun control and registration laws in certain states to restrain crime; busing to achieve social integration.

For many years the United States had difficulty with its diplomatic corps because diplomats were not trained to perceive the context of culture. American citizens traveling abroad were also criticized and considered "ugly" Americans because they were perceived as behaving boorishly. Anthropologists have contributed information which may correct this situation. Communication is affected by cultural influences. We see and hear subjectively depending upon our experiences—the same television show will affect different cultural groups in different ways. Once again, there are implications for curriculum content.

Implications for Curriculum

Social scientists have identified probable events that will have consequences for the content of education. Shane (1979, 1981) suggests five generalizations derived from those trends as justifiable:

1. Learning experiences should be reality based. Divergent opinion should be explored using inquiry processes. (See Chapter 13.)
2. Students should learn that there are alternative solutions to problems.
3. Students should learn that all solutions have consequences.
4. Solutions are based upon choices which are derived from the learner's values and intellectual insights. Education must provide the learner with socially desirable values.
5. Knowledge and skills are prerequisite to implementing choices. Students should learn group process skills; respect for expertise in specialized fields such as law, medicine, psychology, botany, etc.; and substantive knowledge appropriate to the student's ability and developmental level.

The teacher's challenge will be to design curriculum to encompass these five generalizations so that students will become personally involved and will

- examine social problems
- participate and accept social responsibility
- be willing to make decisions by choosing and valuing, using criteria based on personal and group welfare needs
- recognize the need for lifelong learning.

Purposes of Schools

When Mary Hogan began her teaching career she frequently shared her teaching problems and questions with another new teacher. Together they discussed their beliefs about the process and purpose of education. Their discussion usually focused on their personal beliefs about students, the curriculum, teaching methods, classroom discipline, and the purposes of schools.

Greg Thomas, Mary Hogan's colleague, had slightly different ideas about teaching, and his classroom reflected his beliefs. If we were to listen to their discussion we could probably develop a chart to reflect the differences in their orientation. The following is an example.

GOALS OF EDUCATION[1]

Hogan	Thomas
Schools should teach problem-solving skills and procedures.	The purpose of the school is to preserve and transmit culture.
Schools should develop the students' personal capacities so they can learn for themselves and become self-sufficient.	Schools need to socialize the child.
	We need to teach an appreciation of our institutions.

THE CURRICULUM

Hogan	Thomas
By utilizing contemporary problems and issues of interest to the students, scientific methods of problem solving should be taught.	We need to teach students to be good citizens.
Basic skills subjects are important.	We should stress the 3 Rs.
Behavioral and social sciences should be a part of the curriculum; the social sciences can be taught by utilizing contemporary problems and issues of interest to students.	History and political science should be taught, as well as some of the natural sciences.
Most of the natural sciences need to be taught in the elementary school.	The school needs to stress moral education.
Humanities instruction should also be planned as a part of the curriculum.	Physical education and health are important.
The teacher should emphasize an activities approach in teaching these subjects.	

THE STUDENTS

Hogan	Thomas
I believe that each student is unique.	Students need firm guidance.
Instruction should be differentiated according to the needs, interests, and abilities of each child.	Children are fundamentally all alike; they need basically the same things.
Students need practice in accepting responsibility and directing their own education.	We need to discipline students so that they will become responsible, law-abiding citizens.
Students are naturally caring and good.	

[1] Based upon the comparative overview of educational ideologies in William F. O'Neill, *Educational Ideologies* (Santa Monica, Calif.: Goodyear, 1981), pages 296–309.

INSTRUCTIONAL METHODS

Hogan	Thomas
Individual and group problem-solving approaches and inquiry methods should be stressed.	Teacher-directed lessons are the most effective and efficient way to teach.
The teacher should act as a guide to facilitate group work and develop group process skills.	Students need lots of drill and practice.
Motivation is extremely important so that students will be interested and attend to what is being taught.	Discussions are important, but they should be directed by the teacher.
Students should be involved in meaningful activities.	Competition motivates students to participate and to learn.
Projects can be useful to evaluate what students have learned.	Paper-and-pencil tests are best, and the tests should be fact oriented.
Essay tests are better than objective tests.	

DISCIPLINE

The teacher should be a democratic leader.	The teacher should be strict and stress proper behavior.
Students should be held accountable for setting goals and for accomplishing them.	I expect the students to conform and be good citizens.
If I teach my children to act in a reasonable and intelligent manner they will behave in a moral manner.	Character training is part of a teacher's responsibility.
	The school is responsible for moral education.

When Hogan and Thomas first began to teach, had they been asked, "What is your philosophy of education?" they probably could not have responded. However, their philosophy is reflected in their choices of subjects to emphasize, teaching methods, and classroom control, and in their perspective about children. Thomas' ideas of the purpose of the school is based upon an abiding respect for the past. He does believe, however, that education should be useful for present-day society, and he considers it important to teach respect for political and social institutions. He probably does not expect students to contemplate change; he wants to develop character and intellectual discipline. He chooses the more practical disciplines, such as history, political science, biology, and physical science because he considers them more important for students to study than some of the newer disciplines such as archaeology, anthropology, or psychology. Thomas would probably be called an educational conservative.

Hogan has a different perspective on the purpose of the school. She wants students to be self-sufficient and believes that this goal can be accomplished only if they are taught problem-solving skills to serve them now and in the future. Since students need to get along well with others, she emphasizes group process skills. In Hogan's classroom, knowledge is used as a tool to solve present-day problems. Although there is still some factual memorization, learning how to inquire, or discover what one needs to know, is of primary importance. Hogan begins with students' own needs and interests to teach what students will need to know to be personally effective. She believes that if each student develops to his/her fullest potential then that student will be able to deal with present and future problems. She appears to be liberal in her educational beliefs, or what some educators would describe as an experimentalist.

Incidental Education vs. Deliberate Education

Thus far in this text, the words "education" and "school" have been used interchangeably. They are not precisely the same, and if we are to think about the purposes of the school, then we need to differentiate between them. John Dewey distinguished between deliberate and incidental education: "There is . . . a marked difference between the education which everyone gets from living with others . . . and the deliberate educating of the young. In the former case the education is incidental; it is natural and important, but it is not the express reason of the association" (Dewey, 1967, p. 6).

About schools, he stated: "We are thus led to distinguish within the broad educational process . . . a more formal kind of education—that of direct tuition or schooling" (p. 7). Dewey noted that in the creation of schools, adults are consciously controlling the education of the young by purposely setting an environment for learning. He identified three functions of the school:

1. To provide a simplified environment arranged to facilitate response from the young and progressively sequenced as the child matures.
2. To select the social customs that are worthy of transmission and weed out the undesirable achievements of society.
3. . . . to balance the various elements in the school environment, and to see that each individual gets an opportunity to escape from the limitations of the social group in which he was born, and to come into living contact with a broader environment (p. 20).

Dewey believed that the purpose of the school was the social, emotional, and mental development of the learner.

Educational Goals

Educational goal statements have been defined through the years. The Educational Policies Commission of the National Education Association (1938) identified four goals: self-realization, human relations, economic efficiency, and civil responsibility. For each of these goals the Commission established objectives. For example: the goal for self-realization included objectives related to the teaching of skill subjects; human relations included respect for and cooperation with others; economic efficiency included objectives related to occupational choices and consumer information; civil responsibility included objectives related to social participation. This same commission modified its aims in 1944 and wrote a report entitled *Education for All American Youth*. Ten imperative needs were identified.

Educational goal statements are broad and in the last several decades there have been slight shifts in emphasis as the schools reacted to crises and public pressures. For example, the White House Conference on Education (1955) urged the schools to develop the abilities of the gifted. A later commission (1960) suggested through goal statements that the schools emphasize the teaching of mathematics, science, and foreign language. Congress legislated the necessary funds to accomplish these goals. During the 1960s the focus was on disadvantaged students, and during the 1970s there was renewed interest in basic skill goals.

This text began with the challenge of the future. The futurists tell us that we can no longer clearly define the skills and subject matter content that will be needed in the coming decades. How will their images of the future affect educational goals?

Critics of the Schools

Some educational writers have talked about "deschooling" society because they believe that the educational institution no longer fulfills its purpose. Dewey believed that the school coordinates the diverse influences to which every individual is subjected (family, community, work experiences, religion) and provides a broader context and a unity of outlook as children of different races, religions, and customs intermingle. But critics of the school dispute whether the school still serves society. They question:

- Have the schools equalized opportunity for all?
- Have the schools been agencies for social control and inhibited access to opportunity by lower socio-economic groups?

- Have the schools inhibited social change by mirroring society?
- Can the schools be instrumental in effecting social change?

These questions challenge both the aims of education and the purpose of schools. It is important for teachers to be aware of the many fine accomplishments of the American school. For instance, the schools have achieved a high level of literacy among the American people, acculturated immigrant populations, provided vocational education, fostered appreciation for American institutions and democratic processes, and made education available for the majority of students. But teachers *also* need to be aware of the criticism. The goals of education must be relevant to the times, and the schools need to adapt to change. Perhaps the most classic illustration of schools not adapting to change was portrayed in Harold Benjamin's *The Saber-Tooth Curriculum* (1939). Benjamin's satire portrayed a society characterized by its dependency upon fish for food, the need to frighten away the saber-tooth tiger and the need to club horses. So the schools taught these three skills to the children (catching fish, scaring the tigers, and clubbing the horses). But as time went on, the society's needs changed. The saber-tooth tigers and the horses vanished, and there were no longer any fish because the streams had dried up; yet the schools continued to teach the same curriculum. Curriculum change only happens when teachers plan for it.

- Do you believe contemporary schools are fulfilling Dewey's functions? Why or why not?
- If you were asked to write the purposes of schools, what would they be?
- Would Shane's generalizations be compatible with your purposes?

The twelfth annual Gallup survey (1980) of the attitudes of Americans toward their public schools provides some significant information concerning the opinion of the public about the importance of schools. This question was asked in the 1973 poll and once again in 1980:

How important are schools to one's future success— extremely important, fairly important, not too important?

	National Totals %	No Children in Schools %	Public School Parents %	Parochial School Parents %	National Totals 1973 %	National Totals 1980 %
Extremely Important	82	80	85	84	76	82
Fairly Important	15	16	13	15	19	15
Not too Important	2	2	2	—	4	2
No opinion	1	2	—[a]	1	1	1

[a] Less than 1%

Further breakdowns for 1980 follow:

	Extremely Important %	Fairly Important %	No too Important %	No Opinion %
National Totals	82	15	2	1
Sex				
Men	79	17	2	2
Women	84	14	1	1
Race				
White	81	15	2	2
Nonwhite	82	16	1	1
Age				
18 to 29 years	77	19	4	[a]
30 to 49 years	87	13	[a]	[a]
50 & over	80	15	1	4
Community Size				
1 million & over	82	15	2	1
500,000–999,999	85	11	1	3
50,000–499,999	81	16	2	1
2,500–49,999	80	15	3	2
Under 2,500	80	17	1	2
Education				
Grade school	77	17	2	4
High school	84	13	2	1
College	80	18	1	1
Region				
East	86	11	2	1
Midwest	80	17	2	1
South	84	15	[a]	1
West	75	19	4	2

[a] Less than 1%

How much confidence do you, yourself, have in these American institutions to serve the public's needs—a great deal of confiidence, a fair amount, or very little?

	Great Deal %	Fair Amount %	Very Little %	None Volunteered %	Undecided %
The church	42	40	15	2	1
The public schools	28	46	20	3	3
The courts	19	45	28	5	3
Local government	19	51	23	4	3
State government	17	52	24	4	3
National government	14	47	31	5	3
Labor unions	17	38	30	9	6
Big business	13	42	36	5	4

While the schools may have many critics, it does not appear that the American public desires to "deschool" our society. In fact, the poll reveals that Americans have a better opinion of the public schools than they have of most other public institutions.

Alternative Schools

Peter Schrag (1970) has been a critic of the public schools. He believes that children should not be forced to attend a particular school. He contends that there should be choice of school, subjects, and teaching style. Schrag discussed alternatives to the public school system, and in fact there are many alternative schools within public education systems as well as private and parochial alternatives.

Although the roots of alternative education can be traced back to early American history, many of today's alternative school programs developed from the humanism movement of the 1960s. Critics of education, of government, and of society provided leadership for these programs. One of the first alternative schools (1969)—the Parkway Program—began in Philadelphia. The Parkway Program has been called "the school without walls."

The purpose of the Parkway Program was to change the social and administrative organization of the Philadelphia school system (Bremer and Von Moschzisker, 1971). It was first envisioned in 1967 by Clifford Brenner, a newspaperman and one-time press secretary to Philadelphia mayor Richardson Dilworth. It was Brenner's idea that the four-year high school be created without buildings. The school program would use existing city facilities—public and private—such as the pool and gym at the YMCA, the city's Museum of Art, the Academy of Natural Sciences, Bell Telephone, General Electric, and the like.

In mid-1968 John Bremer developed Brenner's program concept and became Parkway's first director. Bremer sent a letter to all of the city's high school students advertising the program. Students applied and were chosen by a series of lotteries, and care was taken to ensure that the ratio would be 60 per cent black and 40 per cent white. The faculty was recruited from the Philadelphia school system.

The students at Parkway are organized into tutorial groups of about 15 students. A faculty member and a university intern are assigned to each group. The tutorial program is the only compulsory component of the curriculum. The tutorial group provides counseling for the students and assures the faculty that students are making progress in basic skills.

All other state requirements are met in a variety of ways as students determine *how* they will earn their credits. For example, English credits can be earned by taking a Shakespeare course, or by taking a course in magazine writing, or in one of many other ways. Courses may be taught by the Parkway faculty, or by community resource people, or even by faculty from the neighboring colleges.

Formal school concepts such as class periods, school days, school weeks, and school years are abandoned at Parkway. The learning requirements of the situation determine the student's schedule, and the student's own learning needs determine the process and activity.

Public Alternative Schools

Presently, there are more than 10,000 public alternative schools and an estimated three million students attending them (Raywid, 1981). Most alternative schools attempt to be different in one or more ways from the standard school. Although research on the effectiveness of the alternative schools has been limited—the Ford Foundation found "no significant difference"—some studies suggest a number of constants:

- a higher percentage of students from alternative schools tend to go on to college when compared to students in comparable schools in the same district;
- students attending alternative schools have a positive attitude about school and about themselves (Raywid, 1981).

Case (1981) analyzed a number of successful alternative schools to see if there were any common characteristics. She found five basic factors that contributed to success and survival.

1. *Programs:* The programs were developed to serve a specific need of a community group. The programs are unique, featuring individualized instruction, or open design, or community-based learning. The programs are continually evaluated and modified. There appears to be a balance between stability and experimentation.
   Program feedback is sought from students, staff, and parents.
2. *Goal Focus:* The philosophy of the school is clearly defined. The school's purpose is precise—to carry out the goal focus—and all changes are evaluated in terms of the goal focus. The clearly stated goal allows staff to defend the school when it is attacked.
3. *Legitimacy:* The successful schools have won support of the professional education community. Although most of the public alternative schools began as an experiment, they have accomplished their anticipated outcomes, thereby proving that they "work."
4. *Reliable Funding:* Although many of the alternative schools began as an experiment and were funded by private grants, federal money, or funds from state governments, the successful schools have made the transition from soft money to hard money. In other words, they are presently funded by the district board of education.
5. *Positive School Climate:* Both students and staff agree that the school is a pleasant place to be. Both groups are enthusiastic about their programs and appear to have a positive feeling about themselves. Case's research indicated that students felt a high degree of control, felt that they were cared about by the school staff, and felt that the school curriculum met their needs (Case 1981, p. 554–557).

Alternative Schools in the 1980s

Alternative schools have been accepted both by the public and by the teaching profession. In 1975 California became the first state to pass a law mandating a variety of educational modes within the public school systems of the state. The California Teachers Association supported the development of alternative public schools.

RESEARCH FINDINGS

Smith, Gregory, and Pugh (1981) compared seven alternative and six comprehensive high schools in four states.

Their findings indicated that students in the lowest scoring alternative school were more satisfied that their school met their needs than were the students of the highest scoring conventional school.

In all 13 schools, teachers and students of the alternative schools indicated that their schools did a better job satisfying: needs for security, esteem, self-actualization, and social needs.

Florida (1978) passed the Alternative Education Law which demanded that local school systems develop alternatives to the conventional education offered in the standard school. New York, Minnesota, Illinois, and Pennsylvania have all encouraged the development of alternative schools within the public schools.

Alternative schools have been credited with a number of successes (Barr, 1981):

1. They have helped to reduce school violence. This fact may be related to school size. There is less anonymity in smaller schools. Barr relates a high positive correlation between small school size with low teacher/student ratios and reduction of school crime.
2. Alternative schools have assisted in the desegregation of urban schools by offering students an attractive choice.
3. The alternative schools compete with private academies and parochial schools, thereby reducing urban flight.
4. Both the highly gifted student and the dropout student do well in the alternative school.
5. Teachers can choose a program that they believe will be best for them.
6. Alternative schools have been used to reform public education by providing an environment in which to experiment with ideas such as peer tutoring, internships, out-of-school programs, and conferencing rather than report cards.
7. Student self-concept improves in alternative schools, as does student involvement in school life.

Why Do Teachers Choose Alternative Schools?

The author interviewed teachers who have worked for more than 5 years in public, private, and parochial alternative schools. All of the teachers were former public school teachers in standard schools. They were asked two questions: "Why did you leave the standard school and/or the Los Angeles Unified School District," and "What are the 'rewards' for teaching in an alternative school?"

"Why did you leave the Los Angeles Unified School District and/or the standard school?"

- "I was always the only one doing these different curriculum things. I felt there was no support from colleagues or from my principal."
- "I was attracted to the philosophy of the alternative school. There was no philosophy where I was teaching."
- "I needed to teach a half day versus the whole day and the school district wasn't flexible enough to allow me to do that."
- "I was tired of travelling so far to my school; the district didn't care and refused to reassign me closer to home."

"What are the rewards for teaching in an alternative school?"

- "The principal is committed to quality education and her philosophy is consistent with mine. I work to achieve the very best I can do when I teach, and I can pull it off here!"
- "There is continuity of goals here. They don't keep changing. The children belong to all. At the end of the semester, you don't have to stop caring about the kids. You can provide information and help to your colleagues about how best to help the children. That's what I mean by continuity."
- "You don't feel isolated here. There's a parallel feeling. Teachers support each other; we have the same philosophy."
- "A personal approach with parents and children is acceptable here. I really get to know the children and their parents, too. My evenings are often spent talking to parents. I would never have done this in the public schools. I can reach out to the parents!"
- "We are encouraged to go off in unique directions. I get highly motivated and so do the children. It is great to be able to experiment with curriculum and with different ways to teach."
- "There is flexibility and there is innovation here. I can try something new and not be afraid of failure. It's OK to fail because you have learned something that you didn't know before."
- "There is a smaller teacher/student class ratio and that is very important to successful teaching."
- "Everyone is involved—parents, teachers, students, (even the consultants!), secretaries, custodial help. Why, I remember when the custodian in my public school classroom complained because I was doing art work. The result was I had to give up most of the art activities."

From these interviews it is apparent that teachers leave the standard school (or the school district) for philosophical professional reasons as well as for a number of personal reasons. That there are many rewards for teaching in the alternative environment is obvious. Teachers repeatedly commented on the joy of collegial and administrative support in an environment where the goals and philosophy are consonant among the members of the professional staff. Other reasons included the opportunity for innovation, problem solving, and experimentation. Curriculum flexibility was a positive factor, as was the involvement of all members of the school community. Comments about students included that students were more *interested* to learn, and their parents were more *concerned* that they learn.

The Challenge of Accountability

A schoolmaster during the nationalistic period of American history (1776–1823) agreed to the following contract:

- Must teach 25 students for 80 days.
- The school term will begin the first week after Thanksgiving.
- Must be honest and of high moral character.
- Each child must be taught as much as he is capable of learning.

- At the end of the term a report identifying student progress in each subject must be submitted to the trustee (Lemlech & Marks, 1976, p. 8).

American nationalism influenced not only the development of the school and the curriculum, but during this period teacher contracts specified the number of children to be taught and the fact that the children were expected to learn as much as they were capable of learning. The roots of the accountability movement can be traced to this period in American history.

What Is Accountability?

Accountability focuses on the results of student achievement. Teacher accountability means that the teacher is judged by his/her ability to produce behavioral change in a group of students. Leon Lessinger, a staunch advocate of teacher accountability, explains that "the concept rests on three fundamental bases: (1) student accomplishment, (2) independent review of student accomplishment, and (3) a public report, relating dollars spent to student accomplishment" (Lessinger, 1980). Lessinger believes that accountability will reform and renew school systems.

Robert Bundy believes that accountability is self-defeating. The term was originally borrowed from management and Bundy believes that using it in education means applying an industrial consciousness concept to nonindustrial problems. He contends that the concept is used as a "red herring" to distract attention from those issues that presently confront the schools (Bundy, 1980).

California was the first state to require teachers to be accountable in terms of student performance. Under the Stull Act provisions teachers are evaluated on a continuing basis, at least once each year for probationary teachers and at least once every other year for permanent personnel. Stull Act provisions included: (a) the establishment of standards of expected student progress in each area of study and of techniques for the assessment of progress; (b) assessment of certificated personnel competence as it relates to the established standards; (c) assessment of other duties normally required to be performed by certificated employees as an adjunct to their regular assignments; (d) the establishment of procedures and techniques for ascertaining that the certificated employee is maintaining proper control and is preserving a suitable learning environment.

The Stull Act in California was motivated by public dissatisfaction with the cost of education as well as public alarm over the results of standardized tests in reading and math and over the reports of high school graduate illiteracy. The concept of accountability is unpopular with teachers because there are many factors that are related to student achievement beyond teachers' control. (Teachers cannot control family background, social class, language, students' attitudes, intelligence, peer group pressure, etc.) Many believe that accountability puts an unfair burden on teachers.

Minimum Competency Tests for Students

The emphasis on teacher accountability has shifted slightly in the last several years to minimum competency tests for students. Presently, more than forty state legislatures have required minimum competency testing of secondary school students. Complaints from parents and employers about students' inability to read, compute, and fill out simple employment forms gave impetus to the competency test movement. However, there are a number of problems related to literacy testing. Van Til (1978) anticipated many of these current problems. They include (a) higher rate of failure for minority students, (b) high dropout rate for students who fail the test, (c) tendency of teachers to teach for tests, (d) lawsuits against literacy testing, (e) ineffectiveness of remedial classes and lack of funding for them, (f) the expectation that competency tests for teachers will be implemented. Each of these problems will be discussed briefly.

Minority Students Fail Literacy Test. Most of the literacy tests are designed to verify eighth grade competence. In 1979, New York City's high schools anticipated that 7,000 seniors would fail the test. New York City has an 85 per cent black population. Since 1979 New York has increased its standards and planned an even tougher test. The director of New York City's high schools anticipated that tens of thousands of New York high school seniors would fail to graduate in June of 1981.

Albert Shanker, president of the United Federation of Teachers in New York City, has been in favor of accountability. He believes that a study of student achievement in the schools will reveal that teachers are being unfairly held accountable for declining test scores because he feels it is unrealistic to expect teachers to overcome the large influx of disadvantaged students who have migrated to the New York City schools (Lieberman, 1980).

In Florida the failure rate for minority students was predicted to be two and one half times the rate for white students. At a black vocational school, Stanton High School, only 6 per cent of the 1,000 students passed the math portion of the literacy test and 48 per cent passed the verbal portion (Van Til, 1978). Florida seniors who fail the test, but have completed attendance requirements, receive "certificates of completion" instead of a high school diploma. Since the unemployment rate for minority youth is excessive, these young people will be severely punished for not having attained at least a high school diploma.

In Detroit, Michigan, minimum competency tests are being used to improve instruction. Detroit educators, along with citizen groups and the UCLA-based Instructional Objectives Exchange, designed a 12-component proficiency program to improve basic skills instruction. The tests were first administered to 10th and 11th graders in the spring of 1980. The results showed that 81 per cent of the students passed the reading test, 55 per cent passed the written test, and 49 per cent passed the math test. Students who fail all three tests do not receive an endorsed diploma. But Detroit has been unique in the development of remediation strategies and instructional resource materials for teachers. Subject matter specialists have incorporated the 12 competencies into the K–12 curriculum, and Detroit educators anticipate that in time all students will master the proficiency program (Popham & Rankin, 1981).

High Dropout Rate. Van Til and other educators across the nation are concerned that failure to pass the literacy test will induce many youngsters to quit school. Despite social and economic hardships, many high school students, prompted by parents and concerned counselors, have managed to stay in school (in the high school vernacular, "to hang in there"), but the prospect of receiving certificates of completion will not persuade students to continue their education. Remedial help for 11th graders is too late; only systems that detect potential failure during the crucial late elementary or junior high school years will be beneficial.

Teaching for the Tests. An old adage in education may be useful to explain this problem. It has been said, "let me prepare your tests, and I will have designed your curriculum." Since teachers are aware that the public holds them to blame when test scores decline and when students fail, the temptation may be great to structure all learning experiences to prepare students to pass the literacy test. Seeley (1979) commented, "the link between student accountability and teacher accountability is no doubt what makes many professional educators so fearful about the competency movement." This fearfulness may spur teachers to teach to the test instead of using the tests to validate their own judgments concerning students' instructional needs.

Are Literacy Tests Biased? A survey of the highest and lowest scoring counties in Florida revealed the socioeconomic effects on the test results. Florida minority groups questioned whether the literacy test was culturally biased and discriminated against blacks. A class action suit was initiated in 1978, and in 1979 the Florida State Department of Education was prohibited from using the literacy test results as a discriminating factor for graduation. The court ruled that Florida students, parents, and teachers should have been given advanced warning of the function of the literacy test; therefore, the judge ruled that the test results could not be used as a graduation requirement until at least 1983.

Detroit educators took steps to ensure that there would be no test bias. Test items to be used in the High School Proficiency Program were subjected to intense examination by minority affairs specialists, by citizen groups, and by Detroit educators. Any item suspected of reflecting cultural or racial bias was removed. Items that did not reflect the Detroit curriculum or the Detroit cultural setting were not approved for use.

How Do You Help Failing Students? Many of the state legislatures have required testing programs beginning in grade three and continuing every two to three years. Basic skill deficiencies can be detected when students are still in elementary school. To help the students, funds need to be provided for remedial programs and teachers need preparation programs to develop the skills to provide remedial assistance. State legislatures have been very willing to fund testing programs but less willing to remedy the weaknesses discovered as a result of the testing programs. If the minimum competence test is used as a means (a) to identify failing students, (b) to provide them with the encouragement to stay in school, and (c) to offer the remedial assistance to correct deficiencies, then it has value; but if tests are used as means to separate and cut off failing students, then teachers and society have failed. The key to success is instructional improvement.

Should Teachers Be Tested? At least ten states now use some form of competency testing of teachers; many more states are developing tests or considering the use of existing tests for teachers (E. F. Northern, 1980). Florida, in 1978, was the first state to require teacher applicants to pass a test before licensing; however, for many years large school districts in the United States have screened candidates for teaching positions through preliminary tests. The Los Angeles Unified School District has required competency testing in subject fields and in pedagogy since the 1940s.

RESEARCH FINDINGS

Andrews, Blackmon, and Mackey (1980) examined the relationships among undergraduate gradepoint averages, student teacher performance, and scores on the National Teacher Examination (NTE). They found:

1. The NTE is a valid test of academic preparation. Students with higher grade point averages achieved higher NTE scores.
2. The NTE is *Not* useful as a predictor of the teacher's classroom effectiveness. Factors evaluated by supervising teachers are not the same factors evaluated in the NTE.

The Dallas Independent School District gave a minimum competency test to new teachers; fifty per cent of the Dallas candidates failed the verbal and quantitative ability tests at the tenth grade level. Most of these candidates were minority teachers. While most professional groups disapprove of testing certified teachers because of the widespread feeling that tests are not valid indicators of effective classroom performance, the testing of new teachers has been favored, most notably by Albert Shanker, President of the AFT (Ornstein & Levine, 1981).

Obviously nobody wants a teacher who is not literate beyond tenth grade reading and mathematics; however, we do not know the relationship between high level knowledge scores and classroom practice. The public's concern about getting and retaining good teachers is reflected in the response to the 12th annual Gallup poll question, "Do you think a one-year internship for teachers is a good idea or a poor idea?"

ONE-YEAR INTERNSHIP FOR TEACHERS

A number of persons interviewed in this twelve-year series of surveys complain about the difficulty of getting "good" teachers, enough to place this problem among the top ten "most important problems facing the local schools." This may explain, in part, why the public favors the idea of an internship of one year at half pay for those who wish to enter the teaching profession. On the other hand, an internship at half pay may discourage many young persons from entering this profession, which is already losing some of its appeal.

The question:

Teachers now receive certificates to teach upon completion of their college coursework. Some people believe that teachers should be required to spend one year as interns in the schools at half pay before they are given a certificate to teach. Do you think this is a good idea or a poor idea?

	National Totals %	No. Children in Schools %	Public School Parents %	Parochial School Parents %
Good idea	56	56	55	56
Poor idea	36	35	37	42
Don't know	8	9	8	2

Analysis of the vote by groups indicates that the most recent graduates—those eighteen to twenty-nine years of age—are most in favour of the internship proposal. Those who are over fifty are most opposed.

The movement toward testing of teachers' basic skills gained impetus as a consequence of public dissatisfaction with students' performance on competency tests. However, there are a number of other questions related to professional standards that should be considered in the discussion of teacher accountability.

Professional Standards

A number of studies indicate that teacher candidates tend to have low grade point averages in college, but as noted earlier there is a question whether there is a positive correlation between effective classroom performance and high grade point average. Both the public and members of the profession have challenged: *Who* should be admitted to teacher preparation programs? Tests designed to screen out those candidates who have not achieved desired standards of literacy would be of value to facilitate the selection of candidates for admission to teacher preparation programs.

Another problem is: How should subject matter preparation be evaluated? Since there is a lack of congruence between subjects taught in higher education and the subjects taught in the K–12 curriculum, it is difficult to test teacher candidates for subject matter preparation. Knowledge gained in the college classroom provides depth and background for teaching, but it does not necessarily correlate with what needs to be taught at lower levels of education.

The public fails to recognize and accept the need for strong professional preparation. As a consequence, a third problem confronting educators who are concerned about professional standards is that pedagogical preparation for teachers has often been kept to a bare minimum. In California, legislation has imposed a limitation on the number of units allowed for pedagogical study. Since the legislation also requires that teacher education institutions provide a four-year credential program, most California teachers study methods for teaching reading and have only one (general) methods course for all other subjects. With these limitations it is impossible to provide new teachers with the necessary skills for classroom practice.

A problem closely related to pedagogical preparation is the question of how to evaluate the teacher candidate's field experience. Minimum professional standards for performance of specific generic teaching competencies have not been set. Teacher candidates are rarely required to demonstrate their competence in developing questioning strategies, to demonstrate alternative means of developing concepts, or to apply the teaching of skills to a variety of subject fields.

A fifth problem related to professional standards has to do with the expectation by many young teachers that, "Now that I have my credentials, I have completed my professional study." Competence to teach is a developmental process; there is no specific moment when one is completely competent. Additional advanced studies in subject fields, collegial support and interaction, and inservice programs are all needed for purposes of renewal and continuation in the profession. Standards for continuing education to assure effective classroom performance need to be established.

In California (1981–1982) the problems related to professional standards are being studied by a national panel of experts and by a state appointed panel of California educators to develop recommendations leading to a proposed system of standards for California teaching. Other states are considering similar actions.

Bilingual Education

Educators as well as society as a whole appear to be divided between those who believe that bilingualism is an asset and those who believe it to have negative effects on a child's academic development. Both pro- and antibilingual forces seek solid evidence that bilingual education enhances a child's self-concept and improves academic achievement.

Minority communities are as divided as the rest of society. For minority parents the issue has greater impact. Minority parents are particularly concerned about the lack of guidance from educators concerning language use at home. Should minority parents reinforce the dominant native language at home or should second language use be encouraged at home? Should the native language be eradicated?

In the schools educators ask many of the same kinds of questions. For instance, do students need a certified bilingual teacher throughout an entire school day in order to become proficient in the second language? Or should students be subjected to the *immersion* strategy by participation in a monolingual program that employs only the second language?

Landmark Decisions

The Bilingual Education Act was passed by Congress in 1968 as Title VII of the Elementary/Secondary Education Act. Over half a billion dollars has been provided for bilingual education since 1968.

In 1974 the United States Supreme Court ruled that the San Francisco Unified School District had to provide equal educational opportunities for all students. In *Lau vs. Nichols*, the court required the San Francisco school district to provide bilingual education to the Chinese speaking students of the district. The decision required school districts to rectify those English language deficiencies that exclude students from effective participation in educational programs.

Later that same year, Congress extended bilingual education to include bicultural education. Congress stated that bilingual education must be given with an appreciation of the cultural heritage of the target group. The expansion of the Title VII Act recognized the intimate relationship of language, culture, and ethnic identity.

Transition vs. Maintenance

As bilingual education was originally conceived, the idea was that children should be taught basic skills in their native language so that they would not fall behind academically. At the same time they would be given some English language experiences. When their oral language development in English was sophisticated enough, then they were to receive their instruction in that language. The *transition stage* refers to this period when the limited-English speaking student or the non-English speaker receives instruction in the basic skills in some language other than English.

The concept of bilingual *maintenance* was conceived out of a concern that the native speaker of languages other than English would lose his/her native identity. Maintenance programs reinforce the worth and dignity of the student's native heritage even after the minority student has acquired English speaking ability.

Elementary teachers often voice concern that they do not know precisely when to discontinue native language instruction. Most agree that the original intent of Congress was that native language instruction should last for about two years and that at the end of that period the students should be ready to resume their education in English.

Teachers raise the following questions:

1. Does bilingual instruction hinder the acquisition of English language skills?
2. Could instructional time be better spent teaching English since most minority students lack fluency in their native language as well as in English?
3. Is academic retardation of bilingual students a consequence of transition programs when the native language instruction is discontinued?

Some bilingual specialists raise even more controversial questions. They ask: Is bilingual education a goal of public education? They believe that if bilingualism is considered an asset to the individual and to society, then schools should encourage the acquisition of many languages—as many as the student can acquire. Therefore, these educators do not believe that one should question the value of a maintenance program because only through a maintenance policy can scholarship in more than one language be attained.

Research in Bilingual Education

Troike (1978) pointed out that since 1968, when bilingual instruction was first approved, less than one half of one per cent of the appropriated funds was spent for research. It is for this reason that there is very little evidence concerning the effectiveness of bilingual education.

Troike verified the comments of other researchers that thus far bilingual research has suffered from a number of failings: These include:

- no control for socioeconomic status of the students
- inadequate sample size, improper techniques, high attrition of target group
- no control for native language dominance
- significant differences in teacher qualifications or characteristics.

As a consequence of these and other shortcomings, Troike and other researchers disapprove of the American Institute for Research, Palo Alto, study of the impact of Title VII programs. In this study Malcolm Danoff (1978), the principal research scientist, stated that Title VII students performed more poorly than non-Title VII students of similar background in English reading and at about the same level in mathematics. Over 85 per cent of the students in the study were in projects implementing a maintenance bilingual program rather than the transition program mandated by Title VII legislation.

Educators and the lay public will continue for some time to debate the value of immersion programs, transition programs, and maintenance programs. Perhaps in the near future researchers will resolve some of the questions that have been raised. The 12th annual Gallup poll asked another question—whether students should be required to learn English in special classes before they are enrolled in the public schools. Their question and the responses are on page 22.

RESPONDING TO THE CRITICS

- Critics of bilingual education claim that Congress is rewarding failure and that bilingual-bicultural programs actually prevent students from becoming literate in English and from learning a common culture.
- Proponents of bilingual education claim that no state provides bilingual-bicultural programs for all of the students who need them and that those children who are in bilingual-bicultural programs do not receive the benefits of a maintenance education which recognizes the value of two languages.

HOW WOULD YOU RESPOND TO THE CRITICS?

Many families who come from other countries have children who cannot speak English. Should or should not these children be required to learn English in special classes before they are enrolled in the public schools?

	National Totals %	No. Children in Schools %	Public School Parents %	Parochial School Parents %
Yes, they should	82	82	83	80
No, they should not	13	13	13	18
Don't know	5	5	4	2

FURTHER BREAKDOWNS:

	Yes, They Should %	No, They Should Not %	Don't Know %
NATIONAL TOTALS	82	13	5
Sex			
Men	83	13	4
Women	81	14	5
Race			
White	82	14	4
Nonwhite	80	9	11
Age			
18 to 29 years	89	10	1
30 to 49 years	81	15	4
50 & over	77	16	7
Community Size			
1 million & over	83	14	3
500,000–999,999	91	6	3
50,000–499,999	83	12	5
2,500–49,999	79	16	5
Under 2,500	79	15	6
Education			
Grade school	74	17	9
High school	84	12	4
College	82	15	3
Region			
East	82	15	3
Midwest	86	10	4
South	80	14	6
West	79	16	5

Mainstreaming: The Least Restrictive Environment

Conceptually, the intent of special education programs was to meet the needs of students who had physical handicaps or learning problems. These programs attempted to provide a basic education to these students in an environment that would be free from academic competition and free from discriminatory behavior of peers.

However, special education classrooms often were used as a dumping ground for students who were labeled "exceptional." The special education classroom served to isolate special students from peers who exhibited more socially acceptable behavior.

During the late 1960s special education teachers and educational researchers began to question the effectiveness of special education placement, and minority parents questioned the validity of IQ tests that labeled their children retarded. Many children whose primary language was other than English, when placed in a monolingual immersion situation, appeared to have learning problems. Teachers unable to detect non-English speaking children from children with genuine learning handicaps placed them in special education classrooms. Mercer (1971) verified that special education classrooms were populated with a disproportionate number of minority and low-economic-background children, labeled mentally retarded.

Parental dissatisfaction with special education placement led to a number of court cases in Pennsylvania (1971), District of Columbia (1972), and California (1972). The judicial decisions in each of these cases declared that the constitutional rights of children had been disregarded. The courts, and later legislative enactments, recognized the cultural bias of IQ tests and the testing milieu, prejudicial attitudes that resulted from labeling students "exceptional", and educators' contradictory evidence of effectiveness of special education placement.

Full Educational Opportunities

Congress in 1974 passed the Education Amendments (PL93–380) to the Education of the Handicapped Act, which specified criteria for funding special education programs. This Act established a goal to provide full educational opportunities to all handicapped children. Provisions specified that "to the maximum extent appropriate, handicapped children in public or private institutions or other care facilities are educated with children who are not handicapped and that removal from the regular classroom occurs only when the handicap is of such severity that educational services cannot be achieved satisfactorily" (Education Amendments, 1974).

In addition PL93–380 specified that testing and evaluation materials used for the purpose of classifying and placing the handicapped child be "selected and administered so as not to be racially or culturally discriminatory."

Individualized Educational Program

Cited as a bill of rights for handicapped children, Public Law 94–142 was enacted by Congress in 1975. The law has implications for all children, both handicapped and nonhandicapped, because it specifies the use of an individualized education program (IEP) to identify individual needs and capacities. The Act guarantees that handicapped children are to receive special education and related services, free and appropriate, conforming to the nature of their handicap.

In accordance with PL94–142, the IEP must specify

- the student's present educational achievement level
- appropriate educational goals, annual and short range
- special services to achieve or implement the goals
- extent to which the handicapped student can be placed in a regular classroom
- annual review of instructional goals, progress, and implementation plans.

The IEP plan must be signed by the student's parent or guardian to indicate that the parent or guardian participated in the planning conference and agreed with the proposed program.

Mainstreaming

The bill of rights for handicapped children did not mention the word "mainstreaming." Instead, the law specified that handicapped students must be educated in the "least restrictive environment."

The term mainstreaming refers to the normalization of the classroom so that it represents a true learning community of heterogeneous individuals with equal educational opportunities.

Through mainstreaming, teachers can help students (handicapped and nonhandicapped) learn about human variability and function as members of a democratic society. PL 94–142 does not do away with special education classrooms or the need for special education teachers. The specification of the least restrictive and appropriate setting means that many physically handicapped students and many students formerly labeled "handicapped" can return to the regular classroom and participate for at least a portion of each school day. However, if the handicapped child needs special instruction or tutoring or special services, then it is the intent of the law that these services be furnished free and appropriately.

Glick and Schubert (1981) described the characteristics of successful programs that have implemented mainstreaming:

1. Good communication existed between regular and special education teachers.
2. Meetings between the special and regular teachers tended to be informal rather than formally scheduled conferences.
3. Teachers were provided with administrative support.
4. Students' schedules were flexible and changed to accommodate the student's needs as s/he shifted gradually into the regular classroom.
5. Teacher expectations for success in mainstreaming the handicapped child were positive.
6. Successful programs had begun mainstreaming children before PL 94–142 was mandated; therefore, they were backed by years of experience.
7. The special education teachers were an integrated part of the school faculty; they were not physically isolated from the rest of the school.
8. The special educators had a positive attitude about the success and desirability of mainstreaming and worked hard to accomplish it.
9. Regular students accepted their handicapped peers; regular students had been prepared for the experience by their classroom teacher.

Glick and Schubert observed that the implementation of successful mainstreaming programs depends upon communication, administrative support, time, and inservice.

- What professional issues should be considered before implementing mainstreaming programs?
- Since so much attention is being given to the atypical learner, do you believe that the average student is ignored?
- In what ways does the average student have individual needs?

Teacher Stress

The issues presented in this chapter are but a few of the daily challenges and demands placed on teachers. While most teachers are well qualified to teach in their respective grade levels or academic fields, new requirements, federal and state mandates, isolation, discipline problems, new curriculum, or the pressure of paperwork all contribute to the phenomenon known as teacher stress and burnout.

Stress refers to the individual's pressures and the individual's emotional responses to traumatic events in his/her personal, interpersonal, institutional, and societal life. The body responds emotionally to stress, whether the stress is good or bad. Good stress is distinguished by the term *eustress* (Selye, 1974). Desirable stress can be caused by peak experiences such as an aesthetic experience, or a compliment from a colleague, or the birth of a child. Some individuals delight and thrive on such stress for personal and professional goals. Other individuals go out of their way to avoid all stress and, thereby, seem to increase it.

Bad stress is often referred to as *distress*, and too much of it causes *burnout*. We do not really know whether teaching is more stressful than other professions; however, in Chicago (1977) 56.6 per cent of 5,500 teachers who responded to an AFT survey claimed physical and/or mental illness as a direct result of their jobs.

Symptoms and Reactions to Burnout

Cardinell (1980) analyzed teacher burnout and provided the following list of symptoms:

Physical
1. fatigue and physical exhaustion
2. headaches and gastrointestinal disturbances
3. weight loss
4. sleeplessness
5. depression
6. shortness of breath

Behavioral
1. changeable mood
2. increased irritability
3. loss of caring for people
4. lowered tolerance for frustration
5. suspiciousness of others
6. feelings of helplessness and lack of control
7. greater professional risk taking (pp. 9–10).

Absenteeism has been a typical reaction to burnout. Another reaction has been to walk out at the end of the day without any sense of commitment to students, colleagues, or professional responsibilities. Many teachers with this reaction ultimately abandon the profession. Some teachers have physical ailments which affect them as a result of the pressures they cannot face, some turn to alcohol, others have an abnormal desire for holidays. Low self-esteem has been another common reaction. Burnout has affected teachers of all ages; it has not been attributed only to midlife crises. Teachers in small Alaskan school districts are just as likely to be affected by burnout as teachers in large urban areas.

Stress Reducing Conditions

Although we are quite aware of the symptoms of and reactions to burnout, we know very little about the causes and ways to alleviate it. Some studies have indicated that one of the reasons teachers are subject to burnout has to do with a lack of conditioning to share professional problems with others. Teachers have been loners.

Collegial Support. Most studies indicate that a supportive environment not only helps to alleviate pressures but helps to prevent distress. Although an administrator can initiate a supportive environment in a school, teachers can foster a support system on their own. Complimenting colleagues, expressing interest in collegial ideas, sharing examples of student excellent, and visiting each other's classrooms all help to develop loyalties and to raise morale.

The teachers' faculty room and workroom should be furnished so they are comfortable and cheery. These rooms should facilitate communication and relaxation. Colleagues can also help each other by stimulating humor. Kossack and Woods (1980) note that it is impossible to harbor negative feelings while you are laughing. Laughter develops comraderie, and good-natured teasing facilitates a balanced perspective.

The AFT has developed a number of programs to confront the causes of stress. Knowing that the implementation of the mainstreaming legislation had stress potential, the AFT developed an information network to assist teachers. Under a $150,000, two-year grant from the National Institute of Education, AFT is studying the problems of stress at three schools in New York City and three schools in Chicago.

Discipline and Stress. Discipline has been known to be one of the major problems related to teacher stress. Bloom (1980) suggests a program to reduce conflict between teachers and students. The approach is called "Creative Effective Discipline" (CREED) and there are three goals:

1. Adults should minimize stress and disruption.
2. Adults should act so as to relieve stress, not intensify it. ("Don't make it worse!")
3. Adults should be rational and reasonable.

Bloom notes that good behavior management means acting in a nonjudgmental way and making rules judiciously. The disciplinarian using the CREED approach intervenes in a low-intrusive manner whenever possible. Bloom also suggests the use of humor as often as possible to defuse tensions.

Time Management. Learning to manage time is essential if teachers are to avoid burnout. New teachers, particularly, tend to take all their paperwork home each evening and on weekends with the result that they work at least 18 hours each day. Not only does this mean that the teachers surround themselves with their work at home and at school, but it means that mates and children get as tired of the "teacher-work" as does the professional.

Teachers need to learn to budget time by carefully evaluating the tasks to be accomplished and finding ways to involve students in doing some of the less essential paperwork. Goodall and Brown (1980) suggest that teachers examine their work tasks and perform pleasant tasks 75 per cent of the time and unpleasant tasks 25 per cent of the time. They also suggest performing more pleasurable tasks first.

Exercise Relieves Tension. Exercise and play are very important if one is to cope with the vicissitudes of life. Appropriate exercise relieves tension. Professional fitness leaders recommend at least thirty minutes of exercise three times a week to improve muscle tone. Exercise improves body functions and reduces stress by releasing physical tension. Prudden (1975) suggests a number of tension-relieving exercises to be performed during the course of the workday. She suggests shoulder shrugs performed by pulling the shoulders to the ears and counting for three seconds. Another exercise suggested by Prudden is headrolls beginning with the chin resting on the chest. In this exercise the head is moved slowly and gently from the center to the right, back to the center of the chest and to the left, then back to the center again.

Walking briskly instead of riding, climbing stairs instead of using elevators, and jogging are other Prudden suggestions. Exercise leaders at most YMCAs can suggest personal fitness programs. Fitness classes at most Ys accommodate teachers' working hours. Chapter 7 provides some ideas for exercises to be performed in classrooms to relieve both adult and student tension.

RESEARCH FINDINGS

Esposito (1981) investigated teachers' perceptions of their schools' psychological climate. He categorized each school's climate using an open/closed continuum.

Open schools were those in which teachers were not burdened by busywork, enjoyed working together, and expressed job satisfaction. Principals were perceived as models and leaders.

In the closed school climate, teachers expressed little job satisfaction. Teachers in these schools had trouble working together. In the closed school the principal was perceived as aloof and impersonal and not concerned with teachers' welfare.

Esposito compared the attendance record of the teachers at the open and closed schools. His analysis showed that there was a significantly lower absence rate for teachers at schools perceived as having an open psychological climate.

Stress Reduction in Tacoma, Washington. The Tacoma, Washington, school district in 1978 became the first system to offer a program for reducing stress and to provide teachers with insurance coverage for long-term disability resulting from burnout. A joint committee from the school district and the Tacoma Association for Classroom Teachers developed a stress reduction program.

RELIEVING STRESS

- Make a list of teaching experiences that were successful for you during the last month.
- Make a list of your personal and professional strengths exhibited during the last month.

To stimulate interest, teachers at the building level were provided with fitness and nutrition information. Guest speakers encouraged teachers to develop individual fitness programs. At some schools faculty members developed charts to report progress and show which teachers had cut down on smoking or lost weight. Aerobic workshops were jointly sponsored by the school district and the teachers' professional association, and weekend trips were organized to encourage teachers to relax. The school district also made a commitment to provide a counseling program to teachers in need of it (Young, 1980).

Chapter Summary

The future is challenging; it is both predictable and unpredictable. Teachers need to cope with a variety of issues related to preparing students for tomorrow. Teachers are challenged to improve education and demonstrate equity in education.

A discussion about the future initiated this chapter because it is important to consider the future as you develop a perspective about the purposes of schools and educational goals. Critics of the schools challenge the aims of education and the purposes of schools. In response to the critics, alternative forms of schooling have developed. The term *alternative* school implies that there is a difference among schools and that students, parents, and teachers have a choice of deciding among schools. Alternative schools exist at both elementary and secondary levels.

Public demands for better schools have led to minimum competency tests for students and teachers. The issues of professional standards and literacy testing are related to the challenge of accountability and discussed in this section of the chapter.

Bilingual instruction has been challenged by those who believe bilingualism is an asset and those who believe it to have negative effects on a child's academic development. Public opinion about bilingual education and educators' concern about transition versus maintenance strategies are discussed in this section.

Teachers are challenged to develop individual educational programs for mainstreamed children. The meaning of mainstreaming and the characteristics of successful programs are discussed in this section.

The chapter concludes with a discussion about a new professional phenomenon, teacher stress. Symptoms and reactions to burnout are described, and suggestions are made to help teachers cope with stress.

There are many other issues that could have been selected for emphasis in this chapter. The reader is urged to read widely in professional journals and the daily newspapers to identify current and future problems that will affect teachers and teaching.

Classroom Application Exercises

1. Visit an elementary classroom and observe the teacher or observe in the classroom of a colleague. How does the room environment reflect the teacher's educational philosophy? Identify the teacher's beliefs about the purposes of the school, the curriculum, instructional methods, students, discipline.
2. Read the metropolitan news section of your daily newspaper. Choose issues that would be of interest to your students. How could you use some of these issues in the subjects that you teach?
3. Develop a student activity using TV to motivate students' thinking about the future.

4. Visit an alternative school and compare it with a standard school. Compare the subjects taught, students' school responsibilities, teaching methods, materials and resources, facilities, parental involvement.
5. Choose a current professional journal and read two articles. Analyze them and list the underlying objectives for elementary education assumed by the authors.

Suggested Readings for Extending Study

Armstrong, David G., Kenneth T. Henson, and Tom V. Savage. *Education—An Introduction*. New York: Macmillan Publishing Company, 1981.

Benjamin, Harold. *The Saber-Tooth Curriculum*. New York: McGraw-Hill Book Company, 1939.

Charles, Cheryl and Bob Samples, Editors. *Science and Society: Knowing, Teaching, Learning*. Bulletin 57. Washington, D.C.: National Council for the Social Studies, 1978.

Combs, Arthur W. *A Personal Approach to Teaching: Beliefs That Make a Difference*. Rockleigh, N.J.: Allyn and Bacon, Inc., 1982.

Counts, George S. *Dare the Schools Build a New Social Order?* New York: The John Day Co., Publishers, 1932.

Dewey, John. *My Pedagogic Creed*. 1897. Washington, D.C.: Progressive Educational Association, 1929.

Fitch, Robert M. and Cordell M. Svengalis. *Futures Unlimited: Teaching About Worlds To Come* Culletin 59. Washington, D.C.: National Council for the Social Studies, 1979.

Gephart, William, ed. *Accountability: A State, a Process, or a Product?* Bloominton, Indiana: Phi Delta Kappa, 1975.

Good, Thomas L. and Jere E. Brophy. *Looking in Classrooms*. New York: Harper and Row Publishers, 1978.

Illich, Ivan. *Deschooling Society*. New York: Harper & Row, Publishers, 1971.

O'Neill, William F. *Educational Ideologies*. Pacific Palisades, Calif.: Goodyear Publishing Company, Inc., 1981.

Toffler, Alvin. *The Third Wave*. New York: William Morrow & Company, Inc., 1980.

Webb, Rodman B. *Schooling and Society*. New York: Macmillan Publishing Company, 1981.

Chapter 2

How Children Differ

After you have completed the study of this chapter, you should be able to accomplish the following:

1. **Identify ways in which individuals differ.**
2. **Explain why teachers should be aware of developmental stages.**
3. **Identify and discuss the social factors that influence learning.**
4. **Identify teacher behaviors that affect learning and educational aspiration.**
5. **Explain why it is important for a teacher to recognize how a student learns.**
6. **Suggest ways to utilize learning style information.**

"I know," and the boy stood up and raised his fist; "It's *this* big." Again he emphasized his fist. The teacher laughed. "Yes, Barry, you're right. Everyone raise your fist. Good, now you all know the size of your heart." The teacher continued the lesson, demonstrating by using a plastic model of the heart. While most of the class was as excited and animated as Barry, there were several children in the room who appeared bored. One youngster was staring out of the window, and another student was reading a comic book hidden inside a science textbook. Individuals differ in a variety of ways. We all have cognitive, affective, and psychomotor abilities. These aptitudes are influenced by social class, cultural group, age, sex, prior experiences, places of residence. The individual's interests, motivation to learn, readiness to learn, and efficiency in learning are affected by that person's characteristics. In the school setting there are other factors that also influence learning, such as the teacher's characteristics and teaching style, the nature of the learning task, the classroom environment, and the student's peer group. Each of these forces affects the individual in unique ways, and so it is not surprising that while some of the children in Barry's class were enthusiastic and attentive, others found the learning task less interesting and perhaps even dull.

How Students Differ: Developmental Patterns

Knowledge of developmental patterns allows the teacher to match subject matter, teaching methods, and the child's conceptual level. All the students in a fifth-grade classroom are not at the same conceptual level, *and* the children's ability to handle different subject fields may depend upon the particular subject that is being taught. Barry, in the example above, may be able to work at a high level in science and health, but he may have a great deal of difficulty with mathematics.

Barry's teacher needs to know whether Barry needs concrete materials to work with or whether he can handle abstract symbols. The teacher needs to know whether a fifth-grade student can understand and use appropriately abstract concepts such as freedom, democracy, and manifest destiny, or whether these concepts need to be acted out. Does Barry understand the concept of time—immediate, past, and future?

Jean Piaget, a Swiss psychologist, developed a framework for understanding age-level changes or developmental stages as children mature. Since all children pass through these stages, it may seem peculiar that these developmental stages are included in a section about individual differences; however, since students mature at different rates it is important to recognize that all students in a given classroom will not be at the same cognitive developmental stage at the same time.

Piaget studied developmental patterns of intellectual growth. He found that each of the patterns identified general behavioral characteristics. The stages are as follows:

1. Sensorimotor (0–2 years)
2. Preoperational (2–7 years)
3. Concrete Operations (7–11 years)
4. Formal Operations (11–16 years)

Sensorimotor Stage

The sensorimotor stage is the prelanguage stage and it is vital to the development of thought. During this stage the infant and toddler demonstrate intelligence prior to speech. The baby loses interest in any object that is not in sight, but by the end of the first year the baby will search for a vanished object. Before leaving this stage the baby will learn through experience the rudimentary concepts of space, time, causality, and intentionality.

Preoperational Stage

True language begins during the preoperational stage. In the beginning all vehicles that move may be "cars" and differentiated by the words big or little. All four-legged animals may be dogs, but as the child structures reality and participates in imitation and symbolic play, s/he begins to conceptualize more accurately by breaking down classes into subclasses through the process of categorization. The child in this stage needs concrete objects to manipulate.

The preoperational child has difficulty managing the concept of reversibility. A typical problem in a second grade classroom may have to do with understanding the concept of conservation. The teacher has two pint containers on the demonstration table. Each of the containers is of a different shape. The children are asked whether the liquid in one of the containers (the tall skinny one) will fit into the other container (the squat one). Invariably the children will respond that the liquid will not fit into the squat container because the tall skinny container is higher and bigger! The concept of conservation is an example of the difficulty experienced by children during this stage in understanding reversibility. During this stage the child will begin to grasp the concept of conservation.

The preoperational student has difficulty focusing on several details at the same time, perhaps because of the need for concrete representation, and this accounts for the inattention to the similarity of size of the two containers.

The concept of egocentrism is particularly important in order to understand the preoperational student. During this stage the student is unable to perceive viewpoints other than his/her own.

> Egocentrism . . . denotes a cognitive state in which the cognizer sees the world from a single point of view only—his own—but without knowledge of the existence of viewpoints or perspectives and, *a fortiori*, without awareness that he is the prisoner of his own. (Flavell, 1963, p. 60).

The student is not role oriented to others or reflective because of the lack of consciousness and awareness of others' ideas. Since it is so vital that a student be able to perceive his/her own illogical thought in order to progress beyond egocentrism, the student must encounter others and be forced to accommodate his/her thinking process to that of others. Only through repeated and forced social interaction does the child learn to be reflective and to relinquish egocentric thought.

Concrete Operations Stage

During the concrete operations stage the child resolves most of the prior problems with conservation and can think logically about concrete problems. For example, if the teacher told the child that the two containers in the conservation problem were of the same size (a pint) and then asked whether the liquid could be transferred from one to the other, the child in this stage would reason logically "yes" even though s/he did not perceive the two containers as being equal. However, the student during this stage is dependent upon personal experience; therefore, experiences must be appropriately arranged and must be concrete. For instance, the concept of a rural environment can best be understood by an urban child who sees a picture depicting farms, tractors, barns, and the like, rather than hearing a verbal definition only.

Formal Operations Stage

During the formal operations stage the child is no longer tied to concrete reasoning about objects. The child can begin abstract thought; skill in scientific reasoning increases. Data can be organized by classifying, seriating, and corresponding. The results of these operations facilitates the student's thinking logically and subjecting thought to inference, implication, identity, conjunction, and disjunction. The student can now reason hypothetically and enjoys "if-then" types of problems.

Classroom Applicability

Developmental models assist teachers in deciding what to teach, when to teach it, the sequence of teaching, and the scope of teaching. Sigel (1969) provided some insight concerning the use of Piaget's theory:

1. The stage of development provides information about cognitive modalities. Block play is important for the primary child to acquire information; the adolescent can learn by listening to others.
2. Cognitive growth is a dynamic process and proceeds with surges and a leveling off. Although growth is continuous, it may proceed at different rates.
3. Students need practice in expressing themselves. Language is a tool to convey meanings. Since children do not know all the words they need, they have difficulty expressing meanings. For this reason, students need to define in their own terms the concepts they are learning.
4. Egocentricity is expressed in thoughts and in actions. Interaction is significant in Piagetian theory. The teacher needs to plan social, physical, and conceptual confrontations so that students can learn cooperative behaviors to progress from egocentrism to sociocentrism.
5. There are behavioral indications of each stage, and because development is sequential, the teacher can observe when students are "ready" for what is to be presented. Activities should be chosen so that they "fit" with the developmental stage; they should allow interaction, experimentation, manipulation, or higher-level thought operations.

APPLICATION OF RESEARCH

Moses (1981), in a lierature review of Piagetian based principles of learning and problems of the learning disabled, warns that although it may be a temptation to provide instruction on how to perform Piaget's tasks with the goal being cognitive development, this approach is considered by special educators as inappropriate. The teaching of cognitive development is ineffective because children must achieve cognitive development themselves as they acquire the necessary cognitive structures that enable them to perform the Piagetian tasks on their own.

Using Piagetian theory, the teacher is careful to arrange the classroom environment to conform to developmental levels of students. Content is chosen based upon the individual child's conceptual level.

Experiences are selected on the basis of the child's need for concreteness or abstractness. Activities are purposeful and sequential. Interaction allows children to learn from others who may be at a more advanced conceptual level. Confrontation with others and/or with data assists the child in realizing the illogical nature of his own point of view and brings about a state of disequilibrium. Each new conceptual stage subjects the child to disequilibrium, thus forcing the child toward conscious thought to accommodate and justify his/her own reasoning process to others.

Brain Development

Myelination is the name given to the process of nerve fiber maturation. The maturation of the nerve fiber system has been related by researchers to the maturation of children's cognitive powers. The researchers believe that the physiological myelin stages of development correspond to Piaget's cognitive development stages (Sinatra, 1983). Myelination affects physiological capability to perform language tasks which require hemispheric integration. It has been reasoned that visuospatual/manipulative activities stimulate myelin growth which in turn promote the integration of the hemispheres.

The left hemisphere of the brain dominates language expression; the right hemisphere is superior in visual/spatial processing. The maturation of the fiber systems between the two hemispheres and among the brain systems affects the coordination of the hemispheres and the integration of verbal and nonverbal learning.

According to Sinatra the stimulation of the right hemisphere during preschool and primary grades may be the foundation for literacy learning in verbal modes during the middle and upper grade levels. If children have not had adequate life experiences during early childhood, they will not have the basis for the ideas and conceptualizations needed for reading and writing. Sensory exploration of the environment appears to be vital for reading and writing ability. Some educators, notably Eisner (1981), have speculated that children who have been deprived of sensory stimulation are unable to gain information, process it, and express meanings. Educating the senses appears to be critical for the development of literacy.

Moral Development

Lawrence Kohlberg, a Harvard psychologist, developed the theory of moral development. It is a cognitive-developmental theory and like Piaget's theory of development proceeds through a series of qualitatively distinct stages. Kohlberg believes that the structure of thought can be separated from the content and that development proceeds in a universal sequence. However, individuals of the same age may differ in their level of development and, ultimately, in their *final* level of development. Unlike Piaget's stages of development, Kohlberg's stages extend into the middle or late twenties before the individual achieves full moral maturity. According to Kohlberg many individuals never reach the highest stages of development.

Levels of Reasoning

Kohlberg identified three levels of reasoning about moral issues. Within each level there are two stages, thus making a total of six stages or moral reasoning.

Preconventional Level. The individual at the preconventional level typically is a preadolescent. At this level the individual is characterized by a concern for the consequences of rules and behaviors. "Right" behavior serves one's own interests or the interests of someone close. One behaves in the "right" way to avoid punishment, as a deference to power, to serve oneself, or in exchange for a favor. The child is obedient because s/he is afraid of the consequences. The stage I individual is sensitive to obedience and punishment; stage II individuals are instrumental-relativists and may be responsible to others if being so will ultimately affect their own needs. At this level of moral development loyalty, gratitude, and justice are not considered, and fairness, equality, and reciprocity are considered only when practical.

Conventional Level. Chronologically, the individual at the conventional level is an adolescent. At this level the individual is capable of moral reasoning which considers family or peers. The stage III adolescent aspires to please others in order to achieve their approval. The individual at this stage judges others in terms of whether or not they are perceived as meaning well. The stage IV individual is concerned with upholding societal rules, expectations, and roles. Right behavior is performed because the individual is motivated to act in a manner approved and expected by society rather than arising out of a concern for punishment.

Postconventional, Autonomous, or Principled Level. The individual at this level is of adult age; however, less than 20 per cent of adult society act at the principled level. Universal principles guide the individual's orientation. The stage V individual critically examines laws and acknowledges that they can be changed. Rights are determined by the society of which the individual is a member. The individual considers that s/he has a social contract with society to uphold the rights of others and that the individual should act in accordance with ethical values. Arbuthnot and Faust (1981) note that stage V and stage VI individuals base their actions upon morality rather than social practices. Arbuthnot and Faust related a typical dilemma used to assess one's moral reasoning stage:

> In Europe, a woman was near death from a very bad disease, a special kind of cancer. There was one drug that the doctors thought might save her. It was a form of radium that a druggist in the same town had recently discovered. The drug was expensive to make, but the druggist was charging ten times what the drug cost him to make. He paid $200 for the radium and charged $2,000 for a small dose of the drug. The sick woman's husband, Heinz, went to everyone he knew to borrow the money, but he could only get together about $1,000, which was half of what it cost. He told the druggist that his wife was dying, and asked him to sell it cheaper or let him pay later. But the druggist said, "No, I discovered the drug and I'm going to make money from it." So Heinz got desperate and broke into the man's store to steal the drug for his wife (p. 50).

The preconventional child (age eight) would respond to this dilemma by stating that it was all right to steal the drug because otherwise the wife would die and there would be nobody to take care of the children. Also, if the husband didn't love his wife he wouldn't take the chance of getting caught. At this stage of development the child is not concerned with the welfare of others. The wife is important because she is needed to take care of the children.

The conventional leveled child (age ten) would respond that the husband should steal the drug because he "would want to take care of her. He would be a bad husband if he didn't. It'd be okay to steal it because he's doing something good, but the druggist is being mean and selfish" (p. 60). At this level the child recognizes the marital contract; thus the husband acts in the "right" way even though stealing is prohibited.

At the principled level (age 17) the individual would respond that the husband should steal the drug though he is breaking the law. At this stage the individual would acknowledge that the law was not appropriate because it was "protecting property at the expense of a human life. The value of human life takes precedence over that of property." The individual also concedes that laws should be based upon the values of fairness and justice. "I'm sure that a judge and jury would understand Heinz's decision in this case, even though in general they would not condone stealing. Whether he loved her or not is irrelevant; a human life has value apart from personal relationship" (p. 51).

The principled response is based upon the universal right to life because in this case the law did not serve its function. Therefore, it was acceptable to disobey it, and the community would accept the rightfulness of the act.

TABLE 2.1. The Six Moral Judgment Stages.

	Content of Stage		
Level and Stage	**What Is Right**	**Reasons for Doing Right**	**Social Perspective of Stage**
LEVEL I—PRECONVENTIONAL Stage 1—Heteronomous Morality	To avoid breaking rules backed by punishment, obedience for its own sake, and avoiding physical damage to persons and property.	Avoidance of punishment, and the superior power of authorities.	*Egocentric point of view.* Doesn't consider the interests of others or recognize that they differ from the actor's; doesn't relate two points of view. Actions are considered physically rather than in terms of psychological interests of others. Confusion of authority's perspective with one's own.
Stage 2—Individualism Instrumental Purpose, and Exchange	Following rules only when it is to someone's immediate interest; acting to meet one's own interests and needs and letting others do the same. Right is also what's fair, what's an equal exchange, a deal, an agreement.	To serve one's own needs or interests in a world where you have to recognize that other people have their interests, too.	*Concrete individualistic perspective.* Aware that everybody has his own interest to pursue and these conflict, so that right is relative (in the concrete individualistic sense)
LEVEL II—CONVENTIONAL Stage 3—Mutual Interpersonal Expectations, Relationships, and Interpersonal Conformity	Living up to what is expected by people close to you or what people generally expect of people in your role as son, brother, friend, etc. "Being good" is important and means having good motives, showing concern about others. It also means keeping mutual relationships, such as trust, loyalty, respect and gratitude.	The need to be a good person in your own eyes and those of others. Your caring for others. Belief in the Golden Rule. Desire to maintain rules and authority which support stereotypical good behavior.	*Perspective of the individual in relationships with other individuals.* Aware of shared feelings, agreements, and expectations which take primacy over individual interests. Relates points of view through the concrete Golden Rule, putting yourself in the other guy's shoes. Does not yet consider generalized system perspective.
Stage 4—Social System and Conscience	Fulfilling the actual duties to which you have agreed. Laws are to be upheld except in extreme cases where they conflict with other fixed social duties. Right is also contributing to society, the group, or institution.	To keep the institution going as a whole, to avoid the breakdown in the system "if everyone did it," or the imperative of conscience to meet one's defined obligations. (Easily confused with Stage 3 belief in rules and authority; see text.)	*Differentiates societal point of view from interpersonal agreement or motives.* Takes the point of view of the system that defines roles and rules. Considers individual relations in terms of place in the system.

TABLE 2.1. (continued)

	Content of Stage		
Level and Stage	**What Is Right**	**Reasons for Doing Right**	**Social Perspective of Stage**
LEVEL III—POST-CONVENTIONAL, OR PRINCIPLED Stage 5—Social Contract or Utility and Individual Rights	Being aware that people hold a variety of values and opinions, that most values and rules are relative to your group. These relative rules should usually be upheld, however, in the interest of impartiality and because they are the social contract. Some nonrelative values and rights like *life* and *liberty*, however, must be upheld in any society and regardless of majority opinion.	A sense of obligation to law because of one's social contract to make and abide by laws for the welfare of all and for the protection of all people's rights. A feeling of contractual commitment, freely entered upon, to family, friendship, trust, and work obligations. Concern that laws and duties be based on rational calculation of overall utility, "the greatest good for the greatest number."	*Prior-to-society perspective.* Perspective of a rational individual aware of values and rights prior to social attachments and contracts. Integrates perspectives by formal mechanisms of agreement, contract, objective impartiality, and due process. Considers moral and legal points of view; recognizes that they sometimes conflict and finds it difficult to integrate them.
Stage 6—Universal Ethical Principles	Following self-chosen ethical principles. Particular laws or social agreements are usually valid because they rest on such principles. When laws violate these principles, one acts in accordance with the principle. Principles are universal principles of justice: the equality of human rights and respect for the dignity of human beings as individual persons.	The belief as a rational person in the validity of universal moral principles, and a sense of personal commitment to them.	*Perspective of a moral point of view* from which social arrangements derive. Perspective is that of any rational individual recognizing the nature of morality or the fact that persons are ends in themselves and must be treated as such.

Source: L. Kohlberg, "Moral Stages and Moralization: The Cognitive-Developmental Approach," in *Moral Development and Behavior: Theory, Research, and Social Issues*, edited by Thomas Lickona. (Copyright © 1976 by Holt, Rhinehart and Winston. Reprinted by permission of Holt, Rhinehart and Winston, pp. 34–35.

Classroom Applicability

Arbuthnot and Faust (1981) identify three basic goals of moral education.

1. Movement from a lower stage to a higher stage of development
2. Application of more advanced reasoning
3. Implementation of more advanced reasoning in everyday behavior.

The first goal can be achieved by having students confront other students who are one stage in advance of their own level. Blatt and Kohlberg (1975) report the successful use of moral dilemma discussions on junior-high-school-aged children in ghetto schools, suburban schools and working-class white schools. In each of the classrooms students were identified at three developmental stages. The classroom discussions yielded moral development change to a higher stage of development.

The second goal can be achieved by having students identify dilemmas that occur in their daily life. Newspapers, radio and television news, or existing community problems can be used as a basis for discussion. After identifying the dilemma, students should be asked how to apply their newly acquired reasoning in order to achieve the goal.

The third goal is achieved when students identify dilemmas in their everyday lives and suggest appropriate personal action. The third goal cannot be directed by the teacher. It occurs because students understand and accept social responsibility. Actual teaching strategies for moral development can be found in Part III of this text.

Social Factors Influence Learning

Family Influences

The family is the primary agency for the socialization of the child. The family transmits religious identity, cultural identity, occupational identity, race, social class, family name, nationality, and ethnic affiliation.

> The parents, through their decisions, are partially responsible for the manner in which community and institutional forces impinge on the child. The parents decide where to live, where the family goes on vacation, whom the child may invite to the house, and often to which evening programs the TV set is tuned (Elkin, 1968, p. 48).

Bloom (1964) concluded that the early years of family life are crucial for the child: 50 per cent of the child's potential intelligence is developed from birth to age four; 30 per cent is developed from ages four to eight, and the balance occurs between eight and seventeen.

Ornstein and Miller (1980) group family and environmental interactions with the child into three categories: stimuli, rewards, and encouragement. Interests are motivated by the richness of the home environment: books, games, colors, objects, music, furniture, pictures, people. Rewards and punishments affect the child's personality. When children behave as the parents desire, they are rewarded with an affectionate pat, a smile, a knowing look, or a compliment. Undesired behavior may be punished physically, by eye contact, restraint, or verbal abuse. Middle-class parents typically reward their children for learning to delay their "wants" to a later time or a more convenient moment.

Status expectations and ultimately educational aspiration are learned in the family group. Experiences with siblings affect the child's expectations. The middle child has a different experience than the oldest child or the youngest. The "only" child has a significantly different experience than the child who has five siblings. The responsibilities of mother in the home (cooking, cleaning, dressing the children, working outside the home, gossiping with neighbors, playing bridge) provide status expectations. The work of father (handling the finances, working with tools, fixing the television, cooking or not cooking, etc.) provides a role model. The interactions between child and every other family member influence future behavior.

If the child hears parents disparage the plumber, the carpenter, or the postal worker s/he picks up subtle messages about the value of these occupations, and in this way the child's role aspirations are influenced. Jencks (1972) studied the effect of the family and schooling. He noted that middle-class and lower-class families have different educational aspirations. Middle-class children are pressured by their parents to choose higher occupational roles; these choices necessitate the middle-class child's staying in school longer.

The stability of the family affects academic achievement. Lack of role models in the home means that the child does not learn the social behaviors and attitudes needed to develop self-discipline, training, maturity, and self-control. As a consequence, experience in school is dull and uninteresting. The child may become anxious and frustrated, or even experience cultural shock. However, children of one-parent families who are *not* economically depressed do not have the same problems as those whose economic status is low. Obviously the problems of a low economic family are more severe with regard to the children.

Sex Roles and Socialization

"Boys and girls come to learn their sex identities and expectations of behavior through differential observations, treatment, and emotional attachments" (Elkin, 1968, p. 53). Sociologists have consistently observed differences in the ways families socialize boys and girls. Socialization of the girl to assume domestic chores and child-bearing responsibilities and socialization of the boy to assume job responsibilities has been the typical pattern. Other agencies such as school, church, scouts, "Y"s, media, and other societal groups also reinforce sex roles.

Learning a sex role was supposedly important in order to emancipate the boy from a dependent relationship with his family, particularly with his mother; sex role identity and role behavior was also considered important for the female. Girls typically have had a role model in the home, but boys rarely saw their fathers at work; thus the socialization of the male was considered more crucial.

In recent years the wisdom of sex role socialization has been questioned. Changing sex role patterns and an awareness of the limitations of sex role socialization have led to an understanding of the harmfulness of what in fact was sex role stereotyping. Stereotyping is an oversimplified or generalized opinion about a group or race of people. Sex stereotyping made the following types of uncritical judgments:

- Women are emotional, flighty, domestic.
- Men are aggressive, strong, capable of managing any situation.

Past images of the female characterized her in roles of nurse, teacher, secretary, and social worker; whereas the male had a full range of occupational and professional choices. These stereotypes were reinforced by the school through differential treatment of boys and girls. Teachers conferencing with parents would be heard to comment: "Rodney is *all* boy. He isn't doing too well in reading, but he certainly can pound the baseball across the playground."

Teacher Expectations. Boys were expected not to communicate as well as girls and to be less interested in the arts and in music, but they were expected to be better than girls in math and science. The boys rarely disappointed teacher expectations, which until recently were not questioned.

Girls, on the other hand, have consistently done poorly in math. A recent survey of high school counselors revealed that girls were rarely encouraged to go beyond the geometry course; yet most professions base their admission decisions on higher level math ability. Since girls were not encouraged to take trigonometry and calculus, there have been fewer girls enrolled in professional programs.

Sex Differences—Real or Stereotypic? Many individuals believe that sex differences in adult life may in fact be related to the reinforcement of sex role stereotypes by the school and by society in general. The National Assessment of Educational Progress by subjects reveals very little differences between the sexes. During the early elementary years, girls do better; during adolescence, boys gain and continue to excel as they grow older. Small variations exist in achievement throughout the elementary and high school years, but in adulthood the difference is significant with males achieving 10.4 percentage points better than females in mathematics and 9.9 points better in science. In both of these fields males are encouraged to continue their studies while females are discouraged.

- What are the disadvantages of gender roles and stereotypes?
- How do gender role expectations affect men in adulthood and old age?
- How does the "empty nest syndrome" affect career women?

Sexism in the Classroom. Trecker (1971) analyzed male and female dominance in history textbooks and found that there was an "unquestioned dominance" of male activities in history texts. Barnett (1977) studied basic reading textbooks and found that men were demonstrated in 147 role possibilities while women were demonstrated in only 25. In social studies texts for grades 1–3, Barnett found that men were portrayed in 100 roles, women in 30. In high school government textbooks, there were 1,103 entries for men as compared to 33 entries for women.

The key issue is how to provide a nonsexist education for students. In the first grade when students study families in their own community or in other communities, teachers should encourage students to examine the responsibilities and interdependence of family members. In the sixth grade when students study world cultures, the study can focus on the roles of women in different cultures.

Textbooks should be examined and should not be chosen unless they are nonsexist. (Criteria will be found in Chapter 14). Classroom interaction can be recorded and analyzed to verify that all students get an equal opportunity to respond to questions and to initiate discussion. Attention needs to be directed at the "hidden" curriculum of the school. Does the school reinforce sex role stereotypes? In what ways does the school contribute to sex role socialization? Researchers do not know whether or not differences typically related to gender, temperament, and ability are real, imagined, or anticipated; teachers should certainly scrutinize these ideas and theories and ensure that the school does not perpetuate bias.

Differences Related to Social Class

Social scientists distinguish socioeconomic strata by evaluating the amount of wealth, influence, prestige, and opportunities a group possesses. Social scientists identify five social classes in the United States: (1) a lower-lower class of unskilled workers, many of whom are at the poverty level; (2) an upper-lower class of semiskilled and blue-collar workers; (3) a lower-middle class of skilled blue-collar workers and white-collar office workers; (4) an upper-middle class of professionals and business executives; (5) an upper class whose wealth has been inherited.

Social Class and Children's Experiences

The child's family and community experiences affect the child's interpretation of his/her world and personal self-concept. Children are conditioned by interactions with peers, siblings, parents, and important others. Poverty children who wait to be fed beyond the time when they feel hunger have a different feeling about food than children who are fed whenever they ask for it or who know when breakfast, lunch, and dinner will be served.

Children who have responsive adults nearby have a different perspective than those who are cared for by an older sibling or no one at all. Unless children are deaf, dumb, and blind they perceive their physical and social environment quite accurately. They know when adults cannot pay the bills, or cannot find a job, or cannot face reality.

The family's economic situation affects the child's daily experiences. Consider the following: the amount and quality of food the child eats, the clothes and personal possessions the child has, supervision and role models, physical comforts and social enrichment, recreation and hobbies, health care and other social services.

The poverty child's experience (lower-lower class) may include pessimism and hopelessness as a consequence of observing and listening to the adults in the home. Children "learn" despair from their parents who do *not* want to transmit optimism or hope that the future will be better than the present. They do this to prepare their children for the hard reality of existence.

Poverty children, however, are surprisingly resilient. Robert Coles, a psychiatrist, has noted that educators and sociologists who study the poor are often so intent upon classifying what the poverty child misses and needs that they fail to take stock of the povery child's strengths.

Coles (1967) identified the following positive characteristics of some disadvantaged children: sense of humor, loyalty, expressive qualities, lack of competitiveness, and cooperative attitudes.

Child Rearing

Practices among the social classes are naturally different because of differences related to lifestyle. If caring, accessible adults are always available to the child to "watch over" and play with him/her then obedience, affection, and punishment will be different than for the child who sees adults sporadically or whose parents are overcome with economic pressures. So it is fairly natural that a poor parent bringing up children in a congested urban area will limit the child's exploratory instincts in order to insure physical safety. Of necessity the poverty parent may develop strict rules to govern the child's behavior and physically punish the child if s/he does not comply with the rules.

In contrast, the middle-class parent may have time to express warmth and affection and to ask questions and reason with the child about behavior. Physical punishment may not be as prevalent because the parent with time is more likely to be interested in the child's motivation and as a consequence attempt to attain obedience through the withholding of love and affection rather than physical punishment. However, the reader should realize that all of these behavior characteristics of the classes are really generalities about patterns of behavior. For example, *all* social classes have been known to abuse their children. (The lower class has no monopoly on child abuse.)

In the wealthy child's home, the child may have a surrogate parent providing supervision with the consequence of less parent-child interaction and less warmth and affection. This child may still experience a more child-centered approach than the poverty child, and like the middle-class child, obedience will be accomplished through psychological approaches that appeal to the child's need for love and security.

Values

Children learn the values of the family. The lower-lower-class child learns that what s/he wants or does makes little difference because the individual has little control over the future. The child's survival may be dependent upon physical strength and endurance. The child is taught to obey and to conform.

The middle-class child is taught to reason, to question, to develop social interaction skills, to be competitive and to be independent. The child is urged to set goals, develop self-control, and internalize the concept of delayed gratification. A positive outlook about the future is transmitted.

The upper-class child is expected not to disgrace the family. This child is taught that the world can be conquered; the future belongs to those who develop social graces and sensitivity. The child is expected to be intelligent, to reason, and to maintain high standards.

Social Class and Education

Different home environments and differential aspirations for children affect students' success in the schools.

> **RESEARCH FINDINGS**
>
> Labeling is a form of discrimination. Mercer and associates (1971) learned that teachers inaccurately labeled minority students more often than Anglo students as "mentally retarded." The teachers based their perceptions on the following:
>
> Low academic competence + poor adjustment + low competence in English + few friends = perceived low mental ability = mental retardation

There *is* widespread recognition by all social classes of the value of education, but motivation to stay in school and job-career aspirations differ (Cloward & Jones 1963). Historically, the school has reflected middle-class values, used middle-class textbooks and tests, employed teachers who were middle class or aspired to be, and the language of the school is middle-class. As a consequence lower-class children have not achieved highly, and many school critics insist that school discriminates against the lower classes.

> **RESEARCH FINDINGS**
>
> After observing fifth and sixth grade classrooms, Friedman and Friedman (1973) decided that teachers reinforced the behavior of middle-class students significantly more than they reinforced the behavior of lower-class children.

The research of Labov (1974) provides an interesting example of how false assumptions can be made about children when there is a conflict of values. For many years black ghetto children were considered verbally deprived. The reason justifying this assumption was that the urban black children were consistently poor in basic skill subjects. Labov tested the theory that a hostile testing environment influenced the children's performance. He reasoned that a white adult interviewer would tower over young children and would be especially threatening to a black child. First he tried a black interviewer who was knowledgeable about the values and experiences of the children, but no change in performance occurred. During the second interview he asked his black interviewer to SIT DOWN and be at eye level with the children. The interviewer also changed his own speech by introducing some "naughty" words; then he sat and listened: Labov concluded that there was "no connection between verbal skill at the speech events characteristic of the street culture and success in the schoolroom" (Labov, 1974, p. 143).

Labov' experiment emphasized that the school's normal settings and procedures were not appropriate for testing lower-class black children, and as a result the generalizations made based upon those procedures were false and inappropriate for decision making when applied to educational programs for the lower-class black children.

> **RESEARCH FINDINGS**
>
> Rist (1970) studied a group of children from the time they entered kindergarten through the second grade. Rist noted that the teachers grouped the children in kindergarten based on registration forms and interviews with mothers and social workers. Higher status children were seated near the teacher and labeled "fast learners."
>
> Grouping for these children remained fixed through the second grade, and their teachers were concerned about providing instruction for the fast learners. The lower status children were described as slow learners, and the teachers were concerned about controlling and disciplining them.

The lower grade teachers involved in the Brophy and Evertson Texas Teacher Evaluation Study (1976) represented both low and high Social Economic Status (SES) schools. Their perspective concerning "what works best" as it relates to teaching methodology is of interest. A list of what the two groups of teachers stated to be important follows.

High SES Schools
Important to allow students to talk out
" to provide enrichment materials
" to develop rapport
" to praise frequently
" to use peer tutoring
" to keep interest high
" to avoid rote memorization
" to ask frequent questions
" to avoid lecturing

Low SES Schools
Important to diagnose learning problems
" to evaluate and record information about it
" to develop teacher-made tests versus standardized tests
" to allow time for thinking and relaxing
" to teach facts before generalizations
" to communicate the purpose of assignments
" to remind students to ask questions

Obviously a great deal of research is still needed to learn how to become a more effective teacher for all children. The discussion of social class bias in the classroom leads us to yet another classroom problem: racism and prejudice.

RESEARCH FINDINGS

Morris (1979) reports that early childhood teachers believe that young children's attitudes toward the racially different are innately positive. Children will grow up without prejudice unless they are indoctrinated with racist attitudes.

Race and Cultural Differences

Some behavioral differences in the classroom can be attributed to racial and cultural orientations. For instance, Navaho children freeze when looked at directly because Navaho children are taught that a direct look implies anger (Hall, 1974). Black children will often look downcast when spoken to because they are taught that a direct look from child to adult is disrespectful. Mexican children respond similarly. Black culture also allows individuals in the same room to communicate without demonstrating a listening posture; as a consequence blacks and whites often have a value conflict when working together (Hall, 1974). These and other cultural conflicts affect interaction in the classroom between teacher and children because often teachers are not prepared to work with minority children. Sometimes as a consequence of these conflicts teachers hold negative attitudes about minority-group students.

TABLE 2.2. Equitable Treatment Checklist.

	Always	Sometimes
1. Are all children favored indiscriminately when instructional materials are dispensed?		
2. Are all students encouraged to express themselves when they are angry or unhappy?		
3. Are all students "cued" when they cannot respond to discussion questions?		
4. Are all students encouraged to ask questions when they are uncertain or puzzled?		
5. Are all students in the classroom encouraged to initiate a class discussion?		
6. Are assignments differentially made to challenge the capabilities of each child?		
7. Are the talents and interest of all children considered?		
8. Are the classroom rules predictable and fair for all? (Are they equitably enforced?)		
9. Are all students treated equitably and talked to individually?		

Racism and Prejudice

Sedlacek and Brooks (1976) provide behavioral definitions of individual and institutional racism: "Individual racism is an action taken by one individual toward another, which results in negative outcomes, because the other person is identified with a certain group. Institutional racism is action taken by a social system or institution which results in negative outcomes for members of a certain group or groups" (p. 5). Prejudice is the result of an unsubstantiated prejudgment. Allport (1958) defined prejudice as "an avertible or hostile attitude toward a person who belongs to a group simply because he belongs to that group, and is therefore presumed to have the objectionable quality ascribed to the group" (p. 8). Although values are said to be "caught not taught," prejudice is a learned phenomenon.

In the classroom, racism is practiced in a number of ways.

1. Textbooks: Some textbooks stereotype cultural and racial groups through statements or caricatures that are demeaning. Another variety of text practices prejudice more subtly because target groups are omitted. For instance, the African heritage of black Americans may be omitted from the text.
2. Curriculum: Ethnic studies units or programs (multicultural education) are often initiated without proper planning and without the necessary supplementary materials. Often these courses have been taught to and designed for students from specific ethnic groups where in reality all students would benefit from the program.
3. Teacher Attitudes: Unfortunately teacher behavior may reinforce negative attitudes in the classroom. Petrie (1980) claims this occurs in the way a teacher handles interpersonal relationships in the classroom. *Routines* may be such that certain students are always discriminated against; *delegation* of tasks and trust may be differentially bestowed; *clarification and reinforcement* may not be dispensed to all children; *stimulation and individuality* may not consider the needs, interests, and talents of all children; *value clarification* may be used to discourage openness rather than clarify problems and ultimately lead to misunderstanding between teacher and student or teacher and a group of students.

Table 2.3 (Blumenberg, 1979, p. 25) suggests strategies to respond to racism and prejudice.

Figure 2-1. Kolb's Concept of Learning Styles.

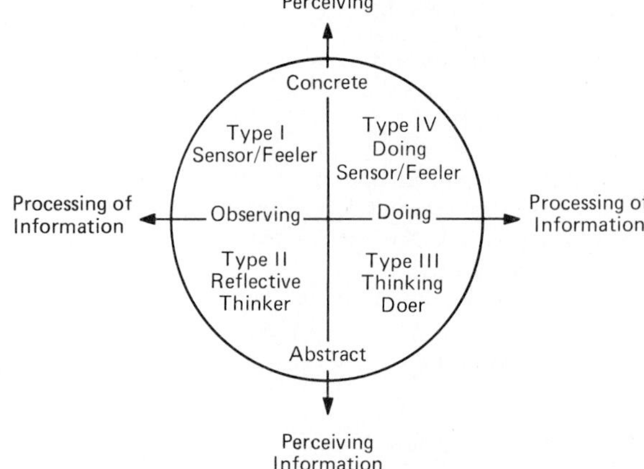

Differences Related to Learning Style. Learning styles emanate from natural, inborn inclinations. The individual's learning style manifests itself through preferred senses and personality characteristics. Students' behavior, if carefully observed, will tell the teacher how the student learns.

Kolb (1976) specifies two dimensions in determining how people learn:

1. Information is perceived along a continuum from concrete to abstract. Those individuals who are more concrete sense and feel their experiences. Individuals who are more abstract tend to think about an experience.
2. Once received, information needs to be processed. Some people process information by reflecting and observing; others process information by performing.

Kolb's research indicates that the two dimensions are paired and four learning styles emerge. Figure 2.1 exhibits the Kolb concept of the two dimensions juxtaposed to form four learning styles. Kolb believes that the schools teach mainly to the Type II learner which makes up 28–30 per cent of the population.

Dunn and Dunn (1978) studied how children and adults learn using educational, industrial, and psychological research. They isolated 18 elements that encompass learning style. Their investigation indicated that learners are affected by their immediate environment, their own emotionality, sociological preferences, and physical needs. Elements related to each of these preferred ways of learning include:

Environment
sound
light
temperature
physical design

Physical Needs
perceptual strengths (sight, touch, sound)
intake (food, drink)
time of day (morning, afternoon)
mobility (needs to move around, can sit still)

Emotionality
motivation
persistence
responsibility
need for structure or flexibility

Sociological Preferences
works best alone
works best paired with someone else
works best with peers
works best with adults

TABLE 2.3. Strategies for Responding to Racism and Prejudice.

Program and Practice	Focus	Objectives	Strategies
Multicultural education	Cultural groups which experience prejudice and in the United States.	To help reduce discrimination against stigmatized cultural groups and to provide them equal educational opportunities. To present all students with cultural alternatives.	Creating an institutional atmosphere which has positive institutional norms toward victimized cultural groups in the United States.
Multiethnic education	Ethnic groups within the United States	To help reduce discrimination against victimized ethnic groups and to provide all students equal educational opportunities. To help reduce ethnic isolation and encapsulation.	Modifying the total educational environment to make it more reflective of the ethnic diversity within American society.
Ethnic Studies	Ethnic Groups within the United States.	To help students develop valid concepts and theories about ethnic groups in the United States, to clarify their attitudes toward them, and to learn how to take action to eliminate racial and ethnic problems within American society. To help students develop ethnic literacy.	Modifying course objectives, teaching strategies, materials, and evaluation strategies so that they include content and information about ethnic groups in the United States.

Source: Eleanor Blumenberg, "Responses to Racism: How Far Have We Come?" in *Racism & Sexism: Responding to the Challenge*, NCSS Bulletin 61, ed. by Simms & Contreas, (National Council for the Social Studies, 1979), p. 25.

Kenneth and Rita Dunn recommend that teachers ask students to diagnose their own learning style by responding to the twelve factors in Table 2.4. After observing and interviewing students or using the Learning Style Inventory, the Dunns suggest that teachers create an environment that matches each child's preferred way of learning. For example, if a student is identified as extremely mobile, perhaps it would be possible to allow that child to get up and stretch when needed. Another possibility would be to arrange a schedule for the youngster so that s/he can attend a learning center, then work with a group of other students, and then move to where the teacher is for a directed lesson. Each component of the child's schedule should allow movement every 10 or 15 minutes.

The reason learning styles are so interesting is that if they are identifiable, it should be possible to match appropriate instructional approaches to the learning style need of the individual. Renzuilli and Smith (1978) identify learning styles by approaching the problem through preferred instructional modes. These researchers ask students to identify the instructional strategies they prefer. Their Learning Style Inventory measures students' instructional preferences. Students are asked their preferences about nine ways that they can interact with curricular materials: (1) projects (2) drill and recitation, (3) peer teaching, (4) discussion, (5) teaching games, (6) independent study, (7) programmed instruction, (8) lecture, (9) simulation. The Learning Style Inventory yields a score that the researchers translate into individualized programming practices.

TABLE 2.4. Learning Style Diagnosis.

Factor	Question
1. Time	When is the student most alert? In the early morning, at lunchtime, in the afternoon, in the evening, at night?
2. Schedule	What is the student's attention span? Continuous, irregular, short bursts of concentrated effort, forgetting periods, etc.?
3. Amount of sound	What level of noise can the student tolerate? Absolute quiet, a murmur, distant sound, high level of conversation?
4. Type of Sound	What type of sound produces a positive reaction? Music, conversation, laughter, working groups?
5. Type of Work Group	How does the student work best? Alone, with one person, with a small task group, in a large team, a combination?
6. Amount of Pressure	What kind of pressure (if any) does the student need? Relaxed, slight, moderate, extreme?
7. Type of Pressure and Motivation	What helps to motivate this student? Self, teacher expectation, deadline, rewards, recognition of achievement, internalized interest, etc.?
8. Place	Where does the student work best? Home, school, learning centers, library media corner?
9. Physical Environment and Conditions	Floor, carpet, reclining, sitting, desk, temperature, table lighting, type of clothing, food?
10. Type of Assignments	On which type of assignments does the student thrive? Contracts, totally self-directed projects, teacher-selected tasks, etc.?
11. Perceptual Strengths and Styles	How does the student learn most easily? Visual materials, sound recording, orinted media, tactile experiences, kinesthetic activities, multimedia packages, combination of these?
12. Type of Structure and Evaluation	What type of structure suits this student most of the time? Strict, flexible, self-starting, continuous, occasional, time-line expectations, terminal assessment, etc.?

Source: Rita and Kenneth Dunn, *Practical Approaches to Individualizing Instruction*, (Copyright 1972 by Parker Publishing Co., Inc. Published by Parker Publishing Co., Inc., West Nyack, New York), pp. 29–30.

Teacher: "Boys and girls, why do you think we have laws? Jerry, what do you think?"
Jerry: "Uh, uh, I don't know."
Mildred: "I know, Miss Henry."
Teacher: "All right, Mildred, tell us."
Mildred: "Because we would get into fights without them."
Ron: "Laws don't stop us from getting into fights."
Teacher: "Jerry, would you like to tell us now what you were thinking?"
Jerry: "Well, I think we have laws to help us settle our disputes."
Teacher: "Boys and girls, Mildred said we have laws so that we will not fight; Jerry said we have laws to settle disputes. Are they both right?"

Yando and Kagan (1968) studied the psychological dimension of reflection versus impulsivity. During classroom discussion and during the reading process, some children tend to respond quickly or impulsively; others like to reflect and take their time. In the example above, Jerry is a reflective responder while Mildred is impulsive. Teachers can help both Jerry and Mildred improve their thinking processes. For example, the teacher should have "stayed with" Jerry by giving him more time to answer and even cuing him with another question if necessary. Probably a nonverbal look or hand motion could have slowed Mildred down and helped her think a little more about what she wanted to contribute.

The research of David Hunt and his associates (1971) characterizes the individual's personality development. Hunt has identified three stages of conceptual development. Each stage corresponds to the individual's structural needs. In Stage A the individual needs high structure; in Stage B the individual conforms to moderate structure, and in Stage C the individual requires low structure. Hunt determines the student's conceptual level by having the subject respond to a stimulus given in a paragraph completion test. The subject's responses correspond to Hunt's developmental stages. The stages are matched with an appropriate instructional environment. Hunt's research with conceptual levels indicated that students in Stage A performed better with a lecture method of instruction whereas a student who preferred low structure (Stage C) performed better when the teacher used the discovery method.

The social learning theory of Rotter (1966) contributes another perspective about individual personality differences. Some individuals hold others to blame if they fail an examination, forget their homework, or are late to school. These individuals have what psychologists call an external locus of control. Other individuals believe that if they fail an examination, it is their own fault; if they are successful in an endeavor, they credit themselves with working to be successful. These individuals have an internal locus of control.

The individual with an internal locus of control views himself as having control over his environment and his fate. S/he perceives a relationship between personal behavior and consequences.

TABLE 2.5. Characteristics of Stages and Matched Instructional Environment.

Stage (Conceptual Level)	Characteristics	Environment
C	Self-responsibility Multiple alternatives Capacity for integration	Low-structure Discovery Rule: example Student-centered
B	Authority-oriented Concerned with rules Categorical thought	High-structure Lecture Rule-example Teacher-centered
A	Self-protective Immature self-centeredness No alternatives	

Source: David E. Hunt et al., *From Psychological Theory to Educational Practice: Implementation of a Matching Model* (Washington, D.C.: Educational Resource Information Center, U.S. Office of Education, April 1968), ED 068 438,34P.

- How does Hunt's conceptual-level system compare with Kohlberg's stages of moral development?
- How could a teacher encourage a Stage B individual to develop to a higher level (Stage C) and still provide an appropriate environment for the Stage B person?

The individual with an external locus of control is just the opposite. This individual believes that s/he has no control over consequences and views others as responsible and controlling events and circumstances.

RESEARCH FINDINGS

Stallings (1976) in a national study of Follow Through and Non-Follow Through Classrooms found that students in more flexible classrooms took responsibility for their own success but not for their own failure; students in structured classrooms believed their successes were due to their teacher's ability, whereas, their failures were their own fault.

Some research indicates that locus of control is influenced by parental behavior. Parents who are continually critical of their children may develop children with an external locus of control, while parents who are accepting and approving may develop the internal factor in locus of control.

Coleman et al. (1966) believed that locus of control affects school success. He and his associates found that black children with an internal locus of control were more likely to be successful in school. Battle and Rotter (1963) found that black children and low socioeconomic status children were more likely to have an external locus of control. Middle and high socioeconomic children and white children were more likely to have an internal locus of control.

- How might a teacher's personality affect teaching style?
- How would the student's locus of control relate to instructional needs?

Weiner and colleagues (1974) have developed an attributional model of achievement motivation. They have identified four causal attributes which affect the individual's perceived reasons for success and failure. They theorize that the individual believes personal success or failure, and predicts future success or failure, as a consequence of four elements: ability, effort, task difficulty, and luck.

Ability and effort are internal elements which the individual can control, while task difficulty and luck are beyond the control of the individual; thus they are external elements. Also, ability and task difficulty are stable or invariant dimensions, while luck and effort are elements of change and thus unstable.

Using the Weiner model, a student who successfully performs a science experiment could explain the achievement by saying either it was the result of personal ability or it was the result of luck. If the student believes it was ability, his/her confidence will increase, but if the student calls it luck, then success will be less meaningful and self-confidence probably will not enhance future efforts. The self-confident, success oriented individual believes that future success will be positively related to personal effort and ability.

TABLE 2.6. Attribution Model of Achievement Motivation.

Stability	Locus of Control	
	Internal	External
Stable	ability	task difficulty
Unstable	effort	luck

Source: B. Weiner, *Cognitive Views of Human Motivation* (New York: Academic, 1974), p. 52.

Chapter Summary

The teacher is challenged to respond to the uniqueness of each student. In this chapter the work of Piaget was reviewed to help teachers understand developmental patterns. The importance of helping students develop a conceptual base for reading and writing through visual/motor activities was discussed in the section on brain development. Lawrence Kohlberg's research was also reviewed to provide some insight into levels of reasoning and to form a basis for discussion of moral development.

The young student's socialization is affected by many groups—including the school. Status expectations and educational aspiration are learned in the family group.

In recent years changing sex role patterns have led to new understanding and new expectations. Social class differences account for differences in value orientations. The school appears to reflect middle-class values; school critics claim that the school discriminates against the lower class.

Researchers define learning styles in a variety of ways, but most agree that instructional approaches should be matched to students' learning styles.

Classroom Application Exercises

1. View five TV commercials. Using the information related to social class differences, decide:
   - Which social group(s) is the target audience?
   - Why was this group chosen?
   - What are the underlying value assumptions made about the target group?
2. Observe a student you consider to be successful and one you consider to be unsuccessful. In what ways are their responses and attitudes different?
3. Identify appropriate experiences for kinesthetic, visual, and auditory learners.
4. Plan a learning experience for preoperational students to help them understand viewpoints other than their own.
5. Explain why we should or should not have the same instructional expectations for all primary children.

Suggested Readings for Extending Study

Allport, Gordon W. *The Nature of Prejudice*. New York: Doubleday & Company, Inc., 1958.

Arbuthnot, Jack B., and David Faust. *Teaching Moral Reasoning: Theory and Practice*. New York: Harper & Row, Publishers, 1981.

Biehler, Robert F. and Jack Snowran. *Psychology Applied to Teaching*. 4th ed. Boston, Mass.: Houghton Mifflin Company, 1982.

Bigge, L. Morris and Maurice P. Hunt. *Psychological Foundations of Education: An Introduction to Human Motivation, Development and Learning*. 3rd ed. New York: Harper and Row Publishers, Inc., 1980.

Dembo, Myron. *Teaching for Learning: Applying Educational Psychology in the Classroom*. Pacific Palisades, Calif.: Goodyear Publishing Co., Inc., 1981.

Gagne, Robert M. *The Conditions of Learning*. 3d ed. New York: Holt, Rinehart and Winston, 1977.

Good, Thomas L. and Jere E. Brophy. *Educational Psychology*. 2nd ed. New York: Holt, Rinehart and Winston, Inc., 1980.

Havinghurst, Robert J. and Daniel U. Levine. *Society and Education*. 5th ed. Rockleigh, N.J.: Allyn and Bacon, Inc., 1979.

Labinowicz, Ed. *The Piaget Primer: Thinking-Learning-Teaching*. Menlo Park, Calif.: Addison-Wesley Publishing Co., Inc., 1980.

Seefeldt, Carol. *Teaching Young Children*. Englewood Cliffs, N.J.: Prentice-Hall, Inc., 1980.

Spitzer, Dean R. *Concept Formation and Learning in Early Childhood*. Columbus, Ohio: Charles E. Merrill Publishing Company, 1977.

Chapter 3

How Children Learn

After you have completed the study of this chapter, you should be able to accomplish the following:

1. **Define and contrast allocated time and academic engaged time.**
2. **Discuss the research related to direct instruction.**
3. **Identify classroom management skills that facilitate on-task behavior.**
4. **Explain the concept of task signals and the concept's relationship to behavior.**
5. **Identify factors that affect task signals.**
6. **Explain the importance of substantive academic feedback.**
7. **Explain the classroom management behaviors of: "withitness," "overlapping," "transition smoothness," "ripple" effect.**
8. **Identify the advantages and disadvantages for small and large group instruction.**
9. **Suggest classroom activities to develop a sense of belonging and to foster democratic behaviors.**
10. **Anticipate potential classroom management problems during small and large group instruction by identifying the problems and suggesting means to avoid or alleviate them.**
11. **Explain why it is important to allow time for both content and group work evaluation.**
12. **Suggest a variety of classroom activities to develop school success oriented behaviors.**

Eleanor Bryant taught second grade in a middle-class school in Ohio. She was a serious, businesslike woman with seven years of teaching experience. She enjoyed teaching and liked the students she taught. For reading instruction she used the McGraw-Hill programmed readers, and her daily class schedule indicated that she taught reading for 60 minutes each day.

Ms. Bryant's classroom was highly structured. When students were not working, she went over to them to find out if they needed help. Her students were actively engaged in reading instruction and appropriate follow-up work 80 per cent of the time. This means that the class averaged 48 minutes of reading time per day.

Rona Berry taught second grade in the same school as Eleanor Bryant. She was a warm, enthusiastic young woman with five years of teaching experience. Her classroom was more casual than Bryant's. Her students knew the rules of the classroom and were allowed to move about freely to obtain reading games, library books, or go to the reading centers. She, too, used the McGraw-Hill readers.

Ms. Berry's daily schedule indicated that she set aside 90 minutes per day for reading and centers work. Her students were actively engaged 65 per cent of the time. This means that the class averaged 58.5 minutes of reading time per day.

At the end of the semester when the two classes were tested in reading vocabulary and reading comprehension, Ms. Berry's students' achievement gains were greater.

To understand the reason why one class did better than the other, we need to review some of the current research and to define some terms. In the daily schedule for each of the teachers, there was a designated period of time for the teaching of reading (60 minutes for Bryant and 90 minutes for Berry). This period of time, so designated, is defined as the *allocated time*. The percentage of time that the class actually worked rather than

Students Enjoy Computer Instruction, Perhaps Because of the Immediate Feedback the Computer Provides During Skill Instruction.

fooled around, waited for the teacher's help, or moved about, is designated the *academically engaged time*. There can be quite a difference between the allocated time and the academically engaged time.

Stallings and Kaskowitz (1974) studied first and third grade reading and mathematics achievement in follow-through programs. They learned that the students' achievement reflected the academically engaged time that the students were involved in those subjects throughout the day. In other words, students who were actively engaged in reading or math activities gained more in achievement than students who were not actively engaged in the academic tasks.

The Beginning Teacher Evaluation Study (BTES) observed students in grades two and five throughout the entire day. (The students were observed for five days between October and December and twelve days between January and May.) The observers took note of *all* reading and mathematics activities even when these activities occurred in subjects other than reading and math. They found that the students were engaged for 63–84 minutes in relevant activities in reading and 26–31 minutes in mathematics. The overall engagement rate was 70–78 per cent of the time. In this study the researchers found that the teachers who allocated more time to reading and math also had the highest engagement rates. A higher engagement rate was positively associated with higher gains in achievement.

It is important to remember that the more time a teacher spends teaching a subject, the more content is attended to, and as Rosenshine (1979, p. 39) has noted, "What is not taught in academic areas is not learned."

This brings us to the concept of *direct instruction*. Direct instruction relates to those activities in which (a) the goals are clear to students, (b) the tasks are appropriate to the content to be covered, (c) student involvement is high, (d) instructional materials are appropriate to the students' ability levels, (e) student performance is monitored, (f) feedback is immediate and academically oriented, and (g) the classroom environment is democratically structured. Now let's look at a classroom involved in direct instruction.

Rod Marcus teaches fourth grade in a low-middle class and upper-lower class school. During reading instruction he arranged his students into three groups. While he teaches one group, another group works at a skill reinforcement reading center and the third group works at their desks at a task related follow-up activity. Each activity period is 25 minutes long.

Teacher	**Skill Center**	**Follow-up**
Group A	Group B	Group C (25 Min.)
Group B	Group C	Group A (25 Min.)
Group C	Group A	Group B (25 Min.)

While the students work with the teacher, they are seated in a semicircle in front of him with their backs to the rest of the class. As he directs them to read silently, he will get up and walk behind them, scanning the rest of the class, observing to see if anyone needs his help. If he detects that a student has a problem or is not "on task," he will go over to find out what is happening. He immediately provides information to help the student continue to work and now and then he cautions students not to disturb others.

Marcus does not have a great many rules in his classroom, but the students know what is expected of them. If students need help they will raise their hands shoulder high until the teacher acknowledges that he sees them; then they wait quietly until he can come over. If a student needs to leave the room s/he writes his/her name on a corner of the chalkboard (but only one student at a time) to identify departure from the room.

Since pencil sharpening is too noisy during reading, there are extra sharp pencils provided on a back table. The student merely exchanges the broken pencil with the sharp one.

All of the materials needed at the skill center are right there. The center is changed each day and so at the beginning of reading time Mr. Marcus introduces the center to all of the children. Each group's special tasks at the center are kept in a box with the group's name on it. When the child finishes the group work, there is another box provided at the center in which to place the completed assignment.

Follow-up task materials are explained in the reading group, and each student is given the necessary materials at that time.

Some of the students finish their work at the reading skill center or their follow-up work faster than others. For these students Mr. Marcus encourages the use of library books and reading skill reinforcement games. Students may get out of their seat to obtain these materials, but they may not disturb others. At the end of the reading period, Mr. Marcus provides information so that students can correct their own follow-up work. As they do so, he walks around to see how well the students accomplished their work. A student who has had a problem is immediately detected. Mr. Marcus will conference with this student to diagnose the problem.

Marcus has a good sense of humor, and he is genuinely kind with the students. He has communicated to the students that reading time is to be "businesslike" and that there is little time for small talk. Yet the room is quite relaxed; if one student quietly assists the student next to him, s/he is not afraid that Marcus will be angry. In fact, Marcus will let the students know, nonverbally, that it is OK.

Piaget stated that children should learn "to invent and discover" and that teachers should create possibilities for this to occur. How can a teacher do this? Is this goal compatible with the concept of direct instruction?

To summarize: direct instruction occurs when the teacher plans precise instructional goals, chooses appropriate learning materials, verifies that students are involved in the assigned tasks, monitors progress, provides necessary academic feedback, and maintains a friendly but structured environment. Additional information related to direct instruction as an expository teaching approach can be found in Chapter 12.

Direct Instruction and Effective Classroom Management

Many of the elements of direct instruction really relate to classroom management skills and good sense. An analysis of Marcus' reading plan indicates that he demonstrated the following classroom management skills:

Planning Curriculum
- planned academic instructional goals
- planned reading center skill reinforcement tasks
- planned reading group follow-up work
- chose appropriate instructional materials

Arranging the Environment
- arranged reading in a semicircle
- decided where to place the reading center, library books, reinforcement games

Organizing Procedures and Resources
- reading center with boxes provided for special group-related tasks
- reading center with box provided for completed work
- box with sharpened pencils
- follow-up work distributed during reading group time
- library books and games available

Monitoring Student Progress
- observed and gave assistance to whole class while teaching small group reading
- developed a system to correct follow-up work and to detect individual problems

Anticipating Potential Problems
- system communicated for obtaining teacher help
- system communicated for leaving room
- system communicated for what to do with completed work
- system communicated for what to do if finished earlier than others.

Classroom Management

In the definition of accountability it was stated that a teacher is judged by the results of student achievement. Classroom management is the dominant factor that affects the teacher's instructional expertise and, therefore, influences accountability. "Classroom management is the orchestration of classroom life: planning curriculum, organizing procedures and resources, arranging the environment to maximize efficiency, monitoring student progress, anticipating potential problems" (Lemlech, 1979, p. 5). Teachers who are successful classroom managers have mastered techniques for planning activities and maintaining high levels of student involvement in those activities, for enriching the classroom environment, for anticipating organizational and behavioral problems, and for monitoring students' progress. The research pertaining to classroom management will be discussed using the following categories: planning instructional activities, organizing procedures, monitoring students' progress, and structuring the learning environment.

APPLICATION OF RESEARCH

The Cognitive Levels Matching Project emphasizes the application of Piaget's model of cognitive development. The inservice project helps teachers understand cognitive development, assess students' cognitive levels, and match educational experiences to the students' cognitive abilities. By matching tasks with abilities through structuring of curricula, environments, activities, and interactions, it is hypothesized that cognitive development will be facilitated (Brooks, Fusco, Grennon, 1983).

Planning Instructional Activities

In recent educational history, concern about classroom management originated with the work of Jacob Kounin (1970). Kounin defined successful classroom management as "producing a high rate of work involvement and a low rate of deviancy in academic settings" (Kounin, 1970, p. 63). Kounin studied teacher behaviors that produced high and low work involvement of students. He noted the importance of motivation before teachers change activities and the need for variety and challenge in the tasks demanded of students.

In later research Kounin and Doyle (1975) found that greater involvement and less deviancy occurs when students receive task signals that are carefully sequenced to support appropriate behavior. Teacher-directed formal lessons were more likely to deliver high continuity of task signals than were informal lessons.

Kounin noted that certain types of lessons produce continuous appropriate signals while other types produce lags which encourage deviant behavior.

Greg Thomas is teaching reading to a small group of nine students. He begins by introducing new words to the students and playing a simple drill game to help them remember the words. Next, he asks them a question and they begin to read out of their books to find the answer. As each child discovers the answer he or she sits quietly looking up at Thomas expectantly. Thomas calls on a child—in no particular order—to read the appropriate passage. Then he asks a new question and the process continues.

This example models the concept of continuity. The children know what to expect in terms of the reading lesson and the teacher acts as a signal source. This format produces a continuing signal and, according to Kounin's research, yields high involvement of the students.

Low involvement of students often occurs when the lesson format is dependent upon multiple shifting signal sources. For example, when the format of the lesson requires a large group discussion, the signal sources are the children themselves. In classrooms where the students have not mastered the technique of group discussion, there will be many lags; the signals are inadequate and continuity waivers.

Kounin and Sherman (1979) note that the success of a formal lesson is dependent upon the delivery of signals which support appropriate behavior and the deterrence of signals that motivate inappropriate behavior.

Another type of lesson that may yield high involvement of students is the art experience or the individual construction lesson. Individual lessons are dependent upon precise directions, preplanning of material needs and resources, and the capability of the student to perform the appropriate actions or tasks. The source of signals in this lesson is the child's own actions as s/he moves from one task to the next in a continuous flowing manner. The total absorption of the student in his/her own work isolates and inhibits the intrusion of others, thus providing high task involvement and very little deviant behavior.

Music and movement lessons need a great deal of planning. Kounin and Sherman (1979) learned that these lessons provide a continuing source of signals from the teacher or from records or tapes; however, since props may also be involved, students are subject to intense stimulation. As students participate by singing, playing instruments, or moving they send signals to each other, thereby making these lessons vulnerable to deviant behavior.

Kounin and Sherman concluded that recitation-discussion lessons and role plays were the least successful lessons and that music performance or singing lessons were subject to off-task actions. They did *not* conclude that these lessons should not be used. The implications of the research indicate that the content of a lesson is but one aspect to be considered in the total planning. The teacher must consider whether the lesson is more appropriate for a small group or a large group; s/he must determine the motor activities involved, the resources needed, the props to be used, the physical space needed;

and finally—most important of all—the teacher must adapt teaching techniques to all of these distinctions.

The California Beginning Teacher Evaluation Study (BTES) observed second- and fifth-grade students studying mathematics and reading. Researchers focused on teaching behaviors that fostered student learning in those two subjects. They found that when teachers provided a great deal of academic feedback, there was higher student involvement; academic feedback and substantive academic interaction were related to higher student engagement in work activity. Similarly, when students received substantive direction for follow-up activities (seatwork), there was greater student engagement. If, however, students received discipline-related feedback, then there was a low engagement rate in work activity.

RESEARCH FINDINGS

The Beginning Teacher Evaluation Study originated the term Academic Learning Time (ALT). They defined it as "the amount of time a student spends engaged in an academic task that s/he can perform with high success. The more ALT a student accumulated, the more the student is learning" (Denham & Lieberman, *Time to Learn*, 1980, p. 8).

Bill pondered this problem on his math paper:

$$\begin{array}{r} 17 \\ - \\ \hline 8 \end{array}$$

Although he wrote in the difference correctly, he looked uneasy. His teacher had been observing him. She proceeded to ask him:

T.: "Bill, how many tens do you have?"
Bill: "One."
T.: "How many ones do you have?"
Bill: "7"
T.: "If you were to change a dime to pennies, how many would have have?"
Bill: (Smiling) "Ten"
T.: "If you change one unit of ten to ones, how many do you have?"
Bill: "I'd have ten. I understand now."

Bill's teacher had provided substantive academic feedback. She detected, by observing Bill as he worked, that he was insecure even though he worked the problem correctly. the BTES indicates that Bill will be more fully absorbed in his work as a consequence of the feedback provided to him. Academic feedback is more consistently related to achievement than any other teaching behavior.

Since the BTES findings are based on students who scored in the 30–60 per cent achievement range, would you expect high and low achieving students to have similar needs for:

- more substantive interaction with teachers?
- less substantive interaction with teachers?
- more review time?
- less review time?
- more challenging error rate?
- less challenging error rate?

Organizing Procedures

Experienced teachers typically consider the first three weeks of the school year as the most important. It is at this time that elementary teachers socialize their students to conform to the rules and procedures of the classroom. Evertson and Anderson (1979) confirmed that more effective classroom managers develop specific procedures and communicate them to the children. Examples of such procedures are how to obtain assistance, how to line up at the door, how to work in a group, standards for seatwork, where to put seatwork. These procedures are taught just as if they were part of the content.

Researchers who have studied effective teachers also note that these teachers are precise and clear in their directions to students; they communicate well, listen intently, and express feelings to students. Perhaps the most striking difference between effective and ineffective classroom managers is the knack for anticipating potential problems. The effective teacher anticipates resource and material needs, physical space needs, individual and group needs, noise constraints, traffic flow problems, affective and cognitive student reactions. Having anticipated these possible problems, the effective teacher preplans to avoid pitfalls. Examples are given in Chapter 4.

Another characteristic of effective managers is the ability to set clear expectations. Emmer and Evertson (1980) found that junior high school teachers were able to set expectations for behavior, standards for students' academic work, and classroom procedures.

Monitoring Students' Progress and Behavior

Kounin (1970) described a number of teacher behaviors related to managerial success. Experienced teachers are able to communicate to students that they as teachers are aware of what is going on. Sometimes they do this with a special "look," or a raised eyebrow, or by standing up, or touching, or walking over to a student. In these ways the teacher conveys the message to desist—or else! Kounin called this awareness behavior "withitness."

Another behavior that successful teachers manage is paying attention to more than one event at a time. For instance, the teacher may be working with a small reading group when someone walks into the room with a message, and a child raises his hand at his seat for assistance. The teacher leaves the reading group very quietly without disturbing the students, examines the message, whispers a response, helps the child having difficulty, and continues directing the reading lesson without skipping a beat! This behavior was called "overlapping" by Kounin.

A characteristic related to managerial success is knowing when an activity needs to be changed and managing that change so smoothly, because irrelevancies are disregarded, that students continue in the same manner without the lesson's losing momentum. Kounin called this "transition smoothness." Arlin (1979) also studied transitions between activities and found that if teachers monitored what was happening in the classroom and provided clear directions so that the transition was structured, then off-task behaviors were reduced.

Kounin (1970) concluded that there are a number of consequences related to teachers' behavior that are often not anticipated. When a teacher disciplines a child in front of other children, there is a "ripple" effect. The ripple effect is influenced by the type of desist the teacher emitted. An angry desist produces emotional conflict—sometimes embarrassment—and does not produce conformity by other members of the class.

It is interesting to note that Kounin found in his 1970 research with kindergarten children that, by increasing repetition of an activity, the activity changed from being liked to being disliked. He concluded that variety and challenge, initiating and maintaining movement, smoothness, and momentum were very important in elementary classrooms. A provocative comparison can be made between this conclusion and the implied finding of the BTES researchers that the more time spent in academic activity the higher the achievement.

In Kounin's kindergarten study he also found that when teachers clarified their meanings by providing information (feedback) to the deviant child along with the desist, the result was more conformity from other children. Firmness, the "I mean it" factor, also produced more conformity than nonconformity in witnesses.

Brophy and Evertson (1976) contrasted successful and less successful teachers and noted that the successful teachers maximized their teaching time with children by monitoring individual effort and providing immediate feedback information to the students. These successful teachers appeared to accept personal responsibility for their students' achievement.

Learning Environment

The classroom environment influences students' behavior. This should not be a surprise to any college student who has sat in a lecture hall and automatically whipped out a notebook and pencil. Seating arrangements in rows, in small groups, in a circle, in the front of the room or the back—all influence interaction of students with each other and with the teacher. When seated in an auditorium or a library, in a gymnasium or a reading circle, students' behavior is affected by the environmental setting and the resultant expectations.

The management of the classroom is similarly affected by the environmental setting. Kounin and Sherman (1979) described the fit between preschoolers' behavior and the environmental setting. Preschoolers, who were not imposed upon by adult structure, used a free-play setting and 95 per cent of the time played without dawdling, wandering, crying, or fighting. The author has similarly observed preschoolers in a free-play setting, not constrained by adult pressure, acting totally involved. Kounin and Sherman concluded that the preschoolers behave "schoolish" and act appropriately when the setting fits the activities.

When the classroom environment does not support the activities a teacher chooses, management problems arise. For example, in a classroom where the tables are in straight rows and all of the physical space is consumed by those tables, it would be very difficult to develop students' discussion skills. If students do not face each other when they talk, then interaction becomes a back and forth process from student to teacher. As a consequence, the students will not be listening to each other; they will be waiting for the teacher to "call" on them. This type of lesson is really a recitation period rather than a class discussion. The effects of this lesson will be student boredom, lags between responses, off-task behavior (horseplay), and teacher frustration.

MANAGEMENT PROBLEM

The students were crowded at lunch tables—about 16 children to each table. They ate their bagged lunches and banged elbows with each other. Some spilled milk; some exchanged sandwiches and desserts. Papers and lunches were flying through the air. The lunch area was dirty and excessively noisy.

The lunch supervisors blew their whistles. "Unless you stop talking and clean up, we will not excuse you to play on the playground."

Do you think the supervisors were right to ask the students to be quiet?

How would adults act in the same setting?

Discuss what you would do to improve this situation.

WHAT WOULD YOU DO IF . . . ?

Unbeknown to its captor, the small lizard escaped from its cardboard prison and slithered across the room toward the learning center. Charlie, the lizard's owner, had placed the cardboard box on the floor under his seat. Charlie was what his teacher described as "hyper," and he kicked the lid off the box without being aware that he did so. Charlie had not bothered to tell his teacher that the lizard was visiting the classroom.

It was 10:10 AM and many of the students began to close their books (noisily) in anticipation of recess. The teacher ignored the disturbance, but noted the time and began to give directions to prepare for recess. As the teacher did so, Bonnie saw the lizard and screamed; Erik fell over as he tried to capture it, and Charlie came running. "It's mine," he screamed.

The teacher hollered, "Everyone stop. Right now. Don't move."

What can you infer from this incident about this teacher's classroom management skills? Think about:

1. Classroom organization and rules
2. Student responsibility and discipline
3. Teacher behavior: withitness, clarity, firmness

If you were this teacher, would you discuss the problem(s) with the whole class or with just Charlie?

What would you say to Bonnie and Erik?

Would you do anything about the students who noisily anticipated recess? If so, what?

Grouping for Instruction

Current research on grouping appears to associate large group instruction with formal, traditional classroom teaching and small group instruction with flexible, more open teaching approaches. In fact, the effective classroom teacher uses both approaches throughout the school day. The skills involved in managing group behavior are basic to classroom management and effective instruction.

Why Group?

Students attending my classes are often surprised by the fact that I will group them in clusters of five to seven students on the first or second day of class and present the groups with a problem or an issue for discussion.

During the 15 or 20 minutes that the groups meet (out on the lawn, in adjoining rooms, and in our lecture room) I will tour the groups: to listen to their discussion, to observe them, to make a suggestion if it appears to be needed.

Having given the groups a designated time to come back and meet as a whole class, I return to the classroom to await their entrance.

The change in their behavior is remarkable. They had left the room as individuals; they straggled out, wary and a little apprehensive about doing something that is not typically done in a college classroom. But their return was different. They come in noisily, companionably, and invariably they sit together as comrades.

The debriefing of the activity occurs in two stages. Stage I is substantive. Whenever possible I try to motivate a little bit of conflict among the groups so that the reports are not "group" reports but, in actuality, a whole class discussion.

Some Students Work Better Independently; Others Perform Better in Group Situations.

As voices rise and adults forget their discussion manners—interrupting each other—I nonchalantly ask, "By the way, is there anyone who did not talk in their small group discussion?"

They look around and sheepishly acknowledge that "everyone contributed." This initiates Stage II, in which we discuss my behavior as teacher and their behavior as learners.

I usually end this session by asking the students, "What did you learn from working in a small group that was valuable?" Invariably they will respond with some of the advantages of grouping:

1. they felt less inhibited about talking out
2. they learned from their classmates
3. they felt involved

Every teaching approach has advantages and disadvantages. The effective teacher chooses the teaching strategy that best meets the needs of the teaching situation in order to accomplish the desired outcomes. Before reading the discussion of group work, study the charts of specified advantages and disadvantages for small and large group instruction.

Discussion: Large Group Instruction

Careful study of the two tables should reveal that each strategy has both conflicting and contradictory values. For example, for large group instruction Table 3.1 states that advantages include teacher-centered authority and single continuous signal source; this means that control should be facilitated. Yet at the same time it states that task involvement *may* be reduced and that the teacher *may* be tempted to make an example of disruptive students. What is the explanation of this?

According to the research of Kounin and Sherman (1979), certain environmental settings have more holding power than others. Large group settings have the potential to decrease social ineffective behavior; therefore, if the teacher can hold students' attention, the teacher will be the sole and continuing "signal" source. If the lesson does not lag and the teacher can manage the disparate interests of the group, high involvement can be achieved.

The BTES study emphasized the efficiency of large group instruction because when a new skill is to be taught the teacher can introduce it to all students at the same time. The skill can be modeled by the teacher, and controlled practice can occur under the teacher's watchful eyes. Proper implementation of this approach facilitates keeping the students "on task," thereby increasing academically engaged time.

Why, then, may control problems be more difficult during large group instruction? The discussion in Chapter 2 on the ways in which children differ should have provided some insight into why this approach is not always successful. Hearing and vision problems or the physical size of some students may be a factor. When students cannot hear or see, they cause problems. Learning style differences are not provided for when all students must

TABLE 3.1. Large Group Instruction.

Advantages	Disadvantages (possible)
1. Efficient means for input: lecture films, guests, demonstration	1. Reduces individual responsibility
2. Develops sense of belonging	2. Subordinates individual needs to whole group needs
3. Facilitates teaching of new skill	3. Impedes differentiation of instruction
4. Promotes teacher-centered authority	4. Impedes social participation
5. Provides single continuous signal source	5. Increases physical problems (vision, hearing)
	6. Increases impersonality of teaching/learning
	7. Reduces task involvement
	8. Tempts teacher to make an "example" of disruptive student

TABLE 3.2. Small Group Instruction.

Advantages	Disadvantages (possible)
1. Facilitates communication	1. Excites students
2. Promotes interaction	2. Wastes time, if students' group skills are poor
3. Motivates involvement	3. Wastes time, when introducing new skills
4. Encourages assisting others, accepting responsibility	4. Subordinates high and low achiever needs to accomplish group goals
5. Teaches bargaining, negotiation	5. Subordinates academic content for group process skills
6. Promotes decision making	6. Extroverted, aggressive students may overrule and subordinate introvertive students
7. Necessitates listening to others' viewpoints	
8. Necessitates sharing own values	
9. Promotes cooperation, group production, and group learning	
10. Allows differentiation of instruction	
11. Frees teacher to observe, listen, diagnose.	

attend in the same way. Disinterest of some students will be a consequence. (Remember Barry's classmates at the beginning of Chapter 2?) Large group instruction assumes that all students need the same "lesson," but this may not be true. Large group instruction is impersonal and so can decrease involvement. Finally, the spatial arrangement of the students during instruction may cause problems. If students are spread too far away from the teacher, they can pursue their own interests without teacher monitoring; or, if students are seated too close together, the result may be disruptive behavior. A typical mistake of the beginning teacher is to get upset when students begin to fidget and "mess around." In an uncontrolled burst of temper, the teacher is tempted to lash out at the disruptive student or at the student the teacher thinks is disruptive. This behavior results in embarrassment for others as well as for the "target" of the outburst and is known to decrease students' achievement.

A Sense of Belonging in Classroom and in School Motivates Attendance, Cooperative Behaviors, and Enhances the Ability to Learn.

Sense of Belonging. It is very important for students to feel a sense of identity with their classmates and their teacher. A sense of belonging motivates attendance at school, encourages cooperative behavior, and enhances the ability to learn. Classroom management is facilitated when students learn to care about others and about their own role in the group. At the beginning of the school year, this sense of belonging has to be cultivated. Each teacher works to develop pride in group identity. Both schoolwide and classroom activities are used to develop this ego-satisfying behavior.

Large group activities have the potential to develop this important characteristic. Experienced teachers develop it in a variety of ways.

The following examples will illustrate:

Ms. Brown wrote the words to a song on the board. She seated her third-grade students on the floor in front of her. Then, using the autoharp, she began to sing. After singing the whole song through, she taught it line by line to the students. After several minutes of singing and when the students knew the words, the teacher encouraged them to put their arms on the shoulders of their classmates and sing and sway to the music.

In this way Ms. Brown developed what human relations specialists call *oneness*. Choral speaking is another fine strategy to develop group cooperation. A sixth-grade class (the author's) learned the words to "America Singing" and performed it in choral fashion. This selection requires four groups of children and a narrator or soloist.

AMERICA SINGING*

SOLOIST: I hear America, America singing.

North
South
East
West

(Each group calls out its designation in turn, in unison, in clear staccato tones.)

SOLOIST: A song of praise, a song of work, a song of freedom's making.

NORTH (in unison): Here are forest trails, shining waters, broad wheat fields.

Farmers
Workers
Business
Pleasure
Deer
Fish
Birch bark
Snow
Hills
Forests

(Each of these is called out rapidly, one at a time, by first one and then another of the 10.)

NORTH (in unison): Hear the ring of axe, the grind of tractor, the lap of water. See the smoke of business, hear the noisy clatter—in this land of sky and water, this land of tall tales.

* Berne Caroline Thune, *Elementary English*, Vol. XXV, March 1948.

SOUTH (in unison): A place of warmth and sunshine, cotton fields, plantations, song and laughter.

Oil
Peanuts
Cotton pickers
Share croppers
Planters
White pine (Separately by 10, one at a time)
Coconut
Palm
Alligator
Mesa

SOUTH (in unison): Hear the song of workers, the sigh of wind through pine, pueblo; the mating call of alligator—in this land of field and canyon, where the warm sun shines.

EAST (in unison): Feel the tang of salt spray, hear the muffled fog horn, taste the deep sea scallops!

Rocks
Sea horses
Cotton mills
New York
Appalachians
Fields (Singly by each of the students)
Streams
Homes
Fishermen
Whirr of wheels

EAST (in unison): Over the mountains white clouds blowing, over the cities smoke clouds louring; turn of wheel and quiet spaces, land of rock and ocean.

WEST (in unison): Plains and mountains, forests and deserts. Rugged land and rugged people.

Snow-capped Rockies
Timberline
Rushing water
Far horizons
Orchards
Oranges
Redwoods
Indians
Cowboys
Ten gallon hats

WEST (in unison): Space and height, long trails winding, cry of coyote, place of rugged beauty.

(Once again each group separately calls out its designation in unison in clear staccato tones.)

North
South
East
West

Now all four groups speak together for the first time: Oh! land of plenty, land of fruitful harvest, land of contract, land of promise, land of freedom, land we love.

SOLOIST (with reverent feeling):

Vision for the worker,
Vision for the employer,
Vision for the statesman,
Vision for today and tomorrow and tomorrow.

Rhythmic and physical activities performed in a group also have the potential to develop strong group feeling. The King (1975) text provides a fine resource for group activities that will help accomplish group identity. One such activity encourages the exploration of body movements and necessitates working together. Students are divided into four groups. Two of the groups, holding hands, are required to exhibit a shape or movement with their bodies. They are required to hold the position while continuing contact with each other. Once the position is formed, the other two groups are required to fill in unused space within, around, or under the first two groups. The activity can be repeated changing the order of the groups.

It is extremely important that group activities such as these be evaluated. Depending upon the nature of the activity, the teacher should ask questions, such as the following:

- How did you depend upon others?
- How did your classmates help you?
- How did you help others?
- What did you like best about this activity?
- What was difficult about the activity?
- What skills did the activity require?

Activities should be chosen on the basis of their potential to develop group cooperation, responsibility, respect, and dependence upon classmates. More sophisticated activities that are of longer duration are also appropriate. For example, an activity that takes students out into the community to perform a service in their own neighborhood has the potential for developing group solidarity and oneness.

Discussion: Small Group Instruction

Rosenshine (1977) noted that large group direct instruction can make the classroom a very grim place to be. It is apparent from the research on direct instruction that to accomplish creative goals, intuitive thinking, discovery, exploration, and inquiry, small group instruction with less structure is more suitable.

Small groups can be arranged to take advantage of student diversity as well as homogeneous needs. The heterogeneous group can be arranged by the teacher to take advantage of students' special abilities (thereby increasing the likelihood of peer modeling and assistance) or, on some occasions, the students can choose their own group arrangement. (This affects student motivation to participate.) For teaching and monitoring specific skill development, the group should be arranged homogeneously, but in social studies, science, health, art, music, or physical education, the heterogeneous group is appropriate.

Small group work facilitates the differentiation of instruction. It is more difficult for teachers to manage group behavior while individualizing instruction; utilization of small group instruction provides a means to correspond instruction with the precise needs of the individual. It also allows students to learn from each other and to develop respect for classmates.

Sometimes in the modern classroom we lose sight of the fact that a major purpose of the school is to foster democratic behaviors. If we expect young adults to participate meaningfully in our society, then they need appropriate experiences that teach social participatory skills. These skills can only be

TABLE 3.3. Management of Small Group Instruction.

Potential Problems	Means to Avoid
1. Need for structure	1. Appoint or direct students to choose a leader, recorder and/or reporter.
2. Need for a system of rules	2. Define appropriate behavior; define operating procedures. Chart the rules.
3. Need to communicate group problems	3. Ensure that students know how to get your assistance.
4. Need to share problems and accomplishments	4. Provide evaluation time at the end of each work period.
5. Content should not be subordinate to process	5. Evaluate substantive findings, then group process; do not focus on individual behavior.
6. Group size	6. Uneven number of students facilitates compromise; optimal group: 5–7.
7. Material and resource needs	7. Anticipate, monitor, and provide necessary materials.
8. Groups fail to "get started"	8. If it is a continuing activity begin by asking all of the groups to identify what they intend to accomplish. If it is a one-shot or new activity, verify that each group understands what is expected.
9. Physical space	9. Provide and designate a working space for each group so that groups do not intrude upon each other.
10. Deviant behavior (individual)	10. If behavior cannot be corrected with a reminder, decide what you will do: (a) Have the disruptive student watch another group and report during the evaluation period: "What makes groups function smoothly, what inhibits effective group work." (b) Assign the deviant an individual project; monitor its completion. (c) Share information with and ask for assistance from the parents.
11. Deviant behavior (group)	11. Assess whether the problem is a consequence of misunderstanding about the objective. If so, clarify and provide information to refocus group thinking. If there is a nonacademic reason, conference with the group using the best "I mean it" expression; let them know what you expect of them; then monitor their adherence to class rules. Assess whether or not the combination of students in the group should be changed.

taught when students are confronted by each other and forced to work together. Young children who always get their own way become unsocialized beings; the moment that they are forced to relate to others necessitates the identification of areas of agreement and disagreement with others. This in turn motivates confrontation (see Piaget and Kohlberg, Chapter 2), and the use of persuasion, negotiation, and cooperation. Self-control is learned in the process, but it is a developmental process.

Management Suggestions for Small and Large Group Instruction

Preplanning (anticipating the potential problems) will alleviate most of the difficulties involved in either instructional approach.

TABLE 3.4. Management of Large Group Instruction.

Potential Problems	Means to Avoid
1. General disinterest	1. Choose lesson needed by most students; motivate interest.
2. High or low achievers' disinterest	2. Provide special information to interest the highs; comfort the lows by stating that you will be available to give additional assistance after the lesson.
3. Deviant behavior due to space problems (crowding)	3. Direct the less mature students to places where they will not be trouble to others. Arrange the room to accommodate this type of instruction.
4. Inattention due to space problems (class too spread out)	4. This happens most frequently when students are at tables or desks and the teacher does not establish eye contact. Have students arrange chairs in a three-sided square to face you, or seat students on floor in front of chalkboard. Do not start lesson until all students have directed their eyes on you.
5. Deviant behavior as a consequence of physical problems	5. Provide for individual needs. Seat handicapped students appropriately.
6. Impersonality of instruction	6. Involve students by using short and frequent questions. Wait, and encourage responses.

How to Begin Small Group Instruction

Regardless of the subject, small group instruction necessitates specific teacher and learner behaviors. The next episode should provide you with some ideas about how to begin small group instruction.

Mr. Atwater had some of his first graders on the floor in front of him; the rest were seated on chairs behind the group on the floor. On a low table in front of the group, Mr. Atwater had a large horseshoe magnet and a number of objects with it: paper, pencil, scissors, crayon, rubberband, penny, nails, eraser, paper clip, ball, and string.

Motivation

T.: Who can tell us what this is? (He holds up the magnet. Many hands go up, and the teacher chooses one student to respond.)

Sue: I bet it's a magnet.

T.: What does a magnet do?

Sue: It picks things up.

T.: How could we find out?

Bert: See if it will pick those things up that you have on the table.

T.: Good idea, Bert. (He uses the magnet to try to pick up the string.)

Jean: Magnets won't pick up string; only certain things.

T.: What do you mean, Jean?

Jean: Well I know string won't work.

T.: Come show us what will.

Jean: (Jean uses magnet and picks up a pin, nail and paper clip.)

T.: All right, we can see that Jean made the magnet pick up three items. We also know that it did not pick up the string. In what way are these three items alike? (He holds up the magnet with the pin, nail, and clip.)

William: I think they must all be made of metal.

T.: What kind of metal will magnets pick up? (The teacher looks around, and students appear to be unsure.)

Assignment

Today, I thought you might like to be scientists and explore a problem. I am going to ask you to work in small groups. Each group will have some magnets and a bag of objects. Your job is to find out what the magnet will pull and to make a rule about the objects that magnets will pull. If your

RESEARCH FINDINGS

Stallings (1976), in a national study of Follow-through and Nonfollow-through classrooms, related a number of cognitive and affective aspects of instruction to grouping procedures in the first- and third-grade classrooms.

Cooperation: Cooperative behaviors were more likely to occur in classrooms where children selected their own groups part of the time and participated in a wide variety of activities throughout the day.

Independence: Independent behavior was more likely in classrooms in which students selected their own seating and groups part of the time, participated in a wide variety of activities, and utilized an assortment of audiovisual and exploratory materials.

Absence: Students were absent less frequently when they worked in more "open" classrooms where there was a high rate of independence, individualized instruction, open-ended questioning, child questioning, and adult response.

Reading: First-grade students achieved higher gains when taught in small groups; third-grade students achieved higher gains when taught in groups of about nine students.

Math: First-grade students achieved higher gains when taught in small groups; third-grade students achieved higher gains when taught in large groups. Nonverbal problem-solving skills improved when students were taught in more flexible classrooms using manipulative materials.

group makes its rule before the other groups are ready, I will come over and suggest another problem to investigate. When you think your group is ready, or if your group has a problem, have your group leader raise his hand and I will come over and listen to your rule or give you some help.

Organization

Mr. Atwater distributed magnets and bags of materials to six different locations in the room. The bags contained a penny, nails, wire, screws, pins, and hair curlers. Then he said:

T.: We will need to work together cooperatively. I think we had better make some group work rules. What should they be?

Joe: I think we better have a captain or a leader.

T.: Good idea, Joe; I will write the rules on the board. What else?

Mary: We need someone to write down *our* ideas.

T.: Yes, but since writing may be a problem, how about if each group chooses a group reporter for our discussion? (Students nod, and teacher writes another rule.) How will you decide what to do when you are in your group?

Ben: I guess we better plan.

T.: Good point, Ben. We need to plan the experiment. Suppose I write, "Plan the experiment."

Sam: Then we need to do the experiment.

T.: OK, so number 4 should be, "Perform the experiment." What will number 5 be?

Terry: We better discuss what we found out.

T.: OK, number 5 should be, "Talk about the experiment," and number 6 better be, "Prepare for class discussion." Is there anything else?

Midge: Cleanup?

T.: Yes, indeed. Let's read our group work rules together.

Group Work Rules

1. Choose a group leader.
2. Choose a group reporter.
3. Plan the experiment.
4. Perform the experiment.
5. Talk about the experiment.
6. Prepare for class discussion.
7. Clean up.

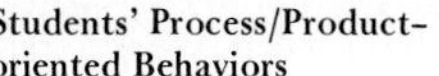

Figure 3.1. Group Work Behaviors.

T.: Now, boys and girls, when I call your names please go to the area I designate for your group. Remember to move quietly so that the students who are waiting can hear their names called. If I need your attention I will flash the lights. (Each group is quietly dismissed to go to work.)

As the groups worked, Mr. Atwater walked around and observed their progress. Each group had several different types of magnets as well as their bag of materials. As Mr. Atwater observed each group, he would suggest to them: "Arrange the objects in two groups, those that the magnet will pull and those that the magnet will not pull. Find out if all magnets pull the same things."

When the groups thought they were finished, Mr. Atwater would listen to their rule. Sometimes the students were not quite accurate, and that would lead to Mr. Atwater's telling them the names of the metals in the objects that they were testing.

For the groups that were right on target, Mr. Atwater had prepared an additional experiment. He asked them to find out if magnets can pull objects through other materials. He suggested that they find out by using books, paper, cardboard and anything else that was not too thick.

Evaluation

After about ten minutes, the students appeared to have concluded their work. Mr. Atwater flashed the lights and all students looked up expectantly. Next he suggested that they leave their magnets and bags on the table, and he invited each group back to the front of the room to discuss their experiments.

T.: Did you test all of your materials and all of your magnets? Sharon, I know you are the reporter for your group; tell us how your group planned its work. (Each group contributes its planning steps.) What did you do next? (Several groups mention that he has suggested that they arrange their objects into two groups—those that pulled and those that did not.) Well, what did you find out? Which objects belonged together? (He writes two headings on the board:)

Objects Magnet Pulled *Objects Magnet Did Not Pull*

The students completed the list classifying the objects. Then Mr. Atwater asked: "Did all the magnets pull the same objects?" The students responded positively. "Well, then, it's time to find out what we learned." One student tentatively raised hand and said, "Magnets pull metals." Mr. Atwater went to the two lists on the board and wrote in the names of the metals or metal alloys in each. Then he asked again, "Will magnets pull all metals?" William responded, "No. Magnets only pull objects that have iron or steel in them."[1]

Mr. Atwater smiled and said: "By golly, you have stated a good rule about magnets and he wrote it on the board. Now boys and girls, what did you think about your first experience working in small groups during science? Let's talk about it. Mr. Atwater led the discussion so that students responded to the following questions:

Group Work Evaluation

- When you do group work, should everyone get to talk? (yes)
- Is it possible for all members of the group to agree? (No.)
- How did you decide what to do when you did not agree?
- Why was it a good idea to try the experiment in different ways?
- Why is it important to listen to all members of the group?
- What was most difficult about group work?
- What was easiest?
- In what ways was your group successful?
- If you were to work in groups tomorrow, what would you want to remember?

Reviewing the components of Mr. Atwater's lesson using small group instruction, we note that there were definite steps involved in the process. These included:

1. Large Group Instruction and Motivation
2. Communication of the Assignment
3. Organizing for Work
   - Standards for Group Work
   - Providing Materials
   - What to do if the group needs help
   - How the teacher can get students' attention, if needed
   - Time Constraints (if any)
   - Assigning work settings
4. Small Group Instructional Process
5. Evaluation
   - Content Evaluation
   - Group Work Evaluation

What Do Children Learn?

Among all the other things that the school teaches, children learn to recognize success and failure. The student who has difficulty learning to read experiences failure. After repeated failure in reading, everything the child does is affected. Lack of success in reading affects other subject fields, and after a period of time peers and teacher recognize the student as a loser. If the child perceives this conception by others, s/he learns to play the role of a loser and accepts and anticipates extended failure.

Effective, conscientious teachers can avert the disaster of recurring failure by de-emphasizing reading. This is not to suggest that reading lacks importance, merely that appropriate goals can be set and legitimate rewards bestowed so that all children can earn praise from peers and teacher and experience success. This means that many activities that utilize abilities other than reading skills will be planned throughout the school day and that these activities will be recognized as important. Table 3.5 identifies four sets of behavior needed by children to *feel* successful at school. If activities are developed to promote each of the behavioral goals, students will have the opportunity to be successful at one or more activities throughout the school day. Activities should focus on "doing" and reasoning.

[1] Content for this lesson was based upon information in Peter C. Gega, *Science in Elementary Education*, 3d ed. (New York: Wiley, 1977), pp. 112–113.

TABLE 3.5. School Success-oriented Behaviors.

		Means to Achieve	
Emergent Behaviors	**Behavioral Goals**	**Teacher Behavior**	**Learner Behavior**
Ego-satisfying behaviors	Self-confidence Self-respect Optimism Security Status	Define class organization, structure, requirements, constraints. Provide motivation, acceptance, clarification, reinforcement, evaluative procedures. Provide appropriate learning and responsibilities.	With knowledge of class organization, structure, requirements, and constraints, develops personal goals for work, companionship, leisure. Chooses both independent and group activities. Acts as a leader and a participant.
Learner-assertive behaviors	Questing Seeking Searching Defining Analyzing Conceptualizing Evaluating	Develop challenging tasks for independent and group inquiry. Develop problem-solving skills and social conscience skills utilizing conflict situations.	Utilizes vocational research, value clarification skills in large and small groups, and independent tasks. Participates in buzz groups, dramatics, construction, exhibits, debates, interview, panels, reporting.
Independence-oriented behaviors	Initiation Decision making Individuality Creativity Dependability	Provide time, space, materials for independent projects; environmental, creative, skill oriented.	Defines goal, decides means, develops projector specific task. Participates in cartooning, crossword puzzles, cooking, modeling, sewing, reading, picturemaking hobbies.
Group-satisfying behaviors	Cooperation Rationality Responsibility Respectfulness	Develop group projects and tasks: research, conflict problems, art projects, music making, science experiments, group roles in simulations.	Participates as both leader and group member in small group projects, discussions, games, simulations, art and music works, experiments, choral speaking, listening activities, puppeteering, plays, service projects.

Source: Johanna K. Lemlech, *Handbook for Successful Urban Teaching* (N.Y.: Harper, 1977), p. 58.

The important point is that there be a wide range of activities provided so that in the course of the day every student can be good at something.

It is especially important that students rotate roles. Billy should not always be a group leader or a demonstrator of skills. Mabel should not always be the "tutee". If students are to feel successful, they must perceive that others are aware of their strengths. This will only occur through peer interaction, and it must be programmed by the teacher.

In a fifth-grade classroom, Ms. Henry noted that although Bert was able to observe every detail in a picture, he read poorly. Bert was often aggressive, and she recognized that he had a very low self-concept. It occurred to her that it might be possible to utilize Bert's visual strengths to build his self-confidence and ultimately develop reading skills. She asked Bert if he owned a camera. When he responded positively, she suggested that the two of them conference about a project. (Before the conference, Ms. Henry contacted Bert's mother to obtain her permission to initiate a visual literacy program for Bert.) Bert developed a project that involved his photographing the community around the school and interviewing homeowners and business people that he knew. He presented the

RESEARCH FINDINGS—MAINSTREAMING

Slavin (1981) described Student Team Learning (STL): After teacher presentation of a lesson, students are grouped in teams of four or five; together the students try to master worksheets on the lesson; the students take individual quizzes on the material; students' scores are based upon the improvement they achieve over their own past average; this improvement score becomes a team score. Using this strategy, Madden and Slavin (1980) learned that Student Team Learning would help nonmainstreamed students accept their mainstreamed classmates.

Positive effects of working together using the Student Team Learning model were also achieved by Cooper and others (1980) in a study of the acceptance of mainstreamed learning disabled children.

project to his classmates. Bert learned about the community using a camera and a tape recorder. Other members of the class learned about the community by reading and utilizing resource materials. Bert's activities were developed with Ms. Henry's assistance. The behavior Ms. Henry was focusing on and the activities used to achieve the performance components are as follows:

Ego-Satisfying Behavior	**Activities to Achieve**
Self-confidence	Chooses to take neighborhood pictures with own camera.
Self-responsibility	Pursues task and completes pictures.
Optimism	Plans and sets goals.
Security	Communicates plan to classmates.
Status	Demonstrates how to take pictures, use of light meter, focusing on center of interest.
Learner-Assertive Behavior	
Questing Seeking Searching Defining Analyzing Conceptualizing Evaluating	Interviews homeowners and business people. Tapes interviews. Edits tapes and pictures. Prepares tapes and pictures for classroom demonstration.
Independence-Oriented Behaviors	**Activities to Achieve**
Initiation Decision making Creativity Individuality Dependability	Mounts pictures on poster board. Develops a second tape of background music. Coordinates interviews with background music; sequences pictures. Presents project to class and answers questions about it.
Group-Satisfying Behaviors	
Cooperation Rationality Responsibility Respectfulness	Works as a small group leader to discuss community problems and to plan a community service project.

When Bert and other members of his class were engaged in small group work, they had to listen to each other and take turns talking. Group work in Bert's classroom was practiced almost daily. Students rotated roles of group leader and recorder. Ms. Henry taught them to participate. As a result of repeated experiences with group work, the students were actively engaged in constructive reasoning.

By changing the typical projects in this classroom, Ms. Henry manipulated the evaluative feedback that each child receives. Bert was perceived by his classmates as a conscientious, creative, rational person and Bert began to look at himself as a leader. In time, Ms. Henry will have Bert talk about his pictures and write stories about them. The stories will be typed and Bert will develop reading skills by using his own instructional materials.

RESEARCH FINDINGS

Cohen (1981), speaking before the Association for Supervision and Curriculum Development national conference, noted that her research and the research of others had determined that more student participation and effort equaled more active learning behavior.

Chapter Summary

The concept of direct instruction has implications for the teaching of essential basic skills. Effective skill instruction is characterized by small group instruction, teacher direction, academic focus, and orientation to the individual in the group.

Open teaching approaches are more appropriate for inquiry/problem solving. The teacher's choice of instructional approach should be based on who is to be taught and what is to be taught.

Studies of teacher behaviors have identified approaches that lead to more effective management of the classroom. Planning curriculum, organizing procedures and resources, arranging the environment to maximize efficiency, and monitoring student progress all contribute to successful teaching.

Effective classroom teachers use both large and small group teaching approaches throughout the school day. The skills involved in managing group behavior are basic to classroom management and effective instruction.

Social participation skills need to be taught in order to foster democratic behavior. Responsibility for the management of large and small group instruction was discussed with instructional guidelines stated for beginning small group work.

Children learn to recognize success and failure. Success behavior can be taught in school by setting appropriate goals and bestowing legitimate rewards. Activities that utilize a wide range of abilities need to be planned throughout the school day. Every student should be (and can be) successful at one or more activities each day.

Classroom Application Exercises

1. What are the classroom management procedures exhibited in Mr. Atwater's science lesson? Use the following categories to make your list:
   - Planning
   - Arranging the Environment
   - Organizing Student Progress
   - Anticipating Potential Problems
2. If you were Mr. Atwater, what would you teach the students about magnetism the next time you have a science lesson?
3. Work with a learning disabled student. Develop a problem that will provoke questions in order to develop the student's problem-solving ability. (Provide the student with manipulative materials to solve the problem.)

   Example
   $$\begin{array}{r} 8 \\ -\square \\ \hline 4 \end{array}$$
4. Plan a group activity to develop group identity and a sense of belonging.
5. Identify some challenging tasks to develop learner-assertive behaviors.

Suggested Readings for Extending Study

Gage, N. L., and David C. Berliner. *Educational Psychology*. Chicago: Rand McNally & Company, 1979.

Lemlech, Johanna. *Classroom Management*. New York: Harper & Row, Publishers, 1979.

Maslow, Abraham H. *Toward a Psychology of Being*. New York: D. Van Nostrand Company, 1962.

Miller, John P. *Humanizing the Classroom.* New York: Praeger Publishers, Inc., 1976.

Newmark, Gerald. *This School Belongs to You & Me.* New York: Hart Publishing Co., Inc., 1976.

Postman, N. and C. Weingartner. *Teaching as a Subversive Activity*. New York: Delacorte Press, 1971.

Reilly, Robert R. and Ernest L. Lewis. *Educational Psychology*. New York: Macmillan Publishing Company, Inc., 1983.

Rosenthal, Robert, and Lenore Jacobson. *Pygmalion in the Classroom.* New York: Holt, Rinehart and Winston, 1968.

Williams, Joyce W. and Marjorie Stith. *Middle Childhood.* New York: Macmillan Publishing Company, Inc., 1980.

Chapter 4

Planning and Guiding Learning Experiences

After you have completed the study of this chapter, you should be able to accomplish the following:

1. **Identify and discuss professional responsibilities of teachers.**
2. **Discuss the purposes of learning and interest centers.**
3. **Develop a daily time block schedule for teaching the elementary curriculum.**
4. **Anticipate scheduling needs and priorities for mainstreamed children.**
5. **Identify important tasks for the first day of school.**
6. **Suggest means to get acquainted with students and community.**
7. **Explain the relationship of educational goals to instruction.**
8. **Write instructional objectives at varied cognitive and affective levels.**
9. **Ask questions at varied cognitive and affective levels.**
10. **Select and sequence learning experiences related to objectives utilizing suggested criteria.**
11. **Plan a lesson utilizing suggested procedures.**
12. **Explain the importance of integrating subject fields.**
13. **Identify the daily tasks of the teacher.**

The Day Before the Children Came

The teachers' meeting was scheduled for 8:30 AM the second Monday in September. Both Mary Hogan and Greg Thomas were nervous; both had arrived early at the Martin Luther King elementary school. Thomas had taught at another school in the district, but he still felt a bit insecure. Hogan had student teaching experience in a nearby inner-city school, but this was her first "real" teaching assignment.

Mary and Greg were the only new teachers at the school, so it was not surprising that they became instant friends as they began the task of moving in and acclimating themselves to their new environment. Both were eager to see their classrooms. Mary knew that she would be in the main building; Greg's classroom was a bungalow.

The principal presented the schedule of classes at the meeting. Mary was to be responsible for 31 second graders; Greg would have 36 fifth graders. The school secretary handed out the students' cumulative records, personal health records, and new attendance cards for the coming school year. Mary and Greg learned that all textbooks had been returned to the book room when school closed in June, so they would need to go and pick up their books. Workbooks for spelling and reading would be available, but the teachers were urged not to begin workbooks until the third week of school when the final organization of the classrooms would be set.

When Mary Hogan arrived in her classroom, she noted that the tables were stacked in the middle of the room; there were four bookcases and two taller display tables; there was also a television, one tape recorder, and an old phonograph machine. On top of one of the cupboards Mary saw a chart rack, and in the closet area there was a chart box on wheels apparently available for Mary's use. Mary decided to go to the teacher's room and change into her "grubbies" so that she could begin the task of moving furniture.

She arranged the furniture first, putting the bookcases under the windows and setting several tables under bulletin boards to serve as interest centers. She organized the tables to accommodate the 31 children using an "E" formation. Figure 4.1 illustrates Hogan's room plan. Her plan would

Figure 4.1. Hogan's Room Plan.

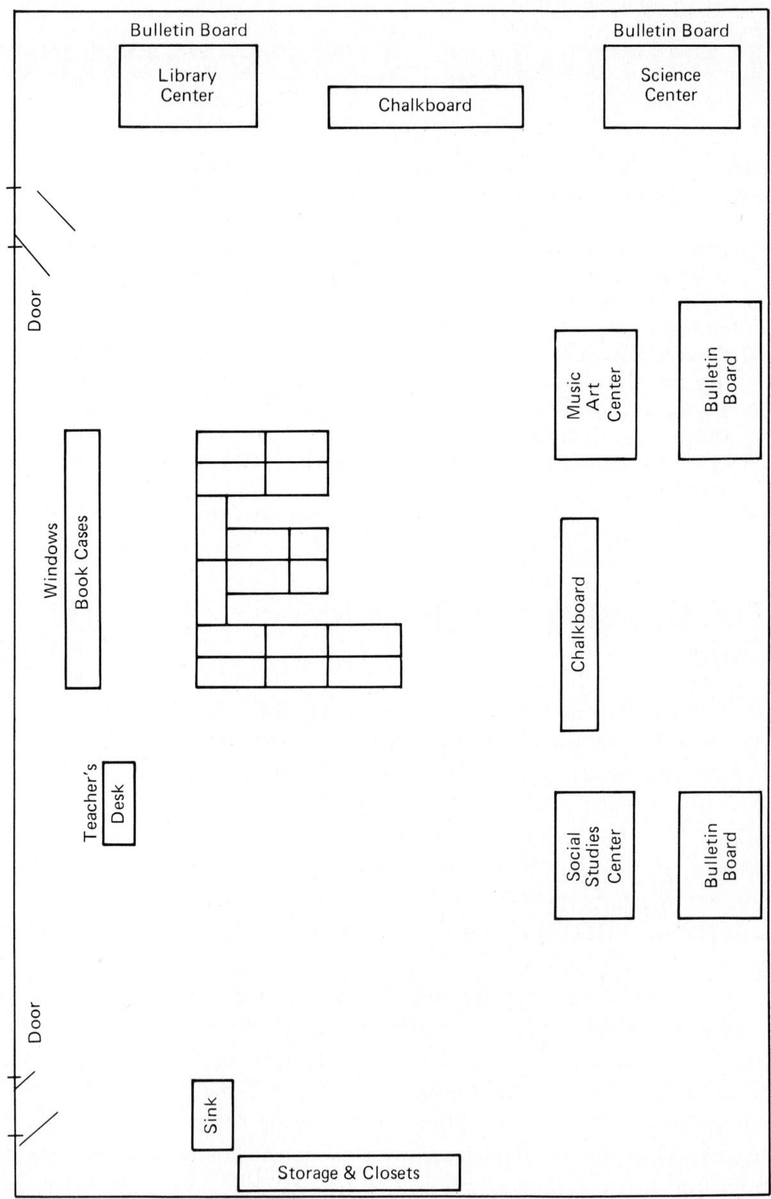

encourage some social interaction among the children. She knew that at times this might be a disadvantage. (The importance of the physical arrangement of the classroom for class discussion is emphasized in Chapter 12). Hogan moved her desk so that it would not impede the traffic pattern in the classroom, nor would it be a focal point.

With the room somewhat organized, Hogan began the task of reading the students' cumulative records. She wanted to find out what reading texts the children had used last semester so that she would have a guide in the choice of appropriate books for this semester. The "cum" card in some school districts provides information about students' past experiences in school, such as achievement test scores, reading textbooks used, and past social studies units. Although Mary Hogan knew that she would do diagnostic testing during the first week of school to pinpoint the children's precise ability levels, she felt it was important that the students begin to read on the first day of school.

Slowly she determined her textbook needs. She conferred with a colleague next door and then began the laborious task of carrying the different books into the classroom. She reviewed pencil, crayon, and paper needs for the room and brought in chart paper and other supplies for herself. As the room began to take shape, she turned her attention to the bulletin boards.

Room Environment

Mary Hogan recognized the value of a cheerful and thought-provoking environment. She wanted to establish interest centers that would support and encourage students to explore and discover, and she hoped that the centers would provide for individual

A Cheerful, Thought-provoking Classroom Environment Encourages Students to Explore and Discover.

differences. As she surveyed her classroom, Mary decided that she would need a science center, an art and music center, a social studies center, and a library center. The library center was the easiest. She hung a beautiful poster of children reading books on the bulletin board. Then, in the bookcase below it, she put out some of her own books which she had begun to collect. On top of the bookcase, using book stands, she opened several books to display a picture of the beginning of a story. On the floor next to the bookcase she put a small round rug and a beanbag cushion. She knew that such furnishings would attract the students.

Science Center. She perused the science text to see if any of the units corresponded to some of her own interests and to see if she had supportive materials to set up a center. She decided to begin with a unit about rocks and minerals because she had done a similar unit in student teaching and she knew she could encourage the children to bring in their favorite rocks. On a table by the bulletin board she placed several baskets. In one basket she placed rocks with different textures, and she decided to write a sign asking the students, *How do these rocks feel*? In another basket she placed rocks that were unusual in color, and near this basket she wrote the sign, *How many colors do you see?* She would plan lessons to encourage the students to categorize the rocks by both texture and shape.

Art and Music Center. On the bulletin board Mary Hogan hung a painting of children dancing. Below the picture she displayed the second-grade music books and her own autoharp. She anticipated that she would also display other instruments, but she felt it might be better to develop room standards before she put out too many temptations.

Social Studies Center. Mary Hogan decided that she wanted to display a series of pictures depicting people's basic needs. She had some pictures of her own, and she thought she would take a look at the school's resource center to see if there were some pictures that she could borrow. Ultimately she decided on one picture depicting a shelter in New Guinea, another picture of farmers irrigating a field, and a third picture of a home vegetable garden. Underneath the pictures appeared the caption, *What do all people need?* Near the bulletin board she placed a small picture file so that the students could browse through the file for other pictures that would help them answer the bulletin board question. Social studies books were also displayed.

Interest Centers and Learning Centers. Mary Hogan knew the difference between the two types of centers and was well aware that she had created interest centers, not learning centers. The learning center is designed to motivate, reinforce, and support students' learning needs. A center approach allows the teacher to differentiate instruction so that individual ability levels and learning style needs can be met. The interest center attempts to lure students, to coax them, and to appeal to their natural inquisitiveness.

Although the day was getting late and Mary Hogan was rapidly becoming exhausted, she had two more important tasks before she left school that first day. She still needed to establish a seating chart so that she could learn to identify the students quickly, and she needed to develop the daily program. She also anticipated taking several of her books home that day and working on specific lesson plans for the first day of school.

Seating Chart. Using her class list and her health cards, Mary began the task of establishing a seating chart. First, she sorted through the health cards to identify students with special problems. She noted that she had one child with a partial hearing loss and another student identified as having a limp because one leg was shorter than the other. She decided on their placement in the classroom first. Then she began to cluster the rest of the children. The principal had told her earlier that she had one student who sometimes had difficulty

A Center Approach Allows Teachers to Differentiate Instruction to Provide for Individual Ability Levels and Learning Style Needs.

working with others; she seated this student so that he only had a neighbor on one side of him instead of on both sides. She did *not* seat students by reading groups, having decided that this practice often had a negative effect on motivation to learn.

The Daily Schedule

In the development of a daily schedule Mary Hogan had studied the elementary curriculum and divided the subjects into major time blocks for teaching purposes. For example:

Language Arts and Reading would include reading, speaking skills, written skills, spelling, listening skills, handwriting, and literature.

Social Studies/Science would include geography, history, political science, economics, psychology, anthropology, sociology, and the science of living things, matter and energy, the study of the earth, and the study of the universe.

Physical Education/Health would include physical fitness, motor skills, and rhythmic experiences, along with personal and community health.

One of Hogan's main concerns was to intermix active experiences and concentrated experiences so that students would not be sitting too long a period of time without the opportunity to move around and stretch. In Hogan's school, first and second graders were at school for five and one-half hours; she was aware that this was a little longer than was customary, and so she wanted to make a special effort to interweave activities carefully. She also intended to use the longer periods of time for integrating subject fields. She knew that there would be occasions when she would want to use the period of time after recess or after lunch for special projects.

Hogan developed the following schedule for her second graders:

8:30–8:40	Class Business/Sharing
8:40–9:40	Reading
9:40–10:00	Lower-Grade Recess
10:00–10:25	Reading/Language Arts
10:25–10:45	Spelling and Handwriting
10:45–11:10	Physical Education/Health
11:10–11:40	Mathematics
11:40–12:40	Lunch
12:40–12:55	Literature/Music
12:55–1:55	Social Studies/Science/Art
1:55–2:00	Cleanup/Sharing/Dismissal

Greg Thomas's schedule provides a contrast. Remember that his students were fifth graders and were at school from 8:30 to 2:30 PM. Greg's daily schedule looked like this:

8:30–8:35	Class Business
8:35–10:00	Reading
10:00–10:20	Upper-Grade Recess
10:20–11:20	Social Studies/Science/Art
11:20–12:00	Language/Spelling/Handwriting
12:00–1:00	Lunch
1:00–1:40	Mathematics
1:40–2:10	Physical Education/Health
2:10–2:30	Music/Literature/Language

APPLICATION OF RESEARCH

Research on the allocation of time (Chapter 3) indicated the importance of providing a moderately high amount of time for language arts (reading) and mathematics. Both Hogan and Thomas were apparently applying this research in their schedule of allocated time.

The Daily Schedule and Mainstreamed Students

Mary Hogan had two handicapped children who were in her classroom part of each school day. As she planned her daily schedule she thought they would be able to participate during recess, physical education/health, lunch, and the afternoon program which included literature, music, and social studies. She knew that she would have to consult with the special education teacher, and that it might even be possible for the special education children to join the second graders for mathematics.

Greg Thomas had also accepted and considered several handicapped students. He anticipated that these students would join the rest of his group during recess, lunch, social studies/science/art (10:20–11:20), and possibly the entire afternoon when he had mathematics, physical education, music/literature/language.

Both teachers knew that the essential skills of reading and math were often individualized for the handicapped student and taught in the special education resource room.

APPLICATION OF RESEARCH

Planning cooperative group activities so that handicapped and nonhandicapped students pursue common goals is vital to the success of social integration for handicapped and nonhandicapped students.

The First Day of School

Mary Hogan's principal had cautioned the teachers that it was likely there would be a number of new pupils enrolling the first day of school. As a consequence she suggested that teachers plan academic tasks of a review nature so that the teachers could monitor how well students were working and yet be "free" to give attention to a new student if the need arose.

Using the *reading* group lists that she had compiled, Hogan chose fairly easy stories to review with the students during reading. She manuscripted the key words in the stories on tagboard and planned to use them in a "pocket" chart. She developed follow-up materials for each group and wrote the follow-up on large pieces of newsprint. She developed some "extra" tasks for fast workers.

In *math*, she wrote out a worksheet to be duplicated in the morning. She did not intend to group the students for math that first day. She also wrote the answers to the problems on a piece of newsprint because she wanted to begin immediately to prepare the students to correct their own work.

For *spelling*, Mary decided to teach the spelling of her own name to the students plus the words *class*, *room*, *school*, and *game*. She intended to emphasize manuscript writing as the children studied spelling.

Knowing that the students were likely to get restless the first day after summer vacation, Hogan chose several fun books to read to the class. She also planned some rousing songs to develop group feeling.

For *language*, she chose a number of simple words that the students could learn to alphabetize. She would write these words on the chalkboard and explain to the students how and why alphabetizing is important. If there was any spare time, she intended to read some poetry and choral verse to the students.

She planned to talk to the students about the bulletin boards. She would help them read the captions and ask them to identify what interested them. Her intent was to begin the *science unit* that first day by asking children to name the colors they saw in the rocks. She would also ask the students to describe how the rocks felt, and then introduce the concept of "texture." She hoped that they would identify the words *smooth*, *rough*, *slippery*, *jagged*.[1]

[1] J. Lewis and I. Potter, *The Teaching of Science in the Elementary School* (Englewood Cliffs, N.J., Prentice-Hall, 1970), pp. 63–65.

For *physical education* she would play the game, "Around The World." The children would be organized into two concentric circles. The inside circle sits down on the playground, while the outside circle stands behind a seated player. The teacher gives a direction ("skip") and the outside group follows the direction (skips) around the circle until the teacher blows a whistle. Then the outside circle must scamper to stand behind one of the seated players. Several "extra" children are in the center of the circle, and when the whistle blows they, too, try to find a place behind a seated player. After a few minutes the two circles change places. Hogan remembered that this was a very active and exciting game for second graders, and she hoped that it would extract some of the wiggles from the students!

Setting Standards

With most of her plans made for the first day of school, Mary turned her attention to classroom management details. She thought about her room arrangement and pondered the traffic pattern. She would discuss exiting and entering patterns with the students. She was also concerned about the need for classroom monitors, so she prepared a pocket chart for that purpose. She expected the students to be able to handle classroom routines without her direction. The following monitoring jobs would have to be performed by the students: door, lights, play equipment, office, window, lunch count, library, art, paper, attendance, books, flag, centers. Some of the jobs would require more than one person.

Since control problems would be less likely if she could name students quickly, she decided to make name cards that would stand up in front of each student.

She anticipated classroom problems that could be alleviated if the students were encouraged to develop class standards or rules. She decided that the following problem areas should be discussed:

- Walking in the classroom
- The use of quiet voices

- Respecting classmates' right to work
- Putting work aside when the teacher has something important to share
- Maintaining a clean and neat environment
- Pencil sharpening
- Use of the classroom fountain
- Sharing materials (books, games, equipment)
- Listening to others' viewpoints

Discussion of these problems would occur as the need arose. For example, before recess would be an appropriate time to discuss the traffic pattern for leaving the classroom. Also, sometime during the morning she ought to talk to the students about fire drill routines.

"Quiet voices" and most of the other routines would be discussed when they began their reading group work. The class "rules" would be recorded on the chalkboard until the end of the day at which time Hogan would transfer them to a chart.

WHAT WOULD YOU DO IF . . . ?

Brian Johnson was teaching fourth grade. It was the first day of school, and it was recess time. The bell rang and the students looked up expectantly. Johnson said, "I guess it's recess time boys and girls, let's line up at the door."

Some of the students ran to the front door and some ran to the back door. There was a great deal of pushing and shoving.

Make a list of the room standards that Johnson forgot to develop with his students.

Getting Acquainted

Mary Hogan recognized that the cumulative records and the health cards provided her with just a bare outline of information about each child. In order to personalize her teaching technique for each student, she wanted to become better acquainted with the interests, attitudes, and personality of each of her students. To begin this task she would read a story to her students about hobbies. After motivating the students to talk about their personal interests, she would have each student write and draw a book called "All About Me." This project would initiate an integrated language and art program.

Other Get-acquainted Techniques. As Hogan observed her students playing at recess and lunchtime she would learn about their capacity for cooperative play and teamwork. During the first couple of weeks she would test their physical skills through skill-related tasks at physical education time (see Chapter 10).

She planned "get acquainted" sessions and would invite small groups of children to eat lunch with her in the classroom. The informality of the small group lunch session would provide her with new insights about each student.

She would introduce a puppet family to the students and have different students role-play family decisions related to specific problems:

Maya was not doing her homework.
Benjy was ill. Who would stay with him if he could not go to school?

They would also role-play family celebrations: Susan's birthday, Dad's commendation from the police department for bravery.

Mary Hogan would use a variety of diagnostic tests to assess students' ability levels, but she was just as concerned with learning about students' self-reliance, social skills, and sense of belonging. For these capacities she would need to rely on her own observation skills and some sociometric measures (see Chapter 17).

Getting Acquainted with the Community

Mary Hogan and Greg Thomas planned to get together during the first week of school to drive around their school community. To understand the students they were to teach, they recognized the importance of visiting in the community in order to learn about the problems, interests, services, and cultural priorities of the residents around the King Elementary School.

Hogan and Thomas had a list of questions they would use to facilitate their observation.[2]

Community Questions

1. Who lives in the community?
2. What is the residential pattern (apartments, single homes)?
3. How does the natural and manmade environment contribute to or detract from the community?
4. What businesses appear to flourish in the community? What businesses appear to flounder?
5. Are there social services within the community available to assist residents (hospital, clinics, police, fire, legal aid)?
6. Do recreational facilities exist within the community (for children, for adults)?
7. Are there distinctive cultural characteristics apparent (speciality shops, restaurants, cultural sites, unique patterns or environmental characteristics)?
8. Are there businesses, places of interest, or sites for field trips?
9. Are there resource people available in the community to assist in the classroom?
10. What kinds of work opportunities exist in the community?
11. What special problems are apparent in the community?
12. If there are businesses in the community, does any one type predominate?
13. What special interests are obvious in the community? Do these interests relate to cultural priorities?
14. How might your own interests and talents be of assistance in the community?

Curriculum Goals and Instructional Objectives

Members of the lay public as well as professional educators hold varied philosophical beliefs. These beliefs do influence to some extent the choice of curriculum goals. Curriculum goals, in general, are derived from three sources: the child, society, and subject matter specialists. From the child the curriculum developer learns about needs, interests, and ability levels; from society the curriculum worker derives information about the needs of contemporary life, tradition, eternal values and aspirations; from subject matter specialists one learns what knowledge is of the greatest importance. Figure 4.2 illustrates the relationship of instruction to educational goals.

Educational goals are broad statements concerned with establishing the purpose for instruction. Examples of educational goals are statements such as the following:

- To aid students to become aware of and assume their future life role in American society
- To arouse students' interest in studying other people's cultures
- To develop an understanding of common art elements
- To promote the appreciation of lyric poetry

In contrast to the goal statement, an instructional objective is a precise statement that tells what the student will be able to do as a consequence of instruction. Examples of instructional objectives are statements such as the following:

- After reading the section in this book on social economic status, the reader will view five TV commercials and identify the target socioeconomic group for each commercial.
- After studying harmony, the student will construct and play three chords on the tones of major and minor scales.
- Given an example of a subtraction problem, the student will identify the minuend, subtrahend, and the difference.
- After instruction and given a subtraction worksheet, the student will solve and complete 100 subtraction problems in 30 minutes.

[2] Adapted from J. K. Lemlech, *Handbook for Successful Urban Teaching* (New York: Harper, 1977), pp. 100–101.

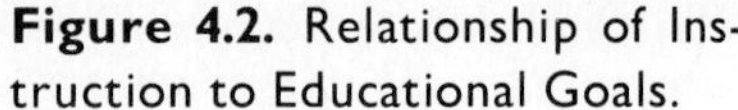

Figure 4.2. Relationship of Instruction to Educational Goals.

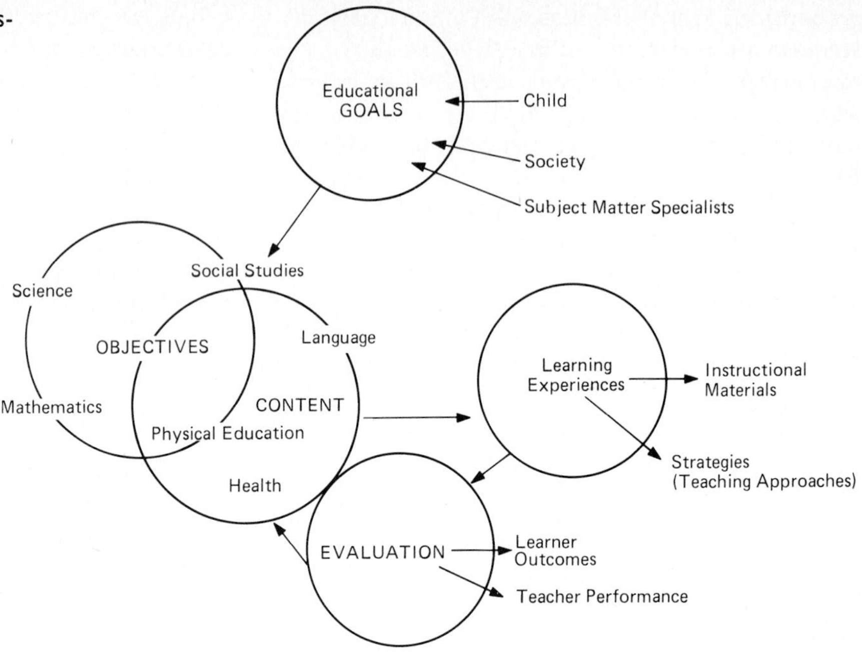

Instructional objectives identify three important elements about learner behavior:

1. The *task* that is required of the learner
("... the reader will *view* five commercials and *identify*. . . .")
("... the student will *construct* and *play*. . . .")
("... the student will *solve*. . . ."),
2. The *condition* under which the behavior will be performed
("After reading the section in this book. . . .")
("After studying harmony. . . .")
("Given an example of a subtraction problem. . . .")
("Given a subtraction worksheet. . . ."),
3. The *level of performance*
("... the *target* SES group in *each* commercial.")
("... *three chords on the tones of*. . . .")
("... *complete* ... *in 30 minutes*.").

RESPONDING TO THE CRITICS

Suppose a reporter said that only trivial objectives could be stated in behavioral terms. What would you respond?

The important element in *defining the learner task* involves the identification of the precise behavioral term to express the desired outcome of instruction. The purpose of identifying the behavioral outcome is to *limit* the interpretation of what the learner will be doing. Examples are as follows:

to identify	to play
to draw	to compose
to compare	to state
to contrast	to list
to differentiate	to categorize
to sing	to solve

The condition describes the limitations or constraints which will affect the student's performance of the task; for instance, "after studying harmony . . . ," "given an example of . . . ."

The *level of performance* identifies the evidence desired in order to be confident that the learner has achieved the objective, as in the following:

"must complete in 30 minutes,"
"three chords on the tones of the major and minor scales,"
"the target group in each commercial,"
"at least 85 per cent accuracy,"
"four out of five cultural characteristics."

In most school situations, teachers are provided with a description of subject goals and a selection of representative objectives. But since students in elementary classrooms are so diverse in abilities, interests, and attitudes, most teachers tend to write their own objectives.

Bloom et al. (1956) classified cognitive objectives in the *Taxonomy of Educational Objectives (Handbook I: Cognitive Domain)*. This guide is helpful because it categorizes intellectual objectives on a continuum from simple to complex behaviors. The categories are hierarchical:

Evaluation ↑
Synthesis
Analysis
Application
Comprehension
Knowledge

Figure 4.3 provides an outline of the cognitive domain with illustrative statements or questions based upon the categorical system (Bloom, 1956).

Krathwohl et al. (1964) classified affective objectives in the *Taxonomy of Educational Objectives Handbook II: Affective Domain*. This handbook organizes objectives hierarchically involving values, attitudes, and interests.

Characterization ↑
Organization
Valuing
Responding
Receiving

Figure 4.4 provides an outline of this domain with illustrative statements and questions (Krathwohl et al., 1964).

The Relationship of Objectives and Content

Objectives are often stated in terms of instructional intent. For instance, Greg Thomas, teaching fifth-grade social studies, might develop a chronological list of topics to be covered: exploration period, colonial period, prerevolutionary conflict, and so on. This type of list exhibits what Thomas intends to teach but not what the outcome of learning will be. The content outline is useful for the teacher and important for the student and the public, but it cannot be viewed as appropriate for the statement of learning objectives.

Tyler (1949) depicted the relationship of content and objectives by illustrating the topics to be covered in an academic course in one column and the objectives overlaid on that column and stated in broad behavioral terms.

Figure 4.5 demonstrates Greg Thomas' content using Tyler's two-dimensional illustration. For each topic an appropriate behavioral objective needs to be developed.

> Do you believe that behavioral objectives dehumanize the teaching process? Why or why not?

Figure 4.3. Illustrative Statements/Questions.

1.00 *Knowledge* (pp. 201–207)	
1.0 The learner recalls specifics (facts, terminology), a pattern structure, or a setting. The emphasis is on remembering. Recall involves the process of "data retrieval."	
1.10 Knowledge of Specifics	
1.11 Knowledge of Terminology	
1.12 Knowledge of Specific Facts	Name seven large cities in the world.
1.20 Knowledge of Ways and Means of Dealing with Specifics	
1.21 Knowledge of Conventions	
1.22 Knowledge of Trends and Sequences	What are some causes of Poverty?
1.23 Knowledge of Classifications and Categories	
1.24 Knowledge of Criteria	Which of the following cities are considered large?
1.25 Knowledge of Methodology	
1.30 Knowledge of the Universals and Abstractions in a Field	
1.31 Knowledge of Principles and Generalizations	What do we need to know about poverty?
1.32 Knowledge of Theories and Structures	
2.00 *Comprehension*	
2.0 The learner "hears and understands what is being communicated. This is a relatively low level of understanding.	
2.10 Translation	In what ways does poverty affect the rich?
2.20 Interpretation	What causes some cities to become dense population centers?
2.30 Extrapolation	
3.00 *Application*	
3.0 The learner remembers, understands, and applies ideas, rules, methods, or theories. The learner uses the known and may apply it to an unknown situation.	How would you explain the growth of a city? In what ways are the causes of poverty similar worldwide?
4.00 *Analysis*	
4.0 The learner will take apart the various components or elements of an idea in order to clarify or organize the elements for communication.	
4.10 Analysis of Elements	Why might a population center expand and then decrease at a later date?
4.20 Analyses of Relationships	What is the relationship between a cycle of poverty and change?
4.30 Analysis of Organizational Principles	
5.00 *Synthesis*	
5.0 The learner puts together components or elements into a whole and perhaps devises an original way for communication or produces a new plan.	
5.10 Production of a Unique Communication	What steps could be taken to break the cycle of poverty?

Figure 4.3. (continued)

5.20 Production of a Plan or a Proposed Set of Operations	
5.30 Derivation of a Set of Abstract Relations	If you were a demographer, what signs of change would you look for?
6.00 *Evaluation*	
6.0 The learner judges quantitatively and qualitatively, using personal criteria or criteria given to the learner.	
6.10 Judgments in Terms of Internal Evidence	How will changes in population affect public services, major industry, agriculture?
6.20 Judgments in Terms of External Criteria	How would the elimination of poverty in other nations affect us?

Source: Taxonomy of Educational Objectives: Handbook I: Cognitive Domain by Benjamin S. Bloom et al. Copyright © 1956 by Longman, Inc. Reprinted by permission of Longman, Inc., New York.

Figure 4.4. Illustrative Statements/Questions.

1.0 *Receiving (Attending)*	
1.0 The learner is passive. The learner may be aware and attending but is neutral.	
1.1 Awareness	
1.2 Willingness to Receive	
1.3 Controlled or Selected Attention	
2.0 *Responding*	
2.0 The learner demonstrates willingness by responding to a suggestion, complying with a rule, or raising hand to communicate. For instance, the leader might say, "How many agree?" The learner in this situation would hold up a hand to agree.	
2.1 Acquiescence in Responding	Name seven large cities in the world.
2.2 Willingness to Respond	Describe how living in a farm community would affect you and your family.
2.3 Satisfaction in Response	
3.0 *Valuing*	
3.0 The learner commits by assuming responsibility, debating a point of view, expressing own feelings or convictions.	
3.1 Acceptance of a Value	Debate the advantages (disadvantages) of large-city life vs. small-town life.
3.2 Preference for a Value	
3.3 Commitment	

Figure 4.4. (continued)

4.0 *Organization*	
4.0 The learner organizes own and others' ideas or values into a system for analysis.	
4.1 Conceptualization of a Value	In what ways would population expansion or decline cause changes in the way of life of your family?
4.2 Organization of a Value System	
5.0 *Characterization by a Value or Value Complex*	
5.0 The learner internalizes personal values and adapts own behavior so that actions are consistent with beliefs.	
5.1 Generalized Set	Explain why you would prefer to live in a large city, small city, rural community.
5.2 Characterization	

Source: *Taxonomy of Educational Objectives: Handbook II: Affective Domain* by David R. Krathwohl et al. Copyright © 1964 by Longman, Inc. Reprinted by permission of Longman, Inc., New York.

Figure 4.5. Behavioral Objectives.

Topics	*Identify Facts and Principles*	*Apply Concepts*	*Interpret Historical Data*
Exploration Period	(see Example #1)	+	+
Colonial Period	+	(see Example #2)	+
Prerevolution Conflict	+	+	(See Example #3)

The objectives cannot be separated from the content; the content provides the framework for the objectives. The following illustrates how this can be done:

Example 1. After studying air, wind, and ocean currents, students will identify facts and principles related to the exploration period of history.

Example 2. Using the concept of migration, students will provide three reasons why colonists chose to come to North America.

Example 3. Using data from both American and British history textbooks, students will identify conflicting viewpoints and interpret value positions of the Americans and the British during the prerevolutionary period.

The Relationship of Objectives to Learning Experiences

Tyler (1949) defined the term "learning experience." The term "learning experience" is not the same as the content with which a course deals nor the activities performed by the teacher. The term "learning experience" refers to the interaction between the learner and the external conditions in the environment to which he can react. Learning takes place through the active behavior of the student (p. 63).

Tyler's viewpoint that the learner learns through active involvement in the learning process is certainly compatible with the research concept of "active engagement" time presented in Chapter 2. The teacher's problem appears to be to choose learning experiences that will foster active involvement in order to accomplish the desired learning outcomes. Tyler suggested five principles for selecting learning experiences.

1. The learning experience must give students the opportunity to practice the desired behavior.
2. The learning experience must give the student satisfaction. (This means that the student must be successful as s/he practices the behavior; otherwise satisfaction is not achieved.)
3. The learning experience must "fit" the student's needs and abilities. (In other words, if the student is unable to perform the task, then it is not appropriate.)
4. Many learning experiences should be appropriate for use. (This means that the teacher is limited only by her/his own creativity. At any given time there are probably an infinite number of ways to accomplish a given objective.)
5. The learning experience should accomplish several learning outcomes. (This means that experiences should be broad so that students can integrate knowledge from several fields or satisfy more than one learning need. Several objectives may be accomplished through the use of one learning experience.)

Looking again at one of Greg Thomas' objectives, let us illustrate several learning experiences that will help Thomas attain his objective.

The objective: After studying wind, air, and ocean currents, students will identify facts and principles related to the exploration period of history.

The Learning Experiences[3]

1a. Students discuss heat at the equator and cold at the poles.

1b. Students observe or participate in a science experiment using a cold glass and a warm glass. Students see that smoke rises in the warm glass and falls in the cold glass. Students discuss the direction of air movement. (Punk is used to produce smoke.)

2. Students construct individual sail boats (yachts). They plan, measure, saw, plane the boats.

3. Students use large world map and identify area called the *Doldrums*. Students hypothesize what would happen to a sailing ship in the Doldrums.

4a. Students sail boats in a pond on a day when there is no wind and another day when it is windy.

4b. Students respond to: What would happen to a sailing vessel in the Doldrums before the days when engines were available.

Figure 4.6 abbreviates Tyler's principles and uses them to evaluate Thomas' learning experiences.

[3] A fine source to accomplish this objective is William W. Fisher, *Geo-Cepts* (Chicago: Denoyer-Geppert, 1977).

Figure 4.6. Evaluation of Learning Experiences Using Tyler's Principles.

1. *Practice*	2. *Satisfaction*	3. *Fit*	4. *Multitudinous Experiences Available*	5. *Accomplish Several Outcomes*
Students practice: acquiring information, problem solving, cooperative behaviors, discussion skills, map skills	Diverse interests encouraged through experiments, construction	Diverse interests and abilities provided for: construction, map skills, discussion, experiment	Observation, discussion, problem solving planning, measuring, sawing, sailing, experimenting	Broad integration of subject fields: Science, mathematics, social studies, language skills, social participation

Sequencing Learning Experiences

Both Mary Hogan's rock lessons and Greg Thomas' wind, air, and ocean current lessons were a part of a "unit" plan. Learning experiences need to be organized into a systematic program, course, or unit. The unit is typical in the elementary school. For learning experiences to be effective, they must be organized in a manner so that each lesson complements what came before and what will come next (Reread Thomas' learning experiences). Each lesson reinforces the prior lesson. Sequencing of learning experiences means that the organization is such that there is a natural progression to the lessons, that complexity increases, and that each lesson broadens the learner's vision by integrating information across subject fields. Using Mary Hogan's rock unit, the concept of sequence is demonstrated.

WHAT LEARNING EXPERIENCES WOULD YOU CHOOSE?

1. Suppose that you were teaching Hogan's rock and mineral unit. What learning experience would you choose after the students had learned to classify the rocks by hardness, color, texture, shape, holes, layers, and weight?
2. Where in Hogan's outline of teaching experiences would you inject an experience with fossils?
3. What learning experience could you choose to have students learn how fossils became imprinted in rocks?

Outline of Learning Experiences—Rocks and Minerals

1. Students classify rocks:
   - by hardness
   - by color
   - by texture
   - by shape
   - by holes
   - by layers
   - by weight.
2. Students discuss the properties of rocks.
3. Using tools, students try to change the shape of rocks.
4. Students see film of natural forces which affect the shape of rocks.
5. Students experiment with ice and thawing of water; students observe plants growing in rocks. Students discuss the effect of temperature.
6. Students read to find out how people depend on rocks and minerals.
7. Students see film on mining. Students discuss strip-mining and open-pit mining.
8. Students write stories about why people need rocks and minerals.
9. Students chart the uses of rock and minerals.
10. Students evaluate why rocks and minerals are resources.

Mary Hogan will be integrating her science unit with her social studies instruction as she discusses both resources and basic needs of people. Hogan also uses her language time to write stories dealing with science and social studies content. During spelling she will include words to be studied from both science and social studies.

Lesson Planning

Upon completion of student teaching, most teacher candidates comment, "Hurray—no more lesson plans." But in reality the effective (and experienced) teacher continues to utilize a lesson plan. However, the plans differ in the degree of specificity. In this section we will take a look at the lesson plan of a student teacher (Figure 4.7), the lesson plan notes (Figure 4.8) of an experienced teacher, and a teacher's weekly plan (Figure 4.9). Long-term planning in social studies and science is discussed in Part III of the text.

As teachers become more experienced, they are able to anticipate what students will say and their own responses as well, and so the experienced

Figure 4.7. A Student Teacher's Lesson Plan.

Subject: Mathematics—Fifth Grade

Objectives: Students will measure the perimeter of a rectangle.
Students will use a formula to find the perimeter of a rectangle.
Students will draw a square.
Students will define perimeter, reactangle, square.

Materials: Ruler, Paper, Cardboard Shapes, Guinea Pig and Cage

Procedure:

1. *Motivation:* Display a guinea pig in a cage. Comment that cage is too small, but—"I did not know what size to buy since I didn't know the size of this cage."
   "How can I find out the size of this cage?"
   (Students will respond—"Measure it.")
2. Allow several students to measure cage.
3. Have students draw size of cage on board.
4. Have students label "length" and "width".
5. Have all students draw a small "cage" on their own paper.
6. Observe students' work.
7. Ask: "Do you know the shape of the cage?" (Introduce word "rectangle" and define it.)
8. Ask: "Do you know another shape in which all four sides are the same?" (Introduce concept of "square" as a rectangle with equal sides.)
9. Have children draw a square and label it. (Observe students.)
10. Ask: "If I want to know the distance around the guinea pig's cage, how can I find out?"
11. (Students respond—"Add the lengths and widths.")
12. Have students do it with the chalkboard example.
13. Explain that the word "perimeter" means the distance around the outside of a geometric shape.
14. Ask: "Can you think of a shortcut to find the perimeter of a shape?" (Give clues if they cannot.)
15. "Let's see if the shortcut works. Let's use the size of the cage to experiment." (Cage size = 12″ × 18″? 2 × 12 = ? 2 × 18 = ? "Now what do we do?") Pause for suggestions. ("Yes, add them together.")
16. Give students formula: 2 × L + 2 × W = Perimeter.
17. Hand out cardboard geometric shapes to students.
18. Have students practice measuring and using formula to find perimeter.
19. Students trace shapes on their own paper; measure and label widths and lengths; use formula to solve the question.
20. *Evaluation:*
    (a) Review meaning of perimeter.
    (b) Ask students for formula for finding perimeter.
    (c) Ask students for definition of square and rectangle.
    (d) Have students report on perimeter of the cardboard shapes.

teacher does not have to write these things into the lesson plan procedures. Provision for interaction, discussion, the thinking process for problem solving no longer appear under procedures, because the experienced teacher automatically provides time for these things to happen. For discussions to be effective, however, even experienced teachers have to plan their questioning approach prior to instruction and have a cue card ready for use.

Some teachers like to file their lesson plans into a loose-leaf notebook or a 4″ × 6″ box. The advantage of doing this is that it is easy to refer to when a student returns from absence or when a parent comes in for a conference.

Figure 4.9 exhibits Mary Hogan's weekly planning schedule. This form appears in a special booklet entitled Weekly Planning Forms. The booklet was given to Mary by the principal, at the first faculty meeting. Mary Hogan still needs lesson planning notes for some subjects, but the weekly plan will help her remember special events and document subject matter preparation through the course of the semester. It will also be a handy guide for the substitute teacher if Hogan is absent.

The Integration of Subject Fields

In the discussion concerned with selecting learning experiences, it was noted that one of Tyler's prin-

Figure 4.8. Experienced Teacher's Lesson Plan Notes.

Subject: Math
Objectives: Measure, draw, define rectangle, square, perimeter. Use formula to find perimeter.
Materials: Guinea Pig Cage (for motivation), ruler, shapes.
Procedure:

1. *Motivation* (use cage with guinea pig!)
2. Introduce L., W.—use cage.
3. Have students draw; observe.
4. Define rectangle, square.
5. Have students find P. of cage.
6. Explain formula.
7. Have students practice using shapes.
8. Evaluate objectives.

ciples was that learning experiences should accomplish more than one purpose. An example of this principle would be a class discussion that occurs during social studies. The discussion would no doubt focus on social studies content, but for the discussion to be purposeful, students would have had to acquire pertinent information. This skill necessitates one or all of the following: reading, listening, observing. These activities are all related to the language arts. Thus, an effective class discussion is dependent upon *other* learning experiences. The class discussion as a learning experience becomes a means to integrate broad subject fields. The class discussion to be effective is also dependent upon students' respect for others' viewpoints and their skills in social participation.

Another example of integration would be the activity planned by teacher Greg Thomas to have his students construct sailboats. This activity was the means by which Thomas integrated mathematics, science, and history and accomplished more than one learning outcome.

The advantage of integrating subject fields is that it applies the principle of what Ausubel (1969) called *integrative reconciliation.* This means that students' prior experiences are utilized as new ideas are integrated with previously learned knowledge. Instead of knowledge being fragmented or compartmentalized in a single subject approach (like a textbook), ideas are broadly related across subject fields. This permits the elementary teacher to develop a balanced curriculum. The daily schedule, at first glance, appears to be designed to meet only single subject objectives. This observation occurs because it is necessary to specify time commitments for each subject in the curriculum; but the daily schedule should *not* be interpreted so strictly that it would hinder the integration of subject fields or reflect an unbalanced curriculum.

To illustrate the concept of integration of subject fields, the social studies-science unit "Water" was designed for grades four through six. This unit can be found in the Appendix. Additional suggestions for unit planning and instruction can be found in Chapter 14.

WHAT WOULD YOU DO IF . . .

A parent accused you of not teaching social studies or science? In fact, you were integrating science and social studies into the daily program. How would you prove to the parent that you were teaching a balanced curriculum?

Daily Tasks of the Teacher

This chapter has focused on a variety of teaching responsibilities, such as arranging an attractive classroom environment, planning the daily program, planning goals and instructional objectives, anticipating management needs, and selecting learning experiences. Most of these tasks can be subsumed into two major headings of teacher responsibility: instruction and management. A third area of responsibility, not yet discussed, is the teacher's leadership role. Each of these divisions of responsibility is briefly outlined in terms of the daily tasks of the teacher. (Instruction and leadership will be treated in depth in later chapters of this text.)

Figure 4.9. Weekly Planning Schedule.

	Monday	Tuesday	Wednesday	Thursday	Friday	Special Notes
Reading	*Blue:* Select picture with long vowel sound. Read: 35–39 of GMC *Red:* Identify designated sight words on 101–105	Select nonsense word with long vowel; Read 40–44 Read orally	Select initial → consonants; Read orally; Retell story orally. Read 106–110	Read 45–49 Select phrases to correspond to pictures Read orally	Read 110–114	Use reinforcement centers and a free choice center
Reading and Language Arts	B.B.W. *White:* Sequence pictures → related to story; Read 55–59 of W & G Draw picture for "All About Me" White Story →	Read 60–63	Select final punctuation marks; Read Orally	Identify number of syllables in 1 & 2 syll. words; Read 64–68 Finish Pictures & Stories	Read Orally Share: "All About Me"	
Spelling and Handwriting	New words: story, read, word, picture, color, clock, where, when Introduce words; Practice spelling words Practice handwriting:	The alphabet →	Write story using words		Spelling Test	
Physical Education/ Health	Teach Side Throw → Play: Caboose Dodge Ball →		Play: Circle Relay	Rhythms: Teach* Hokey-Pokey; Practice: Skipping	Nutrition: Use Health Book—Ch. 1.	*Borrow record from Miss Smith
Math	Use flannel board for story of 5; Use sticks; Draw Story of 5	Practice addition facto through 5	Tell number stories Use flannel board	Teach Hours; Use → individual clocks; → Use practice sheets on clocks →		
Literature and Music	Teach: Grey Squirrel → Sing: Old favorites →		Read: Horton Hatches An Egg	Teach: American Review Songs	Read poetry from speech book	
Science, Social Studies (SS), Art	*Science:* Work in groups to classify rocks; Discuss properties of rocks	*Science:* Use tools to change shape of rocks; Discuss	*SS:* Initiate unit; (Use arranged environment) "What do all people need?"	*SS:* Research** "Basic Needs" Use picture file; filmstrip, chart, books	*Art* Finger painting	**Use reading groups
Special Notes	Send note home with Billy M. for parent conference			Remind children to bring aprons for art lesson		

Instructional Role Decision. Students' success in school is dependent upon the teacher's accurate assessment of cognitive and affective learner needs. "Students learn more when teachers know more about what their individual students can and cannot do" (Fisher et al., 1980, p. 24). Daily, the teacher must gather data to assess academic progress and decide where the student is and where the student ought to be. Sometimes cognitive data are inadequate. Students whose frustration level is low or whose success-rate needs are high must be programmed in such a way that self-concept needs are not sacrificed.

Data Gathering. Assessment occurs in a variety of ways. First, the teacher must decide what it is s/he needs to know about students. Skills, concepts, attitudes, and values should be specified. Once this is done, the teacher can decide what techniques or procedures to use for the assessment.

Simple checklists can be used to evaluate skill sequences, specific behaviors, or interests and concepts. (See Chapter 17 for examples.) Teacher observation of students' interests, skill performance, and on-task behavior can be recorded on an observation card. Anecdotal records, conferences, and diaries contribute to the assessment processs. Teacher's own paper-and-pencil tests as well as standardized achievement tests will provide data for interpretation. Once the data have been gathered, the teacher must diagnose needs. An accurate diagnosis is the sine qua non for appropriate instructional planning.

Diagnosis. This term is often used in education in a fashion similar to the medical model. Assessment provides the data, the symptoms, and the signs. Using the data, the teacher interprets the condition of learning and the situation most likely to facilitate the learning process. Technical descriptions based on the data can be recorded, although it is not always necessary to do so.

Prescription. While diagnosis is the interpretation of the data, prescription refers to the plan the teacher will use to carry out instruction. Mary Hogan, our fictitious second-grade teacher, decided that Charlie, a second-grade student, was continually frustrated working in the high reading group. She shifted him to a slightly lower group where he could excel. The result was that Charlie expressed delight in his own progress and began to make great strides in other subject fields. Hogan's "prescription" was obviously accurate and appropriate for Charlie.

Grouping decisions such as the one Mary Hogan made should always be based on accurate data. For example, at the Lincoln School, teachers were told to move five students from an all fifth-grade classroom to a fourth/fifth combination room and to move five fourth-grade students to a third/fourth-grade combination room. Without any data about the students, the teachers made their choices. The result in both cases was that the third-grade students were superior in achievement to the fourth-grade students in the third/fourth-grade combination class and the fourth-grade students were superior in achievement to the fifth-grade students in the fourth/fifth-grade combination room. As a consequence, there were a lot of highly frustrated students whose egos were affected negatively, as well as control problems for the teachers.

WHAT WOULD YOU DO IF . . . ?

You are teaching third grade and you have a group of students who read below grade level. They are all boys, and several of them are considered "trouble-makers." You also have two reading groups at grade level. Your principal asks you to choose three students to move into a second-grade classroom.

Which students would you choose? Why?

If the teachers had reviewed the evidence before making their decisions they would have placed average fourth graders with low to average third graders and average fifth graders with low to average fourth graders. An appropriate prescription is one that provides for a "reasonable instructional program corresponding to students' needs." Selection of the appropriate learning experiences is also based on the "prescription." Instruction is based on the assessment, the diagnosis, and the prescription. These three components comprise the planning stage for instruction.

Instruction. The term "prescription" was used broadly in the previous section to signify the "plan" for teaching. That plan should also include methodological decisions about teaching strategy and instructional materials. Actual direct instruction by the teacher or indirectly through discovery approaches, is considered to be the "presentation." Presentation decisions will be based on grouping needs, individual skill levels, the nature of the learning task, and the appropriateness of the instructional materials. In the classroom, the teacher mediates instruction using the plan that was preconceived before the beginning of the school day. The greater the teacher's skill in the presentation of instruction, the greater will be the engagement rate of students. (In other words, the students will pay attention!) The carefully planned and structured lesson facilitates students' understanding of what they are expected to learn and how they should go about it. Discovery approaches need to be planned and structured just as carefully as a direct instructional lesson in reading or mathematics.

Monitoring. Monitoring is considered to be an instructional task component. As the teacher teaches, s/he must keep track of student progress. By checking students' progress during the instructional act, the teacher knows whether to deviate from the plan or to carry on. Monitoring is closely related to assessment. If the original assessment provided inaccurate data, then the diagnosis and the prescription will be wrong. The teacher monitors instruction by circulating around the room during "practice" periods or while students are working in small groups. During a direct instructional episode, teachers frequently monitor progress by asking questions.

Reinforcement. As the teacher monitors instruction, s/he gives feedback to the student(s). Students' engagement rate is higher when teachers let them know whether they are right, wrong, or on the right track. Academic feedback has been closely related by researchers to students' achievement.

Teachers reinforce the purpose of instruction and reinforce good study habits by providing time to correct seatwork or homework. At learning centers, reinforcement is provided by developing a system whereby students can correct their own work or find out if their work is "on target". Some curriculum materials and programmed textbooks also provide immediate feedback to the student.

Evaluation. Formative (ongoing) evaluation need not be distinguished from monitoring and reinforcement because an ongoing type of evaluation helps keep students on task and provides immediate feedback so that the students know if they are progressing. Summative evaluation is also a progress report to both teacher and student (as well as parents), but it does not monitor instruction in the same interactive way.

Management Decisions

The three components management, instruction, and leadership should not be separated as if they were distinct entities. The teacher who is not an effective classroom manager will not be an effective instructor; nor will this individual be able to provide leadership. It is only for the purpose of opening up and viewing the varied tasks of the classroom teacher that these three components are isolated as if they were distinct occurrences. The following seven items should provide some insight into teachers' daily management decisions.

Classroom business. Attendance, lunch count, collecting money for milk or fund raising, PTA collections, handing out notices, collecting parent responses—these are but a few of the daily tasks that teachers perform under the heading called "classroom business."

Scheduling. Coordinating the work of other teachers such as the music teacher, the special reading teacher, and the special educator may fall under the heading of arranging the daily schedule. Facilitating the work of these professionals and coordinating their work with your own existing schedule is an important but sometimes wearing task.

Arranging the Environment. Another management task that must be attended to daily is arranging seating for special instructional strategies. How should children be seated during a classroom discussion? What should you do with the tables for a construction lesson? Should the chairs be stacked during finger painting so that students will not touch them? How can a learning center be made more attractive? Should the bulletin board display be changed? These and countless other questions are attended to as teachers make environmental decisions.

Anticipating Instructional and Organizational Problems. One of the most important decisions that teachers make on a daily basis has to do with grouping students for instructional activities. For physical education, how can you ensure that there will be balanced teams and that less skilled students will not end up with hurt feelings? For small group project or planning experiences, students should be grouped heterogeneously. Should you, the teacher, choose the group that is to work together, or will you allow students to choose? How will you group for the science experiment and the social studies research lesson?

Today is "rhythms" day, but the auditorium is not available. Should you rearrange the classroom, or have rhythms outside, or change the activity? Yesterday it appeared that the students did not understand the math concepts that you taught. Should you reteach or continue on and hope for the best?

Your students have written a class play and will perform it for the other third-grade classrooms, but Billy, the star performer, has a temperature. Should you let him stay and perform, reschedule the play, or attempt it without him?

Supplies. One of the most frustrating but typical problems of the new teacher is the failure to anticipate material needs. Paper for writing or math work, pencils, art supplies, colored paper, and tagboard for charts, all need to be surveyed before instructional time. The teacher who constantly bothers classroom neighbors to borrow materials becomes very unpopular. The need for reference books, such as dictionaries or textbooks, also needs to be anticipated before class time. Audiovisual equipment is another common supply item that is forgotten until needed. Successful teaching is dependent upon having the right equipment and supplies *on hand* when needed.

Routines. While many classroom routines can be set on a weekly or monthly basis (monitors, group leaders), others need to be anticipated almost on a daily basis. For example, a learning center for language arts and art experiences had the children making masks. This activity required the use of colored paper, scissors, and paste. The teacher needed to anticipate where the students would put their wastepaper and how they would clean their hands after using paste. A simple paper bag, thumbtacked to the bulletin board, served as a waste container, and because the classroom had no sink the teacher brought in a pail of water and had paper towels next to it.

Establishing and communicating routines concerned with collecting seatwork, self-correcting center work, or handing out paper and other supplies need to be reinforced daily by the classroom teacher.

Monitoring Behavior. Monitoring instruction has been cited as an instructional component; monitoring behavior is specified as a management component. Again, the line is too fine between these two classifications. A key task during instruction is to maintain academic interest and involvement of the students. Research has indicated that the higher the engagement rate, the higher the achievement. Substantive feedback is important in instructional monitoring, but *just* as important is the teacher's expression of "withitness." The teacher who communicates awareness of what is happening in the classroom knows precisely when to stand by a student and demand attention, when to smile or make eye contact with a student, when to nod approval or disapproval, and when to change activities.

All of these seven tasks comprise daily management responsibilities, and each needs to be carried out in an efficient manner. The reader is urged to review the research on classroom management cited in Chapter 3.

Leadership Decisions

Coordinating the Work of Auxiliary Personnel. It is not uncommon in elementary classrooms for there to be one or more parent volunteers, teacher aides, or paraprofessionals assuming nonteaching tasks. The classroom teacher is responsible for preplanning the work assignments of aides, explaining and providing guidance to them, and evaluating nonteaching performance (Lemlech, 1979). The teacher must exercise leadership skills and provide appropriate work tasks for the nonprofessional. The teacher needs to provide time both at the beginning of class and later in the day to guide auxiliary personnel in their work and to offer feedback at the end of the day. The nonprofessional may also contribute a great deal of insight to the teacher concerning learning activities.

Assuming Professional Responsibilities. Responsibility for special programs at a school or for the development of bulletin board displays for the office or hallways are typical assignments for teachers. Other duties may include responsibility for school safety, playground chores, cafeteria tasks, or choosing staff development leaders. Whatever the assignment, there are daily planning tasks and it is assumed that every teacher will participate and accept leadership roles.

The teacher who has classroom aides is responsible for the professional development of auxiliary personnel. For instance, knowledge about special classes for aides or workshops to improve the skills of aides is important to communicate. Sometimes the teacher must provide training for the aide. Often the insight needed to perform daily classroom chores cannot wait for the paraprofessional to be trained by others, and it is up to the classroom teacher to identify the needed skills and to improve the understanding of nonteaching personnel.

Meeting Professionally with Others. Teachers meet with other teachers on a daily basis. Collegial interactions are very important. It is extremely necessary to communicate information about students, school problems, and ways of teaching. But professional interactions must not divulge personal information communicated by children, nor should it reveal privileged information shared by parents. However, when teachers have mainstreamed special children in their classrooms, there is a great deal of information that must be shared by the special education teacher and the regular teacher; it is a professional responsibility to provide time to do so. Professional association meetings also provide many opportunities for communication and for leadership. This is discussed in Chapter 18.

Chapter Summary

This chapter was designed to provide practical information on ways to arrange the classroom environment, plan an instructional program, select learning experiences, and integrate subject fields.

Very specific information was provided about curriculum goals and the development of instructional objectives. Criteria for the selection of learning experiences were cited, and the plans of two fictitious teachers were used to demonstrate the selection and sequencing of learning experiences.

The components of a lesson plan were explained, two daily schedules were provided, and a weekly schedule was exhibited.

Teachers' responsibilities were expanded in this chapter to include instructional responsibilities, management responsibilities, and leadership responsibilities.

Classroom Application Exercises

1. Draw a classroom floor plan. Illustrate the arrangement of tables, bookcases, and centers.
2. Develop a daily schedule for primary students and another one for upper-grade students.
3. Explain how you will integrate several mainstreamed children into your program. Use your daily schedule to explain.
4. Plan a first day of school. What will you teach? What standards will you develop?
5. Make a list of "get acquainted" strategies to use with your students.
6. Use the suggested Community Questions to guide your own observation of your school community. Share your observation with others.
7. Write several instructional objectives in both a basic skill area and in a subject field area.

Suggested Readings for Extending Study

Bloom, B. S., ed. *Taxonomy of Educational Objectives: Handbook I: Cognitive Domain*. New York: David McKay Co., Inc., 1956.

Callahan, Joseph F., and Leonard H. Clark. *Teaching in the Elementary School: Planning for Competence*. New York: Macmillan Publishing Company, 1977.

Gronlund, N. E. *Stating Objectives for Classroom Instruction*. 2d ed. New York: Macmillan Publishing Company, 1978.

Jarolimek, J., and C. D. Foster. *Teaching and Learning in the Elementary School*. 2d ed. New York: Macmillan Publishing Company, 1981.

Hunkins, Francis P. *Curriculum Development: Program Improvement*. Columbus, Ohio: Charles E. Merrill Publishing Company, 1980.

Krathwohl, D. R., B. S. Bloom, and B. B. Masia. *Taxonomy of Educational Objectives. Handbook II: Affective Domain*. New York: David McKay Company, Inc., 1964.

Mager, R. F. *Preparing Instructional Objectives*, 2d ed. Palo Alto, Ca.: Fearon, 1975.

Piechowiak, Ann B. and Myra B. Cook. *Complete Guide to the Elementary Learning Center*. Englewood Cliffs, N.J.: Prentice-Hall, Inc., 1980.

PART **TWO**

UNDERSTANDING THE CURRICULUM

The seven chapters in Part II focus on major content experiences provided by elementary schools. The content areas by themselves are *not* the curriculum. The curriculum can be defined as all the experiences the school provides for children. This encompasses the learning experiences and activities, procedures, and resources planned for students.

Each chapter defines the content field and identifies goals, concepts, programs, teaching approaches, ways to evaluate growth, and relevant issues. Integration of the content area with other content fields is discussed in each of the chapters. Mainstreaming and classroom management, although discussed generically in Chapter 3, are included with specific applications in most of the chapters of Part II. Ideas for learning centers in each content area are provided. At the end of each chapter is a list of suggested readings to extend the reader's study of the content field.

A few of the states have curricula frameworks that provide teachers with a basic structure for the scope and sequence of instruction. The framework helps teachers select appropriate instructional experiences and instructional materials. In most of the chapters the California framework has been cited. This should be used as a springboard for discussion of the content field and as a basis for comparison with your local school district and/or state guidelines.

Although reading is a language arts component, due to its importance in the elementary school, a separate chapter has been devoted to this skill area.

Chapter 5

Teaching Language Arts

After you have completed the study of this chapter, you should be able to accomplish the following:

1. **Explain how the language arts are interrelated.**
2. **Identify the sequence of language development.**
3. **Discuss the importance of language, and explain why language changes.**
4. **Cite factors that affect language development.**
5. **Identify the ways in which language arts are taught.**
6. **Identify the language arts components.**
7. **Explain the effect of classroom environment on oracy skills.**
9. **Identify several factors that influence students' writing ability.**
10. **Suggest ways to facilitate mainstreaming during language arts.**
11. **Suggest ways to assist the nonstandard speaker of English or the bilingual student.**
12. **Create a language arts learning center.**

"I would go to Mars and land and walk all around."
"Not me. I would go to the moon and see the things that the astronauts got to see."

"I'd take my laser gun and me and my machine, we would fight off creatures like Darth Vadar."

Eagerly the first graders shared where they would go with their very own flying machines. The oral language lesson had been motivated by the reading of the children's book *Me and My Flying Machine*, by Mayer. After sufficient time had been allotted to the oral lesson, the teacher directed the students' attention to the collage-type materials set up on several tables in the classroom. The oral lesson was to be followed by an art experience in which the students would make their own "flying machine." The teacher explained that each student was to make a flying machine on a piece of colored paper which would then be used as the cover to his/her very own creative writing book. Collage materials for the lesson included popsicle sticks, colored pieces of plastic, propellers, string, straws, rubber bands, and small blocks of wood. Over the course of several weeks the students would be drawing pictures and writing stories about where they would go and what they would do in their flying machines.

This teacher demonstrated the interrelatedness of the various language arts and the way in which language arts can be integrated with other subject fields.

What Are the Language Arts?

The purpose of language is communication. Language is a tool we use to express ourselves. Through speaking or writing we convey ideas and feelings; the reception of those thoughts occurs through listening or reading. The children in the episode about the flying machine listened to a story first; then they had the opportunity to speak and practice oral language skills. Next, they will write about their ideas, and finally they will read their own thoughts and the thoughts of others.

Communication between two individuals means that those individuals are sharing ideas, feelings, information. The language arts curriculum can be defined as those activities that occur throughout the school day in which communication happens through reception (listening and reading) and expression (speaking and writing). In some school districts language arts is called "the English language arts" or "communicative arts."

The Language Arts Are Interrelated

The receptive and expressive language arts are interrelated. Success in reading is dependent upon an adequate oral foundation. For this reason most early childhood classrooms and primary classrooms stress oral language skills and reading readiness activities. Teachers who hurry to place children in books are often frustrated because they fail to recognize the importance of speaking and listening skills.

LANGUAGE PROGRESSION

	↑
Writing	(Encoding—Expressive)
Reading	(Decoding—Receptive)
Speaking	(Encoding—Expressive)
Listening	(Decoding—Receptive)

During infancy and early childhood children spend most of their time listening. Since speaking skills are "modeled" during this period, the quality of the child's models are critical to development. Competence in listening varies among children. The process of listening involves decoding speech meanings. The process of speaking involves encoding sounds so that they are meaningful. In writing, the individual must encode sounds into graphic symbols; reading involves decoding those graphic symbols to attain meaning.

The children in the oral language lesson were sharing ideas. Because they all had the same experience (listening to the story), their thoughts were meaningful to each other. Communication really means to share common meanings for the words that are spoken or written.

> The professor asked the student why he had been absent for the last several class meetings. The student responded, "My daddy passed." The professor walked away, mystified. Did professor and student have a consensus about the meaning of the word "passed?"

Differences in language meanings are often related to culture, values, generation, and socioeconomic status. Certainly if the student had used the term "passed away" or "deceased" or "died" the professor would have understood. Sometimes slang expressions and new fads present problems in communication between the "in" group and the "out" group. For instance, this conversation was overheard in the beauty parlor:

> The beautitian asked his customer, "Which soap do you prefer?" The customer responded, "The Days of Our Lives."
>
> The beautitian was astonished until he finally realized what the customer meant.

Rubin (1980, pp. 6–7) states that effective communication depends upon understanding that:

1. Language is manmade.
2. Language changes.
3. Language is a system of sounds.
4. Sounds are arranged into words.
5. The method of sound production helps to convey meaning.
6. Words are made up of vocal sound plus meaning.
7. Words are organized into patterns which convey unique meanings.
8. There are no right or wrong words for things, but common usage is employed in word meanings.
9. New words are derived as a society advances.

Why Is Language Important?

Through language we communicate meanings. We make our own meanings based upon our perceptions of reality. When the young child goes home from school and tells mother that the teacher is "mean," the student is probably perceiving the teacher as "mean" or "unfriendly" based upon the *behavior* of the teacher toward the child. We use language to express our conception of reality, but by the same token, we are imprisoned by the language that we use. Postman and Weingartner (1969) make the point that what we typically call knowledge is really language. Their example is that if we were to extract all of the words that biologists use from our langauge, then we would not have the science of biology.

Another example of language as the way in which we see the world is this classic passage from *Through the Looking Glass* (Carroll, 1923):

"I don't know what you mean by 'glory,'" Alice said.
Humpty Dumpty smiled contemptuously, "Of course you don't—till I tell you. I meant 'there's a nice knock-down argument for you!'"
"But 'glory' doesn't mean 'a nice knock-down argument,'" Alice objected.
"When I use a word," Humpty Dumpty said in rather a scornful tone, "it means just what I choose it to mean—neither more nor less."
"The question is," said Alice, "whether you *can* make words mean so many different things."
"The question is," said Humpty Dumpty, "which is to be master—that's all" (p. 213).

Language is related to personality. Through language the child expresses emotions and thoughts, and as facility is gained, so is self-confidence in the ability to put into words one's own ideas. Social competence is aided by the individual's use of appropriate language. Language also "gives us away." The words we choose, the things we say, the way in which we say them, and those things that we do *not* reveal contribute to the picture we transmit and that others receive.

Language is also used to relieve tension. Psychologists have confirmed that the use of occasional swear words relieves personal stress. When you drop the open pitcher of frozen orange juice on the floor (and you are hurrying to work), an expletive may help!

Another purpose of language is the sharing of culture. The literature of our own society and of other societies is available to us and serves to convey information about the human experience. Without language we would have no means to transmit our experience or to profit from the experience of others.

Nonverbal Communication

Teachers need to interpret nonverbal behavior. All individuals communicate nonverbally, and some nonverbal communication is culturally related. Nervousness is often conveyed by hand-writing mannerisms, excessive movement, fidgeting, or drumming with the fingertips. Anger may be expressed by the clenched fist, the raised arm with the clenched fist, the shaking of the index finger, pounding the table, expression of the eyes, or body posture.

Misunderstanding occurs in the classroom when teachers are unable to read nonverbal signs. Almost classic in the stories of the urban school are the incidents related to attention. Teachers are accustomed to students looking directly at them when they are talking. But Mexican-American, Indian, and black children rarely direct their eyes at an adult. In these cultures it is considered impolite to stare directly at another person. However, in these same cultures, when an individual is angry s/he will look directly into the eyes of the person causing the anger. If teachers are unaware of these cultural characteristics, there can be management problems in the classroom.

Body language is very expressive. During a role-play situation, the author observed a female student's disdain for a statement made by the person next to her. As a result, this individual turned completely around in her seat so that her back was to the person she wished to isolate. Certain physical movements are culturally realted. Some Japanese people still bow to greet each other; sometimes black males will do a back-to-back dance when greeting an old acquaintance on the street. Teenagers will often do a special handshake to indicate club membership. Hand movements (kinesics) while speaking are also expressive and typical of many European peoples.

Teachers frequently use nonverbal communication to control behavior in the classroom. A raised eyebrow or a finger to the lips can be a very effective means to forestall misbehavior, and a commiserating look or a smile of encouragement may be successful in motivating students to continue work or to try harder.

Factors Affecting Language Development

Individual differences need to be considered in the development of the language arts program. Readiness for the language arts may be affected by sex differences, although many of these differences have been culturally induced. Research indicates that girls mature earlier than boys. Readiness for reading is affected by maturity. The child who can sit still longer can usually listen more efficiently, and listening skills are positively related to success in learning to read. Verbal ability favors girls at young ages. This means that young females are more skillful at expressing themselves than young males. Also, the incidence of stuttering among girls is less than with boys.

Language or dialect differences also affect success in the language arts. School English or standard English may cause communication problems for children accustomed to speaking a dialect that is different from the standard structure. Dialect differences are often a result of geography. Where a person has lived affects speech sound, expressions, and usage.

When the primary (home) language is different from English, children may have a great deal of difficulty—even if they are working in a bilingual program. The sounds of English are different from the sounds of other languages, and the ear needs to be trained to hear the appropriate sounds. Aural development in a language needs to precede the development of reading and writing skills. Teachers must remember that in adulthood social competence—the ability to speak standard English—and economic success are closely related.

The child's first language models are in the home. Socioeconomic class, cultural priorities, and the number of siblings in the family affect the encouragement and reinforcement the child receives. Parents who encourage the development of language do so by modeling language and by listening attentively to the child's speech. Children who do not have language models will be at a disadvantage in school. Differences in child rearing related to socioeconomic status should be reviewed (see Chapter 2). These differences will affect success in the language arts.

RESEARCH FINDINGS

Lesser et al. (1964) studied the cultural traits of Negro, Puerto Rican, Chinese, and Jewish first graders. The Jewish children exhibited superior verbal skills; the Chinese students were superior in visual and spatial relationships. Lesser et al. concluded that cultural subgroups foster skills and abilities prized by their own group.

The child's ability to reason abstractly also affects readiness for reading. The wide range of ability levels in every classroom should be considered in the design of the language arts program. IQ tests, in the main, test verbal ability. For this reason they may not provide an accurate index of the ability to do well in school for many students. Most intelligence tests seem to be valid only for middle-class English-speaking children. Language development appears to be affected by both sociocultural environmental factors and individual neurophysiological factors. Preschool experience or lack of it also affects language development. Perception, cognition, language, and motivation are all affected by these out-of-school influences and individual difference factors. If a child has difficulty learning to read, the nature and range of individual differences must be evaluated critically along with the specifics of the reading or language problem (Sawyer & Lipa, 1981).

Children learn language and concepts by listening to others' verbal descriptions, associating words to objects, practicing language with others listening (all the while receiving reinforcements through encouragement and praise), and ultimately expanding their repertoire of language with longer sentence patterns. Concept development and language learning go hand in hand. The organization and integration of words into groups or categories (concept development) allows the child to increase knowledge and learn progressively abstract understandings.

How Are the Language Arts Taught?

While linguistics is the study of language, language itself has no natural content. Thus, when teachers provide language arts instruction they are teaching skills and tools of communication. For this reason the skills must be taught so that they are meaningful within other fields of study. In most school districts teachers rely on the following to facilitate the teaching of language arts:

- District-developed skills continuum to assist in the systematic teaching of language arts skills
- Use of language arts to interrelate curriculum fields; skill instruction applied to all curricula
- Informal use of language in all subject fields
- District-developed goals for each language arts component
- District or state recommendations for the allocation of time devoted to language arts instruction
- Basal reading textbooks for reading instruction
- Spelling workbooks (typically grades 3–6)
- Handwriting manuals (typically grades 3–6)
- Language textbooks for the teaching of grammar (grades 3–6)
- Literature textbooks—not always available

Although selected textbook series differ, language arts programs are remarkably similar from district to district. Primary classrooms tend to be informal and more dependent upon teacher creativity than upper-grade classrooms. The lower-grade teacher takes advantage of students' personal experiences to create a more individualistic type of program. Lower-grade teachers rarely rely on textbooks except for the teaching of reading.

Middle and upper-grade classrooms are more formally oriented. Teachers are able to rely on textbooks for the teaching of grammar, spelling, and handwriting. In some districts literature books are also available.

Differentiation of Instruction

Student differences in terms of maturation, interests, and abilities necessitate that some instruction be individualized. To differentiate instruction simply means to recognize individual needs and to provide instruction based upon those needs or variations. Individualization does *not* necessarily mean that teaching becomes a one-to-one situation in the classroom. In practical terms it usually means that students are grouped in small clusters to improve instruction. An example:

Mary Hogan was teaching reading to her second graders. She had a group of ten students sitting in a semicircle in front of her. After reading a story, Mary suggested that they play a game that she called the "Sequence Game." She asked the child at one end of the semicircle to begin to retell the story orally. Each child, in turn, was to add the next event in the story. As the story progressed around the semicircle, it was apparent that three of the students were unable to recall events in the order that they had occurred in the story.

When the game (and story) were concluded, Mary assigned a follow-up activity which also required sequencing skills. The three children who had difficulty with the activity were asked to remain in the reading circle. For these three students Mary told another story. This time she used flannel board pictures of the story. She asked the three children to take turns arranging the pictures on the flannel board in the order that they had occurred in the story. Using the tangible pictures, the three children were successful. Since they then understood what was expected of them, Mary assigned the three students to a learning center to obtain additional practice.

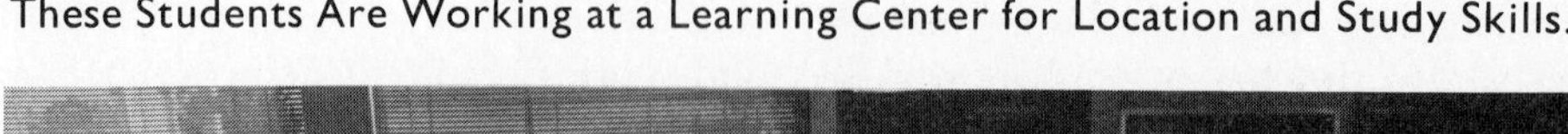

These Students Are Working at a Learning Center for Location and Study Skills.

Mary Hogan recognized that three of her students needed additional instruction; she recognized learning style needs (concrete materials for manipulation), and she provided special practice at a learning center where once again the students would use special materials. Hogan had differentiated instruction to accommodate individual variation.

Personalizing Instruction. Mary Hogan let her students know that she cared about them. By personalizing the lesson, Hogan communicated that three of the students needed "teacher" time. Students in Hogan's classroom learned to be unselfish because they were accustomed to receiving the attention of the teacher when they had special needs.

Decision Making. Another element important to the differentiation of instruction is the idea of personal choice. There ought to be occasions during the school day when students may choose "how" to learn. Mary Hogan accomplished this with the design of optional learning centers. Since objectives can be accomplished in a variety of ways, Hogan arranged an array of learning experiences—all related to the same objective. Students had to make decisions about how they would meet the objective

Hogan was not an indulgent type of teacher, and she did not believe that learning experiences should be unstructured; however, she recognized the advantage of student decision making, and whenever possible she provided opportunities for student choice.

Peer Tutoring. By teaching students to accept responsibility to help others, teachers can extend the concept of individualization in the classroom. The pairing of students must be done with a great deal of insight so that a reciprocal relationship exists between tutor and tutee; each recognizing the advantage of the helping relationship. The primary advantage of peer tutoring is that individual rates for learning can be accommodated. Peer tutoring for mainstreamed students is a meaningful way to provide individualized assistance. (See mainstreaming in this chapter.)

By acting as tutor, students learn to program instruction step by step for a friend; in so doing they become proficient themselves. However, teachers must be careful to monitor the instructional process to verify that instruction is modeled appropriately, and, if the step by step plans of the tutor are not correct, then the teacher must take time to develop the process for the tutor.

An expectation in peer tutoring is that every student will have the opportunity to be both tutor and tutee. In the normal course of events this should happen as students become proficient in evaluating their own skills to determine whether they can give assistance or need to receive help. Once again, teachers need to monitor individual proficiency and be mindful to assure that every student has the opportunity to play both roles.

Interactive Instruction

Communication involves more than one person. We talk with others, and we write for others. Although reading and writing may be solo activities, we pursue them so that others may take advantage of what we know, so that we may learn from others, and so that we may enjoy literature and dramatics. Although sometimes teachers rue the fact that students can talk, in actuality speech only improves through practice with others. This means that speech practice must be planned just as reading skill development is planned.

Since students do not view peers as authority figures, they often learn more from peers than they do from teachers. Picture second graders stretched out on the floor as an example of the contagious nature of reading in groups. See these students enjoying recreational reading. At first just one student will sit on the rug with a library book; soon others will arrive, and they posture themselves in the most comfortable ways!

Plan for Interaction

Language experiences need to be planned. By grouping students or allowing them to work in a partner situation, students will stimulate each other to accomplish routine chores, homework, or projects they would never accomplish working alone. Since language activities are basically skill activities, they need to be practiced. The teacher's role is to choose activities that are worthwhile and which will provide appropriate practice opportunities. For example, if students need practice in oral communication, then the teacher needs to choose activities which will allow students to

- hold conversations and discussions
- give informal and formal talks or reports
- participate in dramatic activities
- participate in choral recitations.

If students need practice in written communication, the teacher can choose among the following activities:

- write notes, reports, outlines
- write letters
- write stories and plays
- write summaries
- write advertisements and publicity
- write diaries, descriptions, histories.

The rationale for interactive instruction is consistent with the findings of Cohen (1981) reported in Chapter 2, that more student participation and effort leads to more active learning behavior. Oral communication really has two components: listening and speaking. Since both need to be practiced, group work is essential. Active learning behavior can be translated into active engaged time in academic tasks.

Integration of Experience

The child's primary language or dialect has been identified as a factor in language development affecting school success. If school and home are in conflict, the child's language development suffers. Although every child needs to learn standard English, it is important that the student not be made to feel that his/her home dialect or language is rejected. To integrate the child's experiences and facilitate language learning, teachers need to draw upon the child's cultural life. If a child has no one to relate to—in the textbooks, peer group, or teacher-model—interest in learning will be nil. The teacher's task is to find ways to allow each child to contribute information, stories and interests and build these elements into the language program.

Integration of experience has another meaning. In the elementary school, subject fields are "melded" even though we still talk about teaching science, math, history. We do this because students learn more efficiently if experiences fit and build upon each other rather than if those experiences are compartmentalized. Since language is used in all of the subject fields, language is taught throughout the school day. Students need to learn the "special" language of math (subtrahend, minuend, difference) and the special language of social studies (interdependence, migration, democracy). Although we may schedule a time for creative writing, we teach writing skills in every subject. Reading can be taught while using the social studies textbook, reading cartoons in a magazine, playing games, or watching filmstrips.

When students interview others as part of their social studies lesson, they are accomplishing language objectives and social studies objectives. When students describe a science experiment, they may be reasoning deductively for science, but once again they are languaging and learning to write "records." The use of data-gathering tools in the disciplines work naturally to integrate those subject fields with the language arts. The reader is urged to preview the teaching unit in Chapter 14 and the Appendix and review the section on the integration of subject fields in Chapter 4.

The Language Arts Components

Approaches to Listening

Students are requested to listen more than 50 per cent of the school day. A listener has no control over the tempo of speech. If school language is different from home language, listening problems are compounded. Listening is considered the basis for the other language arts components. The child who hears "bus" for "boss" obviously is not going to understand what has been said. Similarly the student who hears "git" for "get" may not be able to read or write the word "get". Discrimination of sounds is critical to learning language and to communication in general.

Listening requires decoding what is heard. We hear sound symbols. These sound symbols are called *phonemes*. When phonemes are combined into a pattern, the phonemes become a *morpheme*. The morpheme is a word unit. Morphemes are combined in order to form a sentence. If the individual does not discriminate among phonemes, then it will be impossible for that individual to interpret what has been said. We know that students differ in their auditory discrimination, and that auditory discrimination is subject to the maturation process. Frequently students do not mature in the development of this skill until they are about eight years old.

There is a positive relationship between poor auditory discrimination and reading. The student who does not hear well will not learn to read well. However, Ramsey (1972) studied the relationship between listening and dialect and found no significant difference in the children's ability to answer questions about a story they had heard.

Levels of Listening

Auding is considered to be the highest level of listening. To aud means that the individual perceives what has been said and is able to think about it critically. The individual who is auding listens to a message and begins to ask himself/herself questions about it. For example, the other night on radio the newscaster stated that Americans were asked to leave Libya. Critical auding of this message would mean that the listener would ask the following types of questions:

Who has requested that Americans leave Libya?
Are Americans in danger in Libya?
What provoked this request?
In what ways have relations changed between Libya and the U.S.?
To what extent is our information about Libya reliable?

Innumerable questions could be added to this list. The point is that auding involves the skill of detecting bias, examining what has been heard in terms of the listener's own experiences, and ultimately making a judgment.

Below auding is the ability to *listen*. In listening the individual identifies and recognizes sound. Listening involves concentration. Environmental conditions affect the ability to listen. The temperature of the classroom may affect attention; noise or movements may distract the listener; the comfort of listeners in chairs or on the floor may facilitate or inhibit good listening. Other factors affecting listening may include hunger, lighting, acoustics, interest, the speaker's voice and/or gestures, and enthusiasm.

The lowest level of listening is *hearing*. Hearing is affected by physical factors. Auditory acuity is the ability to detect sound vibrations at various intensities. Individuals with ear damage will not be able to hear properly. Other problems affecting hearing include auditory fatigue, which occurs when the ear has been exposed to loud noises over an extended period of time. For example, the author attended a basketball game in which the student body continuously pounded their feet and yelled. The noise was so pervasive and intense that hearing became difficult. Another hearing problem occurs when the individual hears more than one conversation simultaneously. For instance, at a cocktail party, the listener must decide which conversation to receive. What happens is that each ear receives a different message and so confusion or fatigue sets in; the listener must be able to direct both ears to one speaker and one conversation in order to listen. Another factor affecting hearing may be background noises. Classrooms that face the playground are affected by playground sounds that mask what is being said in the classroom. Schools that are close to freeways are troubled by masking sounds that affect hearing in the classrooms.

APPLICATION OF RESEARCH

In the cloze test words are omitted from sentences in order to determine whether or not the reader can determine the missing word or the meaning. When used as an individual treatment, the procedure can be effective in improving reading and listening skills (Kennedy and Weener, 1973).

Listening Skills

The following guidelines may be useful in the development of listening skills:

- The teacher should model listening skills. When students speak, let them know through eye contact and response that what they say is important.
- Ask students to clarify, amplify, or explain their thoughts when they have miscommunicated.
- Ensure that the classroom environment facilitates listening; attend to noise, temperature, and comfort.
- Set listening objectives. If students are to listen, explain the purpose for the activity.
- Help students to become discriminating listeners in order to detect bias, stereotyping, emotion.
- Set listening standards. Consider asking students to take turns during a discussion *without* raising hands.

Activities to Develop Listening Skills

1. Oral games: Simon Says or Follow the Leader. Students should take turns being the leader.
2. Musical instruments: Have students repeat rhythm patterns. Use rhythm sticks or drums, or oatmeal boxes.
3. Nonsense sentences: Recite nonsense sentences and have students listen and correct the sentence. Example: "Drink a Jennie wants."
4. Listening to a tape: Students pantomime what they hear.
5. Recitation of rhymes and poems: Teacher recites familiar rhyme or poem and students fill in missing line.
6. Listening to a story and observing pictures of the story: Students identify what was *not* in the story; students arrange pictures in sequence of the story; students retell the story in their own words.
7. Records of city sounds, country sounds, animal sounds: Students identify what they hear.
8. Dance: Students dance the "Hokey Pokey."
9. Listening to a story: Students express emotion, telling how they would feel if they were the characters in the story.
10. Listening to words: Students count the syllables heard.
11. Listening to sentences: Students listen for a new word; then they name it and use it in a new sentence.
12. Listening to sentences: Students listen to present and past tense sentences and identify the differences in meaning.
13. Taping a discussion: Students critique their own discussion. Criteria and guidelines should be used. (See Chapters 12 and 17.)

Additional suggestions for using and relating listening skills will be found in the other approaches to the language arts components.

Approaches to Oral Language Development

Oral language is really the result of "learning by doing." Speech is generated from the experience of listening. Although speech is a natural development, it is affected by the substance of the child's environment. An only child can be expected to have advanced language development. The language development pattern is qualitatively affected by the child's enriched experiences. Oral language also reflects the child's emotional and social adjustment. Children who lack adult contact and love fail to extend the quality of their language.

School-age children typically produce sentence or main clause patterns that conform to the following:

Subject + Verb + Direct Object (Transitive)
The cat likes hot milk.
He hit Billy.
Subject + Linking Verb + Predicate Nominative
The cat is black.
He is silly.
Subject + Verb (Intransitive)
The cat sat on the mat.
The birds are flying (De Stefano & Fox, 1974, p. 55).

Studies of school-age children indicate that in most cases children's oral language growth increases around the five- to six-year-old level and once again when the child reaches ten to twelve years old. During the years in between (grades two through five), growth appears to be much slower. While the developmental sequence of syntactic structures appears to be consistent among children, the ages where it occurs is inconsistent.

> Should students' oral language be evaluated? If yes, how would you do it? If no, why?

Chomsky (1974) described her research on syntactic constructions with different age groups. Using the following sentences children from five to ten years of age were asked to analyze the meaning of each set of sentences.

a. The doll is eager to see.
b. The doll is easy to see.
c. The girl told the boy what to paint.
d. The girl asked the boy what to paint.

> Should all third-grade students be at the same syntactical level? Why?

Chomsky found that six- and seven-year-old children interpreted sentence *b.* to mean, "It is easy for the doll to see," and at the same age the children interpreted sentence *d.* as meaning, "The girl told the boy *what* to paint" or "The girl asked the boy what *he* was going to paint." Not until the children were over the age of eight were all of them able to explain sentence *b.* correctly. Sentence *d.* was not interpreted correctly until age nine, when two thirds of the children explained it correctly.

> In what ways could a second-grade teacher use Chomsky's research as a basis for oral language activities?

Classroom Environment

Wilkinson (1974) described the skills of listening and speaking as "oracy" skills. (Literacy skills are writing and reading.) Oracy skills influence personal, social, and intellectual development. Wilkinson stated that elementary teachers can be very influential in the development of a child's vocabulary because (1) the elementary classroom can facilitate a warm relationship between teacher (or other adults in the classroom) and student, (2) the seating arrangements in elementary classrooms can facilitate interaction, and (3) oracy skills can be developed throughout the school day in all subject fields. However, in some classrooms children are not allowed to talk even though oral communication and the improvement of speech are very important components of the elementary school curriculum. As Wilkinson indicated, in some classrooms the physical environment is conducive to speaking; in others it is not. Rows of chairs arranged so that students cannot see each other will *not* facilitate good speaking habits. For children to feel self-confident in volunteering what they have to say, the social and emotional climate must be friendly and accepting.

To improve oracy skills, the following guidelines have been suggested by elementary teachers:

1. Arrange classroom furniture to encourage eye and voice contact. During a class discussion, arrange chairs to facilitate listening and speaking.
2. Prepare students for speaking and listening by calling attention to "models." (The teacher is the best model.)
3. Utilize tape records and language masters in the classroom so that students can listen to themselves as well as others, and practice speech habits.
4. Plan a variety of activities to encourage speaking and listening.
5. Create a stimulating classroom environment to encourage speech.
6. Consider the students' personal experiences and needs in planning the program.
7. Base remediation activities on individual needs.
8. Lessen drill time; increase informal speech times (Lemlech, 1977, p. 214).

To encourage speaking and listening, the following activities are suggested:

- Dramatics. Students can make up plays, participate in role-plays and dramatic representation.
- Art experiences. Students can participate in art activities and then describe the experience to others.
- Small group interaction. Students can work together to plan a project or resolve a conflict.
- Interviewing. Students can interview peers or others. They can tape the interviews and play them back for classmates.

The Puppet Theater Helps Kindergarten Children Develop Oral Language.

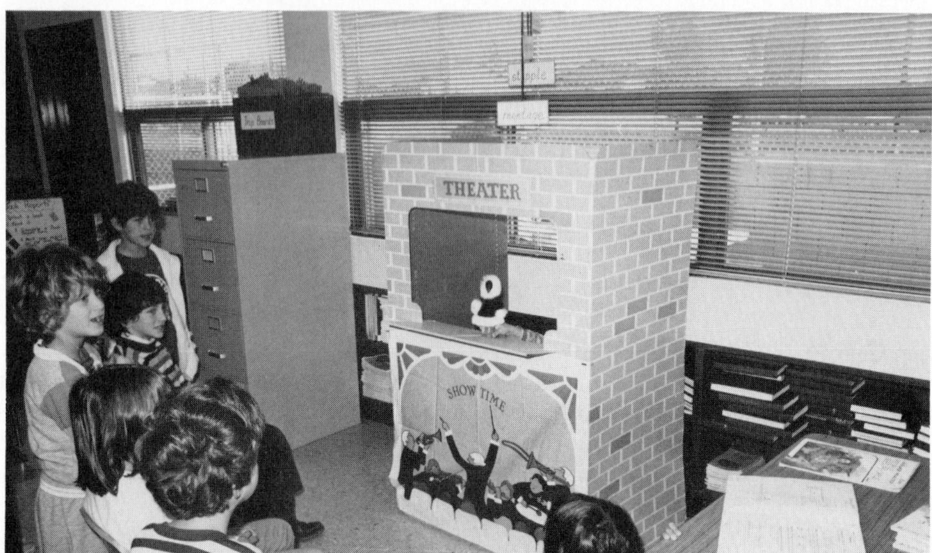

- Storytelling. Students can listen or read a story and then retell the story to others.
- Puppetry. Students can make hand puppets and use them for dramatics.
- Singing. Students can sing current favorites and rewrite the words.
- Choral verse. Students can participate in group speech activities.
- Touch and tell. Students can describe what they feel: hot, cold, soft, rough, smooth, sandy.
- Listen and tell. Students can listen to strange sounds and then describe them.

Approaches to Reading Instruction

Due to the importance of reading in the elementary curriculum, a separate chapter (Chapter 6) has been devoted to reading instruction.

RESEARCH FINDINGS

- Listening vocabulary and reading vocabulary are effective predictors of inference, deduction, and interpretation—the three components of critical thinking (MacNaughton, 1976).
- Fifth-grade boys and girls do not differ in their ability to think critically (Harris, 1975).

Approaches to Written Language Development

For some time now both educators and the public have been concerned that we are producing nonwriters in the schools as a consequence of assignments that require multiple choice selections, short answers, and worksheet responses. Even more critical is the fact that in making such assignments, teachers organize and synthesize information, thereby depriving students of the value of planning, organizing, and communicating meanings (Applebee, 1981). The development of written composition skills needs to occur throughout the school day; these skills are basic to the entire curriculum. For this reason the writing component is emphasized in this chapter.

To some extent writing may be the most difficult language arts component to develop. Students typically have a large listening vocabulary but a much smaller speaking vocabulary. The child is dependent upon the speaking vocabulary for written expression. For this reason, the speaking component should be emphasized before students are expected to write. Students who do not use correct sentence patterns or expanded sentences in speech will certainly have difficulty in writing. The writing process is dependent upon the ability to use a pencil and to write legibly and the ability to spell and appreciate word usage.

To write effectively, students need to understand the relationship of words to thoughts. Writing involves ordering words into a logical pattern for self-expression. When primary-aged children draw pictures, their teachers usually ask them to "tell the story of your picture." The oral composition of a story should precede the written composition. Quality of written work is dependent upon the quality of thought.

Effective writing requires knowledge of writing mechanics, such as punctuation, capitalization, spelling, and sentence structure. Young children are rarely aware that in oral speech their facial expression, stress, pitch, or foot stomping help clarify their communication to others. Punctuation serves to clarify written expression in the same manner, and so students need to discover how writing is affected by punctuation, capitalization, and sentence structure.

How Is Writing Taught?

The purposes of the writing program include:

1. The development of functional writing to communicate ideas
2. The development of creative writing to express thoughts
3. Skill development in the mechanics of writing.

These three purposes are developed through student activities such as letter writing, creative writing, informational writing, recordkeeping, note taking, outlining, research, and proofreading. These activities and the mechanics of writing will be discussed.

Letter Writing. To enable students to recognize the importance of letter writing, personal letters and business letters should be taught as an integral part of the regular program. For example, if there is to be a school open house, students can write personal invitations to their families and friends; if a classmate is ill, students can write greetings or friendly letters. If special information is needed, students can write business letters requesting information or materials and then follow up the request with a thank-you note when the purpose has been accomplished.

Many occasions can be used to generate a letter-writing session. The purpose of the letter, the form, punctuation, and capitalization—even the way in which a letter is folded—should be taught at the moment of need rather than as a special language lesson. During any discussion of letter writing, students will need to learn sensitivity to the timing of letters, appropriate greetings and closings, and the amount of detail a letter should contain. All writing that is individually derived is creative. During creative writing teachers should allow students to attend to the content of their work rather than spoil the creative effort by insisting on correct form. When creating, students should use any words they desire, without concern for correct spelling. If students ask for assistance, the teacher can provide it by writing the desired word on a slip of paper for the student's dictionary word box or writing the word directly into a dictionary notebook maintained by each student.

At the beginning of this chapter there was an example of an oral language lesson that began with literature, then class discussion, an art lesson, and ultimately creative writing. These students have their own writing book in which they will write imaginatively about themselves and a flying machine. The creative writing will occur periodically over several weeks. After a student completes a story, the teacher will "correct" it. The corrections will be talked about between teacher and student. The students will *not* be asked to change their stories to adhere to the teacher's form; but as the students continue to write new stories in their creative writing book, their stories will naturally reflect what they have learned about punctuation, capitalization, and word usage.

Since motivation is extremely important to initiate creative writing, the first-grade teacher, whose students will be writing creatively over a period of time, will need to re-motivate each time the students are to write about their flying machines. Part of the time s/he will do this by having individual children read their stories to the class; the students will serve to motivate each other.

APPLICATIONS OF RESEARCH

Written language achievement is positively effected by prewriting activities . . . which involve time to think, to experience, to discuss, and to interact with language . . . (Silverman et al., 1981, p. 95).

Creative Writing. Creative writing may involve writing about personal experiences or feelings or make-believe. Poems, rhymes, and stories are all appropriate.

> You have edited your fourth-grade students' creative writing compositions. Do you believe that the students should rewrite their compositions? Explain the value of each position.

Note Taking. Note taking begins at the personal level to meet the needs of the individual. The notes may be used for studying purposes or, eventually, to write a report or to communicate orally to others. Young students rarely know "how" to take notes. The skills involved in note taking have much to do with the act of studying. For example, the note taker needs to know:

- Purpose/importance of the assignment or task
- Background knowledge
- Organization of the materials to be used

1. The significance of note taking for preserving information for future reference, or for evaluating print or nonprint information, or as a basis for future outlining, needs to be communicated to students. If students are to take notes in order to study for an examination, then the students will also need to know whether the examination is to be essay type, multiple choice, or true-false. If students are to use the notes for an oral report, the notes will be different than if they are to be used as evidence citations during a discussion. The purpose and the importance of the assignment must be communicated to students.

2. Note taking skill may be dependent upon prior knowledge and information about the topic to be researched. When Greg Thomas' students (Chapter 13) researched architecture and furniture produced during the colonial period, they had to have some background experience recognizing early American furniture and architecture. The students in the furniture group also had to know that their notes would be used to develop a retrieval chart about colonial and European furniture. This knowledge would influence their research and the type of notes they would preserve.

3. Note taking is influenced by the nature of the materials to be used. An art history book may be organized in a different way than a science or health textbook. Students need to be alerted to the author's use of headings or questions as an organizing structure. If students are to take notes about slides they have viewed or if they are to take notes during an interview situation, they will need to have a way to judge what is important and valuable to record.

Taba (1967, pp. 130–131) identified a number of learning activities to develop note taking skills. These include:

- making charts (classroom rules, procedures about "how-to," recipes)
- writing captions (for students' stories or pictures)
- listing (events, changes, problems)
- recording information (utilizing resources both written and oral and media resource materials)
- diagramming (flow charts, sequence studies, family structure)
- classifying (developing conceptual categories using the yellow pages of the telephone directory or other reference tools)
- tabulating (votes, opinions, survey information, textbooks used).

Teachers can help students learn to identify what is important for note taking by demonstrating the skills on the chalkboard as the whole class works together reading or viewing a specific area of content and practicing the skill.

Moffett and Wagner (1976) describe another type of note taking called *sensory writing*. Sensory writing involves observational notes obtained by seeing, hearing, and recording sensations. Observational notes are particularly useful for keeping science journals and for studying behavior in social studies and health education. Difficulties sometimes encountered by students with observational notes have to do with controlling the speed of the input when using an oral source and with developing a code for personal use during note taking. Sometimes young children also have difficulty maintaining attention because they are subjected to stimuli overload.

A fine technique for improving students' note taking skills is to group the students after the sensory experience. Let us assume that a group of fourth graders observed a discussion in another classroom. During the discussion they took notes. Back in their own classroom, working in small groups, the students shared their notes with each other. They can compare their notes in terms of capturing the important points in the discussion, and they can compare their observations and impressions of the speakers' moods, enthusiasm, attitudes, voice tone, and gestures.

APPLICATION OF RESEARCH

Sinatra (1983, p. 12) recommends that teachers cultivate and reward the nonverbal mode of expression. By praising the nonverbal strengths used for invention and art and music expression, teachers can help restore the dominant role of the right hemisphere of the brain in creativity and in language development.

In the evaluation of the assignment the whole class discussion can be focused on whether the observers were objective or in fact wrote very personal reactions. The tendency to write whole sentences, lists of what happened, or emotionally laden expressions can be discussed.

In helping students develop note taking skills, it is important to communicate that note taking is a personal aid to learning and, as such, requires each person to develop an individual notation style.

Outlining. Students need to learn the purpose of an outline and the structure of an outline. The skills identified by Taba for developing note taking competence are useful to help students make the discriminations necessary for organizing information into an outline. Rubin (1980) identified readiness skills for outlining. Kindergarten students learn to group items that belong together, such as scissors, doll clothes, paints, puzzles. At the first-grade level, students may be able to separate items, discriminating between real and make-believe, or foods to be cooked and foods that can be eaten raw, warm weather clothing and cold weather clothing. At the second-grade level students continue grouping activities but are able to make finer discriminations among items. For example, the second grader may be able to identify the different compositions of rocks or different classifications of plants. Third graders become even more sophisticated and learn to classify ideas in a more organized fashion. The third grader may categorize using several different headings and become fairly adept at developing a table of contents for stories and pictures.

Formal structural rules for outlining can be taught beginning with the fourth grade. However, once again, the outline should be related to the area of study and taught when outlining will be useful to the students. Donoghue (1979, p. 395) suggested the following structure:

I. Main Topic with Roman numeral
    A. Subtopic indentation and capital letter
        1. Detail indentation, Arabic numeral
            a. Sub-detail—indentation and lower case letter
        2. More detail on same topic—Arabic numeral
    B. Subtopic with capital letter
II. Additional main topic with Roman Numeral
    A.
    B.
        1.
        2.
            a.
            b.
    C.
        1.
        2.

Since the structure of outlining is confusing to students, Rubin (1980) suggested that the structure be described by students in their own words and displayed on a classroom chart for reference purposes. To help students recognize the relationship between classifying and outlining, she recommended the use of organizing exercises. For example, lower-grade students could be asked to write the main topic (or family name) for items and upper grade students might be asked to fill in an outline about rocks.

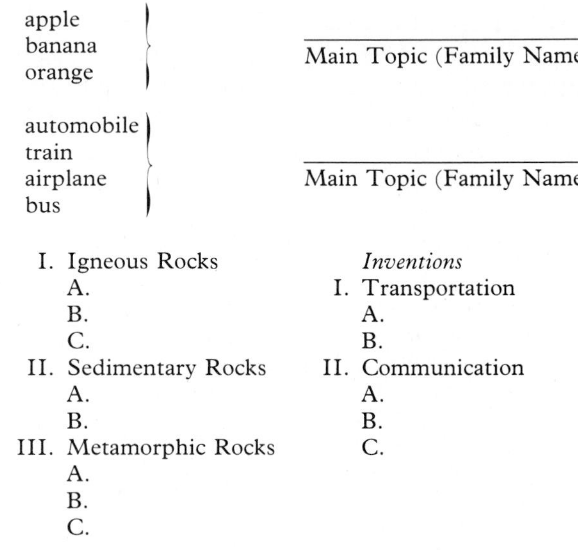

Perhaps these students would be searching for the information using their science textbook or experiments in the classroom. As upper grade students become more sophisticated, they could develop an outline about rocks that would identify other attributes and require finer discriminations so that details would be added to the outline.

Informational Writing. Informational writing includes the writing of reports, personal experiences, new articles. This type of writing may communicate information or personal feelings. Students need to learn how to organize a report to make it interesting and they need to adhere to a specific form. The development of the form may be decided by the teacher, or guidelines for the report may be developed by the class. Unlike creative writing, informational writing demands that spelling and punctuation receive prominent attention. A class or school newspaper is a particularly motivating way to teach informational writing. Since a newspaper has so many different types of stories, students have the opportunity to choose special interests and styles.

Writing Descriptions and Observations. Students need a great deal of practice communicating information about events that have happened. Remembering and reporting objectively (who was involved, what was involved, where it occurred, and the length of time of the event) are extremely difficult tasks. Yet every time there is a problem in the schoolroom or out on the playground, teachers ask students: "What happened?" "Who did what to whom and why?"

Strategies for teaching objective writing can be practiced by assigning students to be reporters, historians, judges, or scientists. School or classroom newspapers or magazines are popular ruses to develop observational skills. Other useful activities for practicing these skills include writing up science-health experiments, making a procedural accounting of "how to" make something, or giving a report of what happened in Room 28 yesterday with students asked to stress accuracy and objectivity.

Sharing descriptions with others is valuable for broadening students' perspective. As in the note taking strategy, if students have the opportunity to share their observations in a small group of others who have witnessed the same event or activity, they will be surprised by the differences in their observations. Differences in choice of vocabulary, phrasing, use of descriptive words, length of sentences, and types of comparisons can be shared. These differences, however, are not evaluated in terms of "good" and "bad" or "correct" and "incorrect."

RESEARCH FINDINGS

Graves (1975, p. 235) researched students' writing behavior and concluded:

(1) Informal environments and unstructured assignments motivate students to write more and in greater length than specific assignments in a formal environment.
(2) When students are required to write in a formal classroom environment, girls will do better than boys; in informal environments, boys will write at greater length than girls.
(3) Assigned writing restricts the range, content, and amount of writing produced by both boys and girls.

Recordkeeping. A variety of activities throughout the school day provide opportunities to learn this type of writing. A small group planning session requires a group "recorder." This person takes the minutes of the meeting by recording the "plans." Individual, group, or class science experiments require a different type of recordkeeping. In some classrooms, students take turns writing the daily news on the chalkboard. Writing individual or class diaries provides another type of experience in recordkeeping. First graders may just begin to record facts or experiences, while fourth graders may be expected to record information in outlines. Through recordkeeping, students learn the value of accuracy, a sense of time, continuity, cause and effect, and the need for attention to detail. Records should always be written in the students' own words rather than in adult language.

Research. The style of writing used in research papers is similar to the writing of informational papers. The main difference involves the skills that are taught. First graders may begin to learn research skills by filing words in a dictionary box. Third graders may be expected to use picture dictionaries and a table of contents and an index to locate information. Fifth graders can be taught to make and use bibliographies, utilize several sources of information, write questions about what they want to research, and take notes to answer the questions they have developed.

Proofreading. Proofreading skills need to be modeled as well as taught. Few adults know how to edit their own work, so it is not surprising that students seldom reread their own reports or compositions for the purpose of self-editing. Teachers can model proofreading by acknowledging to students: "Just a minute, let me reread this," or the teacher may say to students, after recording something on the chalkboard, "Does this say what we wanted it to say? Do the sentences fit together?" Students can be asked to help develop proofreading criteria. For example, students might develop criteria to call attention to punctuation, capitalization, topic sentences, paragraphing, and conclusions. Or perhaps the criteria will suggest rereading to determine whether the story has a good title, an exciting beginning, and a good climax.

Mechanics of Writing

Composition skills include capitalization and punctuation, sentence processing and paragraphing, spelling, and handwriting. These skills are best taught in a meaningful situation rather than as isolated lessons. During the primary grades as students write, the teacher provides independent help while circulating and observing the students at work. By the middle grades, students can begin editing their own work.

Punctuation and Capitalization. As a general rule the young child will tend to over-punctuate and over-capitalize. The relationship between punctuation and speech needs to be demonstrated to the students. By the end of second grade most students recognize the need to end sentences with a punctuation mark, begin sentences with a capital letter, and capitalize the personal pronoun "I." By the end of the middle grades most students have mastered the use of capitalizations in abbreviations, in the first word of greetings, in topics in an outline, and in the first word of a direct quotation. Commas used in a series, in writing the date, and between city and state have typically been mastered by the end of the fourth grade.

Sentence Processing Skills. In the primary grades sentence processing skills begin with students demonstrating understanding of word order in a sentence by unscrambling simple sentences. Sentence transformations begin in the second grade, and the ability to expand a simple sentence is typically mastered by the end of the primary grades. Independent writing of simple sentences is usually mastered by the third grade. Simple paragraph writing occurs during the middle grades.

Word Usage. Selecting and using nouns, pronouns, verbs, and adjectives are typically mastered by the end of the third grade. Students can also recognize the use of synonyms, antonyms, and homonyms during the middle grades.

Style. It is extremely difficult for an elementary student to develop writing style until compositional skills have been mastered. Sentence structure, logic, and clarity come first; however, teachers need to exercise care that, in their editing and assisting zeal, they not discourage students from expressing themselves in unique ways. Sometimes students want to use slang in order to express their individuality. To some extent this tendency can be curbed by demonstrating to students the temporal quality of slang terms and the meaninglessness of words when they are no longer commonly understood. When students learn to use figurative language, development of writing style appears. During the middle grades students begin to use metaphors and similes. The frequency of writing and the encouragement provided to students facilitates the development of style in writing.

What Influences Students' Writing Ability?

In a review of research studies on students' writing ability, Donoghue (1979, pp. 247–249) reported the following factors to be influential in writing performance:

1. *Verbal Ability.* Verbal ability is significantly related to composition writing. Superior students write more and perform at a higher level of development.

2. *Reading Ability*. Reading ability is positively related to writing ability. Better readers tend to write more complex sentences.
3. *Grade Level*. As students advance in grade level and are chronologically older, average and above average students write longer sentences with more variations than their younger classmates. For low-ability students, as grade level advances there is a greater variation with the national performance in expressive writing.
4. *Classroom Environment*. (Review the Graves study in this chapter.)
5. *Handedness*. Verbal and nonverbal tests indicate that left-handed students do better than right-handed students; therefore, left-handers have an advantage in writing ability. However, left-handed students may need special assistance because of the physical difficulty of performing in most classrooms. Without provisions made for left-handed performance, the student may be inhibited from experimenting syntactically.
6. *Socioeconomic Status*. Students in the higher socioeconomic groups have an advantage over those in lower socioeconomic groups; their written papers are more expressive and imaginative as a rule, and the students use more variety in choice of words.
7. *Sex*. Generally, girls write more than boys and their compositions have been judged to be of a high quality. Seven-year-old boys write more about an expanded environment away from the home.
8. *Teacher Attitude*. Students produce more writing, make fewer errors, and develop more ideas in classrooms where the teacher encourages expression. Neither positive nor negative criticism appears to affect students' output.

APPLICATIONS OF RESEARCH

Silverman et al. (1981) reported in a study of written language that students do not spend enough time practicing the expression of their ideas in written form. These authors recommend that teachers in basic education and special education allocate more time to creative writing.

Teaching Spelling

Students have the opportunity to learn and to use spelling words whenever they are expressing themselves in written form. A daily planned spelling period is usually provided by the time students are in the second grade. During the spelling period teachers typically use methods and techniques which include observing the word to be studied, hearing it, saying it, defining it in the student's own words, and practicing it by writing.

The spelling period habitually involves:

1. Presentation of words
2. Definition of words
3. Study of words
4. Using words in sentences or exercises
5. Practice and drill.

Pretest, posttest, and review of words customarily occurs on predetermined days of the week. Students who pass the pretest should be provided with vocabulary-building activities or other extended experiences.

Words are selected for study from approved source books or state or district spelling textbooks. Words are also selected from the list of words that children request most often, from social studies and science content, and from words that students miss most frequently in their written work.

Dependent upon the grade level and maturity of the students, spelling skills to be taught include phonetic analysis, diacritical marks, syllabication, suffixes and prefixes, and dictionary skills.

In kindergarten and grade one students engage in readiness activities and language experiences rather than a formal and systematic spelling program. Activities that facilitate language development include block work, art work (finger painting, clay, paints and crayons, crafts), rhythm activities, field trips, and use of audiovisual materials. Spelling habits are encouraged by providing opportunities for students to dictate letters and stories to adults or older children, by writing signs and labels to identify work areas or dramatic activities, and by observing the teacher writing charts and stories on the chalkboard.

Spelling games. Spelling games can be used to enrich the spelling program. Some commercial games such as Scrabble for Juniors, Anagrams, and Spelling Lotto are popular with elementary students. Many games (crossword puzzles, word wheels) can be created by the teacher to encourage students to use the dictionary and to study spelling words.

Teaching Handwriting

The purposes for teaching handwriting include:

- The development of legible and fluent manuscript and cursive writing
- The development of pride in neatness and correctness of writing

Handwriting is taught beginning in the first grade, but its mastery is dependent upon the age of maturity of the individual student. The transition from manuscript to cursive writing is customarily accomplished in the third grade; however, school districts vary as to when they suggest beginning cursive instruction. Many students are not ready for cursive writing at the beginning of third grade.

Readiness for handwriting is determined by eye-hand coordination and the ability to differentiate the forms of letters. The use of manipulative materials facilitates readiness for handwriting. These experiences may include the use of clay, tempera, finger paint, and physical activities involving motor skills.

Handwriting Skills. In the primary grades handwriting skills include the development of arm and hand coordination and eye-hand coordination. Students need to learn directionality in order to be aware of the left-to-right progression used in writing. Young students often have difficulty detecting the size and spatial relationship between letters and words. In upper grades students should practice the correct form and size of letters and the proper alignment on the page including correct margins. The spacing and slant of writing should be observed and practiced so that it is uniform and legible.

Handwriting Program. A planned program for handwriting should include:

1. Opportunity to develop muscle coordination.
2. Appropriate materials (large pencil and paper for primary children).
3. Guidance concerning correct posture and positioning of paper. This is particularly important for left-handed students.
4. Opportunity to study the correct form for manuscript and cursive writing.
5. Opportunity to practice the correct form for manuscript and cursive writing using words, phrases, and sentences rather than isolated letters.
6. Opportunity to compare their own handwriting with the correct form of handwriting.
7. Supervision and individual assistance during handwriting.

Teaching Literature

The primary purpose of a literature program is to create awareness and enjoyment of all types of books. As students progress through the elementary grades they should be aware of the different types of literature—including the classics—and they should develop an appreciation for reading. The literature period can be a designated time when young students are read to, or it can be a time when students choose their own books for recreational reading. The literature program can be planned to supplement teaching in the content fields by exposing students to specialized information and the ideas of scholars interested in specific academic fields.

Teacher tasks during literature include modeling enthusiasm for reading, providing for a wide range of interests, encouraging variety in reading choices, assisting students to interpret what they read, and developing library skills. The literature period should be planned as an integral part of the reading program although it does not have to share the same time slot. (Review Hogan's and Thomas' daily schedule in Chapter 4.)

Moffett and Wagner (1976) suggested that teachers allow students to discover the different types of literature rather than defining it for them. By providing appropriate reading selections, students can discover the difference between myths and legends or between fables and parables. These authors also suggest that students rewrite stories in different forms. For example, students could take a comic strip story and write it as a short story or change a nonfiction story or article into a fictional narrative or fictional autobiography. Science fiction could be transformed into an historical novel framework. The literature program can be used to encourage creative writing.

Special Concerns in the Language Arts

Evaluating Growth in Language Arts

Language arts growth can be evaluated by means of actual learning activities as well as through standardized tests. Although it is not possible to know how well students are listening or how much students comprehend when they are reading, it is possible to evaluate growth when students produce a product. Receptive growth can be measured by expressive acts. When students discuss, dramatize, or use written materials to produce something, comprehension can be evaluated. If students need to interpret written directions while working in a learning center, their comprehension is assessed.

Informal teacher-made tests, observation of students' learning behaviors, learning activity products, and standardized tests should all be used to identify students' levels of ability. Once assessed it is the teachers' task to diagnose learning problems, if they exist, and proceed to design instruction to facilitate the learning process. Students should also be involved in the evaluative process. It is important for students to be aware of their own strengths and weaknesses. However, it is also important that they not be overwhelmed with failures. Particularly in the area of reading, it is significant to conference with the student and develop goals jointly for future progress.

Oral language skills should be evaluated for speech defects, such as: lisping, poor articulation, stuttering, baby talk, unpleasant or inappropriate pitch. Speech performance in small groups, whole classes, and with one or two peers should be evaluated. The ability to converse with adults should also be assessed.

Students' writing can be evaluated in terms of content (relevancy, clarity, originality, interest) and in terms of form (organization, style, punctuation, capitalization, word usage, legibility, appropriateness). Specific writing skills such as the ability to write a business letter or a personal letter can also be evaluated.

Although we never know when students are listening, it is possible to recognize their readiness to listen by observing external signs. It is a teachers' responsibility to see that students get themselves ready for listening and then to test through expressive means whether students attended. This is accomplished by checking whether students can identify details, sequence elements, distinguish relevant from irrelevant information, recognize supporting facts after the receptive experience. Checklists for doing this will be found in Chapter 17.

Mainstreaming

Typically, elementary classrooms have a wide range of ability levels which include gifted children and slow learners. The addition of physically handicapped students or students with learning problems can also be expected in most classrooms. Customarily mainstreamed children are provided with individualized instruction for their language arts components; however, appropriate instruction can occur in the regular classroom provided an Individualized Educational Program has been developed with instructional materials and supportive services available to student and teacher.

An advantage to regular classroom placement is the availability of peer tutors. Working with a partner, mainstreamed children can practice reading and oral language skills. Proper reinforcement with peer tutors can have a positive effect on motivation and interest.

Research on direct instruction is applicable to the teaching of academic skills to handicapped students. The reader is urged to review and preview the following sections in the text:

1. Mainstreaming information in Chapter 1
2. Direct Instruction in Chapters 3 and 12
3. Table 7.3 in Chapters 7.

Nonstandard English

It is especially important in the teaching of language arts that teachers demonstrate to students their acceptance of all languages and language differences. There is no conclusive evidence that speaking nonstandard English has any effect on learning to read or learning to spell. Cultural gaps between school and community appear to be responsible for most learning problems. Moffett (1976) observed that speakers of nonstandard pronunciation automatically adjust for dialectical differences in pronunciation, grammar, and vocabulary.

To assist the nonstandard speaker of English (or the bilingual student), teachers should provide many opportunities for oral language. Auditory discrimination exercises can be used to improve the speech of the nonstandard English speaker. Examples of exercises follow:

1. Select and pronounce pictures with the same beginning sound as the key picture. (The teacher makes a chart with a key picture and many other picture examples of the same beginning sound. If the key picture is a banana, other pictures include: book, barn, bear, cat, apple, ball, pear, boot.)
2. Select and pronounce words that sound alike (cat, bat). Explain in what way the words are alike.
3. Select and pronounce words that are unlike each other (cats, houses).
4. Identify initial, medial, and final consonant sounds.

Initial	*Medial*	*Final*
pan	apple	lap
pear	hamper	map
pie	happy	ship

5. From a list of words, students select initial consonant blends.

blouse	beat
black	blood
bear	blend

Learning Centers

Learning centers in the language arts are used as an integral part of the instructional program. The center facilitates reinforcement of skill development and offers an opportunity to individualize instruction.

Figurative Language Center

Language Arts, Social Studies
Upper Grades

Objectives: To improve comprehension of word meanings, appreciate language, use figurative language, develop cooperative work skills.

Materials: An envelope or box to contain the figurative expressions, a direction card.

Evaluation: Observation and discussion.

Procedures:

1. Direction card explains that students are to take turns choosing an expression from the "box" or envelope. Each student is to pantomime an expression while the other members of the group try to guess the expression.

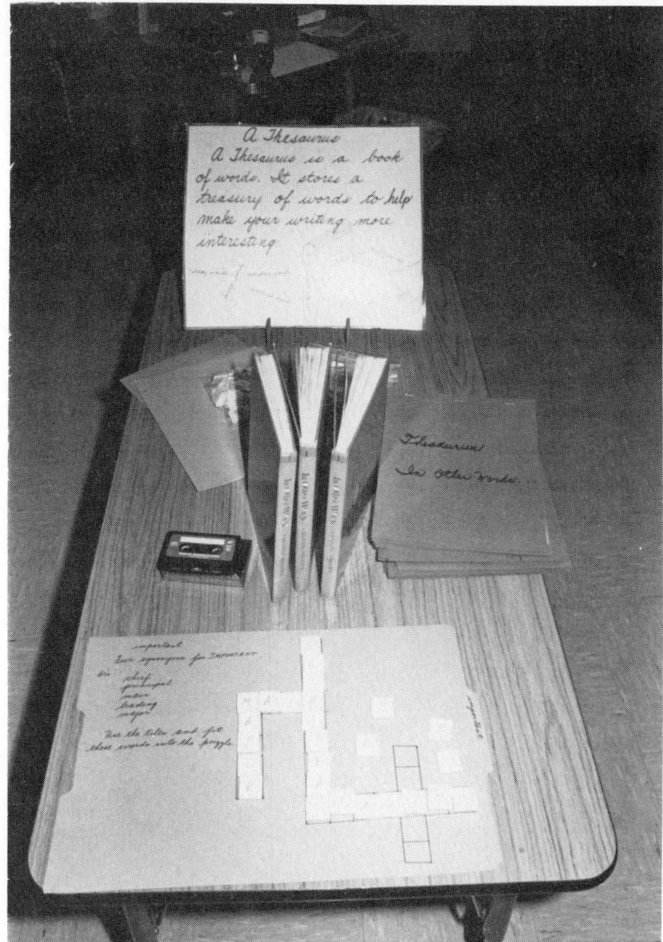

In This Classroom the Learning Center Was Used to Expand Students' Vocabulary.

2. Expressions may include the following:
   - arm of the law
   - on the face of it
   - put on the dog
   - eye of the storm
   - cat got your tongue
   - out of the woods
   - horsing around
   - leg of the journey
   - painted the town red
   - jumped on her high horse
   - check bounced
   - into the frying pan

To Simplify: Students may work with a partner to pantomime the expression.

To Extend: Students may write their own expressions and hand them out for others to act out.

Listening Center
Language Arts
Lower Grades

Objective: To improve listening skills; to sequence pictures related to a specific story.

Materials: Story record, flannel board pictures.

Procedures:

1. Students listen to a familiar story.
2. Students take turns retelling the story using the flannel board pictures.
3. Students self-evaluate by turning pictures over and checking the number sequence.

To Extend: Familiar routines are identified on the tape. Students take turns dramatizing, sequentially, these routines.

Examples: Making breakfast, getting ready for school, bike-riding, painting a picture, making ice cream, making tortillas.

Category Center

Language Arts, Art

Lower Grades

Objective: To categorize objects in order to improve comprehension.

Materials: Picture file, scissors, paste, paper.

Evaluation: Students share pictures and identify category and objects.

Procedures:

1. Students sort pictures by categories such as pets, fruits, animals, toys, transportation, vegetables, clothing, shelter.
2. Students cut out pictures and make a collage to demonstrate one selected category.

Comic Strip Center

Language Arts

Middle and Upper Grades

Objective: To improve creative writing, expand writing skills.

Evaluation: Students share composed comic strips.

Materials: Variety of comic strips with the dialogue eliminated, pencils.

Procedures: Students choose a comic strip and compose and insert the conversation in the appropriate spaces.

To Extend: Students may draw and write their own comic strips.

To Simplify: Students may work with a partner to compose the dialogue.

Information Center

Language Arts, Science, Social Studies, or Health

Middle and Upper Grades

Objective: To improve informational writing skills.

Materials: Taped stories, paper and pencils.

Evaluation: Students share stories with others.

Procedures:

1. Students listen to an incident and take notes.
2. Students write a news report of the story identifying:
   - Who is involved?
   - What happened?
   - How did it happen?
   - What were the results?

To Extend: More than one incident can be used; students may dramatize the story; students may take the roles of reporter and interviewees.

To Simplify: Students write stories with a partner. Less complicated taped incidents may be used.

Chapter Summary

The receptive and expressive language arts are interrelated; components reinforce and complement each other. Success in reading is dependent upon an adequate oral foundation. Identified in this chapter were teaching methods, activities, and research for teaching listening, oral language, writing, literature, spelling, and handwriting. The teaching of writing was emphasized. Suggestions were provided for mainstreaming and for working with bilingual or nonstandard English speakers. Learning center ideas were provided. Growth in the language arts can be evaluated through the use of standardized tests, teacher-made tests, observation, and actual learning activities.

Classroom Application Exercises

1. Plan a field trip for a group of students at the primary, middle-grade, or upper-grade level. Identify the new words that this experience could provide.
2. Plan a creative writing lesson based on a children's book of your choice.
3. Design a learning center to integrate language arts and another subject. Use the learning centers in this chapter as a guide.
4. Observe a group of students participating in block work or dramatic play. Describe your observation and explain what value this experience had for the participating children.
5. Begin to develop a file of ideas and games to use in learning centers to stimulate students to write.
6. How can you help students to develop their personal code for note taking?
7. Plan a science lesson and identify the communicative choices students will have to present their data.

Suggested Readings for Extending Study

Brizendine, Nancy Hanks and James L. Thomas. *Learning Through Dramatics: Ideas For Teachers and Librarians.* Phoenix, Ariz.: Oryx Press, 1982.

Cihak, Mary K. and Barbara Jackson Heron. *Games Children Should Play—Sequential Lessons for Teaching Communication Skills in Grades K-6.* Glenview, Ill.: Scott, Foresman & Company, 1980.

Lee, Doris M., and Joseph B. Rubin. *Children and Language Reading and Writing, Talking and Listening.* Belmont, Calif.: Wadsworth Publishing Co., Inc., 1979.

Moffett, James, and Betty James Wagner. *Student-Centered Language Arts and Reading, K-13. A Handbook for Teachers.* 2d ed. Boston; Houghton Mifflin Company, 1976.

Norton, Donna E. *The Effective Teaching of Language Arts.* Columbus, Ohio: Charles E. Merrill Publishing Company, 1980.

Petty, Walter T., and Julie M. Jensen. *Developing Children's Language.* Boston: Allyn & Bacon, Inc., 1980.

Rosenberg, Sheldon D. *Sentence Production: Development in Research and Theory.* New York: Halsted Press, 1977.

Rubin, Dorothy. *Teaching Elementary Language Arts.* 2d ed. New York: Holt, Rinehart and Winston, 1980.

Wehmeyer, Lillian Biermann. *Images in a Crystal Ball.* Libraries, Unlimited, Inc., 1981.

Willbrand, M. L., and R. D. Rieke. *Teaching Oral Communication in Elementary Schools.* New York: Macmillan Publishing Company, 1983.

Chapter **6**

Reading

After you have completed the study of this chapter, you should be able to accomplish the following:

1. **Explain how reading ability contributes to both personal and societal goals.**
2. **Describe the reading process.**
3. **Identify and discuss four purposes of reading.**
4. **Explain why each individual has a different level of readiness.**
5. **Suggest ways to develop reading readiness.**
6. **Describe several approaches to reading instruction; cite advantages and disadvantages of each approach.**
7. **Suggest classroom activities to encourage reading in the classroom.**
8. **Clarify grouping patterns for reading instruction.**
9. **Define a skill management system.**
10. **Suggest ways to use classroom aides during reading.**
11. **Define and describe a developmental reading program.**
12. **Identify skills used for decoding words.**
13. **Suggest classroom activities for skill development.**
14. **Create a learning center to enrich or reinforce skill instruction.**

Why Is Reading Important?

Individuals who can read with understanding hold the key to all of the stored knowledge of civilization. They are able to enter a limitless arena of thought, imagination, exploration, and enjoyment; to stop and reflect on what is read, leading to more intensive critical thinking about a given subject; to organize ideas from many sources; and to fulfill personal needs and interests (*Reading Framework*, California Public Schools, 1980, p. 3).

Reading instruction or the lack of instruction is purposeful. Literacy skills have typically been used to accomplish national purposes. During the colonial period of our history, children were taught to read to satisfy religious goals because it was considered important for children to read the Ten Commandments, the Lord's Prayer, the Bible, and other religious statements. During the nationalistic period of our history, reading was used to develop patroitism and citizenship responsibilities.

In this country during the pre-Civil War years, black children were rarely taught to read because the majority society in the South believed that literacy was not important for slave populations. In some Northern colonies prior to the Revolutionary War, and in other nations of the world, children of the poor did not attend school. Typically, indigent populations were not taught to read; however, in twentieth-century Cuba, Castro recognized the need for an informed citizenry and developed a literacy campaign to teach illiterates to read in order to accomplish political unity (Kozol, 1978).

Reading ability contributes to societal and individual goals. Economic competence is directly related to the ability to utilize written information for vocational training, technical applications, professional development, and personal interests. Reading contributes to thinking ability and stimulates the individual to create, critique, and develop intellectually. It is an extremely important aspect of life. People read for a variety of reasons: to obtain information, to solve problems, for personal satisfaction, for recreation, to satisfy curiosity, and to protect their safety, health, and interests. The reasons overlap and are not intended to be exclusive.

What Is Reading?

Reading differs from speaking and writing in that it is a comprehension activity. It is a receptive form of communication. (Review Chapter 5.) Listening, which is also a receptive form of communication and a comprehension activity, requires the listener to translate speech into thought. In reading, the reader must (1) decode print into speech, and (2) decode speech into thought; thus the reader must perform two different activities simultaneously (Moffett & Wagner, 1976). Reading is difficult because it is dependent upon visual processing as well as comprehension. Researchers do not know how the reader joins the two functions.

In the teaching of reading, teachers are teaching the communication process. Reading instruction is dependent upon oral language proficiency and experiential background along with the self-confidence and motivation of the beginning reader. To understand reading as a communication process, the beginning reader must take an active role in the learning process.

To learn to read, the beginner must discriminate between letters that often look alike. Therefore, it is important that the reader discover the critical attributes that discriminate between these letters. It is almost impossible for a teacher to tell students what to look for in order to discriminate between various letters such as "b" and "d." The student must be sophisticated enough to know what distinctive features to look for.

Smith (1978) differentiates between learning to read and fluent reading. The beginning reader must first learn to discriminate the critical features and translate these into an identification system of letters, and then into a given word name. The fluent reader discriminates the critical features and moves immediately to the word name or word category. Since the beginning reader must learn to identify words and store these words in a memory bank in order to make sense out of what is being read, the process of making sense is often tedious. It is for this reason that the beginning reader must be motivated to learn to read and have the necessary self-confidence to proceed with a trying task. Reading materials for the beginning reader should use short sentences so that the memory system is not burdened unnecessarily during this beginning stage. Beginning reading, therefore, is more difficult than fluent reading because in learning to read one must first identify words before attaining meaning, whereas the fluent reader obtains meaning directly from the visual features.

In explaining the reading process, Smith, a psycholinguist, states that immediate word identification and comprehension are accomplished by the fluent reader by using the skill of redundancy or alternative sources of information. By this he means that the skilled reader reduces the number of letter or word possibilities that could exist in a given context. The reader relates the possibilities to the frequency of use of words in a specific sequence, on prior knowledge, or to the words surrounding the key word.

A frequent controversy in the teaching of reading has to do with whether a meaning approach or a skills approach to the teaching of reading is more effective for the beginning reader. Those who favor the skills approach are usually advocating an emphasis on phonics. Phonics advocates claim that phonics instruction speeds up the word identification process for the beginner, but psycholinguists contend that the skill focus tends to fractionate the reading process, interfering with comprehension (Carroll, 1978).

RESEARCH FINDINGS

Beginning readers are not assisted in the early stages of learning to read by knowing the alphabet letter names. Reciting the alphabet has no relationship to the process of learning to read (Samuels, 1972).

Approaches to Reading Instruction

Silent Reading Purposes. Students are urged to read for a variety of purposes. Silent reading is usually performed during the teaching of reading when students are asked to read to accomplish a very specific objective. The silent reading time is usually preceded by a short discussion. New vocabulary words are presented during an oral discussion, and then the teacher asks the students to read in order to clarify, predict, understand, or determine sequence, or for some other purpose.

Oral Reading Purposes. After a passage has been read silently, the teacher asks students to read the same passage orally. During oral reading the teacher verifies understanding by the way the passage is read. Expression, intonation, and rhythm are practiced during oral reading. Sometimes the oral reading is used as the evidence to prove or verify what the students were looking for in their silent reading. Listening to others read and following the text as others read are also objectives for the oral reading session.

Work/Study Purposes. One of the most advantageous ways to teach reading skills occurs when reading is the tool for obtaining information—reading maps, charts, or graphs—and for problem solving. As students progress through school, work/study reading becomes more important and more closely tied to school success. The ability to read within different subject fields and for a variety of purposes needs to be taught and practiced throughout the school day. During work/study reading time students should be taught

- to adjust speed of reading to purpose and subject
- to locate information using a variety of source materials
- to extract and interpret information from a variety of sources (charts, maps, cartoons)
- to compile and organize information using a variety of sources.

Recreational Purposes. Reading for recreational purposes should be like the frosting on the cake. If students are to develop lifelong interests in reading, their enthusiasm must be cultivated by providing a variety of reading materials to satisfy diverse interests. Students need to have the opportunity to share with others something that they have particularly enjoyed. Even recreational reading needs to be modeled. If students are not accustomed to observing adults enjoying reading, they will not choose to read. In some classrooms teachers will set aside a special time for recreational reading and proceed to model reading. In one classroom where the author visited, the teacher chose a selection and began to chuckle as she read. After about five minutes the teacher asked the class if she could share "something funny." The teacher read to the class the amusing passage and then asked the students if there was anyone who would like to share something that s/he had enjoyed. This procedure became a common happening in the classroom, and as a result the students looked forward to their recreational reading period.

APPLICATIONS OF RESEARCH

The reader is urged to review the research on direct instruction and "Time on Task" in Chapter 3.

How Is Reading Taught?

Reading Readiness. Before charts or books are used to teach reading, the teacher's first task is to determine whether or not the child is ready for formal reading instruction. Readiness has different meanings to different people. Some believe that readiness is indicated when the child expresses the interest or desire to read. However, interest and motivation are not the prime determiners of readiness—at least in this text.

Physical factors such as the ability to discriminate visual differences and the ability to hear likenesses and differences affect learning to read. Eye-hand coordination affects reading. Understanding directions and differentiation of right from left are important because print is directional; the child who has difficulty with directions will have similar problems in learning to read.

Children unable to follow instructions or with poor memory retention or poor attention span will not have the mental maturity needed for reading. Social-emotional factors also affect learning to read. The child who cannot sit still or who lacks self-confidence and the child who cannot work cooperatively with others may have difficulty during reading.

Experiential factors also affect success in reading. Awareness of environmental signs is an example of the background experience needed by children learning to read. If the child does not perceive the difference between a stop sign and a school crossing sign or a railroad sign, s/he is not ready to read. The child with limited concepts and information will have difficulty understanding reading textbooks.

> How can a teacher determine if a child is "ready" to read?

The assessment of readiness for language arts is an important teacher task. If the teacher judges that the student lacks readiness for instruction, then it is the teacher's responsibility to create learning experiences to develop readiness systematically in those areas in which the student lacks the prerequisite capacities. The student may need activities to develop visual or auditory discrimination or work habits, or vocabulary and concepts. It is also important that the teacher plan a conference with parents to prepare them to assist in the process.

Experience Charts. Ricardo, a first grader, brought his hamster to school. It was in a cage, and the teacher asked all of the children to sit on the rug in the front of the room so that Ricardo could tell about his hamster. But Ricardo was too shy, so the teacher said to the class: "Boys and girls, why don't you ask Ricardo questions about his hamster?" The children asked questions and learned the hamster's name, that the hamster was gentle and clean, and that he ate lettuce, carrots, cabbage, and peanuts. The teacher added to the information by explaining to the students that hamsters needed to be kept in metal cages because they were able to gnaw their way out of a wooden cage. After talking and watching the hamster for several minutes, the teacher suggested that the class compose a story about Ricardo's hamster. The students readily agreed, and the story was written on the chalk board.

T.: Who came to school today?
S.: Pepe came to the school today.
T.: Who is Pepe?
S.: Pepe is a hamster.
T.: What do hamsters eat?
S.: Hamsters eat lettuce, carrots, cabbage, and peanuts.
T.: What else do we know about hamsters?
S.: Hamsters are gentle and clean.

The story written on the board was ready for the students to read.

> Pepe came to school today.
> Pepe is a hamster.
> Hamsters eat lettuce, carrots, cabbage, and peanuts.
> Hamsters are gentle and clean.

The children took turns reading the story. If they had difficulty, the teacher would prompt them with the original questions that motivated the story. ("What else do we know about hamsters?") Since the children had just "experienced" the story they were able to read it easily. The story can be rewritten on a piece of tagboard and hung on a chart rack for use during reading and science throughout the semester. Usually teachers allow students to draw a picture to place on the experience chart or use a commercial picture to help the students recall "Pepe, the hamster."

Language Experience Approach. The language experience approach to reading instruction is based on the idea that what you can think and say, you can read. For example, the students who wrote the experience story about the hamster will be able to read that story because they just composed it. The story can be used for reading instruction with a group of students or with an individual child. The students in that second-grade classroom could be asked to draw pictures about Pepe, the hamster, and then write personal stories about him.

The student's stories could be taped or dictated to an aide. The aide (or teacher) will type the story for the student, who will then practice reading it aloud. This approach is quite motivating for students since they are reading about their own experiences. The language experience approach has been particularly successful with urban students and students with reading problems because the approach is more meaningful and based upon the student's own vocabulary and interests.

The major problem with this approach is that vocabulary and skills are not necessarily developed sequentially. This means that the teacher has greater responsibility to assess students' needs and provide the appropriate skill instruction. The language experience approach integrates all of the language arts components, and this is its major advantage.

Kinesthetic Approach. This approach utilizes the language experience approach to reading. Each child is given a "dictionary box" which is kept on the table in front of him/her. When the child is ready to write a story s/he uses the dictionary box. During the writing period, the teacher is circulating. When a student raises his/her hand asking for assistance with a word, the teacher comes over and writes the requested word on a slip of paper. The child *traces* the word with the index finger; then turns the slip of paper over and writes the word from memory. (If the child cannot do so, the word is retraced.) Next the word is utilized in the story, and when completed, the student files the word in the dictionary box for future use.

Reading is taught by using the student's own stories. Spelling is based on the personal words in the student's dictionary box. All of the language components are integrated using the student's experience stories.

Individualized Approach. Another extremely motivating approach to reading instruction is an individualized reading strategy. By providing for a wide range of choices and interests and having on hand many books, students self-select what they want to read. This approach assumes that students will naturally select what they are able to read. However, this is not always true, and teachers do need to provide some guidance to students in the selection of an appropriate book. Jeannette Veatch (1959) suggests the "rule of thumb" approach. This idea is that students are told to scan a page in their chosen book. For each word that they cannot read they should raise one finger beginning with the little finger. If they get to the thumb while on the same page, then the book is too difficult and they should choose another book to read.

Using the individualized approach, the teacher meets with each student individually to check comprehension and skill needs. Skill instruction is usually taught in a small group as the teacher identifies common learning needs. Students progress at their own rate; they do not have to "cover" any specific number of books. Since they choose their own books, interest is usually high. Students will read individually two or three days per week, conference with the teacher at least once during the week, and have a skill lesson at least once during the week.

This Child Is Learning Letters by Writing in Sand. Which Reading Approach Advocates the Tracing of Letters and Words?

Teachers differ greatly in the ways in which this approach is implemented. Some teachers "individualize" every day; others use basal reading texts in conjunction with their individualized program.

Record keeping is the most important aspect of the approach. Each child has a personal record card in which the student marks what books have been read and the teacher keeps track of skill needs and skill mastery. Often a skill continuum is used, with the teacher checking when the skill need is manifested and when it is accomplished.

Basal Reader Approach. Most teachers use the basal reader approach to reading instruction. This occurs for the following reasons:

- A great variety of text series are available.
- The texts provide for a logical, sequential development of vocabulary and skills.
- The teacher manuals provide assistance in the organization of the reading program.
- The manuals guide the teacher in framing key questions to motivate reading and assistance in the assessment of skills and the evaluation of skill mastery.

Because of their ease of use, basal readers are appreciated by teachers, but this does not mean that the basal text must be the only way in which reading instruction is provided in the classroom. The basal reader approach may be combined with any other system.

The basal reader approach has been criticized because authors tend to write for a "typical" student. As a consequence, the text may be unappealing to minority youngsters or rural students or any special interest group.

Since the vocabulary is carefully controlled, the writing pattern in the basal text tends to be stilted. This is another reason why this approach is ridiculed.

The creative teacher can take advantage of the organization and systematized arrangement of the basal text and implement a variety of teaching materials to enrich reading instruction. When teachers design their own reinforcement materials to follow up the reading instructional period, students are more motivated and instruction tends to be more appropriate for the specific group of students. Problems occur when teachers feel the need to utilize all workbook suggestions and take advantage of every commercial ditto that accompanies the text. When this happens, reading instruction becomes rigid and lacks the necessary individualization; all students do not need the same skill follow-up activities.

Additional Approaches. There are many advocates of *"phonics" approach* to the teaching of reading. Few teachers would ignore the advantages of teaching children to use phonetic clues as a tool for learning to read words; however, those that advocate this approach to the exclusion of other instructional methods are attempting to present letter sounds and rules governing those sounds *before* students learn words by sight. Phonics programs teach letter sounds for all 26 alphabet letters, 70 phonograms, 13 phonic rules, and 26 spelling rules (Austin and Morrison, 1963). Teaching phonics has the advantage of giving the students a tool to use in the analysis of words and reduces the necessity for a controlled vocabulary. But when this approach is used as a separate program, the disadvantages may outweigh the benefits. For example (1) students often lack interest in reading because of the large amount of time devoted to drill, (2) lack of interest in reading results in lack of attention, (3) comprehension skills are not developed because of the large amount of time spent on sound drills and rules, (4) the oral reading of "phonics students" often lacks expression because comprehension has not been emphasized and the students are attending to word sounds.

The *Initial Teaching Alphabet* (i.t.a.) is another approach based upon the correspondence of sounds (phonemes) and symbols (graphemes) for teaching reading. This approach uses 44 symbols—a symbol for every letter of its alphabet. The letters are similar to the traditional alphabet except that the letters *g* and *x* are not used. The larger alphabet permits consistent correspondence of symbol to sound. Since there is only one possible sound for each symbol, the student is never confused. The i.t.a. approach is used only in the beginning stages of reading instruction. After students have learned to decode, the transition to the traditional alphabet is made. Children seem to make the transition to conventional reading materials easily. However, there are several disadvantages: (1) students using this method need special reading materials; (2) adults frequently find it difficult to read using the i.t.a.; (3) some children do have a difficult time making the transition to traditional orthography.

Approaches to Reading: Conclusion

Research on beginning reading has failed to show how students learn to read and which approach to the teaching of reading is better or more efficient than the others (Lotto, 1978). Rarely does a classroom teacher attempt a "pure" form of one specific approach. Most teachers use aspects of several approaches. In most classrooms the basal reader will be used two or three days per week, phonics will be taught as an integral part of a skill lesson, and two days per week the teacher may individualize, use the language experience approach to reading instruction, or choose some other approach.

To encourage reading in the classroom and to facilitate the understanding of printed materials the following activities are suggested:

1. *Reading to Students.* By listening to "good" readers, students develop their own interest in

reading. When teacher reads an adventure story to students and needs to continue the story over several days, it is not uncommon for students to ask if they may borrow the book and read it on their own throughout the school day. By modeling oral reading techniques, teachers teach pronunciation, intonation, punctuation, enthusiasm, and the fun of reading.

2. *Listening Centers.* A listening library can be created in the class room. Moffett and Wagner (1976) cited two important reasons for the development of a listening library: recordings can be purchased in a variety of dialects and styles to enrich students' listening experiences; records are available throughout the school day whenever students have time, and they provide for the individualization needed by students. Recordings can also be used with library books. Students often enjoy following along by reading in the book as they listen to the story. By listening to a story read well, students improve their own oral reading technique.
3. *Recreational Reading.* A supplemental library in the classroom with books that cater to students' diverse interests and reading levels will serve to reinforce the reading habit. Many teachers create informal areas of the room to encourage students to relax with a book. Beanbag cushions, large pillows, or a thick rug appeal to young students.
4. *Oral Reading.* Silent reading is improved when students have the opportunity to perform orally and listen to themselves read. Oral reading can be performed in the small reading group after silent reading. Sometimes it is a good idea to allow students to rehearse what they are going to read orally. This can occur by having students work with a partner. Each student practices what s/he will read to the group. The partner offers suggestions for improving the performance.

APPLICATIONS OF RESEARCH

After reviewing the research on reading skills, Bussis (1982) concluded that an overemphasis on reading skill instruction was displacing actual classroom reading.

In contrast, the classrooms of successful teachers are characterized by the following practices:

1. Teachers provide a range of reading materials for students' use in the classroom.
2. Teachers provide time for students to choose books to read or to look at each day.
3. Teachers program a time for students to write at least several times each week.
4. Teachers read aloud to the class each day and vary the selected literature.
5. Teachers provide time to work individually with each child in order to listen to the child read or to talk about what the child has read (p. 241).

Organizing the Reading Program

Classroom Environment and Classroom Management

As in other subject fields, the learning environment of the classroom affects students' ability to attend to instruction. A classroom that is too warm may make students lethargic. A room that is noisy may affect concentration. A classroom that is cluttered or too filled with distracting displays may make it difficult for students to settle down and study. Space, temperature, ventilation, aromas, orderliness, and light may influence learning and students' adjustment to instruction.

The arrangement of furniture and the placement of materials are important considerations in preparing to manage reading instruction. For example, the teacher must decide where instruction will take

RESEARCH FINDINGS

Exposure to noise impedes learning. Researchers have found that rate of learning, attention span, and reading levels suffer negative effects when children are exposed to noise over a prolonged period of time (ASCD UPDATE, November 1982).

place. Will the students move their chairs to a designated place for instruction, or will the teacher move from group to group? If the teacher is to move, will students be seated throughout the school day in their designated reading group? If the students are to move, there needs to be a space in the classroom for the reading group large enough to accommodate the materials for instruction. Young students will need to use a flannel board, charts, and other motivating devices; the chalkboard will probably be needed for all age groups.

The arrangement of learning centers, if they are to be used, must be considered in the overall planning of the reading program. Accessibility of the learning stations, movement patterns to and from the station, and availability of electrical outlets, if needed, should be preplanned.

The location of books, pencils, paper, and workbooks should be studied to be certain that students can avail themselves of these materials as needed. Classroom management considerations include whether or not students should sharpen pencils during reading instruction. If pencil sharpening is distracting during reading, then what alternative decisions will be needed to provide for "emergency" situations?

Appropriate utilization of time is a major consideration in the reading program. The minutes

Reading Is Contagious When Children Can Assume Informal and Comfortable Positions.

used for organizational or procedural purposes as children change places for group instruction can detract measurably from the achievement of reading goals. For this reason movement patterns and classroom rules should be jointly decided and agreed upon by teacher and students. Care must be taken to provide for the physical movement needs of primary children. Perhaps there should be a place in the classroom where restless energy can be expended. A place in the classroom to stretch out or curl up may be necessary for restive students.

Grouping Patterns

Skill Grouping. Grouping students for skill instruction is one of the major teacher tasks in organizing the reading program. Typically, students are flexibly grouped for a limited period of time according to special skill needs. An effective reading lesson can be provided to several students at the same time, if student needs and skills are matched.

Teacher observation and informal assessment as well as a skills management system or a criterion-referenced test can be used to facilitate the grouping of students for skill instruction. The advantage of skill grouping is that direct instruction can be provided in an area of need and students who are proficient in the skill are not bored with unnecessary instruction. The disadvantage to skill grouping is the amount of time needed to assess skill development; however, accurate instruction is dependent upon the identification of specific skill needs.

Interest Grouping. Sometimes it is advantageous to group students by interests. When students need to perform research on a specific topic or to obtain special information, it is helpful to bring students together in a small group to accomplish the specific objective. For example, in a first-grade classroom the students were studying about animals, and the teacher grouped the students according to the animal to be studied. Grouped by interest, the students were able to share ideas and printed and nonprinted materials. However, when grouping students by interests, care must be taken that learning materials are adequate for the task involved so that students at different achievement levels can contribute to group progress.

Interest groups are more frequently used when subject matter fields are integrated. Projects in health, science, social studies, and art may require a grouping pattern based on interests or specific subject matter needs rather than reading skill needs. But if students are to utilize reading materials, the teacher must be alert to provide a large selection of appropriate materials.

Joplin Plan. In some schools a departmentalized plan is used for reading instruction. Reading is scheduled at the same time in all classrooms, and students are grouped for instruction without consideration of grade level. The students are grouped homogeneously utilizing reading achievement information. During reading instruction time the students may leave their own classroom and attend reading class in another classroom with other students at the same developmental level.

Achievement Grouping. Achievement grouping is probably the most common intraclass grouping plan that exists. Informal assessment or standardized reading achievement scores are used to group students for instruction. Typically, the classroom is arranged in three instructional groups. In the lower grades the span of achievement can usually be accommodated by three reading groups; however, in the upper grades the range of ability may be greater, and more groups are sometimes necessary.

Skill Management Systems

A skill management system is a defined program with several basic elements: testing program to assess skill development, skills continuum, a retrieval system, a record-keeping system. The purpose of a management system is to facilitate the diagnosis, prescription, evaluation, and record-keeping tasks involved in reading instruction.

A skill management system is based on the assumption that certain identifiable skills must be mastered if students are to progress. The system sets a mastery level; usually 80 per cent is the criterion, and progress is determined using tests included in the management package.

The program may be purchased from a publisher or developed by the local school district. The advantage of local development is that the chosen skills and objectives will fit the population to be taught. Large management systems produced by publishers are designed to fit a preconceived "average" population and may not be appropriate for children with special needs or children from specific ethnic populations.

Since there is little agreement by reading specialists concerning which subskills are to be taught or the sequence of subskills instruction, it is important to choose and order the skills considered essential for the children in the local community. Otto, Rude, and Spiegel (1979, p. 55) suggest the following:

1. During reading instruction, teach only those skills that are reading-related.
2. Sequence the chosen skills realistically. If the sequence of skill development does not work, modify it.
3. Be frugal in identifying essential skills. Skill lists have a tendency to become too long and unwieldy.

Management systems have been developed to assist the classroom teacher individualize reading instruction. The system should provide information to meet individual needs. Use of the system should enable the teacher to diagnose skill needs, prescribe for remediation, and keep track of individual progress. It is not the purpose of the system to have students work alone. Small group skill instruction should be possible.

It is extremely important that teachers be familiar with and understand the system to be used. The management system should be introduced and thoroughly explained either by the publisher or by the reading specialists in the school district. Effective utilization of the system requires knowledge about the skill continuum, the sequence of skills, and the various components of the system.

Utilization of Aides, Volunteers, and Tutors

The assistance of other adults or student tutors in the classroom enables the classroom teacher to individualize instruction and to increase the opportunities for students to interact with others. Aides, volunteers, and tutors should be directly supervised by the classroom teacher, and they must be trained to assist in reading instruction. It is important to define precisely what it is they are to do. The following tasks are frequently assigned and can be performed by noncertificated personnel:

- Reading to small groups of students
- Listening to students read aloud
- Tutoring specific skills identified by the teacher
- Recordkeeping chores
- Duplicating materials
- Providing bilingual reinforcement
- Recording dictated stories
- Setting up or taking apart learning centers

Developmental Reading Programs

A developmental reading program is a *plan* to provide sequential instruction to students in order to ensure growth. Typically, the plan is created for students of diverse backgrounds, interests, and needs. The major component of the plan is a skill continuum that spirals skill development from readiness levels through higher levels of complexity.

The major advantage of the developmental plan is that it provides a means to assess students' proficiencies. In a modern, mobile society the scope and sequence for reading instruction is extremely important if students are to continue development while moving from one school and one community to another. The developmental plan facilitates the identification of deficiencies and proficiencies.

Skill Instruction Is Facilitated by Placing Students in Small Reading Groups.

The Reading Framework for California Public Schools (1980) encompasses three levels of reading competence: Learning to Read, Reading to Learn, and Reading for Life. The three levels are considered continuous and interrelated. In California the State Framework proposes 12 components to ensure language growth. The components are as follows:

- Reading Readiness
- Listening Improvement
- Oral Language Development
- Writing
- Vocabulary and Concept Development
- Comprehension Development
- Decoding/Language Processing
- Reading in the Content Areas
- Study Locational Skills
- Flexibility, Rate, Purpose
- Reading and Literature
- Personal Reading

Content. The process skills make up the content for the developmental plan. The skills should be taught not only during reading, but throughout the school day utilizing the content of the disciplines. Students should be aware of the skill(s) being emphasized to ensure understanding of its use in the content fields.

Materials for Instruction. Teachers can use a wide range of materials because the skills are predetermined and are the constants of the program. Students may change schools and instructional materials because skill levels are assessed, and instructional materials should be chosen to teach or reinforce specific skill needs.

Grouping for Instruction. Grouping should be based on similar skill levels and instructional needs. Groups are correlated to teaching the skills rather than teaching the book. Lesson planning is based on skill needs. (Review "Grouping Patterns" in this chapter.)

Assessment. Both paper-and-pencil tests and informal assessment should be used to determine skill levels. Skill proficiencies can be demonstrated by students throughout the school day as skills are used in various subject fields. The ability to apply the skill in different situations should be the critical evaluative measure.

Skills. The following skills are typically identified in developmental reading programs: readiness, structural analysis, phonics, contextual skills, comprehension, location/study, and critical reading. Illustrative objectives and classroom activities are provided for each skill. It should be remembered that researchers do not agree on the appropriate sequence for reading subskills. The order and priority of subskills should be determined by the school district, teachers, and community.

Skill Instruction

Readiness Skills

The reader is urged to review the earlier section in this chapter on reading readiness. Teachers who recognize the importance of readiness factors utilize a variety of approaches and materials to develop readiness skills. The primary objective of readiness activities is for students to develop a positive attitude and appreciation for reading as a resource. Identified skills focus on visual discrimination, visual memory, auditory memory, names for objects and auditory and visual stimuli, directional words and prepositions, and a variety of other readiness skills.

Typical Objectives

- Discriminating and matching of geometric shapes
- Identifying objects that are alike and different
- Recognizing left-to-right orientation of reading and top-to-bottom concept
- Recreating shapes and letters (tracing)
- Identifying missing parts and objects
- Discriminating sounds; identifying sounds
- Repeating words, songs, phrases, stories, rhymes
- Identifying up/down; before/after; in/out; under/over
- Identifying colors, shapes; sorting and classifying
- Following directions
- Retelling and sequencing stories and story elements
- Dictating own stories; drawing pictures for stories

Classroom Activities

To encourage sensorimotor development, it is important that the classroom environment be enriched so that students can be challenged by objects to manipulate and compare and by sounds to distinguish and match. Moffett and Wagner (1976) state that comparison is the most important element. Students need to be active and to touch and play with a variety of toys, games, tools, and materials. Music should be a significant part of the primary program. Interaction with peers through talking, playing, and listening is vital for emotional and experiential readiness. Auditory and visual discrimination lessons are high priority lessons to develop readiness. Whenever possible gamelike activities are helpful.

> Identify some materials and activities for making instruction meaningful for visual learners.

Decoding Skills

Decoding involves three aspects of language: grammar (syntax), meaning (semantics), and sounds (phonology). Skills used to decode words include letter-sound relationships, whole word recognition, structural analysis, contextual clues, and spelling-pattern/sound relationships. The fluent reader uses these word identification strategies interactively and unconsciously. Basically, decoding requires the reader to utilize phonics concepts, structural analysis, and context clues.

The fluent reader uses word identification strategies to reduce uncertainty. Smith (1978) called this using the "skill of redundancy." Goodman (1976, p. 497) described the process as a "psycholinguistic guessing game" in which the reader uses language cues in order to make tentative decisions that are then confirmed or rejected as reading proceeds. It is at this point in the learning to read process that students who lack confidence may have difficulty. These students are often fearful of taking risks; they do not trust their own knowledge or instincts, and thus they fail to use the cues properly and are afraid to commit themselves to choice.

Otto, Rude, and Spiegel (1979) call attention to another attitudinal problem. They note that success in reading is dependent upon self-monitoring of what one decodes. Some students read sentences without concern for meaning. The consequence is nonsense reading. For example, the student who reads, "Billy eats peanut butter and *jar* on his bread," is not concerned about appropriate semantics.

In teaching decoding skills, reading specialists warn that isolated word and letter study or phonic generalizations should not be dwelled upon and taught apart from language context. Strategies that are taught in isolation can rarely be applied by the student when "real" reading is to be performed.

Strategies for Decoding Words. The beginning reader utilizes several skills to decode words. Word attack strategies include one or more of the following techniques: phonics, structural analysis, the use of context clues, and punctuation clues.
Procedures used by students differ; some students appear to rely more on one strategy than on others. The more effective students utilize several strategies in combination. Word attack strategies should be taught to students during reading instruction. Each strategy is defined with examples of several objectives and classroom activities.

RESEARCH FINDINGS

After observing students perform reading seatwork, researchers from the Institute For Research On Teaching concluded that first graders spend 40 per cent to 60 per cent of their reading time doing seatwork, but that it does not help them learn.

* * *

They recommend that teachers explain the content-related purpose for the work to be performed; remind students about the purpose of the assignment; and reiterate what was to be learned at the conclusion of the lesson (*Communication Quarterly*, Summer 1982, pp. 2–3).

Context. To utilize context clues for decoding purposes, the reader obtains meaningful information (clues) from the surrounding words in the reading passage. Context clues are obtained from the meaning of the passage and are therefore sometimes dependent upon the students' knowledge and prior experiences. The importance of context clues needs to be emphasized to students. Awareness of context clues begins during initial readiness lessons. For example, the teacher may be reading a Halloween story to students about a little boy who is frightened of a ______. The teacher says to the class, "What do you think Billy saw that frightened him?" If the students fail to respond, then the teacher can show them the picture of the *ghost*. The students soon learn that both story context and pictures provide clues about the story.

Students should also be taught that authors give themselves away by providing clues about action, ideas, beliefs. For example, in the story Caps for Sale, the author, Slobodkina (1947), tells about a peddler who sells caps. When the peddler cannot sell his caps he goes for a long walk in the country and sits down under a tree and falls asleep. After awakening the peddler feels "refreshed and rested." The sentence begins, "When he woke up, he was . . ." Students can be helped to guess how the peddler would feel when he awakens. (How do you feel after a nap?) The story continues with the peddler realizing that while he slept a bunch of monkeys had stolen his caps and put them on. As the peddler hollers, gestures, and stomps, pleading with the monkeys to return the caps, the monkeys imitate him by mimmicking, gesturing, and stomping. Finally in disgust the peddler removes his only remaining cap and throws it away. At this point the teacher should ask the students, "What do you think the monkeys did?" (The monkeys removed the stolen caps and threw them away!)

Classroom activities for teaching contextual analysis skills include reading stories to students at all grade levels and asking content-related questions. Another technique is to teach students key words that provide clues as to what type of word will follow. For example, students can be shown that words like *what*, *how*, *where*, *when*, *why*, and *who* will trigger a question. They can also be encouraged to discover in their books what kinds of words will signal that the next word is likely to be a noun (*the*, *a*, *this*, *our*).

Sentence completion activities can be helpful in teaching contextual analysis. The missing words can be given to the students as a forced-choice, it can be left open, or it can be partially given to the students.

example: The mother cat fed her_____ (mittens, kittens). (Note that the students would also be forced to examine the initial consonant sound.)
example: The mother cat fed the _____.
example: The long slow train puffed and ch_____.

Objectives for Teaching Contextual Analysis

Students will

- Recognize synonyms in a definition
- Utilize picture clues
- Identify the relevant word(s).

Phonics. Auditory discrimination begins as a readiness skill. During the prereading stage, teachers help students discriminate likenesses and differences in sounds. Students may practice saying words which begin alike, or they may identify the word that is different. Students can listen to jingles and rhyming verse; they can be encouraged to find objects in the classroom or pictures in magazines that begin with the same sound as a predetermined word or object.

As students learn to read, auditory discrimination is extended to include understanding of phoneme-grapheme relationship as students learn that letters represent sounds. Phonics instruction is provided by teaching students initial consonant sounds, blends, digraphs, silent consonants, and medial and final consonant sounds. Vowel sounds are also taught.

Otto, Rude, and Speigel (1979, pp. 115–117) suggest guidelines for teaching phonics generalizations to students:

1. Students and their parents should be cognizant that all words cannot be sounded out.
2. As a word attack strategy, phonics should be applied with other strategies (grammar and meaning).
3. Care must be exercised that phonics rules are not taught in isolation of real reading. Students should be helped to apply rules during reading instruction.
4. Teachers need to be aware of dialectal differences among students. These differences may affect the utility of teaching vowel sounds. For example, the pronunciation of Boston residents differs from a Midwestern pronunciation in the short *a* sound, as in the word *bath*. It would be useless to ask students to apply a phonics rule that is not consistent with the students' normal pronunciation.
5. Care must be exercised when pronouncing isolated consonant sounds to ensure that an artificial "uh" is not produced after the target sound. Example: the *t* sound should not be sustained so that it sounds like "tuh," or students will not be able to use the sound properly to sound out *tip* or *took*.

Phonics Generalizations. Along with those activities designed to develop auditory discrimination, students can be taught certain phonics generalizations which facilitate word identification.

Rules such as the silent *e* at the end of one-syllable words such as *kite* or the short vowel sound when it is in the middle of a one-syllable word such as *his* help develop word attack skills; however, it must be emphasized that rules should be taught and applied during reading, not as isolated facts to be memorized.

Teaching Consonant Sounds. Since consonant sounds are more useful and more regular than vowel sounds, most reading specialists suggest that they be taught prior to vowel sounds. The following phonics rules governing consonant sounds are typically taught:

1. Initial consonants should be taught first.
2. A consonant digraph is the pairing of dissimilar consonants that, when put together, represent a single sound. Consonant digraphs include the following sounds: *sh, ch, th, qu, wh.*
3. Variant consonant digraphs should also be taught: *gh* as *g* or *f*, *ph* as *f*, and *dg* as *j*.
4. Silent consonants should be taught so that students learn that when they cannot identify a word, perhaps they need to try deleting the consonant sound. Examples include: *kn* as in *knot*, *ght* as in *might*, *tch* as in *batch*, *b* in *doubt*, *t* in *hasten*, *h* in *honest*, *wr* in *write*.
5. Consonant blends are clusters of two or three consonants. The resultant sound is a combination of each individual consonant. Examples: *scrap, throw, string, glad, grand, branch.*

Teaching Vowel Sounds. Learning to identify vowel sounds may be more difficult for students than identifying the consonant sounds. Vowels have not only long and short sounds, but many variations. Students also need to be taught that sometimes *y* (*may*) and *w* (*know*) are vowel substitutes. Otto, Rude, and Spiegel (1979, pp. 121–123) recommend that the following rules governing vowel sounds should be taught to students:

1. A vowel has a short sound when the word contains only one vowel and the vowel is positioned at the beginning of the word or in the middle (*up, it, tap, met, pop, elf, mist*).
2. When a vowel is positioned at the end of a word and it is the only vowel in the word, it usually has a long vowel sound (*be, me*).
3. If the vowel is positioned at the end of a syllable, it usually has the long vowel sound (*fever, minor, rotate*).
4. When a word or syllable contains two vowels and the second vowel is an *e* at the end of the word, the first vowel will have a long vowel sound and the *e* will be silent. (We formerly told students that the silent *e* makes its friend say its own name!) (*make, mule, hike, hope.*)
5. When two vowels are adjacent in a word or a syllable, the first vowel has a long vowel sound and the second vowel is silent (*seat, boat, main, boast, may*). ("When two vowels go walking, the first one does the talking!") However, there are many exceptions to this rule.
6. A vowel followed by the letter *r* is controlled by the letter *r* (*bar, worm, burn, shirt, her*).
7. In certain cases a pair of vowels will lead to a completely new sound. Since the new sound is unpredictable, the pairs must be taught as special cases. Examples: *mew, mouse, toy, how, toil, pause, raw.*
8. Students need to be taught to recognize the schwa (ə) sound as in *banana, kitten, divide, lemon, circus.*

Syllabication is also considered phonics instruction. Typically, it is taught in the following order: rules, prefixes and suffixes, compound words, doubling final consonants, and accent marks.

Classroom Activities. Sorting activities, in which students identify the beginning letter sound from pictures or objects in the classroom, have been mentioned as a means to develop auditory discrimination. Imitation of environmental sounds and animal sounds can also be used in the prereading program. A variety of games can be made to help students identify target sounds. These games may be of the "Lotto" or "Bingo" design or could include a game board in which students use a spinner and move spaces along the "sound" path.

Practice materials of a game nature encourage students to sound out unfamiliar words and to practice specific sounds. Figure 6.1 illustrates a clock-style game made of chipboard. The child moves the spinner with the beginning sound to be

Figure 6.1. Phonics Practice Game.

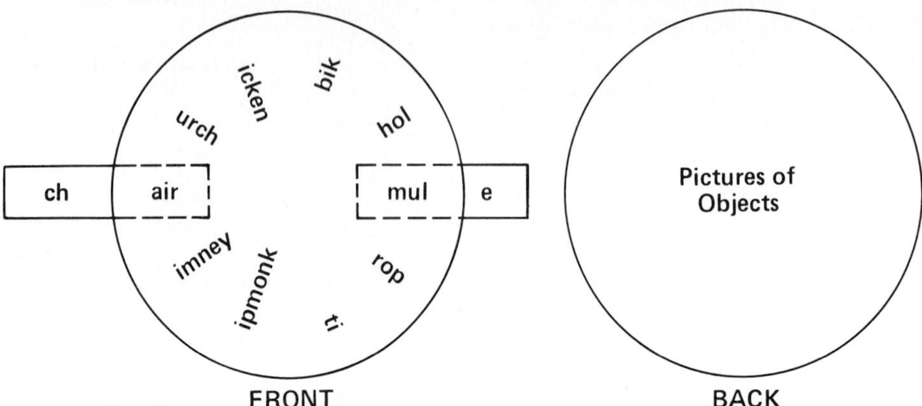

placed in front of certain words and the ending sound at the end of others. After practicing, the student turns the card over and the pictures of the objects on the back verify the student's word identification "guesses."

Drill activities that focus on auditory discrimination should be included in each reading lesson to provide students with practice and feedback immediately after skill teaching. These activities may occur while students are in the reading circle. For example, after teaching consonant blends, the teacher might pronounce several words to the group and instruct them to listen for the sound of the consonant blend and be prepared to name the word with the sound. The words might include: *draw*, *drink*, *door*. Young students will have difficulty concentrating and remembering more than three words at a time.

> What are some activities and materials for teaching reading to kinesthetic learners?

Another procedure for practicing the target skill might make use of the chalkboard and provide skill practice in both auditory and visual discrimination. The target sound can be written on the board. Then additional words can be written. The students should be asked to pronounce the sound and go to the board and underline the consonant blend. Each phonics skill should be practiced in the same manner.

After verifying that students understand the phonics skill through small group practice, appropriate follow-up seatwork can be assigned. For example, after verifying that students hear and can reproduce the sound of *ph*, the follow-up activity could ask students to underline letters indicating that sound. The word lists may use the sound in different positions and include some words where the target sound does not appear. Examples of words with the *ph* sound include: *phone*, *biography*, *orphan*, *phrase*, *autograph*, *telephone*, *nephew*.

The teaching of vowel sounds is more difficult because the rules are less often "true"; the vowels change sounds in different words. For this reason it is sometimes better to program instructional activities so that sounds are taught in families. To teach the short *i* sound, for example, you could include the following families:

ding	chill	wig	ship	tick
wing	hill	dig	rip	sick
sing	mill	big	hip	wick
spring	till	pig	sip	pick

Whenever possible, students should be asked to generate additional words using the target sound.

Foreign speakers of English have the greatest difficulty with Americans' use of the schwa (ə) sound. In words of more than one syllable, we tend to soften the vowel sound. The effect of this is to make all vowel sounds somewhat alike. Some linguists call this the American "Tarzan" sound, "uh." The result is that in words like the following, the vowel is indistinguishable:

Sənatra—Sinatra
bedləm—bedlam
bottən—button
barrən—barren

Teaching activities for the schwa sound should include correct pronunciation along with an understanding that this occurs because the syllable is unstressed.

Phonics activities should include practice in pronunciation, listening, and visual discrimination. Whenever possible, students should be given opportunities to generate additional words using the target sound(s). After supervised practice with feedback, students may be assigned follow-up tasks, but these tasks should be of a limited nature and should not be of the "busywork" variety.

Objectives for Teaching Phonics

Students will

- identify the target sound(s)
- recognize the target sound in words and read words containing the target sound
- recognize spelling-pattern and sound-pattern relationships.

What are some activities and materials for enhancing instruction for auditory learners?

Structural Analysis. Word identification through structural analysis assumes that the student hears and can reproduce inflected endings for different sentence needs. Structural analysis is dependent upon appropriate use of oral language. Unlike phonic analysis, which is dependent upon letter-sound relationships, to utilize structural analysis for decoding purposes, the student must recognize units of meaning in the word. Root words, suffixes, prefixes, compound words, and contractions are all important structural elements in word identification.

During reading instruction, as students encounter structural differences, the teacher should call attention to these differences and ask students to explain what is different and what it means. For example, when students see *boy* and *boys* used in different sentences, they should be asked to explain their use. The beginning reader also encounters these common endings: *-ing*, *-ed*, *-es*, *-er*, *-est*. Each needs to be explained. The teacher should call attention to the doubling of the final consonant before endings as well as the dropping of the final *e*.

drop → dropped	run → running
hope → hoping	write → writing

Structural changes are best taught using a semi-discovery approach. Once such words are encountered, students should be asked to identify the base word. Then the students should be asked to apply the structural elements to the base word. Structural generalizations can be taught during reading, language, and spelling. Typically, students understand and use prefixes before suffixes. Since prefixes do not change the spelling of the base word, they are somewhat easier for the student. Also, there is a tendency for some students not to see the addition of a suffix to a word. This is particularly true of suffixes such as *ful* and *ment*. Inflected endings do not carry specific meanings, which is another reason why students tend to ignore them; however, some suffixes, such as *ful* and *ment*, do carry meaning clues, and it is important that students understand the meanings and use them for structural clues.

Classroom Activities. Students will need practice in identifying plurals, past tense, continuous tense, and comparisons. These four are usually described as inflections. Since spelling changes may also occur, students will need special instruction in order to know how to change the word endings.

Compound words are often taught by listing the two parts of the word in different columns. Students are then asked to put the two parts together. They need help in defining the new word that results from the two parts. Sometimes students have difficulty with compound words because they tend to break up many words into distinct parts (to-get-her); this may occur as a consequence of phonic analysis. To rectify this problem, students should be reminded that a compound word is made up of two words with distinct and different meanings that are combined to form a new word with a new meaning.

Contractions should be taught by first encouraging students to find the missing letter and to identify the two parts of the word. Pronunciation of the contraction is another important instructional activity for primary students.

Sentence completion exercises help students recognize inflections. It is also a good idea to have students underline the base word when using inflections.

In the middle grades a good technique for teaching structural analysis is to have students build words using inflected endings. The students can be given a list of endings and another list of root words.

At the upper-grade level, McNeil, Donant, and Alkin (1980) recommend that students collect groups of words with common origins; for example: *hero*, *heroic*, *heroine*, *heroically*; *commune*, *community*, *communicate*, *communicative*. This activity will contribute to both word attack and comprehension skills.

Objectives For Structural Analysis Skills
Students will

- recognize and use word parts such as compound words, verb endings, plurals, possessives, contractions, inflectional endings reflecting tense, prefixes, suffixes, and words of comparison.

Summary: Decoding Skills

Reading specialists advocate the use of several strategies for decoding words. Specialists have expressed concern about the emphasis placed on the different skills, the amount of time given to decoding activities, and the memorization of rules. The following guidelines have been suggested:

1. Word analysis skills need to be used in combination; too much reliance on any one method will inhibit fluent reading.
2. Meaning is achieved when whole words are read as a unit. Letter sounds do not provide meaning.
3. The beginning reader needs a number of known sight words in order to begin the reading process. The goal of reading instruction is to facilitate the recognition of words as a whole. Recognized words are "sight" words, and they do not need to be, nor should they be, analyzed for identification purposes.
4. Knowledge of sight words facilitates seeing and hearing similarities between recognized words and new words to be learned.
5. The learning of complicated rules for sounding out words inhibits the beginning reader; therefore, rules should be introduced gradually as students progress through the primary grades.

Reading For Comprehension

Reading involves the communication of ideas, thoughts, and feelings. Learning to decode words helps students translate graphic symbols into speech, but it is the process of decoding speech into thought that relies on comprehension processes. We have all heard individuals read words without expression; this occurs because the individual does not infer punctuation signs and does not understand what s/he is reading. The ability to pronounce words accurately does not mean that the individual reads with understanding.

A number of taxonomies of comprehension skills have been developed by different reading specialists. Most specialists agree that reading comprehension begins at the literal level. Literal comprehension means that students understand the meanings of the words in a written message, are able to follow the directions of the message, and can answer explicit questions about information contained in the message. Beyond the literal comprehension level the various taxonomies of skills vary. Nila Smith's (1969) levels of comprehension have been most commonly accepted. Summarized, the levels include:

1. Literal comprehension
2. Interpretive
3. Critical reading
4. Creative reading

Literal Comprehension. Before progressing to higher levels of comprehension, every individual needs to begin with the basic, literal message received through either reading or listening. At this level the individual becomes aware of specific information, general tone, sequence, setting. After reading a story about a lost dog, the teacher asked the following questions:

- What was the dog's name?
- Who lost the dog?
- Where was the dog lost?
- What did the dog do when he was chased?

Correct responses to these questions require the student to remember the basic ideas and sequence of the story.

Interpretive Reading. The most common type of thinking activity at the interpretive level occurs when students are asked to retell the story in their own words, thereby reflecting their own interpretation (Wilson & Hall, 1972). By asking students to sequence the events in the story in order of importance, teachers achieve interpretive thinking about the message. Thoughtfully asked questions are needed if students are to progress from the literal to the interpretive level of thinking. Appropriate questions could include:

- Tell us what you think the author meant when he said . . . ?
- In order of importance, describe the events of this story.
- If you were ______, how would you feel?

In interpretive thinking, students relate events to their own experiences. Both the literal level and interpretive level are prerequisite to critical thinking.

Critical Reading. The critical reader grasps the author's message and reflects upon it by comparing it with personal experience and knowledge or other information that has been read; the information is then restructured and evaluated by comparing it to personal knowledge. The reader actively takes part in considering the message and accepting, rejecting, challenging, or reflecting upon it. The reader asks him/herself:

- Is this information relevant/irrelevant?
- How does this information compare/contrast with other information?
- How can I apply this information to . . . ?

Creative reading involves divergent thinking. Through reading the student is encouraged to involve him/herself in formulating new ideas, alternative solutions, or extended thinking. The information may be applied in a new and different manner to a personal, group, or societal problem.

The individual may be stimulated to create a totally new product or project. The teacher can stimulate creative thinking through appropriate questions:

- If you were ______, how would you solve that problem?
- Suggest a different conclusion for this story.
- Write an imaginary conversation between the two characters in this story.

Classroom Activities. Reading for comprehension is stimulated by asking appropriate questions and promoting higher levels of thinking. Students can be asked to report on current events, engage in oral discussions, or utilize printed materials to develop personal projects. If literal comprehension is desired, then students can be asked to reread to find specific information. If interpretive thinking is the objective, then students should be asked to summarize a story in their own words. For critical and creative thinking levels, students should be asked to apply what they have read to a different problem, or they might be asked to evaluate a decision made in the story. Students can also be asked to compare the story or book or article with other information.

Peer interaction can motivate interpretive, critical, and creative thinking. By participating in small group activities to share information read, plan a project based upon prior reading, or make a decision about shared information, students will gain from each other by engaging in joint thinking activities.

Objectives For Comprehension Skills
Students will
- identify main ideas/details
- utilize punctuation in reading orally
- sequence information
- identify cause and effect
- identify and interpret emotion reactions
- predict outcomes
- compare and contrast information
- identify opinion/bias
- write own endings to stories.

Location and Study Skills

Location and study skills enable the student to find, order, and use information from a variety of sources in their studies for learning purposes. Location and study skills assist the student to achieve thinking, valuing, and participatory goals.

Students' success in school is dependent upon the effectiveness and efficiency of their study habits. Effective study skills allow students to pursue independent learning. The independent learner is able to choose materials judging both the difficulty and the appropriateness of the material.

Essential skills include the ability to locate information using the card catalog and other library resources. The student learns to use reference materials such as dictionaries, periodicals, and encyclopedia. The student utilizes the table of contents, index, and glossary within books.

Maps, graphs, and tables are used to interpret information. Utilizing these source materials requires special skill instruction. Some students who have difficulty reading textbooks enjoy the use of these materials because of the pictorial representation.

Skimming is another study skill that needs to be taught. In order to preview both content and resource, students need to learn how to skim and scan reading materials. Different subject fields require different rates of reading dependent upon the difficulty and purpose of the material being used. Students must learn to read with flexibility. For suggestions about reading in content fields, the reader is urged to preview the "Reading in Social Studies" section of Chapter 7.

Since each subject field has a special vocabulary, attention must be given to unfamiliar words and concepts before students begin to read. The organization of study material also affects the student's ability to use materials efficiently. To facilitate subject field reading, teachers should provide insight into the organizing structure of the content textbook.

Classroom Activities. Study skills are common to all subject fields, and opportunities for development and practice occur throughout the school day. Whenever students use textbooks, they can be asked to demonstrate the function of the organizational parts of the textbook. When in the library they can be given the opportunity to develop reference skills by using multireference materials, the card catalog, and the Library of Congress System or the Dewey Decimal System, the *Readers' Guide to Periodical Literature, The World Almanac,* and *Bartlett's Familiar Quotations.*

In the classroom students can learn to read airlines and bus schedules, the Yellow Pages, and a variety of maps such as city street maps, freeway and highway maps, weather maps, product and political maps. Students can also be given special preparation for studying through systems like SQ3R (Robinson, 1946). The study approach teaches students how to organize for independent study. Briefly summarized, the components of SQ3R involve the following procedures:

- Survey: Organize for reading by surveying the material to be read. Read the title, introduction, headings, and key information provided by the author such as italicized words or a summary; note pictures, graphs, and captions.
- Question: Practice self-motivation by asking oneself questions about the materials to be read. Questions come from the previous survey of the reading material. Questions set the purpose for study.
- 3R—Read, Recite, Review: Read everything that has not already been read in order to answer the questions posed. Recall the main ideas in preparation for recitation and class discussion. Review material to ensure that main ideas have not been overlooked; prepare for test or discussion.

Another formula for study that can be taught to students is *PQRST* (McNeil, Donant, and Alkin, 1980). This formula specifies that the student preview, question, read, survey, and test. It is considered an independent study technique.

Objectives For Location and Study Skills
Students will
- identify and use parts of a book
- utilize reference materials in all subject fields
- alphabetize by first, second, and third letters
- interpret maps, graphs, and other pictorial data
- adapt speed of reading to content
- select and evaluate information and material.

APPLICATIONS OF RESEARCH

Armbruster and Anderson (1981) synthesized the research on work/study skills. They reported that students should be taught appropriate study techniques. These techniques involve four factors:

1. *The Nature of the Task.* Students should receive information on the goal or task involved and then receive assistance in determining the best strategy for studying.
2. *Organization of Materials.* Students should be helped to use the organizational pattern of the materials such as the headings, topics, summaries, opening and concluding sentences.
3. *Student Characteristics.* Students need to recognize and utilize their own experiences and relate them to what is to be studied. They need to be taught the relationship of personal motivation, ability, and background information and how each contributes to the ability to learn.
4. *Study Techniques.* Students need to be taught appropriate study techniques dependent upon what is to be learned. Successful students learn to focus on relevant information, relate the new material to personal experiences and memory, monitor understanding, assume responsibility to obtain help, or relearn if comprehension fails.

Choosing a Reading Series

When a school district has a diverse academic student population, more than one reading series should be selected. The texts need to provide for the diverse academic needs of the student population. The chosen materials must correlate with the skills continuum developed by the district. In addition, the materials must consider the multicultural needs of the population to be served. Each school in the school district should select one or more reader series which meets the needs of the student population in the school. Selected readers should provide continuity and sequence of reading skills. In addition, there should be ancillary materials such as worksheets, skill activities, and duplicated materials chosen to facilitate and support the basal reading series. Supplementary reading books should also be selected to enrich and reinforce the reading program. Criteria and suggested procedures for evaluating reading textbooks can be found in Chapter 16.

Readability Formulas

Textbooks vary in readability levels, sometimes as much as three years within the same book. There are several readability formulas available to assist teachers in assessing the approximate grade level of subject field reading materials. Two criteria are used to assess the difficulty of the written materials: word difficulty and sentence length. Word difficulty is based on the number of unfamiliar words in a reading selection. Sentence length is judged by the number of words and syllables and the complexity of the sentence. For example, the *Fry Graph For Estimating Readability* is based on the average number of syllables per one hundred words.

Teachers need to consider a number of factors affecting readability, not just sentence length or word difficulty. The reader's interest and past experiences affect readability. The size of the print, organizational factors, size of book, color of paper, and typeface may all be pertinent to whether a book is suitable for a specific group of students. Although publishers identify the reading level of subject field textbooks, the great variance within a text plus other factors account for the difficulty that students frequently have with books other than the basal reader.

Learning Centers

Learning centers during reading instruction should be used to reinforce and/or enrich instruction. The reinforcement center contains materials for practicing the objectives of the directed reading lesson. Enrichment centers extend the directed lesson and provide opportunities for applying what has been learned during directed instruction. The following types of centers are suggested for reinforcement or enrichment of skills:

- Library
- Dictionary Skills
- Reference Skills
- Writing Skills
- Viewing Activities
- Phonic Skills
- Manipulative Materials
- Games
- Read Aloud Center

Auditory-Visual Center #1

Reading—Lower Grades

Objectives: To improve auditory and visual discrimination; to develop word attack skills; to reinforce phonics skills.

Materials: Pictures.

Procedures:

1. Illustrative picture is pasted at the top of a piece of chart paper or on a piece of chipboard. Picture is identified with name, and the target letter sound is underlined (*book*).

Figure 6.2. Graph for Estimating Readability-Extended, by Edward Fry, Rutgers University Reading Center, New Brunswick, N.J. 08904.

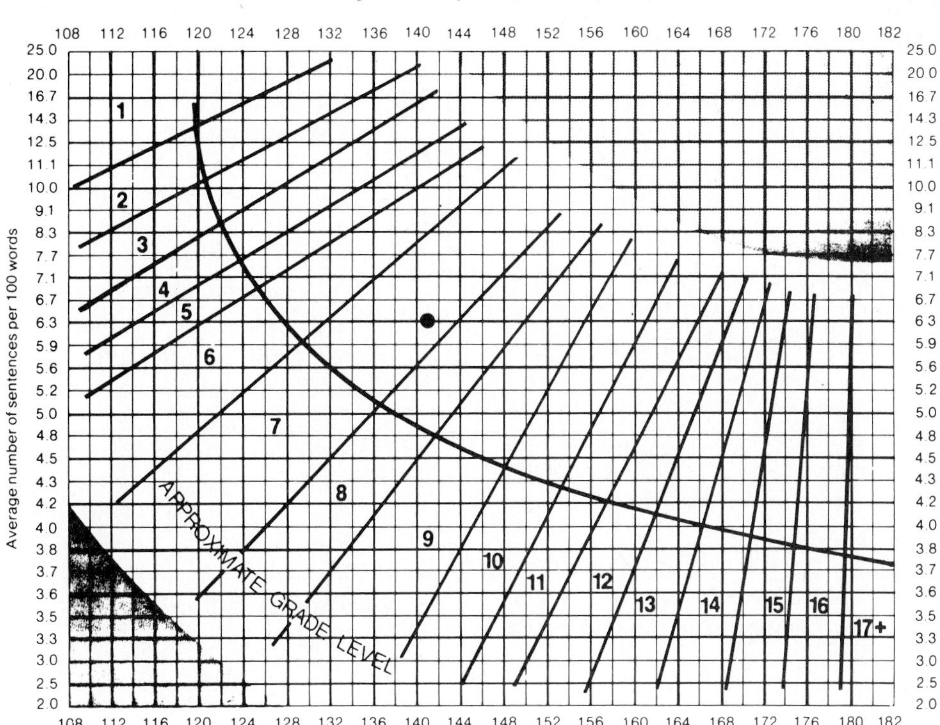

Expanded Directions for Working Readability Graph

1. Randomly select three (3) sample passages and count out exactly 100 words each, beginning with the beginning of a sentence. Do count proper nouns, initializations, and numerals.
2. Count the number of sentences in the hundred words, estimating length of the fraction of the last sentence to the nearest one-tenth.
3. Count the total number of syllables in the 100-word passage. If you don't have a hand counter available, an easy way is to simply put a mark above every syllable over one in each word, then when you get to the end of the passage, count the number of marks and add 100. Small calculators can also be used as counters by pushing numeral 1, then push the + sign for each word or syllable when counting.
4. Enter graph with *average* sentence length and *average* number of syllables; plot dot where the two lines intersect. Area where dot is plotted will give you the approximate grade level.
5. If a great deal of variability is found in syllable count or sentence count, putting more samples into the average is desirable.
6. A word is defined as a group of symbols with a space on either side; thus, *Joe*, *IRA*, *1945*, and & are each one word.
7. A syllable is defined as a phonetic syllable. Generally, there are as many syllables as vowel sounds. For example, *stopped* is one syllable and *wanted* is two syllables. When counting syllables for numerals and initializations, count one syllable for each symbol. For example, *1945* is four syllables, *IRA* is three syllables, and & is one syllable.

Note: This "extended graph" does not outmode or render the earlier (1968) version inoperative or inaccurate, it is an extension.
(REPRODUCTION PERMITTED—NO COPYRIGHT)

2. The center should have a number of letter sounds and pictures for students to identify.
3. Students choose pictures with the same beginning sound to place under the target picture(s).

Evaluation: Students self-evaluate by comparing their choices with an answer card that illustrates the appropriate choices.

Auditory-Visual Center #2

Reading—Lower Grades

Objectives: To improve auditory and visual discrimination, to develop word attack skills.

Materials: Pictures, word cards, paper, pencils.

Evaluation: Self-evaluation, teacher observation.

Procedures:

1. Picture(s) with target digraph(s) are identified on a word card or chart. Target digraph is underlined.
2. Duplicated sheets at the center provide students with a list of words. Students underline the target digraph. Example: Chicken

   show lake
   church choose
   shall chop
   whiz witch
3. Students self-evaluate work with an answer sheet at the center.

Game of Fish

Reading—Lower Grades

Objectives: To improve auditory and visual discrimination; to develop word attack skills.

Materials: Deck of cards designed by teacher.

Evaluation: Group success.

Procedures:

1. Word cards the size of a deck of cards are designed to focus on vowel or consonant sounds.
2. Four students may play the game together.
3. The object of the game is to get rid of all your cards.
4. Six cards are dealt to each player; the remainder of the cards are arranged in a stack.
5. First player calls on another player to provide word cards with desired sound (word cards with the consonant digraph *sh* as in *shout*).
6. If the designated player does not have any cards to give, the player responds "Go fish." The caller must then select a card from the top of the deck.
7. If the caller is successful in obtaining cards, s/he may continue to request desired sound cards from other players. When a set of four cards with the same sound is collected, the player stacks the set on the table.
8. The game ends when all players have successfully stacked their cards on the table in groups of four.
9. The winner of the game is the first person to get rid of all of his/her cards.

Vocabulary Center

Reading—Middle Grades

Objectives: To reinforce comprehension skills; to develop vocabulary.

Materials: Motivating pictures, sentence strips.

Evaluation: Self-evaluation using an answer sheet at the center.

Procedures:

1. Motivating pictures are displayed on small individual charts. Each picture chart is numbered.
2. Sentence box contains more sentences than there are picture charts.
3. Students choose an appropriate sentence for each picture chart. The sentence "labels" the main idea of the picture.
4. Correct sentences are checked by looking at an answer sheet with the picture numbers matched to the correct sentence strip.

To Extend:

1. Pictures and sentences may be made more complex.

2. Students may write their own sentences to match with the pictures.
3. Students may draw pictures to match with sentences.

To Simplify:

1. Use easier pictures and sentences.
2. Allow students to work with a partner.

Critical Reading

Reading—Upper Grades

Objective: To improve critical reading skills identifying adjectives, facts, opinions.

Materials: Commercial product boxes and/or advertising pages from newspapers and magazines.

Evaluation: Group evaluation, class discussion.

Procedures:

1. Products and/or advertisements are displayed at the center.
2. Students write out the descriptive advertising slogans, adjectives, gimmicks used by the advertiser.
3. Students compare their answers with each other.

To Extend:

1. Students write their own advertising slogans for products.
2. Students identify the target audience for the product and the advertising.

To Simplify:

1. Limit the quantity of products.
2. Simplify the advertising to be read (write your own).

Chapter Summary

Reading ability contributes to both individual and societal goals. Reading is a receptive form of communication. In the teaching of reading, students are learning the communication process. Approaches to reading instruction were identified. Methods for organizing the reading program were provided; the importance of the classroom environment, grouping patterns, skill management, and the utilization of aides was emphasized. The components of developmental reading programs were discussed. The special focus on skill instruction included classroom activities and teaching objectives. Suggestions for choosing a reading series were provided, and readability formulas were explained.

Classroom Application Exercises

1. One of your students has had a great deal of difficulty learning to read. You have just discovered that this student owns a camera and has taken a number of pictures of the neighborhood. Which approach to the teaching of reading would use this interest advantageously? How would you go about instruction?
2. A parent has complained that you are not teaching reading using phonics. Prepare a discussion about how decoding skills are taught. Explain why a "sight" vocabulary is important to the beginning reader.
3. Develop a reading center to reinforce reference skills.
4. Plan a lesson to broaden students' reading interests.
5. Several students have stated that they "hate" reading. Identify motivating techniques that could be used for lower-grade students, middle-grade students, upper-grade students.

Suggested Readings for Extending Study

Chall, Jeanne. *Learning to Read: The Great Debate*. New York: McGraw-Hill Book Company, 1967.

Cooper, J. David, and Thomas W. Worden. *The Classroom Reading Program in the Elementary School: Assessment, Organization and Management*. New York: Macmillan Publishing Company, 1983.

Dishner, Ernest K., Thomas W. Bean, and John E. Readence. *Reading in the Content Areas: Improving Classroom Instruction*. Dubuque, Iowa: Kendall/Hunt Publishing Company, 1981.

Karlin, Robert. *Teaching Elementary Reading: Principles and Strategies*. 3rd ed. New York: Harcourt Brace Jovanovich, Inc., 1980.

Lapp, Diane, and James Flood. *Teaching Reading to Every Child*. 2nd ed. New York: Macmillan Publishing Company, 1983.

McNeil, John D., Lisbeth Donant, and Marvin F. Alkin. *How to Teach Reading Successfully*. Boston: Little, Brown and Company, 1980.

Otto, Wayne, Robert Rude, and Dixie Lee Spiegel. *How to Teach Reading*. Reading, Mass.: Addison-Wesley Publishing Co., Inc., 1979.

Ransom, Grayce E. *Preparing to Teach Reading*. Boston: Little, Brown and Company, 1978.

Readence, John E., Thomas W. Bean, and R. S. Baldwin. *Content Area Reading: An Integrated Approach*. Dubuque, Iowa: Kendall/Hunt Publishing Company, 1981.

Smith, Frank. *Understanding Reading*. 2nd ed. New York: Holt, Rinehart and Winston, 1978.

Tunjes, M. J., and M. V. Zintz. *Teaching Reading/Thinking/Study Skills in Content Classrooms*. Dubuque, Iowa: William C. Brown Publishing Company, 1981.

Chapter 7

Social Experiences: The Nature of the Social Studies

After you have completed the study of this chapter, you should be able to accomplish the following:

1. **Identify the three criteria for selecting social studies experiences.**
2. **Explain why social studies is considered "basic" education.**
3. **Describe three perspectives or conflicts related to social studies instruction.**
4. **Identify your conclusions about what students should learn in social studies.**
5. **List the typical grade level sequence for social studies instruction in the United States.**
6. **Identify several topics or programs frequently taught during social studies time.**
7. **Identify resources for teaching social studies.**
8. **Identify and describe several strategies for teaching social studies.**
9. **Name three categories of social studies skills and suggest classroom activities to develop each skill category.**
10. **Identify ways to evaluate social studies growth.**
11. **Suggest ways to facilitate mainstreaming during social studies.**
12. **Create a learning center to teach social science concepts.**
13. **Cite advantages of multitext reading during social studies.**

When did the status of citizen fall from grace? At what point in our history did people cease to be proud of being a citizen? It was not always so. At one time people believed that to be a citizen of a republic was a special blessing. In contrast, subjects were to be pitied because they had no opportunity to govern themselves or to determine the rules by which they lived. Who debased the concept of citizenship? What events led many Americans to conclude that being a citizen was no longer an honor and a privilege? (Mehlinger, 1977, iii).

Why Do We Teach Social Studies?

In no other curriculum field are the challenges that elementary teachers face more apparent than in the teaching of social studies. With the emphases on reading and math, social studies has not been considered important by the public. As a consequence social studies receives very little financial support in school districts. In some schools it is not unusual for teachers to use textbooks and other materials that are more than twenty years old. Interestingly, while the public responds to Gallup poll interviewers that social studies is an "essential subject," it is perceived as less useful in later life. In the 13th Annual Gallup Poll, 1981, when asked about the quality of instruction in nine different subject fields, 42 per cent of the public rated social studies "A" or "B," but this was the second lowest rating of the nine different subjects.

Concern about "basic" education (reading and math skills) has led many elementary schools to deemphasize or even to eliminate entirely the teaching of social studies in grades 1–3. While it is true that mastery of reading and math are basic to the study of all other subjects, it is also true that

The question:

Using the A,B,C,D, and FAIL scale again, please grade the job you feel the public schools here are doing in providing education in each of the following areas.

The interviewer then read a list of nine subject areas, asking the respondents to rate each subject in turn.

	A or B Rating	D or FAIL Rating
	%	%
Physical education	61	6
Music	49	11
Reading	48	16
Mathematics	47	14
Writing	46	18
Science	44	10
Art	42	11
Social studies	42	11
Vocational training	35	21

social studies contributes to the development of comprehension skills in reading and math. Certainly it is not possible to research discrete information, to take notes, prepare an outline, write a report or deliver it orally without competence in basic skills. However, reading activities cannot be performed without a subject matter base. The integrated teaching of social studies and other subject fields is advocated by most curriculum specialists. But the fact that teachers are teaching reading during social studies does *not* mean that social studies objectives are automatically achieved. The essential characteristic of social studies has to do with the word "social." Let us find out what is essential about social studies.

Jarolimek (1978, pp. 32–33) questioned what was basic about social studies and identified criteria for selecting basic experiences in the social studies as those values, skills, processes, experiences, or subject matter that

1. teach the learners to participate in the common culture,
2. develop a commitment to shared, general values,
3. develop the learners' effectiveness in functioning in a group,
4. increase the learners' capacity to engage in decision making.
5. develop the learners' willingness to live according to the norms that govern individual and group behavior,
6. prepare the learners to engage in those activities that are essential for societal continuity.

Common Culture. It would be ludicrous if our schools in the United States prepared students to participate in Russian Society, or if we attempted to prepare students to live in Iran. It would be just as ridiculous if we did *not* prepare students to participate meaningfully in the affairs of our own society. While there are diverse people and cultures living within the United States, we share a common mainstream culture. This culture has to do with our economic system, our political and judicial systems, and our American heritage. United States citizens should be able to speak English, and students should be educated to participate in the social, economic, and political life of our country. Participation in the mainstream culture can be considered a basic need if one is to live in the U.S. Social studies is the subject field responsible for the achievement of this goal.

Shared Values. Parents teach certain behaviors that they value in family life. These behaviors may be that the family always gathers together for Sunday night dinner or celebrates birthdays together or plans holiday or vacation observances together. Society also has values that are shared. Loyalty, unity, respect for others' rights, innocence until proved guilty—these are but a few of the general values that are shared in our society. These values are communicated in a variety of ways through the schools. For example, we study the Bill of Rights to teach rights and responsibilities; we study about our branches of government so that students are aware of and appreciate American democracy; we use the symbol of the flag and the Star Spangled Banner to promote group unity; we holiday on Lincoln's birthday, but before we do, we teach students about our country's accomplishments. The development of these shared values typically occurs during the social studies time.

Outdoor Block Work Provides an Opportunity for Students to Participate in Cooperative Planning.

Group Effectiveness. The child comes to school relatively unsocialized. Group experiences are usually limited to the family, small groups in the nursery school (if the child attended), or in the neighborhood. Learning to work in a group and utilizing group process skills, being an effective leader and participator are developmental processes. The interaction that occurs when working in a group is different from what occurs in the family group. The assumption of a group "role" cannot be learned unless one experiences social organization. Reading and math group experiences are much different than group experiences where students are grouped heterogeneously for the purposes of discussion, planning, and listening to others' viewpoints. Interaction in groups requires understanding and adherence to group norms, roles, and social control.

Decision Making. Stemming from our colonial history, the saying "no taxation without representation" illustrates the essential characteristic of American democracy. Americans elect officials to represent them, but expect those officials to poll constituents' attitudes and interests regarding key issues. The process of decision making needs to be taught. The process includes the definition of key terms, an awareness of diverse values, the use of objective data, an understanding of the tentativeness and ongoing quality of decisions, and a realization of the necessity for active involvement in the process. The content of social studies emphasizes the importance of personal involvement and participation as students study about key periods of American history, legislation, and court decision.

Social Control. At school we guide children to develop self-control. We prize individuality, variations in thinking, creativity, and intellectual freedom. But at the same time we promote social order and conformance with established norms. We do this by guiding rational inquiry. We study social institutions (the family, church, fraternal associations), the development of civilizations, famous Americans, law, and justice. Once again, social studies is instrumental for achieving this goal.

Societal Continuity. Educational experiences, activities, ceremonies, and rituals are all directed to ensure that each new generation will continue the tradition of the past. The study of social functions is typical to most social studies programs. These functions include: (1) producing goods and services, (2) distributing goods and services, (3) transporting goods and services, (4) consuming or using goods and services, (5) communicating with others, (6) protecting and conserving human and natural resources, (7) expressing aesthetic and religious impulses, (8) providing for education, (9) providing for recreation, (10) providing for government (Jarolimek, 1978, p. 31). Social studies programs facilitate inquiry into the ways in which each society organizes itself to perform these functions, thereby preparing students to engage in essential activities for societal continuity.

Why Do We Teach Social Studies? Through the teaching of social studies we prepare students to participate in a democratic society. We facilitate the development of humane, rational, and understanding individuals so that we will preserve and continue our society. To be effective citizens we recognize that there are specific skills, knowledge, values, and attitudes necessary for social participation and that these goals direct the social studies program.

What Are Students Expected to Learn (What Is Social Studies?)

Although there is considerable disagreement about what content to select for the teaching of social studies and about how to teach social studies, most educators accept that the overarching goal of social studies is citizenship education. Barr et al. (1977, p. 69) defined the social studies as "an integration of experience and knowledge concerning human relations for the purpose of citizenship education." To achieve this goal, objectives must be developed to

1. provide *knowledge* about human experiences in the past, present, and future,
2. develop *skills* to process information,
3. develop appropriate *values* and *beliefs*,
4. provide opportunities for *social participation*.

This definition of the social studies differs from an oft-quoted one written by Edgar Wesley. When Wesley was asked, What is social studies? he responded that "the social studies are the social sciences simplified for pedagogical purposes" (Wesley & Wronski, 1958, p. 3).

APPLICATION OF RESEARCH

Schwartz (1975) studied the political socialization of preschoolers and found that children aged three through six believe that the policeman "helps you most, knows more than anyone, and is the most important" person. The teacher, according to the preschoolers, "makes people do things."

More consistent teaching about political concepts, according to the researcher, would be beneficial. Teaching about the United States should occur by utilizing music and literature along with social studies.

Using both of these definitions of the social studies, we can see that Barr's "integration of experiences and knowledge" really means knowledge from the social sciences. These social sciences are history, geography, economics, political science, anthropology, sociology, and psychology. Wesley's "pedagogical purposes" means simplified for the purpose of teaching. While Wesley's definition is broad in its intent, the Barr definition is specific in detailing the primary goal of the social studies.

TABLE 7.1. The Three Social Studies Traditions.

Social Studies Taught as Citizenship Transmission	Social Studies Taught as Social Science	Social Studies Taught as Reflective Inquiry
Purpose—Citizenship is best promoted by inculcating right values as a framework for making decisions.	Citizenship is best promoted by decision making based on mastery of social science concepts, processes, and problems.	Citizenship is best promoted through a process of inquiry in which knowledge is derived from what citizens need to know to make decisions and solve problems.
Method—Transmission: Transmission of concepts and values by such techniques as textbook, recitation, lecture, question and answer sessions, and structured problem-solving exercises.	Discovery: Each of the social sciences has its own method of gathering and verifying knowledge. Students should discover and apply the method that is appropriate to each social science.	Reflective Inquiry: Decision making is structured and disciplined through a reflective inquiry process which aims at identifying problems and responding to conflicts by means of testing insights.
Content—Content is selected by an authority interpreted by the teacher and has the function of illustrating values, beliefs, and attitudes.	Proper content is the structure, concepts, problems, and processes of both the separate and the integrated social science disciplines.	Analysis of individual citizen's values yields needs and interests which in turn form the basis for student self-selection of problems. Problems, therefore, constitute the content for reflection.

Source: Robert D. Barr, et al., *Defining the Social Studies* (NCSS, Bulletin #51, 1977), p. 67.

Conflict in Social Studies. An analysis of the conflicting perceptions about what should be taught in the social studies and how to go about teaching it provided Barr and his co-authors with three basic traditions in the social studies (Table 7.1). To some extent the history of the teaching of social studies can be traced by using the three traditions.

Social Studies Taught as Citizenship Transmission

Every nation of the world is faced with the need to develop cultural unity. In our own country this need was perceived soon after the revolutionary war. Our early citizens were concerned that future generations should know about our history and that young citizens be taught "patriotism." This traditional conception of citizenship transmission is dependent upon the adult's passing on the cultural heritage to the youth. This seems to necessitate that the adult "transmitter" be a strong and partisan teacher. The method of teaching is primarily inculcation. This means that the teacher has a clear idea of what a good citizen is supposed to be able to do and attempts to transmit it, in order to help the young become loyal citizens. While this conception of the social studies was more pervasive during our early history, it is still a viable concept today.

The content in the classroom of a teacher who believes in citizenship transmission is a combination of the "hidden" curriculum and the textbook or state-prepared curriculum guide. The teacher frequently exhorts students to "share," "take turns," "all bright eyes looking this way," "sit up tall," and "close your lips when a visitor comes into the classroom to talk to teacher." These socializing techniques may comprise the hidden curriculum, and the textbook and the teacher's own beliefs, mainstream values, norms, obedience to laws, social participation, and perception of the ideal society together comprise the content of social studies. The central goal of citizenship transmission is the focal point and serves to organize the curriculum.

Social Studies as the Social Sciences

The fifth-grade students returned to their classroom after recess and found a number of display centers. There were pictures of pioneers, pioneer homes, and the interior of a pioneer cabin. There were several wall maps illustrating the Oregon and Santa Fe Trails and other pioneer routes West. There was a filmstrip about soapmaking. There were exhibits of a covered wagon, a loom and spindle, a Flintlock rifle, and pioneer clothes. There were personal letters obviously written by family members who had traveled westward and a diary written by a young pioneer girl.

The classroom buzzed as the students excitedly wandered about looking at the centers. The teacher watched and listened. After a while the teacher went to the chalkboard and wrote two sets of questions. On one side of the chalkboard he wrote these questions.

- What happened to the pioneers as they moved westward?
- How did the pioneers travel westward?
- Why did the pioneers move westward?

On the other side of the chalkboard he wrote these questions:

- What are primary sources of information?
- What are secondary sources of information?
- How does an historian determine "what happened"?

The students returned to their seats. Many looked puzzled. The teacher acknowledged their puzzlement by asking several students: "What's the matter?"

"Why are these things on display?" "What are we going to study?" These were the questions that the students asked. The teacher responded, "We are going to pretend that we are historians. Who can tell me, what is a primary source of information?"

The teacher will teach about social science inquiry, and using a westward movement unit of study, the students will learn about human behavior during the early nineteenth century as the American pioneers moved westward. When social studies is taught from the perspective of a social scientist, it is expected that students will come to understand human experience by learning the kinds of problems studied by social scientists and the assumptions and techniques used by social scientists. Students learn to ask intelligent questions similar to what the historian or the sociologist, or perhaps the political scientist, might ask. In this way students will learn to reason and to become effective citizens.

The social science approach, although rooted in early historical practices before 1900, really became meaningful during the 1960s through the work of the Social Science Education Consortium and the varied social science projects that were funded by the National Science Foundation. Many contemporary textbook series reflect the social science orientation. The changing emphases of the social science disciplines are reflected in the questions that social scientists ask and in the expansion of social studies to include some of the newer disciplines, such as social psychology and anthropology. This approach to social studies teaching was stimulated by the post-Sputnik concerns of the 1960s.

APPLICATION OF RESEARCH

The research of Peterson (1979) provided evidence that open teaching approaches facilitate problem solving. Since teachers should use a variety of teaching approaches, this means that when teachers want to develop critical thinking skills they will need to choose a problem that is genuinely puzzling to students and create a classroom environment that promotes stimulating inquiry.

Social Studies Taught as Reflective Inquiry

Both the social science perspective of social studies and the reflective inquiry perspective expect students to make intelligent decisions. In the social science tradition, the teacher chooses what the student will study and sets the stage for inquiry.

How Students Learn Is As Important As What Students Learn. These Students Are Involved in Building a Community.

However, when social studies is taught as reflective inquiry, the teacher expects the *students* to choose what to study. The major difference is that the problem selected may be more relevant to the students. It is usually more personal in its focus. The reflective inquiry teacher will try to spotlight several problems that have potential for puzzlement, for a conflict in values, or for social implications, and some sources for data concerning the nature of these problems.

In a reflective inquiry classroom, the teacher might bring in a newspaper story for the students to read. An example would be the story about the Vietnamese fishermen who were physically attacked by American fishermen and the Ku Klux Klan. All three groups lived in Galveston, Texas. The Vietnamese were recent immigrants, and fishing was their way of life in Vietnam. They utilized the same fishing techniques in Galveston Bay as they had in Vietnam, but they fished seven days a week. The American fishermen only fished five days a week, and their techniques were slightly different. The Americans believed that the Vietnamese were guilty of poaching and that they took unfair advantage by fishing seven days of the week.

The teacher using this story would first have the students read the story and then ask the students if they saw a problem. If the students acknowledge that there *is* a problem, the teacher asks them to hypothesize about how to study the problem. In the example given, the students might hypothesize that there is a conflict of values. The next step would be to have the students define all aspects of the problem, such as what is meant by the term *values*.

Next, the students would suggest ways to study the problem. During the study stage the students would be gathering facts and evidence to support or refute the hypothesis. Finally, the students would come to a decision about the social implications of the problem or how the problem could be resolved.

The teacher's purpose in this classroom is to help students understand that all individuals are motivated by personal needs, interests, and values. As citizens we have to make rational and informed decisions; reflective inquiry teaches inquiry skills and helps students make choices and deliberate decisions.

What Is Social Studies? The three approaches to teaching social studies provide information about what some professional educators believe students should learn in the social studies. The conflict about the question "What is social studies?" is concerned with several issues:

- Should social studies be solely responsible for the development of citizenship goals?
- What content in social studies is of most worth?
- What method(s) should be used to teach the social studies?

APPLICATION OF RESEARCH

In a study of 550 fourth-grade students, Barrows and Jungleblut (1976) concluded that the students had a "we-they" perception of other nations and other people. The fourth-grade students characterized the U.S. as the strongest, nicest, and largest nation and Russia and China as small nations with fewer people than in the United States.

Culture studies of other nations along with the teaching of map skills appear to be needed.

The three approaches presented can be summarized as follows:

1. Cultural Heritage Approach to Content: This approach teaches knowledge and understanding about the past; inspirational heroes and heroines are often selected as foci; patroitism is emphasized; traditional textbooks are selected for use. Content should cultivate citizenship and loyalty.

2. Social Science Approach to Content: This approach teaches concepts, generalizations, and processes used by social scientists; student-centered teaching techniques are utilized. Citizenship goals are to be achieved through a better understanding of the world.

3. Reflective Inquiry Approach to Content: This approach teaches students how to think, how to process information in order to make informed decisions, and how to participate effectively in groups. Content is considered relatively unimportant; it is selected on the basis of "mileage." The selected content should provide sufficient data for students to practice problem-solving and group participation skills.

Although the three traditions in social studies education express philosophic orientations to content selection and methods of teaching, all elementary teachers do not necessarily choose a specific approach and adhere to it in the classroom. It is more likely that teachers utilize a little bit of this approach and a little bit of that approach!

Selecting and Organizing Content

Whenever curriculum experts discuss the "what" of curriculum, they are discussing the *scope* of the curriculum pattern; when experts discuss the "order" or grade level of the pattern, they are referring to the *sequence*. Surprisingly, there is very little variation in the United States from school to school as to what is taught in the social studies.

Expanding communities is the name given to the most typical pattern found in elementary schools. The pattern developed as a response to the developmental needs and interests of young children. Figure 7.1 represents the approach illustrating the widening perspective and sequence of social studies as students move away from their own egocentric world to study human behavior in far-off places.

The intent of the curriculum design was to introduce students, through inquiry, to social science generalizations underlying each of the communities of which the student is a member. Beyond sequence considerations, Hanna (1965) organized the scope

Figure 7.1. Expanding Communities. (Source: Paul R. Hanna, "Revising the Social Studies: What Is Needed?" *Social Education*, **27**:4 April 1963, p. 193.)

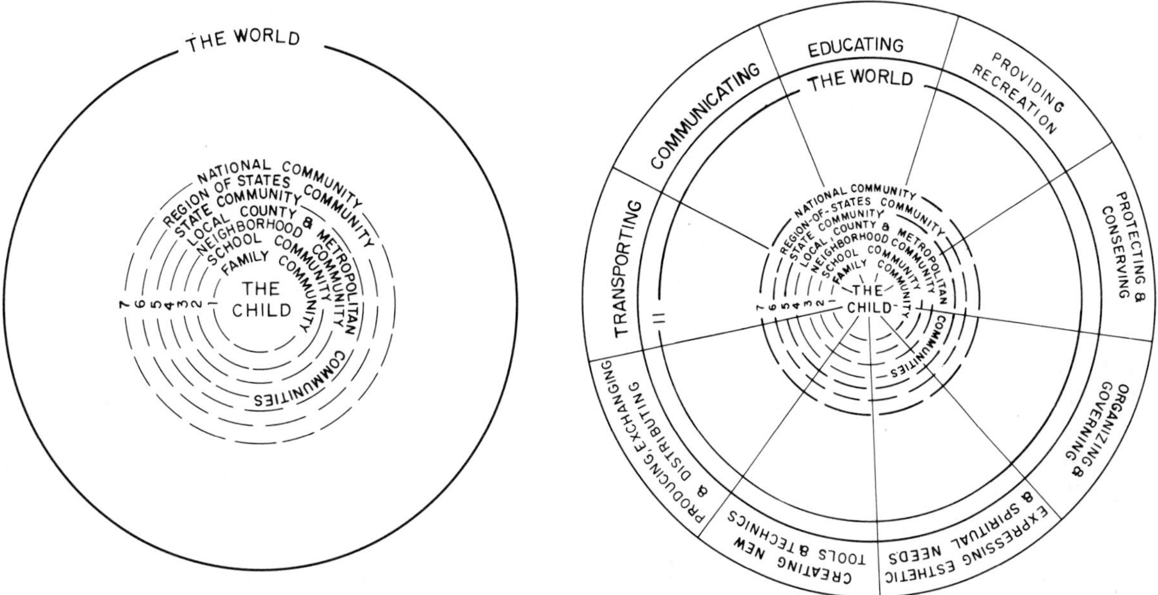

of the program into categories of basic human activities. Two dimensions coordinated the design. The expanding communities represented the sequence, and the basic human activities the scope. Figure 7.1 illustrates the two dimensions.

The expanding communities design was often interpreted too narrowly by teachers and social scientists. Since the advent of television, students view people in remote areas of the world, travels in space, behavior that may be less than exemplary. As a consequence, teachers may need to incorporate conceptual content and skills related to controversial problems, societal issues, or student concerns.

Many states adopt their own guidelines to provide a basis for determining the scope and sequence of the social studies program. In California the State Board of Education adopted a History-Social Science Framework for California Public Schools (1981) in order to provide guidelines and recommendations for teachers and publishers of materials and curriculum developers. The framework is intended as a policy statement and as a guide for designing curricula and courses of study. It also serves as a base from which criteria for instructional materials can be developed. Each grade level in the California framework has a specific recommendation for a major setting or topic, and then a number of subtopics are recommended. The major topic appears below, and several subtopics have been selected to provide insight into the nature of state frameworks.

> As you read the framework, decide in what ways the scope and sequence conforms to the expanding environments approach to the organization of content. How has the plan encouraged teachers to exercise choice in the selection of content? In what ways does the framework differ from the expanding environments point of view?

The California History-Social Science Framework (1981):

Kindergarten—Myself and Others in My World
- The uniqueness of me: my similarities and differences
- Finding my way in my world (map skills)
- Cooperation and conflict between friends and classmates through work and play

Grade One—People at Home and at School
- Roles people play in my family and at my school
- Families—my own and others in the community and in the world
- Who is an American?

Grade Two—People as Members of Groups
- Groups to which I belong
- American ethnic groups: their roles and contributions
- Rules, responsibilities, and group norms
- How art, music, and dance influence and enrich group life

Grade Three—People as Members of Communities
- What is a community?
- The diverse cultures and peoples who make up and contribute to our community
- How does our community compare/contrast to other communities in the United States and in the World?

Grade Four—The People of a Region: California
- California: its land and its environment (e.g. regional setting, major physical features, economic and cultural geography, current environmental concerns)
- Californians all: men and women who have made significant contributions to our social, political, economic, and cultural life
- California: its place and role in the United States and in the world

Grade Five—The People of a Nation: The United States of America
- We, the people of the United States, today
- Explorers and settlers in America—north, south, east, and west
- The United States and its people: their place/roles in the world today

Grade Six—Our World, Its Diverse Peoples, and Their Societies
- Earth as home for human beings—the world's water, land, climate, and natural resources and how they affect where and how peoples live
- The world's diverse peoples and the reasons for differences in appearance and behavior
- The role and importance of language in all human societies

Grade Seven—The Changing World
- Knowledge about the geography of the world and how it has changed over the centuries
- Selected case studies of great civilizations in the Western and non-Western worlds.
- When peoples meet: conflict, controversies, cooperation, and cultural change

Grade Eight—The American Experience
- Old World/New World: continuity and change
- The colonial experience viewed from a variety of perspectives
- Contributions of men, women, and groups to the political, economic, social, and cultural development of the United States

Only several of the subtopics at each grade level have been included here. However, even with this brief view of the California framework several observations about what Californians expect students to learn can be generated.

- Which topics in the California framework adhere to the citizenship transmission approach to social studies?
- Which topics in the California framework adhere to the social science approach to social studies?
- Which topics are appropriate for reflective inquiry?

The Spiral Curriculum is another approach to the selection and organization of content in the social studies. Developed by Hilda Taba (1967), basic concepts are structured in such a way that they are used at different levels of abstraction dependent upon the age and ability of the students. Figure 7.2 illustrates the concepts of interdependence, cultural change, and differences. The hierarchical arrangement allows each level to be prerequisite to the subsequent level. Concepts must be taught at increasing levels of complexity and abstraction as they thread their way through the curriculum from grades 1 to 6.

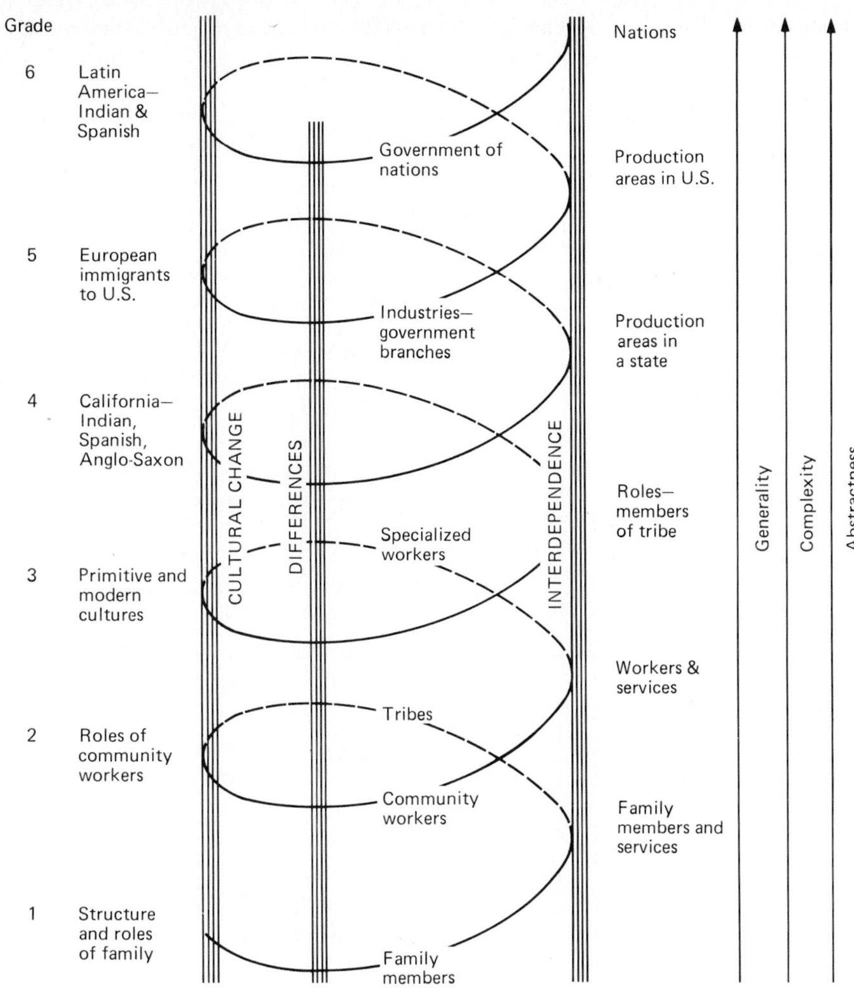

Figure 7.2 The Spiral of Concept Development. (Source: Taba, *Teacher's Handbook for Elementary Social Studies*, © 1971. Addison-Wesley, Reading, MA. Figure 1. Reprinted with permission.)

How does the focus of the spiral curriculum differ from the focus of the expanding environments curriculum?

Diversity of Topics and Programs

If you have not guessed it already, the social studies curriculum encompasses almost everything that society is concerned about: multicultural education, ethnic studies, career education, consumer education, global education, law education, moral education. The teacher is continually faced with making choices about what to include in the relatively short period of time devoted to social studies. Let us take a brief look at the modest proposals for some of these topics.

Law Education. Gallagher (1977, p. 111) has suggested that elementary students need to understand the nature and function of law. The basic premises for laws can be studied.

- Law reflects social values.
- Law is a means to govern human behavior.

- Law assumes voluntary compliance.
- Law is a means to justice.

Gallagher suggests the use of role-plays, mock trials, or simulations (see Part III) to clarify the purpose of laws. Field trips and neighborhood walks are also valuable so that students can observe the use of laws in their daily lives. In the neighborhood walk students can observe the following:

- the use of street signs to assure orderliness
- the observance of traffic regulations by pedestrians and motor vehicles
- rules that protect the environment
- rules that regulate business use
- rules that regulate residential land use.

Consumer Education. Advocates of consumer education believe that children are subject to more intense advertising pressures than adults. By teaching economic concepts such as needs and wants, supply and demand, scarcity, surplus, labor, and services, students will be able to make more intelligent choices and be more competent as consumers. Little (1975) recommends teaching about truth in advertising and combining such a study with a study of law.

Career Education. Career education programs in the elementary school focus on the world of work. Their purpose is to acquaint young students with the diverse occupations that are available as career choices. The program's aim, primarily, is to develop awareness of occupations that may be beyond the child's immediate experiences. Teachers who choose to develop career education programs are particularly careful to avoid sex-role stereotyping. The special skills and training that different occupations require make up the substance of the program.

Global Education. Anderson and Anderson (1977, pp. 139–140) identified four major objectives of global education programs in the elementary school:

1. Competence in perceiving one's involvement in global society. A global education program should help students realize the ways in which humans are linked: culturally, ecologically, biologically, technologically, historically, psychologically.
2. Competence in making decisions. We are affected by worldwide conditions, and these conditions necessitate decisions that affect our ways of life. The decisions that we make have a reciprocal effect on the rest of the world. Creative adaptation to worldwide conditions demands competent citizens capable of making informed decisions.

RESEARCH FINDINGS

Mitsakos (1978, pp. 12–13) investigated the effect of a strong global education program on third-grade children's views of foreign peoples. The program evaluated was the "Family of Man." He concluded:

1. A carefully designed primary-grade social studies program with a strong global education dimension can have a significant impact on the formation of attitudes that children develop toward foreign peoples.
2. A carefully designed primary-grade social studies program with a strong global education dimension can have a significant effect on the understanding that children develop of other nations and other peoples.
3. A carefully designed primary-grade social studies program with a strong global education dimension can achieve other important objectives.
4. An organized social studies curriculum that has well-defined objectives, specific materials, and some sequence achieves better results than a social studies program that is not well-defined or structured.
5. Effective techniques can be developed to measure primary-grade children's views of other nations and other peoples.

3. Competence in making judgments. Interrelated global problems necessitate that citizens be able to manage cultural diversity, conflict and violence, cultural change, problems of inequality, population growth, and human-biosphere relations. These judgments require competent analytical skills along with judgmental maturity.
4. Competence in exercising influence. Students need to be taught how to influence others through negotiation, bargaining, and compromise. The concept of power can be taught so that students appreciate and value political activity.

   The focus on global education need not be confined to the sixth or seventh grades; aspects of it can be incorporated into the total program throughout the grades.

Moral Education. The work of developmental psychologist Lawrence Kohlberg has been influential in motivating interest in moral education programs. A strategy developed at Carnegie-Mellon University has been quite successful in the classroom. The teaching plan, described by Galbraith and Jones (1975), is as follows:

1. Presentation of a Moral Dilemma. The teacher chooses a dilemma, presents it by reading it; or the students may read it or view it on film. The teacher assists the students to clarify and define the concepts presented in the dilemma.
2. Problem Definition. The students are asked to state what the problem is. The teacher encourages the students to express the values inherent in the problem. Sometimes the students are asked to write down what they think is the problem and then to discuss it. During this stage the teacher asks for a hand-show to determine how many believe that there *is* a problem and how many do not perceive the dilemma as a real problem. If the students do not feel that the situation is a dilemma, then the teacher chooses a new problem situation.
3. Reasoning Stage. The students are grouped and asked to develop reasons for actions. The students may be grouped with all of the members of the group in agreement, or the groups may be composed of members in disagreement. If the group members agree, then they decide on the two best ways to deal with the problem. If the group members disagree, then they are to choose the best defense for each position.
4. Evaluation. Each group presents its conclusions. Groups may disagree with each other; discussion is encouraged. Closure is not an objective, and there is no "right" answer. The goal is confrontation and the reasoning process.

The teacher's role during moral education strategies is that of a facilitator. The purpose is to encourage discussion and help students learn to reason.

RESEARCH FINDINGS

Selman and Lieberman (1975) investigated moral education in the primary grades. Moral dilemmas were presented using sound filmstrips, after which teachers would encourage discussion and debate among the second-grade children.

The researchers found that small group discussion, used to resolve interpersonal and moral conflicts, effected greater change in posttest moral development levels.

Multicultural Education and Ethnic Studies. Many school districts expect teachers to teach multicultural education. Frankly, this author has never been sure what that means. However, the intent, as in most of the other special interest programs, is that it be taught during the social studies. Investigation of multicultural education reveals great divergence in program implementation. Some teachers design a program about our "multicultural" heritage. This seems to mean that they teach about the diverse cultural groups who live in the United States. Other programs focus on ethnic groups and attempt to sensitize students to black history or to the contribution of Hispanics or other minority groups. The ethnic studies programs usually emphasize one specific group at a time, but at the elementary level this is unusual. Obviously the goal of multicultural education is to help students appreciate the contributions of all the peoples who are a part of our cultural life. This end can be achieved most effectively in a total, integrated social studies program rather than in a fragmented program called "multicultural."

Man a Course of Study (MACOS). This program is often taught in either grade 5 or 6. Since it is virtually a self-contained program, packaged with all of the instructional materials and teaching suggestions, it is presented here as a special social studies program. To use the materials and teach the program, teachers are required to have special training from the developers or from other teachers who have had the thirty required hours of special instruction.

The program uses the spiral curriculum approach by choosing several key concepts and developing them in greater complexity throughout the year of instruction. The concept of "life cycle" is developed as students study about salmon, herring gulls, baboons, and ultimately the Netselik Eskimos. Other concepts include "learning" and "humanism." The basic organizing questions in the MACOS program are: What is human about human beings? How do humans differ from animals? How can people become more human? These questions are pursued as students compare the human life cycle and human learning with the animal studies.

The MACOS program has been subjected to a great deal of criticism because it alerts students to societal problems such as infanticide, trial marriage, and senilicide. When teachers deal with these issues sensitively, in the total context of the program, generally the public is accepting. The study of human behavior can be controversial, but this is what social studies is all about.

Family of Man and MATCH Programs. Of lesser depth and of shorter duration, these two

These Students Are Planning and Constructing an Environment As They Participate in the MACOS Program. They Are Studying the Concept of Adaptation.

programs have been developed for grades K–6. The Family of Man program was developed by Edith West as part of a K–12 social studies project at the University of Minnesota. The program does not conform to the expanding environment curriculum format. Units include: The Kibbutz Family, the Ashanti Family, Hopi Indian Family, Japanese Family, Russian Family in Moscow, Family of Early New England. The programs were designed with the intent of helping students become both nation- and world-minded. The units emphasize concepts, generalizations, skills, and attitudes focused on cultural understanding. The program is interdisciplinary, utilizing concepts from anthropology, sociology, geography, history, economics, and political science.

The MATCH (Materials and Activities for Teachers and Children) program was developed by the Boston Children's Museum. The units include The City, Indians Who Met the Pilgrims, Paddle to the Sea, Medieval People, A House of Ancient Greece, The Japanese Family. The House of Ancient Greece has been the most popular. It was designed for use in grade 5 or 6 and requires about four weeks of class time for an in-depth study. The teacher using the kit needs no special training. The disciplinary structure of the program is based on archaeology with minor strands emphasizing geography and history. Using the program, students should develop an appreciation of life in an ancient Greek household. The students study ancient societies using archeology as a learning tool. The program requires students to gather and analyze evidence and formulate conclusions about life in ancient Greece. Students are divided into six teams and, using the artifacts, photos, books, and filmstrips, each team simulates the activites of archeologists. Each team keeps records, examines evidence, studies the pictures, maps, and household implements, and ultimately develops conclusions which are shared with the other teams.

The special programs of MACOS, MATCH, and Family of Man utilize concepts from the social sciences. These programs also encourage reflective inquiry. The subject matter of the special programs functions as a mechanism by which students can contrast their own experiences with the knowledge presented.

How Is Social Studies Organized for Instruction?

The organization of related and sequenced segments of work in the elementary school is usually described as a "unit" of study. Units in the social studies may be as short as a week or as long as the semester. The selection of a unit of work usually conforms to school district or state framework guidelines and is designed to meet the needs and interests of a specific group of students. The social studies unit is usually planned so as to integrate subject fields. The content for the unit focuses on social science concepts, but the theme or topic will probably conform to school district or state recommendations. Illustrative topics were identified earlier in the chapter. The actual unit planning process is outlined in Chapter 14. The following is a list of concepts typically taught in elementary classrooms:

culture	acculturation
multiple causation	enculturation
adaptation	technology
assimilation	conflict
environment	scarcity
resources	land use
needs and wants	roles
groups	immigrant
rules	family
norms	socialization
law	cooperation
government	norms
power and authority	competition
motivation	communication
interaction	artifacts
interdependence	citizenship
change	justice
behavior	freedom
space	property
time	privacy
diversity	social control
supply and demand	migration
community	emigrant

How Is Social Studies Taught?

Competence to teach social studies is a developmental process. Of course, this is true of all subject fields, but more so, perhaps, for the social studies. A number of factors are more critical for success in social studies than in teaching skill areas. These factors will be briefly summarized.

In the skill areas of reading and mathematics, once the teacher has diagnosed students' needs, textbooks can be depended upon to facilitate a consistently sequenced program. This is not necessarily true in social studies. It is important in social studies for the teacher to prepare a teaching unit, as Greg Thomas did, (see Chapter 14) and then to utilize textbooks and other materials for resources. Purposeful teaching is dependent upon the teacher's long-range planning in social studies.

Strategies for teaching social studies need to be refined. Again, unlike the skill areas where direct instruction is to be favored, social studies requires greater depth and versatility.

Diagnosis in social studies is dependent upon teacher judgment and informal means of assessment. This does not mean that there are no standardized tests in social studies—just that available tests are not always appropriate, nor do they test the range of knowledge, skills, values, and social participation components that teachers need to know.

Another area of difference is the classroom environment. Skills in reading and mathematics can be taught at the kitchen table, if necessary. The latitude of social studies activities and experiences is so great that an extended environment needs to be considered. The environment for social studies is not only for motivation but to provoke inquiry or to be used as a resource for learning. Each of these factors will now be discussed in greater detail.

Resources for Teaching Social Studies

Resources for teaching social studies are almost too numerous to mention. Nonprint materials include pictures, films, tapes, television, realia, records, resource persons, and places. Print materials include textbooks, newspapers, workbooks, and computers.

Obtaining and utilizing resources requires anticipation of classroom needs. This is an important management prerequisite for successful social studies teaching. Since it is fairly easy to anticipate what your social studies unit will be, advanced planning of resources is not as difficult as it might seem. For example, the teaching of a unit on the community can include some slides taken by the teacher of the immediate neighborhood. Photos can also be utilized. Magazine pictures can be collected. Travel agencies and large corporations are often quite willing to supply teachers with pictures. Groups like the dairy council or the meat industry welcome teachers' requests. Many teachers utilize their vacation travels to take pictures of places that will be useful in teaching social studies.

Great care needs to be exercised in selecting people to serve as *resource guides*. Although it is not difficult to identify individuals who have specialized knowledge, the problem is to ascertain whether or not the individual is able to communicate that knowledge to children. A good idea before finalizing your commitment to an individual is to provide the person with a guide of what to expect in terms of students' questions and in terms of what you want the person to communicate.

Field trips should also be preplanned. The teacher should know what students will see and what they may do on a field trip. The best way to assess this is to take the trip yourself before you plan to take the students. Before the field trip, students should be programmed with questions about what to observe. A walking trip through the neighborhood can be a valuable experience, but only if students are directed to observe some specifics. Students visiting a dairy might be programmed with the following types of questions:

- How are cows milked?
- See if you can describe the steps for milk production—from cow to market.

- What other products besides milk do dairies produce?
- How are other dairy products made?

Realia can be collected bit by bit and purchased when funds allow. Quite often friends have special objects such as tapestries, knickknacks, or items from personal travel experiences that they are willing to share. Realia can often be borrowed from teacher resource centers. For example, in Los Angeles the museum of natural history has a teachers' resource center. From this center teachers may borrow all types of realia (including taxidermic animals), slides, and pictures.

Records, tapes, and films can usually be ordered from the school district or county school offices. Many large libraries also allow teachers to borrow media, but orders have to be placed well in advance of need.

Print materials include books, maps, graphs, charts, newspapers, *My Weekly Reader, News Ranger,* and the computer. Reading during the social studies will be discussed under the category of "strategies." When considering the use of textbooks in the social studies it is important to remember that grade-level designations are not necessarily pertinent. It is possible to do a community study at almost any grade level, and it is possible to study other societies at many grade levels. This means that social studies books should be shared rather than designated for a particular classroom and stored on a closet shelf. For preparation purposes the teacher needs to survey what is available at the school and what is useful for teacher resource purposes and for students' resource needs.

Diagnosis

Teachers need to diagnose what a child knows (knowledge), what a child can do (skills), students' learning characteristics, attitudes about learning and working with others, and ability to work cooperatively with others. Greg Thomas will need to know whether his students understand the concept of adaptation. One of the easiest ways for Thomas to find out is to ask his students the meaning of adaptation. If his students can define it and provide examples of the concept, then Thomas may feel relatively confident that the concept of adaptation can be used by the students as a tool to study human behavior. Although it is fairly simple to write a paper-and-pencil test to find out what students know, it may not be necessary for diagnostic purposes.

The ability to use study skills is easily diagnosed. Given charts, tables, pictures, or cartoons, if students are able to extract and interpret information, then the teacher can be confident that students have mastered a certain level of competence. On the other hand, if students are unable to utilize reference materials to locate information, then the teacher knows that reference skills will need to be taught. Critical thinking skills can be similarly diagnosed. Given evidence about certain events, students are asked to suggest probable conclusions. If they cannot do so, then they have not mastered that skill. Skill diagnosis should be systematically performed by the teacher. This can best be done with the use of checklists. Chapter 17 will provide examples for use in the social studies.

Interpersonal or social participation skills, such as listening and respecting others' opinions or recognizing one's own and others' biases, can be diagnosed by observing students. During a class or small group discussion, the teacher is able to observe the way students work with their peers. The observation of students at lunch or on the playground will also reveal a great deal about social participation skills.

Classroom Management

Classroom management during social studies is no different than during reading or math in the sense that the teacher still needs to perform planning, organizing, anticipating, arranging, and monitoring tasks. However, certain aspects of classroom management may be more significant in terms of making a difference when teaching in a subject field like social studies. For example, if students are to use a variety of instructional materials (books, media, pictures, and the like) and use them in different places in the classroom because of grouping arrangements, then all of the classroom management components assume greater importance. The teacher needs to anticipate what learning materials students will need, where these materials will be used, how students will be grouped, and how evaluation will be handled. Monitoring behavior and learning needs become crucial to the success of the lesson.

The teaching episode in this chapter about the fifth-grade students observing the "arranged" environment, provides an example to analyze for classroom management problems. The episode does *not* tell you about the following:

1. Why did the students *not* misbehave as they wandered about observing the artifacts and instructional materials?
2. How did the teacher get the students to their seats?
3. How did the teacher get attention so that a discussion could take place?

These are the kinds of questions a teacher would have to ask before attempting this strategy. The episode lets us know what the teacher did *not* do; now let us think about what must have really happened.

1. The teacher had *many* items on display, and they were distributed around the room so that students would not crowd as they looked at the materials.
2. The students were allowed to *touch* the materials. Since children need to touch (so do adults) what they are looking at, any admonishment not to do so would only *create* a problem.
3. The teacher provided enough time to satiate interest; the students had no need to beg for more time.
4. The teacher began to write on the chalkboard. This signalled the students that it was time to return to their seats. (The teacher observed the students carefully and knew they had observed for a sufficient amount of time.)
5. Probably the students were accustomed to nonverbal suggestions; the teacher may have gestured or made some expression of the need to begin the discussion.

The "trick" to social studies classroom management is the anticipation component. The teacher needs to think out:

- where students will work
- what resource tools will be needed
- how the lesson will be motivated
- how much time will be needed
- what problems might be anticipated
- how evaluation will be accomplished.

Strategies for Teaching Social Studies

Strategies for teaching are diverse and numerous. They range from reading and discussion to construction, dramatics, and role playing. There is emphasis on critical thinking and analytic skills; reading and research are featured. Values and human relations skills are often taught through games and simulations. Interviewing and case studies are used. Arts and crafts, music and dancing are all integrated in the social studies. Since Part III of the text is devoted to instructional strategies, many of the aforementioned techniques will be explained in the later chapters. In this section the emphases will be on several strategies that are germane to the teaching of social studies.

Initiation, Development, and Culmination

In a social studies teaching unit, strategies are planned to initiate, develop and culminate the unit.

An *initiation* may be extremely simple or complex. Thomas initiated with a film about the different groups of people who settled in the New World. This beginning was quite simple, and since the film is provocative, it will be effective. At the beginning of the section about "social studies as the social sciences" is a description of an arranged environment. The arranged environment is a more elaborate way to develop students' interests in the teaching unit. The purpose of the initiation is to motivate inquiry and to provide a fruitful way to find out what students know and what they need to learn.

Developmental activities are all those experiences that move the unit from beginning to end. If students' interest lags during the course of the unit, the teacher may have to find a way to initiate new interest. *Culminating* activities serve as a means to evaluate what has been learned and to end the unit. Thomas ended his unit with the production of a class mural. Sometimes dramatic play is an appropriate means to culminate a social studies unit. Often parents enjoy observing the culmination of the unit when students participate in dramatic play. The production of a play, a mural, or a project provides a fine way to let parents know what their children are learning in the social studies.

Reading in Social Studies

During social studies, teachers have the opportunity to develop a variety of reading skills: location skills, reading for details and specific facts, skimming, note taking, proofreading reports and projects, choosing reading selections to fit specific historical time periods. These skills can be taught more efficiently using subject field textbooks and materials than using basal readers. However, the reading of subject field materials presents special problems. Johnson (1973) described several of these problems.

Frequently, the organization pattern of social studies, science, or other subject field texts use too few questions and subheads. Major and minor content foci cannot be differentiated by immature readers. As a consequence young readers cannot make sense of what they are reading, and they quickly lose interest. Preplanning by the teacher can counteract this problem. By providing task instructions to facilitate structuring of the material and by helping students to frame questions about what they are to read, a content outline will emerge and students will then have the necessary insight and motivation to read.

Another problem has to do with the concept load. Words like interdependence, culture, and change are not easily defined by students; therefore, they do not understand what they are reading. The remedy is the same as what teachers do during reading instruction. By prescanning the selection to be read and noting the concepts that students will not understand, the teacher can provide assistance, giving examples to the students and allowing the students to generate their own examples of the concept. Research indicates that when the content of the textbook assignment is discussed prior to reading the assignment, better results are obtained (English, 1977, p. 106).

A third problem has to do with the use of abstract time and space terms typically found in social studies material. Again, by helping students define these words, the problem will not exist.

The reader is reminded to review the readability graph and the discussion about reading for comprehension in Chapter 6.

In *Using Social Studies Instructional Materials* Patton (1980) suggests that old textbooks can be updated with new pictures (maps, graphs, cartoons, charts, photos) and with new information, but that outdated material should not be thrown away. By using old and new information and pictures side by side, teachers can help students make comparisons and develop interpretive skills.

In lower-grade classrooms many teachers develop picture files related to their teaching unit. These files are not for bulletin board use, but rather for students' research activities. Sandler (1980) noted that pictures can be used to facilitate the development of the following social studies skills:

- gather data'
- group data
- form generalizations
- make inferences
- make predictions.

However, it would be a mistake to believe that students can use pictures without guidance. For example, to group data it is necessary to develop classifications for sorting.

> Pretend that you were given a box of apples. Observe the apples carefully. What categories would you suggest for grouping the apples?

As students get better at classifying data, they will learn to develop their own categories; but young primary children would certainly need help. A classification example was given in Chapter 4 when Mary Hogan had her students classify rocks.

Sometimes pictures disagree with each other. Paintings of early revolutionary battles that appeared in English and American history textbooks are remarkably different. These pictures, now available, can be used for students to form generalizations or to make inferences based upon the data. This lesson is most interesting if the students are not told the source of the data.

The reader is urged to review the information about the use of context clues in Chapter 6.

Small Group Research is a very effective teaching strategy in the social studies classroom. Students can be grouped either by reading ability or heterogeneously. Let us suppose that in Mary Hogan's third-grade classroom the children are studying about cities. She has grouped the students into five groups, and each group is to study a different city in order to answer the question: Why do people live in cities? On this particular day, she has grouped the students by reading ability and so the students are using the following types of materials:

- Group A is using a social studies textbook about Japan.
- Group B is viewing a filmstrip about London.
- Group C is using teacher-written information about the city of New York.
- Group D is using a picture file developed by the teacher after her visit to Honolulu.
- Group E is using some chart material with the teacher directing the lesson.

Note the following: (1) only one group is using a textbook; (2) two groups are using teacher-prepared materials; (3) two groups are using non-reading types of materials.

Why did Mary Hogan group the students instead of having the whole class read the same material? Why did she use five different cities? Mary Hogan knows that it is important for all students to contribute to a class discussion. For this to happen, the students need "unique" information. If all groups used the same material, there would be limited contributions during the discussion, and these contributions would be made by a chosen few.

Hogan chose to study five cities because she wanted the students to be able to generalize about: In what ways are all cities similar? In what ways are cities different? This was a personal teaching decision, not a decision that was absolutely necessary.

What About Heterogeneous Grouping for Research? Suppose Mary Hogan had asked the students to "plan" a city. This lesson would probably follow the preceding lesson. She would group the students heterogeneously and remind them to choose a group leader and a recorder, and then she would designate places for the groups to work.

The students would begin their task by reviewing what each student knew about the characteristics of cities. If they needed to verify their information, they would be responsible for finding the resources in the classroom. Their work would be enriched by the fact that some had used different resources for the previous lesson, and their work would be enriched on this occasion by their own diversity. Since at least one student in each group could "read well," they would not have a reading problem.

IF YOU WERE THE TEACHER . . .

Your second graders are studying about Kibbutz life in Israel. Develop a data retrieval chart for their data.

Data Retrieval. For Mary Hogan's students to get to the point where they can make generalizations about the nature of cities, there would have to be a system to amass the data that each group brought to the class discussion about "Why do people live in cities?" Hogan's system was to write the pertinent information on the chalkboard and then to guide the students to develop categories and accumulate the data for later use. With her students she developed a data retrieval chart.

Teaching Social Studies Skills

The California State Framework (1981) identified three categories of skills: Study skills, critical thinking skills, and social participation skills. Many subskills can be identified for each of these skill areas. These three categories are descriptive of the major skill areas in the social studies. Study skills and critical thinking skills have been discussed in Chapter 6.

Study skills are those skills that have to do with acquiring information: locating the information, organizing it, interpreting it, and communicating what has been learned. They are best taught at the propitious moment. For example, when students encounter a graph that they cannot read, the teacher might say: "Just a moment, boys and girls, some of us may have a difficult time reading this

TABLE 7.2. Data Retrieval Chart.

	Tokyo	London	Honolulu	New York	Atlanta
Types of Housing	Apartments Houses			Apartments Townhouses Houses	
Types of Work					
Types of Services		Police Health Fire Schools			
Types of Recreation					
Types of Transportation				Subways Bus Taxi Auto	

graph. Let's all put our pencils down and look up here while I explain how to read a graph."

Study skill needs in the social studies should also be anticipated. If students are to be required to gather information from a variety of sources, then they will need research competencies in order to locate information in textbooks, encyclopedias, and other reference materials. These skills may be taught during social studies or during reading, because these competencies are critical to many subject fields.

APPLICATION OF RESEARCH

Citizenship education, according to the Citizenship Development Program (Quarterly Report, Mershon Center, 1977) should challenge students to widen their perspective of global education and interdependence. Decision making and problem solving should be taught as open-ended processes in order to create independent thinkers. Active involvement in school organizations, youth groups, and the family will help to prepare students for citizenship responsibilities.

Critical thinking skills, like all other skills, need to be practiced. They include both convergent and divergent thinking. The development of critical thinking skills in social studies include the abilities to

- compare and contrast ideas, happenings, objects, or periods of time
- set criteria to group data
- formulate appropriate questions
- use evidence to make inferences
- formulate hypotheses
- detect bias, stereotyping, ethnocentricity
- make decisions and judgments.

Social participation is another important skill area in the social studies and is considered a major social studies goal. Literature on social participation indicates that students should be involved in group decision-making activities which necessitate:

- cooperation with others
- observing and sharing observations with others
- listening to others' viewpoints
- planning individual and group research or projects in school and community
- voluntarily assisting others; accepting assistance from others
- accepting responsibility and recognizing the need to act
- identifying and interpreting group agreements and disagreements
- using persuasion to influence others
- negotiating and bargaining to influence intergroup action (Lemlech, 1976, p. 45).

Activities that emphasize social participation help the elementary student become aware of how people participate in rational decision making, how social change occurred in the past, and how it will occur in the future.

Social participation strategies are action oriented; they utilize both small and large group participation. Content typically springs from students' personal experiences in the neighborhood and at school. The newspaper, student council, and the playground are good sources of information for choosing relevant problems for student investigation.

What research validates the need for social participation skills in order to diminish egocentricity? (See Chapter 2.)

IF YOU WERE THE TEACHER . . .

A new family moved into a house across from school. One of the children was in your third-grade class. During their first week in the new neighborhood, their trees were "papered' by a neighborhood gang. If you were the teacher, how could you use this event in a positive way in a social participation strategy?

Evaluating Social Studies Growth

Social studies growth can be measured by standardized tests. For example, the *Comprehensive Tests of Basic Skills* (McGraw-Hill) has a test of reference skills and a test of social studies. The reference skills test measures the student's ability to use library procedures; the social studies test measures the student's understanding of certain concepts, generalizations, and inquiry skills for problem solving.

Achievement test batteries can be used: *Metropolitan Achievement Test Battery* (Harcourt), *Iowa Test of Basic Skills* (Houghton Mifflin), *Sequential Tests of Educational Progress: Social Studies* (Educational Testing Service). Standardized tests can be helpful when they are used to identify areas of skill deficiencies. However, standardized tests have several limitations:

1. The test may be testing reading ability instead of subject matter content.
2. The test is often used to "label" students' ability levels instead of being used to diagnose skill deficiencies.
3. The norms established for standardized tests often do not represent minority populations.
4. Low-level objectives are easier to measure; therefore, what the test measures may not be of great importance.
5. Standardized tests may not express what the classroom teacher taught. The diverse nature of what is taught in social studies makes it a difficult subject to test with a standardized battery.

How else can a teacher measure social studies growth? Chapter 17 will provide ways to evaluate change. In social studies, teachers can use checklists, paper-and-pencil tests, sociometric devices, teacher and student observation, projects that students have produced, participation, discussions, simulations and other dramatic representations, and personal interviews.

It is important to remember that a test must measure what was actually taught; otherwise, it is an invalid test. In Chapter 4, Figure 4.2 illustrated the relationship of objectives, learning experiences, and evaluation. The evaluation strategy must approximate the original intent of the lesson(s). The major problem in social studies evaluation of elementary students is that students' communication skills often impede precise pencil-and-paper tests. For this reason, it is necessary to utilize a variety of ways to evaluate growth.

Special Techniques for Teaching Social Studies

Mainstreaming

Social studies time clearly provides the optimal environment for mainstreaming. The social studies goal of accepting others' diversity, values, and skills certainly is applicable to the philosophy of mainstreaming. Greg Thomas had several students who worked part of each day in his classroom. For each of his students, along with health information and test scores, he had specific performance information to help him plan an individual educational program. Table 7.3 illustrates the information that Thomas had about Myrna. Using the performance information and other insights he had about the student, Thomas developed the following objectives for her:

Individualized Educational Program (IEP) for Myrna

In social studies Myrna will learn to

1. Express voluntarily her own ideas and viewpoint
2. Listen to others' viewpoints
3. Cooperate with others
4. Share responsibility for group tasks
5. Choose appropriate instructional materials for self-use
6. Use tape recorder to communicate what she has learned from instructional materials
7. Use tactile maps to identify the United States, oceans, and mountains

TABLE 7.3. Performance Information for Mainstreaming.

1. What is the functional level of the student in

reading?	3.5
mathematics?	4.0
spelling?	3.3

2. What kinds of work tasks can the student perform successfully in:

reading? / mathematics?	Cannot work beyond tested functional level
handwriting?	Needs large lined paper
social studies?	Discussion in a small group
science?	Simple experiments
art?	Enjoys tactile experiences
music?	Enjoys singing.

3. To what extent can the student interact successfully with other students in

	Great Deal	**Little**	**Not at All**
small committee/group work?	✓		
class discussions?		✓	
one to one?	✓		
team sports?			✓
large group games?			✓

4. To what extent will the student accept/respond to

	Average	**Poor**	**Not at All**
waiting?	✓		
praise?	✓		
criticism?		✓	
touching?	✓		
questioning?		✓	
responsibility?	✓		
student-directed work activities?	✓		
self-directed work activities?		✓	

5. How can the student be tested?

	Yes	**No**
paper and pencil?		✓
oral?	✓	
cassette tapes?	✓	

6. Does the student tend to respond easily/quickly to

	Yes	**No**
anger?		✓
laughter?		✓
embarrassment?	✓	
fear?	✓	
helpfulness?	✓	
non-verbal communication?		✓

7. Does the student have special material/resource needs?
   - paper (extra large✓, lined✓, unlined)
   - pencils (primary✓, regular)
   - books (large print, pictures✓)
   - workbooks
   - cassettes for taping✓
   - seating accommodations (hearing, vision)

TABLE 7.3. (continued)

8. Does the student have physical coordination problems?

	Yes	No
Can the student		
dance?	✓	
jump?		✓
run?	✓	
skip?		✓
hop?		✓
throw a ball?	✓	
write on lined paper?	✓	
write within small spaces?		✓
use puzzle materials?		✓
saw?		✓
hammer?		✓
button clothes?	✓	

9. Does the student have speech problems or atypical mannerisms? *No*
10. Does the student dress appropriately? *Yes*
11. What skills should be stressed with the student?
    Motor skills
    Verbal skills
12. Are there instructional approaches that are more effective than others with the student?
    Visual
    Kinesthetic

Source: J. K. Lemlech, *Classroom Management* (New York: Harper, 1979), pp. 145–146.

8. Use a map of the community to identify school, market, gas stations, drug store, and department store
9. Use junior dictionary to define selected words
10. Use *World Book* to locate information about selected topics
11. Recall several details from a visual presentation
12. Sequence several events from an informational article or visual presentation
13. Use pictures to gain meaning and make inferences
14. Ask appropriate questions

Although Myrna was identified as a learning disabled student, she is not necessarily different from many other students who become bored when lectures and discussion strategies are overused. Myrna has poor memory retention, particularly when information requires auditory attention. Her memory is much improved when she uses tactile materials or when she observes a visual presentation. Her motor coordination skills are poor and affect her ability to take notes, take tests, and perform on handwritten projects. She can use a tape recorder quite effectively to communicate what she has learned. Since she is shy and unused to working in a large class situation, Greg Thomas realizes that she will be more effective when placed in small working groups.

Instructional strategies for Myrna will involve using small groups for her to work with; individualization, so that she can record her work rather than be required to write it; the use of learning centers; tactile or visual materials whenever possible; and print material at a third-grade level. Most of these strategies will not need to be created for Myrna alone, since many of the students in the classroom will benefit from the same types of instruction.

APPLICATION OF RESEARCH

Understanding of map symbols is dependent upon the ability to coordinate perspectives. Cobb (1977) studied K–6 children using an experiment patterned after Piaget's three-mountain experiment. Data from The Test of Map Conceptualization revealed that children improve with chronological age. Cobb concluded that teachers should assess students' spatial relations skills and teach spatial conceptualization.

Learning Centers in Social Studies

The learning center provides a means to enrich and expand social studies teaching. The center technique can be used to reinforce skills, teach concepts, and differentiate instruction to accommodate learning style needs. The center may be planned for use by an individual or for small group work.

The Direction Game

Social Studies, Mathematics
Lower Grades

Objective: To reinforce spatial directions (north, south, east, west).

Materials: Gameboard constructed of tagboard, twenty pictures, spinner, playing pieces.

Evaluation: Cooperative play, recognition of directions.

Procedures:

1. Construct a square game board of tagboard with 120 squares.
2. Collect twenty small pictures of places in the neighborhood (gas station, stores, fire station, homes) to place on twenty squares.
3. In the center of the gameboard designate a square for START.
4. Write a Rules card.
   a. Place the pictures on the game board. Space them around the board.
   b. Take turns to spin the spinner. Tell the other players the direction you will move your playing piece.
   c. If you land on a picture, you may take it.
   d. The person who has the most pictures, wins the game.

New Business

Social Studies, Language Arts
Upper Grades

Objective: To reinforce reference skills, decision making, social participation.

Materials: Task card, fictional yellow pages, want-ads, map of a city, books about "how to" study a community, pictures of businesses in a fictional city.

Evaluation: Group evaluation of social participation skills (see Chapter 17). Provide time for group sharing of decisions after all groups have used the center. Provide an evaluation card with a list of possible choices, if desired.

Procedures:

1. Task Card instructions:
   a. If you were to start a new business in the fictional city of Abercrombie, what would it be? List the steps your group will follow to make the decisions.
   b. Choose a recorder and a group leader.
   c. Decide what each person will do to gather data.

To Simplify: Use easier materials; control the data.

To Extend: Increase the data to be used.

Choose a Role

Social Studies, Language Arts
All Grade Levels

Objective: To reinforce communication skills, data gathering skills, comprehension skills.

Evaluation: Class discussion after center has been used about the importance of insightful questions and the authenticity of role playing.

Procedures:

1. Role Card Instructions
   a. Choose a role
   b. Study the role using pictures, books, information sheets.
   c. Play the role when you are interviewed.
2. Interviewer Card Instructions
   a. Write questions for an interview.
   b. Play the role of an interviewer.
   c. Guess the role of the person you are interviewing.
3. Develop roles related to a historic time period (pioneer in colonial America, surveyer, ship builder, mill owner, pirate) or to careers in contemporary society such as community helpers for primary children.
4. After students play the role of the interviewer and the interviewee, they should exchange task cards with a new role chosen and with the new interviewer writing new questions to ask.

Characteristics of Learning Centers in Social Studies

1. Learning centers in social studies integrate fields of study. The Direction Game uses social studies and counting skills in mathematics.
2. The learning centers are *social.* While it is true that a center can be used to individualize instruction and that it is possible to design a learning contract for a student using a center, the purposes of the centers proposed here involve goals related to social studies. These centers are for two or more students, and they promote interaction, communication, and decision making.
3. The center provides an element of fun and satisfaction. The use of the center should be different from typical classroom activities.
4. The center is arranged to attract and motivate the students. Materials do not have to be elaborate, but they can be colorful and appealing. The center can utilize bulletin board space, or a special area can be designed to create the illusion of privacy.
5. The center is purposeful and meaningful. Gimmicks are not needed. The activities should be designed to accomplish specific learning objectives.

APPLICATION OF RESEARCH

The content of elementary social studies textbooks tends to sanction and justify institutional arrangements. The books foster acceptance and support of our social institutions. Elementary textbooks fail to develop critical thinking about social matters (Anyon, 1978). If students are to be more than passive members of society, teachers will need to encourage critical evaluation of our institutions and our ideals.

Multitext Reading

The use of more than one textbook to study the content of social studies is characteristic of most classrooms. Perhaps the custom originated because many school districts failed to buy enough textbooks for each child to have a copy. However, when studying historical events it is much more valuable to read what different authors have to say in order to detect bias and to compare the authors' interest in the event. Another good reason for appreciating more than one social studies textbook is that most students cannot read at the same level. By utilizing more than one textbook, it is much easier to find print material appropriate to students' ability levels. Since the social studies book is a resource, each text is a little bit different; by utilizing more than one textbook the students learn research methods.

Mary Hogan's small-group research strategy demonstrated the appropriate method for using more than one research tool. Obviously, Mary Hogan could not find enough textbooks to satisfy her students' needs, *or* she was concerned about accommodating different learning modalities. Multitext reading is a fine approach to adapt textbook reading to ability levels and to teach research skills, but it does not respond to learning style differences.

Chapter Summary

The social studies curriculum provides essential knowledge, skills, and values for citizenship participation in our democratic society. In social studies, beginning in the primary years students learn about the history and culture of the United States and the world; they study geography, government, economic theories, social institutions, global relationships, and intergroup and interpersonal relationships. Beliefs in our democratic society are developed through an understanding of due process, equal protection, and civic participation. Skill competencies depend upon systematic practice; study skills, critical thinking, and social participation are essential and contribute to the four major purposes of education in the United States: self-realization, human relationships, economic efficiency, and civic responsibility (Education Policies Commission, 1938).

There is a wide range of content and teaching approaches applicable for social studies teaching. The overriding concern is that teachers prepare students for participation in the democratic system and that students understand and can help solve problems in an increasingly diverse, interdependent, and complex world.

Classroom Application Exercises

1. Design a social studies learning center to accommodate students who prefer auditory learning.
2. Make a list of personal decisions that elementary children typically make.
   Examples: "I forgot my homework, what shall I do?"
   "Mabel doesn't know the answer; I do. Should I show off?"
   "Bill lied. Should I tell what really happened?"
3. Your fourth-grade students are studying the concept of culture. Develop a data retrieval chart using the components of culture.
4. Privacy is a basic value in a democratic society. Develop a rule-making activity focused on privacy needs. Decide how to divide the class into groups so that each group will develop its own rule. Decide how to motivate the activity and how to evaluate the rules generated by the groups.
5. Develop a list of ideas on how primary- and middle-grade students can participate in their community and how upper-grade students can participate in school, city, or state affairs.

Suggested Readings for Extending Study

Allen, Jack. *Education in the 80s: Social Studies.* Washington, D.C.: National Education Association, 1981.

Beyer, Barry K., and Robert Gilstrap. *Writing in Elementary School Social Studies.* Boulder, Colorado: Social Science Education Consortium, Inc., 1982.

Chapin, J. R., and R. E. Gross. *Teaching Social Studies Skills.* Boston: Little Brown and Company, 1973.

Dunfee, Maxine. *Social Studies for the Real World,* Columbus, Ohio: Charles E. Merrill Publishing Company, 1978.

Ellis, A. K. *Teaching and Learning Elementary Social Studies.* 2nd ed. Boston: Allyn & Bacon, Inc., 1981.

Gross, Richard E., Rosemary Messick, June R. Chapin, and Jack Sutherland. *Social Studies for Our Times.* New York: John Wiley & Sons, Inc., 1978.

Hovinen, Elizabeth L. *Teaching Map and Globe Skills.* Chicago, Ill.: Rand McNally & Company, 1982.

Hunkins, Francis P., Jan Jeter, and Phyllis F. Maxie. *Social Studies in the Elementary School.* Columbus, Ohio: Charles E. Merrill Publishing Company, 1982.

Jarolimek, J. *Social Studies in Elementary Education.* 6th ed. New York: Macmillan Publishing Company, 1982.

Joyce, B. R. *New Strategies for Social Education.* Chicago, Ill.: Science Research Associates Inc., 1972.

Joyce, W. W., and J. E. Alleman-Brooks. *Teaching Social Studies in the Elementary and Middle Schools.* New York: Holt, Rinehart and Winston, 1979.

Moffet, J. B. *Teaching Elementary School Social Studies.* Boston: Little, Brown and Company, 1977.

Seif, E. *Teaching Significant Social Studies in the Elementary School.* Chicago, Ill.: Rand McNally Company, 1977.

Servey, Richard E. *Elementary Social Studies A Skills Emphasis.* Boston: Allyn & Bacon, Inc., 1981.

Welton, D. A., and T. Mallan. *Children and Their World: Strategies for Teaching Social Studies.* 2nd ed. Boston: Houghton Mifflin Company, 1981.

Chapter **8**

Mathematics Education

After you have completed the study of this chapter, you should be able to accomplish the following:

1. **Identify two purposes of the mathematics program.**
2. **Explain why the use of concrete materials is important to develop mathematical ideas.**
3. **Give an example of the Piagetian concepts of reversibility and transitivity.**
4. **Identify content strands in mathematics.**
5. **Write several objectives for each content strand.**
6. **Describe the sequence of mathematics instruction in a lower grade classroom.**
7. **Explain why mathematics specialists advocate discovery learning.**
8. **Discuss the conflict between behavioral and developmental psychologists related to math content and method.**
9. **Make a list of instructional materials available for use in the math program.**
10. **Suggest ways to use calculators and computers in the classroom.**
11. **Discuss the research about sex-related differences in mathematics achievement.**
12. **Identify planning considerations for teaching mainstreamed students in math.**
13. **Identify ways to evaluate progress in mathematics.**
14. **Create a math learning center to reinforce a math concept.**

Learning Mathematics—What Are the Goals of Instruction?

A sound mathematics program considers three factors: how children learn mathematics concepts, the logical structuring of mathematical ideas, and the functional application of mathematics content to the world of the child. Through the study of mathematics, students learn to work with and communicate quantitative relationships. Mathematics can help students solve real-life problems by providing them with an abstract model for analysis. The study of geometrical and numerical ideas should encourage the solution of practical problems and contribute to students' personal satisfaction.

The mathematics program should focus on logical reasoning and independence of thought rather than the production of correct answers. Learning experiences need to progress from the concrete to the abstract with an emphasis on real-world problems to develop students' interests. The mathematics program should provide an understanding and appreciation for mathematics concepts, structure, and terminology.

How Do Children Learn Mathematics Concepts?

The child's ability to think logically affects the learning of mathematics concepts. Copeland (1982) linked Piagetian stages of development with mathematics learning. At the preoperational level the student uses sensory impressions when confronted with the question, "Are there more objects in one set than in the other, or are the sets the same?"

○	○	○	○	○
○○○○○				

At this level of development, the student would respond that there were more objects in the first set than in the second. The critical element is the spacing of the two rows. Only by making the two rows of equal length will the student believe that the two sets are equal. Not until the concrete operational stage will the child recognize that the number is *conserved* or *invariant* and the arrangement of the set does not affect the number of objects.

Primary teachers need to know that even though the primary student counts the number of objects in each set, the student may believe that the spaced row of objects has more objects than the set that is not spread out.

Students are ready for formal abstract level mathematics at approximately eleven years of age, when the child can think at the formal operational level. However, Copeland cautioned that most eleven- or twelve-year-old children still need experiences with concrete materials to understand many mathematical ideas.

The concepts of reversibility and transitivity are useful to understand how children learn mathematics concepts. At the preoperational level students do not realize that number is not affected by the ordering process. Students will count objects from left to right and right to left before discovering that the set is the same from both directions. Not until students are six to seven years of age, at the concrete operational level of thought, will they understand the logic of reversibility.

Figure 8.1. At the Concrete Operational Level of Thought the Student Will Recognize That If Two Glasses Contain an Equal Amount of Water, When Water from One Glass Is Poured into a Tall, Skinny Glass, the Amount of Water Will Not Change.

Transitivity means that the individual can coordinate a series of relations using physical objects. For example, if students have several sticks of varying length, they can respond which stick is longest, shortest, longer than, and shorter than. They will be aware that there is a relationship among the sticks making one stick longer than the preceding stick, but shorter than the successive stick.

According to Piaget (1969), physical and logico-mathematical experiences with objects are significant foundations for the development of deductive thought. Concrete activities with objects should begin during the nursery school years. Cardinal ("one," "two," "how many") and ordinal ("first," "second") usage of numbers begins during the preschool years. Activities during both the preschool and primary school years should focus on matching objects, using one-to-one correspondence, in order to determine which group has "more" or "fewer" or "as many" objects. Number names ("one," "two") can be associated with the matching activity. Instruction in reading and writing numerals should begin following the matching relations (Lamb, 1977).

Experiences with logical thinking should begin with concrete activities. Children will not learn seriation through observation; they must have the opportunity to order objects from large to small or tall to short. Varied experiences are necessary for logical thought development.

Lamb (1977) suggests that experiences with geometry in the elementary classroom should focus on exploration. Students should be encouraged to construct their own objects and figures using a variety of materials.

Measurement ideas should be developed through

activities of sorting and comparing lengths. Children should be encouraged to verbalize about what they perceive ("This stick is shorter than, or longer than . . . .") Opportunities need to be provided for students to develop concepts of conservation and transitivity of length (Lamb, 1977).

> **APPLICATIONS OF RESEARCH**
>
> Concrete activities should be structured so that there are frequent links between physical and symbolic representations (Hiebert, 1981).

Mathematical ideas are dependent upon discovering and creating patterns and classifying and comparing physical objects. Students lacking these experiences during the preschool years will need direct experiences during the primary school program. The primary program should be characterized by informal and exploratory experiences. Observation of students as they work with physical objects should reveal whether or not they can compare and classify objects and whether they understand symmetry and balance. The primary child should be encouraged to verbalize about experiences involving numbers and to ask questions about activities. Many primary teachers find that cooking experiences develop vocabulary and natural interest in mathematics; for this reason it is a favored primary activity.

Content of Mathematics Programs

How Are Mathematics Programs Structured?

The elementary mathematics program has typically been organized into major content strands. The California State Framework in Mathematics (1980) identified seven strands with an overarching emphasis on problem-solving applications for all of the strands.

- Arithmetic Numbers and Operations
- Geometry
- Measurement
- Calculators/Computers
- Probability and Statistics
- Relations and Functions
- Logical Thinking

} Problem-Solving Applications

Arithmetic Numbers and Operations. This strand emphasizes computational skills. Experiences include counting and comparison activities using concrete sets of objects. Basic addition and multiplication facts are presented. Manipulative materials are used to motivate the development of computational algorithms. To develop students' abilities to work with abstract symbols, informal experiences are provided with physical models. Suggested activities include: building with blocks, sorting objects of different shapes and sizes, sorting and classifying objects, fitting objects into each other, arranging objects by size and shape, experimenting with balance, recognizing positional relationships and symmetry, and discovering patterns.

The California State Framework in Mathematics emphasizes the following topics in this strand: counting, operations, place value, patterns, nature of numbers, properties.

Geometry. Geometric concepts of line, point, plane, and three-dimensional space are developed. Once again manipulative objects are used for investigation, exploration, and discovery. Awareness of geometry in the environment is encouraged by utilizing art forms from business and industry, from nature, and from cultural experiences. Major topics include: geometric figures, reasoning/logical thinking, coordinate geometry, measuring geometric figures.

Measurement. Measurement is considered a key strand in the elementary program because understanding of measurement permeates our daily lives. Simple measurement tools are used to develop concepts of measuring distance, capacity, and the passage of time. Topics include: arbitrary units of measure, standard units of measure, approximate nature of measurement, and estimation in measurement. The purpose of arbitrary units of measure as instructional content is to encourage students to measure with differing units in order to discover the need to compare objects using common properties and accepted units of measure. Techniques of measurement used during the arbitrary units are utilized when students recognize the need for standard units. As students use measuring tools, the concepts of approximation and estimation are taught. The development of the "educated guess" skill needs to be expounded as students practice measurement using measurement tools and observation skills.

APPLICATION OF RESEARCH

Sharma (1981) believes that mathematics is a bona fide second language; successful solution of word problems is dependent upon language understandings such as the following:

1. Translating the problem into one's own words.
2. Comprehension of the specific mathematics concepts involved in the problem.
3. Translating mathematics language into English in order to understand which operation is to be performed.
4. The ability to solve the mathematics equation.
5. Translating the answer into practical terms (p. 62).

Probability and Statistics. Appreciation of the human achievement and a healthy skepticism of capital "T" type truths necessitates understanding, interpreting, and analyzing data that affect our everyday life. Statistics involves collecting, organizing, interpreting data, and making inferences from data. Experiences beginning in the kindergarten should involve gathering, organizing, and analyzing data. (Examples are provided in Chapter 14.) Topics include: collection, organization, and representation of data; interpretation of data; counting techniques; and probability. Problems in science, health, physical education, and social studies should provide good content experiences for students to use in the collection, organization, and representation of data.

Relations and Functions. Topics in this strand include: patterns, relations, functions, and graphs. *Patterns* refers to painting, drawing, woodworking, collages, and models. Pattern activities provide opportunities for discussing symmetry, repetition, counting, ordering, and pattern discovery. *Relations* refers to the associations that are made as objects are counted or compared or related in some way with other objects or pairs. Verbalization in mathematics allows students to talk about sets, numbers, pairs, collections, and sequencing. Function is taught to elementary students when they study number facts. Learning to graph information is essential for students in order to record and communicate observations. Teaching the reading and recording of graphs may occur during other subjects as well as during mathematics instruction time.

Logical Thinking. During the primary grades, the teaching of logical thinking is informal; beyond the third grade, students learn to be precise. Logical thinking is supposed to be a natural outcome of mathematics instruction. Topics in this strand include patterns in mathematics and formal and informal reasoning. Mathematical patterns are taught through problem-solving activities. For example, the teacher might write the following on the board:

3 . . . 7 . . . 11 . . . 15 . . . ?

Students are asked to guess the next numeral and explain the basis for their decision. Discussion focuses on the recognition of a pattern. Students should be encouraged to recognize patterns in music, nature, and history. Formal and informal thinking occurs as students are encouraged to use and explain terms such as *if, then, and, all, some, sometimes.* Students should be helped to see the value of using language precisely.

Problem Solving

Problem solving is viewed as the most important and central aspect of the mathematics program. The Mathematics Framework in California views problem solving as the "umbrella" for all content strands. There are four components to problem solving/applications skills. These are:

1. formulating the problem,
2. analyzing the problem,
3. finding the solution,
4. interpreting the solution.

Each component is discussed.

(1) *Formulating the problem.* How many times were you as a student asked, "What do you think is the problem?" How frequently do you ask your own students to identify the problem situation? Both the recognition of existing problems or perplexing situations and the statement of the problem in a form that can be studied requires practice and special skills. The formulation of mathematical problems is similar to writing sentences. Both require precision, organization, and divergent thinking.

(2) *Analyzing the problem.* Students need to be taught to plan a strategy for "attacking" the problem. Quite frequently students are overwhelmed by a problem and cannot understand how to sort out the important information. A number of tactics can be taught to students, but the most critical aspect of problem analysis is the planning process, and it must be emphasized that the same tactics will not work in all situations. For this reason it is valuable to have students share their strategies so that poor problem solvers will perceive that there are many ways to go about the task. Some suggested tactics to be taught students include the following:

- Guess and observe the results; if it works, you don't have to go any further.
- Draw or graph the problem and see if that helps to understand the relationships involved in the problem.
- Sort out similar and dissimilar elements.
- Identify known and unknown information.
- Identify the operations involved; translate the information using mathematical symbols and notation.
- Act out the problem.
- Construct or use physical objects to represent the problem.
- State the problem in your own words.

APPLICATIONS OF RESEARCH

Hiebert (1981) proposed an alternative to direct instruction by providing students with opportunities to develop their own solution processes. Problem-solving strategies invented by students are more likely to be meaningful to them.

(3) *Finding the solution.* A variety of skills are needed to find the solutions to problems. It is important that students realize that some problems may have more than one solution or perhaps no solution. It is at this stage of problem solving that students should perceive the value of anticipating the results by using estimation. In addition to the typical operational skills needed, students may also have self-confidence to take risks and attempt to solve problems in new and imaginative ways.

4. *Interpreting the solution.* This problem-solving component should say to the student, "So what?" If the solution is meaningless and the answer does not provide insight, then there was no purpose to the exercise. In interpreting the solution, the student needs to consider the original problem in order to judge the validity of the solution. The problem and the solution should consider the following questions:

- Was the answer reasonable? Expected?
- Was the strategy appropriate?
- Were all the facts considered?
- Is the solution accurate?
- Can the strategy be used with other problems?
- If some of the number components were changed, how would it affect the answer?

Choosing Appropriate Problems For Applications

In a second-grade classroom the children wanted to celebrate the end of the semester by going out to lunch together. The teacher used their interest to teach problem solving. The teacher wrote this question on the board:

Should we celebrate the end of the semester by going out to lunch, *or* should we make a lunch for the entire class at school?

To *formulate the problem* the teacher guided consideration of these questions: Does it cost more to eat out at a restaurant than it does to make a lunch at school? Which restaurant would they select? How would the children get to the restaurant? Does it make a difference what they choose to eat? Could all of the children afford to eat out?

Analysis of the Problem. After the students tentatively decided that perhaps they could walk to a neighborhood Mexican restaurant and that they would choose to eat quesadillas (tortillas with cheese), they realized that now their problem was to compare the cost of eating out with making the same lunch at school.

Finding the Solution. The teacher encouraged the children to guess how much it would cost to eat quesadillas at the restaurant and how much it would cost to buy flour tortillas, cheese, and vegetable shortening at the market. The students soon realized that they had no idea how many tortillas come in a package; nor did they know the price of cheese, shortening, tortillas. To find the solution the students decided to walk to the market and price their ingredients *and* to call the restaurant and ask the price of eating the quesadillas there. After they had all of their information, they knew they would have to add the costs and compare eating out with making the lunch.

Interpreting the Solution. The teacher was well aware that the second graders would not be able to perform the addition necessary to work out the cost for an entire class; however, by breaking the cost down for the students so that they could compare the cost of one lunch at the restaurant with making the same lunch, the students were able to make a judgment. Their evaluative discussion focused on the following:

- Were their guesses accurate about the cost of eating out and making the same lunch?
- Is it cheaper to eat out or eat in?
- How would it make a difference if they had selected a variety of lunches at the restaurant to compare with the prepared lunch at school?
- Why does food cost more at a restaurant than if they make the same food at home?

Problem-solving investigations need to be meaningful to students and encourage a range of problem-solving strategies. The selected problem should motivate the development of skills and improve students' decision making. Good problems integrate subject fields and encourage investigations that expand students' knowledge, skills, and values.

> What science, social studies, and health questions could be studied by the second graders along with the comparison of lunch costs?

Representative Objectives for Mathematics Instruction

The mathematics program should provide opportunities for each student to work at his/her own ability level. Most school districts identify a hierarchy of skills to be developed during mathematics instruction. Mastery levels should be reasonable for most students at the defined grade level, but the identified skills should not be considered either as minimum levels or as limits for students with better than average abilities.

Skill levels are typically defined for each of the strands in the mathematics program. Examples of representative objectives for each of the content strands at the fifth- and second-grade levels have been selected (Los Angeles Unified School District Mathematics Continuum, 1979):

Problem Solving
Writes a number sentence to describe a real-life situation. (Grade 2)
Makes up a real-life problem from a number sentence and solves. (Grade 5)
Statistics
Collects, organizes, and interprets data in pictograph form. (Grade 2)
Collects, organizes, and interprets data in bar graph form. (Grade 5)
Relations/Functions
Recognizes and extends number patterns. (Grade 2)
Identifies, extends, and creates number patterns. (Grade 5)
Geometry
Identifies geometric shapes: circle, square, triangle, and rectangle. (Grade 2)
Identifies solid figures: cone, cube, sphere, cylinder, prism, and pyramid. (Grade 5)
Measurement (Length)
Measures length in nonstandard units by counting. (Grade 2)
Estimates and measures, using inches, feet, and yard. (Grade 5)
Numeration (Fractional Numbers)
Identifies one half, one fourth, and one third of a whole. (Grade 2)
Identifies and finds equivalent fractions. (Grade 5)
Counting and Place Value
Counts by tens and fives to 100. (Grade 2)
Rounds off to the nearest 10. (Grade 5)

How Is Mathematics Taught?

In a first-grade classroom the students were seated in a group in front of the flannel board. Their teacher, Jed Benson, was telling them a story using five flannel-made airplanes.

> These airplanes belong to the daring Navy pilots known as the Blue Angels. These pilots often fly their planes in formation like this. (Benson demonstrated on the flannel board.) Let's count the airplanes together. (One . . . two . . .) Now let's see if we can tell some stories about the numeral 5 using the airplanes.

Benson arranged the airplanes to tell the story of the numerals 2 and 3. He called on the students to verbalize about what they were seeing. Then he called on different students to arrange the airplanes into the various subsets of 5. When the students seemed confident with this activity, Benson passed out counting sticks to each student and sent them to their tables. He told them to arrange the sticks in a straight line in front of them and to count them. ("How many do you have?") After verifying that the students recognized that they had five sticks, he said: "Let's see if you can group your sticks to tell the story of 5 with subsets of $3 + 2$."

"Now do $2 + 3$." As the students worked, Benson observed their manipulation of the sticks. In making the transition from $3 + 2$ to $2 + 3$, Benson watched to see if the students reversed the arrangement of the sticks or had to count each stick individually. If a student had to count the sticks in order to make the transition, Benson knew immediately that the student did not understand the relationship of subsets to the original set of five and probably lacked the concept of reversibility.

After the manipulative experience, Benson went to the chalkboard and presented the information visually again—this time using dots. Then he presented it using numerals (1, 2, 3, 4, 5) and symbols (+ , =). Following the visual representation, he passed out practice sheets for the students to use. Students were encouraged to use their counting sticks to help them as they worked with the abstract numerals on the practice sheet.

Benson's lesson had the following components:

- Motivating visual story of the numeral 5; verbalization

- Concrete manipulative experience using counting sticks
- Visual presentation using numerals
- Reinforcement of the manipulative and visual experiences with abstract numerals.

During each stage of work, Benson had monitored the students' performance and provided both positive and negative feedback.

Instruction in mathematics is enhanced by the use of objects or pictures. Elementary students learn best when they work with real objects and when they deal with realistic problems. It is more effective to introduce new concepts and skills with concrete referents than with paper and pencil exercises. Mr. Benson's teaching sequence was appropriate; he began with a concrete experience that appealed to the students' senses. He provided objects for manipulation. He then moved to the visualization stage and concluded with the abstract symbol stage of representative mathematical ideas. In the following episode a teacher introduces fractions using a physical object.

In Greg Thomas' fifth-grade classroom the children were asked to bring egg cartons to school. Thomas provided the students with dry beans. He asked the students to fill one half of the carton with beans and leave the other one half empty. Then he had the students compare the different ways in which their classmates arranged the beans in order to fill one half of the carton. The lesson continued with directions for the students to represent one third, one fourth, two thirds, three fourths.

Throughout the lesson, Thomas had the students compare their arrangements and talk about the number of ways each fraction could be depicted. As the students improved, Thomas had students go to the chalkboard and write the fractions.

On successive days, to extend ideas, Thomas had the students use Cuisenaire rods and sets of tangrem pieces, and finally the students were asked to bring in some simple cooking recipes to help reinforce the applications of fractions. These activities preceded formal abstract work with fractional numbers. Thomas was aware that it was not until about the age of ten that students could use an operation approach to study fractional numbers.

Discovery Learning

Most mathematics specialists advocate learning by discovery in mathematics. Copeland (1979) contrasted "knowing" and "knowing how-to." "Knowing how-to" involves plugging in a formula and performing an operation based on having learned certain rules. For example, the young student may learn to add $18 + 3$ without understanding the principles of place value or base 10.

"Knowing" consists of conceptualization of a physical action or a mind-picture that is then translated to the abstract level. Logico-mathematical knowledge is internal to the student rather than external.

Discovering patterns is much more difficult for students than writing answers. The former involves the process of thinking and requires that the student discover which particular pattern will apply to a specific situation. Discovery learning is enhanced by peer interaction. Communication between student and teacher and among students encourages students to share a variety of ways to solve problems, express creative thinking, and obtain creative results.

Problems should be selected by the teacher to foster discovery learning. This means that motivation is an important element in mathematics teaching. Students need to feel that the problem is relevant and interesting to them as well as challenging.

The process of discovery may involve the use of unsophisticated (rudimentary) procedures. As the student directs his/her own learning s/he will apply familiar procedures until the point when s/he is ready to speculate about or guess a new pattern or a new way to approach the problem. Discovery occurs in the form of applying the discovered generalization.

The teacher's role during discovery teaching is to ask questions, encourage students to make guesses, focus the search when needed, and select appropriate situations to apply the new ideas.

Repetition, Reinforcement, Application

There is a great deal of controversy between behavioral and developmental psychologists over what should be taught in mathematics and how it should be taught. These conflicts are discussed in the next section. Teachers need to be cognizant of the dialogue and research in mathematics education concerning these practices and make decisions related to the following questions:

- To what extent does drill and practice facilitate "knowing" or "knowing how-to"?
- To what extent should drill and practice be used for the correction of errors?
- In what ways does drill and practice affect motivation?
- To what extent does drill and practice facilitate the application of concepts to new and varied situations?

> If students lack the concept of reversibility, will drill on basic addition facts help students master the concept of addition?

Active Learning

Active learning involves working with physical objects to transform them in order to learn through real experience what happens when you transfer, for example, a liquid from one vessel to another or manipulate clay from one shape to another.

Active learning also means involvement in group discussions and verbal clashes with classmates over which solution is right. The group discussion should focus on the thinking process so that students are forced to clarify why they believe that their solution is correct. An encounter about mathematical ideas can be as important as a discussion carried out in science or social studies.

Summary: How to Teach Mathematics

Mathematics instruction should develop both an understanding of numbers and number systems and the skills for using numbers to solve problems. In general, instruction should correspond with the following sequence:

1. manipulation of physical objects (concrete experiences),
2. visualization of the number problem (drawings),
3. abstract representation using number symbols.

> **RESEARCH FINDINGS**
>
> In a study of fourth-grade mathematics, Good and Grouws (1981) report that teacher effectiveness was associated with the following behavioral clusters:
> 1. clarity of instruction,
> 2. task-focused environment,
> 3. relaxed learning environment with limited use of praise and criticism,
> 4. higher achievement expectations,
> 5. relatively few behavioral problems,
> 6. whole-class teaching
>
> The researchers observed that the teachers demonstrated alternative teaching approaches, emphasized the meaning of math concepts, and systematically reviewed learning (pp. 84–85).

Behavioral vs. Developmental Perspectives

Mathematics Content and Method

Mathematics Content. The developmentalist focuses on mathematical ideas. The emphasis is on understanding mathematics concepts and processes. Kamii (1982) stated that writing correct answers does not prove that students understand the underlying thinking process. She provided an example of a young student who had spent three years using the Individualized Instruction Program in mathematics and "learned that arithmetic consisted of figuring out how to make his method and answer conform to the method and answer in the key" (p. 248).

The behaviorist emphasizes traditional teaching of mathematics content. Correct written and verbal responses control the scope of instruction. The behaviorists rely on behavioral objectives and tests. The back-to-basics movement is typical of the focus of content.

Mathematics Methods. The developmentalist utilizes inductive and deductive discovery techniques. The emphasis is on active thinking (not to be equated with activities). Experiences are provided to move the student to form new concepts utilizing structures already understood. The developmentalist believes that repetition will not teach concepts and processes unless the student understands the basic underlying concept involved. Application of learning will occur only if the student has developed and structured the concept him/herself and gained the basic mathematical concepts of conservation, commutativity, and transitivity.

The behaviorist advocates mastery learning. This approach is based on systematic instruction. It is designed to help all students learn by defining mastery instructional objectives. The objective is converted into a criterion-referred examination. All errors that a student makes are corrected, and mastery practice time is provided. The assumption is made that all students can learn—given enough time. When an error is made, the teacher guides the student back to an instructional alternative and the student begins mastery practice. Copeland (1982) commented that repetition becomes the correctional mode.

Block (1980) outlined the mastery learning sequence:

- Instruction is systematically designed. (Instructional components are chained.)
- Mastery objectives are defined.
- Teacher provides appropriate guidance during learning.
- Teacher anticipates appropriate amount of time for learning.
- Students are oriented to mastery learning.
- Teacher varies instructional method as needed and varies amount of time for practice depending upon mastery.
- Mastery learning is graded using preset performance standard (p. 103).

Application of learning to new situations occurs if the new situation is identical to the practiced sequence. The behaviorist believes that transfer of learning occurs only if there are enough similar elements.

RESEARCH FINDINGS

An analysis of test data in reading, math, and science by the National Assessment of Educational Progress (1983) revealed that the lowest-achieving students improved the most scholastically in reading, math, and science during the 1970s. The top quarter of achieving students dropped the most scholastically.

The national assessment program periodically samples the achievement of students at ages nine, thirteen, and seventeen. The 1983 report concluded that the heavy emphasis on basic skill development improved the performance of the bottom fourth of the students, but that minimum competency requirements adversely affected the motivation of top students to take advanced courses in math and science and impeded the acquisition of higher-level thinking skills.

Both the developmental and behavioral theories for math education will have great impact on new math programs. Professional educators as well as the public will continue to debate the issues.

Instructional Materials for Teaching Concretely

There are a variety of instructional materials available for use in the mathematics program. These learning "aids" enrich the climate of the classroom, serve to arouse students' interest, and encourage experimentation.

Materials are needed for counting, sorting, comparing relations, measuring, and practice purposes. Most of the materials are relatively inexpensive or can be made by the teacher. Examples follow:

Size Relations. Objects such as wooden blocks, buttons, nails, wooden rods (Cuisenaire), string and ribbons, or rulers can be used to help students observe size relations. Students may be asked to determine "Which is longer?" "Which is shorter?" "Which is wider?" "Which is smaller than . . . ?" "Which is taller?"

Weight Relations. Students estimate and measure ounces, pounds, grams, and kilograms. The measurements can be performed using a balance scale. Suggested materials for weighing include beans, marbles, stones, coins, buttons, and sand.

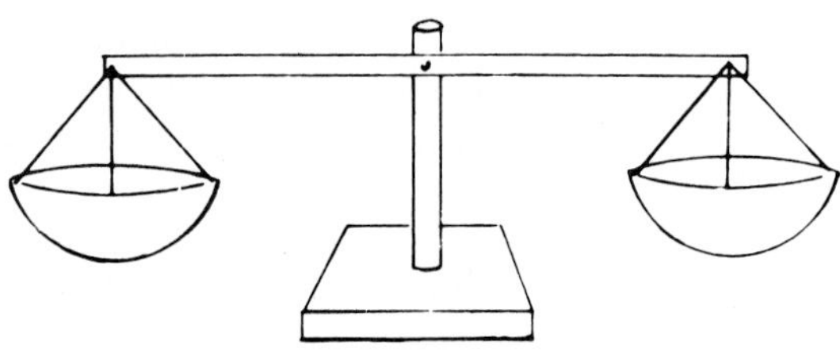

Volume Relations. Different sized containers need to be available in the classroom so that students can experiment with volume relations. These may be plastic containers of various shapes and sizes. Students should measure capacity using cups, pints and quarts, liters and milliliters.

Time Relations. To explore time relations students will need to use model clocks, a sun dial, and a calendar. Many teachers like to make clocks from paper plates. The hands can be made of chipboard and attached with a brass brad. Teacher-made sun dials for use outside are usually adequate for demonstration purposes.

Temperature. Both Fahrenheit and Celsius thermometers should be provided for students to learn to measure temperature.

Counting. For counting and to learn place value, the following materials are recommended: ice cream sticks, beans, straws, counting frames, the abacus, soroban, small wooden blocks, coins, place value chart, number chart. The abacus can be made using coat hanger wire, a wood frame, and counting beads. The abacus and soroban are used to teach place value. They were first used by the ancient Romans, Chinese, and Japanese and are still used in banks and businesses in the Orient. Contests in Japan between individuals skilled in the use of the soroban and other individuals using calculators have demonstrated that the soroban can be used more rapidly than a calculator.

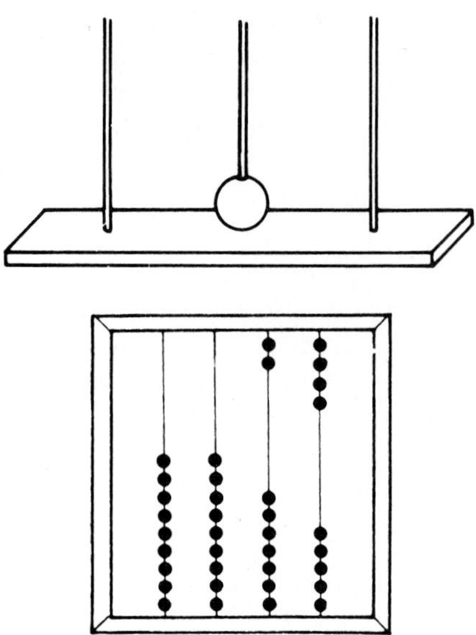

The pocket chart that is used so frequently in reading is also useful in mathematics. Teachers usually make their own place value charts. The pocket chart is labeled for place value use in mathematics.

Hundreds	Tens	Ones

The number chart (0–100) is displayed in most primary classrooms. It is used to help students identify numerals, learn to write number symbols, discover patterns in the base 10 system of numeration, and perform addition and subtraction.

0	1	2	3	4	5	6	7	8	9
10	11	12	13	14	15	16	17	18	19
20	21	22	23	24	25	26	27	28	29
30	31	32	33	34	35	36	37	38	39
40	41	42	43	44	45	46	47	48	49
50	51	52	53	54	55	56	57	58	59
60	61	62	63	64	65	66	67	68	69
70	71	72	73	74	75	76	77	78	79
80	81	82	83	84	85	86	87	88	89
90	91	92	93	94	95	96	97	98	99
100									

The number line is a useful semiconcrete tool in the classroom. Use heavy tag or chipboard, all that is needed is a straight line with points and arrows pointed in both directions to convey the number continuum. It is a good idea *not* to write the numerals on the number line. When the number line is displayed on the chalkledge, numerals can be written in at designated points. The number line can also be used on the classroom floor.

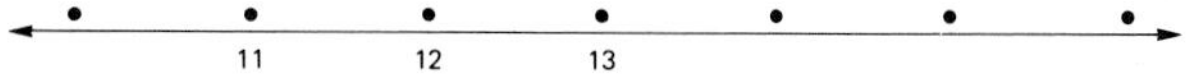

Commercially made rods are functional in the primary classroom. The rods are of varied lengths and colors. Students learn quickly that if they want to make 6, the 6-rod will be as long as the 2-rod plus the 4-rod or two 3-rods.

The arithmetic blocks are advantageous to help students perform subtraction. The blocks allow students to visualize the changing of hundreds to tens and tens to ones.

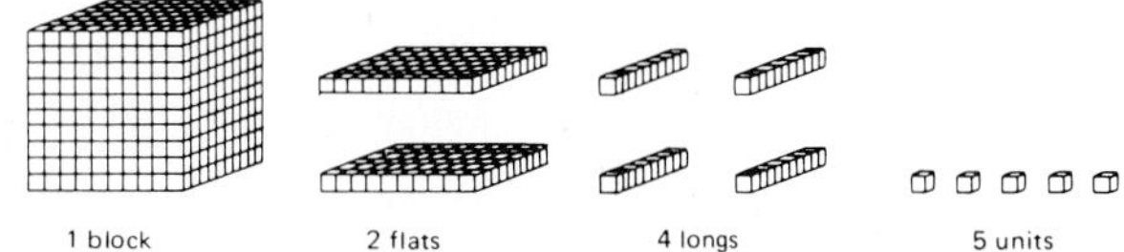

Students enjoy using puzzle cards to practice their basic facts. These can be made out of chipboard or out of wood for long-standing use. The card should have pictures or dots for counting, along with the abstract numerals.

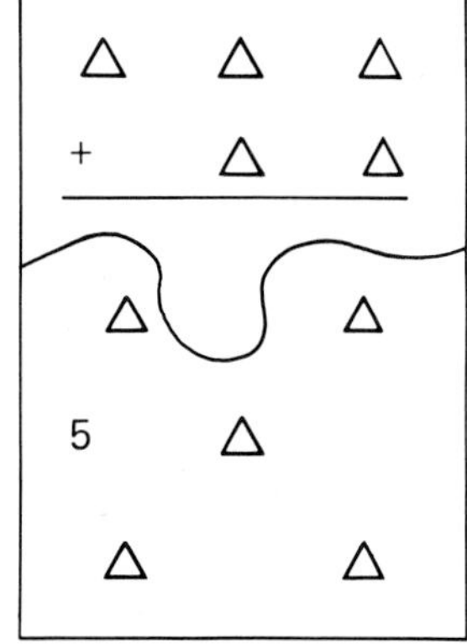

Geoboards can be made or purchased commercially. A square piece of wood is used with nails spaced one inch apart, vertically and horizontally. The geoboard is used to explore geometric figures, shapes, and relations. By stretching rubber bands around some of the nails, students study geometric concepts, relations, and measurement.

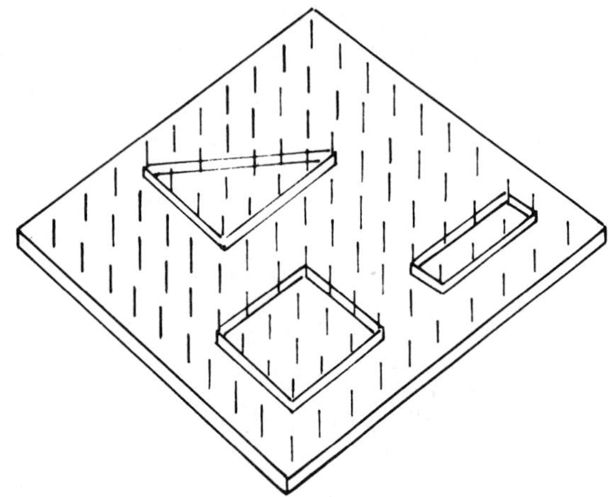

Game materials for practice and drill purposes can be bought or made. Useful items include number cards, Lotto- or Bingo-styled games, Dominoes, "Old Maid," or "Fish." The game of Battleship has been popular in middle-grade classrooms to help students use a number grid.

Dominoes can be used for sorting and learning number facts.

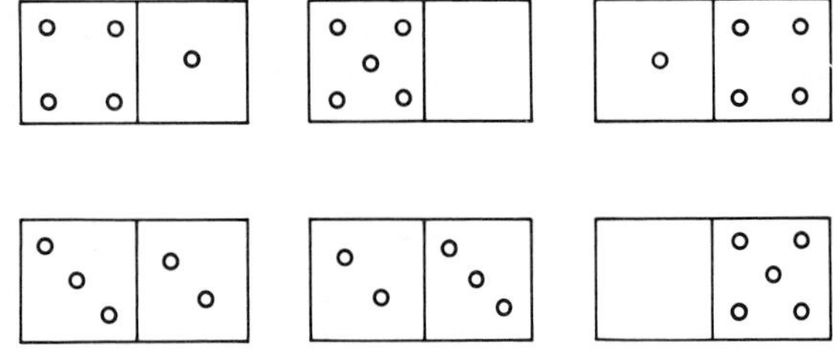

Rummy-type games are popular in the lower grades and easy to make from tagboard.

FOUR	o o o o	4

The Battleship game's Ocean Grid teaches graphing and location skills as students graph and plot the opponent's ships through a series of "hits" and "misses" (Milton Bradley Co., Springfield, Mass.).

	1	2	3	4	5	6	7	8	9	10
A										
B										
C										
D										
E										
F										
G										
H										
I										
J										

Calculators and Computers in the Classroom

The California Mathematics Framework (1980, pp. 77–78) listed eight ways in which the calculator can be used in classrooms:

- *Motivation:* Children of all ages react enthusiastically when given the opportunity to use the calculator to experiment with mathematical ideas. The students become more inquisitive and creative when allowed to use the hand calculator.
- *Discovery:* The calculator is useful for the investigation of concepts and problems that would be too tedious if paper and pencil had to be used.
- *Drill and Practice:* The old "check your answers" can be done very efficiently with a calculator; this enables students to vary some of the more boring tasks when practicing essential skills.
- *Enrichment:* Games and problem-solving experiences can be performed using the calculator; with this tool, students can extend thinking in nonstructured ways.

These Students Are Fitting Rubber Bands to Pegs on the Geoboard to Explore Basic Shapes.

- *Application:* The calculator brings the real world into the classroom. Personal and family problems such as budgeting, balancing the checkbook, and estimating expenses can be applied using the calculator.
- *Problem Solving:* The calculator facilitates the "guessing" or "trial-and-error" stages of problem solving. When students have to project their "guesses" using paper and pencil, it becomes boring because of the time investment. Using the calculator this step is simple, efficient, and fun. Students gain insight into the problem-solving process that would otherwise not be apparent to them.
- *Reinforcement:* The calculator provides instant feedback; as a result, students can locate errors and become more accurate in computation. The calculator can be used instead of flash cards for practicing number facts.
- *Conceptualization:* Calculators help students learn number system concepts such as place value, decimals, and powers of 10.

Copeland (1982) cautioned that students should be introduced to the basic operations using physical objects prior to learning to use a calculator; however, the calculator can be used as a recorder of what the students have experienced. Calculators can be used in primary-grade classrooms, but their use is more typical in the middle and upper grades.

To use the calculator productively, the student needs to know what operations are necessary to

RESEARCH FINDINGS

Does the use of calculators in elementary classrooms inhibit the learning of basic facts? *No.* Results indicate that children benefit from using the calculator (Weaver, 1981).

The Geoboard Is Useful to Explore Geometric or Spatial Relationships.

perform in a given problem. The calculator only helps the student speed up the computation step. The student needs to plug in the operation(s); therefore, it is important that teachers require students to think through the correct operation or sequence of operations.

Time magazine (Janaury 3, 1983) reported that there were more than 100,000 computers in United States schools. It has been found that children are often better at using the computer than adults. The computer has been used by children to play rather unusual games ("cracking corporate security and financial secrets, playing games on military networks, inserting obscene jokes into other people's programs" p. 24). The computer may motivate thinking; using the computer students can be encouraged to formulate a problem, analyze it, find a solution and interpret the solution. In mathematics education the computer has been used successfully to assist in instruction (Computer Assisted Instruction—CAI) and manage instruction (Computer Managed Instruction—CMI).

CAI has been used for drill and practice programs, instruction in mathematical concepts, problem solving, and computer programming. Developers from the Computer Curriculum Corporation's CAI program report the following research results:

1. Time spent at CAI is positively related to achievement gain.
2. Actual achievement gains exceeded expected gains.
3. Grade placement as determined by the CAI program was highly correlated with grade placement as determined by standardized achievement tests.
4. Students and teachers had a positive attitude about CAI (DeVault, 1981).

In reviewing the research evidence that evaluates CAI, Davis (1981), director of the Madison Project, warns that tests to evaluate how well students have progressed using computer programs may be deceiving. His concern is similar to that expressed by Kamii (1982) already discussed in this chapter. Mathematics test scores may provide evidence about how many correct answers students can write, but they do not provide adequate descriptions of how students are thinking. Davis is concerned that "we have not been testing what we have thought we were teaching" (p. 151).

APPLICATION OF RESEARCH

How are calculators used in elementary classrooms?

1. For checking computational work originally done with pencil and paper.
2. Gaming, to provide additional motivation.
3. Calculation, after operations have been defined, and in conjunction with the regular textbook or program.
4. Exploration, to teach mathematical ideas (Suydam, 1978).

Sexism

Careers in the late 1980s and the near future require greater numerate capabilities. It has been estimated that by 1995 one out of every five people in the United States will use computers. Concern about the impact of technological developments generated the interest of mathematics educators to find out why so few females were enrolled in higher-level mathematics courses. These courses were considered prerequisite to career advancement and to new careers in technology and the professions.

In a speech about sex-related differences in mathematics achievement, Fennema (1978) came to these conclusions:

1. When both sexes study the same amount of mathematics, differences in achievement are minimal.
2. Fewer females choose to study mathematics.
3. The failure to choose mathematics courses appears to be related to lack of confidence in learning mathematics and the belief that mathematics is a male domain.
4. Differential treatment of the sexes by teachers may also contribute to the failure of females to choose mathematics education.
5. There are no inherent reasons for females' failure to learn mathematics at the same level as males.
6. Intervention programs can be designed to increase female participation in mathematics programs. These programs must include male and female students and their teachers.

More recent studies of female enrollment patterns in mathematics education reveal that in the states studied, female seniors (12th grade) are less prepared than males (Fennema, 1981).

In a study of mathematics achievement reported by Fennema (1981), the California State Assessment of Mathematics revealed that sixth-grade girls do better than boys in computations and one-step word problems. Boys outperformed the girls on items dealing with spatial relationships and reasoning ability. In geometry, girls outperformed the boys on questions that required the recall and identification of geometric shapes. In measurement the girls scored higher on problems that dealt with money, but the boys did better than girls on all other questions.

From the review of research concerned with sex-related differences in mathematics education, it is apparent that fewer females enroll in higher level mathematics courses that are prerequisite to, or will prepare them for, advanced careers in technology and the professions, and fewer females are encouraged by their teachers to enroll in higher-level mathematics courses. Fennema concluded that sex-related differences can and should be eliminated.

Mainstreaming

Although frequently skill instruction for exceptional children occurs in special education classrooms, students with special learning problems or physically handicapped students can benefit from mathematics instruction in the regular classroom. Instructional planning for the mainstreamed student should focus on the following considerations:

Learning Style

- For the kinesthetic learner, provide more manipulative aids than is typically done. Be sure that students have counting sticks and other aids for computation tasks.
- For the auditory learner, record math facts on a cassette; record skill activities.
- For the visual learner, utilize individual chalkboards for students to write and draw on; suggest that students draw problems; use the Language Master for math facts.

Motivation

- Choose situations that are relevant to the mainstreamed child to motivate skill development.
- Explain the practical use of the skill (calculating gasoline consumption, identifying health risks).
- Vary activities to increase interest.
- Reinforce strengths; do not just dwell upon deficiencies.
- Program instruction in short segments so that the student does not sit too long.
- Allow the child to work with a friend who will be of assistance.
- Reinforce positive accomplishments with realistic praise.

Instruction

- Diagnose needs carefully. Identify the precise need or error to be corrected.
- Determine the missing link in the chain of understanding. Reteach using concrete materials.
- Verify understanding verbally. Provide appropriate practice.
- Utilize math learning centers for reinforcement activities.

Instructional Materials

- Clarify instructions and verify that students understand instructional tasks.
- Be certain that materials are clear and understandable. Some students may need large print.
- Verify that students can read the instructional materials and understand the math operations and processes.
- Avoid burdening the student with too many worksheets at one time.

Time

- Monitor the amount of time the child is working to ensure that activities are varied, movement needs are provided for, length of assignment is reasonable, individualized, and motivating.

Evaluation of Learning

Progress in mathematics learning can be evaluated by teacher observation, teacher-made tests, standardized tests, and conferences between student and teacher. As Mr. Benson observed his students manipulating the ice cream sticks, he was able to detect which children had not attained the concept of reversibility. Students' interest and enthusiasm for working with math concepts can usually be detected through observation. Observation of students as they work is usually the first step in evaluation of growth. For example, if a student appears to be confused, the teacher can then engage the student in a discussion.

Questions during the discussion (informal conference) can focus on: "Show me how you found the answer." "How do you know that you should (multiply) first?" "Explain the pattern to me."

Teacher-made tests can focus on math vocabulary, the identification of processes, estimation, explaining problems, performing computation. The tests can be completion, multiple choice, or matching. It is important that the mathematic's test not be a test of reading skills. Teacher-made tests in math have greater content validity than formal standardized tests because teachers should know "what they have taught." The tests can be designed to gather information about the concepts and skills taught and practiced during the mathematics program.

The test can be a creative endeavor with pictures for young children and symbolic information for the more mature students.

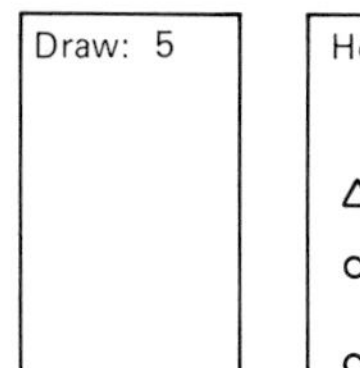

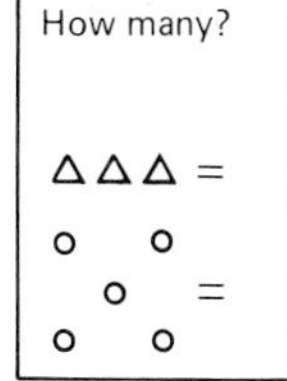

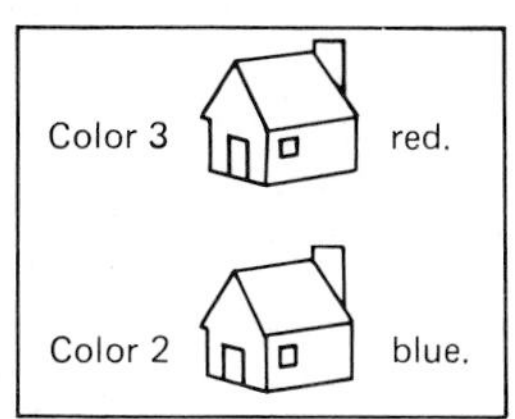

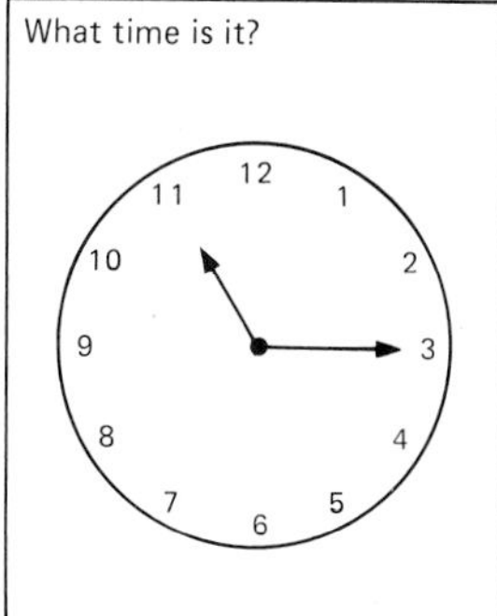

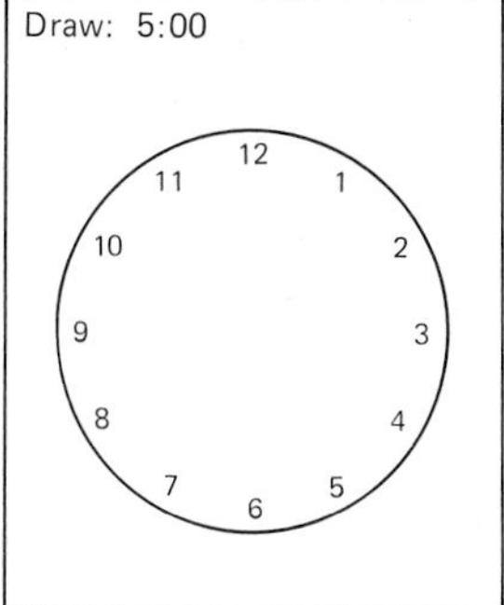

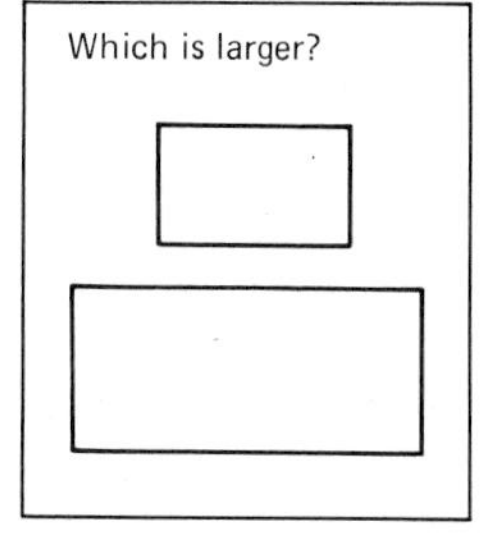

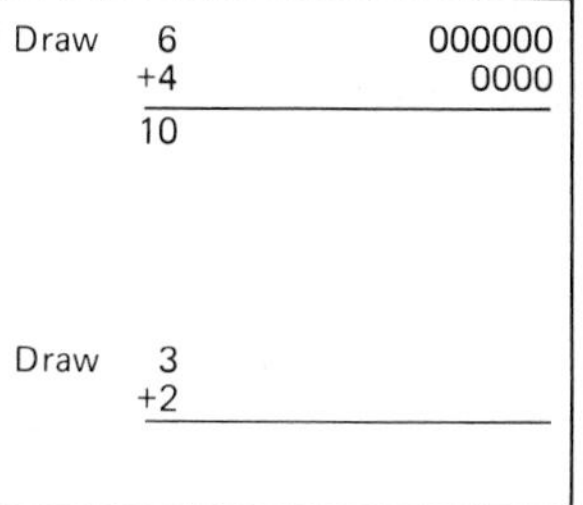

With young children, care needs to be exercised that they can read and understand the directions.

The interpretation of students' math tests should provide information for future teaching. Careful analysis will reveal whether students need reinforcement of a concept or perhaps additional teaching using a different approach. Frequently the test should be followed with an individual conference to determine the "missing link" in the student's understanding.

In reporting progress to parents, it is important to remember that the isolated mathematics test is meaningless unless it is accompanied by an explanation of the concept that was taught. If all the parent sees is a test sheet that informs him/her of a score (5 out of 12), the parent will focus on the number of correct answers instead of gaining a perspective on what the child understands. Communication about a student's progress in mathematics is best achieved through a parent-teacher conference rather than through test papers.

Parental help should be solicited when students perform poorly in math. Home experiences can include the use of concrete materials. Teachers can suggest appropriate experiences and practice materials that can be used at home. However, as in other subject fields, it is important to warn parents not to overdo the "practice" time.

RESEARCH FINDINGS

Good and Grouws conducted an experimental program in fourth-grade classrooms (Missouri Mathematics Effectiveness Program) involving the following instructional system:

1. Instructional activity was initiated and reviewed in the context of meaning.
2. A substantial portion of each lesson was devoted to content development.
3. Students were prepared for each lesson stage to enhance involvement.
4. The principles of distributed and successful practices were used.

Results indicated that experimental students performed better than control students and had a better attitude about mathematics instruction (1981, p. 86).

Learning Centers

Learning centers in mathematics are used to reinforce math concepts, individualize instruction, and provide for special needs. Center use can be an integral part of the instructional program.

How Much Does It Weigh?

Mathematics
Lower Grades

Objectives: To practice estimation; to compare weights.

Materials: Two-pan balance scale, small objects (rocks, erasers, blocks).

Evaluation: Observation, weight, discussion, self-evaluation.

Procedures:

1. Student(s) arrange objects from light to heavy or heavy to light on the table top.
2. Items are weighed and compared with original guesses.
3. Objects are rearranged on table top if original estimation was incorrect.

Which Container Holds a Cup? Pint? Quart? Liter?

Mathematics
Lower and Middle Grades

Objectives: To compare different-sized and shaped containers; to use standard and metric units; to estimate volume.

Materials: Plastic containers of different sizes and shapes, sand, plastic drop cloth and/or newspapers, large spoon or scoop, measuring units.

Evaluation: Observation, discussion, self-evaluation.

Procedures:

1. Table and surrounding floor area are protected with the drop cloth or newspapers.
2. Students should be encouraged to guess how much each container will hold before measuring.
3. Students use standard measuring units to fill plastic containers with sand in order to determine how much each container holds.
4. Containers are compared and estimation validated.

Congruent Figures

Upper Grades

Objectives: To identify and draw congruent figures and line segments.

Materials: Rulers, paper, pencils, task cards, examples for self-evaluation.

Evaluation: Self-evaluation with peers.

Procedures:

1. Set of task cards explains what students are to do. Example: Draw two congruent geometric figures. Draw two geometric figures that are not congruent. Draw the radius and diameter of a circle. Label each. Draw and label: an angle, ray, line segment, isosceles triangle, parallelogram, trapezoid.
2. Compare your drawings with examples at center.

Congruent Figures

Lower Grades

Objective: To identify and draw geometric figures.

Materials: Crayons, paper, examples of different sizes and shapes, ruler.

Evaluation: Teacher observation, self-evaluation.

Procedures:

1. Find three objects (in the center) that are rectangles. Draw them.
2. Find three objects that are circles and draw them.
3. Find three objects that are triangles and draw them.
4. Draw two squares that are different sizes.

Problem Solving

Mathematics
Middle and Upper Grades

Objectives: To identy problem components; practice problem solving; develop the ability to generate data; participate in peer discussion of problem components and processes.

Materials: Problems, box, paper and pencil, guide card.

Evaluation: Answer sheet; discussion of processes, patterns, and probability.

Procedures:

1. Prepare a guide card to remind students how to solve problems. The guide card should ask:
   What do you need to find out?
   What facts are given?
   What processes do you need to use?
2. Students may choose the problems from a special shoe box or "fish" for the problems.
3. Students should first identify the information, draw the problem, and/or use manipulative materials.
4. Write the problem and solve it.

Illustrative Problems

Pretend that you have $300 for a vacation. Travel will cost you 1/4 of your total; food will cost you 1/5 of the total; accommodations will cost 1/3 of the total. How much will you have left for entertainment and gifts?

Make a chart of class absences for the month of October. See how many ways you can illustrate the information.

Week 1	Girls	Boys	Week 3	Girls	Boys
Mon.	2	3		3	4
Tues.	2	2		3	4
Wed.	2	1		0	1
Thur.	3	2		2	3
Fri.	3	3		3	3
Week 2			**Week 4**		
Mon.	3	4		3	5
Tues.	1	2		3	4
Wed.	0	0		2	2
Thur.	1	2		3	1
Fri.	1	2		4	2

Were there more boys or girls absent during October? Did absences increase or decrease during October? What reasons might account for this? Which day of the week had the most absences? The least? What reasons might account for this? Is this pattern typical of other classrooms at school?

In a fourth-grade classroom, 7 children had birthdays in the month of December; 14 children had birthdays during the months of January, February, and March; 5 children had birthdays in April; 4 children had birthdays in May; and 2 children had birthdays in June. None of the children had birthdays during the summer or fall months. Was this distribution of birthdays unusual? How could you find out?'

In this problem, students should be encouraged to organize the data, suggest ways to detect a pattern, interpret the solution. Is this pattern of birthdays typical of other fourth-grade classrooms? Fifth grade? Sixth grade?

Weather Chart

Mathematics, Science
Upper Grades, Middle Grades

Objectives: To observe, record, and predict weather conditions; to make inferences from graphs, peer interaction and discussion.

Materials: Weather instruments (mercury thermometer, alcohol thermometer, mercury barometer, wind vane, anemometer), pencil and paper, weather charts.

Evaluation: Compare predictions and measurements with other students, weather bureau, newspaper.

WEATHER RECORD

	Temperature	Air Pressure	Wind Direction	Wind Velocity	Prediction
Mon.					
Tues.					
Wed.					
Thur.					
Fri.					

Procedures:

1. Students use weather instruments to observe and measure weather conditions.
2. Students record information.
3. Students make daily predictions of the weather.

Money

Mathematics
Lower Grades

Objectives: To identify value of coins; to find equivalent sets of coins.

Materials: Charts, paper and pencil, manipulative coins, task cards.

Evaluation: Self-check with charts at the center.

Procedures:

1. Task cards should identify a set amount of money that is to be illustrated. Example: Draw all the ways you can make 42¢ (53¢) ($1.00).
2. Students are to use the coins to help them find the answers.
3. Students are to draw their answers.
4. Students check their answers with prepared charts at the center.

Chapter Summary

How children learn mathematics was discussed and linked to the Piagetian stages of development. Seven strands for structuring the mathematics program were identified, and an example of the problem-solving process was provided. Representative objectives for each strand were identified.

The varied perspectives of developmentalists and behaviorists concerning the content and method for teaching mathematics were highlighted. Discovery learning, mastery learning, repetition, and drill were discussed as teaching methods. A sequence for teaching mathematics was provided and illustrated through classroom teaching examples.

Contemporary issues in mathematics education were emphasized through the discussion of sexism and modern technology. Suggestions for mainstreaming and learning centers were provided.

Classroom Application Exercises

1. Perform conservation tests with different-aged children and describe stages of development.
2. Prepare a speech for a PTA meeting on the value of using concrete materials in mathematics. Explain the use of Cuisenaire rods.
3. Prepare a lesson to teach subtraction that requires renaming tens to ones. Use concrete materials.
4. Plan a mathematics learning center to reinforce the understanding of fractional parts.
5. A student's response is totally irrelevant to the given problem; how will you discover what the student knows and what s/he does not understand?

Suggested Readings for Extending Study

Copeland, R. W. *Mathematics and the Elementary Teacher.* 4th ed. New York: Macmillan Publishing Company, 1982.

Copeland, R. W. *How Children Learn Mathematics.* 3rd ed. New York: Macmillan Publishing Company, 1979.

Cruikshank, D. E., D. L. Fitzgerald, and L. R. Jensen. *Young Children Learning Mathematics.* Boston: Allyn & Bacon, Inc., 1980.

Gerber, H. *Mathematics for Elementary School Teachers.* Philadelphia: W. L. Saunders Company, 1982.

Lerch, H. H. *Active Learning Experiences for Teaching Elementary School Mathematics.* Boston: Houghton Mifflin Company, 1981.

Miller, C. D., and V. E. Herren. *Mathematical Ideas.* 4th ed. Glenview, Ill.: Scott, Foresman and Company, 1982.

Shumway, Richard J., ed. *Research in Mathematics Education.* Reston, Virginia: National Council Teachers of Mathematics, 1980.

Underhill, Richard G. *Diagnosing Mathematical Difficulties.* Columbus, Ohio: Charles E. Merrill Publishing Company, 1980.

Underhill, Richard G. *Teaching Elementary School Mathematics.* Columbus, Ohio: Charles E. Merrill Publishing Company, 1980.

Vigilante, N. J., ed. *Mathematics in Elementary Education.* New York: Macmillan Publishing Company, 1969.

Chapter **9**

Science Education

After you have completed the study of this chapter, you should be able to accomplish the following:

1. **Identify purposes for teaching elementary science.**
2. **Identify the content for elementary science programs.**
3. **Describe several ways of teaching science.**
4. **List several national science programs and what these projects emphasize.**
5. **Make a list of science materials and equipment for classroom use.**
6. **Identify and discuss ways to evaluate science learning.**
7. **Create a science learning center emphasizing discovery learning.**
8. **Explain why mainstreamed students need a "hands-on" approach to learn science concepts.**
9. **Identify classroom management considerations when teaching science.**

The Wump World was a small world, very much smaller than our world. There were no great oceans, lofty mountains, giant forests, or broad sandy deserts. The Wump World was mostly grassy meadows and clumps of leafy green trees with a few winding rivers and lakes. But it was perfect for the Wumps, who were the only creatures living there (Peet, 1970, p. 1).

Mary Hogan continued to read The Wump World to her students. When she finished she showed her students several globes with only water and land masses on them. She asked the students, "What covers most of the earth's surface?" In this way Hogan introduced a unit of study on the earth and the environment.

Hogan enjoys teaching science, but many elementary teachers feel insecure about their science knowledge and their understanding of science concepts (Stake & Easley, 1978). Elementary teachers surveyed for the National Science Foundation status studies on precollege science, mathematics, and social science indicated that they "typically spend about 20 minutes each day on science in grades K–3 and 30 minutes in grades 4–6" (Weiss, 1978, p. 51). The teachers surveyed indicated that science was of low priority in the elementary curriculum. That elementary teachers emphasize reading and mathematics is no surprise, but the reaction of the National PTA to the status studies should be of professional interest.

Though emphasis on acquiring basic skills is at the heart of the educational process, there is a distinct possibility of basics becoming the curriculum rather than just part of the curriculum. Another problem with an overemphasis on basics, is a tendency to teach children only those things for which they will be tested, a tendency that leads to mediocrity (National Congress of Parents and Teachers, p. vii of NSF Report, cited by Weiss, 1978).

For a nation that was shocked by Sputnik in the 1950s and determined to lead the world scientifically and technologically, it is somewhat alarming to think that science is not considered (by teachers) important in the elementary curriculum. In a report to the President of the United States by the National Science Foundation and the Department of Education (1981) several points were emphasized:

- The role of science and technology is increasing throughout our society.

- The declining emphasis on science and mathematics in our school systems is in marked contrast to that of other industrialized countries.
- The commitment to excellence in science, mathematics, and technology has lessened in the United States.

What Are the Purposes of Elementary Science?

Science is an essential and fundamental subject within the curriculum. Elementary science provides students with opportunities to (a) think critically and practice methods of inquiry, (b) develop science concepts which facilitate understanding of the biological and physical environment, and (c) develop appropriate attitudes and skills essential for democratic citizenship.

Science offers unique opportunities to interrelate curriculum areas. Language development is facilitated when students have an experiential base to practice reading, writing, listening, and speaking. Science provides relevant situations for the integration of other subject fields such as social studies and mathematics. The problem-solving skills learned in science and social studies facilitate the development of decision-making capacities that enable students to accept citizenship responsibilities.

Through the study of the natural environment students develop principles, processes, and generalizations of science. As students learn the application of these principles, organized knowledge becomes meaningful.

Why is science considered a basic subject?

Science teaching is concerned with *content* (facts, concepts, theories, generalizations) and with *process* (observation, measurement, classification, comparison, inference, generalization, theory-building).

RESEARCH FINDINGS

Johnson and Johnson (1979) studied a cooperative interaction pattern and found that small group work was effective in building students' positive attitudes and particularly appropriate to the teaching of science.

Content of Elementary Science Programs

Both content and process are intertwined in the elementary program using the content as the subject of the inquiry. The emphasis of the science program is on discovery so that students will develop problem-solving skills and scientific attitudes. Most science units and textbook series focus on three major divisions in the natural sciences: living things, the earth and the universe, matter and energy. Units are often developed using topics such as the following:

Living Things
Organisms
Life cycles
Plants and animals
Human body
Health and disease
Our senses
Fossils
Dinosaurs
Ecology
Environmental issues
Conservation
Recycling
Natural resources
Pollution
Food chains

Matter and Energy
Molecules and atoms
Physical and chemical properties
Temperature, heat
Solar energy
Machines
Magnetism and electricity
Sound
Light
Space travel

EARTH AND UNIVERSE

Rocks and minerals
Earthquakes, volcanoes
Erosion
The changing earth
Sun and the planets
Stars and the universe
Air and weather
Wind
Sun, air, water

How Is Science Taught?

How students learn science is just as important as what students learn. In the teaching of science, a major objective is to develop students' problem-solving capacities. To do this, learning experiences must be structured to provide students with opportunities to participate in processes of discovery.

For example, in Chapter 3 there was an episode about first-grade students studying magnets. First the children *observed* the teacher using a horseshoe magnet, then they themselves used them. Their problem was to find out,

"What will magnets pull?"

As the children *experimented* with different objects that magnets attract, they *discussed* their observations in their small groups. They *hypothesized* in the sense that they tried out different explanations for what they were observing. They continued to experiment until they were satisfied with their *explanations*. The students *classified* their data by grouping their objects into those that were attracted to the magnet and those that were not. With the teacher's assistance they formed a *generalization* about their experiment.

There are a number of problem-solving skills that can be taught during science, but every science lesson will not feature all of these skills. The foregoing explanation is not intended as an all-encompassing list of the processes involved in discovery.

Students' Attitudes

One of the purposes for elementary science identified at the beginning of this chapter was to develop appropriate attitudes and skills essential for a democratic society. A scientific attitude is considered essential in our society. This means that students will learn to accept the "tentativeness" of certain evidence; they will be willing to subject their ideas to testing; they will understand that it is "OK" to change their minds and that hypotheses often need revision.

In science teaching, teachers have the responsibility to encourage curiosity and to confront students with interesting problems to stimulate an investigation.

In a sixth-grade classroom, the students were disdainful about washing their hands before lunch. Jim's attitude was typical of many of the students: "Phooey, all we've been doing is sitting and writing."

Teacher: "All right. How could we find out if it makes a difference?"

Rhoda: "What happens to food or to us if our hands are dirty?"

Teacher: "Why don't we design an experiment to find out?"

Jim: "Well, most of us eat sandwiches, maybe we should preserve one touched by us unclean ones and another one by the cowards who wash up!"

Teacher: "Well, Jim, I'm not impressed with your terminology, but I think you are on the right track."

Sean: "If we preserve a whole sandwich, how will we know whether what ever happens is a result of dirty hands or natural food spoilage?"

Tina: "Maybe we should just use bread without anything in between that would spoil."

Rod: "Yeah, Tina, that's a good idea. But there's another problem."

Tina: "What's that?"

Rod: "Even the air can contaminate; we still won't know if it's dirt or bacteria in the air."

Bart: "We could enclose the bread in some air-tight jars."
Jan: "Ah, Good. Why don't we get two jars with lids and put the bread inside?"
Susan: "Wouldn't we need to sterilize the jars?"
Rod: "That's a good idea."
Teacher: "Boys and girls, you are doing great. It sounds to me like you have developed a good test to see if dirty hands really make a difference."

The next day the teacher brought bread and jars to class. The students talked about sterilization, and several students were appointed to take the jars to the school cafeteria for sterilization. The students refined their procedures and decided that each slice of bread would be handled by several students. One jar was labeled "dirty" and the other "clean." Three students were assigned the task of washing with soap and three were chosen at random to touch the piece of bread to be labeled "dirty."

As the week progressed the students were rewarded by being able to record how the presence of mold changed the bread in the jar labeled "dirty," while the other piece of bread showed no noticeable change.

This teacher demonstrated confidence in her students. She gave them enough time to think about how the experiment could be designed. She herself modeled a scientific attitude by allowing the students to discover instead of telling them or having them read to find out the answer. As the experiment progressed, the students observed, questioned, and developed generalizations. Ultimately the students' curiosity led them to their textbooks to study about mold and bacteria.

Open-Ended Teaching

The teaching of science provides a marvelous opportunity for teachers to release their own and students' creativity. By asking questions like, "What would happen if . . . both pieces of bread developed mold simultaneously (heaven forbid) or someone sneezed on the bread as they touched it . . . ," new ideas for experimentation are explored.

If the sixth-grade students had not thought about the possibility of bacteria in the air contaminating their experiment, the teacher might have said, "How can we make sure that the only variable affecting the bread is dirt?"

Open-ended science teaching is similar to inquiry teaching, which is discussed in Part III. It is important to identify the ways in which science can be taught most successfully. For this reason, examples of open-ended science teaching will be cited.

Several fifth-grade students had been working on a time line of great inventions through the ages. When they shared their work with their classmates, the teacher realized the children had little conception of how magnetism was converted to electricity even though the students were discussing the inventions of Faraday, Henry, and Oersted.

The next day in class the teacher provided the following materials: dry cells, insulated copper wire, sandpaper, large nails, and paper clips. The students were divided into small groups. Each group had the following problems to solve:

- How do you make an electromagnet?
- How do you change the strength of the electromagnet?

Through experimentation the students learned that an electromagnet is made by winding the wire tightly around the nail and connecting the ends of the wire (which have been stripped of insulation, using the sandpaper) to the dry cell. Further experimentation led to the discovery that the strength of the electromagnet was affected by the number of turns of wire on the nail. (More coils of wire increased the strength of the magnet.)

While this is relatively uncomplicated, many of the students did not realize that the wire had to be stripped at the ends before attaching to the dry cell; nor did they realize that the amount of wire would affect the outcome. Many had no idea that the dry cell had both negative and positive poles and that both would be required to make the electromagnet.

Students Study Electricity by Constructing Their Own Motors, Telegraphs, and Radios.

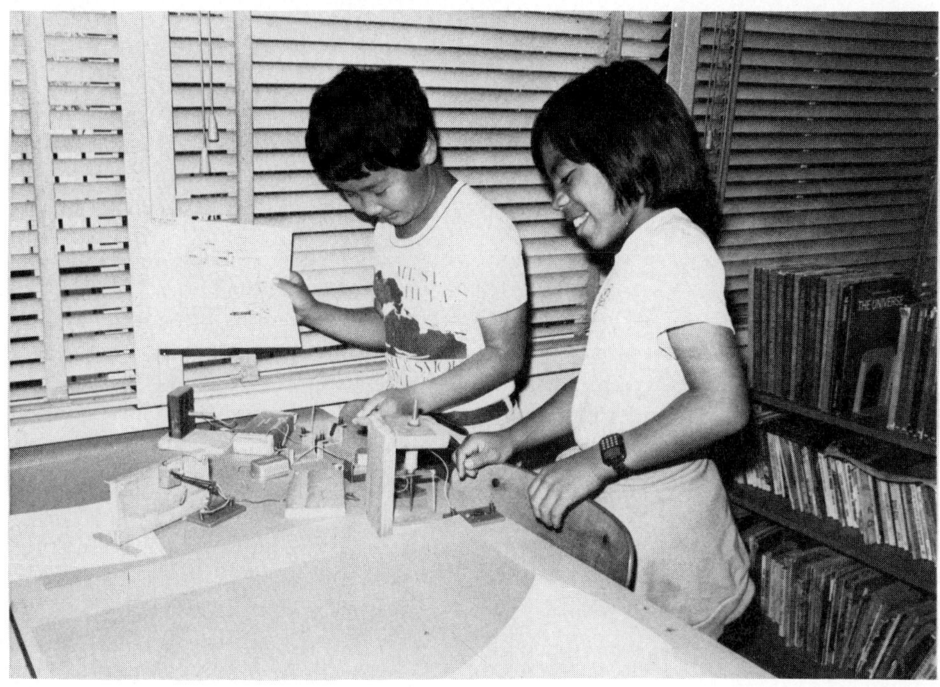

By comparing the electromagnets made by different groups of children, students were encouraged to find out "who made the strongest magnet?" (A simple way to find this out is to see which magnet picked up the most paperclips!)

The homework assignment for this class was to make a list of ways that electromagnets are used at home. Students were so enthused with their experiments that the teacher presented them with a list of projects they could make to continue their study of electricity. The list included the following: A Telegraph System, A Lifting Crane, A Motor, and A Crystal Radio. The students chose their projects and were divided into project teams for the planning stage. Each student was required to draw a plan and list the specifications for the intended project. The students had a variety of pictures of telegraphs, motors, cranes, and radios. They were able to choose which model they wanted to make.

To make the models the teacher provided wood for the bases, tin from tin cans, nails, copper wire, sandpaper, coat hangers for the "station finder" on the radio, empty spools of thread, thin sticks, corks, masking tape, different types of clips, tubes from aluminum foil for winding coils, diodes for the radios.

The projects motivated students to read about electricity and experiment with their projects. For example, students asked the following questions:

- Does it make any difference if you use more than one dry cell? (If two are used, how do you go about it? A connecting wire is needed!)
- Will radio waves pass through different materials? Which ones?
- How can we make our radio louder or softer?
- How do you send messages using the Morse Code?

- How does an electromagnet differ from a regular magnet? Do they both pick up the same things?
- How can we make the motors faster? Slower?
- How much weight will our crane pick up?

The students' own questions rather than the teacher's questions became the focus of individual experimentation. Their questions served to expand their interests and "open up" the study of electricity.

Construction

The students were encouraged to work with a partner during the construction stage. On the first day of construction the teacher demonstrated correct tool safety procedures. These included the use of saw horses, bench hooks to hold the wood, and the "C" clamp; how to measure using T square and a ruler; how to nail two pieces of wood together; where to store tools when not in use. The students also needed to learn to use tin snips to cut tin from the cans and how to wind wire evenly for the coils.

Purposes of Construction

Construction is considered a creative and a socializing experience. During construction students attempt to create a likeness to the original model. Projects are evaluated for authenticity even though "authentic" materials may not be used. Projects to be constructed require:

- group planning
- selection of materials
- manipulative skills
- sharing of materials and ideas
- cooperative problem solving
- measurement skills
- experimental attitude
- continuous evaluation
- appropriate use of tools and materials
- research related to use and function.

Construction Satisfies Students' Natural Urge to Produce Something of Their Own.

As an activity, construction satisfies students' natural urge to produce something of their own and provides a means to motivate research about the real thing or product. Social and scientific concepts are learned when construction is carried out in a purposeful manner.

Reading During Science

Reading is used as a way of teaching science when

- students need to "find out" something (research)
- students need to extend their information and experience
- a substitute for original investigation and experimentation is wanted.

Reading is a particularly natural means to learn about science. Even though it is considered important for students to inquire on their own and experiment because of the benefit in terms of scientific attitudes, reading materials provide classroom resources that are not available in any other way.

In Mary Hogan's classroom when the students began to discuss the environment, one of the students asked, "What is a desert like?" Hogan in her best teacherly fashion responded, "How could we find out?" When the students asked if there were any books in the classroom about deserts, Hogan suggested a number of different resources. She identified the characteristics of the different resources:

- This book shows the author's interest in plants and animals of the desert.
- This book has many pictures of deserts.
- Our own classroom picture file will provide some information about desert sands and rocks.
- This resource may provide some information about the temperature of deserts.

Hogan then directed the students to "choose their own resource for research about deserts and plan to have a classroom discussion about deserts in about ten minutes." To facilitate the students' reading, she wrote several questions on the board:

1. What is a desert?
2. Why can some plants live in deserts?
3. What are some desert plants?
4. What animals can live in deserts?
5. What is the name of a place in the desert where water can be found?
6. Why is a camel suited to desert travel?

Reading during science (or during any other academic subject) should be purposefully directed. If students will be reading unfamiliar words or concepts, they should be introduced and explained before the students are to read on their own. Science reading should *not* be a session where the teacher directs students to "take out your science book and reader Chapter 5."

Reading during science as during social studies is far more effective when several resources are utilized. This method provides different viewpoints and perspectives on what is to be investigated *and* it provides for individual differences in reading ability.

Utilization of different resources also develops students' research and location skills. Teachers can identify the resources available as Hogan did for her third graders, but it is a good idea for students to find the appropriate pages through the use of the table of contents and the index.

Demonstrations

Should teachers ever demonstrate an experiment? Certainly. There are occasions when it is more appropriate for the teacher to demonstrate a science concept or perform an experiment with students observing than to have individuals perform the experiment. Some experiences are beyond the manipulative skills of students and may in fact be unsafe for students to perform. Under these circumstances it may be wise for the teacher to perform the experiment and have students observe.

Sometimes the purpose of a teacher experiment is to motivate new areas of interest or to evaluate students' observation skills, attitudinal growth, and conceptual understanding. Here again a demonstration may be the most efficient means to accomplish the purpose.

Gathering Data, Record Keeping

If students are to improve in their ability to use scientific processes, they need to learn how to gather data and describe their observations in order ultimately to decide "why" something happened. All kinds of records for writing up experiments can be devised.

Table 9.1 is an example. Students should be encouraged to devise their own records for writing up experiments. For young children it is often a good idea to create a large chart to record class observations. Sometimes the data can be recorded using "smiles" or "frowns" or other pictorial means to reflect the observation. The emphasis should be on describing "what is," not "what ought to be." If an experiment does not come out as teacher and students anticipated, then the discussion should focus on "why not?" Sometimes an experiment should be duplicated for verification purposes. This, too, can be explained to children.

Field Trips

Field trips may be simply a walk through the neighborhood to observe something special, or a field trip may be a real excursion that requires planned transportation. Whichever it is, the field trip must be planned and be an integral part of an ongoing science program. Students should be prepared for the trip with information about what they are to see and what they are expected to do. If they are to take notes, this too must be communicated. If specific students or groups of students are to be responsible for particular information, then this should be assigned before the trip commences.

The field trip should be evaluated in terms of "What did we learn that we didn't know before?" "What surprised us?" "What did we verify?" and

TABLE 9.1. Third-Grade Experiment Record.

Problem: Miss Hogan's plant looks sick.

Hypotheses: (1) She did not water enough. (Plants need a lot of water.)
(2) She watered too much. (Plants need a little bit of water.)
(3) There was not enough sunshine. (Plants need sunlight.)

Materials: New Plants

Procedures:

1. Plant #1 will be watered daily and placed on the windowsill.
2. Plant #2 will be watered twice a week and placed on the windowsill.
3. Plant #3 will be watered daily and kept on Miss Hogan's desk.
4. Plant #4 will be watered twice a week and kept on Miss Hogan's desk.

Results (Observations)

Plant #1	#2	#3	#4
3rd Day			
5th Day			
8th Day			
11th Day			
15th Day			

Conclusions:

TABLE 9.2. Science Activities for Data Collection and Data Evaluation.

Discussing	(Planning, Reporting, Sharing)
Recording	(Record Keeping, Listing, Describing)
Writing	(Fiction, Reports, Information)
Constructing	(Making Gadgets, Science Equipment, Projects)
Expressing	(Talking, Singing, Drawing, Painting)
Reading	(Fiction, Science Information, Reports)
Experimenting	(Soil, Magnets, Sound, Light, . . .)
Observing	(Animals, Plants, Events, Experiments . . .)
Dramatizing	(Role-Plays, Plays)
Collecting	(Pictures, Plants, Rocks, . . .)

"What did we enjoy?" It is important to discuss the field trip and accurately record essential information, but it is not necessarily important that the field trip be written up individually by students.

Summary of How to Teach Science

Science teaching utilizes scientific concepts and focuses on the processes used by scientists. Discovery learning is featured because it motivates students' curiosity and interest in scientific subject matter and provides opportunities to practice the skills of observing, measuring, classifying, comparing, generalizing, and theorizing.

The teacher's role as a resource person and facilitator is featured in science teaching in contrast to the teacher as an authority figure. Science teaching attempts to develop students' skills in other subject fields such as mathematics, social studies, language arts. There is an effort to integrate cognitive, affective, and psychomotor behaviors. Learning "how" to learn science is as important as learning the content of science.

RESEARCH FINDINGS

Stake and Easley (1978, pp. 13:5–13:6) found that teachers persist in a common pattern of instruction in science teaching: assign—recite—test—discuss.

Materials developed for science teaching and most studies of science teaching suggest student-centered and hands-on instruction.

How Is Science Organized for Teaching?

Teaching Units

On a rainy day in West Los Angeles, some first graders entered their classroom and asked their teacher if she had seen the rainbow. She responded, "Yes; do you know how to make a rainbow?" The students were perplexed. It had not occurred to them that it was possible to "make" rainbows. Their teacher took them outside to observe the rainbow once more. This time she asked them to name the colors they observed and the sequence of the colors (violet, blue, green, yellow, orange, red). She asked them to observe the way the colors merged. Once more the teacher asked the students, "How can we make a rainbow? What do we need?" Observing the rainbow across the sky, the students realized that they needed sunlight and water. The next day the teacher provided jars and suggested that the students take them outside to see if they could make rainbows. With the teacher's assistance, the students soon learned that they would also need mirrors to reflect the sunlight through the water-filled jars. The student's interest and curiosity for light and colors led the teacher to develop a teaching unit that integrated science, art, and mathematics. Some of the science generalizations included the following:

- Sunlight is a mixture of many colors.
- Rainbows are made because water changes the direction of the light.
- Some colors change direction more than other colors do.
- Color depends upon the light that is reflected.
- Light that is not absorbed is reflected.

- White light is composed of the colors of the rainbow.
- A sundial can be used to tell time.

Science discovery lessons included:

- Using magnifying glasses and mirrors
- Making, mixing, and matching colors
- How shadows help us tell time.

The teaching unit developed by this teacher effectively integrated science, mathematics, and art, but as the unit progressed, the teacher realized that health could also be integrated by having the students study the care and use of their eyes. The development of a teaching unit in science is similar to the development of a unit in social studies. It is important to identify the concepts to be taught and the possible learning experiences. By identifying the activities to achieve the unit objectives, the teacher can anticipate equipment, material, and resource needs. Culminating activities should also be planned. It is advantageous to use a unit plan in science because it ensures that important concepts are taught rather than trivia, and it provides the teacher with a format to see that there is continuity in the lessons planned.

Although social studies teaching units may be limited to one or two a semester, it is customary in science to have a series of short units progress through the semester. Also, in science it is possible to include many science experiences that have nothing to do with the unit of study. This happens because it is advantageous to include experiences that may arise as a result of students' interests.

Science Textbooks

The teacher should be the one to decide what is to be taught during the semester. Science books are not organized, necessarily, to be followed in sequence. Although the content of the book is organized in unit form, it is up to the teacher to choose the sequence of the units. Most textbooks emphasize discovery learning and suggest appropriate experiments to help children understand the science concepts.

RESEARCH FINDINGS

Scientific concepts such as time, distance, gravity, and life-maintaining requirements of the living organisms are among the most basic ideas that one can imagine. The fact that natural science is not considered a "basic" is probably a reflection of some of the misconceptions held about the sciences by society at large (Smith, 1980, p. 67).

National Science Programs

Developed by scientists and science educators, curriculum improvement projects were created for use in the elementary school. These projects emphasize

- inquiry learning
- sequenced experimentation by students to learn science concepts
- understanding the underlying science disciplines
- understanding the environment
- development of mathematics skills.

Four of the national projects will be discussed.

1. *Science Curriculum Improvement Study (SCIS)*. This project focuses on science concepts concerned with matter, energy, organism, and ecosystem. Twelve units were developed for the project. Teachers using the SCIS materials are to guide children in their exploration of the science materials and to encourage the students to investigate, discuss, and ask questions. The purposes of the project include the development of scientific literacy, investigative experience, and scientific attitudes. The materials designed by SCIS are available from Rand McNally & Company, Chicago, Illinois.

2. *Conceptually Oriented Program in Elementary Science (COPES)*. This project developed a spiral curriculum for grades K–6 using five conceptual schemes: The Structural Units of the Universe, Interaction and Change, Conservation of Energy,

Degradation of Energy, The Statistical View of Nature. All five schemes are used concurrently from K–6. The learning activities are designed to help students learn the concepts through active involvement. Skills such as analysis, classification, communication, experimentation, and interpretation are used repeatedly during the activities. The materials are available through The Center for Field Research and School Services at New York University.

3. *Elementary Science Study (ESS).* Schools may select and sequence the ESS science units to develop their own curriculum. The units in this project are designed to promote investigation through construction activities. The purpose of the activities is to have students develop a sense of satisfaction and confidence that they control a bit of their world by inventing and making something that really works. All of the suggested activities use simple everyday materials. An example is the student book for the ESS unit *Batteries and Bulbs* which contains pictures and descriptions of gadgets and projects that can be made by students. The purpose of the book is to interest the student in the wide range and variety of gadgets that can be made using simple tools and "scrounged" materials. Fifty-six units have been developed for grades K–8 and are available through McGraw-Hill Book Company, New York City.

4. *Science—A Process Approach II (SAPA II).* SAPA II is a revision of the original project which was developed by the Commission on Science Education of the American Association for the Advancement of Science. The K–6 project focuses on science processes instead of science subject matter, based on a belief that the scientific method for acquiring knowledge is essential to the education of all students. For this reason students participate in the activities that scientists would perform. Science lessons begin with the process of identifying the problem, proceed with ways to find solutions, and end with a group evaluation to determine whether or not the students have achieved the specified objectives. Blough and Schwartz (1979, p. 51) describe the project and comment that students "are not asked to learn and remember particular facts or principles about objects and phenomena." Instead, they learn "how to infer internal mechanisms in plants, how to make and verify hypotheses about animal behavior, and how to perform experiments on the actions of gases."

> Open-ended experiences are typical of the National Science Programs. Do you believe that open-ended experiences conflict with an emphasis on exactness? Why?

Materials and Equipment

Science materials and equipment should not be a problem for the imaginative teacher. Common, everyday materials and equipment from the immediate environment can be used to enrich the science program. In the ESS project students are urged to use materials typically found around the house, school, or street:

- corks
- the cylinder from paper towels
- frozen juice cans
- tin cans
- scissors
- emory board
- spool from thread
- toothpaste boxes
- milk cartons
- string
- tinkertoy parts
- rulers
- glue
- hammer
- paper clips
- flashlight
- bottles
- springs
- pulleys
- screw driver
- wire
- scrap lumber
- apple boxes
- crates

Blough and Schwartz (1979, p. 67) suggest studying the school environment for a source of problems to investigate and materials to use for the investigation. Their list includes:

- The school furnace
- fuses
- circuit breakers
- insulators
- conductors
- meters

- lights
- switches
- water pipes
- window glass
- paper
- fire extinguishers

Students and their parents can also be counted on to help equip the science program. Frequently students can bring to class the following materials:

kitchen ingredients (vinegar, baking soda, food items, food coloring)
magnets
thermometers
barometer
pulleys
pans
bulbs
seeds
balance
balloons
bicycle pump
lenses
tools
nails, tacks
jars
measuring cups, spoons
musical instruments
plants

Iron filings, used frequently when students are studying magnets, can be obtained by sending students to the school sandbox with a magnet and an envelope to store them in. The teacher's main problem is to develop science "kits" for the different investigations or science units. Apple boxes, obtained at the produce department of large markets, make marvelous storage containers for the science materials and equipment.

> Why is it important in science teaching to have a variety of manipulative materials for students to use?

Science Specialist Teachers

In some elementary schools a science specialist teacher is responsible for the entire school science program. This teacher's classroom is equipped as a science laboratory. The specialist teacher organizes and plans the science teaching units for each grade level. The classroom becomes a science center, and all the materials are stored in this facility. Students come to the center two or three times each week with their regular teacher accompanying them. The regular teacher serves as a "team member" with the science specialist teacher performing the major teaching tasks. Follow-up teaching and reinforcement of science concepts occur in the students' regular classroom. In this way other subject fields are integrated, and the science program is not fragmented and apart from the real life of the children.

Science Centers

Some schools set up one classroom as a science center. The center is scheduled for use by the teachers, and each teacher is responsible for keeping the center equipped and ready for the next person's use. The center may also be used by a science club or students with special interest in science activities. The major advantage of a science center is that equipment and materials can be shared by many teachers instead of each teacher's being responsible for obtaining personal resources.

Resource People

The science program, whether it is taught in the self-contained classroom or in a science classroom, should utilize resource people at school and in the community. The school custodian is probably an expert electrician, plumber, and carpenter; the custodian may be willing to share his or her skills in the classroom and thereby help translate textbook content into real-life problems with practical solutions.

The community itself should provide resource places and people valuable to the science program. For example: museums, the fire station, industries, the weather bureau, ecology groups, the city engineers' office, the sanitation department—all may be a source of information and a source for classroom consultants. The advantage of using community resource people or visiting in the community is that it adds a sense of reality to the study of science, so that students do not think that textbook problems never occur. However, it is important that teachers verify that the "expert" knows how to talk to students. Before turning a resource person loose in the

These Students Are Enjoying Working in a Special School Science Laboratory.

classroom, the teacher should verify what is to be communicated and how it is to be communicated. Young students may not react positively to the parent photographer who wants to lecture about the use of light meters; however, these same children may be very interested in how to build their own camera.

How Should Science Learning Be Evaluated?

Three purposes of elementary science were presented at the beginning of this chapter. These purposes should be used to guide the evaluation of science learning.

Evaluation of Critical Thinking and Methods of Inquiry

Observation of students' performance as they engage in group discussions, experimentation, group work, and individual projects will provide information about how well students are progressing in using methods of inquiry. For example, a checklist (Table 9.3) will provide a format for observation of inquiry skills.

What we really want to know about the student is whether or not s/he thinks scientifically. We can collect this type of evidence by observing the student performing in the aforementioned ways. We can also learn about the student's progress through teacher-made tests.

> How can you verify that students are "observing?"

Suppose that some upper-grade students were studying about sounds. Their teacher brought a megaphone to class. To determine whether or not

TABLE 9.3. Critical Thinking, Inquiry Skills Checklist.

	Names of Students			
	Bill	Jean	Sue	Rick
1. When presented with a problem situation, does the student attempt to identify and define the problem?				
2. Does the student identify relevant information?				
3. Does the student suggest possible solutions or raise questions about cause and effect?				
4. Does the student suggest means to test or find ways to explain the data?				
5. Does the student attempt to gather data, observe or collect evidence in a variety of ways?				
6. Does the student accurately report/observe the evidence?				
7. Does the student interpret the data accurately?				
8. Does the student recognize the need to validate the experiment/research?				
9. Does the student attempt to generalize, make inferences, or theorize based on the interpretation?				

the students could think scientifically, the teacher asked them the following questions on a test:

1. How can we make a megaphone?
2. How is a megaphone used?
3. How can a megaphone help us hear?

The students in this class were expected to identify the materials needed to make a megaphone and to identify how they would go about discovering its use. They were also expected to suggest ways to find out how the megaphone would improve our ability to hear sounds. This type of test measures the application and use of methods of inquiry. It does not focus on facts or scientific concepts.

The Los Angeles Unified School District (1979, p. 105–106) science continuum identified the following competencies to be evaluated for student participation in scientific inquiry:

- By questioning, identifies and delineates a problem by forming questions likely to be answered through investigation.
- Proposes a possible answer to identified problems.
- Plans an experiment or an appropriate science investigation.
- Generates, records, and organizes data.
- Analyzes, evaluates, and interprets data, reaching a judgment about situations or events.
- Summarizes experiences and relates them to others.

Evaluation of Scientific Concepts

If those same upper-grade students had made megaphones and discovered their use and determined how a megaphone could be used to help them hear better, their teacher could develop a test to determine whether or not the students understood the concepts associated with sound energy. The test could be short answer, essay, or multiple choice. In this test the teacher might ask:

- Why does a megaphone conserve sound energy?
  (A megaphone reflects sound in a specific direction.)
- Explain how a megaphone works.
  (A megaphone concentrates the sound waves instead of allowing the sound waves to spread out equally in all directions.)
- Does it make any difference which end of the megaphone you use? Explain.
  (The large end "gathers" the sound; the small end magnifies the sound.)

Students can also demonstrate knowledge of scientific concepts by what they say during an evaluative discussion or by what they write when they interpret an experiment. After studying organisms, the teacher should expect students to know that living things are interdependent and that organisms may be classified by similarities and differences in characteristics. Concepts such as these should be generated by the students after performing experiments or reading about the adaptation of organisms.

> **RESEARCH FINDINGS**
>
> The teacher is critical in instituting change in science teaching. Science teaching is dependent upon what the teacher "believes, knows, and does" (DeRose, Lockard, & Paldy, 1980).

Evaluation of Students' Attitudes and Skills for a Democratic Society

A scientific attitude describes the individual's skills development and willingness:

- to be open-minded (unbiased)
- to use reliable sources of information
- to validate information from a variety of sources
- to be curious
- to examine evidence and to deliberate
- to interpret on the basis of evidence
- to understand the significance of multiple causation
- to reject superstitions.

These behaviors can be evaluated by critically observing students' performance on work tasks, group participation, and the kinds of things that students choose to do or to share. For example, the student who chooses to participate in a science fair, pursues science hobbies, or suggests a class experiment certainly is expressing personal choice and a scientific attitude. A scientific attitude is vital in a democratic society because the individual is more likely to believe in and practice:

- questioning results
- searching for causal relationships
- using several resources
- accepting responsibility
- critically evaluating own and others' work
- contributing thoughts and opinions
- applying scientific methods to a variety of situations.

Further discussion of evaluation procedures can be found in Chapter 17.

Learning Centers for Science

Science learning centers may be a part of the ongoing science unit or an added dimension used to reinforce skills during reading or mathematics. The centers may be used by a group of students working together or by an individual alone. Following are four "experiments" that can be used in a science learning center.

Soil Testing
Science, Language Arts
Upper Grades

Objective: To observe and participate in a simple investigation to determine the composition of soil; to explain how the composition of soil affects the growing of crops.

Materials: Blue and red litmus paper, soil samples from different places, paper cups, bottle of water, bottle of limewater, teacher-information sheets or science books about soils and farming.

Evaluation: Discussion: How does the composition of soil affect the growing of crops? Self-evaluation of experiment using teacher-prepared exhibit of acid, alkaline, neutral litmus paper.

Procedures: Task Card

1. Place a soil sample in a paper cup. Prepare at least four samples.
2. Add small amount of water to each sample to dampen the soil.
3. Test samples with the litmus paper.
4. After five minutes, remove the litmus papers and observe their color.

(Blue litmus paper turns red or pink in an acid soil; red litmus paper turns blue in a alkaline soil. If each paper stays the same, then the soil is neutral.)

5. How do your soil samples differ?
6. If one of the soil samples is acid, change it to a neutral condition using the lime water.
7. What difference does the composition of the soil make to a farmer? Read and find out.

Making Magnets

Science, Mathematics

Middle Grades

Objective: To compare the strength of temporary magnets; to generalize about temporary magnets.

Materials: Iron nails, steel pins, steel screwdriver, head of a hammer, iron bolt.

Evaluation: Discussion and self-evaluation using teacher-prepared answer sheet.

Procedures: Task Card:

1. Brush the nail with a magnet.
2. Use the nail to pick up the steel pins.

Find Out:

3. How can you make the nail stronger? (Brush the nail longer.)
4. How do you know when it is stronger? (It will pick up more pins.)
5. Does it matter how you brush the nail with the magnet? (Brushing the nail in one direction makes the nail stronger.)
6. Try the experiment with other objects. Record your results. (It will be more difficult to magnetize steel than iron; however, the students should also discover that the steel once magnetized will retain magnetism longer.)

Life Cycles

Science, Social Studies, Language Arts, Mathematics

Lower Grades

Objective: Observation of life cycle; sequencing the life cycle in appropriate order.

Materials: Tank of tadpoles in different stages of development, garden exhibit in different stages from seed to mature plant, duplicated pictures of the two exhibits, scissors, paste, paper.

Evaluation: Students may compare their life-cycle sequence with a teacher-prepared exhibit.

Procedures: Students are to observe the two exhibits. Students cut out pictures and paste them in sequential order to illustrate the life cycle of the frog and of a plant.

Visual Arts

Science, Art, Language Arts

All Grade Levels

Objectives: To observe and describe accurately; to improve art skills; to enjoy an aesthetic experience.

Materials: Weeds, flowers, leaves, and branches or fish, insects, and pets; drawing or painting materials.

Evaluation: Self-evaluation and group sharing.

Procedures:

1. Observe the exhibit.
2. Describe the exhibit.
3. Draw or paint what was observed.

Mainstreaming During Science Teaching

Science teaching, as described in this chapter, emphasizes student participation in discovery learning. Mainstreamed children need a "hands-on" approach to learning and a great deal of individualization. This makes science ideal for facilitating their acceptance, both personal and by peer mates, into the regular classroom.

Since most science activities are group oriented, the mainstreamed student can work in a carefully selected small group or be programmed to work individually. The experiences themselves should be of high interest to the student since most students enjoy the study of animals, plants, magnetism, and the solar system. Manipulative experiences tend to be therapeutic, thus increasing the significance and attraction of science. Experimentation is particularly appealing, and the use of the senses in science enhances the study experience.

Classroom Management Reminders for Science Activities

Classroom management considerations in science are similar to the concerns expressed about social studies. Anticipatory planning is of greater significance when students are to perform experiments in small groups that are not under the immediate supervision of an adult. The teacher needs to make plans thinking about the students' safety, work space, and need for material resources. The modeling aspect of experimentation should also be considered. Suggestions are as follows:

1. Safety: Before students use science equipment or tools, they should be given specific instruction in their care and use.
2. Work Space: Before students are dismissed for work, the work space area should be designated and consideration should be given to providing sufficient work space for each group.
3. Resources: Equipment, materials, and textbooks should be inventoried to ensure that they are of sufficient quantity to meet study or experiment needs of students.
4. Modeling: Modeling by the teacher of open-ended, inquiry oriented learning is important so that students recognize that it's "OK" if an experiment fails, *and* that most experiments need validation.

Chapter Summary

The development of science as a way of thinking is of primary importance in the teaching of elementary science. Greater emphasis on experimentation and inquiry oriented teaching has made the process of teaching science as important as the content of science.

Science enlarges the student's perspective on the world and its environment. Science experiences are varied and appealing to the natural interests and curiosity of most students.

There are innumerable possibilities for science units; the choice can be based on the interests and maturation level of a specific class of students. Teaching units typically reflect an interdisciplinary approach to the teaching of science and attempt to integrate subject fields.

Teachers can help students appreciate scientific principles and the processes of science by modeling a scientific attitude and demonstrating the methods of inquiry.

Classroom Application Exercises

1. Identify scientific concepts and processes to be taught at a specific grade level. Describe three learning experiences to teach the concepts and processes. Describe experiments precisely.
2. Develop several science kits for use in science experiments. List the equipment and materials to be found in each of the kits.
3. Your upper-grade students have discovered how to light a bulb using wire and a dry cell battery. What additional open-ended experimentation could they perform?
4. Your lower-grade students are studying plants. Suggest some experiments they could perform to learn about seeds, plant growth, and plant propagation.
5. You have been requested to explain to parents why inquiry teaching is important in the teaching of science. What will you say?

Suggested Readings for Extending Study

Blough, G. O., and J. Schwartz. *Elementary School Science and How to Teach It*. 6th ed. New York: Holt, Rinehart and Winston, 1979,

Butts, David P., and Gene E. Hall. *Children and Science: The Process of Teaching and Learning*. Englewood Cliffs, New Jersey: Prentice-Hall, 1975.

Carin, Arthur, and Robert B. Sund. *Teaching Science Through Discovery*. 4th ed. Columbus, Ohio: Charles E. Merrill Publishing Company, 1980.

Crescimbeni, Joseph. *Science Enrichment Activities for the Elementary School*. Englewood Cliffs, New Jersey: Prentice-Hall, Inc., 1981.

De Vito, A., and G. H. Krockover. *Creative Sciencing: A Practical Approach*. Boston; Little, Brown and Company, 1976.

Esler, W. K. *Teaching Elementary Science*. 2nd ed. Belmont, Calif.: Wadsworth Publishing Co., Inc., 1977.

Gega, P. C. *Science in Elementary Education*. 4th ed. New York: John Wiley & Sons, Inc., 1982.

Good, Ronald G. *How Children Learn Science*. New York: Macmillan Publishing Company, 1977.

Hounsell, Paul B., and Ira Trollinger. *Games for the Science Classroom*. Washington, D.C.: National Science Teachers Association, 1977.

Lowery, Lawrence F. *The Everyday Science Sourcebook: Ideas for Teaching in the Elementary and Middle School*. New York: Allyn & Bacon, Inc., 1978.

Navarra, J. C. T., and J. Zafferoni. *Science in the Elementary School*. Columbus, Ohio; Charles E. Merrill Publishing Company, 1975.

Nelson, Leslie W., and George C. Lorbeer. *Science Activities for Elementary Children*. Dubuque, Iowa: William C. Brown Publishing Company, 1976.

Roche, R. L. *The Child and Science*. Washington, D.C.: Association for Childhood Education International, 1977.

Rowe, M. B. *Teaching Science as Continuous Inquiry*. New York: McGraw-Hill Book Company, 1978.

Victor, Edward. *Science for the Elementary School*. 4th ed. New York: Macmillan Publishing Company, 1980.

Chapter **10**

Physical and Health Education*

After you have completed the study of this chapter, you should be able to accomplish the following:

1. **Perform with a friend the Kraus-Weber tests of physical fitness.**
2. **List the content areas for physical and health education.**
3. **Define physical fitness and state the purpose of physical and health education.**
4. **Describe stabilizing, locomotor, and manipulative movements.**
5. **List factors that contribute to low fitness.**
6. **Suggest classroom activities to foster a positive self image, and explain how play activities foster appropriate social behavior.**
7. **Discuss ways to develop health education goals.**
8. **Identify and describe the instructional sequence for teaching both a directed and indirect lesson in physical education.**
9. **List the instructional sequence for teaching skills.**
10. **Suggest movements appropriate for warm-up, vigorous exercises, and cool-down.**
11. **List equipment appropriate for physical education.**
12. **Identify ways to evaluate growth in physical and health education.**
13. **Suggest ways to teach health education.**
14. **Suggest ways to integrate the teaching of health education with other subjects.**
15. **Identify classroom management considerations when teaching physical education.**

Importance of Exercise

President John Kennedy once commented that we are an "under-exercised" nation. We are spectators rather than participants; we tend to ride instead of walk. In recent years there has been an alarming incidence of coronary heart disease among children. Coronary heart disease has been associated with a lack of exercise in the adult population. Physical educators and health service professionals have been concerned that children rarely perform physical activities with high intensity. This means that the heart rate never reaches levels higher than 180 beats per minute. In a study of eighty boys between the ages of eight and ten years Gilliam (1978, p. 41) noted that even though half the boys were involved in competitive ice hockey, their "involvement in high intensity physical activities seldom occurred."

In a technological society such as ours we have *decreasing* demands for physical exertion, but increasing opportunities for spectator and non-physical recreation, e.g., video games and television sports. In urban America children rarely climb trees, play sand lot or street ball, or even walk to school. On physical fitness tests American students fall behind the rest of the world.

Physical Fitness Tests

The Kraus Weber tests were medically validated at the Presbyterian Hospital, New York City. The six tests were designed to test the key muscle groups in the body. The tests are performed in the following way:

In *Test One* you lie on your back on the floor with hands clasped behind head. Keeping the knees straight you are

* The author is indebted to Sue Wood, director of Touch of Fitness, Van Nuys, California, for suggestions and review of this chapter.

Kraus-Weber Test #1: Sometimes It Is Necessary to Demonstrate How to Perform an Exercise. In This Exercise the Hip Flexors Are Tested.

Student Is Performing Test #1.

Kraus-Weber Test #2: Hip Flexors and Abdominal Muscles Are Tested.

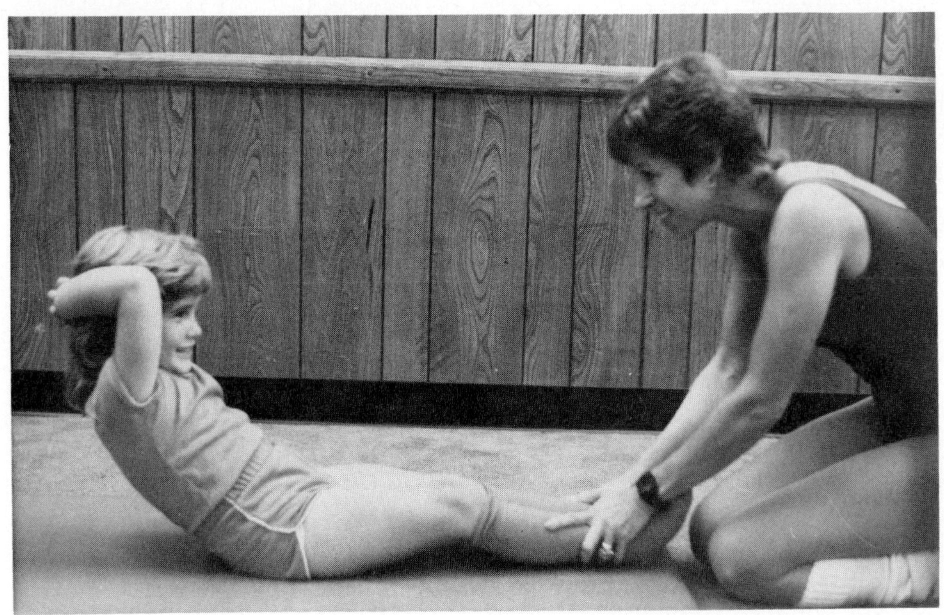

Kraus-Weber Test #3: Abdominal Muscles Are Tested with the Bent Knee Sit-up.

Kraus-Weber Test #4: Upper Back Muscles Are Tested in This Exercise.

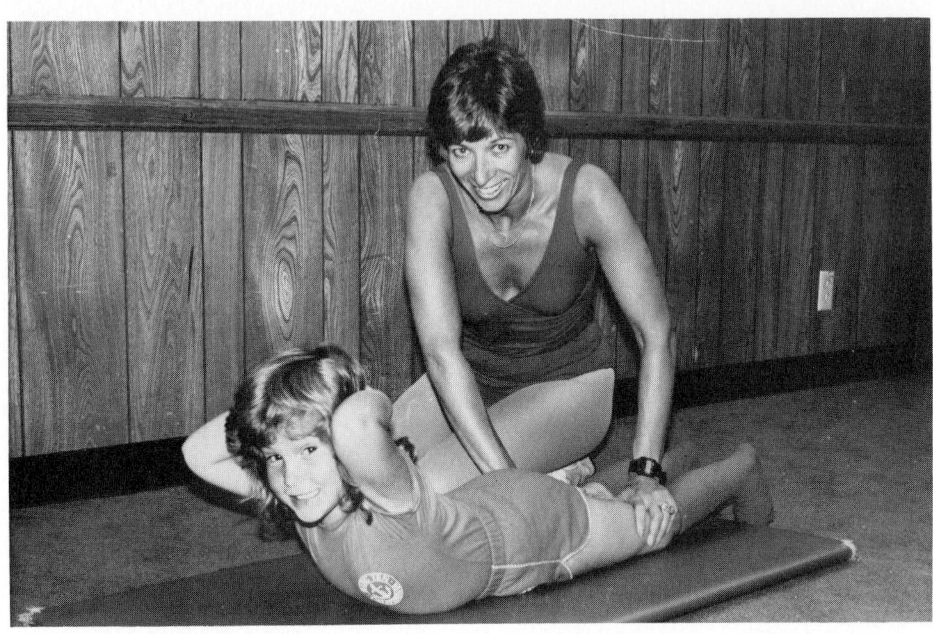

Kraus-Weber Test #5: Lower Back Muscles Are Being Tested.

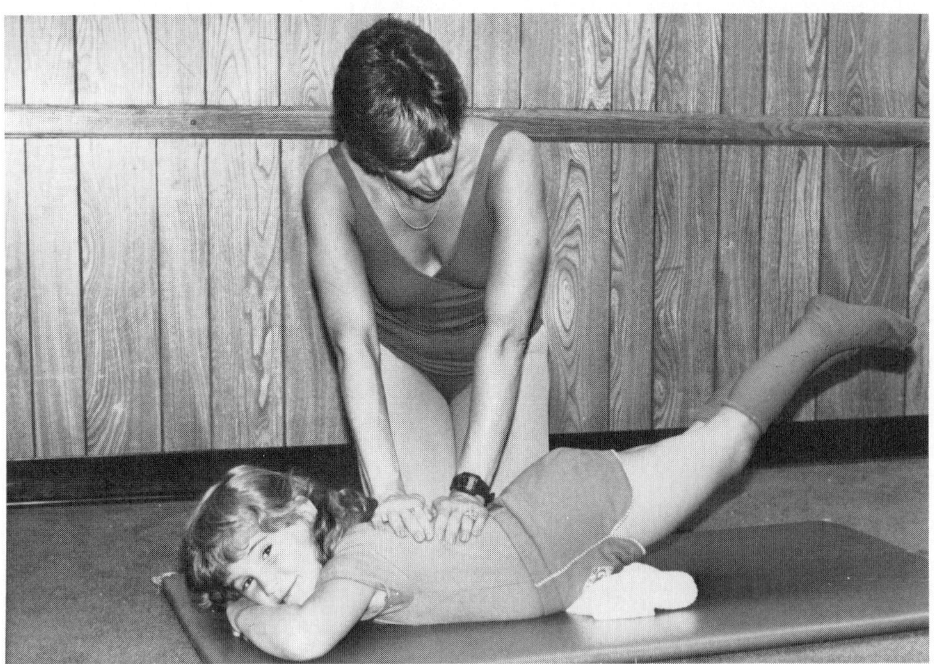

Kraus-Weber Test #6: Flexibility of Back Muscles and Hamstrings Are Tested.

required to lift your feet so that the heels are ten inches above the floor. You must keep this position for ten seconds. Test One indicates the strength of the hip flexors.

Test Two is similar to Test One; once again you lie on your back on the floor with hands clasped behind head. Another individual should hold your ankles. The test is passed if you can roll up into a sitting position—just once. The test shows whether hip flexors and stomach muscles combined can handle your body weight.

In *Test Three* you assume the same position, but this time the knees are bent and the heels are placed close to the buttocks. With your ankles held down, you must roll up into a sitting position. Stomach muscle strength is thus tested.

In *Test Four* you lie on your stomach with a small pillow or a rolled towel under your abdomen. You clasp your hands behind the neck and have someone else place a hand on the small of the back and on the ankles to hold you steady. Now you lift your upper trunk off of the floor and hold that position for ten seconds. Back muscle strength is tested in this way.

In *Test Five* you retain the same position, on the stomach with the pillow under the abdomen, and have someone else hold your back with two hands to keep you steady. Now you lift your legs, keeping the knees straight and holding the position for ten seconds. Lower back muscles are tested with this maneuver.

In *Test Six* you stand up straight and without bending your knees and with feet together, you lean over and touch the floor with your finger tips. This tests the flexibility of the back muscles and the hamstrings. (The hamstrings are those muscles in the back of the thighs.)

The Kraus-Weber tests were designed for all age groups and reveal whether the key muscle groups of the body can handle body weight and have the flexibility to match the body's height. In 1952 when these tests were administered to children ages six to sixteen all over the world, American youth had the highest failure rate (57.9 per cent). Italian youth had the lowest failure rate (8 per cent); Swiss students had an overall 8.8 per cent; Japan 15 per cent (Prudden, 1965; Kraus, 1969).

RESEARCH FINDINGS

Using the six Kraus-Weber tests, a physical fitness pretest-posttest evaluation of 388 elementary students in grades 2–4 was performed to evaluate the YMCA Feelin' Good Program in Van Nuys, California.

At the second-grade level, 30 per cent passed all six tests on the posttest as compared to 8 per cent on the pretest.

At the third-grade level, 36 per cent passed all six tests on the posttest as compared to 12 per cent on the pretest.

At the fourth-grade level, 50 percent passed all six tests on the posttest as compared to 16 per cent on the pretest.

The pass rate for American youth ages 6 to 16 in 1952 was 42.1 per cent (Lemlech & Wood, 1982).

APPLICATION OF RESEARCH

To reduce the risk of coronary heart disease, elementary children should be involved in physical education programs and sports that provide opportunities for vigorous participation. (Gilliam, 1978)

It is perhaps interesting to note that malnutrition and poverty are prevalent in Guatemala and India, a fact that certainly may account for their students' poor showing. But what was our excuse? Bucher (1975) found that approximately 60 per cent of our students do not participate in a vigorous physical education program on a daily basis. Only 28 per cent of our schools have an adequate health and physical education program, and only 8 per cent of our elementary schools have gymnasiums.

Upon learning the results of the Kraus-Weber studies, President Eisenhower created the President's Council on Youth Fitness; Kennedy continued the work of the Council but changed its name to the President's Council on Physical Fitness; President Lyndon Johnson changed the name once again. This time it was called the President's Council on Physical Fitness and Sports. The Council under the direction of Charles B. Wilkinson, who was appointed by Kennedy, developed and organized a program of physical fitness for the schools. Excerpts of the basic beliefs advocated by the Council (1971) include:

- Daily programs for K–12 children emphasizing physical fitness and sports skills
- Regular vigorous exercise during school years
- Mastery of skills to participate safely in sports
- Knowledge of the relationship of activities to lifelong health; basic elements of the physiology of exercise; continuing activities throughout life to be stressed; development of desirable attitudes concerning the values of participation in vigorous activities
- Adapted physical education offered for students with special needs
- Programs planned to include physiological fitness goals and educational aims to meet the developmental needs of students; activities adapted to individual needs in order to increase energy utilization and heart rate
- Developmental and conditioning activities, appropriately sequenced and planned at each grade level
- Continuing supervision by family physician and dentist as well as by school personnel; health appraisal procedures implemented.

The Youth Fitness Test Project was initiated in 1957 by the American Alliance for Health, Physical Education, and Recreation (AAHPER). Directed by Paul Hunsicker, the first national fitness survey was published in 1958. Results confirmed what the worldwide Kraus-Weber tests had indicated: American youth ages 10–17 were not physically fit as compared to children in other nations.

In 1963 a second survey was initiated to see if there was any improvement in physical performance by American youth. Slight improvement in the national norms was obtained in six of the seven tests. The tests included: pull-ups (boys only), straight leg sit-ups, shuttle run, standing broad jump, 50-yard dash, and 600-yard run-walk. The softball throw for girls was eliminated (Hunsicker & Rieff, 1975).

In 1975 Hunsicker once again undertook a national follow-up survey using the six-item fitness test. The norms for 1975 showed no significant difference with those established in 1965. In interpreting the results, Holbrook (1977) found them disappointing. Holbrook's conclusions indicated two possibilities: (1) fitness levels of school-aged children may be maintained at the 1965 level, but it may not be possible to improve performance beyond that level; (2) school physical education programs were *not* sustained at the 1965 levels. Holbrook was not able to support either conjecture.

Physical education is required by 46 states. Not all of the 46 states require it in grades 1–12. In California elementary schools, physical education is required to be taught for 200 minutes every ten days. The purpose of this provision is to encourage flexibility for program planning. The AAHPER recommends that elementary students participate in an instructional program for 150 minutes per week. In 1974, New York adopted a plan requiring 120 minutes per week (Grover, 1975). Ideally students should participate in a planned exercise program five days per week; however, most surveys of the schools seem to indicate that the median number of days for physical education is three.

Health and Physical Education Programs

Health and physical education are interrelated and need to be coordinated in order to attain a complete school and community health program. Foundation disciplines for both subjects come from the life sciences, medical sciences, physical sciences, and the social sciences (Michaelis et al., 1975). Content for both subjects is organized in the following way:

Physical Education

- Self-testing Activities
  - Physical Fitness Activities
  - Movement patterns and Skills
  - Stunts
  - Tumbling
  - Use of Apparatus
- Games
  - Sport Activities (individual and team)
  - Lead-up Activities
  - Games and Relays
- Rhythms
  - Creative and Dance Activities
- Aquatics

Health Education

- Personal and Family Health
- Emotional and Mental Health
- Community Health
- Environmental Health
- Diseases and Disorders
- Safety and Accident Prevention
- Nutrition
- Use and Misuse of Tobacco, Alcohol, Drugs, Narcotics.

Physical and health education programs emphasize the development and maintenance of total body fitness. To medical specialists fitness means freedom from disease. To social scientists, particularly psychologists, fitness has to do with mental health; physical educators describe fitness in terms of the individual's physical performance. The physical educator determines fitness by testing muscular strength, muscular endurance, flexibility, circulo-respiratory endurance, and body weight and composition.

Both subjects are taught as separate lessons and as integrated lessons within other subjects such as language arts, science, and social studies. Incidental learning, unrelated to a particular health or physical education unit, can be provided advantageously. For example, when the first graders were studying about light and color (described in Chapter 6), health instruction focused on light and posture for reading and the care of the eyes. Health and physical education lessons may come about as a consequence of safety needs, class discussions, school or community concerns.

Purposes of Physical and Health Education

Physical Education

While the basic purpose of physical education is to provide students with movement experiences, the underlying goal is optimal growth and development consistent with each individual's characteristics, interests, and abilities. Physical education experiences should be of a developmental nature so that students progress competently. Physical education goals as defined by the *California Physical Education Framework* (1973, p. 38) include:

1. *Motor skills.* To develop efficient and effective motor skills and to understand the principles involved and to develop an appreciation for the aesthetic quality of movement.
2. *Physical fitness.* To develop and maintain the best possible level of performance, understanding, and appreciation for physical fitness to meet the demands of wholesome living and emergency situations.
3. *Self-image.* To develop a positive self-image which includes awareness and understanding of the performance of one's body, the use of the body as an important means of expression, and the body as an instrument for self-realization.
4. *Social behavior.* To develop socially desirable behavior involving movement in interactions with others.
5. *Recreational interest.* To develop interest and proficiency in using the skills essential for successful participation in worthwhile physical recreation activities.

Health Education

The purpose of health education is to prepare students to accept responsibility for applying health principles in their daily lives and to promote family and community health. Health education should develop positive habits and patterns that enhance healthful ways of living. Goals include:

a. Self-awareness so that students develop a positive self-concept
b. Decision making so that students recognize health problems and seek positive solutions
c. Coping action so that students can adapt to their environment and manage life problems by participating effectively in social situations (Los Angeles Unified School District, 1979).

How Are Physical Education Goals Developed?

Motor Skill Development

Movement abilities advance in a sequential manner. Gallahue et al. (1975, p. 6) identified six stages from simple to complex movements:

- Reflexive behavior—infancy to 1 year
- Rudimentary movement abilities—0–2 years
- Fundamental movement patterns—preschool to 7 years
- General movement skills—8–10 years
- Specific movement skills—11–13 years
- Specialized movement skills—14-adulthood.

Children's movement abilities are progressive: while each phase is distinct, the child may be advancing through more than one phase at a time. Motor skills may be categorized within three sets of movement activities: stabilizing activities, locomotor activities, and manipulative activities. Students improve in these categories of movement through practice. At school this practice is mediated through the content of physical education (self-testing activities, games and sports, rhythms, aquatics). As in other subjects of the curriculum, the teacher's task is to sequence learning experiences appropriate to the students' developmental levels. Primary students (K–2) need basic movement experiences for each of the categories of movement; middle- and upper-grade students need both general and specific movement skills within each category of movement.

Stabilizing Activities

Maintenance of stability is considered the most basic of all human movements. Although we may place our body in a variety of positions which may include axial movements and varied postures, the trick is to control equilibrium. Both locomotion and manipulative activities are dependent upon stability.

Stabilizing movements are those in which the body maintains balance, changes posture, and/or engages in axial movements. Stability includes axial movements and postures. Axial movements are those which involve the trunk or limbs. Postures are concerned with the maintenance of balance. Examples of axial movements include bending, turning, stretching, swinging. Examples of postures include standing, rolling, stooping, dodging.

Problems with Stabilizing Movements

While each movement may have special problems for an individual based on individual characteristics or abilities, teachers need to be aware of these more typical problems.

1. Most individuals need to see a movement performed before they can perform it.
2. Lack of flexibility will affect the performance of the movement.
3. Concentration on performance is necessary.
4. Controlled movements, as opposed to jerky, ballistic type movements, need to be stressed.
5. Speed is difficult to develop, and changing tempo during a performance is difficult for many individuals.
6. Maintenance of balance causes difficulty.

Locomotor Activities

Locomotor movements are progressive and involve the body in changing its position relative to fixed points on the ground. Locomotor activities include running, walking, hopping, skipping, jumping, climbing, leaping, galloping, sliding.

Typical Problems With Locomotor Activities

Teachers need to be alert to the following types of problems:

1. Students need to be able to alter their performance based upon circumstances peculiar to the movement situation. For example, a faster or slower pace by others means that the student must be flexible in order to change the original movement.
2. Locomotor activities are often combined with stabilizing or manipulative movements and may cause difficulty because of the combined movements.
3. Students sometimes exaggerate arm or leg movements.
4. Rhythm needs to be established for most movements.
5. Some students have difficulty alternating feet and using both sides of the body; it is difficult for some students to begin a movement with both feet.
6. When running, some students tend to land on heels first; some students tend to run on toes only.

APPLICATION OF RESEARCH

Lack of flexibility contributes to accidents. Teachers need to plan a variety of activities to develop muscular flexibility. Increased flexibility may prevent injuries as students get older (deVries, 1966).

Manipulative Activities

Manipulative movements involve giving or receiving force to and from objects. Activities include kicking, striking, throwing, catching, bouncing, rolling, trapping, volleying. These activities are dependent upon locomotor and stabilizing movements. Manipulative activities combine one or more movements (locomotor and/or stabilizing) and use those movements together with other movements. For example, in throwing an underhand toss, the performer must assume a stable position with one foot ahead of the other, bend slightly, project the ball forward and upward, release the ball, and follow through with arms in the direction of the propelled ball. Manipulative movements are more difficult than stabilizing or locomotor movements and are dependent upon the performer's understanding and integration of space, time, force, and flow.

In teaching manipulative movements, the teacher needs to be aware of and anticipate the following problems:

Typical Manipulative Problems

1. Students do not develop proper follow-through in movements.

2. Timing—the object is released too soon or too late.
3. Position of feet—some students tend to place feet together instead of one ahead of the other when throwing or kicking.
4. Some students have difficulty shifting their weight as they kick, trap, or throw.
5. Lack of coordination of arms and body movement due to poor rhythm causes a problem for some students.
6. The failure to maintain balance when throwing or kicking is a typical problem.
7. Maintenance of eye contact with target when catching, trapping, or kicking is a common problem.

If you were the teacher, what three things would you teach students about maintaining their balance?

Physical Fitness

The interrelationship between health education and physical education is most apparent in the shared goal of total fitness. Total fitness encompasses fitness for play and exercise and fitness for learning and appreciating life. Sherrill (1977, p. 210) identified ten factors that contribute to *low* fitness:

(1) obesity, (2) underweight, (3) asthma and other chronic respiratory problems, (4) susceptibility to infectious diseases including the common cold, (5) poor nutrition, (6) inadequate sleep, (7) a lifestyle which does not encompass physical exercise, (8) a repugnance toward perspiration, dirt, wind, and other environmental factors surrounding physical activity, (9) fear of failure and/or embarrassment, and (10) a genetic predisposition toward low fitness.

The YMCA "Feelin' Good" project (Kuntzleman, 1978) is an example of a unified approach to teaching about fitness. This program is taught in selected elementary schools by YMCA personnel. The program is comprised of two components: a classroom instructional component, which focuses on health education, and an activity component, which emphasizes cardiovascular fitness. The "Y" instructors integrate both the health and physical components of the program so that students appreciate the interrelationship of nutrition, good health practices, and exercise.

The *Physical Education Framework* (California State Department of Education, 1973) identifies five basic components of physical fitness: (1) muscular strength; (2) muscular endurance; (3) muscular explosive power; (4) cardiorespiratory endurance; (5) flexibility.

APPLICATION OF RESEARCH

Boys exhibit less flexibility than girls, but this is not due to anatomical differences. Flexibility diminishes due to a lack of activity (Gallahue, 1976).

Muscular strength, endurance, and explosive power are to be developed through participation in developmental exercises using apparatus such as rings, horizontal bar, horizontal ladder, and without equipment performing push-ups, sit-ups, and the standing long jump.

Cardiorespiratory endurance is to be developed through participation in activities which are of a continuous and vigorous nature. Suggested activities include rope jumping, continuous exercises to music, rhythmic actions, running, jumping, and hopping.

Flexibility can be developed through stretching, bending, twisting, stopping, and squatting exercises, and through movements which involve a total range of motion for specific body joints.

Agility, speed, and balance are important fitness components to be developed through exercises, rhythms, games, rope jumping, sprinting, use of kinesthetic sense, body control exercises, and stabilization of body weight over the center of gravity.

An appreciation of fitness along with knowledge about fitness should be developed through planned

Strength, Coordination and Balance Are Taught Through Individual and Partner Stunts.

lessons emphasizing the importance of sleep, rest, nutrition, and physiology of exercise. The California Framework (1973) stresses that students should be guided "in the development of self-discipline, mental toughness, pain tolerance, and goal attainment."

Self-Image

The goal of a positive self-concept can be fostered by providing students with opportunities to learn about self and about others, to learn to face adversity, and to overcome problems. Self-image is enhanced through planned experiences and opportunities:

- to learn about the body, its parts and functions
- to perform physical movements in a successful manner appropriate to individual characteristics, interests, and abilities
- to understand and accept personal capabilities and limitations
- to explore movements
- to experiment and to be physically challenged
- to express ideas and emotions through body movement and physical exercise
- to choose, to demonstrate, and to satisfy personal skills and recreational interests.

APPLICATION OF RESEARCH

Teachers' comments may serve to stereotype sex roles. Ulrich (1973, p. 113) noted that teachers typically designate boys to move equipment. Stereotyping include "some girls can hit baseballs as well as boys."

Certain customs in elementary classrooms can have a negative effect on the self-concept. Frequently upper-grade students are allowed to elect captains and choose teams. The student who is not well coordinated will be the last one to be selected with the natural psychological consequence to the child's ego. The following excerpt describes an incident in a fourth-grade classroom where the teacher anticipated the problem and found a way to develop a student's self-concept and promote social behavior (Lemlech, 1979, pp. 238–239).

Drew was considered the best athlete in the fourth grade. The children in his classroom consistently chose him for captain. After the election process, Drew and the other three captains would go through the formality of selecting their teams. If asked, Ms. Wellesly, the fourth-grade teacher, could have listed the order in which each child would be chosen, and that was precisely what was troubling her. She knew that Ben would be the last to be selected because out on the playground he was uncoordinated. Ben seemed to be going through a trying period; he did quite well in the classroom, but then his ego seemed destroyed when he came in from recess or lunch.

Ms. Wellesly decided to delay the selection process until later in the day so that she could think about the situation. Sometimes she had the captains use the attendance cards and select their teams outside, away from the class, in order to spare hurt feelings; yet as soon as the teams were written on the board, the students would know instinctively who had been chosen first and who had been chosen last.

As she watched the children work on their spelling, she observed that Ben was quizzing Drew. She saw Ben shake his head as Drew made a mistake; she went closer and heard Ben tell Drew a trick for remembering the word. Drew nodded and said, "Hmm, I think that will help. Thanks, Ben."

It occurred to Ms. Wellesly that the two boys worked well together and seemed to have a genuine friendship, yet they were rarely together on the playground because of Drew's physical prowess. Ms. Wellesly decided to talk to Drew. She asked him if he had ever wanted to do something and had tried very hard but had failed because he lacked the necessary skills. Drew recalled that he had wanted to ski with his older brother but had been unable to do so. Ms. Wellesly then explained how much Ben wanted to do well in sports and that he needed someone to have confidence in him and to assist him.

Drew confided that he really liked Ben and felt sorry for him when he wasn't selected for a team. "Ben helps me a lot in class. Do you think he would really like me to try to help him on the field?" The teacher assured the boy that Ben would be "pleased."

Just before lunch Ms. Wellesly settled the class, called the captains to the front, and said, "OK, now is the time to choose your teams."

When it was Drew's turn to make his first selection, he said, "I want Ben to be on my team." Ben was shocked, but he walked to the front to stand next to Drew, as was the custom. Drew put his arm around Ben's shoulders and whispered, "Who shall I choose next, Ben?"

Physical education offers rare opportunities to develop both self-image and social behavior. Ms. Wellesly modeled both humanistic and respectful behavior. Students imitate teacher behavior; in the preceding episode Drew modeled compassion.

Social Behavior

Play activities serve to help the child move from egocentric behavior to social behavior. During the primary-grade years, students play most cooperatively with a single partner or in a small group. As physical skills improve, students can play in small groups and in teams. Competitive play during the middle-grade years is enjoyed by students; however, students should compete with others of similar ability rather than with older students or adults. Successful group behavior occurs when students have opportunities to be both a group leader and a group participant.

Social behavior can be developed by providing opportunities for students to assume leadership responsibility. Students can be score keepers, umpires, referees, and play leaders for younger children. They can be in charge of equipment; they can demonstrate and teach specific skills to a friend or a small group of students, and they can be team leaders.

As group members they can demonstrate cooperative behavior and good sportsmanship. They can offer encouragement to others by their own participation and by praising others. They can accept responsibility for their own behavior.

Recreational Interest

It is quite natural to develop interest in activities where there is some proficiency and in activities that are particularly enjoyable. Physical education activities can be extremely satisfying to students when a relaxed atmosphere is created for participation. Activities that are paced so that students experience a "warm-up," a period of vigorous exercise, and a period of "cool-down" will usually result in relieving classroom stress and providing students with a feeling of ease and good health.

Teachers can help students identify play areas for after-school participation (parks, playgrounds, community facilities), and encourage students to suggest appropriate games and sports for after-school recreation.

How Are Health Education Goals Developed?

School health programs encompass health guidance, health instruction, and the development of a healthful school environment. Health guidance begins with obtaining a health history when the child first enters school. Information concerning immunization, school rules about attendance, vision and hearing screening tests are usually performed in a preschool admission program. Health guidance continues throughout the elementary years.

Teacher observation of students should be performed daily. Teachers are often the first to detect signs of illness and signs of child abuse. Teachers along with other members of the school staff (doctors, nurses, principal) should prepare reports and solicit cooperative assistance from other social agencies to ensure the health of the child.

A healthful school environment includes teaching about sanitation and the use of school facilities such as the drinking fountains, the lavatories, and the cafeteria, and the maintenance of a healthful classroom environment. Students are asked to accept responsibility for:

- opening windows to provide appropriate ventilation
- controlling lights and window shades to provide for visual health
- emptying trash
- placing clothing and lunches in the proper place
- washing hands before meals and after bathrooming
- maintaining the classroom so that it is orderly and attractive.

Health instruction goals are accomplished by expanding the students' awareness from self to family to others. Development of awareness begins as the student shares his/her own feelings of "wellness." The primary-aged student is helped to differentiate between health and illness. Knowledge about individual needs for rest, sleep, and relaxation are introduced during the primary grades.

Nutrition and dental care are emphasized throughout the grades, and teaching strategies focus on providing students with food choices and consumer information about food nutrients appropriate to their grade level.

Food choices influenced by culture and ethnicity are featured in the health program so that students learn to accept and understand other students' likes and dislikes.

Fitness and cardiovascular health are developed by teaching about the body and how it works, and physical activity is related to the increase of pulse and breathing rates. The school nurse along with the classroom teacher may provide fitness counseling and guidance in order to develop positive attitudes about fitness and exercise.

Family and community health problems focus on student responsibility for maintaining personal good health. The value of regular health and dental care is advocated, and the utilization of community health resources is encouraged. Students may be asked to demonstrate ways that the family takes responsibility for good health practices. Laws affecting health practices are studied, and the responsibilities of health agencies are identified.

Heredity and genetic disorders are studied during the upper grades. Students learn to differentiate between the effects of environment and heredity on human organisms, and knowledge of the traits that are inherited are studied and contrasted to those traits that are acquired.

Mental and emotional health goals are developed by providing opportunities for students to make decisions and learn to cope with stress and anxiety. Through the realization that a person feels better when feelings of happiness, anger, and frustration are expressed, students learn to analyze the positive and negative aspects of stress.

The health program is responsible for providing instruction about alcohol, drugs, narcotics, and tobacco and relating the use and misuse of these substances to family and community health. Responsibility of individuals in the prevention of the misuse of these substances is the focus of instruction.

Disease prevention and control are studied during health education. Often community resource people are invited to the school for special programming. The school shares responsibility with the community for providing information about communicable diseases and ways to control such diseases. Through the education of the children, parents can be encouraged to use immunization programs and other preventive measures. Students can also be instructed in self-observation for symptoms of illness, and instruction can focus on microorganisms that cause or affect the spread of communicable diseases.

Environmental studies are integrated with both social studies and science. Students learn about ecological conditions that affect the environment and how a healthful environment affects the quality of life. Water, soil, air, and noise pollution are appropriate areas of study to develop understanding that living things are interdependent with others and the environment. The conservation of human resources along with natural resources may be integrated into a health/science unit to develop understanding that people can control, change, and improve the environment for the benefit of all.

How Is Physical Education Taught?

Planning

Planning physical education instruction should be based on the purposes to be accomplished and the students' characteristics, interests, and abilities. Unit planning for instruction is appropriate in physical education just as it is in other subject fields. Greg Thomas developed weekly plans for physical education, and whenever possible he correlated his physical education activities with other subject fields. For example, since he used the water unit (see Appendix) with his students and taught them the Israeli song "Mayim," he also taught them the dance called "Mayim" that required learning the grapevine, running step, and hop (Hall et al., 1980, p. 157).

> If you were the teacher, would you mainstream handicapped children in physical education? Why?

Thomas' students were learning to play softball. The students were organized into four teams. The students knew the rules and were in their second week of a three-week unit on softball. On Monday Thomas worked with teams A & B to practice batting, catching, throwing, and running skills. Team A was in the field. Four students played first and second bases, shortstop and catcher; the other students positioned themselves in the field. Team B was lined up at home plate using a batting tee to hit the ball. The students in the field rotated positions practicing throwing and catching, and the students at home plate each had three turns batting and running to first or second base. To teach more effective base running, Thomas had placed cones on first and second bases so that the students would try to increase their rate and their efficiency. Thomas stood near first base coaching the catching, throwing, and batting. He also timed the batter in the batter's run to first base. On Tuesday he would

Working with a Partner and a Dowling Makes Stretching Hamstrings Fun.

TABLE 10.1. Weekly Schedule for Fifth-Grade Physical Education.

Monday	Tuesday	Wednesday	Thursday	Friday
Teams A & B	A & B Softball	Exercise Relays		
Skills Work-up;				
Batting,			Individual and Partner Stunts:	Square Dancing
Catching,		(Whole Class)	1. Russian Dance	1. All-Amer, Promenade
Throwing			2. Turnover	2. Mayim
Running			3. Rooster Fight	3. Virginia Reel
Teams C & D	C & D	Exercise Relays		
Softball	Skills Work-up			

provide the same instruction for teams C and D, while teams A and B played an actual game of softball.

On Wednesday the whole class would participate in exercise relays. Thomas would draw three lines on the playground 15, 30, and 45 feet in front of the start/finish line. The teams would be in four lines. Each team member would perform three exercises: one on the 15-foot spot, another on the 30-foot spot, and the third on the 45-foot mark. The player would then run back to the starting line and tag the next person on the team. The exercises chosen by Thomas were sit-ups, jumping jacks, and half knee bends.*

[1] The relay suggestions were adapted from Charles T. Kuntzleman and Beth A. Kuntzleman, *Fitness With Fun* (Spring Arbor, Mich.: Arbor Press, 1978) 102–110.

Use of the Apparatus Promotes the Development of Flexibility, Agility, Endurance, and Coordination. Students Need to Be Taught Body Control, Balance, Posture, and Safety Skills.

On Thursday Thomas would teach individual and partner stunts. He would borrow resting mats from the kindergarten rooms for use in this activity. He chose the V-Seat exercise, the Russian Dance, the Rooster Fight, and the Double Bear (See Hall et al., 1980, and Kuntzleman & Kuntzleman, 1978).

On Friday the students would use the auditorium and Greg would teach rhythms. The selected

TABLE 10.2. Weekly Schedule for Third-Grade Physical Education.

Monday	Tuesday	Wednesday	Thursday	Friday
½ Class Apparatus Teach Skip Ring Travel on Horizontal Ladder		½ Class Teach Catching, Throwing, and Kicking Skills		
——	(Teams reverse Monday's activities)		(Teams reverse Wednesday's activities)	
½ Class Small Group Skill Games Ishigetigoko Jumping Fancy Duck on the Rock		½ Class Play Kickball		Rhythms Whole Class

dances correlated with the social studies and the science units. Each week, Thomas taught one new dance and practiced two familiar routines. He would allow the students to select another dance when time allowed.

Teacher-Directed Instruction

Mary Hogan's students enjoyed playing sockball and kickball, but Mary observed that they needed to improve in catching, pitching the kickball, and kicking. She planned a skills work-up session for half the class on Monday and the other half on Tuesday. Before going out to the playground Mary explained to the students where she wanted them to stand while she demonstrated the skills, so that they would be able to see and hear her. Half the students were assigned to play a game of sockball; the other half would receive the skill instruction. Once out on the playground, she demonstrated the correct performance for catching, pitching, and kicking. She emphasized how to hold the hands for catching, how to focus on the ball as it approached, the position of the feet for pitching, and the correct follow-through for kicking. Then she set the students up in groups of four and helped each group establish a drill formation to practice the skills. As the students practiced, Hogan observed them and assisted those students who were having difficulty. Throughout the drill session she encouraged the children to proceed quickly. She praised them and gave them instructions: "Watch the ball"; "Look at the target", "Extend your fingers"; "Follow through".

Hogan's directed lesson had the following components:

1. *Instruction*
   Organization instructions;
   instructions about skills to be taught.
2. *Demonstration*
   Hogan demonstrated the skills to be practiced.
3. *Practice Period*
   The students had the opportunity to practice the skills that were demonstrated.
4. *Reinforcement* (Evaluation)
   As the students practiced, their teacher encouraged them and offered suggestions for the improvement of their performance.

Hogan was careful to offer only positive feedback. If Mary Hogan had not been satisfied with the students' performance then she would have repeated steps 2–4.

Student Exploration

"How many boys and girls know how to play hopscotch? (Students respond *yea!* and *nay!*). Good, let's all get up and show each other movements for playing hopscotch."

Greg Thomas observed the students as they jumped on two feet and did some hopping. He noted that many of the students had difficulty landing on two feet simultaneously, and very few could move from the two-footed jump to a one-footed hop.

Thomas chose several students to demonstrate the jump and the hop; then he suggested that all the students try once again. This time he suggested that they jump and then hop on the left foot. Next he had them practice jumping and hopping on the right foot.

After the students had practiced, he asked them which had been easier, the right- or the left-footed hop. The students discussed the movements and decided that much depended upon whether or not they were right-handed or left-handed. (Thomas followed up with a lesson on dominance in their health books.)

Children (and adults) learn more effectively when there is an opportunity to experiment (explore) with the movements involved. After experimenting with the movement, the students begin to watch others to see if they could correct their own performance. Thomas observed his students to detect when it would be appropriate to demonstrate the desired skill. He was careful to allow the students to move through the exploration

For Some Students Hopscotch Is Difficult.

stage and be motivated for a demonstration. His sequence of instruction was as follows:

1. Experimentation (exploration)
2. Observation of others
3. Demonstration by others
4. Practice
5. Evaluation

RESEARCH FINDINGS

Public school children like contact sports: judo, boxing, wrestling, karate.
Private school children prefer noncontact sports: swimming, skiing, tennis, golf (Seefeldt and Haubenstricker, 1978).

The advantage of the indirect approach used by Thomas is that it allows students to satisfy their own needs, curiosity, and creativity, and decide upon their own actions. It is less structured than the directed instruction lesson even though Thomas suggested the movements for exploration.

Small Group Activities

Dividing students into small groups, squads, or teams is advantageous in physical education because it allows students greater participation and less waiting for turns. A variety of activities can be planned so that all of the groups do not need equipment for play. For example, primary students may be grouped so that one group is playing on the apparatus, another group is involved in a circle game that requires a ball, and a third group is participating in stunts and skills. The activities can be rotated during the class period or on successive days. The small group strategy allows the teacher to provide individualized instruction to a small group of students who are able to see and hear and respond to the teacher. Instruction to a large group on the playground sometimes involves management problems. Mary Hogan chose small-group skill games when she was teaching half her class an apparatus skill.

Skill Instruction

Students do not necessarily learn a skill just because they play a game that requires the skill.

Skills need to be taught, *and* they need to be practiced. The movement skills described earlier in the chapter are developmental; the student must learn to maintain balance, change direction, adjust to environmental problems. The student's safety may be dependent upon the movement skills learned at school.

The teacher's task is to demonstrate the desired skill or have it demonstrated by students who perform the skill correctly. When observing students practicing the skill, it is important to observe whether the students are implementing the key elements involved in the skill. The third task is to provide feedback to correct the student's performance or to reinforce correct achievement.

1. Model the Skill
2. Skill Practice
3. Feedback

Skill instruction can begin as an exploration lesson or as a direct instructional lesson.

Physical Education Instruction in the Classroom

There are many occasions when it is more propitious to teach physical education inside the classroom. This may be necessitated by inclement weather or by students' physical need for activity. Typically, physical education in the classroom has meant low-involvement activities that provide teacher and students with a change from the normal routine, but nothing vigorous enough to elevate the pulse rate. There is nothing wrong with choosing low-intensity activities for the classroom; however, when students sit for several hours during the school day, they will feel more alert and more joyful if they are involved in activities that require muscular strength and endurance and aerobic exercise.

There are many movements that can be taught inside the classroom to help students relieve tension by stretching, exercising vigorously, and then relaxing to prepare them for academic study. The following classroom episode will suggest appropriate movements for achieving physical fitness goals. (Numbers designate movements)

T.: We're going to do some warm-ups. Spread out so that you are not touching anyone else,

(1) Let's reach up first. Come on—way up. Way up. Arms overhead—stretching. OK. Good. Like you're picking apples. Make yourself taller. Stay up there. Keep your arms up high. Super.

(2) Now let's make big circles with our arms. Good. Take a big breath. Inhale. Let the breath out through your mouth. Continue to make big circles. (You're not getting tired already!)

(3) All right. Reverse the circles with your arms. Backswim.

(4) Now, let's all push our right arm out across our body to the left. Good. Come on press the palm of your hand out, like you're pressing the wall. Good. Now let's use the other arm and move to the right. Press. Press.

(Six major muscle groups *should* be warmed up before vigorous exercise: Neck, Shoulders, Arms, Hips, Legs, Ankles.)

(5) Now let's go back and forth. Press with the right arm, palm out; Press with the left arm, palm out. Bend forward as you press.

(6) Let's do some shoulder lifts. Come on, shrug your shoulders; Life them up and down. Shake them loose.

(7) Now, with your legs straight and feet apart, bend forward from the hips. Pretend that you are swimming. Swim to the front. Good. Now let's swim to the right. Good. Now swim to the left. Keep your legs straight. We're doing great.

(8) Put your hands on your hips and let's do a half knee bend. This way. Good. Let's do a few of these.

(9) All right, now do a deep squat and place the palms of your hands on the floor. Good. Isn't this fun? Hold the position.

(10) Now slowly straighten your legs. Keep your hands on the floor. Good. Can you bend and straighten? Bend; straighten. Keep your hands on the floor.

(11) Now, slowly, with your head down, come up to a standing position. Keep your head down until the very end. Wow, that's good!

(Note that the teacher made only positive and encouraging comments.)

Movement #7: The Dry Swim Is a Good Warm-up Stretch Movement.

Movement #9: The Squat Is Used to Warm-up the Lower Body.

(12) Now let's do some leg lifts. Lift your right leg straight—and try to touch it with your left hand. Now lift your left leg and touch it with your right hand. Move your arms up and down with your legs. That's the way.

(13) Now we're going to march in place and lift our knees high. Oh, very good. I like the way you are doing that. Now that we're warmed up, I'm going to put some music on.

(14) Let's play hopscotch. Jump with two feet just as if you were jumping into two boxes. Now hop on your right foot as if it were a single box. Now jump on two feet and hop on the right foot again.

(15) Now let's change the pattern and jump with two feet and then hop on our left foot. Good. Keep doing it. That's the way. Is this difficult?

(16) Now see if you can do this. Jump on two feet and hop on the right foot. Then jump on two feet and hop on the left foot. Keep alternating the feet for the hop. Good. I see people doing it easily. Listen to the music. Should we be doing this fast or slow?

(Vigorous exercise should follow the warm-up period.)

(17) OK, bend your upper torso forward and pretend that you are running. Make your arms do the running. Wow are we going fast! Good.

(18) Now make your arms go from side to side. Keep your torso bent forward. Good.

(19) Now we're going to jog in place. Make your arms push out toward your neighbor. Push. Push. Keep your arms pushing while you jog. Good. Now push with your arms down. Push. Push. Now push with your arms in front of you. Push. Push.

(20) Now, boys and girls, let's use our chairs. Hold on to the back of the chair. Let's do some more knee bends. Not all the way down, just half way. Good.

(21) Now, holding on to the seat of the chair, lift your left leg behind you. Good. Lift. Lift. Keep doing it. Now lift your right leg. Lift. Lift. Lift.

(22) Now sit down on your chairs. Don't lean back. (Are you tired? *Noooo.*) Hold on to the seat of the chair and let's make our feet jump up and down. Good. (Not so loud!) Now, jump from side to side. Only your legs are moving. Pretend that the floor is hot.

(23) Jump with your legs only, but turn your toes in. (Still seated) Jump. Jump. Good. Now turn your toes out. Jump. Jump.

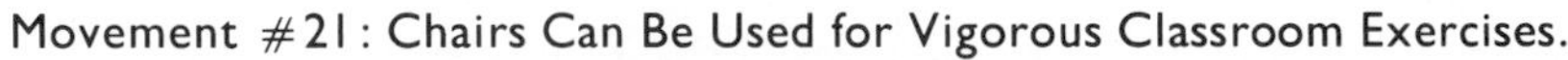

Movement #21: Chairs Can Be Used for Vigorous Classroom Exercises.

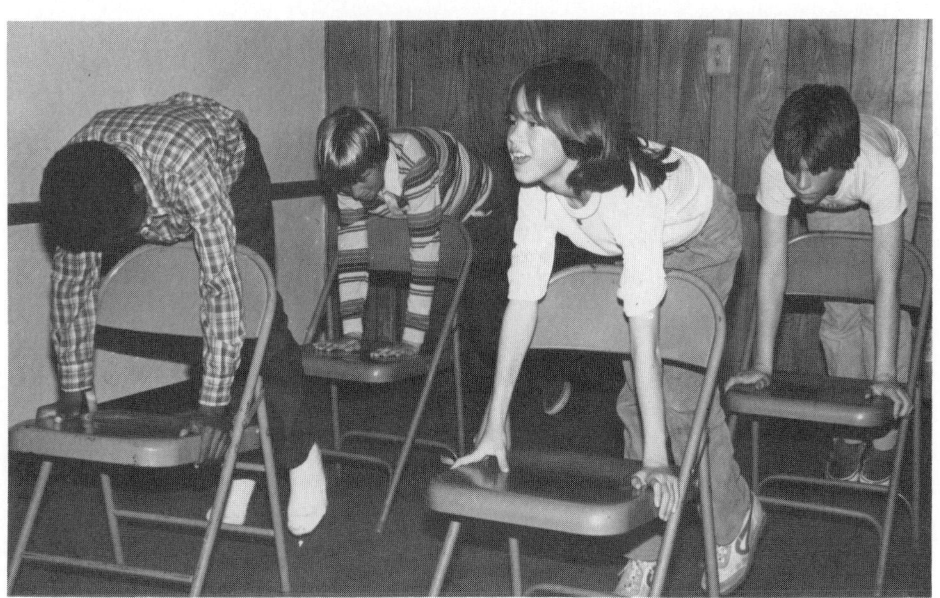

(24) Now lift your legs and put your knees together. (Still seated) As you move your legs to the right, move your arms to the left. Now swing, back and forth, legs to the left, arms to the right. Keep moving.
(25) All right, let's all go to the walls of the classroom. Face the wall and place your hands on the wall. Extend your arms straight out with your hands apart, the width of your shoulders. Now let's do some push-ups. Your feet are together and straight. Good.
(26) Now with your hands in the same position, place your left foot to the wall, bend your left knee. Place your right foot behind you with the leg straight. Your feet should be in a straight line. Now push with your hands on the wall. Good.
(27) Now change feet. Place the right foot to the wall. Push. Be sure that your right knee is bent and that your left leg is straight.

(Cooling down is as important as warming up. The cool-down exercises may be the same as the warm-up exercises.)

(28) Now keep your palms on the wall. Let's do some heel lifts. Up and down. Up and down. Good. Be sure that your feet are together, not one in front of the other.
(29) Rock from heel to toe. Good. Keep going.
(30) Face the center of the room. With your legs together and straight, bend forward and stretch to the floor. Good. Hold that position. (Doesn't that feel good?) OK. I think we're ready for mathematics. Let's put our chairs back and . . . ."

Suggestions for Classroom Exercise

Music. Themes from the Disney movies are good. Dr. Doolittle is excellent with primary children. Popular songs are fine with older students. Allow them to choose themes from TV series and record them on tapes for the exercise period. Have students suggest movements appropriate to the music. Be sure that the music has a good beat. Change the music for the cool-down period to help quiet and relax the students.

The Use of Props Provides Variety and Makes Exercise Fun.

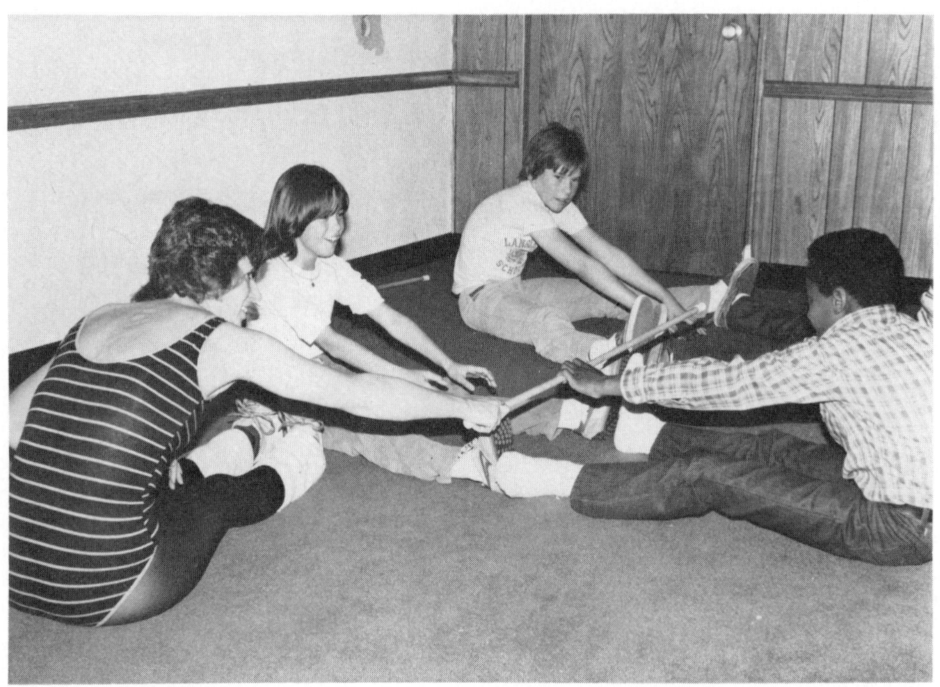

Props. The use of chairs or other props enhance the exercise period. Dowling or short ropes can be used to keep the arms straight for bending exercises. Ropes or dowling can be used with a partner for resistance movements. Paddles or wands are great for attaching strips of cloth. Use the paddles with the cloth for swinging exercises or scissor exercises. Books can be used for weights. Use one book in each hand and perform arm lifts. The purpose of props is for motivation.

Space. Obviously if there is an empty classroom or the auditorium available, this would be optimal; however, in the normal classroom students can be arranged in staggered formations around the room. The important point is that they are able to see the teacher model the exercises and that they will not touch another student as they exercise.

Exercises. Students will always complain that they are tired. Use good judgment as to the number of repetitions for each exercise. Always model the movement to be performed. Encourage smooth movements using the full range of motion. Physical fitness periods should have three distinct stages: warm-up, vigorous exercise, cool-down.

Clothing. If the exercise period is to occur on a set day of the week, ask girls to wear pants on that day. However, since one of the objectives for classroom physical education is to relieve tension, you really do not know in advance when you might want to engage in an exercise session. The problem can be solved if girls will keep a pair of shorts in the classroom to be put on under skirts for this activity. (Parents readily approve of this idea!)

The Bent Knee Stretch Protects the Lower Back, and Is a Good Movement for Either a Warm-up or a Cool Down.

Walking on the Toes Strengthens Calf Muscles. Follow the Leader Games Make Cardiovascular Activities Fun.

Equipment for Physical Education

The following equipment facilitates the physical education program:

1. Balls—6-inch, 9-inch, and 13-inch for volleyball, kickball, basketball, football. One for every two students is considered optimal.
2. Jump ropes—single, double, and one 20-foot rope for each class.
3. Beanbags
4. Soccer pins
5. Hoops
6. Mats
7. Bats
8. Playground Apparatus
9. Paddles or racquets with balls or birds
10. Horseshoes, shuffleboard cues, and discs
11. Table tennis equipment
12. Tubes, Tires, Stilts
13. Vaulting boxes and horses
14. Percussion instruments and records for rhythms and dance, record player
15. Cones

Evaluating Physical Education Growth

Evaluation in physical education should be based on individual growth and development. Students should be apprised of their personal progress so that they can relate progress to practice and personal goals. Since both the potentials and the abilities of students differ, students should not be compared with each other.

It is important to identify the individual needs and abilities of each student. This may be accomplished through observation, interviews, and physical fitness tests. The following procedures may be used:

1. Observe the student as s/he relates to other students to determine basic needs and interests.
2. Test the students using the Kraus-Weber tests described in this chapter, or for students over age 10, you may use the AAHPER test.
3. Review and analyze the student's health record; review vision and hearing records.
4. Evaluate growth (weight and height) using standard growth charts.
5. Observe the student performing movement activities.
   - Can the student exercise vigorously and recover quickly, or does the student continue to look fatigued?
   - Can the student control body movements?
   - Does the student's performance improve after practice and feedback?
   - Is the student enthusiastic about activity?
   - Does the primary-aged child support his/her weight when using the horizontal bar?
   - Can the primary child climb the Jungle Jim?
   - Does the student share equipment and take turns?
   - Does the student help others or interfere with others?

How Is Health Education Taught?

Experimentation

Many aspects of health education can be taught through the utilization of the scientific method. The students who developed the experiment for testing the effect of dirt on their hands when handling bread were studying health as well as science. Personal health care studies are often motivated and initiated through science experiments. Upper-grade students studying light can construct cameras and microscopes and then go on to the study of the eye. Experiments with food decay, contamination, growth of bacteria are typical of the studies appropriate for health instruction.

Research

The use of actual situations for study has a positive effect on health attitudes and habits. In a sixth grade classroom the teacher initiated a safety unit by asking the students to research safety problems at school. The students analyzed the safety records in the school office and then investigated the areas where accidents were occuring. They observed other students at the bicycle rack area, on the playground, stairways, and sidewalk in front of school. They watched before school, during recess and lunch, and after school. They studied the frequency of accidents, the location, and the activity. Then they recorded their findings and wrote their conclusions. They compared their own study with the school district's study at other schools. Finally the students wrote some plays to dramatize the safety problems. Using their own dramatizations they taught other students at their school about safety.

TABLE 10.3. School Safety Record.

Location and Activity	Frequency K–3 Boys	Frequency K–3 Girls	Frequency 4–6 Boys	Frequency 4–6 Girls
Bicycle Rack Area				
• Fighting				
• Falls				
• Skidding				
Playground				
• Unorganized activities				
• Fighting				
• Running				
• Apparatus				
Stairway				
• Skipping steps				
• Pushing				
• Running				
Sidewalk				
• Carrying too many things				
• Watching others				
• Running				

Resource People

Community resource people are valuable assets to the school health program. Health department professionals, fire and police personnel are usually willing to come to school and perform demonstrations and to lecture. Hospitals frequently have a list of speakers to assist in health education. Community service organizations sometimes have health specialists who are experienced with working with children. Organizations like the American Heart Association have instructional materials available for classroom teaching. The American Heart Association has developed two kits for teaching about the heart and exercise. The kits contain filmstrips, cassette tapes, and an instructional booklet for the teacher. The materials are in both Spanish and English, and one is appropriate for lower grades, the other for upper grades.

Health and Guidance and Examinations

Students are usually examined several times during their elementary school years by the school nurse and/or doctor. This can be a learning experience if the students are prepared for the examination, knowing how it will be performed and what will be learned from the examination. Students can study growth charts from health textbooks. They can study problems of underweight and overweight. Nutrition and food habits can be the focus of a unit. Dental hygiene can be studied in conjunction with the dental examination.

Demonstrations, Discussions, Textbooks

Audio-visual resources, exhibits, and models are useful for demonstrating health concepts. Many materials can be borrowed from community resources; however, student-made models and exhibits are most meaningful. Pictures and posters are readily available from health organizations and the National Safety Council.

It is extremely important in health education that the teaching approach be positive, calmly presented, and as objective as possible. Issues in health education may elicit emotional reactions from different segments of the community; thus it is important that the teacher help students discuss problems in a nonthreatening classroom climate.

Textbooks are available for grades 3–6, and most textbooks integrate science and health concepts. Textbooks should be used for resource purposes.

Evaluating Health Education

Health education should be evaluated in the same ways that growth is assessed in other subject fields. Paper-and-pencil tests may be designed to test health concepts. If students produce projects, models, or dramatizations, then these may be used. Attitudes and habits may be observed to see if there is continuous and consistent growth. Since much of the learning in health education should be organized so that students engage in inquiry and discover for themselves, the use of scientific methods and attitudes should be evaluated.

Integration of Health and Physical Education with Other Subjects

Whenever possible subject fields should be integrated. Physical education experiences can be used to enhance other curriculum fields. For example, the teacher can give auditory directions that require students to remember a sequence of directions and rhythmically produce it. The rhythm can be orchestrated by the teacher. Students might be asked to clap hands overhead, snap fingers, shake fingers, and roll arms. The students could even be asked to remember a set number of repetitions.

Students can listen to records and act out stories or sounds. Students (kindergarten age) can be asked to shape their bodies to look like whole numbers. Animal movements are particularly motivating for primary age children: to walk like an elephant; to do a cat walk; to make your back look like an angry cat; to walk like a crab (on hands and feet with hands behind you—walking backward).

Mathematics can be enhanced by having students learn to time their skill performances or measure their running distances.

For science, Newton's laws of motion can be taught:

a. Bodies in motion tend to stay in motion or bodies at rest tend to stay at rest unless acted upon by some outside force.
b. An object will change its speed when acted upon by a greater force; the greater the object, the smaller the acceleration.
c. For every action there is an equal and opposite reaction. (Illustrate by bouncing a ball against a wall or dribbling the ball.)

For social studies integration, teach regional and cultural games and dances. Music and art integration are discussed in Chapter 11. Health education integration has been discussed throughout this chapter.

Mainstreaming in Physical Education

Whenever possible students with handicaps should participate in the physical education program. However, participation should be guided and modified when necessary. Hall et al. (1980, pp. 491–494) identify twelve handicapping conditions and suggestions for activities.

1. *Accidents:* Depending upon the seriousness of the accident, students can participate, while convalescing, in shuffleboard, horseshoes, darts, Ping-Pong, and board games.
2. *Cardiovascular disorders:* The student's doctor should identify the type and extent of activities.
3. *Cerebral palsy:* Exercises for muscle stretching, antigravity exercise, postural improvement exercises, swimming, and games for those who can execute specific movements.
4. *Emotional disorders:* Normal physical activities should be appropriate unless there are safety restrictions. Students should be carefully observed to see if a modification of activity is necessary.
5. *Mental retardation:* Generally the mentally retarded child can participate in a regular physical education program with classmates.
6. *Muscular disorders:* Health professionals should identify the reconditioning activities for specific muscle injuries. Care should be taken that all muscle groups are exercised.
7. *Nutritional imbalance:* A regular physical education program should be appropriate for both the underweight and overweight student; however, vigorous activities should be suggested to the overweight student (jogging, folk dancing).
8. *Orthopedic disabilities:* Medically approved exercises and activities should be used. A reconditioning program should be designed by the student's doctor.
9. *Postural deviations:* The regular physical education program with classmates is appropriate; additional exercises should be specified to correspond with the functional deviation.
10. *Respiratory disorders:* The regular physical education program with classmates is usually appropriate; however, some students may need to rest after vigorous play, and those students who are too inconvenienced should participate in modified activities such as shuffleboard, Ping-Pong, horseshoes, archery, golf, or weightlifting.
11. *Sensory problems:* Students with minor disabilities should participate in the regular program with their classmates. Specialized programming might include swimming, dancing, track and field, croquet, shuffleboard.
12. *Hyperactivity:* Some hyperactive children can participate in the regular program; others need activities such as yoga, T'ai Chi, and dance therapy.

Students' readiness to participate in physical activities is determined by their developmental level. Students with special problems, whether because retarded or as a consequence of other handicapping conditions, may not be ready to participate in group activities. Handicapped students are often overprotected by parents, peers, and teachers with the natural consequence that they do not have the necessary motor skills to participate with others. Before these students can be integrated with peers in group activities, they should be allowed to progress using self-testing individual sports activities (Sherrill, 1977).

Abdominal Muscle Strength Is Developed Through the Bicycle Activity.

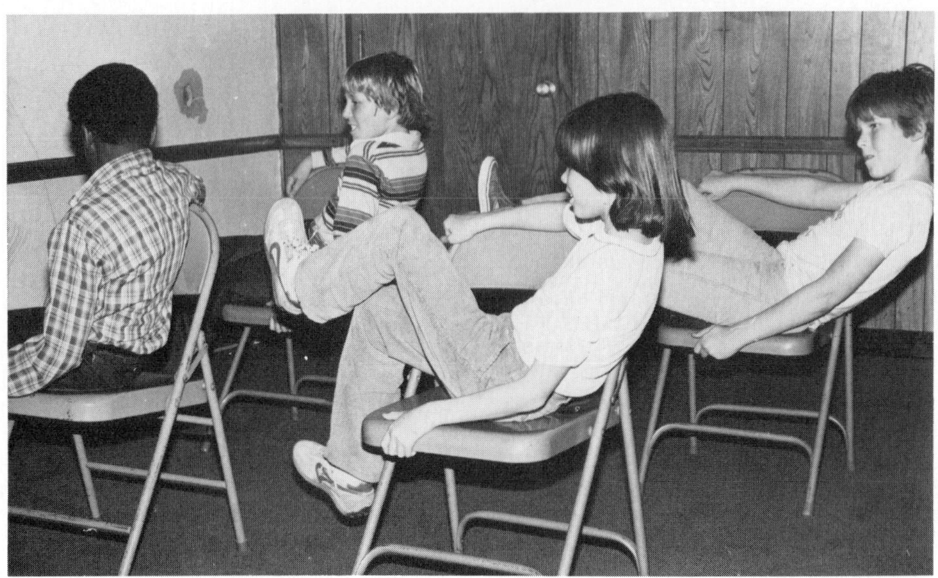

Classroom Management in Physical Education

Classroom management problems occur during physical education because sometimes there is the tendency to let physical education be a "game" or free time period for students, and as a consequence teachers do not perform the planning, organizing, monitoring, and anticipatory tasks that they engage in for other subject fields.

This idea of physical education and play time being one and the same is most evident when teachers tell students, "We are not going to have P.E. today, because you have been too noisy," or "You didn't finish your mathematics on time, sooo . . . ," or "We have had so many interruptions today that we need to skip . . . ."

All of the above comments should be used as the rationale for why physical education is important *every* day. If students are noisy, or less alert than they should be, or harassed, the need for vigorous exercise is all the more evident.

Typical classroom management problems in physical education relate to decision-making concerns: class organization and grouping, equipment, instructional approach.

1. *Class Organization.* Whenever teachers need to change the place where an activity occurs, there will be management considerations. Unless a teacher wants the whole class to surge forward to the door at the same time, s/he should not direct students with the comment, "Let's go out to P.E. now." Directions to students should include the following information: (a) Who is to leave the classroom? (b) When are they to leave the classroom? (c) Where are the students to go to participate in the activity? (d) What equipment will they need? (e) Should they walk, run, skip to the destination? These directions should be stated clearly and concisely. Consideration should also be given to how to get the students back to the classroom. The following decisions need to be made: (a) Should students line up before returning to the classroom? (b) Should they move by groups, games, or all together? (c) Will they go to the bathroom and/or

obtain drinks? (If they do not obtain drinks on the playground, will they want to do so in the classroom?)

2. *Instructional Arrangements.* Another organizational problem has to do with instructional arrangements. If skill or game instructions are needed, will they be provided in the classroom or out on the playground or in the gymnasium and/or auditorium? Game or "rule" type instructions are best handled while students are sitting at their desks. Sometimes a "chalk" talk before students are to participate in an activity is helpful. But if students are to observe a demonstration, then it is important to plan how they will stand or sit in order to see and hear. There are several arrangements advocated by physical education specialists for facilitating skill demonstrations. For example:

- *Semicircle:* Students can sit or stand in a half-circle formation, and the teacher can demonstrate the skill. This is particularly good if only half the class is involved in the demonstration.
- *Circle:* Teacher or model can demonstrate from the center of the circle. However, if the teacher/model is to give instructions verbally, the semicircle is better for talking/listening.
- *Squad/Small Group:* Students stand in short lines by group. This is a good arrangement if students are to practice or give evidence of having attained a skill. The teacher can walk between the groups or stand in a central location to observe performance.
- *Scatter:* If the teacher/model has a megaphone or is standing on a stage, this formation minimizes students' "messing around" tactics. Teachers who use this formation for demonstrations usually assign students to a special spot on the floor. Whenever the teacher calls for a scatter formation, the student moves to the special spot. The scatter formation facilitates students' exploration of movement.

The decision about how to arrange students for demonstrations should also be based on the type of learning situation. Are students to learn via direct instruction, or is the instructional planning based upon student exploration? This decision will need to be made prior to the decision about the type of formation.

APPLICATION OF RESEARCH

Sex stereotyping is reinforced by classroom management practices which:

- separate teams for girls and boys
- persist in separate lines for boys and girls
- change game rules for boys or girls
- select different games to play for boys and girls (Richardson et al., 1980).

3. *Grouping.* A third decision that frequently causes management problems is grouping students for play activities. Should students be grouped by friendship patterns, by size, by ability, or by interest? There are trade-offs involved in each of the choices. Perhaps there should not be one consistent way of grouping students for physical education; instead, it may be a good idea to change the pattern depending upon the games, skills, and purpose of the activity. Whichever pattern is chosen, the decision should be shared with the students along with the objective of the lesson.

4. *Equipment.* In some schools activities must be chosen on the basis of the available equipment. Sometimes there is not enough equipment for an entire class of children to participate in the same game activity. Luckily there are many activities that do not require equipment. The trick is to plan ahead, be knowledgeable about your resources, and present the game plan to the students confidently. A typical error of new teachers is to send students out to the playground and forget to give them equipment. This usually results in students running around to find the teacher and the keys to the classroom and confusion out on the yard.

Most management problems in physical education can be avoided with unit planning and anticipatory thinking about instructional arrangements, grouping, and equipment needs.

Chapter Summary

The close relationship between exercise and physical fitness was emphasized in this chapter. In the elementary school the health and physical education programs are interrelated and need to be coordinated. The organization and goals of both programs were outlined. Teaching approaches were explained in both physical education and health education and examples of weekly schedules in physical education were provided. In physical education, an indirect instructional approach was contrasted with direct instruction, and the instructional sequence for each was provided. Physical education can also be taught *in* the classroom and an exercise sequence was provided to demonstrate how it can be accomplished. Suggestions were provided for physical education equipment, for evaluating physical education growth, and for integrating both subject fields with other elementary subjects. Mainstreaming activities were provided for physical education. Classroom management was discussed focusing on organization, instructional arrangements, grouping, and equipment.

Classroom Application Exercises

1. Identify people, animals, things, and emotions that students could dramatize to music.
2. Compare the motor skills of a handicapped primary-age student and a normal primary-age student. How were the performances similar? Different?
3. Develop a lesson plan for students in grades 3–4 which allow them to explore movements.
4. Visit a YMCA and observe an aerobic exercise workout. Create an aerobic rhythmical sequence for upper-grade students.
5. Use the Kraus-Weber tests and test a group of elementary students.
6. Prepare a presentation for parents to explain the relationship between coronary heart disease and lack of exercise.
7. Develop a checklist for evaluating students' track and field skills.
8. Investigate which social agencies will provide health services to elementary students. Find out how a teacher can obtain help for a student.

Suggested Readings for Extending Study

Bucher, Charles A., and Evelyn M. Reade. *Physical Education and Health in the Elementary Schools.* New York: Macmillan Publishing Company, 1971.

Burton, Elsie C. *The New Physical Education for Elementary School Children.* Boston: Houghton Mifflin Company, 1977.

Gallahue, D. L., P. H. Werner, and G. Luedke. *A Conceptual Approach to Moving and Learning.* New York: John Wiley & Sons, Inc., 1975.

Hall, J. Tillman, N. H. Sweeny, and J. H. Esser. *Physical Education in the Elementary School.* Santa Monica, Calif.: Goodyear Publishing Co., Inc., 1980.

King, Nancy. *Giving Form to Feeling.* New York: Drama Book Specialists, 1975.

Kirchner, Glenn. *Physical Education for Elementary School Children.* 5th ed. Dubuque, Iowa: William C. Brown Publishing Company, 1981.

Lamb, David R. *Physiology of Exercise: Responses and Adaptations.* 2nd ed. New York: Macmillan Publishing Company, 1983.

McAdam, R. E., and Carleen Dodson. *Concepts and Practices in Elementary Activity Programs.* Springfield, Ill: Charles C. Thomas, Publisher, 1981.

Prudden, Bonnie. *Fitness from Six to Twelve.* New York: Harper & Row, 1972.

Read, Donald A., and Walter H. Greene. *Creative Teaching in Health.* 3rd ed. New York: Macmillan Publishing Company, 1980.

Sherrill, Claudine. *Adapted Physical Education and Recreation.* Dubuque, Iowa: William C. Brown Publishing Company, 1977.

Sorochan, Walter D., and Stephen J. Bender. *Teaching Elementary Health Science.* 2nd ed. Reading, Mass.: Addison-Wesley Publishing Co., Inc., 1979.

Werner, Peter H. *A Movement Approach to Games for Children.* St. Louis: The C. V. Mosby Company, 1979.

Willgoose, Carl E. *Health Education in the Elementary School.* Philadelphia: W. B. Saunders Company, 1974.

Chapter 11

Music and Art Education

After you have completed the study of this chapter, you should be able to accomplish the following:

1. **Identify reasons why it is important to teach music and art.**
2. **Identify the purposes of music and art education.**
3. **Discuss the content of art and music education programs.**
4. **Suggest classroom activities appropriate for teaching art.**
5. **Relate art activities to the child's developmental level.**
6. **Suggest classroom activities appropriate for teaching music.**
7. **Identify illustrative objectives for teaching music.**
8. **Make a list of suggestions for teaching music and art.**
9. **Summarize trends in the teaching of the arts.**
10. **Suggest ways to evaluate growth in the creative arts.**
11. **Identify resources and equipment for teaching the creative arts.**
12. **Identify several national programs and projects in the arts and the emphasis of each.**
13. **Suggest ways to integrate the arts with other subjects.**
14. **Discuss mainstreaming in the arts.**

Importance of the Creative Arts

Music and art education contribute to the total development of the individual and increase an individual's ability to communicate with others. The creative arts contribute to the goal of self-realization by helping students to express themselves, to enjoy creative experiences, and to make qualitative judgments.

The visual and aural arts encourage students to explore their own personal responses to creative experiences. The arts enable students to utilize creative imagination, to see and hear clearly, and to express essential feelings. The emphasis on the senses in music and art education motivates consciousness and exploration of aesthetic experiences.

More than other curriculum areas, the aesthetic arts help students to accept the challenges of a pluralistic society. Music and art play an essential role in facilitating and extending the appreciation and understanding of other people and other cultures and thus are valuable in themselves. While both subjects contribute to the development of other subject goals, each is unique. Each allows the individual to make a personal statement. Each provides a continuing and lasting record of a people and is a reflection of a society's way of life. Both provide means to analyze society and culture. Universal communication is facilitated through the arts. As aesthetic experiences, both involve the mind and the feelings.

Purposes of Music Education

Raebeck and Wheeler (1980, p. 2) stated that the value of music in the elementary school is to help the student

- Learn what music is
- Discover what in music is most enjoyable
- Discover personal musical aptitudes and skills
- Learn to value music as an aesthetic experience.

Music Helps to Develop Group Identify and Social Participation.

The Music Framework for California Public Schools (1971, pp. 4–5) identified six purposes:

1. Promote sensitivity to the expressive qualities of music.
2. Encourage musical responsiveness, involvement, and discrimination.
3. Promote understanding of the nature, meaning, and structure of music.
4. Develop skills, including aural acuity.
5. Promote awareness and understanding of music, literature of various periods, and the forms, styles, and idioms that are characteristic of various national cultures including our own.
6. Provide a sound base of musical experience which students can use in making intelligent judgments of musical value.

Land and Vaughan (1978) identify additional purposes for music education:

1. *Individualization.* Music transmits different meanings to each individual. Since individual reactions are encouraged, the child feels "safe" in expressing him/herself. Music enhances the individual's feeling of success; self-esteem is fostered.
2. *Aesthetics.* Music increases the individual's self-awareness and evokes important feelings. Unique satisfactions are experienced. Through participation and expression of feelings, the student learns to make decisions and judgments about music.
3. *Socialization.* Group singing, dancing, playing, and composing develops social behavior. Both leadership and group participation are learned.
4. *Correlation.* Music provides opportunities to use other curriculum fields to study and enjoy music. Similarly other subjects are enhanced because of the musical correlation of song and dance.
5. *Remediation.* Music is successful in helping students with special problems. Both the learning handicapped and the physically handicapped student can enjoy and reap the benefits of musical activities.

It appears that the key purpose of music education is the development of aesthetic sensitivity. This is accomplished by focusing on music concepts, inquiry skills, music skills, and music attitudes and values. These are discussed under the heading: What Should Students Learn in Music Education?

Purposes of Art Education

The basic purposes of art education are to enable students to see clearly, to express feelings, to demonstrate and communicate individuality, and to understand and apply art knowledge.

Art education objectives frequently aim to expose students to art production and art appreciation. Students are to enjoy discovery and be discoverers. The art curriculum should increase sensitivity and heighten perceptual and creative awareness. Art educators want students to integrate thinking, feelings, imagination, and senses in the application of art knowledge to personal experience. Art instruction should help students to perceive visual relationships, produce art, understand the art of others, and judge artistic products.

What Should Students Learn in Music and Art Education?

Art Education

Unlike other curricula areas most art programs of the 1950s and 1960s were limited to curriculum guides or lists of activities with suggestions for the use of appropriate media. Teachers were expected to choose among the activities to develop their own classroom curricula (Greer, 1977). During the late 1960s and early 1970s concern was expressed that students learn art concepts and begin to develop an understanding of works of art.

As a part of a program for educational accountability, Michigan developed Minimal Performance Objectives for Art Education (1974); Florida developed The Florida Catalog of Art Objectives (1974). Other states instituted similar approaches. In California an art framework was developed to provide state guidelines for the teaching of art education. The California State Framework in Art Education (1971) describes four components of art education: visual/tactile perception, creative expression, art heritage, and aesthetic judgment.

Visual/Tactile Perception

The purpose of this component is to sharpen students' sensory awareness of the world around them. The goal is to maximize seeing, feeling, and understanding of form, color, and texture. Illustrative objectives are:

- Students will identify varying colors, shapes, and textures in natural and manmade forms.
- Students will distinguish color qualities by value and hue as well as identify negative and positive shapes and textures.
- Students will model three-dimensional qualities as indicated by overlapping planes, vertical position, size, and color intensity.

Creative Expression

The second component is accomplished by providing students with art media to learn skills and express ideas and feelings in visual form. As students participate in creative exploration, instruction should focus on art concepts and the structure of art. Illustrative objectives are:

Students will draw, demonstrating techniques of action; continuous line; and imaginative, decorative, or realistic styles.

Through art work the student will express his/her own moods and feelings. Students will use media appropriately (drawing, painting, sculpture, graphics) and create two- and three-dimensional art forms.

Art Heritage

Development of art values and understanding of our art heritage is gained as students study works of art and artists of the past and of contemporary times in our own society and in other cultures and societies. Illustrative objectives are:

- Students will identify similarities and differences among works of art produced by different cultures and societies at different times.
- Students will describe the varied uses of the visual arts in modern society.
- Students will express the purposes of art as it relates to the celebration of historical events, conveys beliefs and values, and communicates social practices.

Aesthetic Judgment

Students learn to critique, express preferences, and appreciate art works by learning about the visual, intellectual, and philosophic bases for understanding art and for judging the form, content, technique, and purpose of art works. Illustrative objectives are:

- Students will describe qualities in visual work: line, color, shape, intensity, value, texture, composition, and contrast.
- Students will express preferences in art, comparing sensory qualities, style, art form, and materials.
- Students will critique a work of art, comparing style and function.

Organization of Art Experiences

The research of Lowenfield (1947) has been influential in the organization of art experiences for children. Lowenfield found that there was a progressive pattern to the development of children's drawings. Like Piaget, Lowenfield noted the egocentric behavior of the young child and observed the changes in chilren's drawings from representations of the self in early childhood to objective realism in the later elementary years. Although levels of development should not be rigidly interpreted, the stages do provide a guide to the choice of art activities. Growth is continuous for each child; objectives for art lessons will overlap at the skill levels.

The primary child (K–2) emerging from the scribble stage is in a presymbolic stage, spontaneous, usually nonreflective, and not concerned with reality. The young child loves to express drawings and paintings in vivid terms using bright colors. The child works best using large pencils or large brushes on extra large paper. Content for the primary child typically relates to the child's self and family.

The following activities are considered appropriate for the K–2 child:

- Students enjoy experimenting with a variety of art materials: paint, felt-tip pens, crayons, clay, tissue, chalk, starch, paste, sand, string, yarn, plastic, beads, wood.
- Using the materials, students explore, learning to create line, form, color, texture and patterns; students can recognize two- and three-dimensional forms.
- Students enjoy art experiences and can communicate feelings, observations, the observance of odors, sounds. Students will express reactions to verbal and visual impressions.
- Students can make pictures expressing feelings, moods, imagination, stories, music, physical activity.
- Students will make designs using varied art materials. Designs are typically of borders, sometimes an overall design is achieved.
- Students will make models using clay, wood, and paper.
- Students express appreciation:
  of nature (flowers, rocks, shells, sky, grass, rainbows)
  of order (nature, classroom)
  of appearance (self and others)
  of art works (of others and classics).

The middle-grade student is sociocentric rather than egocentric as in the prior stage and is able to work both independently and cooperatively with others. The student is more oriented to reality and wants to produce art objects that are more truly representative—details are important. The student will describe similarities and differences in shapes and patterns. Color is used more realistically and with more restraint. The concept of space becomes important to the child of this age, and s/he will attempt to express it in landscapes, figures, and in total composition. The following activities are considered appropriate:

- Students experiment with ways of using art materials. The student will use the side and point of crayons and chalk. S/he will enjoy using crayon resist and wet chalk. Mixing and blending colors is explored. Using tempera paint, the student enjoys dripping, spraying, and stippling. Greater manipulative abilities allows the student to use water colors and mix and blend the colors. The child enjoys manipulating clay—punching, pinching, and coiling. The student can use papier-mâché and can cut, tear, fold, fringe, and curl paper.

- Students make pictures of real and imaginative experiences. The student enjoys using a variety of art media; can portray essential characteristics of form depicting *front*, *back*, *behind*, *below*; considers colors, contrast, size, shape, texture, and pattern.
- The student will produce three-dimensional models using clay, paper, and wood.
- The student is more aware of design features and enjoys experimenting, making designs for a variety of purposes.
- The middle-grade student appreciates collections, art objects, bulletin board arrangements. The student will express enjoyment in selecting and reacting to pictures and art experiences.

The upper-grade student's motor skills are more controlled, and so the student can be more mature in his/her art productions. The student can work longer and more intently and is able to work independently. If the student has been exposed to art experiences, the vocabulary will be more developed and art appreciation more sophisticated. The student should be able to compare artists and art works in relation to sensory qualities, style, and materials. Students at this age are more analytical about what they see and more evaluative about what they like. The upper-grade student manipulates art materials with greater control and sophistication. The following activities are considered appropriate:

Crayons: uses side and point; uses pressure to produce light and dark; blends colors; makes transparencies and etchings.
Chalk: blends, uses dry or wet surfaces.
Charcoal: combines with water colors; shades, uses point and side.
Clay: Carves and builds by pinching, pulling out, using slab and coil construction.
Paper: curls, fringes, braids, weaves, bends, folds, rolls, twists.
Papier-mâché: enjoys making masks, covering buildings, frames.
Tempera Paint: Can spray, drip, stipple, spatter; mixes and blends colors.
Water Colors: Can combine with other art materials.

- In making pictures the student can: express feelings and reactions; portray people, events, time, weather, perspective. In using a variety of art media, the student considers composition and color.
- The upper-grade student enjoys lettering—both upper and lower case.
- The student enjoys producing three-dimensional objects.
- The student considers design in overall patterns and in borders and understands principles of design.
- The student expresses appreciation of art objects, pictures, and artists; the student observes line, form, texture, motion, and color, arranges and orders objects and collections, considers personal appearance, visits museums. The student can recognize examples of American, Indian, and Mexican art and of artists they have studied.

Do you believe that it is important for students to have music and art textbooks? Why?

Music Education

Music instruction is typically organized to teach concepts, process skills, music skills, and attitudes and values through the activities of listening, singing, moving, playing, and reading and writing notation. Concepts are related to expressive elements (tone qualities, tempo, and dynamics), to constituent elements (rhythm, melody, harmony, form), and to the structure of music. The process skills interact with the concepts as the teacher asks students to organize data, generalize and make inferences, and apply knowledge. Students develop music skills as they pursue the aforementioned activities. Attitudes and values are developed through the total music experience and are encouraged by motivating students to choose musical experiences and by providing opportunities for decision making.

Illustrative objectives for each of the activities will provide some insight concerning the content of the elementary music period.

LISTENING

- Students will identify a familiar song by listening to its rhythm clapped or beat out.
- Listening to a song or recorded music, students can differentiate major and minor keys.
- Listening to an orchestral number, students can identify instrument families.

SINGING

- After listening to a melody, students will repeat it with accurate pitch.
- After listening to the rhythm of a melody, or after reading the rhythmic notation, the students will reproduce the number singing the rhythmic pattern accurately.
- Reading notation, students will harmonize and sing in two parts.

MOVING

- Students will demonstrate basic conducting patterns with the hand, to lead a melody.
- Using large muscle movements, students will represent rhythmic components of a number.
- Students will demonstrate the tempo of a number by swaying, stretching, sliding, or rocking.

PLAYING (PERFORMANCE)

- Using a variety of percussion instruments, students will create rhythm. Using an autoharp, bells, or other instrument, students will accompany a song.
- Using instruments, students will demonstrate understanding of tempo, dynamics, and tone color.

READING AND WRITING NOTATION

- Given a pattern of melody written in blank notation, the students will identify a familiar song.
- Reading tempo markings, the students will demonstrate understanding by playing or singing a song appropriately.
- Given a staff and appropriate symbols and notes, students will write a pattern of melody in blank notation.

> Since primary-aged children do not *naturally* sit still for very long, how can music be used advantageously to promote academic engagement?

Organizational Guidelines for Teaching Music

Musical activities are planned to correspond to the developmental characteristics of elementary-aged children just as the art activities were. Land and Vaughan (1978) made the following suggestions for planning musical activities for five- to eight-year-old students:

1. Each music lesson should include a variety of experiences chosen from singing, performing, reading notation, composing, listening.
2. There should be opportunity for both individual or small group participation and whole group participation.
3. There should be teacher choice and student choice of music.
4. The vocabulary of songs should be examined to verify that students will understand the words. If they do not, explanations should be given.
5. Music should reflect students' moods and needs for self-image.
6. Music concepts are learned best through movement activities.

Students Enjoy Singing and Acting-out Familiar Songs.

7. Since the young child is imaginative, there should be opportunity for the exploration of movement and dramatization of songs.
8. Music should reflect the community and culture of the children.
9. Students should be asked to identify simple rhythmic patterns.
10. Students should feel successful during the music period.

Activities for older elementary children should be planned with the following considerations:

1. Increased coordination of the older student allows greater freedom in choosing instruments for them to play. They enjoy the ukulele, guitar, autoharp, and recorder, along with percussion instruments.
2. Developmental differences among children in grades 4–6 are great, so the activities should be varied: square and folk dances; participation using instruments, singing, composing, listening.
3. Greater maturity allows the use of music books and the singing of two- and three-part songs. As boys' voices change, they can sing the lower parts. Students of this age can harmonize by ear.
4. Fifth- and sixth-graders enjoy changing the words of popular songs to write their own class songs. They also enjoy performing in musicals and writing dramatizations for performance.
5. Students should be given the opportunity to make choices about what they are to perform and correlate other subject fields in their dramatizations. They should be able to create introductions, codas, descants, and other tonal embellishments.
6. They are able to understand musical terms and symbols such as *cadence, accent, tempo, rhythm pattern, interval, scale, sharp, flat, clef, tonal pattern, underlying beat, phrase, key signature, p—pp, f—ff, crescendo, retard, minor, major.*

How Should Music and Art Be Taught?

A lesson plan for music and for art is used to demonstrate teaching approaches for the aesthetic arts. However, there is a wide range of appropriate techniques for teaching both subjects. As in physical education, both exploration and direct instruction are appropriate.

Music Education

Mary Hogan wanted to teach the concept of rhythmic pattern duration. She would demonstrate to her students that rhythm patterns have long and short sounds and that when a melody uses a rhythm pattern, the words are sung in a long and short rhythmic sound pattern. She chose the Calypso song "Tinga Layo."

Hogan's Objectives:

1. The students will recognize and identify rhythmic changes.
2. The students will sing the rhythmic pattern accurately.
3. The students will clap and produce the rhythmic pattern using coconut shells.
4. The students will recognize the rhythmic pattern written in blank notation on the board.

Materials: Record player, record, four sets of coconut shells.

Procedure:

Hogan: "Yesterday, Benny brought in his Harry Belafonte record and we listened to Calypso music. Who remembers what impressed us about the Calypso music?"

(The students respond that it was the rhythm that was unusual and that they had enjoyed it.)

Hogan: "Good. I thought you'd remember, and since you enjoyed it so much, I brought another Calypso record for you to hear."

(Hogan plays "Tinga Layo" and students listen.)

Hogan: "This time, boys and girls, see if you can clap the rhythm of the song when I give you the signal."

(Hogan provides the cue for the rhythm pattern that occurs six times during the song. Then she brings out some coconut shells and claps them together.)

Hogan: "What does this sound like?"

(The students respond that it sounds like a pony's hoofbeats.)

Hogan: "Yes, who would like to play them when we hear the rhythm pattern?"

(She chooses four students to participate.)

Hogan: "While our friends play the shells, let's have everyone else count the number of times we hear the same pattern."

(After the song, Hogan has the students respond, and several had counted correctly; the pattern was repeated six times.)

Hogan: "I'm going to write the notes on the board; see if you can recognize which are short sounds and which are long sounds."

Hogan: "Let's see if we can sing the pattern." (She leads them by pointing to the notation on the board.)

(Next she teaches the entire song and asks them to match the words to the rhythm pattern written on the board. She asks them to identify the words that represent the short sound and those that represent the long sounds.)

Hogan: "All right, let's give some other people a chance to perform using the shells." (The children pass them to friends.) While some of us are using the shells, let's have the rest of us cup our hands (this way) and clap to make the sound of hoofs.

Hogan: "Well, boys and girls, we have done such a good job with 'Tinga Layo,' who would like to suggest an old song for us to sing?"

Analysis of Hogan's Music Lesson

Hogan chose the lesson because she needed to teach the concept of rhythmic patterns *and* because the lesson fit neatly with the students' prior experience of listening to Belafonte sing Calypso music. She motivated the lesson by having the students recall the previous day's listening experience. To develop the concept she had the students participate in the following activities: listening, singing, movement (clapping), performing (using the coconut shells), reading notation.

Hogan verified understanding of the concept by having the students (1) clap the rhythm, (2) count the number of times the pattern was used, (3) identify the words to fit the pattern.

She would follow the lesson on a successive day by having the students use different instruments (bongos, maracas, claves) to accompany the rhythmic pattern and to compose patterns of their own.

> How did Hogan manage to have all of the children participate?
> How did she ensure that students would be listening to the music while others performed?

Teaching strategies for music should be varied. They may begin with singing, listening, creative movements, or performing. Music may even begin with an inquiry lesson. The important point is to sequence lessons so that they relate to each other and fit the developmental needs of the students. Children should have the opportunity to learn music concepts, to enjoy, to feel successful, and to release emotion.

Art Education

Greg Thomas' fifth-grade students were excited about Halloween. He decided to use that stimulation advantageously. He planned an art lesson in which the students would make papier-mâché masks.

Thomas' Objectives:

1. Students will make a three-dimensional mask using the medium of papier-mâché appropriately.
2. Students will work imaginatively to express and communicate personal feelings.
3. Students will work individually and explore the fanciful and the strange.
4. Students will create movements to characterize their mask.

Materials: Strips of newspaper, paste, balloons, tempera paint and brushes, scissors, plastic spray.

Procedure:

Thomas: "I've been listening to several of you talk about your Halloween plans. I was wondering, how many like to wear a mask on Halloween?"

(Many of the students respond affirmatively.)

Thomas: "How does it feel to wear a mask?"

Students: "I can't breathe when I wear a mask." "I like it because it lets me hide and surprise people." "I like to scare my friends." "It makes me feel different—kinda strong."

Thomas: "Does wearing a mask change what you see or hear?"

Student: "Well, I feel like the character I'm pretending to be."

Thomas: "What do you mean?"

Student: "If my mask is of a pirate, then I feel like a pirate."

Student: "This year I'm going to be the Greatest American Hero."

Thomas: "I thought I would wear this mask when I answer my door this year."

Student: "Wow! Did you make that mask?"

Thomas: "Yes, and I thought that perhaps you folks would like to make masks today."

(Students respond *very* positively.)

Thomas: "All right. Listen carefully: this is what we are going to do. This is a papier-mâché mask. It is made by pasting strips of paper over a balloon. Then it is decorated to suit the character you want to be. When it is dry, it is sprayed to protect the finish. The last step is cutting the balloon in half and cutting openings for the eyes and other features. It is even possible to add other materials, like yarn or paper, as I did on my mask, to obtain special effects and features."

To plan your mask, you must first think about the medium that you are going to use. How can you use it to convey the mood that you want your character to portray? Remember that you must design your mask to fit *your* face. Visualize your own face. Do you have a large forehead? Do you need a big space between your hair and your nose or a smaller space? Make a sketch of the way you want your mask to look. When you are satisfied with your plan, begin work with the paper and the balloon.

> **Thomas:** "I'm going to ask our art monitors to set the materials out on each table, but before you begin to work, I want each table to be covered with newspaper so that you don't spill paste on the table top. Now—everyone look over here at the chart rack. If you have a question about the procedures for working with papier-mâché, you may look at this chart. If you have a question that you need to ask of me, raise your hand and I will come over to your table."

Thomas's art lesson took three consecutive days to complete. On the second day the students cut and painted and decorated their masks. On the third day they sprayed them to protect the finish. At the end of the week, Thomas suggested that everyone put on his/her mask and walk to the auditorium. Thomas carried his own mask with him and asked the students: "How do you think I should act when I wear this mask?"

After students responded, Thomas turned on a special tape of recorded music. He told the students to take their "scatter" positions on the floor and assume a body posture that would be appropriate for the mask that each student was wearing.

Next, the students were asked to create movements that would indicate how each character feels, thinks, and acts. Thomas also brought a number of props for the students to use to help them create their movements and characterizations (Adapted from King, 1975).

(Thomas will also ask the students to write about their characters as a special creative writing lesson.)

> How does an artisan differ from an artist? What is a limner?

Analysis of Thomas' Art Lesson

Thomas was primarily interested in developing creative expression. He motivated this by providing opportunity for the students to talk about how it feels to wear masks. He asked the students to use their imagination, but he also suggested that they plan the design of the mask. He called attention to the spatial organization of the face.

Since every medium poses special problems, Thomas was probably wise in allowing the students to explore the medium instead of giving too much direction about its use. He carefully provided for individual needs by telling the students to raise their hands if they needed assistance, and he also provided a step-by-step procedural chart for using papier-mâché.

Thomas culminated the mask making in an interesting way. Instead of just talking about and sharing their masks with each other, Thomas had them assume the characterization and portray with movements the mask each was wearing. One can assume that Thomas developed aesthetic judgment as well as creative expression through the art, oral language, and physical movement lessons.

Art is taught through direct instruction to develop art concepts and art skills; art is also taught using discovery approaches which allow students to explore a medium and express feelings and individual perceptions. Strategies should be varied depending upon the medium to be used and the concepts to be developed. A great deal of preplanning is necessary for art activities so that when the actual lesson is implemented the teacher is free to observe and express encouragement to children rather than overdirecting the work activities. Although in most subjects the teacher acts as a model for students to observe, during art it is better if students are free to express their own creative nature instead of trying to imitate the teacher.

Summary: Strategies of Instruction in the Arts

During the 1970s and 1980s the trend in teaching music and art appears to be:

a. emphasis on structural concepts;
b. emphasis on movement as a unifying component of music, art, and drama;
c. application of stages of development to the selection of aesthetic experiences;
d. emphasis on enhancing a positive self-concept and self-actualization;
e. utilization of inquiry methodology when appropriate; emphasis on performing, modeling, analysis, and discussion.

Evaluating the Creative Arts

As in physical education, growth must be measured in terms of the student's own progress and performance. The student's contribution to discussions and the student's enjoyment of the arts provide an index of the student's competencies in art and music.

Musical skills, such as listening, reading and writing music, creative skills, and performance skills (playing instruments, moving, singing, conducting), are best evaluated through sensitive observation by the teacher. Students' behavior as they participate in rhythmic activities, singing, or

RESEARCH FINDINGS

Successful arts programs have common characteristics:

- Content includes a wide variety of arts; utilizes a broad range of stimuli, materials, tools, and processes; focuses on historical, ethnic, and formal elements.
- Program utilizes local resources, such as artists-in-residence.
- Teachers model behaviors expected of students during arts programs (Sayegh, 1981).

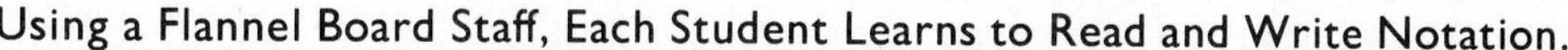
Using a Flannel Board Staff, Each Student Learns to Read and Write Notation.

expressing ideas about music are primarily evaluated by direct observation. A music checklist can be constructed to record information about the student. Listening competencies can be evaluated during a discussion which focuses on identifying the mood of a melody, the instruments, rhythmic patterns, or phrasing. The picture of the children writing notation provides another observational method to evaluate whether or not the student can read and write music.

Art products should be self-evaluated by the child. The teacher's task is to guide the self-evaluation so that the student is not too harsh on him/herself. The teacher should help the child focus on "what's good" about the picture or art object by calling attention to the use of the medium, color, spatial organization, design, or whatever else will encourage the student. With successes recognized, then the teacher can help the child set some realistic goals for the next project.

Group discussions of art work should be handled in a similar manner. Each child should be praised in some way—for creativity, ideas, expression of feelings, discoveries about the use of the media, or solutions to problems. Pictures should *not* be evaluated to choose the "best" picture. Michaelis et al. (1975, p. 414) commented that "It is highly unrealistic and out of step with the character of creative expression to engage in such activities as finding the *best* picture or selecting the *best* artist."

Resources for Teaching Music and Art

Resources for teaching music experiences should include tape recorders, record players, films, slides, videotapes. Audiovisual aids can enhance the music program, but as in all other subjects, good teaching is the most important element for a good program.

Instruments have great appeal to the elementary student. Instruments can be made simply by teacher and students, or they can be purchased. Students enjoy rhythm instruments, percussion, melody and harmony instruments. Typical rhythm instruments include: sticks, triangles, tambourines, castanets, cymbals, bongo and conga drums, claves, and maracas. Students enjoy making unusual instruments out of boxes, bottles, metal containers, and cardboard.

Art materials appear to be limited only by a lack of imagination. There are vast choices available to teachers and students. Materials are needed for modeling, lettering, picture-making, painting, crafts, and design activities.

RESEARCH FINDINGS

Project IMPACT (Interdisciplinary Model Program in the Arts for Children and Teachers) is an art centered model program designed for elementary school children. Objectives of IMPACT include: (1) a balanced school curriculum, (2) a high-quality program in the visual and performing arts, (3) in-service education for teachers and administration, (4) infusion of the arts in the total school program, (5) utilization of artists and performers from the community in the school to improve art experiences for students. Evaluation of the program concluded:

1. Basic skills are learned as well, and in some cases better than before the program was implemented.
2. There was no evidence of a direct transfer of skills; arithmetic skills did not improve as a consequence of learning music notation.
3. The program affected the classroom climate; innovative methods in all curriculum fields led to a more challenging and open classroom.
4. Dropouts and truancy declined; students' self-concepts were enhanced (Boyle & Lathrop, 1973).

This program was tried in Alabama, California, Ohio, Oregon, and Pennsylvania.

Using Natural Materials from the Environment Students Make Their Own Instruments.

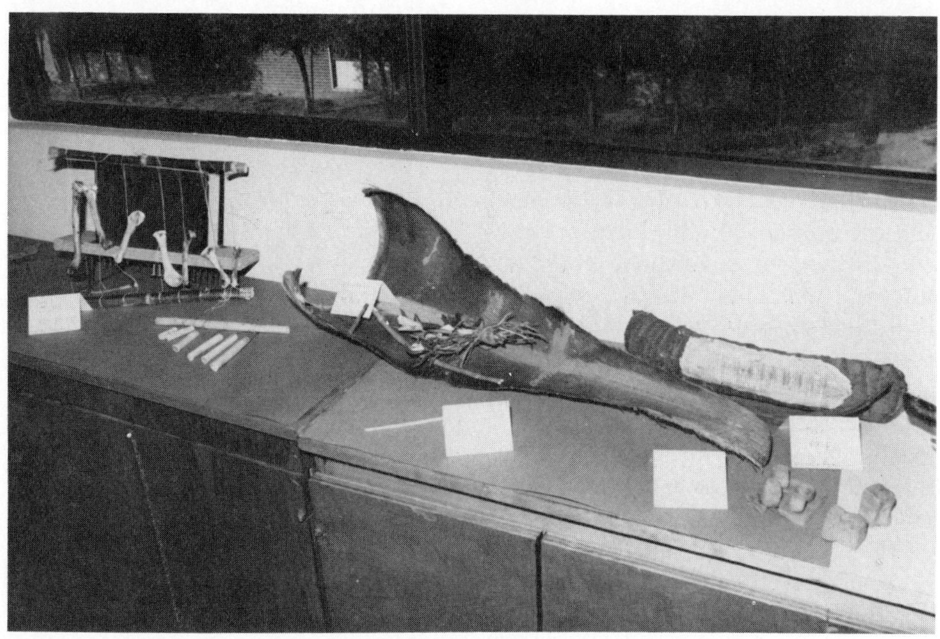

Art materials should be well organized for accessibility and for ease in use. Materials may be stored in boxes, shelves, or drawers. Tin cans, five-gallon ice cream containers, plastic pans, and foil pie plates are all useful for holding art tools and materials.

Work areas for art activities include the floor, table tops, easles, and outside patio areas. The important thing is that newspapers or plastic or oil drop cloths be available to cover any area that is to be used for work or storage. Large work areas available for groups of students are optimal because students can share tools and materials.

Museums, libraries, galleries, music and art centers provide marvelous field trip experiences for students. These community resources usually have docents or artists available to discuss what students will see and/or hear. Local artists and musicians are frequently interested in visiting schools and providing some leadership to young people interested in the arts.

Programs and Projects in the Arts

Education for Aesthetic Awareness (EAA) is a process oriented program for teachers. The program operates in the Greater Cleveland area and was developed by the Cleveland Area Arts Council, funded by grants from several private foundations and by the National Endowment for the Humanities and the Alliance for Arts Education. EAA's purpose is to build confidence and aesthetic literacy among classroom teachers and art specialists. Selected faculty members study—intensively—ways to teach the arts and to develop a school philosophy for the teaching of the arts. Specifically the teachers study melody, rhythm, and harmony in music as well as line, shape, and texture in painting. Along with class lectures in each art form, the teachers study aesthetic philosophy, building curriculum in the arts, advocacy, use of community arts, and the politics of school change (Robiner, 1980).

Arts in Education is a concept that was developed in the United States Office of Education's Humanities Division. The concept has been used to encourage school systems, curriculum developers, arts organizations, and teacher preparatory programs to develop sequential, integrated arts programs in the schools with opportunities to utilize professional artists in the school programs. Programs have been cooperatively funded by private foundations and the National Endowment for the Arts, National Institute of Education, National Endowment for the Humanities, and the Office of Education. The programs are diverse in nature with different states setting different priorities for the Arts in Education. Magnet programs have been established in several states to attract majority students to inner-city schools with strong arts-related curricula. Other states have assigned state personnel to develop strategies for school improvement with a focus on the arts. Another strategy has been the use of the principle of networking. Network members are partners and peers committed to Arts in Education. Professional educators service the network, facilitate program development, and secure community resource personnel to assist in the schools' programs. The chief school administrator is responsible for providing leadership by advocating program development, materials development, and some budgetary support (Fineberg, 1980).

Artists in Schools program has been funded by the National Endowment for the Humanities. The idea is for community artists to participate in the school by working with groups of students in the artist's area of expertise. Involvement by artists in a school residency program has stimulated an examination of the arts curriculum in most school districts where the program operates.

Desegregation Funds that were provided by the Emergency School Aid Act (ESAA) were utilized by the Los Angeles Unified School District to develop programs for the arts, mathematics, and sciences to be used in the district's magnet schools. The program in the performing arts focuses on music, drama, and dance. The first component of the program, entitled "Very General Music," is described thusly:

> The major emphasis of this course is enrichment of the traditional general music class to include the correlation between the visual arts, the sciences, and mathematics.
>
> - Develops an understanding of the common elements in the arts.
> - Develops understanding of the scientific derivation of the elements of music.
> - Encourages positive attitudes and curiosity toward an increased variety of musical examples.
> - Provides opportunities to explore contemporary and avant-garde musical techniques and styles and their relationships to visual arts, science, and mathematics (Los Angeles Unified School District, 1980, p. 1).

The curriculum program written by school district specialists in the arts and consultants in mathematics and science is available to other schools and school districts and can be obtained from the Los Angeles Unified School District.

CEMREL is an aesthetic education program developed by the Central Midwestern Regional Educational Laboratory of St. Louis, Missouri (CEMREL, 1971). Classroom kits have been designed to be used by classroom teachers or art specialists. The teacher is able to select the instructional package or kit needed. There are four components to the program:

- Introduction to Aesthetic Phenomena. This is composed of materials related to the physical elements of the arts (light, sound, time, motion, shape).
- Elements in the Art Disciplines and the Environment. Materials in these kits focus on the interaction of elements within the arts.
- Process of Transformation. These kits focus on the process of synthesizing aesthetic and physical elements in a work of art.
- People in the Arts. These kits are designed to develop an appreciation of the artistic process and understanding about artists and their work.

Comprehensive Arts Program developed by the Southwest Regional Laboratory (SWRL) is a sequenced basic program for elementary students, research based and classroom verified to provide arts concepts and to encourage independent inquiry.

The art program is designed to develop students' awareness and appreciation of the role of artist, the art critic, and the art historian. The program concentrates on visual analysis, art production, and critical analysis.

- *Visual Analysis.* Students observe and analyze objects and illustrations of objects—For example, during the third block of instruction (each block consists of four units). Students will observe and analyze imaginary buildings and figures, trees and animals. They will study size differences that are a consequence of distance and proportion.
- *Production.* Students use a variety of art media to create their own work. Examples provided in the program's scope and sequence at the same level (3rd block) as in the prior example include: crayon drawing, tempera wash technique, sponge painting, cutting paper on a line, and pulling forms from clay.
- *Critical Analysis.* For this component the students observe and discuss the works of artists and begin to analyze and evaluate art works using both a cultural and historical context. During block three, the students analyze American, European, and Asian landscape paintings; Japanese screens in the twentieth century; and sculpture.

The program includes a program guide, a critical analysis guide, filmstrips, and assessment materials.

The music program is organized around six basic music concepts: rhythm, melody, harmony, form, tone color, and dynamic level. Awareness, appreciation, and performance tasks enable the students to understand music in terms of its expressive properties. Program components are performance proficiency, criticism proficiency, and composition proficiency.

- *Performance Proficiency* encompasses singing, playing instruments, reading standard music notation, and moving to music.
- *Criticism Proficiency* includes labeling and describing, analyzing, and evaluating.
- *Composition Proficiency* focuses on writing music notation, elaborating existing music, and composing original music.

The program is organized into 16 blocks of instruction. Each unit of the block is organized around one of the six concepts. For example, during the second block, concentrating on rhythm, the students would learn double and triple meter and for notation they would learn bar line, sets of two quarter notes and sets of three quarter notes.

The music program includes a program guide, assessment materials, song tapes, unit tapes, instrument posters, and notation performance cards for the tone bells and the auto harp along with aids for teaching standard music notation.

Both the music program and the art program are available from Phi Delta Kappa, Bloomington, Indiana 47402.

Manhattanville Music Curriculum Program (MMCP) is an inquiry approach to the teaching of music. MMCP curriculum for children ages three through eight is called "MMCP Interaction: Early Childhood Music Curriculum"; the program for children nine and above is called "MMCP Synthesis." Both use a spiral approach to teaching activities which range from simple to complex. Emphasis is on the structure of music (form, tone quality, dynamics, duration, and pitch). Activities begin with student discovery, then progress to invention, and finally involve composition. For example, in the series entitled "Metal Encounters" from the interaction curriculum during Phase I, students explore a variety of sounds using metal sources. Students are encouraged to add to the "sounds center" with their own metal objects. In the second phase the students contrast sounds from metal objects and discuss sound-producing techniques. During this phase the students identify sounds that are similar to sounds that they recall, such as a ticking clock, a dripping faucet, or a bouncing ball. In the third phase the students practice making sounds and repeating sound patterns. In phase four the students play the game of the "sound machine"—working in small groups the students arrange sound patterns so that they are satisfying to the group, expressive, and meaningful. Teacher materials suggest the foci for discussions and evaluative questions (Nye & Nye, 1974).

Orff. Carl Orff, a German composer, worked with Dorothee Gunther, a movement specialist, to develop a school program that unified dancing and gymnastics. From this experience Orff went on to collect and adapt percussion instruments appropriate for the use of young children. The Orff method for teaching was based on the idea that children are naturally inclined to express themselves with music and with improvisation. The Orff instruments allow children to explore music and sound. Used in elementary schools, the Orff program begins with melodic experiences, encouraging students to improvise, use body movements, sing, and utilize speech sounds and patterns. Favored instruments include the glockenspiel, the metalophone, the six-stringed viola da gamba, and the bordun, which is a bass two-stringed instrument.

Kodaly. Zoltan Kodaly was an Hungarian composer and has influenced music teaching in the United States. Kodaly advocated the use of the John Curwen hand signals, which teach syllables (Do, Re, Mi, Fa, So, La, Ti, Do), and recommended that children be taught to read and write music notation. Kodaly emphasized folk singing and believed that singing experiences should begin during the preschool years.

Dalcroze. Eurhythmics involves the whole body in rhythmic movements. Emile Jacques-Dalcroze, a Swiss teacher, developed this system for teaching music. After eurhythmics experiences, students practice singing using solfège. Dalcroze has been influential in the preparation of music teachers.

RESEARCH FINDINGS

Wright (1980) reported in "The Role and Status of Elementary Arts Programs" that arts education has the lowest status within the overall curriculum along with science and physical education. This conclusion was based on a study of the number of hours devoted to arts instruction and students' and principals' attitudes about arts education. In evaluating the quality of arts programs, the following conclusions were made:

1. There was not a wide array or balance of arts taught in the elementary schools studied.
2. Visual art and music predominated. (They were allotted more time than dance or drama.)
3. There was an emphasis on production and performance activities.
4. There was a similar emphasis on conforming and compliance instruction versus personal expression and creativity.
5. Students rarely chose their own art materials.
6. Students rated art work the easiest of all subjects taught in the elementary school.
7. Teachers rated art instruction as "appropriate" to students' abilities.
8. Primary-age children like art better than music.
9. Older elementary students like the arts and find them more interesting than other subjects.

Integration of Subject Fields and Learning Center Ideas

Interdisciplinary learning can be enhanced through the utilization of music and art as unifying strands throughout the school day. Listed by subject fields, fusion ideas will be cited for music and art. The ideas should also serve as concepts to develop into learning centers.

Social Studies and Art

1. Use art as a visual record of cultural development. Study history through paintings, architecture, occupations, fashion, furniture.
2. Study and reproduce artifacts.
3. Draw historical events.
4. Contrast handcrafts and manufactured products.
5. Draw murals.
6. Research occupations, furnishings, fashion, and the like and keep notes through the use of a sketch book.
7. Study the cultural use of silhouettes—historically.
8. Draw maps

Social Studies and Music

1. Use music as a musical record of cultural development.
2. Interpret social, political, and economic change by listening to and singing songs from different historical periods and different cultural groups.
3. Study customs, beliefs, and values by listening to and singing folk songs, work songs, religious music, sea chanties, recreational music, lullabies.
4. Study ethnic and cultural differences by listening to lullabies.
5. Trace technological development through music. (How many steamboat and choo-choo songs are written today?)
6. Use environmental materials to reproduce early instruments. (See picture in this section of instruments produced by children using natural materials.)
7. Identify a specific culture or society by studying the instruments used in a musical selection.

Science and Art

1. Study and draw natural and manmade environment.
2. Use a sketchbook to record observations of experiments.
3. Draw Darwin's theory of evolution.
4. Study and draw landscapes, rainbows, plants, animals, human anatomy.
5. Experiment, study, draw: light and color, warm and cool colors.
6. Use natural materials to make colors.
7. Use natural materials and make instruments.
8. Record (sketch) observations while looking through a magnifying glass, a prism, or a microscope.
9. Record the development of inventions.
10. Study the human eye, compare with a camera.

Science and Music

1. Find out: What causes sound?
   How does temperature affect sound?
   How does the thickness of bars and strings affect tone?
   How does the frequency of vibrations affect pitch?
   How are vibrations made?
   How do sounds differ?
   Compare the range in octaves of the human voice and instruments.
   How does distance affect sound?
   What happens when you use a megaphone or other devices?
   Through what substances will sound travel?
2. Listen to and identify environmental sounds.

3. Study the human ear; compare it with animals' ears.
4. Make instruments out of different materials and compare sounds.

Language Arts and Art

1. Use art works to stimulate creative writing.
2. Create murals or cartoons with talking people.
3. Use adjectives to describe: warm and cool colors, dull and bright colors.
4. Do the stage design for a play or musical.
5. Draw posters and write slogans.
6. Make puppets for dramatics or puppet shows.
7. Convey moods and feelings of pictures.
8. Draw a book report.
9. Use visual images to communicate.

Language Arts and Music

1. Use music as a stimulus for creative writing.
2. Interpret moods and feelings from music.
3. Interpret lyrics of songs.
4. Compose new lyrics for popular or old familiar songs.
5. Describe the style of musical selections (gay, proud, militant).
6. Read a play and identify stage sounds that will help the audience interpret the plot or understand the characterization.

Mathematics and Art

1. Illustrate math problems involving weight, balance, measurement, or geometry.
2. Illustrate the time of day using the sun and appropriate shadows.
3. Draw designs; divide, using the concept of positive and negative space.
4. Draw patterns.
5. Use symmetry in design work.
6. Plan a board game; divide spaces.

Mathematics and Music

1. Identify the pulse/beat of songs.
2. Study the speed of sound.
3. Measure how sounds differ in decibels.
4. Working in groups, use different number of beats to get to a set distance.

Physical Education, Health, and Art

1. Study space and form in movement activities.
2. Move, identifying positive and negative space.
3. Study and draw the human body.
4. Study health factors related to appearance. Draw good health posters.
5. Study and draw the food groups.
6. Paint a salad bar depicting the salad choices.
7. Use a sketchbook to record observations of experiments.
8. Draw action figures.
9. Study artists who specialize in sports pictures. Paint a sports picture.

Physical Education, Health, and Music

1. Perform folk games and dances.
2. Study body parts involved with making sound.
3. Enjoy creative and interpretive dance movements.
4. Practice singing a phrase in one breath.
5. Study the relationship of exercise and breathing.
6. Perform exercises and stretching to music.
7. Explore space using music.
8. Working in small groups, develop rhythm movement patterns; each group should perform for the other groups.

RESEARCH FINDINGS

Cohen and Gainer (1976, p. 159) studied colors that come from nature. They discovered:

- Juniper berries make a light brown.
- Walnut shells make a dark reddish brown.
- Holly berries make purple.
- Sage brush makes yellow.
- Oak bark makes a purplish brown.
- Red onion skin makes brown.
- Charcoal makes black and gray.
- Soil makes dark brown and sometimes dark red.

Mainstreaming the Arts

The arts can be the great classroom equalizer. Students poor in other subject fields may be talented in the arts. Physically handicapped children frequently perform exceptionally well in music and art. Students with physical problems or psychological problems may find personal satisfaction in the expression of art. The arts program can focus on students' abilities rather than their limitations. Most students enjoy using color, space, line, and textures in art as well as rhythm instruments in music. These experiences allow students to do "different" things and "special" things and at the same time keep in contact with their environment.

Although music and art activities can be individualized, in most situations students enjoy participating in group activities. Small work groups for music or art can accommodate individual differences, special abilities, and varied interests. In music, group work could consist of practicing and learning songs using recordings, planning accompaniments, or composing music. In art work, students may be grouped to use different media; some groups may be experimenting; other groups may be extending an art project; or they may be grouped for special instruction.

When grouping is used as an organizational technique during instruction in the arts, it is very important for the teacher to move from group to group to observe students' progress and to provide the guidance needed to encourage skill development. The mainstreamed student will probably need more guidance and feedback than other students. Motivation and involvement enhances learning in the arts; for this reason, students need small group work as well as whole class involvement.

Summary

The importance of education in the arts was recognized by the United States Congress when it created "The National Endowment for the Arts" in 1965. In addition, educators were encouraged to develop special cultural programs through federal funding under Title III of the Elementary Secondary Education Act.

The creative arts emphasize the development of aesthetic sensitivity as well as personal and creative expression. Child development concepts are used in the planning of curriculum experiences. Instructional programs should emphasize exploration, movement, production, music and art concepts, recognition of artists and works of art, selection of instructional materials and media, and the development of artistic judgment. The integration of subject fields is encouraged so that students experience a total, balanced school program.

Classroom Application Exercises

1a. Develop lessons for teaching the constituent elements of music (rhythm, melody, harmony, form).
1b. Develop lessons to teach the four components of art education: visual/tactile perception, creative expression, art heritage, aesthetic judgment.
1c. Develop lessons for integrating the arts with other subject fields.
2. Identify basic supplies for an art center.
3. Explain why arts lessons may be particularly appropriate for students who are considered discipline problems.
4. How could arts programs "open" the classroom climate and make it more challenging and exciting?
5. What music and art competencies do you believe that students should develop in the elementary school?

Suggested Readings for Extending Study

Brittain, W. Lambert. *Creativity, Art, and the Young Child*, New York: Macmillan Publishing Company, 1979.

Cohen, Elaine Pear, and Ruth Strass Gainer. *Art: Another Language for Learning*. New York: Citation Press, 1976.

Croft, Dorren J., and Robert D. Hess. *An Activities Handbook for Teachers of Young Children*. Boston: Houghton Mifflin Company, 1980.

Dewey, John. *Arts as Experience*. New York: G. P. Putnam & Sons, 1934.

Eisner, Elliot W. *Educating Artistic Vision.* New York: Macmillan Publishing Company, 1972.

Gaitskell, Charles D., and Al Hurwitz. *Children and Their Art: Methods for the Elementary School.* 3rd ed. New York: Harcourt Brace Jovanovich, Inc., 1975.

Haines, B., Joan and Linda L. Gerber. *Leading Young Children to Music: A Resource Book for Teachers.* Columbus, Ohio: Charles E. Merrill Publishing Company, 1980.

Land, L., and M. Vaughan. *Music in Today's Classroom: Creating, Listening, Performing.* 2nd ed. New York: Harcourt, Brace Jovanovich, Inc., 1978.

Linderman, Marlene M. *Art in the Elementary School.* 2nd ed. Dubuque, Iowa: William C. Brown Publishing Company, 1979.

Linderman, Earl W., and Marlene M. Linderman. *Crafts in the Classroom.* New York: Macmillan Publishing Company, 1977.

Linderman, Earl, and Donald Herberholz. *Developing Artistic and Perceptual Awareness: Art Practice in the Elementary Classroom.* 4th ed. Dubuque, Iowa: William C. Brown Publishing Company, 1979.

Lowenfeld, Viktor, and W. Lambert Brittain. *Creative and Mental Growth.* 6th ed. New York: Macmillan Publishing Company, 1982.

Nye, Robert Evans, and Vernice Trousdale Nye. *Essentials of Teaching Elementary School Music.* Englewood Cliffs, New Jersey: Prentice-Hall, Inc., 1974.

Raebeck, Lois, and Lawrence Wheeler. *New Approaches to Music in the Elementary Schools.* 4th ed. Dubuque, Iowa: William C. Brown Publishing Company, 1980.

Regelski, Tom. *Teaching General Music.* New York: Macmillan Publishing Company, 1981.

PART THREE

UNDERSTANDING INSTRUCTIONAL METHODS

After you have completed the study of the introduction, you should be able to accomplish the following:

1. **Name the human and situational variables affecting instruction.**
2. **Identify the three assumptions made about teaching in this textbook.**
3. **Make a list of activities to accomplish "input" and "output" goals.**
4. **Explain the relationship among the following: strategy, learning environment, teacher behavior.**

If you were asked to think about your favorite (and best) elementary school teacher, what would you remember? Do you recall a project that you participated in under the direction of that favored teacher? Is it the teacher's professional competencies that you remember? Are you thinking about the teacher's personal characteristics? The author asked the question to a group of experienced teachers and was surprised by the number of responses that dealt with the personal dimension. Although we know a great deal about the teaching process and professional competencies, it is obvious that there is little agreement about what is good teaching. "Good teaching" is so subjective it appears to depend upon who is doing the describing and who is doing the teaching.

In searching for evidence of the "best" approach to teaching, Joyce & Weil (1980) noted that "whether curriculums are compared, specific methods for teaching specific subjects are contrasted, or different approaches to counseling are analyzed . . . the evidence to date gives little encouragement to those who would hope that we have identified a single, reliable, multipurpose teaching strategy as the best approach" (p. 8).

What works well for one teacher may not necessarily work well for another. Teaching techniques, styles, and procedures need to be adapted to fit the individual teacher's personality and the collective personalities of the students who are being taught. However, even though we cannot predict with certainty what will always work, we do know that certain methods of teaching are associated with specific learning outcomes. Before we examine specific instructional techniques, let us review some of the human and situational variables that affect instruction.

First of all, instruction is defined as the activity which occurs in the classroom setting encompassing the resources or materials used and the teacher and student variables. The human variables include:

Student Characteristics: age, sex, developmental level, social class, language, academic and achievement motivation, intellectual development, cognitive style, self-concept.

Teacher Characteristics: teaching style, age, sex, social class background, preparatory experiences, warmth, enthusiasm, openness, management skills.

Organizational and content variables also need to be considered for instructional planning. These variables include:

Organizational Considerations: size of class, space in classroom, time, class composition.

Content Considerations: subject grade level, objectives, sequence, resources, and materials.

Both human and situational variables affect instruction. The teacher who is cognizant of the variables will use them positively as a guide to planning and implementing instruction. For example:

- If a first-grade teacher wants to have block work, the teacher will need to consider floor space (which may necessitate the moving of tables and chairs), the equipment (blocks and accessories), and specific lesson objectives.
- 9:00 A.M. on Monday morning after Christmas vacation may be a very poor time to have a science experiment. Probably a structured lesson would fit students and teacher better at that particular time.
- The planning of a construction lesson for students you do not know may be inappropriate, but as you become acquainted with the students the construction lesson certainly would be feasible.

In other words, the teacher must use common sense in choosing a teaching method. If the amount of time required for a given lesson is not available or other context variables are wrong, then the teacher must make an alternate decision.

Human and situational variables should be considered for instructional decisions.

Assumptions About Teaching

Three basic assumptions about teaching are made in this section of the textbook. They are:

1. There are a variety of approaches to instruction that are appropriate. If an open-ended science experiment is inappropriate on Monday morning after vacation, there is probably another strategy that will be quite effective.

Instructional Approaches

Expository Teaching	Guided Discussion	Interaction
Lecture Direct instruction	Socratic questioning	Inquiry/Problem solving Case study Group investigation Role-plays Gaming Inductive thinking

2. The method of instruction affects the learning process. This means that although several approaches may be appropriate, each will contribute something quite different. The open-ended science experiment will contribute toward self-development, social participation, and science concepts; reading out of a science textbook will foster science concepts but will not affect social participation or discovery learning.

Interaction of Learning Environment and Teacher Behavior

Environment	Teacher Behavior
Controlled environment, high structure	Teacher controls the dialog; teacher sets the stage and controls student responses. Limited instructional materials are needed.
Controlled environment, moderate to high structure	Teacher initiates discussions and programs questions to elicit desired responses. Teacher controls student interaction to fit discussion. Some supportive instructional materials are needed.
Open environment, moderate structure	Teacher initiates problem or conflict situation. Teacher often guides the problem resolution as it moves from stage to stage. A great deal of student interaction is encouraged. Students are expected to accept responsibility for problem solving. Variety of instructional materials needed.
Open environment, low structure	Teacher facilitates democratic processes. Students define problems and initiate methods for solving them. Teacher provides many resources and encourages students to use resources out of the confines of the classroom.

3. Students react differentially to the instructional process. This means that some students will learn more effectively with some approaches than with others. The student who is visually oriented will not appreciate the teacher

who reads test questions orally to the class. A student's characteristics affect what is learned.

Interplay of Strategy Choice and Learning Environment

Strategy	Learning Environment
Lecture, film, direct Instruction	Controlled environment, high structure important
Guided discussions, questioning, analysis	Controlled environment, moderate to high structure
Role-playing, simulations gaming, dramatizations	Open environment, moderate structure
Discovery, problem solving, group investigations	Open environment, low structure

Types of Teaching Strategies

Visualize a balance scale—on one side of the scale are learning experiences which accomplish "input" goals. These experiences are planned so that students will consume information and learn specific skills. Experiences may include a museum visit, a lecture, films and slides, textbooks, television, records and tapes, use of a workbook, an exhibit, or a demonstration. Student behavior during input includes observation, listening, reading, responding, questioning, and note taking. The student may appear to be passive during input experiences, but in fact, s/he is using the senses to collect information.

On the other side of the balance scale are learning experiences which accomplish "output" goals. These experiences are planned so that the student produces knowledge. Experiences are extremely numerous and may include some of the following:

reports (oral and written)
projects
mapmaking
dramatics, performance, singing
role-playing, simulations, gaming
experiments
discussions, debates
construction
interviewing
committee work

Student behaviors include:

research
exploration

speaking, writing, acting out
manipulative, building
questioning, planning, creating
valuing, decision making

Output strategies require the student to perform in some way.

During output the student is processing information to develop new meanings. There is a reciprocal relationship between input and output teaching strategies. Output strategies are dependent upon prior input; thus the teacher balances teaching approaches to maximize learning.

Organization of Part III

Chapters 12–15 have been organized to facilitate the study of several different teaching techniques. Chapter 12 focuses on the importance of direct instruction and guided discussion for the development of skills. Direct instruction is considered an expository teaching technique. Chapter 13 provides an instructional contrast by illustrating inquiry and problem-solving techniques. Unit teaching, or the project method, and research skills are discussed in Chapter 14. All of the techniques identified in Part III are appropriate strategies for use in unit teaching. Chapter 15 illustrates role-playing, games, and simulations.

Chapter 16 discusses the importance of instructional materials. Procedures for evaluating learning resources are provided along with an example of the process.

Chapter 17 completes the section on instruction by focusing on strategies for evaluating and communicating learning progress. The importance of evaluation as a factor in learning is emphasized.

Chapter 12

Exposition and Discussion Strategies

After you have completed the study of this chapter, you should be able to accomplish the following:

1. **Identify the characteristics of skill instruction.**
2. **Identify and explain the three-step process for direct (skill) instruction.**
3. **Compare direct instruction to open teaching approaches; explain differences in achievement.**
4. **Explain the use of guided discussion during direct instruction.**
5. **Identify the characteristics of oral discussions; explain the use of the classroom environment and discussion roles.**
6. **Identify and define the three types of discussion and corresponding teacher behavior.**
7. **Discuss the research on questioning.**
8. **Practice writing questions to achieve specific purposes.**

In this chapter two modes of instruction are explored: expository and discussion. The expository mode focuses on the teacher. The teacher's task is to communicate information to students. The teacher may do this through lecturing or sometimes through the use of a combination technique of lecture, question, and short-answer response. The main purpose of expository teaching is to transmit knowledge. There is very little interaction among students during expository teaching. The classroom environment is controlled, and there is moderate to high structure. The teacher controls discussion by initiating questions and eliciting short-answer responses.

Direct instruction is a type of expository teaching. Direct instruction defined in Chapter 3, usually conforms to the following format:

- Diagnosis
- Prescription
- Modeling (presentation, lecture)
- Practice
- Monitoring
- Feedback

Direct Instruction

Effective Teaching of Reading and Math Skills

Stevens and Rosenshine (1981) generalized from the research by Stallings and Kaskowitz (1974), Soar (1973), the BTES study (1977), and others that there were four basic characteristics of effective skill instruction:

1. it is group instruction;
2. it is directed by the teacher;
3. it has a clear academic focus;
4. it is oriented to the individuals in the group.

Group Instruction. Since it is difficult, if not almost impossible, for teachers to give one-to-one direction and keep the rest of the class actively engaged in academic work, directed instruction in small groups of three to seven students appears to be the most effective system. The research indicates that if an adult can closely monitor the work of the group, academic engagement and achievement are higher.

Teacher-directed Instruction. The most successful teachers (those whose students achieve highest gains) are strong classroom leaders. They plan their teaching objectives, teach to them in a businesslike way, asking meaningful questions directed to the students, listen to responses, and give immediate feedback.

The less successful teachers are disorganized in the classroom. They play the role of a participant rather than a leader, and they allow too much student choice during the teaching of the essential skills.

RESEARCH FINDINGS

Stevens and Rosenshine (1981) observed that although the intructional methods for teaching basic academic skills was derived from observation in regular classroom settings, the methods suggested for direct instruction appear to be applicable to teaching academic skills to handicapped students.

Academic Focus. Teachers who are able to keep their students task oriented instead of using time allocated for math and reading to play games, read stories, or do arts and crafts, achieve higher gains with their students. However, this does not mean that the teachers who have been successful in the teaching of skills are not warm, democratic leaders. In an ethnographic study of the classroom (a study of the social system of the classroom and the roles of students and teacher), Tikunoff, Berliner, and Rist (1975) observed the successful teachers involved in the BTES study and found that their classrooms were warm, convivial, cooperative, and democratic. In contrast, the teachers of the lowest-achieving classrooms were inconsistent, critical, sarcastic, and demeaning of the students.

Individualization. Individualization in these studies of effective skill instruction does *not* mean students working alone or choosing their own activities. Instead, it means that the teacher directed each child's work, had confidence that each child could learn, and provided the instruction *in the group* to assist the individual through direction, praise, and feedback.

Designated Instructional Practices

The research concerning successful skill instruction is specific. The most efficient method appears to be a three-step process:

1. The teacher demonstrates or models the skill objective.
2. Students practice the skill with the teacher observing and providing immediate feedback.
3. Students practice the skill independently.

During the second step (practice with the teacher observing), it is extremely important that the teacher ask specific factual questions and elicit a student response. The teacher should provide academic feedback during this component. Several studies of low socioeconomic students verify that questions that have single answers during this practice and drill period should be asked and that students should be provided with immediate feedback. Rosenshine and Stevens (1981) note that in most of the studies reviewed the frequency of direct factual teacher questions and the frequency of accurate student responses were positively associated with high achievement.

Success Is Important. The BTES study and other studies emphasize that when students work alone and when they work during the controlled practice period (step two), they need to be successful. Correct answers should be possible for the students at least 80 per cent of the time for low socioeconomic students and at least 70 per cent of the time for students of high socioeconomic status.

During skill instruction, high-level cognitive questions (open-ended questions) do not correlate positively with achievement. The problem with these questions during skill instruction may be related to the students' need for feedback. Open-ended questions do not necessarily have a "right" answer, and so the teacher cannot verify verbally that the student is on the right track. Also, the attack strategy to answer higher-level questions cannot be demonstrated by the teacher, and so the students need to discover and process their responses without teacher assistance.

Monitoring Independent Practice. The independent practice period (step three) usually takes the form of follow-up seatwork during reading instruction or practicing a small number of examples of the skill during mathematics. Since success is so important, the exercises that students do should be relatively easy. As students practice, the teacher should monitor the student's work and provide immediate feedback in the form of positive reinforcement or a short explanation when the student needs assistance. The feedback provided to the student should not take more than about thirty seconds of the teacher's time; if it takes longer, then the teacher can assume that the original explanation was faulty.

The BTES researchers labeled success rate in three ways: high—when the tasks can be readily mastered; moderate—the tasks are somewhat easy; low—tasks are very hard or cannot be mastered. The high rate and to some extent the moderate rate affect students positively whereas the low rate is negatively associated with achievement.

Block (1980) states that success rate can be controlled by the teacher by executing five activities:

1. Diagnosis—the teacher predicts how the student will do based upon present and past performance;
2. Prescription—based upon the teacher's diagnosis, specific learning tasks are designed;
3. Orientation—the teacher clarifies each learning task demonstrating what is to be learned and how to go about it;
4. Feedback—the teacher provides constant information to the student about how she/he is doing;
5. Correction—if a student is not learning, then the teacher provides supplementary instruction (remediation) and begins the process over again.

Block's activities are particularly appropriate for students with learning disabilities.

Is Direct Instruction Ever Inappropriate?

Peterson (1979) used the work of Horwitz (1979) to compare the effects of open versus traditional approaches on student achievement. She concluded that students do slightly better on achievement tests when they have experienced direct instruction, but slightly worse on tests of abstract thinking which validate creativity and problem-solving ability. Open teaching approaches facilitate creative thinking and problem-solving techniques, but students do somewhat worse on achievement tests. Open teaching approaches also improve students' attitudes toward school and teacher and appear to improve students' independence and curiosity.

As Wright and DuCette (1976) discovered, students who feel that they have personal control of their successes and failures do better (achieve more) when the teacher uses an open approach to teaching. Students who feel that others control their successes and failures did just as well in direct and open teaching approaches. Peterson concluded that students who have an external locus of control do better with a direct instruction approach since their learning style matches the controlled setting of direct instruction, whereas the student whose style is self-directed (having an internal locus of control) is frustrated during direct instruction.

Peterson also concluded that the effectiveness of direct instruction depends upon the ability of the students. High-achieving students who are task oriented appear to do worse in direct instruction.

Peterson and Janicki (1979) found that high-ability students did better when the teacher used small group instruction as opposed to large group instruction. The low-ability students did better when the teacher used large group instruction.

It is apparent from the research on direct teaching and open teaching approaches that if the teacher's objective is inquiry teaching/problem solving, then open approaches are superior. If, on the other hand, the teaching objective is essential skill instruction in reading and mathematics, then direct instruction should be used. However, the choice of a teaching approach should also be based on the students to be taught. High-ability students may be frustrated with direct instruction, but low-ability students appear to need the structured environment that accompanies direct instruction.

It is clear from the review of how children learn that there is still a great deal we do not know. Teachers must exercise judgment and make decisions about teaching. Kepler (1980) comments that teachers must find a balance between the following factors:

- High and moderate success rate
- Whole class, small group, individual instruction
- Time allocated to different subject matter goals
- Cognitive and affective concerns
- Coverage and mastery
- Teacher decisions, joint decisions, child decisions
- Absolute attention and realistic inattention
- Standardized criteria of evaluation and idiosyncratic criteria
- Needs of individuals and needs of the group (p. 154).

Guided Discussion and Direct Instruction

Direct instruction is dependent upon students' on-task behaviors. To facilitate students' understanding, involvement, and success, teachers question students during skill instruction. The strategy is really a mixture of expository teaching and guided discussion. The questions are oriented to factual and comprehension information. Responses required from students are short answer. The student is called on during instruction, and the teacher verifies that the student understands. If a mistake is made, the teacher corrects it, thereby providing instant feedback. During small group reading instruction the sequence may be: group question to cue silent reading, teacher question to an individual related to the silent reading, response, teacher question to another student, response; then the cycle begins again.

During instruction of a new skill, the format is similar. The teacher may present or model the new skill or concept. Next the teacher questions students about the presentation. The question is factual and requires a short answer. To verify that others understand, the teacher may continue the question/answer format. Interaction is limited to teacher-to-student and back again to teacher. It is important that students understand the purpose of the lesson when using this format so that they can concentrate on the essential elements.

An Example of Direct Instruction

Let us suppose that in Mr. Atwater's second grade classroom he had determined that several of his youngsters did not understand the use of context clues. He planned a lesson using a short story in the basal reader.

> Boys and girls, today we are going to see if we can play the game of detective. I am going to show some pictures to you and you are to try to guess what is happening in the story from these pictures.

Atwater showed the pictures in sequence to the students. Then he asked specific questions about the action in each of the pictures: "Who do we see in this picture?" "What is Ramón doing?" "How can you tell?" "Why do you think Ramón is crying?"

Atwater guided the students through the story using the pictures. Then he said, "Let's find out if we were good detectives." This time the story was read in the usual manner with silent reading cued by an appropriate question, but once again the questions related to the sequence of the pictures.

When students recognized their success as detectives, Mr. Atwater provided them with another opportunity to practice. He had prepared short, simple eight-line stories. The students worked with a partner. One student told the story using the pictures that were provided, and the other student confirmed the story by reading it. Then with new stories they exchanged roles. Mr. Atwater watched, listened, and provided feedback. Atwater's lesson had several stages:

1. Planning (diagnosis and prescription)
2. Instruction (presentation, activity)
3. Practice (monitoring and feedback)

Another example of direct instruction was provided in Chapter 3.

Discussion Strategies

Characteristics of Oral Discussions

A true discussion involves the sharing of ideas, thoughts, and feelings. An oral discussion is not intended to be a soliloquy. It is a conversation in which two or more individuals participate. During most classroom discussions, it is expected that students will participate equally, and depending upon the type of discussion, the teacher may play an equal role, adopt a leadership role, or choose not to participate at all.

Participants in a discussion utilize background information and experiences and/or data from recently acquired research or study. Although it is possible to participate silently by listening, the individual who does not express ideas, thoughts, and feelings is probably not involved in the discussion.

Classroom discussions may involve the whole class or a small group of students. The discussion may have a discussion leader who may or may not be the teacher. The leader may ask questions to focus the discussion and increase participation, or the leader may act as a moderator.

A classroom discussion should have a purpose. Students are assembled in a group to talk in a meaningful way. This underlying purpose differentiates the classroom discussion from an idle conversation. Discussions should progress through a series of steps; however, the steps are not necessarily sequentially accomplished. A discussion usually begins with a "get acquainted with the topic" stage; it then generally proceeds to a problem definition stage in which the participants focus on the purpose. The discussion may have a data gathering stage, and ultimately the discussion should terminate with a conclusion or a summing up.

Discussion Manners

Discussion manners and skills are crucial to the success of the teaching strategy. If participants in a discussion are "equal," then the flow of conversation moves around the group and encourages individual responses and contributions. But if the discussion is characterized by a back and forth exchange between teacher and student(s) then group interaction is discouraged, the flow of ideas is limited, sense of group belonging diminishes, and positive social attitudes are not developed.

Discussion manners are as important for the teacher as they are for the students, and most are a matter of good sense. However, the manners and skills need to be taught, modeled, and practiced. Good discussions do not happen automatically. The taking of turns—not monopolizing the conversation—is one of the first things that needs to be taught and modeled. For students to grasp this idea, it is important to call attention to it during the evaluation. Although this is just common sense, it cannot be taken for granted.

Listening to others is another common-sense item, but it entails "attending" to the discussion. Its importance is not meaningful to students until they realize that some of the discussion contributions are repetitious and irrelevant.

The importance of not making conversation "asides" to a neighbor or to a limited few needs to be constantly reiterated or the discussion deteriorates into many small purposeless conversations.

That contributions should be meaningful and focus on the topic or purpose hardly needs to be mentioned except that this is a most difficult task for young students.

The ability to synthesize the discussion or to develop a conclusion based upon the discussion is the hardest skill to be taught. The capacity to do this comes through practice. Even adults tend to allow the discussion leader to assume this responsibility; yet, in fact, every discussion participant should be developing the conclusion or synthesis and be ready to challenge and contribute to the culmination of the discussion.

Classroom Environment and Discussion Roles

The classroom environment affects the success of the discussion, and the size of the discussion group influences the skills needed by teacher and students. In a discussion group, students' faces are close together; they see each other easily. They know when someone is about to speak. If the students are motivated by their discussion, they will not be distracted easily, unless they are disturbed by other groups in the classroom. The teacher's role, while students are interacting in small discussion groups, is supportive and facilitative. The teacher walks among the groups, observing, and providing assistance when needed.

In large discussion groups, sometimes students cannot see each other. This occurs at times because the need to see each other has not been anticipated in the planning of the discussion formation. Yet "eyeballing" is crucial in a discussion; in a large group, how else do you know when a classmate is about to speak? We learn a great deal about each

Involvement in a Large Group Discussion Is Often Dependent upon Being Able to See Other Class Members.

other by watching the eyes, hands, posture, and facial expressions. If this is denied to us during a discussion, there is a greater possibility that we will *not* focus in on the discussion or become involved.

The teacher's role during the large group discussion depends both upon the purpose of the discussion and upon the teacher's own personality needs. If the classroom climate is highly structured and the teacher demands rigid control, the discussion will be limited to a select few students. The interaction pattern will tend to be from teacher to student and back to teacher again. However, if the teacher creates an open, warm, encouraging climate for discussion, then the flow of ideas will move among the students and students will learn to listen to classmates and take turns. A moderate environment must be sought; the teacher who is too rigid or too permissive will have a limited discussion monopolized by aggressive students. Taba (1967) states that the teacher who is too permissive and abandons the discussion totally to the students will have a limited and chaotic discussion period.

> How would you arrange your classroom for a discussion? Draw a diagram to illustrate it.

Leadership Role. In all group discussions, a leader is needed. The leadership role may be assumed by either teacher or students. Typically in a small discussion group, a student is designated as the leader. Ultimately, all students should learn to assume the leadership role.

The basic purpose of a discussion is to encourage students to gather and process information by sharing with others and listening to others. This objective helps to define the role of the discussion leader. The leader's attitude influences the discussion. Facilitative behaviors are important to encourage participation. These behaviors include:

- accepting all responses by assuming a nonjudgmental attitude
- encouraging spontaneity by not injecting personal statements or evluative responses
- soliciting feelings and value responses through questioning and asking for clarification
- extending thinking through summative statements.

These behaviors are thoroughly discussed under the category of teacher behavior.

Students can learn to assume the leadership role when they are provided with practice situations and given an evaluation of their leadership performance. Checklists for evaluating discussions can be found in Chapter 17.

The participatory role assumed by most of the students (and occasionally by the teacher) needs a great deal of practice. The very young, egocentric child has difficulty sharing and listening to others. Until the child learns group participatory behaviors, discussions are difficult. Acceptance of group responsibility is a developmental process. Behaviors include:

- sensitivity to others' viewpoints
- listening to others and asking questions of others
- assuming responsibility to contribute ideas, thoughts, and feelings.

It is important to remember that these behaviors are only learned if they are practiced, and they can be learned at any grade level.

The recorder's role is important in most discussions. It is the recorder's job to log the discussion and to be ready to recount it during the evaluative period. Group members should assist the recorder in keeping an accurate chronicle of the meeting. Verbatim minutes are unnecessary; more important are the trends in the discussion and the decisions that are made. The recorder may also assist the group leader by recounting the discussion and summarizing it at different times in order to keep the group "on target."

Discussion Skills Improve with Practice. During a Discussion Students Learn Sensitivity to Others' Viewpoints.

Discussion Problems. It is quite incongruous that on the one hand some teachers complain that students never stop talking; yet when it comes to a class discussion, these same teachers will deplore the lack of class participation! What happens, of course, may be related to several factors:

1. Students have been "successfully" inhibited and feel that participation is undesired by the teacher.
2. Students feel that they are in a fishbowl during a discussion, and they become shy.
3. The teacher or discussion leader or several aggressive students monopolize the discussion and so others do not participate.
4. Students are disinterested in the topic/problem/questions posed for discussion.

If the lack of participation is related to the first factor (inhibition), there is very little that can be suggested except to remind the teacher that at school students are supposed to use language, and the teacher's professional expertise should be used to find as many constructive means as possible to develop language usage. Students who have been turned off to talking can be helped quickly by eliminating the negative influences and by reinforcing positive speech behaviors.

The second factor (shyness) is more relevant to a consideration of types of discussions. Students of all ages are frequently inhibited by the large class discussion. Shyness can be dealt with through the utilization of the small group discussion. In groups of no larger than seven students, everyone participates, and discussion skills can be developed.

If the third problem (aggressiveness) affects participation, then the teacher must develop questioning and involvement strategies to guide the discussion and to encourage interaction.

The fourth factor (disinterest) simply means that the students need to participate in the planning process and help identify meaningful topics or problems.

The Aggressive, Overtalkative Student. If the overtalkative student could hear him/herself as others do, there would be no problem! The trick is to help this student perceive him/herself accurately. One of the most effective means of accomplishing this is to have this student observe another student who has a similar problem. For example, when Greg Thomas had this problem in his classroom, he suggested that Ginger, an aggressive talker, observe another group of students during the discussion lesson. Ginger's task was to provide feedback to the group she was observing concerning participation and progress toward the group objective. Specifically, Ginger was asked to report:

1. Did everyone contribute and participate?
2. Did the group accomplish its purpose?
3. Who helped the group most to accomplish its purpose?
4. What problems did the group have?
5. What suggestions would you make to the group?

Ginger was flattered to be the group observer. Thomas cautioned Ginger not to hurt anyone's feelings. When she reported to the group she observed that one person (Sylvia) had monopolized the conversation on several occasions with the result that the group did not have time to reach a conclusion.

Thomas talked with Ginger about her findings and asked her if she recalled performing in a similar fashion. Ginger recognized that she, too, had often monopolized the conversation. Although Ginger still needed to be reminded during successive sessions, her awareness of the problem improved her own performance.

If Thomas had not had two aggressive talkers in his classroom, he could have accomplished the same objective by taping a small group session and asking Ginger to listen and evaluate using the tape recorder.

The Shy Student. The introverted student can best be helped by providing experiences to talk in a small group situation. This student is usually overwhelmed by whole class participation. Careful group placement with an unselfish group of students will facilitate the shy child's participation. It should be considered extremely unusual if a child does not participate in the small group.

In the large group it may be possible to encourage participation of this child by providing opportunities to contribute prefaced with, "Sally, what do you think about this?" Or, "Rob, do you agree with . . . ?" Or, "Helen, how would you handle this problem?" However, this must be done cautiously because direct questions to the shy student may complicate the problem.

Another thing to remember with the shy child is to provide plenty of response time. Sometimes children anticipate that the teacher will not wait for them to respond; thus, the shy child becomes more inhibited because of the expectation of being cut off before a full response has been made.

APPLICATION OF RESEARCH

Rowe (1974) found that student participation, interaction, and involvement increased when the teachers waited three to five seconds before soliciting another response or before providing additional clues. Teacher silence after calling on a student is an extremely important teaching technique to increase involvement and creativeness.

Types of Discussions

(1) *Unstructured or "free" discussions.* The "sharing" discussion of the kindergarten and first-grade classrooms is an example of an unstructured meeting time in which students simply practice talking, listening, and questioning each other. This type of free discussion has no set purpose other than language usage, the expression of personal feelings, and learning to talk to an audience. The teacher usually refrains from contributing to this discussion in order to encourage spontaneity. The sharing discussion can be made more relevant by suggesting to students that they bring important items to class for the sharing period. These items might include "a book I like," "my hobby," "my collection," "an experiment I performed," "something I made."

The unstructured discussion is also used to initiate new topics or areas of study, such as a social studies unit. The purpose of the free discussion in this situation is to encourage students to identify interests and problems and to find out what students really know about the new topic. The free discussion is typically a large group activity although it does not need to be.

(2) *Semi-structured discussion.* In this type of discussion students are usually reporting progress toward a specific purpose, or exchanging information as a result of a research/problem-solving lesson, or contributing information gained from a field trip or a special experience. The discussion has been structured by the prior activity or by specific instructions. For an example of the semi-structured discussion, review Mr. Atwater's problem-solving assignment concerning magnets in Chapter 3. These primary students were asked to find out: "What will magnets pull?" They were also asked to make a "rule" about what magnets pull. Their small group discussions and their large group evaluative discussion would be characteristic of the semistructured type of discussion.

(3) *Structured discussions.* These are guided discussions which have been preplanned to accomplish specific cognitive functions. The structured discussion is dependent upon a sequenced questioning strategy. The purpose is to facilitate the development of cognitive skills by beginning with a lower-level cognitive skill and moving to the generalization level. The structured discussion can help students develop concepts, make decisions, and learn to solve problems. During the course of the discussion students should be contributing information (data) and, as they listen to others and to the questions they should be processing the data in order to arrive at the concept, a generalization, a prediction, or a decision.

Teaching Tasks and Behaviors

There are two basic ideas to keep in mind when using discussion as an instructional approach. The first is that the students need to learn "how" to discuss, which means that there are skills they need to master in order to discuss "well." The second point is that there is a purpose related to academic content to be accomplished through use of the discussion technique. Thus, at the end of a discussion the evaluation should focus on both the discussion process and on the substantive nature of the subject for discussion. Teacher tasks relate to those two purposes. For example, students will learn discussion skills more easily if they practice the skills in a small group situation. Therefore, the teacher needs to consider the composition of the small group. We have already stated in Chapter 3 that small groups are better if they are composed of five to seven students. Discussion will be facilitated if the group members are *different* rather than alike. Moffett (1968) suggests differences related to dialect, sex, socioeconomic status, verbal ability, and intelligence. His studies indicate that students' speech develops best when it is necessary to explain and clarify meanings. So one of the first tasks of the teacher is to consider the size and composition of small groups when assigning students to a discussion activity.

Discussion Rules and Roles. Another teacher task is the presentation, teaching, and follow-up of discussion rules and roles. Conversing in a group is a difficult cognitive activity. The first thing that students need to learn is to recognize when another speaker has finished talking. Students should be asked, "How do you think you can tell when your friend has concluded speaking?" The basic response is "when they stop." But the next question is the real key, "How can you tell when a friend is ready to speak?" The response should be, "I can tell by the eyes or when the person begins, or . . . ." The bottom line in rule making for discussion is that students must learn to take turns without *hand-raising*. Hand-raising inhibits the flow of conversation and makes the group leader the recipient of all speech.

The teacher must also decide whether to choose the leader and recorder for the discussion group or have the students do so. In the beginning it might be better if the teacher exercises that judgment. But the roles should be rotated on successive days. During the course of the discussion the teacher will need to verify that the discussion leader is encouraging all members of the group to speak. The discussion leader and recorder should be evaluated by the group in an inoffensive manner at the end of the session. During the evaluation session the teacher should solicit from the total group ideas for encouraging all members of the group to contribute. This serves the dual purpose of teaching leadership responsibility to the discussion leaders and participation responsibility to everyone.

Verifying Meanings. Before students are sent off to their discussion group, it is wise to make sure that they understand what it is they are to discuss or accomplish. Then the teacher should verify that they comprehend the meanings involved in what they are to do. For example, Mr. Atwater (Chapter 3) demonstrated what a magnet can do and had the children talk about it before he sent them off to their problem-solving lesson. In this way he prepared them for the group discovery session.

Another aspect of verifying meanings has to do with *establishing the focus*. Children as well as adults tend to digress from the chosen topic. About the best way to deal with this tendency is to be sure that a discussion focus has been set and is understood. This end is accomplished by providing the discussion group(s) with a set of questions. The questions should be open-ended so that there will be many alternatives in terms of the discussion, but there ought to be enough questions so that when you join the group to observe and listen to the discussion you are able to ask: "What question are you discussing now?" Of course, some questions may cultivate enough discussion so that only one is needed. Questions will be discussed later in this chapter.

Refocusing. As you visit the discussion group you may find that the discussion disregards the problem focus. Perhaps the students have misunderstood the meanings, or perhaps they have just strayed from the topic. When this occurs it is the teacher's job to ask a question or make a statement that will bring the students back to the original topic. If Mr. Atwater had found that the students were not discussing the "rule" for magnets when he toured the problem-solving groups, he would have said, "Did you find out what magnets pull?" Or Mr. Atwater might have said, "Do you remember that we were to find out what a magnet can and cannot do? After finding out what a magnet can pull, can you tell us how these items are alike?"

Mr. Atwater also anticipated that some of his groups might complete the assignment earlier than others. As he visited his groups he was prepared to change the focus and extend the experiment by suggesting an additional experiment for the students to perform. This same anticipatory act is necessary even if groups are just talking. Some groups get to the heart of the matter quickly, and they may need to consider the topic in greater depth or to move on to a new topic.

Clarifying and Valuing. Somehow adults have taught children that what they say is unimportant and what adults contribute is to be valued. The consequence of this is that children tend not to listen well to their peers. They anticipate that what their peer has said the adult will repeat, so why bother listening to a classmate? When students reiterate what others have said, it means that they have not been listening. About the only way to deal with this is to say to the repeater, "Roberto already told us about that. Roberto, will you explain to William what you told us before?"

Another typical problem occurs when students do not understand a classmate's comments and so they either just sit there without speaking, or they ask the teacher, "What did Billy mean?" The trick is to get Billy to explain his meanings rather than for the teacher to clarify. Since students become accustomed to the teacher clarifying what has been discussed, they tend not to focus in and listen to their classmates. To take care of this the teacher should ask the original speaker, "Billy, will you tell us what you meant by . . . ?" When the problem is treated habitually in this manner, students will begin to ask questions of their peers rather than of the teacher.

Supportive Classroom Climate. The seating arrangement and structural climate of the classroom has been mentioned; however, there is another type of atmosphere that the teacher must create if the discussion is to be successful. This has to do with the development of an attitude that supports all student contributions even if they are not terribly helpful at that moment. The teacher must be so objective during a discussion that the students will not be able to discern either approval or disapproval of their comments. This does not mean, however, that conceptual errors should be allowed.

When an error in logic or an error involving a specific fact occurs, the teacher should ask the student to clarify the meaning. The teacher should also be soliciting corrections or additional statements from other students when this occurs. By saying, "Boys and girls, what do you think about that?" Or, "Does everyone agree?" Or, "Who has a different idea?" This process must be handled sensitively so that students do not hesitate to make comments because they fear they will make mistakes.

When errors or irrelevant comments occur, the teacher must also make sure that the child making the comment is not attacked by peers. Once again, the supportive climate and encouragement of the teacher is important.

Extending Thinking. The teacher needs to be constantly alert to ways to extend and broaden patterns of thinking. The following may be useful for this purpose:

1. Ask the students to review the major points already discussed, or you may summarize what has been said.
2. After the summary, ask: "What do we still need to consider?"
3. If there has been conflict over definitions or values expressed, ask the class if Billy and Susie mean the same things when they discussed "communication."
4. Remind students that they have already discussed several means of communication. Then ask: "Are there some things we have forgotten?" Or, "How else might we think about . . . ?"

To Evaluate. At the end of the discussion there should be a final recap of what has been discussed and concluded, the main ideas, and/or the areas of conflict. During the evaluation students should be helped to understand what has been accomplished. Students should learn that the discussion will always be evaluated in two ways: substantively in terms of the content and also in terms of the discussion process. They should also learn that personal behaviors will *not* be dwelled upon.

If group observers are used, this is the time they would give their report.

Both group evaluation and self-evaluation may be used at the end of the discussion period.

Questioning Techniques

Purposes of Questioning

Appropriate use of questioning can be the most effective teaching technique used by teachers. Questions can be used to motivate and guide students' study. Questions can be used to orient students to problems and make them aware of values; they can be used to teach students to process information and to facilitate analysis and evaluation. Questions initiate and guide most class discussions.

Questions have many classroom purposes, and research indicates that teachers use questions frequently for both assessment and motivational reasons. In recent years there has been a great deal of debate about whether teachers should ask low-level questions that focus on factual responses or stimulate students to higher-level thinking. Stallings and Kaskowitz (1974) found that low-level questions were more productive than high-level, abstract questions. However, their data were collected during the teaching of reading and mathematics in lower elementary classrooms with disadvantaged students. If students are to engage in reflective thinking, then higher-level cognitive questions will need to be asked. Brophy and Evertson (1976) found that the frequency of questions asked is related to students' learning. These researchers reasoned that the frequency of questions meant that students were involved most of the time in learning-related activities and that their teachers supplemented reading and practice activities with oral activities.

Research on questioning as a teaching behavior provides some guidance about how to use this method most effectively. It is apparent that questions asked should:

1. Stimulate thinking
2. Be formulated so that they are precise and concise
3. Be appropriate to the purpose of the lesson
4. Accommodate the students who are to answer them

To expand these guidelines, a description of each follows:

1. *Stimulate thinking.* An interesting, thought-provoking question will motivate the learner to (a) pay greater attention, (b) reflect about ideas not previously thought about, (c) suggest new avenues for thought, and (d) suggest analysis or synthesis rather than a factual recall of previously learned information. A good question will trigger past experiences and knowledge and motivate new thought.

2. *Precision.* A good question is clear, precise, and concise. The question should tell students how to frame their response. Too often teachers will ask an ambiguous or vague question and then be surprised at the variety of responses. For example, if the teacher wants to know whether or not the students read on the front page of the newspaper an article that is relevant to what they are studying, the question should *not* be worded: "Did you see the newspaper this morning?" Since the class was studying "expansionism," the teacher could have asked: "The front page of the newspaper this morning had an article on expansionism. Who was involved?" Or, "Why was expansionism in the news this morning?"

3. *Purposeful Focus.* Questions should be planned so that they are appropriate to the purpose of the lesson. If the lesson is to be a problem-solving lesson, then the questions must stimulate inquiry. If the purpose is factual recall, then mastery questions should be asked. Suppose that your students have just returned from a field trip. To focus their thinking about the experience, you might ask the following:

- What did you observe?
- What similarities and difference among the incidents did you note?
- Why did these incidents occur?

Since purposeful questioning is often sequenced, it means that the questions were preplanned rather than off the cuff. However, even though the lesson has been planned to focus on specifics, the teacher should be flexible enough to change the questions if students' inquiry moves in a purposeful and fruitful direction.

4. *Meeting students' needs.* Research on questioning and on learning styles indicates that instruction should be differentiated to meet students' needs. Already noted has been the research that disadvantaged students do better with lower-level questions. However, some middle-class students, who do not tolerate a highly structured environment, may do better with open-ended questions. Questions should be adapted to the group of students with whom you are working.

APPLICATION OF RESEARCH

Anderson and Biddle (1975) found that it is advantageous to students' learning if questions pertaining to each point to be mastered are asked during the instructional period, rather than after instruction.

Types of Questions

Some researchers have classified questions according to the thinking process that students are to follow. For example, earlier in this text, the affective and cognitive domains were presented to demonstrate educational objectives. The two taxonomies have been used to classify questions according to their "level" of intent. Examples were provided in Chapter 4. The taxonomies are valuable for assisting teachers to determine the level of educational objective, and they provide a means to study teachers' questions to see if different levels and types of questions are asked in the classroom. However, since some knowledge questions can be extremely complex, the taxonomies may not always be the best tool for sequencing questions for teaching. The reader is urged to review the taxonomies and the question examples.

Taba and her associates developed another system for programming cognitive processes through the sequencing of questions. The questions are used to stimulate the students to process information. The strategy is based on the idea that students need input of content in order to be ready to respond to the questions that are asked. Three cognitive tasks are taught to the students: concept formation, interpretation of data, and application of principles. Each cognitive task requires specific questions.

Cognitive Task I. To facilitate concept formation, the teacher stimulates students to list, group, and categorize items using common characteristics. The questions include (Taba, 1967, p. 92):

- What did you see? hear? note?
- What belongs together? On what criterion?
- How would you call these groups? What belongs under what?

Cognitive Task II. The interpretation of data is taught by asking students (p. 101):

- What did you notice? see? find?
- Why did so-and-so happen?
- What does this mean? What would you conclude?

Cognitive Task III. The application of principles, cognitive task III, is sequenced through the following questions (p. 109):

- What would happen if . . . ?
- Why do you think this would happen?
- What would it take for so-and-so to be generally true or probably true?

These cognitive tasks will be expanded upon in Chapter 13 in the discussion of inquiry and problem solving.

In Mary Hogan's classroom, when she taught a science unit about rocks, she adapted the Taba strategy to teach her students that rocks differ in shapes, colors, and textures and that natural forces cause rocks to change. She asked the following questions:

Questions	**Responses**
Describe these rocks. (What do you see?)	Students described color, shape.
Describe how the rocks feel.	Smooth, rough, slippery, jagged.
How could we arrange these rocks in groups?	Color, shape, texture.
Why do you think these rocks are not the same?	Rocks break. Different types of rocks feel different and look different. Something happens to the rocks to make them different.
What are some things that might affect the rocks? What else?	Sun, heat, cold, water, wind, plants, snow.
What would happen if the rocks were exposed for many years to ice? Or sun? Or water?	(Natural forces) ice, sun and water affect the color, shape, and texture of the rocks.

RESEARCH FINDINGS

Bloom (1980) considers questioning as an "alterable variable." By this he means that teachers can improve questioning skills through study and practice.

WHAT'S WRONG WITH THESE QUESTIONS?

- Don't you think Jesse was scared when she couldn't find her Mother?
- Do you want me to keep you after school?
- Was Franklin Delano Roosevelt a good President?

APPLICATION OF RESEARCH

Anderson et al. (1978) believe that teachers should use a predictable pattern of questioning so that students will know when it is their turn to answer. Other researchers and educators disagree. What do you think?

Common Sense about Asking Questions

Reviews of research on types of questions and levels of questions fail to conclude that learning gains can be correlated with the questions that are asked in the classroom (Dunkin & Biddle, 1974). Some studies report inconclusive results (Brophy & Evertson, 1976). Still, there is a great deal that we do know about the use of questions. The following are some typical questions asked by teachers and some common-sense ideas and advice gleaned from the many research studies.

1. *How can teachers involve students in discussion?*

Several factors are important. First, questions used to motivate the discussion should be asked in a nonthreatening manner. Questions that are interesting and asked in a conversational voice will get the best attention from students. Second, after calling on a student, wait for the response; do not scare the student off. After the student responds, let your eyes observe other students; let them know that you want them to contribute. Call on additional students, without repeating the question; encourage other students to respond by asking: "Anyone else want to comment?" "Who can add to this?" "Well, boys and girls, what else?" Provide feedback through noncommittal, simple responses, such as: "OK," "Good," "Interesting thought," "Hmmm."

2. *What happens when teachers call on specific student before asking question?*

By naming the student who is to respond, the teacher encourages all other students to stop listening. Thus it becomes necessary to regenerate interest through a follow-up elicitation because the class has been effectively inhibited from participation.

However, there are exceptions which merit consideration. If you note that Johnny and Matilda are not paying attention or are misbehaving, it may be profitable to call on one of them and serve notice that you are aware of their inattention and that you will not tolerate it. This lets the inattentive students realize that they had better tune in, and it tells the rest of the class that you are monitoring participation.

APPLICATION OF RESEARCH

Rosenshine (1976) found that teachers should ask questions near the student's ability level for low socioeconomic status children, but above the student's ability level for high socioeconomic status children.

There is another situation that may call for naming the student ahead of time. If there is a very shy student in class who rarely contributes to the discussion, sometimes this student will respond if given extra time to prepare. Decision making along with an extra measure of common sense is needed before deciding whether to focus on a specific student or to ask the question of the whole group.

3. *What types of questions should teachers ask?*

All types. It is important to provide a variety of thinking experiences. Students' interest in answering questions may be dependent upon learning styles and social class background factors. The age of the students may also be a factor. Nevertheless, students need practice in answering a variety of question types, not just those we think are "better" for them. Also to be remembered is that reflective questions are dependent upon prerequisite knowledge. One of the best ways to determine students' readiness to answer a reflective question is to sequence the questions beginning with a factual type.

4. *What happens when teachers use leading questions?*

"Isn't it true that . . . ?" The problem with the leading question is that it is insincere. Students sometimes become hostile because they recognize that they have not been asked a "real" question. Another problem is that students do not pay attention to the leading question, and so good listening habits are not reinforced. Leading questions are frequently used in discipline situations, often with a sarcastic tone of voice. ("You *do* want to go to lunch today, don't you?") This is another reason why these questions are unappealing to students.

5. *What happens when teachers repeat students' comments?*

If students know that the teacher will repeat every student response, they do not need to listen to their peers—just to the teacher. Recall the discussion about interaction patterns during a class discussion presented earlier in this chapter. Students tend to talk to the teacher rather than to their classmates; repeating students' comments reinforces this behavior.

But—another exception: sometimes, particularly with young children, a correct response needs to be vigorously emphasized and reinforced immediately. This occurs most frequently during skill instruction. Under this circumstance it may be necessary to repeat the student's comment in a complete sentence. However, it is critical to acknowledge that the student gave the correct answer, but that it is *so* important, you are repeating it.

6. *Under what circumstances should teachers "cue" students?*

Recall the research about wait-time (Rowe, 1974). This research indicated that teachers should wait about five seconds for a response. Rowe's research (1969) also indicated that teachers are less likely to wait for the low achiever than for the high achiever. Research also reveals that teachers are more likely to "cue" students who they anticipate know the answer rather than students they anticipate do *not* know the answer. What this means, in terms of questioning technique, is that teachers must automatically (a) wait an equal amount of time for both "low" and "high" students to respond, and (b) provide specific content clues to all students who fail to respond after sufficient wait-time.

A probing question represents a special type of cue. For example, you have asked the class, "Why did England send ships to the South Atlantic Ocean when Argentina took over the Falkland Islands?" A student responded that the Falkland Islands belong to England. Next, you ask the responding student, "Under what circumstances do you believe a country will act aggressively?" This question is intended as a cue to the student to extend his/her thinking in a particular direction. Both the student and the content should be considered before a teacher decides to probe.

7. *Why should 'yes-no' questions be avoided?*

The yes-no question usually wastes time. Ask the question for which you really want a response. For example, the questions in this section could have been written as yes-no questions. (Should yes-no questions be asked? Should teachers repeat students' comments?) The problem is that a yes-no response is insufficient and the teacher would have to ask a follow-up question in order to get any information out of the student. Another problem is that the yes-no response tells the teacher very little about the students' thinking and so cannot be used to diagnose needs. Had the author written yes-no questions, a single answer would have been insufficient to provide insight about the problem.

RESEARCH FINDINGS

Singer (1978) advocates that students develop their own study questions. He emphasizes that students are more likely to have a positive attitude about reading and become independent learners when they formulate their own questions.

Other Considerations

Students' Questions and Classroom Management. The questions students ask provide a great deal of insight about the organization and management of the classroom and the effectiveness of instruction. For example, if students ask many, many procedural questions, then it becomes obvious that the teacher has not communicated classroom procedures to the students. (Or, the students have not had the opportunity to have input into planning classroom procedures.)

When students ask what appear to be very elementary instructional questions, they are telling the teacher they do not understand their instructions or that the lesson is too difficult for them. Students who ask questions to receive assurance from the teacher that they are proceeding correctly are probably lacking self-confidence, or they have experienced a great deal of teacher wrath in the past and are presently fearful.

It can be a frustrating experience when teachers have to manage many time-consuming and often pointless questions. For this reason, the teacher must analyze why students' needs are not being met and what kinds of questions are deserving to be asked. The teacher receiving many classroom management (procedural) questions should ask:

- Have the students helped to plan, and do they understand class standards? Do they know what to do when they need paper, when they may sharpen a pencil, when they may get a drink, go to the bathroom, what to do when finished?
- Do they know where to work? Do they know what resources are available to them?
- What should they do if they really need assistance? May they work with a classmate?
- What responsibilities may students assume for their own goal setting?

What kinds of questions should be cultivated in the classroom? Questions dealing with the extension of an instructional task, questions that broaden the area of study, and questions that lend depth to the study should be coveted. Students ask these kinds of questions when they are really motivated with instruction and when they feel that their teacher respects them and wants them to take some responsibility for personal learning. Jarolimek and Foster (1981) commented that students will ask "better" questions when their teacher models appropriate questioning behavior.

What are some ways to help students ask better questions?

Students' Responses. Although commented upon in different ways in other sections of the text, it is important enough to reiterate: language usage is the school's raison d'être, and teachers need to develop students' speech. This can be done by listening to what students have to say and reinforcing it through respect. This means that nonevaluative comments ("OK," "All right," "Interesting") need to be made along with teacher questioning to elicit clarifying responses from students. Teachers may need to use cues and probing questions to facilitate students' replies.

Chapter Summary

Research on teaching indicates that different kinds of knowledge, skills, and attitudes are learned in different ways; certain teaching behaviors are more likely to produce different types of learning than others. Elementary teachers instruct in many different subject fields with diverse instructional objectives. It is therefore important for teachers to have a repertoire of teaching methods, because each contributes to the process of instruction.

In this chapter direct instruction, guided discussion, and questioning methods have been discussed. During skill instruction the importance of teacher demonstration, student practice with corrective feedback, and independent application have been emphasized. Discussion strategies focused on types of classroom discussions, roles, rules, and classroom conditions for discussion. Suggestions were provided for handling typical problems during the discussion period.

For teaching skills, questions should be clear and concise and aimed at what has been taught or what the student has just read. Whenever appropriate, teachers should plan a questioning strategy so that questions are asked in sequence to extend thinking. When teaching the disciplines, questions should be balanced to provide a variety of thinking experiences. All students should be involved in the discussion period by using questions to motivate and distributing them widely. Discussion manners and "roles" need to be taught.

Classroom Application Exercises

1. Prepare a skill lesson using direct instruction. Identify the factual questions you will ask students during the lesson.
2. Make a list of open-ended questions you would use to encourage participation in a large group discussion.
3. Make a list of classroom atmosphere elements that contribute to a good discussion.
4. Record the questions students ask during either the morning or the afternoon. Categorize the purposes for the questions using the following:
   - to extend thinking
   - to obtain permission
   - to clarify tasks
   - to clarify procedures

   What do the questions tell you about your teaching?
5. For a three- to five-day period, record the time you spend with low, average, and high achieving students in your classroom during skill instruction. At the end of the three- to five-days, add up the time and evaluated whether all students receive an equal share of instructional time.

Suggested Readings for Extending Study

Denham, Carolyn, and Ann Lieberman, co-editors. *Time To Learn.* Washington, D.C.: National Institute of Education, 1980.

Ellis, Arthur K. *Teaching and Learning Elementary Social Studies.* 2nd ed. Boston: Allyn & Bacon, Inc., 1981. Chapter 19.

Hunkins, Francis P. *Questioning Strategies and Techniques.* Boston: Allyn & Bacon, Inc., 1972.

Hunkins, Francis P. *Involving Students in Questioning.* Boston: Allyn & Bacon, Inc., 1976.

Hyman, Ronald T. *Strategic Questioning.* Englewood Cliffs, N.J.: Prentice-Hall, Inc., 1979.

Sanders, Norris M. *Classroom Questions: What Kinds?* New York: Harper & Row, Publishers, 1966.

Chapter 13

Inquiry and Problem Solving

After you have completed the study of this chapter, you should be able to accomplish the following:

1. **Describe inquiry learning.**
2. **Discuss the importance of inquiry learning.**
3. **Identify skills needed for inquiry learning.**
4. **Identify the teacher tasks for inquiry teaching.**
5. **Practice inquiry teaching tasks utilizing the exercise in the chapter.**
6. **Suggest ways to evaluate students' problem-solving skills.**
7. **Compare inquiry learning and direct instruction.**

Chapters 13, 14, and 15 focus on "output" teaching strategies and the student as a researcher. Inquiry or problem-solving methods tie these three chapters together, and as you will soon see, the three chapters are dependent upon Chapter 12 because appropriately asked questions are the basis of inquiry methodology.

What Is Inquiry?

Most educational writers define inquiry in terms of the processes involved to resolve uncertainty. While the use of the term is relatively new in educational history, it can be traced to the terms "reflective thinking and critical thinking" as used by John Dewey. Dewey (1933) defined reflective thinking as follows:

> Active, persistent, and careful consideration of any belief or supposed form of knowledge in the light of the grounds that support it and the further conclusions to which it tends (p. 9).

Dewey analyzed the thinking process and differentiated between thinking and reflective thinking. He stated that thinking begins when the individual is aware of an indeterminate situation or a feeling of perplexity. There is a common thread running through reflective thinking. There is consecutiveness of thought, a chaining effect that aims at a conclusion, and an inquiry into beliefs. The difference between thinking and reflective thinking is the ability of the individual to sustain the act while seeking a solution and being critical of the evidence unearthed during the process. The reflective individual subjects the belief and the evidence to reason. The nature of the problem determines the goal to be sought, and the goal determines the process.

Dewey identified five steps in reflective thinking which have served as a basis for all later research into the act of problem solving. They also formed the basis for his theory of reflective thinking. Dewey's five phases are as follows:

1. Suggestions, in which the mind leaps forward to a possible solution.
2. An intellectualization of the difficulty or perplexity that has been *felt* (directly experienced) into a *problem* to be solved, a question for which the answer must be sought.
3. The use of one suggestion after another as a leading idea, or *hypothesis*, to initiate and guide observation and other operations in collection of factual material.
4. The mental elaboration of the idea or supposition as an idea or supposition (*reasoning*, in the sense in

which reasoning is a part, not the whole, of inference).

5. Testing the hypothesis by overt or imaginative action (Dewey, 1923, p. 107).

Hullfish and Smith (1961) also differentiated between thinking and reflective activity. Guided by Dewey's theoretical work, these authors found that the major distinction between thinking and reflection is purposeful thought, directed and controlled. Thinking consists of three interrelated elements: sentiency, memory, imagination. An appropriate and controlled balance of these three elements constitutes reflective thinking. Hullfish and Smith described the reflective situation as consisting of the following aspects:

1. The individual recognizes or is aware of a problem situation.
2. The individual "acts" to clarify the situation—physically or mentally.
3. "If-then" type of thinking occurs: the individual hypothesizes, tests his ideas, modifies them.
4. A decision is made; action is taken, as a result of the previous testing and verification.

Bayles (1960) added to the theory of the reflective process by clarifying the way in which a conclusion can be accepted as final. Bayles described the "principle of adequacy" and the "principle of harmony" (p. 87). The principle of adequacy occurs when the reflector is confident that s/he has obtained all the available information needed to study the problem satisfactorily. The principle of harmony occurs when the reflector interprets his data and reaches a conclusion which is in harmony with all available data. Bayles also used the term "problem solving" and equated it with the term "reflective thinking."

Massialas and Cox (1966) identified reflective thinking as both means and end of classroom method. They defined it as

> the process of identifying problems of fact and value, assessing them in view of the assumptions in which they are grounded, and subjecting them to proof in terms of certain criteria (p. 90).

They distinguished three types of generalizations used in reflective thinking: casual, correlative, and explanatory. Casual generalizations are discovered only after a careful investigation reveals a consequential relationship. The correlative generalization states a relationship between two sets of phenomena. The use of data to describe a relationship in which a particular situation is an example is done through explanatory generalizations.

Suchman (1966) described inquiry as learning that is meaningful and intrinsically rewarding to the learner. During inquiry, the learner attempts to close the gap between beliefs and observations. The learner uses data to organize observations and account for discrepant events. The learner is motivated by a desire for closure (the need to know and understand) and the desire to satisfy curiosity.

Suchman stated the following axioms about scientific inquiry: (1) inquiry is a back-and-forth process between theorizing and data gathering; (2) theories are checked by comparing the theory to the data; (3) all language in the theory is described precisely and meaningfully; (4) limitations are stated for all theories; (5) theories must be consistent to their structure; (6) theories are derived inductively; (7) scientific theories can never be absolutely true.

Suchman called attention to the inductive thought processes involved in stating a theory and proposing hypotheses. However, as students search for evidence and apply and test the gathered data, they are engaging in deductive thought processes.

What Does an Inquirer Do?

The following miniexample of inquiry provides insight into what an inquirer does during the process of inquiry:

I was startled by the sound of the puppy barking. Slowly I opened my eyes. "Was she barking or crying? I wonder what time it is?"

"Only ten minutes after 5:00 AM. Why is she up so early? Is she ill?" "I wonder if she is developing a new habit—waking up earlier each day. Seems to me she woke up at about 6:00 AM yesterday.

Maybe that's it. Still, five o'clock is not six o'clock; something must be wrong with her."

"Well, I'd better get up and find out. OK, puppy, what's wrong? You look perfectly fine. You don't appear to be sick. Let's go outside. Hurry up, so we can both go back to sleep." "Strange, it looks too bright outside for 5:00 AM" "OK, pup, back to sleep." "Hey, she's still barking. Sounds like her stomach is telling her it's breakfast time. I wonder what the other clocks in the house say? Hmm. They agree with the bedroom clock." "Ah ha! I hear the rest of the family. Maybe it's later than I thought." "If our electricity went out, the clocks would all be wrong. I'd better start breakfast." "The microwave clock is blinking. That's *it*!" "I'll call Time and verify. Yep. It's 6:20 AM. Our electricity must have been out for an hour."

Inquiry in the classroom is concerned with more important problems than whether or not the electricity stopped or a puppy has awakened earlier than usual, but just the same this little problem-solving episode will provide a description of the inquiry process. To analyze it, we will review what happened:

	Dog barked "earlier" than usual. Is it really extra early, or is there another reason for the puppy's barking?
Discrepant Event/Fact Problem	(1) The clock is correct; the puppy is developing a new habit. (2) The puppy is ill. (3) The clock is wrong; the electricity stopped.
Evidence Data Gathering	(a) Puppy looks fine; appears in good health. (b) The morning appears to be extraordinarily bright for 5:00 AM. (c) Puppy continues to bark as if expecting breakfast. (d) Others in family are awakening: must be time to get up. (e) Other clocks in house read the same way. (f) Microwave clock is blinking. (It is a digital clock.)
Tentative Conclusion	Clocks in house are wrong. (To verify time is called.)
Conclusion	Electricity stopped. Clocks did not run for an hour during the night.

Since this type of inquiry occurs many times a day, we need to think about why inquiry is important and what value students derive from *planned* inquiry experiences.

Why Is Inquiry Important?

Bruner (1966) characterized the learner who is oriented toward discovery learning and the benefits derived from it:

1. S/he is intellectually more effective. Discovery is made because the individual expects that there is something to be found out.
   The expectation motivates the search, and the learner persists in the search for relatedness. Thinking exhibits connectedness; questions are cycled, and the learner organizes and summarizes.
2. The learner is governed by intrinsic motivation. The individual is more interested in "learning that" something is true than "learning about" something.
3. The learner is heuristically inclined. The individual makes a discovery by practicing problem solving. Problem-solving skills improve through repeated experiences with inquiry.
4. The learner preserves information through superior organization. The individual organizes useful information into a personal cognitive structure, thereby maximizing its retrieval.

Discovery learning, according to Bruner, is the process of using one's own intellect to gain knowledge by discovering concepts and organizing them into a structure that is personally meaningful.

RESEARCH FINDINGS

McKinney (1975) concluded from a study of reflective and impulsive seven-, nine-, and eleven-year-old students that reflective children are more efficient and systematic problem solvers. He found that the cognitive style of the students influenced their problem-solving behavior. However, the developmental level of the student and the type of problem the student was required to solve affected the impact of cognitive style on problem-solving performance.

During the act of discovery, the student "tests" and verifies relationships. The student may be discovering knowledge that is "new" to him/her, but not necessarily knowledge that is unknown to others. During discovery the learner is actively using the mind. The student is totally involved in the learning experience.

Inquiry Skills

As you have probably noted, inquiry learning is a common-sense way of making decisions using the scientific method. Inquiry begins inductively as the student becomes aware of a problem, but as the process continues the student uses deductive processes. Although in practice inquiry is not necessarily a precise process, generally the students proceed through the following stages:

1. Problem Definition
   Students recognize a problem or puzzlement.
   Students narrow and limit the problem to make it meaningful and manageable by asking questions.
   Students attempt to define key aspects of the problem.
2. Hypothesizing
   Students begin to generalize about the problem.
   Ideas are discussed as possible solutions to the problem.
   Students continue to define terms and state hypotheses.
3. Exploration
   Students plan and decide what evidence is needed.
   Students search for evidence to support the tentative solution using the following: observation, field trips, library resources, experiments, interviews, case studies, role-playing, original documents, etc.
   Students gather data on the basis of relevance to the hypotheses.
4. Data Analysis
   Students evaluate data noting objectivity, reliability, source, and bias.
   Data are contrasted; similarities and differences are noted.
   Trends and sequences are noted.
   Data are summarized.
   Data are interpreted.
5. Reaching a Conclusion
   Hypotheses are accepted, rejected, or modified.
   Hypotheses are restated, if needed.
   Students generalize and suggest ways to test generalization in new situations.

Our miniexample of inquiry has all the necessary components: the feeling of perplexity, hypothesizing, exploration, data analysis, and conclusion. However, because it is such a simplistic example we do not see evidence of data examined for "truth" or summarized. For example, it was stated that the 'puppy looks fine; appears in good health." This is a subjective observation. It is acceptable, if its limitation is understood. The fact that the day appears to be especially "bright" for five o'clock is an observation based upon experience of observing the daylight at that hour. Like most observations, it is

APPLICATION OF RESEARCH

To improve problem-solving skills, Whimbey (1980) recommended that students be taught the "habit of patient thinking," accuracy, and willingness to "explain how you obtained the answer."

In studies of good and poor problem solvers, Whimbey found that successful students use a step-by-step approach, are careful, constantly recheck, reread, and review to be certain that nothing is overlooked or that they have not made errors.

Whimbey recommends that students work in pairs or small groups to think aloud and to explain their thinking. Group discussion is especially critical to improve the performance of students working at low levels.

subjective, but it still offers valuable evidence. The rest of the data are more factually based, although they may be subject to error. These are the fine points of inquiry that a teacher needs to communicate to students so that they become efficient problem solvers. Let us look at the teacher tasks during inquiry.

Teacher Tasks for Inquiry Teaching

1. Choosing Appropriate Problems for Study. In planning topics for inquiry, the teacher is confronted with three elements: (a) choosing a problem that provides "mileage" in terms of content, (b) choosing a problem that is of interest to the students, (c) formulating a provocative question. Mileage concerns have to do with selecting problems that have depth, will provide appropriate research skill usage, and "fit" grade level goals and objectives. Whatever problem is selected, it should be useful in meeting the content needs, provide for the development of inquiry skills, and provide for sequential learning of concepts. It is important to remember that the inquiry problem must be significant enough that there is information provided to students as well as questions that motivate skill development.

That the topic must be of interest to students is quite obvious. If students do not perceive that a problem exists, or if it is irrelevant to them, or if it is inappropriate to their developmental level, then students will not be motivated to inquire. Inquiry problems that do not appeal to students will not be successful. Not only must the teacher choose carefully, but it is critical to present the problem in a way that will create controversy and real interest. Some educators advocate choosing a problem that relates to student concerns. Ellis (1981) called this a "real" problem in contrast to a "contrived" problem that has been chosen because of its suitability for inquiry. However, the teacher must be the judge and consider student involvement, skill needs, content needs, and the transfer of learning value.

Formulating an inquiry oriented question is a very important task. Every question that is asked in the classroom should have a purpose. In a sense, there are no "bad" questions, but the problem is to ask a question that will facilitate the thinking appropriate for the task to be accomplished. An inquiry oriented question should motivate inquiry, assist the students in defining the problem, and suggest possible hypotheses.

Consider the following two questions:

1. What is a "Mom and Pop" grocery store?
2. Why are there more supermarkets in modern cities than "Mom and Pop" grocery stores?

Question 1 is really a subquestion of Question 2. Obviously, students will need to define the Mom and Pop grocery store; however, this question is not formulated to inspire inquiry, define the problem, or suggest hypotheses. The second-graders who were asked Question 2 defined the problem and suggested the following hypotheses for investigation:

Problem	**Hypotheses**
Markets in modern cities tend to be larger today than during past times.	1. Modern equipment is too expensive for small grocery stores. 2. Small groceries are not profitable. 3. People prefer "one-stop" shopping.

2. Defining the Problem. In a sixth-grade classroom the teacher began a safety unit with the following question: "What is the relationship between age and auto safety?" The students had difficulty defining the word "relationship." To help them decide what the problem was about, the teacher asked: "How many of you believe that teenagers have more accidents than their parents?" The students (of course!) were incensed at the very idea that teenage drivers might cause more accidents than adult drivers, and they began to justify their belief that teens were good drivers. ("They have faster reflexes." "They take driver training and driver education." "They are more alert.") Finally, the teacher assured the students that their reasons were plausible, but they would have to investigate to find out if they were accurate. "Who can tell us, very precisely, what it is we need to find out?"

The students thought about it and finally came up with the following problem for investigation: Certain age groups have better driving records than other groups and are less likely to have auto accidents.

Next, the teacher asked the students to suggest hypotheses for investigation, and they decided on the following:

1. Senior citizens have fewer accidents than other age groups.
2. Teenagers have more accidents than other age groups.
3. People who cause auto accidents pay more for their insurance.

To help the students define the problem and consider areas for investigation, the sixth-grade teacher in the preceding incident found it necessary to narrow the focus for the students. This was accomplished with the follow-up question about teenaged drivers. Whenever students are unable to open up the investigation and specify the problem, it is necessary for the teacher to probe and facilitate problem definition by narrowing the focus.

3. Data Base. Sources for information are so important in inquiry methodology that most teachers consider the adequacy of their materials and resources *first* before making a decision about an inquiry problem. The second-grade teacher who posed the question about supermarkets had to consider how students would find out why the size of markets had changed in recent years. The teacher's data sources for use by students may include field trip observations, social studies textbooks, resource people, pictures, maps, charts, tables, and informational data written by the teacher. Sometimes data sources are generated by students in the form of interviews, questionnaires, or case studies. Dramatizations or simulations may also be a part of the data sources.

If students are to learn to process information, they need contrasting content so that they will practice and thereby learn to categorize facts, ideas, or events; they will learn to evaluate information for interpretive purposes, and they will develop their own generalization about why something is true, or why something usually happens. As students use data, the teacher assists them by asking questions to help them compare and contrast and make inferences based upon their information.

Newspaper Article

ILLEGAL ALIEN SEARCH DESCRIBED AS CRUDE

The Immigration and Naturalization Service arrested thousands of undocumented aliens last week. Program Director for the International Institute of the San Fernando Valley called the raids "crude" and a violation of human rights.

"The whole thing is a political game to try to make people believe that the fiasco in our economy is a result of undocumented aliens holding jobs that Americans could hold."

"These jobs are minimum wage jobs and American workers are not interested in them," commented Garcia, the Director of the Institute. Garcia also stated that, "it was interesting that the Immigration Service is deporting only Latinos" (*Valley News*, California, May 5, 1982).

1. Write an inquiry question to motivate student interest using the article about the illegal aliens.

   ____

   ____

2. State the problem as you would expect your students to state it.

   ____

   ____

3. Write an hypothesis that you would anticipate your students would propose.

____

____

4. Identify sources for gathering data

____

____

5. How will you have students organize their data? (*What will students produce?*)

____

____

6. How will you evaluate students' inquiry skills?

____

____

4. Creating an Inquiry Oriented Environment. The classroom environment must encourage students to develop inquiry skills. This means that the teacher through planned strategies, modeling, and choice of materials guides students to interact with other students and the environment and motivates students to engage in discovery learning. Students' needs and life experiences should be considered both in the choice of inquiry problems and in the materials arranged for use.

An inquiry oriented classroom is characterized by its ability to sustain reflection. Students and teacher do not hurry to closure, yet at the same time, discussions tend to have a more direct focus. Rather than focusing on a "right" answer in the reflective discussion, the teacher's questions tend to act as a springboard for the discussion. The questions probe instead of elicit.

The reflective classroom uses hypotheses as its discussion focus and relies on factual material to support the hypotheses. Factual recall is not valued, but facts are used to support or reject a hypothesis.

"Time" is another aspect of the inquiry oriented classroom that is used differently than in a more traditional environment. Since material does not have to be "covered" in the reflective classroom, there is no tendency for the teacher to wring hands as the class participates in democratic processes. The act of clarification is important to inquiry. Students need to communicate and search for a consensus of meaning; thus the reflective teacher does not watch the clock.

Joyce (1973) noted that the teacher must create the type of learning environment desired. The teacher must decide whether the environment should be interdependent or unilateral. The social climate should promote social development, and if properly conducted the class environment will promote independence and the ability to establish meaningful relationships with others.

In an inquiry oriented classroom the teacher assumes a less prominent position and attempts to guide children to resources of knowledge. The teacher's central purpose is to arouse interest and raise questions so that students will inquire and learn to draw upon their own experiences. Students should also be helped to perceive discrepancies in their information. The climate of the classroom allows students to gain self-confidence and to direct their own study and thinking.

5. Guidance and Objectivity. The teacher's primary role during inquiry revolves around question-raising. Preplanning of a question strategy and preparation of materials allows the teacher to direct students' hypothesizing to appropriate materials to facilitate their thinking. While students are gathering data the teacher continuously challenges and prods them to explore new alternatives. Student inferences and conjectures are encouraged.

> Make a list of the behaviors teachers will demonstrate using inquiry methodology.

Students will need to be reminded of the temporal quality of knowledge and the fact that authority cannot be trusted as omniscient. The teacher needs to be alert to stimulate students' search for evidence and remind students to challenge an accepted hypothesis.

Taba (1967) contended that thinking can be taught by identifying cognitive skills and devising strategies to give the learner the opportunity to practice each particular cognitive skill. Taba identified the task of questioning as being vital to the teaching of cognitive skills. Questions should be structured by the teacher to accomplish the following: (1) guide the students' search, (2) raise the level of thought, (3) focus on content, and (4) program the study as to sequence and transitions. Taba commented upon the merits of this approach:

> Elements of teaching strategy such as appropriate focusing, pacing, and sequencing wide involvement make considerable difference in the amount of productive thought a class can generate, as well as fostering complex and abstract thought by students who are usually considered incapable of it (p. 48).

In summary, the teacher's major tasks in using inquiry methodology are to stimulate the use of inquiry processes by students, to guide students' choice of materials, and to arrange an appropriate environment and climate for inquiry. The teacher manages participation, provides both cues and feedback, reinforces appropriate behaviors, and directs both formative and summative evaluation of inquiry learning. Now let's take a look at what inquiry instruction is like in different subject fields.

Two Examples of Inquiry Instruction

There are a number of inquiry examples in Chapter 9 (Science) which should be reviewed at this time. Although the main components of inquiry instruction are the same, it should be remembered that varied purposes will change the way in which it is accomplished. Science data gathering usually occurs through experimentation and record keeping. In physical education, discovery may be facilitated through physical movement. In music, discovery learning may focus on the use of instruments or on listening experiences.

Art and Social Studies

Let's pretend that we are back in Greg Thomas' fifth-grade classroom. His students are studying American history, and Thomas is integrating art experiences with the social studies. Thomas asks his students the following question:

> What does the art of the early New England colonists tell us about their cultural beliefs?

On the ledge of the chalkboard, Thomas has displayed photographs and paintings from different periods of American and European history. The students begin to react to the pictures and the question. One outspoken student comments that he doesn't think the American colonists produced much art and therefore there would be little to study. Others react differently by asking questions as to whether only the paintings were to be studied or sculpture and architecture could be included. Another group of students appears to doubt that it is possible to detect cultural beliefs by studying art or artifacts.

After the students have had sufficient time to react, Thomas calls attention to the several different opinions expressed by the group: (1) very little art was produced by the New England colonists; (2) the study should be broad and include handicrafts, art work, architecture, and the like; (3) students doubt that art could be studied to determine cultural beliefs. Thomas asks the students if they think they could suggest a way to reformulate the question into a problem for them to study. After several minutes, they agree on the following problem:

> *Problem:* Using different types of art forms, can we recognize a people's beliefs?

The problem as stated was slightly different than what Greg Thomas had anticipated, but it still would allow the students to study much of what he had preplanned. Next he asked them if they could decide how to go about the study.

Make a list of the behaviors students will demonstrate during inquiry.

As the students suggested ideas for the investigation, the teacher wrote them down on the board. This was their list:

- to look at handcrafted objects from the colonial period
- to look at artists' pictures
- to compare artists' pictures in New England with other artists from other places and other periods
- to examine tools made during colonial days
- to look at the architecture of the period
- to study furniture produced during the colonial period
- to research information about the New England colonists
- to use slides and filmstrips (Thomas told the students he had some)
- to study clothing from the colonial period.

The students agreed that they would draw much of what they observed so that they would have a record of their research.

Some of the students expressed preferences in terms of what they wanted to do. Not all of the students wanted to record their information with pictures; these students would take notes instead. The students chose their work groups and sat down and planned who would do what in their small groups. The study took two weeks and included a visit to the art museum. Several of the students expressed an interest in making tools and chairs identical to those produced during the colonial period.

At the end of each work period, Thomas had the groups report their progress. Each group reported how they had gone about their study during the period, what they had accomplished, problems they had or anticipated, and plans for the next work period.

At the end of the first week, Thomas suggested to the students that perhaps they would need to make a large chart to record the findings from each group. They decided that at the end of the following week, each group would make an oral presentation and then they would discuss the pertinent information in order to analyze the data.

Their data for analysis included the following:

- a list of furniture used in most colonial homes
- a sketchbook of furnishings
- a sketchbook of dress styles
- notes about the New England "work ethic"
- replicated tools and several pieces of furniture (chair, stools)

The group studying colonial furniture used a data retrieval chart similar to Table 13.1.

To organize data, students may make charts and graphs similar to Figures 13.1 and 13.2. Additional materials may include:

- sketches of household utensils
- notes about individual artists' pictures
- pictures of churches
- notes about colonial recreation in New England
- notes about religious interests.

Figure 13.1. Graph Showing Percentages of Handcrafted and Manufactured Products During Colonial Days.

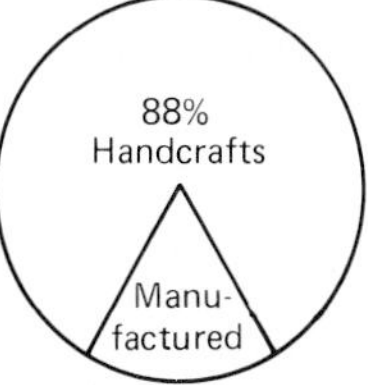

TABLE 13.1. Example of Retrieval Chart—Comparison of Colonial and European Furniture.

	Materials Used	Purpose	Looks	Handmade or Manufactured
Colonial CHAIRS	Wood—Mahogany	Dining, reading	Straight-backed, simple, hard	Handmade
European	Wood/fabric	Relaxing, dining, reading	Ornate, soft	Manufactured
Colonial SOFAS European				
Colonial TABLES European				
Colonial CHESTS European				

Figure 13.2. Histograph of Activities of New England Colonists.

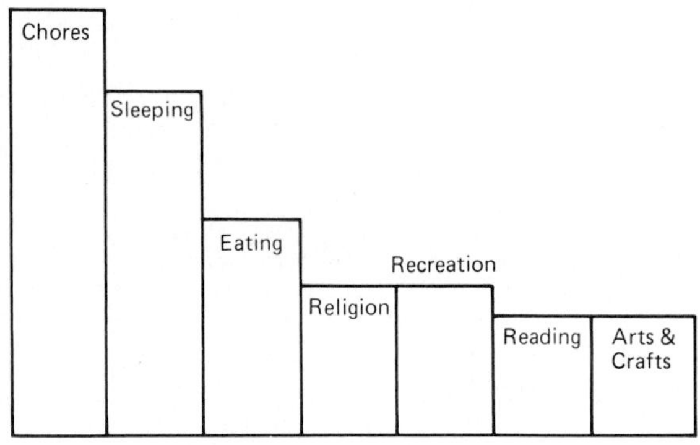

TABLE 13.2. Activities of New England Colonists.

Sleeping	7 hours
Chores	12 hours
Recreation	1 hour
Eating	2 hours
Religion	1 hour
Reading	$\frac{1}{2}$ hour
Arts and Crafts	$\frac{1}{2}$ hour

The class discussion focused on the data and what they had learned. Thomas initiated the discussion by asking: "What do we know about the way of life of the colonists who lived in New England?" This question was followed with a question asking the students to "compare the art forms and styles of the New England colonists with other periods in American history." During the course of the discussion, the students even compared the furniture of the colonial period with the furniture produced in Europe (Table 13.1).

> What was the purpose of Thomas' question: "What do we know about the way of life of the colonists who lived in New England?"
>
> Why did Thomas ask the students to compare the art forms of the colonists with other periods in American history?
>
> How would you initiate the discussion after the students' group investigation?

What Did the Students Learn? Using their data, the students decided that with a fair amount of confidence they could say the following about the New England colonists:

1. They appeared to be a grave type of people.
2. They struggled and worked hard.
3. Their art was practical, functional, symmetrical.
4. Their language was plain and correct.
5. Their household utensils and furniture were plain, simple, functional.
6. Their artists sometimes were house painters and performed other needed chores like painting signs and making decorations for coffins.
7. Their churches were for social gatherings and were designed to accommodate people; they were functional.
8. Their clothes were practical, not fancy.

Greg Thomas was pleased with what the students had learned. He asked them if they were ready to draw a final conclusion about the question he had asked them and their statement about the problem to be investigated. The students responded that they had learned a great deal about the colonists by studying their art and that in fact they really had discussed the colonists' cultural beliefs. The answer to the question posed by the students as to whether it was possible to recognize people's beliefs by studying their art forms was answered affirmatively. Students concluded that art provided a visual record of culture.

The episode that occurred in Greg Thomas' classroom conformed to what Joyce and Weil (1980) described as the Group Investigation Model. As Thomas used the strategy with his students, there were six phases to the inquiry.

Phase One: Thomas posed the question and encouraged the students to react to the question.

Phase Two: Thomas identified the different opinions about the question and asked the students to suggest the problem to be investigated.

Phase Three: Thomas asked the students to suggest ideas for the investigation. Students chose what they wanted to do, organized into groups, and decided on tasks.

Phase Four: Students gathered data independently and in their group situation. Thomas asked for formative evaluations after each work period.

Phase Five: Students gave reports and shared data.

Phase Six: Students concluded by re-examining their original question and problem.

Language Arts

Sara Garcia's third graders were involved in the Program for Intergroup Education (PIE). They were teamed with another class of third graders about twenty miles away. Garcia's students were performing in a play to be presented in the school auditorium the following week. One of the students asked, "Why don't we invite our friends at the Westlake School?" The other students liked the idea; Sara Garcia agreed and suggested that each student be responsible for writing a letter to a friend in the other class.

"What do you think you should say in your letter?" Sara Garcia asked the students while they were still seated together at the front of the room. As students contributed ideas, Garcia wrote on the board. Soon the board was filled with the following information:

Name of Play: "The Capture of Villanova"
Date of Play: May 23, 1983
Time of Play: 1:00 PM.

"Is there anything else we need to tell them?" As the students pondered this question, Garcia sketched out the form of a letter on the board. After a short time, another student commented that their friends would not know where the play was to be given. This information was added to the list and then Sara Garcia asked the students to look at her sketch on the chalkboard and to think about what a letter should look like. Soon the students began to organize the greeting and body of the letter, and someone suggested that they needed to include today's date at the top of the letter.

With the form for a letter outlined on the board, the students were told to write their own letters and compare their letters with the form on the board. As the students began their task, Garcia walked around the room and provided assistance when it was needed.

This strategy emphasized inductive learning. The phases were as follows:

Phase One: A student suggested inviting another class to a play. Teacher and students liked the idea and agreed.

Phase Two: Teacher suggested a letter and asked about the contents of it. Students made suggestions.

Phase Three: Teacher introduced "form" of a letter and asked for organizational details. Students contributed and evaluated suggestions.

Phase Four: Students wrote individual letters.

Phase Five: Students self-evaluated letters by comparing them with the form on the board.

How Can All Students Engage in Inquiry?

Diverse interests and abilities need to be accommodated in most classroom situations. Most of the time there is a wide range of thinking ability in elementary classrooms. In using inquiry teaching we try to develop intellectual skills by providing opportunities for students to observe, to identify, and to hypothesize about problems, to gather and classify data, to analyze, compare, and contrast information, to interpret and verify data, and to come to a conclusion concerning the problem. These tasks can be accomplished by most students.

Inquiry encourages active thinking and seeking rather than rote memorization; appropriately chosen problems will allow students to work at their own ability level. It is important to remember that students are not discovering "new" knowledge; they are only discovering what they themselves do not know. This may mean that the low-ability child will need concrete materials and will need to learn by doing, but regardless of ability the child can engage profitably and successfully in inquiry-related activities. Gega (1977) in discussing open-ended activities for inquiry teaching commented,

> It is this potential for multiple possibilities that sets off an open-ended activity from a close-ended one. Open-ended activities often provide two functions: (1) chances for pupils to discover new examples of an object or event, and (2) chances for them to discover the conditions that might change an object or event in some way (p. 31).

Teachers can create the desire to think and set the proper conditions for thinking. The teacher can assist students to develop curiosity, sensitivity, and habits of subjecting ideas to the test of rationality in order to cultivate the method of inquiry.

APPLICATION OF RESEARCH

In a small pilot study of third- and fourth-grade stimulus-bound and stimulus-free thinkers, Glenn and Ellis (1982) concluded that if teachers want to teach a linear problem-solving model, the instructional strategy should be direct and explicit.

Solving real-life problems can be taught by identifying what is to be learned, teaching the appropriate knowledge and skills, and providing skill practice and reinforcement.

The stimulus-free thinker was judged to be more creative than the stimulus-bound thinker whose responses were limited to the data presented in a test picture or problem.

Evaluating Students' Problem-Solving Skills

It is just as important to evaluate the way in which you, the teacher, went about and accomplished inquiry oriented teaching as it is to evaluate the students' problem-solving skills. In fact, the two components (teaching and learning) cannot be separated; one is related to the other. The purpose and choice for inquiry, the materials, and the conditions in the classroom all affected what the students did and what they said.

Table 9.3 (Chapter 9) demonstrated a checklist for evaluating students' critical thinking and inquiry skills. Other checklists are provided in Chapter 17. Another way to go about evaluating students' skills is to give them an inquiry test problem. Then ask them to write a statement of the problem and to select appropriate sources for data. Students may be asked to suggest ways to gather data and how they would go about analyzing their information.

1. Give students a problem and ask them to write a statement of the problem.
2. Ask students to select appropriate sources for data.
3. Ask students to suggest ways to gather data.
4. Ask students how they would organize data for analysis.

Note that in the list of ways to go about evaluating students' inquiry methods, the final step, concluding, has not been suggested. Practically the only way you the teacher can evaluate students' ability to form an appropriate conclusion is to provide them with specific data in the form of observed or supposed facts. Then ask students to make an inference about the data in terms of whether it is sufficient for making a conclusion. Or give students a number of conclusions and ask them to choose a conclusion that is logical and, beyond doubt, based upon the information given.

Of course, the prime way to evaluate students' skills is to examine the products of inquiry. What students produced while involved in inquiry activities and the discussions that followed inquiry will both provide the most meaningful information about students' performance.

Chapter Summary

An historical perspective of inquiry methodology was provided in this chapter along with examples of the process. Inquiry/problem-solving skills were described. The methodological approach was demonstrated using two teaching episodes in order to provide information concerning teacher behavior during inquiry teaching. The importance of the classroom environment during inquiry was cited. Ways to evaluate students' problem-solving skills were suggested.

The importance of using inquiry methods in the classroom relate to the benefits students derive from inquiry. These benefits include intellectual relatedness, motivation, satisfaction, and involvement in the learning experience.

Classroom Application Exercises

1. Use the information about the sixth-grade classroom studying the relationship between age and auto safety:
   - Write a different inquiry question.
   - Suggest sources for data.
   - Pretend that students have obtained data about auto safety. Write a sequence of questions to help students interpret and apply their data.
2. Choose an article out of the daily newspaper and plan an inquiry activity for your students.
3. Think about the example of the fifth-grade students who studied colonial art in order to learn about the New England colonists' cultural beliefs. Why is it important to distinguish between "activity" and "inquiry?"
4. Which of the following statements would make good inquiry lessons in the classroom?
   - There are fewer farms today than fifty years ago, but American farmers grow more food today than they did fifty years ago.
   - Changes in lifestyle affect language usage.
   - Most students dislike mathematics.
   - People do not work hard anymore.

   (If you chose the first two, you are right. The second two statements would be extremely difficult to research. They are too broad and need clarification.) Suggest data for students to analyze to study questions one and two.

5. Use the following inquiry example to design an investigation.

Inquiry Question/ Problem:	How do the members of your methods class feel about using inquiry methodology?
Sources of Data:	________________
	________________
Gathering Data:	________________
Organizing Data:	________________
Conclusion:	________________

Suggested Readings for Extending Study

Ashton-Warner, S. *Teacher*. New York: Simon & Schuster, Inc., 1963.

Bruner, Jerome S. "The Act of Discovery." In *Readings in Contemporary* Psychology in Education. Edited by C. Edward Meyers and Robert B. McIntyre. New York: Selected Academic Readings, 1966.

Dewey, John. *How We Think*. Boston: D. C. Heath & Company, 1933.

Hullfish, Gordon H., and Philip G. Smith. *Reflective Thinking: The Method of Education*. New York: Dodd, Mead & Company, 1961.

Joyce, Bruce, and Marsha Weil. *Models of Teaching*, 2nd ed. Englewood Cliffs, N.J.: Prentice-Hall, Inc., 1980, Part III.

Joyce, Bruce. *Flexibility in Teaching: An Excursion into the Nature of Teaching and Training*. New York: Longman, Inc., 1980.

Massialas, Byron G., and Benjamin Cox. *Inquiry in Social Studies*. New York: McGraw-Hill Book Company, 1966.

Morine, H., and G. Morine. *Discovery: A Challenge to Teachers*. Englewood Cliffs, N.J.: Prentice-Hall, Inc., 1973.

Raths, Louis E., Selma Wasserman, Arthur Jonas and Arnold M. Rothstein. *Teaching For Thinking Theory and Application*. Columbus, Ohio: Charles E. Merrill Publishing Company, 1967.

Schulman, Lee S., and Evan R. Keislar, eds. *Learning By Discovery A Critical Appraisal*. Chicago: Rand McNally & Company, 1966.

Sigel, I. E., and R. Saunders. "An Inquiry into Inquiry: Question-asking as an Instructional Model," in L. Katz ed. *Current Topics in Early Childhood Education*. Norwood, J.J.: Ablex Publishers, 1979.

Chapter 14

Unit Planning and Research Skill Activities

After you have completed the study of this chapter, you should be able to accomplish the following:

1. **Differentiate the characteristics of the three types of units.**
2. **Write an example of a concept, generalization, and fact.**
3. **Write several "big ideas" for use as a content outline in a subject of your choice.**
4. **Identify the concept(s) and generalization(s) in your outline.**
5. **Follow the sequential development of a unit, performing each task.**
6. **Discuss observation skills; explain why individual observations frequently differ.**
7. **Identify the skills needed for interviewing.**
8. **Differentiate between interview technique and the use of questionnaires.**
9. **List four formats for questions in the interview and questionnaire.**
10. **Suggest ways in which elementary students can organize and analyze data.**
11. **Explain how research strategies can be used to integrate subject fields.**
12. **Identify the purpose of the case study approach.**
13. **Practice the teacher planning tasks for the case study approach.**
14. **Compare the learner tasks during the case study with the learner tasks during inquiry problem solving.**
15. **Contrast the several types of inquiry strategies discussed in Chapters 13 and 14.**

What Is Unit Teaching?

A unit is a plan that organizes ideas and knowledge into a meaningful structure for teaching purposes. Basic concepts within a subject field or across subject fields are selected to achieve specific objectives. The content of the unit facilitates communication. Without content there is very little for students to communicate about for expression and reception purposes. The unit should provide integrative experiences to satisfy students' needs and to develop understandings, values, and skills.

Types of Units

Subject Field Units. Units can be developed for most subjects: science, music, art, health, mathematics, social studies. Science units typically emphasize both the basic concepts and inquiry processes. Social studies units are usually broadly conceived, emphasizing specific social science concepts but providing means to integrate skill instruction in reading and language as well as music and art. Units planned in music and art draw content from social studies and science, and sometimes from physical education and mathematics. Health units frequently integrate content from science and physical education.

A model unit entitled "Water" (see Appendix) was developed to illustrate the integration of subject fields. Although the major conceptual focus of the water unit draws from social science content, the unit features learning experiences from health, science, music, literature, physical education, and mathematics. Skill instruction in the unit focuses on the language arts.

Resource units are often developed at the district level. The purpose of the resource unit is to provide a great deal of information on possible ways to teach a specific topic. The resource unit is usually developed by a committee of teachers or subject field specialists. It is not planned with any specific group of students in mind. Learning activities, resource materials, and evaluation methods, as well as lists of objectives and questions, can be found in the resource unit.

Teaching Unit. The teaching unit differs from the resource unit in degree of specificity; it is focused and planned for a particular group of students and is formulated to teach a limited number of concepts, skills, and values. Before developing a teaching unit, the teacher may make use of a resource unit.

The teaching unit ensures that there is a purpose to the day-by-day lessons. The teaching unit represents long-range planning for teaching the curriculum. Unit activities should include problem solving, reading, language, dramatic activities, and research. All of the instructional strategies discussed in Part III of this text can be utilized in unit teaching.

The first part of this chapter has been designed to illustrate the unit-planning process. To do this a social studies unit has been developed at the fifth-grade level for Greg Thomas' students at the Martin Luther King Elementary School. The second part of the chapter deals with research skill activities.

Unit Planning

The planning process begins with the identification of the organizing "threads" of the unit. These threads relate to the knowledge, skills, and attitudes to be taught.

Concepts, Generalizations, and Facts

The basic organizing structure for content is achieved through the selection of concepts. In social studies the social science concepts tell us which knowledge is of most worth in this particular unit. Concepts are selected on the basis of their organizing value and the amount of information the concept will facilitate learning.

Generalizations tell us what it is about the concept that we want to teach. The generalization supplies direction and narrows the approach. The generalization supplies the main focus of the concept.

The main ideas of the unit can be used as a content outline. The ideas help us organize the topics for coverage. If we know the ideas we want to cover, then we have a basis for eliminating other ideas. The ideas help us determine the significance of our information and lead us to the choice of instructional materials. The ideas determine the scope and depth of the unit.

Facts are the data that the unit deals with. Facts are selected because they demonstrate the main idea and collectively will lead students to the generalization. By themselves, facts have no significance because they become obsolete. Taba (1967) provides an example of this. After one learns the generalization that Argentina is a one-crop country, it makes little difference to know the amount of meat exported by Argentina in any given year (the fact).

(Semester Unit for Fifth Grade—Greg Thomas, Teacher)

THE BIG IDEAS—CONTENT OUTLINE

1. The colonists were motivated to come to the new world for a variety of reasons.
2. The environment and conditions of living in a region affect human behavior.
3. The needs and interests of people differ; events and actions motivate antagonistic behavior.
4. Industrialization affected people's independence and way of life.
5. Conflict, cooperation, and competition occur when cultures meet.

General Objectives

The unit will facilitate students' development of the following concepts, generalizations, skills, attitudes, and values:

Concepts	**Generalizations**
Migration:	People migrate to achieve political or religious freedom or a better way of life.
Adaptation and Culture:	People adapt to and modify their environment; past and present experiences affect ways of behaving.
Conflict:	Different interests and purposes stimulate conflict.
Change:	Survival depends upon awareness of and adaptation to social change.
Interaction:	Individual and cultural differences affect ways of life.

Skills:

1. Gather information through listening, observing, reading; utilize reference materials including maps and graphs; organize and evaluate information.
2. Compare similarities and differences
3. Classify and group data
4. Ask appropriate questions
5. Make predictions; suggest hypotheses
6. Evaluate and make decisions

Attitudes, Values, Social Participation:

1. Acknowledge and communicate own perspective
2. Recognize others' perspectives
3. Acknowledge multiple causation of social phenomena
4. Accept responsibility as leader and group member
5. Exhibit respect for others' opinions and rights

The next step for Greg Thomas was to frame some key questions to guide his choice of learning experiences. Using each concept and his "big ideas," he wrote a tentative list of questions.

KEY QUESTIONS

Migration:

1. Who were the early settlers?
2. Where did they come from?
3. Why did they decide to come? (What reasons influenced them?)

Adaptation and Culture:

1. In what regions did the pioneers settle?
2. What was the physical environment like?
3. How did the early settlers use and change the environment?
4. What different experiences did people have in the various settlements?
5. How did people satisfy their basic needs?
6. How did the ways in which people satisfied their basic needs differ in the Northeast, South, and West?

Conflict:

1. In what ways did the needs and interests of people in the various regions of the United States differ?
2. What disagreements did people in the Northeast, South, and West have?
3. How did the varied needs and interests affect behavior?
4. What events and actions motivated antagonistic behavior?

Change:

1. How did technology affect people's independence?
2. How were workers affected? How were industrial leaders affected?
3. How did the expansion of rail lines affect people's opportunities?
4. In what ways did cities change?

Interaction:

1. How were the American Indians affected by newcomers to the United States?
2. What did different cultures "borrow" from each other?
3. How did different cultural groups feel about land rights, land ownership, farming, education, family life?
4. How did Americans treat new immigrant groups?

Thomas' next task was to select appropriate learning experiences to achieve objectives, to stimulate thinking, and to appeal to students' natural interests.

LEARNING EXPERIENCES (ACTIVITIES) RELATED TO CONCEPTS

Migration:

1. View film about the many faces of Americans (observe and discuss)
2. Map and globe study: locate points of emigration of early settlers.
3. Read and listen to stories about the first newcomers; discuss why they decided to come.
4. Role-play different immigrant groups; identify the reasons that influenced them to emigrate.

Adaptation and Culture:

1. Map and globe study of United States: identify topographic and climatic differences.
2. Use large (floor) map of U.S.: identify and attach mountains, rivers, trails. Discuss direction that rivers flow, elevation; Compute time differences between various settlements.
3. Read and discuss (small group research) regional differences:
   (a) how early settlers used animal life to meet needs
   (b) how early settlers used plant life to meet needs (trees, seeds, fruits)
   (c) how present day farming methods compare with early pioneer farming methods
4. Experiment with plants in small groups. (What do all plants need?)
5. Construct objects to be used to "act out" life of pioneers:
   early settlements (use box board and apple boxes)
   rifles soap
   clothes candles
   tools wagons
6. Measurement lesson using metrics; relate to construction project.
7. Read and discuss (small group research) regional differences in way of life.
8. Dramatic Play: act out pioneer life to verify what students have learned (work activities, recreation, a feast, educational activity, religious activity).
9. Field trip to museum: observe early artifacts and pictures (lamps, furniture, pewter, rifles, clothing).
10. Write "tall tales"—stories typical of pioneer days; develop a class book of tall tales, and/or tape-record stories.
11. Write letters to relations in Europe describing New World experiences.
12. Folk dance: learn and perform regional dances.
13. Sing songs associated with early history.
14. Paint construction objects.
15. Dramatic Play: use completed materials; evaluate whether students understand regional differences in methods of meeting basic needs.

Conflict:

1. Discuss needs and interests of people in Northeast, South, and West; relate differences to environmental adaptation and culture.
2. Read and discuss (small group research): agriculture in the South and trading and manufacturing in the Northeast.
3. Compare regional differences using data from small group research; (discuss) why Southerners thought that trading and manu-

facturing were suitable only for the lower class.

4. Role-play using the simulation "Slave Auction."
5. Read about and discuss: the slave experience, Northwest Ordinance, travel experiences of pioneers as they moved west.
6. Dramatic Play: preparation for moving west, pioneer life on the various trails (Oregon—crossing the Kaw and Platte rivers, hunting, attacks by Indians).
7. Use large (floor) map of United States to identify famous trails and settlements.
8. Using data from small group research, hypothesize about Western attitudes about equality. Verify, using text or teacher-prepared information.
9. Read and discuss (small group research) the main issues that motivated the polarization of sectional attitudes: tariff, states' rights, slavery, Nat Turner Rebellion, Fugitive Slave Law, Dred Scott Decision, Missouri Compromise, John Brown, Kansas-Nebraska Act.
10. Sing famous folk songs from Civil War period; discuss meaning of verses.
11. Develop a time line of events and actions that led to the Civil War.

Change:

1. Read to gather information; develop a time line of inventions.
2. Discuss how technology affected regional life.
3. Read about and discuss (small group research): How did industrialization affect working conditions and employment, the organization of work, where people lived, attitudes of business leaders, the effect on children?
4. Use large (floor) map of the U.S. and affix rail line expansion.
5. Discuss the effect of railroad expansion on people's opportunities.
6. Read about and discuss (small group research) the growth of cities. (Have each group investigate a different city.)
7. Discuss verses and sing folk songs about the industrialization period (John Henry); read poetry and stories of the period.

Interaction:

1. Read about and discuss (small group research) the relations between early colonists and the American Indians. (Study specific tribes—Cheyenne, Sioux, Plains). How did ways of life differ?
2. Role-play cultural conflict between pioneer groups and American Indians.
3. Read about and discuss land ownership, land rights, education, farming, family life. What were regional, group, ethnic differences in attitudes toward these issues or aspects of life? (How did Mexicans of the Southwest feel about land ownership and water rights? How did cattle ranch owners differ from farmers in regard to land rights and ownership? What were the Indian attitudes?)
4. Perform Indian dances and games.
5. Research and chart: What did early settlers learn from the American Indians? What did the Indians learn from the settlers?
6. Discuss cultural borrowing (utilize data from previous lesson).
7. Write stories about how American life is a composite of many cultures.
8. Read about and discuss (small group research) the experiences of different minority groups during different historical time periods. (Assign each group a different minority people.)

   Chinese—1870s   Mexicans—1970s
   Jews—1900s   Vietnamese—1980s
   Irish—1920s

9. Make a class mural depicting immigrant experiences.

Observations About the Teaching Unit

Historical chronology is not of major importance in the unit in the sense that Thomas does not intend to proceed decade-by-decade from prerevolutionary times to modern United States history. This limitation is sensible because it is obviously impossible to include "all" of history. However, this does not mean that Thomas will not teach "time" in relation to history. Each period of history can be connected for the students through the use of time lines in the classroom and by relating significant events to other events that students recall.

Thomas has selected a limited number of concepts to develop in depth. There are others that he could have selected, but his choices do give him "mileage." Again, he is wise in not trying to teach "everything you always wanted to know about American history" to fifth graders.

Although the activities are numbered, the numbers do not mean that each experience necessarily takes only one day. Some of the experiences will not be concluded during one class period (construction, mural, story writing, science experiments). It may also happen that some activities should be repeated the following day. The evaluation of an activity like dramatic play might reveal the need for another repeated experience to clarify concepts. The many research activities may also take more than one class period. It should be noted that the unit is planned as a whole semester sequence.

While the general objectives identified at the beginning of the unit define Thomas' overall purposes, behavioral objectives have not been set. Remember that the list of learning experiences is tentative. When Thomas makes definite decisions about each lesson, he will include the behavioral objective. For example, the activity "to write tall tales about pioneer days" might have the following objective:

After listening to some pioneer fictional legends, students will write individual "tall tale" narratives.

Since each activity tells what the students will be doing, it should be relatively easy to add the behavioral objective.

Teaching the Unit

The initiation, development, and culmination of a social studies teaching unit has been discussed in Chapter 7.

Gathering, organizing, and analyzing data are important search skill activities. Greg Thomas' small group research activities included these skills in his unit teaching plans. These skills contribute to learning in several content fields. The balance of this chapter will focus on research strategies. Field research, using interviews and questionnaires and case study analysis are the specific instructional strategies to be discussed. Other unit teaching activities can be found in Chapters 12, 13, and 15.

Elementary students can be taught research skills, even in the primary grades. However, research skills cannot be developed without utilizing reading, language, and mathematics. The skills to be featured in this chapter will require students to

- observe in an objective manner
- ask questions
- group and classify information
- read
- use oral language skills
- use mathematics.

Observation Skills

To discuss the skills utilized by elementary students—as researchers—we will visit Sara Garcia's third-grade classroom. The students have just finished a session with the YMCA leader of the Feelin' Good program. The leader challenged them by stating that on her next visit the class would check their fitness progress by performing some physical fitness tests.

As the students go out to lunch, Sara Garcia hears them discussing whether girls are more flexible than boys and questioning each other about the fitness tests. During the lunch hour the students get into an argument. Some of the children were performing bent knee sit-ups while others watched.

The "observers" claimed that the children doing the sit-ups were "cheating" and not performing the exercise correctly. The teacher on yard duty had to stop the activity because of the heat of the argument. The yard teacher reported the situation to Garcia.

Sara Garcia asked the students to explain the problem during the afternoon class session. The discussion focused on whether or not the children performing the exercise had performed it correctly. Observers' reports differed. Garcia decided to use the incident to accomplish several purposes: improve understanding of physical fitness, teach research skills, improve playground behavior, and integrate several subject fields.

On the following day Garcia showed a movie in which children were demonstrating exercises. In the discussion that followed, Garcia helped to clarify and emphasize the following ideas:

- All individuals need a daily fitness program.
- Children and adults should exercise.
- Playing games will not necessarily keep children fit.
- Both girls and boys have the same physiological capacity to be flexible.
- Children are not necessarily more flexible than adults.

Many of the students were surprised that all age groups need exercise and that girls are not more flexible than boys. The students' interest provided Garcia with the lead-in she was looking for, and she asked the students if they would like to become "researchers" to find out what others believe about fitness and exercise. The students agreed and immediately one class member asked if they were going to conduct a "survey." Garcia responded that they could do that, but first she wanted to talk about the problem they had on the playground. Garcia asked them if they understood why some of the "observers" disagreed with each other about whether the "performers" were exercising correctly.

The children did not understand why there was disagreement, so Garcia asked several students to demonstrate sit-ups. Then she asked several students to describe what they saw. Once again the reports differed slightly. This time Garcia said, "All right, suppose that we said that when doing a sit-up you must roll up into a sitting position and keep your elbows extended straight from your ears."

Now she had the students demonstrate the sit-up once again. Then she asked the observers for their report. This time the observers agreed about what they saw. "Why did the observers agree this time?" Garcia asked the students. After some discussion, the students realized that this time the observers were all looking for the *same* behavior. They were using the same criteria to describe what they saw.

Using this procedure, Garcia helped her students realize why they had been arguing on the playground. Then she said, "Now that you understand why you had a problem, let's trace the sequence of events that led up to the yard teacher disciplining you." Garcia had the students list the events in the order that they happened. With the list on the chalkboard, Garcia explained to the students that each event was caused by the preceding event, that in fact there was a *pattern of causes.* Then they talked about underlying causes of behavior, such as emotions. As a result of the discussion the students understood that each event was an *effect* of the prior event and that each had caused the final effect of the discipline.

When Sara Garcia felt comfortable about her students' understanding of their own behavior, she suggested that they begin thinking about their research. She told them, "These are some things we need to know in order to begin our research."

About Data. Data means information; data is evidence. The researcher collects data about a specific problem under investigation. Data can be collected by seeing and listening to people, by asking people for information as in an interview situation, and by asking people for a written report as in a questionnaire.

About Observation. Although people may supposedly "see" or "hear" the same event, observations differ. This occurs because some people are more perceptive than others; people differ about *what* they have observed, and sometimes people disagree about *why* something happened. To improve observation and make observations valid, people must observe specific aspects of behavior. To ensure that observations are reliable, several observers must observe independently, and their observations must agree about what they are seeing or hearing. For example: since the observers in Garcia's class had disagreed about the playground performance of the students doing the sit-ups, Garcia had set a standard for skill performance. The next time the observers watched the sit-ups, they were all looking for the same skill performance using specific criteria. This ensured that the observation would be *valid*. To ensure reliability, Garcia used several observers. If the independent observations agreed about what they were observing, they would be considered reliable.

On successive days, Garcia and her students will formalize their research. Using observation skills, interviews, and questionnaires, the third-graders will gather data, organize it, and analyze the results.

RESEARCH FINDINGS

Ellis and Glenn (1977) examined three different approaches to the teaching of economic concepts and the development of problem-solving skills:

1. a real-life interdisciplinary problem
2. a contrived problem using economic simulations and games
3. a discussion workbook experience

They concluded that the problem-solving approach using a real or contrived problem was a more effective instructional means than using a read-recite worksheet approach.

Interviews and Questionnaires

Advantages and Disadvantages of the Interview Technique

There are advantages and disadvantages to both the interview and the questionnaire. Generally, the interview is a more personal way of obtaining information. Face-to-face contact allows questions to be open-ended and determined by the nature of the interaction. Both the respondent and the interviewer have greater leeway in answering questions and in asking them. During the interview the interviewer must make a number of decisions. For example, the interviewer must decide when to probe with a follow-up question or when to change the sequence of questions.

The interviewer must also be careful that the interview situation is objective. Facial expression and voice tone can communicate interviewer bias, thereby affecting the information provided by the respondent. Sometimes the sequence of questions and even the type of question asked can communicate bias. For example, if the interviewer asks a leading question (Isn't it true that . . . ?) the respondent may interpret the question as a biased question or may consider it presumptuous. Yes/No questions should generally be avoided during an interview situation because this type of question does not exploit the advantage of the personal, face-to-face nature of the interview. Exceptions to this will be discussed.

Another advantage to the interview situation is the opportunity for the interviewer to detect respondent hesitance, uncertainty, shyness, and bias. However, to do this, the researcher must know what to look for and be an experienced interviewer.

Difficulties connected with the organization of the interview for analysis are considered disadvantages. A system must be devised so that the interview can be preserved for later analysis. One solution is to tape-record the interview. This can be done if the interviewer obtains permission from the respondent to record the questions and the responses. Very capable interviewers can write down the respondent's answers, but elementary students have difficulty doing this.

Special Skills and Problems. Chapin and Gross (1973) called attention to two skills needed by the interviewer. These are the ability to make the respondent feel at ease and willing to be interviewed, and the ability to restrain personal comments and expressions so that interviewer bias is not apparent to the respondent. Both of these skills should be practiced in the classroom before the interview.

Courtesy to the person being interviewed is another aspect of the interview situation that should be discussed with young students. The interviewer must remember that the respondent is performing a service by permitting the interview. The interviewer should introduce him/herself, explain the reason or purpose of the interview, and be sure to thank the respondent for taking time to respond. Young students should be made aware of the fact that sometimes adults do not like to be interviewed by youngsters. The result is sometimes more positive if students interview in teams.

Structured Interview. Lippitt, Fox, and Schable (1969) recommended a structured interview situation for elementary students. This is an interview in which the questions never differ. They are predetermined and asked exactly as decided upon. They are usually asked in a precise order. Sometimes the respondent is even asked to choose a response from a list of possible answers. The reason these educators suggest the structured interview is that interviewing is really quite difficult to do well and young children need preparation. They suggest—even with preset questions—that the students practice on each other in the classroom before the interview. Their experience has been that the practice period will insure that more data will be collected during the actual interview situation.

Questionnaires. The questionnaire is an example of a measuring instrument. It is more objective than the interview and can be mailed to respondents. Questions should be short and precise. Vague words should be avoided. Care needs to be exercised that each question requires just one response. Inexperienced questioners tend to ask more than one question at a time. A good idea before sending the questionnaire out is to try it with a select audience of friends. Create a "pilot" study to determine if the questions ask what the class thinks they are asking. Although it is possible to ask open-ended questions on a questionnaire, they are more difficult to score and to interpret. Some questionnaries are designed to provide objective measures with forced-choice answers, and some questions are open-ended so that the respondent may add whatever s/he pleases.

Distribution and Sampling. It is important to decide how to distribute the questionnaire. Since postage can be expensive, this may be a major decision. Typically, students decide to hand carry their questionnaires to the respondents and mail only those questionnaires that are going out of town.

Simple sampling concepts should be taught to the students. For example, they can learn that one of the first things the social scientist must do is decide what group of people is to be studied. Then, since it is usually impossible to survey everyone in the group, the scientist chooses a limited number of people. The people s/he chooses are called the *sample*. In choosing the sample, the scientist tries to make sure that the chosen group is *representative* of the total group so that it will be possible to make statements about the total group after the study has been completed. Sometimes scientists make mistakes and choose a biased sample that does not represent the group to be studied. When this occurs the scientist cannot generalize accurately about the total population. An example of this would be the following: A second-grade class wanted to find out if children in the second grade liked dogs. Since they could not ask all second graders, they chose a sample to question. After they finished their study, they discovered that almost all of the children in their sample owned dogs. As a consequence they had what is called a "biased" sample, or in other words a group that was not representative of the total group of second graders.

Choosing the Format for Questions. There are four possible formats for questions in the questionnaire and interview. *Forced-choice* questions require the respondent to choose among alternatives, such as yes-no; always-never; many-few; often-sometimes-rarely. A second type is the *scale* question. This asks the respondent to rate an event, trait, or behavior. For example: I like dogs—

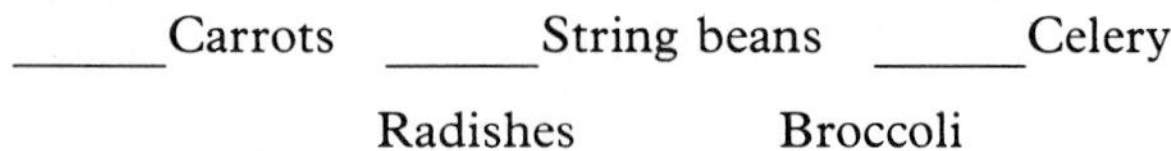

A third type is the *ranking* question. In this question the respondent is asked to arrange events, behaviors, or traits in the order of preference or importance. Ranking items is more difficult for the respondent than answering the forced-choice questions or the scale questions. An example would be: Rank the following vegetables in the order that you like them. Number 5 indicates the vegetable that you like the most; Number 1 the vegetable that you like least.

_____Carrots _____String beans _____Celery

_____Radishes _____Broccoli

Lippitt et al. (1969) recommended that five items be the limit for elementary students. The fourth question type is the *open-ended* question which permits the respondent to say or write anything s/he wants. The open-ended question is the easiest to write, but the hardest to score. However, a great deal of information can be gathered when time is taken to use the open-ended question. An example: What do you enjoy most about teaching?

Before Sara Garcia set her class to work writing questions, she decided that they had better have some idea about how data are analyzed. She knew that this information might influence their decision about the kinds of questions to ask.

Organizing the Data. Forced-choice questions can be tabulated and then analyzed in terms of percentage of persons responding or the frequency of the response. (See Table 14.1.)

Table 14.1 All individuals need a daily fitness program.

	3rd Graders	6th Graders	Adults	Total
YES	20	15	35 (50%)	70
NO	10	10	20	40
No Response	5	10	15	20
Total	35	35	70	140 people

A similar type of worksheet can be designed for the scale-type questions.

Table 14.2. I like exercise.

	Boys	Girls	Men	Women	Total
Very Much	15	10	25	20	70
Much	10	5	1	0	16
Little Bit	2	10	0	5	17
Not Much	3	3	4	5	15
No Response	0	2	0	0	2
Total	30	30	30	30	120 people

Students can be taught different ways to categorize the information. Questions that ask the respondent to rank the items can be tallied in the following way:

Table 14.3.

Points	Carrots	Beans	Radishes	Celery	Broccoli
5	20	8	1	15	2
4	10	10	4	10	5
3	5	5	5	10	20
2	3	10	5	2	10
1	2	7	25	3	3
Totals	163	122	71	152	113
Rank	1	3	5	2	4

Note: The tally was multiplied by the number of points the respondent gave it.

Researchers need to decide on criteria to develop categories in order to analyze open-ended questions. For example, if respondents were asked, "What do you like about exercise?" their responses might be:

"It makes me feel good."
"Nothing."
No response.
"I like sweating."
"I think it is important to do."

To organize this information the researcher would probably establish positive, negative, neutral, and no response categories. Then they would need to provide examples of each category to guide the organization of the data. "It makes me feel good," and "I like sweating" would be examples of positive responses. "Nothing" could be interpreted as a negative response. "I think it is important to do" would be a neutral statement. Sara Garcia's third graders would have difficulty interpreting open-ended responses; capable fifth- and sixth-grade students could probably manage it quite well.

Analyzing the Data. Sara Garcia assisted the students in developing a scale-type questionnaire. The questions were as follows:

1. Do you think it is important for children to exercise regularly?
2. Do you think it is important for adults to exercise regularly?
3. Do you think aerobic workouts are important?
4. Do you think exercise can make people feel better?
5. Do you think it is important to stretch before you exercise vigorously?

The questions would also be used in an interview situation with the interviewer asking one additional question: Do you think exercise is fun?

After the students had tabulated their data, they were given several ways to present the results. Garcia grouped the students into five groups, and each group was told to decide how to *communicate*

Figure 14.1. Histograph. Do You Think Exercise Can Make People Feel Better?

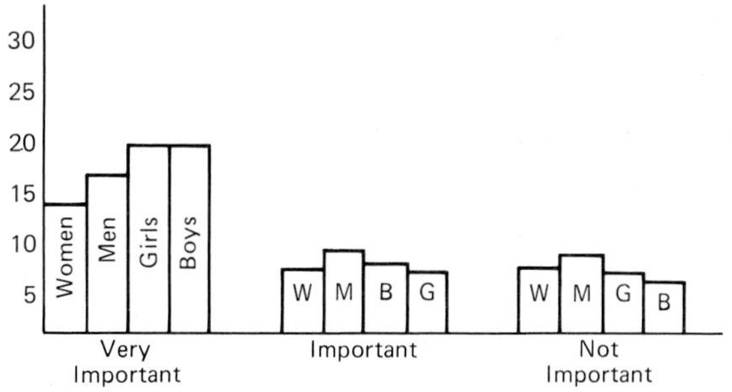

Figure 14.2. Pie Graphs.

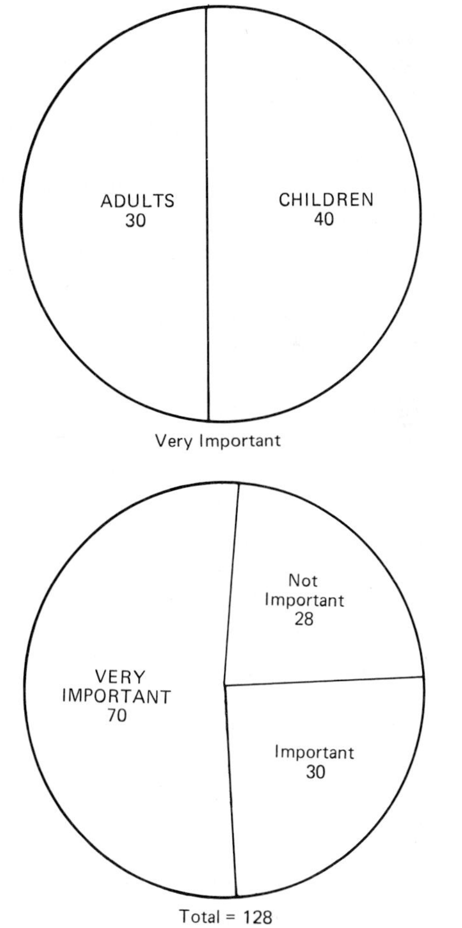

the results to others. Each group worked with just one of the questions. Their choices included a pie graph, histograph, table, or chart. The students had data for boys, girls, men, and women. They were told that they could sum the data or find ways to present the data for each of the four groups. They would have to decide how to communicate the importance of the response. The results as communicated by one of Sara Garcia's groups appears below.

Table 14.4. Do you think exercise can make people feel better?

	Very Important	Important	Not Important
Males	38	18	14
Females	32	12	14
Total	70	30	28

Conclusions. During the summative evaluation, Garcia's students concluded:

1. Children have a better understanding of the importance of exercise than adults.
2. Males appreciate the value of exercise more than females.
3. Adult females were more willing to be interviewed than adult males.
4. Adult males were more willing to fill out a questionnaire.
5. Deciding on the questions to ask and their form was the hardest research task.
6. Choosing their sample was important.
7. They felt shy when doing an interview.
8. It was fun!

What Did the Students Learn?

Sara Garcia used the research study to *integrate subject fields.* She was also concerned about her students' social behavior on the playground. Subject-by-subject, here is a summary of what she accomplished:

LANGUAGE ARTS

Reading: The students read questions, charts, graphs, and the questionnaire. They learned to classify data by sex and to use a scale. They arranged information in sequence.

Oral Language: Students participated in group and class discussions, practiced interviewing, practiced courtesy during interviewing, listened to others, asked questions, expressed ideas.

Spelling: They spelled special words related to the research study, such as *male, female, sample, questionnaire, observations, interview, survey.*

Writing: They wrote questions using capitals and question marks.

RESEARCH REVIEW

In a review of aptitude-treatment interaction studies where two or more methods are allowed to interact with student aptitudes to predict satisfaction and achievement, Clark (1981) concluded:

	High Ability	*Low Ability*
Learn most	Open and permissive instructional approach	Structured approaches
Like most	Structured and directive approaches	Permissive methods of instruction
Research conclusion	Structured approaches interfere with learning and duplicate what the "highs" already know.	Permissive approaches fail to provide cues or model for "lows" to learn.

MATHEMATICS

The students performed addition using two-digit numbers; performed column addition; subtracted two-digit numbers; multiplied two-digit numbers; collected, organized, and interpreted data using charts, tables, and bar graphs.

SCIENCE, SOCIAL STUDIES, THINKING SKILLS

Students used their senses to collect and process data. They developed and used a classification system. They participated in inquiry, identifying a problem and forming questions. They planned an investigation; recorded and organized data; prepared and interpreted graphic material; analyzed, evaluated, and interpreted data; summarized and communicated investigation to others.

SOCIAL PARTICIPATION

They demonstrated curiosity, concern about others, willingness to share data and ideas with others, cooperation with others, participation in group tasks, acceptance of responsibility to distribute and collect data.

HEALTH AND PHYSICAL EDUCATION

Students shared information about physical activities. They considered the relationship of activity to cardiovascular health. They recognized the importance of exercise. They shared negative and positive feelings. They performed exercise activities, explained basic ideas about exercise, discussed physical fitness, participated in fitness testing.

> In field research the students gather the data; in case study analysis the teacher usually collects the data. Why are both instructional techniques considered inquiry?

Case Studies

What Is a Case Study?

A case study is an in-depth investigation of a *single* event, an institution, a decision, an issue, an individual. Case studies have typically been used in business, medicine, law, social work, and therapy. Materials for case studies may include personal records, histories, diaries, graphs, stories—in fact, a variety of data. Although the data may be varied, it is typically relevant only to the single situation for which it was gathered or prepared. The data should lend itself to a systematic analysis. Practice with case study analysis should help students gain insight into similar types of problems or situations. Thinking is usually inductive in nature during the case study.

The case study approach allows the teacher to reduce the amount of data to a manageable size to facilitate analysis. For example, suppose a teacher wanted students to understand our legal system and the way in which the Supreme Court makes decisions. Instead of asking students to research everything about the Court and the decisions the Court makes, the teacher provides data, or has students gather the data, about a single Court decision. Once the data is collected and studied, the students may even role-play the case in order to gain greater insight. The principle illustrated by the case should demonstrate a basic concept that is applicable to similar problems, or in the case of the Supreme Court, it should illustrate the decision-making process of the Court and how the Court relates to a democratic society.

Case studies selected can be about real issues and problems or fictional ones. The studies may be open-ended, involved, or quite simple. Whatever is selected should be motivating and provide an adequate data base in terms of factual information. The open-ended case requires that students make the final judgment about the outcome or at least suggest possible alternatives.

Types of Case Studies

Newmann and Oliver (1967) identified seven basic types of cases:

1. *Story*. The story may be fictional or about authentic events. Literature or history books are appropriate, or the teacher may write an episode or dialogue for study. The story would have a plot and characters.
2. *Vignette*. This type of case would be similar to the story, but shorter, with no plot.

3. *Journalistic Historical Narrative.* A newspaper account of an event is appropriate. The situation may provide an eyewitness account of what happened, or it may be an hour-by-hour description. This case could be about a group or an institution rather than about individuals.
4. *Documents.* Primary resource materials are appropriate for this type of case study. Public records of court trials, hearings, and council reports as well as diaries, letters, and speeches would be suitable for analysis.
5. *Research Data.* Experimental studies and survey data or statistical data would be appropriate. Use of census reports are appropriate for inductive generalizations.
6. *Text.* Text material that describes general phenomena and trends or provides specific information about people may be chosen, if the knowledge appears to be objective.
7. *Interpretive Essay.* The selected essay discusses an abstract issue and provides an explanation or an interpretive conclusion. In contrast to the text, which presents an objective description, the essay is subjective and interpretive. The reader of the essay is supposed to be sophisticated and critical.

Examples of the Use of Case Study

Language Arts. A fourth-grade teacher used the case study method to accomplish both language arts and social studies objectives. The teacher chose the following resources:

- *West from Home*—Letters of Laura Ingalls Wilder
- *A Gathering of Days*—A New England girl's journal, 1830–32
- *The Endless Steppe*—A girl in exile.

The Wilder book provides historical background and information about San Francisco in 1915. The book is composed of letters from Laura Wilder to her husband. *A Gathering of Days* by Joan Blos is a fictional work written in the form of a journal. It is about the rigorous life on a New Hampshire farm in 1830. *The Endless Steppe* is a personal account by Esther Haytzig of her experiences as a girl in exile in Siberia. The story takes place during World War II.

The teacher's goals were as follows:

- To develop an appreciation of authorship
- To differentiate purpose, structure, and style of fiction and nonfiction
- To recognize that personal letters, journals, and diaries are documents—primary resources—and provide a form of autobiography
- To authenticate historical information and background information by reading literature.

The students' assignment was to read the selected portion of the book and be prepared to discuss the following:

1. How does the writer know what really happened?
2. What reasons might the writer have for being prejudiced or for exaggerating?
3. When did the writer or main character live?
4. What event did the writer or main character participate in?
5. What decisions did the writer or main character make?
6. How would circumstances have been different if the story were told by a male?
7. If you were faced with similar conflicts, what decisions would you make?
8. How are you like or different from the author or main character?

Another Example Using Literature

In another elementary classroom the teacher used the story of Goldilocks and the three bears prepared by the Constitutional Rights Foundation. The objective was to teach the concept of privacy. The students read and performed Goldilocks as a play and ultimately discussed whether or not Goldilocks had the right to enter the home of the three bears, eat their porridge, break their rocking chair, and sleep in the bed of the baby bear. In this situation the case study resource was the story of Goldilocks.

A similar case study approach was used by Sara Garcia with her third-grade students. She used the story of the Little Red Hen. Her students discussed the question, "What is fair and equitable?"

Art Education

To develop understanding about the contribution of artists and to help students realize that art changes in time as a consequence of development, interests, and values, a sixth-grade teacher had students study specific artists. Groups were formed in the classroom, and each group was given a different case history and art examples of one artist. From the case history, each group was to respond to the following questions: "What is art as exemplified by . . . (Van Gouch or Picasso or Dali or Degas or Toulouse-Lautrec)?" Each group was to characterize the artist in its case study.

Teaching Tasks Using Case Studies

1. *Is the case study approach appropriate?* In choosing a teaching strategy a teacher must ask: Which approach will be advantageous and facilitate the accomplishment of my objectives? Case studies are appropriate as a teaching strategy when the amount of data about a given problem, situation, or person is so abundant that it would be difficult for students to choose and examine just the pertinent information. When this occurs the case study approach allows the teacher to *reduce* the data, thereby limiting the investigation.

Case studies are also valuable when the data cannot be researched by the students because of the complexity of the issues or the reading levels of the students. In this instance, the teacher may find that it is advantageous to write the case study to fit the students' reading levels.

Case studies are suitable when the situation calls for an open-ended role that makes students decide what the decision ought to be.

Once you have decided that the case study is the right approach and fits the purposes of the lesson, it is time to select the appropriate materials *or* write your own.

2. *Selecting materials for a case study.* The first consideration in choosing case study materials is whether the students will be able to read and comprehend the selected data. Both the concept load and the vocabulary level must be considered. If students do not have the specialized skills needed to read charts, tables, graphs, or maps, then a skill lesson will need to precede the use of the case study materials.

Organizational considerations also affect the choice of the materials. How will students be grouped for instruction? If students are to work in small groups during the intake portion of the lesson, have you prepared or obtained enough materials? If students are working in small groups, can one member of each group be the "reader" for the other group members?

Since media presentations are the easiest to use with young children, films, slides, or tapes should be surveyed. Frequently information can be recorded for use in listening centers. Tapes are advantageous because students can repeat them as often as necessary to obtain needed details.

There is a wide variety of commercial publications available for case study use. In addition, newspapers, textbooks, and literature selections provide a wealth of suitable data. Once you become adept at rewriting materials for your own students, you will find that social studies, science, and health textbooks are a fine source of knowledge.

3. *Motivating the study and organizing study tasks.* As in other inquiry activities, if the proposed case study is not of interest to the students, they will not be motivated to perform the necessary analytic tasks. Therefore, it is important that the teacher determine the relevancy of the assignment before sending students off to study. Once again formulation of the inquiry question will be an important teacher task.

Another area of teacher decision making is: How should students organize the data? Suppose that the case study involved reading about student misbehavior in the Boston school system. The data included charts on federal aid, maintenance and supply costs, and personnel costs. Facts included information about curriculum, students' difficulties, and class distractions. Since the case study will be evaluated during a whole-class discussion, how should students prepare for the discussion?

Table 14.5. Case Study Inquiry Sequence.

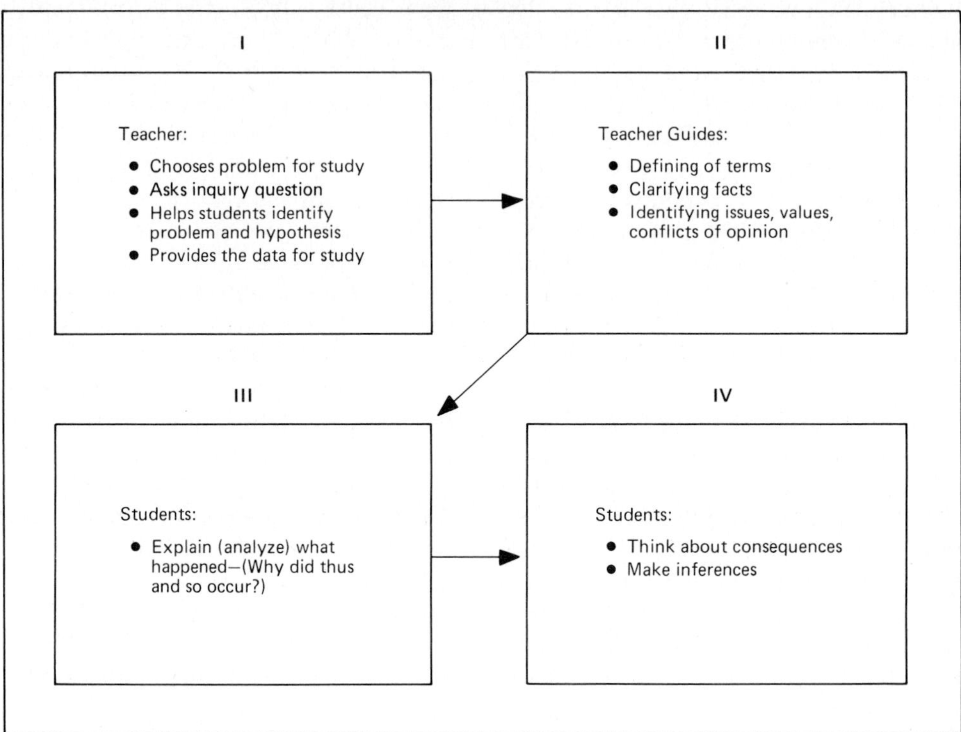

Let us consider the inquiry sequence for a case study. (Refer to Table 14.5.)

> **RESEARCH REVIEW**
>
> In a review of studies on problem solving, Lockhead (1981) concluded that good problem solvers work harder than poor problem solvers. Most studies of thinking find that problem solvers need to be conscious of their own reasoning process by talking or writing down their thoughts.

4. *Debrief using discussion strategy*. Guiding the discussion at the end of the case study is the most important teacher task. During this stage of the study the teacher, through questions, facilitates:

(a) A recap of the definition of key terms. (The teacher or a capable student should record the discussion on the chalkboard.)

(b) Clarification of the facts. The teacher will ask, "What do we know . . . ?" and "How do we know that what we know is reliable?"

(c) Clarification of issues and conflicting values. "What was involved . . . ?"

(d) Whole class participation in the discussion. "What do *you* think . . . ?" "What *else* happened?" "Who can *add* to that . . . ?"

(e) Students' explanation of why what happened occurred. "Why did the Boston school system dismiss 710 tenured teachers?" "Why did the students protest . . . ?" For the final discussion, this step is where teacher efforts should be maximized.

(f) Suggestions for solution. "How can the case be resolved?" "What are the alternatives?" Once again, a list should be recorded for students to see.

(g) Considering implications or consequences for each of the alternatives. "If thus and so occurs, what will be the consequences?" "If we were to manipulate this, what would be affected?" "If you were the main character, what decision would you make?" And finally, "How would this solution apply to similar problems?"

Learning Tasks During Case Studies

Although inquiry is not a precise process and may in fact proceed in a variety of ways, the stages identified in Chapter 13 illustrate the essential ways to teach cognitive skills. Unlike other inquiry strategies, during case studies, students are frequently presented with the problem, the hypothesis, and the data. This means that student inquiry *begins* with data analysis.

During case study analysis students perform the following tasks:

- Students read, observe, or consume in some other way the given information. Their task is to evaluate the information differentiating between facts and opinions. They must evaluate objectivity, reliability, and source of information.
- Students will judge the adequacy of their information.
- If sets of data are available, they must contrast the information, noting similarities and differences.
- Changes in the data should be noted.
- Data analysis will conclude with summarization and interpretation.
- Through discussion, students will share definitional meanings and interpretations.
- Through auding, students will evaluate others' perspectives.
- Through participation, students will share inquiry responsibility.
- To reach a conclusion, students will analyze cause and effect relationships.
- Students will select, from alternatives, the best solution to a problem.
- Students will make predictions concerning the outcome of a particular solution or course of action.
- Students will make choices based on possible consequences.

Chapter Summary

Unit teaching contributes to the integration of students' learning. Unit planning provides sequence and continuity of learning. The unit renders the curriculum operational. In this chapter, a unit was provided to illustrate the planning process and the integration of subject fields.

Research skill activities were discussed with examples of field research techniques using interviews, questionnaires, and case study analysis. Observation skills were featured.

The integration of subject fields was emphasized in selected examples of the use of case studies and in an example of third-grade students' using inquiry skills, math skills, language arts, health and physical education.

Classroom Application Exercises

1. Field research should be planned jointly by teacher and students; however, to practice the skills discussed in this chapter, design a questionnaire to be used by your students. Choose one of the following topics to investigate:
   - Number of languages spoken by families at your school
   - Frequency of moving from one community to another by families at your school
   - Beliefs about sex role differences (make a list: cleanliness, play differences, traits . . .)
   - Jobs performed by children
   - Number of hours of television viewing and number of hours of homework
   - What question type will you use?
   - How will the data be organized?
   - How will you analyze the data?

2. Make a list of input activities that your students participated in yesterday. Consider reading, observing, hearing, and the like.
3. Make a list of output activities that your students participated in yesterday. Consider creative activities, dramatic activities, and products produced.
4. If you were to use the mini-inquiry example about the puppy in Chapter 13 with your students, how would you demonstrate: (a) that cause precedes effect in time, and (b) multiple causation?
5. Using the mini-inquiry example in Chapter 13, make a list of items observed by the sleeper who was awakened, and of the means used to make the observations.
6. Design a learning center that will require the use of observational skills.
7. Select a resource unit from a school district professional library or a university library and develop a teaching unit for your students. Choose learning experiences to integrate subject fields.

Suggested Readings for Extending Study

Joyce, William W., and Frank L. Ryan. *Social Studies and the Elementary Teacher: Promises and Practices* (Bulletin 53). Washington, D.C.: National Council for the Social Studies, 1977.

Kaplan, Abraham. *The Conduct of Inquiry*. San Francisco: Chandler Publishing Company, 1964.

Lippitt, Ronald, Robert Fox, and Lucille Schaible. *The Teacher's Role in Social Science Investigation*. Chicago: Science Research Associates Inc., 1969.

Ryan, Frank L., and Arthur K. Ellis, *Instructional Implications of Inquiry*. Englewood Cliffs, N.J.: Prentice-Hall, Inc., 1974.

Hill, Wilhelmina. *Unit Planning and Teaching in Elementary Social Studies*. Washington, D.C.: United States Department of Health, Education, and Welfare, 1965.

Hanna, Lavone A., Gladys A. Potter, and Robert W. Reynolds. *Dynamic Elementary Social Studies: Unit Teaching*. 3rd ed. New York: Holt, Rinehart, and Winston, 1973.

Chapter **15**

Role-playing, Games, and Simulations

After you have completed the study of this chapter, you should be able to accomplish the following:

1. **Identify the purpose of and skills required for role-playing.**
2. **Identify and explain the 9-step procedures for role-playing.**
3. **Compare caucus group role-playing with the basic role-playing procedures.**
4. **Suggest ways to use role-playing in the classroom.**
5. **Identify the purpose and use of simulations in the classroom.**
6. **Discuss the value of simulations and gaming.**
7. **Design a simulation or board game using guidelines in chapter.**
8. **Identify what teachers can learn about students' learning progress during role-playing and gaming.**
9. **Compare the teacher task requirements during role-playing, gaming, case study, and inquiry problem solving.**

Purpose of Role-playing

Role-playing is a problem-solving method for arriving at a decision which involves diverse interests and values. Similar to gaming and simulations, role-playing uses a symbolic model. Procedures utilized in role-playing progress through problem definition, delineation of alternatives for action, exploration of consequences, and decision making (Shaftel and Shaftel, 1967).

Skill requirements for effective role-playing include: listening, oral language and discussion skills, and inquiry-problem solving skills. During role-play, students must focus on the data and/or issues in the problem situation. Participants explore alternatives by making tentative decisions, and through role-play enactment experience the consequences. Successive enactments of the role-play facilitates the choice of a final decision or conclusion.

Role-playing is primarily used for teaching citizenship responsibilities and for group counseling. Role-playing provides opportunities for students to study human behavior. Joyce (1980) stated that during the process of role-playing, "students (1) explore their feelings; (2) gain insights into their attitudes, values, and perceptions; (3) develop their problem solving skills and attitudes; and (4) explore subject matter in varied ways" (p. 244).

Role theory involves the way in which an individual views himself and others and is specifically concerned with the individual's needs and expectations. Social psychologists have used role theory to study the behavior of the individual in a group and the behavior of a group as it responds to the individual. Role theory can be used to study the structure of the individual or society. Some researchers have used the teaching strategy of role-playing to study the effect of dramatization, involvement, and group influence on attitude change as a result of role-playing participation (Janis and King, 1954;

Culbertson, 1957; Stanley and Klausmeier, 1957). Educators have used role-playing to facilitate learner involvement and interaction in the process of decision making. Research by Michaelis (1968), Dunfee and Sagl (1966), and Massialas and Cox (1966) indicates that role-playing is a valid inquiry technique.

Shaftel and Shaftel (1966, p. 47) stated that role-playing assists students to step out of their "culture shell" and become more "open" to the experiences of others. Through role-playing students learn to explore their own values and the personal consequences. Students choose in the light of consequences and discover causal relationships; as students interact, they may become sensitive to others. Role-playing assists students to attack problems in a "feeling-thinking-acting sequence."

Role-playing Methods

In Greg Thomas' fifth-grade classroom, the students listened to a story about a very poor Mexican family.

The father owns his own farm, but in recent years there has not been enough water for the crops, and as a result the farm has not been profitable. The family owes money to local residents, including the owner of a grocery store and a doctor.

The mother of the family has been helping her husband on the farm. There are two children in the family, a boy who is ten and a girl who is eight. Both attend school.

Recently the father's parents have been living with the family. The grandfather has not been well and cannot work. The grandmother is healthy, but she does not adjust well to change.

The father of the family has heard that there are work opportunities in California. He knows he could sell his farm to pay his debts.

Should the family move to California?

Father: He favors the move, but he is concerned about his parents and family's adjustment. No one in the family speaks English. He is confident that he can find a job in agriculture.

Mother: She has heard that the jobs in agriculture are poor-paying and seasonal. She is afraid that the family will not be able to manage in California. She doesn't want her husband to be a migrant worker and work on his knees picking strawberries and tomatoes. She knows that she will be lonesome for her home in Mexico.

Son: He wonders if he will have to quit school and help to support the family. He likes school.

Daughter: She thinks it will be a grand adventure. She is excited about learning English, but she is worried about leaving her friends.

Grandfather: He does not want to be a "burden" on the family. He hopes that he, too, can find work; he knows that he cannot work in the fields.

Grandmother: She does not want to go to the United States. She has heard that the Mexican immigrants are not treated well in the United States.

What should the family do? According to Shaftel and Shaftel, after the motivation the teacher should select role-players. While the role-players are thinking about their roles and planning their enactment, the teacher talks to the rest of the class suggesting that they think about each of the roles and how they would feel if they were members of the family. Thomas asks the students to think about, "What would you do if you were the father or the son or . . . ?" "How are immigrant groups treated . . . ?"

With the class prepared to listen to the role-play, the role-players arrange themselves in the front of the room in a semicircle. Thomas suggests to the role-players that the father begin the enactment by trying to convince the other family members how important this move would be for the family's welfare.

After about five minutes, it is clear that the students have concluded their enactment, and Thomas turns to the class and suggests that they discuss what happened. The discussion and evaluation focus on how it feels to have to leave your friends and move to a new country (or school), and on the family problems identified by the role-players.

Next, Thomas asks whether there are other solutions to the family's problems. Perhaps the whole family should not emmigrate at once to California. This idea was suggested by one of the class members. Thomas suggests that this alternative be explored, and he chooses new role-players.

Together the new role-players discuss their ideas and prepare for their enactment. After the second enactment the class once again discusses the role interpretations. If new ideas are presented or new interpretations suggested, there can be further enactments with new role-players. If the students have exhausted their solutions, the concluding discussions should attempt to relate the role-playing experience to personal experiences of the class. For example, Thomas might ask: "Has anyone you know had an experience similar to that of the members of this fictitious family?" Or, "Is this a problem that could happen to people today?" Thomas may lead the discussion to a study of the problems experienced by immigrant groups in the United States either historically or in contemporary times.

Basic Role-Play Procedures*

The actual role-playing procedures used by Greg Thomas were as follows:

1. *Teacher sets the motivation.* Shaftel and Shaftel call this the warm-up period. It serves to acquaint the class with the problem. The problem may be read or told to the class, or they may see a film or listen to a tape recording of a problem situation. If it is a story, it may be open-ended, or incomplete. Older students may read the problem or motivating story. In initiating the problem, the teacher may comment to the students that the incident they are to listen to is similar in nature to a problem they have been having.

2. *Selection of Players.* In selecting the first round of role-players it is important to choose students who are involved in the problem or behaviors of the characters. Students who identify with the characters, or students who *ought to* identify with the roles, will make the best actors for the first round. An initial exploratory discussion usually reveals those students who are concerned about the issues or characters. After the first enactment the discussion and evaluation should provide clues for selecting additional players.

3. *Setting the Stage.* Working together as a group or with the teacher, the role-players talk about their roles in order to decide how to begin the role-play. Sometimes an individual may need to be encouraged to pursue certain ideas to see what will happen.

4. *Preparing the Audience.* While the role-players are settling down, the teacher needs to remind the rest of the class to listen. The students may be expected to evaluate the authenticity of the enactment. It is usually a good idea to suggest purposeful things for observation and listening.

5. *The Enactment.* It is important to remember that the role-players are ad-libbing. Their performance will not be perfect; nor should it be. The presentation should be spontaneous and as natural as possible.

6. *Discussion and Evaluation.* The enactment should be evaluated for authenticity, not for theatrics or dramatics. (Would the grandfather really say that or feel that way?) The discussion should focus on the consequences of the solution, or the consequence of certain behaviors. Alternate ideas should be discussed, and as students express ideas for "different" solutions or behaviors, new players are chosen.

7. *A Re-enactment.* The same players may ask to "try it again" with a new solution. Typically, however, a new cast of role-players should be chosen to carry the action one step further or try it a different way.

8. *Further Discussion and Evaluation.* Whenever there is a new enactment, it should be followed with an evaluative discussion focusing on the behavior of the new role-players and their solution.

9. *Generalizing.* When the enactments are concluded, the discussion should help students gain insight into similar problems and situations. The teacher needs to be careful at all times, both during the role-play and the discussions, that students do

* Adapted from Shaftel and Shaftel, 1967, pp. 74–83.

not focus on each other. The students may recognize their own problems or personalities in the situations, but their feelings must be carefully guarded by the teacher. The role-play period should be a time of great sensitivity to the feelings of others.

STUDENT BEHAVIORS

What should a teacher observe during role-playing?

Role-playing Using a Caucus Group

Research by Lemlech (1970) revealed higher participant involvement in role-playing when caucus groups were used. This procedure alleviates the typical classroom management problems because it lessens the "on stage" feature of the basic role-playing procedures. Using the caucus group plan, the class is divided into small groups. Each *group* is assigned one role to portray (father, mother, grandmother, and so on). The procedures are as follows:

1. *Teacher Sets Motivation*
   (Same as in basic procedures)
2. *Students Are Divided Into Groups*
   The teacher arranges the grouping to ensure that the groups are balanced or that a weak child will not be taken advantage of by an aggressive student. Or the students may be grouped with thought about their particular interests. The "role" or issue is assigned to each group by the teacher.
3. *Group Discussion*
   Groups plan their characterization or their consensus viewpoint about an issue or problem.
4. *Groups Choose Spokesperson*
   Each group decides who will be the group representative for the role-play. The group "coaches" the role-player.
5. *The Enactment*
   The spokesperson may improvise and/or use group ideas during the role-play.
6. *Discussion and Evaluation*
   The whole class participates as a group to discuss and evaluate the enactment as in the basic procedures.
7. *Group Meetings*
   Students once again meet in groups to offer advice to their spokesperson based on the prior discussion and evaluation. Groups are encouraged to choose a new spokesperson.
8. *New Role-Play Enactment*
   Based on the discussion and the group meetings, the new role-play should develop alternative solutions and new characterizations.
9. *Discussion and Generalizing*
   Decisions, conclusions, and applications are discussed, or the class may decide that further enactments are necessary.

There are two differences between the two procedures. (1) Using the caucus group, students feel that there is no audience. Since they all participate in group caucus, there is less of a tendency to giggle or feel embarrassed during the enactment; students tend to feel responsible and involved in what happens. The role-players perform with greater freedom because they have a greater sense of personal safety. This too can be attributed to the fact that they have a "back-up" group ready to coach and to provide substantive and moral assistance. Since dialogue is never preplanned during role-playing, the performance is always a personal statement by the role-player. This attribute of role-play occurs during the caucus group role-plays as well as during the basic procedures for role-play.

(2) The second major difference between the two procedures is that students rather than the teacher choose the performers. However, it is important that the teacher observe carefully during the selection stage to ensure that students do not get "railroaded" into being the group spokesperson. This can also be a problem during the basic type of role-play, if students are allowed to call out and "suggest" that friends play a role. Frequently this is accompanied with snickering and gestures.

Moral Education

Role-playing implementing the basic role-play procedures can be used for moral education. The reader is urged to review the discussion of moral development in Chapter 2 and the teaching strategy of Galbraith and Jones (1975) in Chapter 7.

Arbuthnot and Faust (1981) identified four basic principles of moral education:

1. Teachers should facilitate the development of moral education from a lower stage of development to a higher stage of development.
2. Moral development is provoked when the individual experiences cognitive conflict or disequilibrium.
3. Teachers must devise ways to facilitate self-discovery of higher-stage reasoning.
4. Students should not be forced to participate in any phase of moral education. Individuals have the right to choose a personal value system or belief without harrassment.

Moral education procedures often utilize small discussion as well as role-playing. The groups are similar in nature to the caucus groups discussed earlier.

Other Types of Role-Plays

Sara Garcia's third graders practiced to be interviewers by using role-playing during language arts. In a class discussion they decided on some interviewing rules:

1. Introduce yourself and tell the purpose of the interview.
2. Be friendly.
3. Ask the questions just as we decided upon them.
4. Listen to the responses.
5. Ask additional questions if the response is not clear.
6. Thank the respondent for the interview.

Garcia decided that the practice sessions would benefit all the students. She asked the students to choose partners. Each pair was to practice and take turns being interviewer and respondent. As the students practiced, Garcia walked around the room listening. After the students reversed roles, Garcia chose several pairs of students to demonstrate the interview situation to the rest of the class.

In Mary Hogan's second-grade classroom she is experiencing a typical primary-grade problem: tattling. Almost every day several of the children will come in from recess or lunch and complain about others not obeying playground rules. She has tried to listen to both sides of the story and to both participants; she has even tried the "deaf ear" approach, although she knows this is not wise. She has lectured the class about tattling. Since none of these approaches has really solved the problem, she decided to try role-playing. This is the story she told her students:

Instead of joining the game, Mabel watched the other children playing. When recess was over, Mabel went straight to Mr. Clark, her teacher, and told him that the students had not been following the rules for sockball.

Mr. Clark asked the other children how their game went, and they responded, "Just fine."

At lunchtime none of the children would let Mabel play. Once again, she went to Mr. Clark and complained about her classmates, but Mr. Clark ignored her.

The next day during recess, Mabel went to the teacher on yard duty and told her, "Randy pushed me and tore my dress. My mother will punish me when I get home, and it's not my fault." The teacher on yard duty inspected Mabel's dress and promptly went to discuss the matter with Randy.

Mary Hogan asked the children these questions:

a. What do you think happened?
b. Why do you think Mabel has problems with the other children?
c. If you were Mr. Clark or the yard teacher, how would you handle this situation?

The students role-played the story, and after several enactments they concluded:

1. Mr. Clark should have been a better listener.
2. Mabel was a tattletale because she wanted attention.

3. Mabel needed some friends, but she did not know how to be friendly.
4. Mabel probably tore her dress herself.
5. Randy would get in trouble because the yard teacher would not believe him.
6. Mabel's classmates should make an effort to be friends with Mabel and include her in their games.
7. Mabel would feel guilty if Randy got in trouble. She should apologize to Randy.

Using Role-Playing for Diagnostic Purposes

Role-playing sometimes allows teachers to learn more than they really want to know about their students! This occurs because as children "act out" they reveal their own feelings. Antisocial tendencies may be revealed in the solutions that students suggest or dramatize. The child who has problems responding to adults or who has difficulties with younger children may reveal aggressiveness or punitiveness or other insecurities.

> Why is role-playing considered an interactive technique?

Role-playing may serve to help students relieve tensions and insecure feelings and develop greater sensitivity to others. However, whatever the child reveals should be carefully considered by the teacher. Teachers are not counselors and generally not psychologists; role-playing may be used to improve social interaction in the classroom, but it should not be used for individual guidance purposes. When teachers suspect that a student has real personal problems, it is time to enlist the aid of colleagues trained for that purpose, or call in parents, or search out social help agencies.

Getting Started

Classroom Environment. For role-playing to be successful, the classroom must be psychologically open and permissive. Students need to feel free and secure that their ideas will not be summarily rejected. They must feel safe to express their feelings. The atmosphere of the classroom must indicate mutual respect. The teacher needs to be both responsive and respectful so that students have a model to immitate. Students must know that, at least during role-playing, they may express personal feelings even when those feelings are antisocial.

Shaftel and Shaftel (1967) pointed out that role-playing should not be used to coerce students into predetermined behavior.

> (The teacher) is concerned with creating an openness to experience in which all known behavior can be examined, explored for consequences, and pondered on.
>
> The teacher facilitates the open exploration of life situations under the assumption that all possible alternatives are available for examination (p. 90).

Teacher Behavior. The purpose of the role-playing session will determine much of the teacher's behavior. For example, the third graders who were practicing interviewing needed to focus on ways to communicate friendliness, state the purpose of the interview, and then get on with it. Sara Garcia instructed the students to think about an opening statement that communicates who you are, why you need the respondent's help, and appreciation for assistance. Garcia was teaching specific language skills using role-playing.

If the purpose of the session is problem solving, then the teacher must ask questions that will encourage students to focus on the definition of the problem, information, and values. As further enactments are performed, the teacher may ask questions to probe different alternatives. During the discussions the teacher focuses on possible consequences.

Greg Thomas will probably use the immigrant family role-play as an initial study of what happens to new groups in the United States. Additional role-play sessions will be more subject matter oriented, and Thomas will probably begin them by helping students to recall how the Mexican family felt about coming to the United States. Actual sessions may be more "time" oriented for a specific historical period and focus on important issues.

Two Basic Teacher Behaviors

Whatever the purpose of the role-play session, there are two basic behaviors that facilitate leading role-playing: a supportive teacher attitude and an accepting manner. Students should perceive that during role-playing it is OK to express feelings that are normally kept under control, and all suggestions will be listened to and allowed to be explored—even those that sound impractical or antisocial.

Hints for Leading Role-playing

1. Limit your own expectations. Do not expect that your first and/or your students' first role-play session will be a model situation. If you achieve involvement, consider yourself successful. Accept that students' involvement may be characterized by a noisier session than anticipated.
2. Expect students to be self-conscious during their first sessions.
3. Encourage students to focus on problems, characterizations, feelings, and solutions, *not* on silly or self-conscious behavior.
4. Evaluate the realism of the enactment, not the acting ability of the students.
5. Cut the enactment just as soon as you are aware that students have expressed what they feel, know, or want to express. Initial enactments may be less than five minutes long.
6. Discuss *after* the enactment. Expect these discussions to be longer than the enactment. Extend thinking through the discussion.
7. Encourage more children to participate in role-playing rather than using the same actors.
8. Additional enactments should be action-oriented and should explore feelings, issues, and consequences in greater depth.
9. Remember that students will not always get to the generalization stage. This takes practice for both you and the students.

RESEARCH FINDINGS

Teachers can enhance students' self-esteem by

- providing opportunities for students to participate in decision making, interaction, self-discipline
- developing a classroom environment that encourages respectfulness, personal regard, fairness
- providing opportunities for success through team learning experiences
- grouping for a variety of purposes rather than ability grouping only
- facilitating cross-age tutoring and the interaction of young people with older people
- encouraging students to take part in rule setting and teacher-student planning
- encouraging students to self-evaluate progress
- providing instruction aimed at personal and social development (Beane, Lipka, and Ludewig, 1980).

Games and Simulations

Differences Between Games and Simulations

A simulation, like the case study presented in Chapter 14, has a limited and controlled data base. The simulation is a model designed to represent physical or social processes in an abstracted fashion for the purposes of analysis. A game is a simulation, but a simulation does not have to be a game. Neither represent total reality. Games are contrived so that there will be an aspect of competition and there will be winners and losers. Simulations usually have competition, but they are based on the social process that is to be modeled. A simulation does not necessarily have a winner. Social simulations are designed primarily to teach concepts and skills of negotiation, bargaining, cooperation, and compromise.

Role-playing is an aspect of most simulations, but the process of role-playing differs from what has been described earlier in this chapter. During a simulation, students assume roles in order to carry out the decisions and actions of specific individuals involved in the social process that is to be studied. For example, in the simulation game of Legislation, students assume the roles of congressional representatives.

Most educational games use game boards. The best example is the game of Monopoly, created during the 1930s. Monopoly is a miniaturized model of an economy in which the players buy and sell property. The game presents a limited version of reality combined with make-believe. Winning is a combination of luck and decision making. When players lose, they can account for it by blaming their luck, and when players win it is directly related to "intelligent" decision making! Both simulation games and educational games provide a "safe" environment for problem solving, role-playing, and decision making. The individual may always say, "I am playing a role," and in this way, the ego is always spared.

The terms *simulation games, educational games,* and *simulation* are used interchangeably in this chapter to describe interactive game approaches.

Purposes and Use of Simulations in the Classroom

1. *Motivation.* Simulations may be used either to introduce a new unit or to culminate a unit of study. Simulations are extremely motivating to most students, perhaps because they are dramatic, usually exciting, and have an element of suspense. It is possible to participate in most simulations without prior knowledge of the content; however, prior knowledge may enhance the performance of the player or participant. This is why the simulation makes a good initial activity as well as an appropriate evaluative activity. Simulations may also be used developmentally during a unit of study.

2. *Participation.* The stimulating nature of simulations seems to compel involvement rather than passive attention. Game players experience a sense of control over their environment. Their actions are directly related to consequences. They influence what happens. If a poor decision leads to an unhappy consequence, the game player can change his/her strategy. Participation in simulations requires mastering skills in negotiation, bargaining, planning, decision making.

3. *Feedback.* The relationship between actions and consequences is readily apparent during gaming. Feedback is immediate. The Monopoly player who spends all of his assets buying hotels for his property will soon discover the consequences of the savings depletion when he lands on an opponent's property and cannot pay the rent. Role-players in the game of Ghetto learn very quickly the consequences of being an unskilled laborer. Unlike most paper-and-pencil activities, in which students wait for reinforcement, simulation activities provide immediate input.

4. *Goals.* Simulations typically have clearly defined goals and constraints. This results in participants knowing when and under what conditions a game will end. Once again, the motivation to get to the end of the game or to closure helps to sustain interest. In the game of Ghetto, where each round represents a year in the life of ghetto residents, students typically ask, "How many rounds will we play?" The leader's response to that question affects the participants' game strategy. Both having a time limit and playing until you have winners influence short- and long-range goals and overall game strategy.

5. *Interaction.* Simulation activities necessitate students' interaction, and social interaction is often the major purpose for choosing simulations as an instructional strategy. Group-satisfying behaviors are taught as students work rationally with others in a team situation. Communication skills are enhanced as students bargain, debate, and consult with each other. Gilliom (1977) pointed out that the peer interaction during simulations results in a more natural classroom atmosphere.

6. *Relevance.* The acting-out element of a simulation creates a more realistic environment as students are forced to deal with social situations, issues, and problems—even when the simulation represents and focuses on an historical theme. Gordon (1970) stated:

> The operational characteristic of games (decision making in the context of roles) makes them more realistic and relevant to students than, for example, a textbook chapter about a statesman's dilemma in deciding on war or peace. Because the student must make the decision himself, the factors to be considered take on greater importance (p. 23).

7. *Open-ended.* Even though there are rules and frequently winners and losers, simulations are inherently open-ended. Students accept that games represent the real world and, as such, have no predetermined end. The game may focus on a process or a problem, but the end of the game cannot be known in advance. There are no correct answers to a simulation. Perhaps it is the open-ended element of the game that makes it so motivating to students. (The teacher cannot control the outcome!)

8. *Ego-satisfying behaviors.* Since students feel that they can control what happens during the simulation, they also feel more secure and self-confident. Since all students participate in the simulation, everyone has an equal opportunity to shine. Superior academic achievement will not guarantee who will be a winner during gaming. Imaginative solutions, luck, and social skills may prove to be more important during the simulation than verbal skills and reading achievement. Simulation activities provide different leadership and participant roles than typical classroom activities. As a consequence, different leaders may emerge during the simulation than during basic skill instruction. With the opportunity for different classroom roles, students develop optimism, status, self-respect, and self-confidence.

What do you think a teacher should try to accomplish during a debriefing session?

9. *Differentiation of instruction.* Students do not feel that they are being graded during gaming activities, although in fact there are many ways for teachers to evaluate social and academic progress during these activities. Grading pressures are relieved during simulation activities because students can participate at various levels—without hindering others. The superior student may enjoy the flexibility of the game and the opportunity to explore different ideas in an open environment, while the slower academic student will gain from peer interaction and take part at an appropriate personal level. Goals and constraints can be devised to accommodate the diversity of the students in the classroom.

What Do Students Learn During Gaming?

Social Skills. Since everyone is participating in an active fashion, the shy student does not feel "observed" and tends to communicate more freely with peers. The aggressive student is forced to modify interaction habits as new peer relationships develop during the game. Most simulations are dependent upon peer interaction, and students are compelled to share their ideas with others. Social skill development occurs as students are forced to comply to game rules and work with classmates for the benefit of group/team goals.

Knowledge Goals. Every game or simulation requires basic information or a data base. Whether the game is about legislation or the environment, factual information is important in order to participate. Students acquire facts in a variety of ways during a game, and teachers should expect students to recognize the basic concepts and information upon which the game is predicated.

Valuing. Role-playing develops empathy for others as students assume a variety of roles and attempt to play them realistically. Role-playing also requires listening to others' viewpoints; this develops sensitivity to different value positions.

Judging the effectiveness of your own and others' strategies occurs continuously during gaming. Students need to make judgments about bargains, negotiations, biases, or promises, and so they learn to evaluate their own interests and the interests of others.

Problem Solving. Gaming and simulations are problem-solving techniques. Gaming has been used by the military to solve tactical problems and research problems; the business community has used games for training and planning problems. During simulations, students often solve problems instinctively, and after the game is over, strategies can be analyzed so as to improve students' problem-solving ability in other situations.

Choosing Games and Simulations

Games teach a wide variety of skills, including problem solving and decision making. Games are even used to reinforce specific skills. This means that the teacher may select a game to fit the desired objectives. The choice should be appropriate to the interests and abilities of students and the aims of the curriculum. Choice should also be made on the basis of allotted time for the activity. Some simulations may take several class periods while others can be completed during one hour or less of class time. The following are examples of several types of commercial games available.

Gold Rush. This simulation was designed to teach about life in the gold mining camps. Students learn facts about gold and gold mining, decision making and research skills, and an appreciation of the miner's life during the 1850s. The simulation is appropriate for students in grades 4–8. This simulation takes about two and one half weeks to complete. To participate, students are divided into eight mining teams. Each team or company receives one hundred gold nuggets for the purchase of supplies and passage to the gold fields. Each day students rotate roles; roles include leader, recorder, prospector. Each team has specific decisions to make, such as choosing a route to the gold fields, staking a claim, negotiating with other mining companies. Equipment includes "fate" cards with questions for each team to answer. The questions require student research to obtain background information about the historical time period. Cost of the materials package which includes a teacher's guide, work sheets, suggestions, and pretest is about $23.50. Publisher is

Interact Company
P.O. Box 262
Lakeside, CA 92040

Words and Action. These materials are designed for role-playing for students in grades K–2. Objectives are to encourage spontaneity in verbal expression, stimulate students to express feelings in language and gestures, provide intriguing problems to encourage simple inquiry, provide opportunities for dialogue with a sympathetic adult, and provide practice in decision making. The materials include a teacher's manual, twenty role-play photos mounted on Photo-Problem cards. There is no specified amount of time required. The materials, developed by George and Fannie Shaftel, follow their basic role-play methods. The Photo-Problems are introduced by the teacher, and students are encouraged to pantomime and role-play the depicted problems. The program costs about $27.00 and can be obtained from

Holt, Rinehart and Winston
383 Madison Ave.
New York, NY 10017

Powderhorn. This simulation explores the concept of power. Students learn "that the rules that govern a people and the process that created the rules affect how people react to those rules, as well as to one another." The simulation was designed for upper-elementary students and can be played in one and one half hours. Materials include the teacher's manual, trading cards, bonus point cards, headbands, scoring system wall chart, and rule cards. Very little reading is required, but simple arithmetic skills are used. During the simulation students assume the roles of frontiersmen. By trading rifles, traps, and pelts (trading cards), the game is structured so that some participants receive more valued things than others. The result is a three-tiered society with little mobility. After several rounds students discover that the highest tier can rule with absolute power and will do so for their own benefit. The simulation is completed when the two lower-tier groups revolt. The culminating discussion is an important aspect of the simulation, and the teacher's questions used to debrief the game are crucial for success. The cost of the material is $12.50, and it is available from

Simile II
1150 Siverado
La Jolla, CA 92037

An abundance of games is available for classroom use and appropriate for varied subject fields such as science, health, language arts, and social studies. Cost varies from under $10.00 to as much as several hundred dollars when the materials include 16mm films. But frequently the best materials for role-playing and simulation are those created by the classroom teacher to meet the needs of specific boys and girls. Try your own game using the following guidelines.

DESIGN A SIMULATION OR BOARD GAME

1. Specify the grade level of the students who are to play the game. Include special needs and interests.
2. Identify objectives and areas of the curriculum where the game will be used.
3. Decide whether there will be a game board or whether it will be a simulation.
4. Decide whether the game will be for an entire class or for small groups of students.
5. Set the situation and conditions. Will equipment be needed?
6. Determine the goal. Will there be scoring? Will there be winners and losers? How will students know when the game is completed?
7. Decide on rules and constraints that will affect behavior. Establish a time limit so that students will know when the game is over or so that students can plan their strategies.

APPLICATION OF RESEARCH

Iverson (1982) observed a close relationship among play, creativity, and the development of strategies for adapting to changing conditions of modern life. Iverson observed that verbal play (free association) fostered creative combining of ideas whereas predetermined assignments tended to limit children's flexibility of thought and action. Iverson concluded that children need to be taught to "break rules, step out of roles, and assert their own ideas on occasion."

Using the guildlines, the game *School Council* was designed. (1) It is for students in grades 3–6. (2) It can be used as a language arts or social studies learning experience. (3) Objectives include the development of social interaction skills. (4) It is a simulation and is planned for an entire class. (5) The students are to be divided into seven groups. Each group will need the following materials: a Voting Record form, the Group and Council Rules, and the Group Information sheet. Groups may also need pencil and paper for group note taking. During the School Council meeting, a table and chairs will be needed in the front of the classroom. (6) The game is concluded when the School Council makes a decision concerning each proposal. Estimated time is one class period (one hour).

GROUP RULES

1. Choose one person to be the School Council representative.

2. Choose one person to present the group proposal to the School Council.
3. Choose a recorder to transcribe your ideas.
4. Choose one person to be in charge of the Voting Record form.
5. Identify the problem that concerns the group you are to represent.
6. Identify the issues involved.
7. Identify reasons why others may not favor your proposal.
8. Plan the "best" way to present your proposal to the Council.
9. Bargain with other groups in order to obtain support for your proposal.
10. Predict how the Council will vote.

SCHOOL COUNCIL RULES

1. Choose a Council President to keep order and call on each group.
2. Listen to each group's proposal. You may ask the group questions to clarify their suggestions.
3. Discuss the proposals when you have heard all of the seven suggestions.
4. You may agree with the plans, modify them, or reject them; vote on each proposal.
5. The Council President may vote.

Group Information

Group I. You represent fourth-grade students. The physical education apparatus is located on the upper-grade yard, but it is used by grades 1–3. You would like the School Council to ask the Board of Education to move the equipment to the lower-grade yard so that lower-grade students will stop walking through the kickball and dodgeball game areas on the upper grade yard.

Group II. You represent sixth-grade students. The sixth graders would like to be with their friends at recess and lunchtime and do not understand why they should be required to play games in specific areas of the playground. You want the School Council to give them permission NOT to play.

Group III. You represent third-grade students. Upper-grade students are not required to walk in lines to and from the lunch area. You do not understand why third graders or even first or second graders should be required to walk in lines. You would like the School Council to support the same rules for all students.

Group IV. You represent some fifth-grade students. You do not understand why students need hall passes to go to the bathroom. You feel that it is embarrassing to ask the teacher for permission to go to the bathroom.

Group V. You represent some parents. You believe that there should be a school dress code. When you visit the school, you are upset to see children in cut-off shorts and all sorts of apparel.

Group VI. You represent teachers. The teachers would like students to be able to use the school library during recess and lunch time, but the teachers do not want to provide supervision. Administrators claim that the library must have adult supervision and if students are allowed many options, the school will not know where students are during these periods.

Group VII. You represent administration. You want a school rule that students (and teachers) cannot eat in classrooms. You want a clean setting with a minimum need for custodial help.

Council Voting Record

	Promised Votes		Actual Votes	
	For	Against	For	Against
Group I				
Group II				
Group III				
Group IV				
Group V				
Group VI				
Group VII				

Hints for Teachers Using School Council Simulation

1. Circulate among the groups.
2. Remind groups to identify the issues involved.
3. Ask probing questions if the groups have failed to identify the problem.
   For example: How do you feel about differential rules for upper-grade and lower-grade students?
   What would your friends think about a teacher denying a bathroom pass?
   What are your ideas about whether teachers should be asked to work during the lunch hour?
4. Remind students to negotiate with other groups.
5. Communicate to students time limits for their group discussions.
6. Encourage the Council to discuss the issues before voting.
7. Encourage the Council to speak out so that everyone can hear.
8. *Debrief.* Discuss bargaining and compromising. Find out if groups honored their promises. Discuss why political promises are sometimes not honored. Discuss "good" rules and "bad" rules and what should be done when a rule is no longer appropriate. Ask students if they successfully predicted how the Council would vote.
   Find out what issues are important to the students at your school.
   Perform the simulation another time using issues identified by the students.

Teacher's Role During Gaming

Preparation is the first teacher task for gaming. The best preparation is to pilot test the materials to be used. What this means is to find some good-natured friends to play the game with you before using it with students. If this is impossible, see that you are thoroughly familiar with the rules and the goals. If materials or equipment are needed, prepare them in advance. Be sure that you have budgeted enough time to play the game so that you will not spoil it by stopping the game prematurely.

Prepare the class for participation. Choose your role-players and provide instructions in the form of rules or constraints. Be certain that students understand the purpose and goals of the activity. Communicate how much time has been budgeted for the activity.

Observe carefully and circulate during the game or role-play. Remember that first-time gaming experiences are apt to be a bit noisy, but this does not mean that students should be out of control. Maintain your role as a guide and facilitator during the action; remember that students will be learning from each other, rather than from you. However, if role-players ask advice, it is perfectly proper to provide suggestions.

Take plenty of time to *debrief and discuss.* Ask probing questions about the students' gaming experience. If students have ideas about how to improve upon the game or role-play, allow them to try out their ideas or to redesign the game. Discuss the art of negotiation and the reasons for compromising. Discuss how the gaming experience relates to real-life experiences.

Evaluation of Role-playing and Gaming

Observation of students during simulation activities should provide information about students' understanding of concepts and skills, critical thinking and decision making, sensitivity to others, awareness of fate and of consequences, and self-concept.

During evaluative discussions it is possible to gain insight about students' competencies to analyze processes, apply the simulation to other situations, compare and contrast and role-play situation to real-life activities, summarize and make judgments about problems and decisions, and restructure the activity.

Chapter Summary

In this chapter the purposes of role-playing and simulation were discussed. The two techniques were contrasted. Basic role-playing procedures and caucus group role-playing procedures were provided. Classroom examples and uses of role-playing and simulations were given. Ways of getting started with these strategies were suggested. Several commercial games and simulations were reviewed in the chapter, and guidelines for designing a simulation or board game were provided. The guidelines were then demonstrated by the game of School Council. Hints for teachers and the teacher's role during gaming concluded the chapter.

Classroom Application Exercises

1. Design a simulation using the guidelines in Chapter 15.
2. Observe students participating in group activities. Cite examples of ways in which students cooperated with each other, accepted responsibility, demonstrated rationality and respectfulness. List examples of inhibiting factors that affected group behavior.
3. Make a list of affective behaviors that relate to the development of self-concept and self-identity. For example: students voluntarily share successes and failures; students voluntarily assist others in cooperative work or play activities.
4. Identify some core American values that could be taught using role-playing. For example: honesty, fairness.
5. Suppose a parent criticized your use of games in the classroom; prepare a response entitled: Why We Play Games in the Elementary Classroom.

Suggested Readings for Extending Study

Abt, Clark, C. *Learning Theory and General Objectives of Teaching Games.* Cambridge, Mass.: Abt Associates, Inc., 1965.

Boocock, Sarane S., and E. O. Schild, eds. 2nd ed. *Simulation Games in Learning.* Beverly Hills, Calif.: Sage Publications, 1978.

Chapman, Katherine. *Guidelines for Using a Social Simulation/Game.* Boulder, CO.: Social Science Education Consortium, 1973.

Gillespie, Judith, A. "The Game Doesn't End with Winning." *Viewpoints,* Nov. 1973, pp. 21–28.

Gordon, Alice Kaplan. *Games For Growth.* Chicago: Science Research Associates Inc., 1970.

Lemlech, Johanna K. *Handbook for Successful Urban Teaching.* New York: Harper & Row, Publishers, 1977. Chapter 5.

Shaftel, George and Fannie R. Shaftel. *Role Playing in the Curriculum.* 2nd ed. Englewood Cliffs, N.J.: Prentice-Hall Inc., 1982.

Chapter 16

Resources for Learning

After you have completed the study of this chapter, you should be able to accomplish the following:

1. **Explain the effect of the curriculum revolution on instructional materials.**
2. **Identify why instructional materials are important in elementary classrooms.**
3. **Discuss the importance of an evaluation process for instructional materials.**
4. **Practice evaluating a subject field textbook or a basal reader using the categories in this chapter.**
5. **Make a list of learning materials with suggestions for their use.**
6. **Discuss how to improve the use of pictures in the classroom.**
7. **Identify a variety of print materials, and suggest how they can be used with different student groups.**
8. **Begin the development (accumulate, mount, and organize) of your own picture file.**
9. **Practice writing resource information (1-page) for three different reading levels.**
10. **Design a learning center using guidelines in chapter.**

Curriculum Revolution: Effect on Instructional Materials

Historically, teachers have always depended on the textbook for assistance, but until the late 1960s there were few choices available to elementary teachers. During the 1960s a number of factors contributed to a remarkable increase in learning resources accessible to the elementary teacher. These factors are briefly summarized.

Dismay was expressed by the public and professional educators concerning the seeming advantage of Soviet society in launching Sputnik in 1957; this contributed to the setting of new educational goals for quality education and for specialized education. With tremendous technological advances in the decades of the 1950s and 1960s, knowledge exploded in virtually all subject fields. The knowledged explosion, coupled with an input of federal monies for the use of scholars, led to an exchange of ideas among the disciplinarians.

The Civil Rights movement also contributed to both curriculum reform and the impetus for new instructional materials. Concern that all ethnic and religious groups gain recognition in American society and attain equal opportunity to enter the mainstream of American public life led the public and professional educators to realize the need for new curriculum objectives and new instructional materials.

Funding from federal, private, and philanthropic sources facilitated the development of both curricula and instructional materials. Both the new curricula and the new resources developed during this period were different from prior efforts at curriculum reform. The new plans called for greater student participation and involvement in the learning process. The curriculum and the materials were designed to motivate problem solving. There was a new emphasis on concepts and methods of inquiry within each discipline.

Spurred by the "special projects" of the 1960s and 1970s, commercial publishers began to implement changes suggested by the disciplinarians and the professional educators. The new text materials

Learning How and Deciding When to Use Technology Is a Professional Challenge.

were more attractive to students, used more pictures and easier reading print. Questions were used as the dominating organizing structure for the new textbooks and helped make them more interesting for students. The new texts were conceptually oriented and required greater knowledge by teachers of the subject field as well as knowledge of inquiry oriented teaching strategies. Textbooks tended to be more narrowly focused on specific concepts, "doing more about less" than the old "all you wanted to know" broad subject field textbooks. As a consequence of the narrower, in-depth focus, more instructional resources were sometimes needed to provide the data for classroom inquiry. Curriculum materials in the different subject fields expanded to include learning packets, film loops, slides, film strips, tape cassettes, games, realia, and even individualized computer programs.

Importance of Instructional Materials

In the 1980s learning and media centers are typical to most classrooms. These centers utilize both commercial and noncommercially produced products. The array of learning materials available in the modern classroom is somewhat astounding. Studies of classroom life indicate that students use some type of instructional material 90 per cent of the school day.

Teachers need a number of new skills to manage the influx of resources for learning. For example, with the diversity and quantity of materials available, teachers need to be able to identify the most appropriate materials for their students by utilizing information related to geographic factors, cultural factors, and skill levels. Teachers need to be able to evaluate the quality of the materials by using criteria to determine the suitability of the material for the subject field and to determine sex, racial, or cultural bias. In addition, teachers may need special methodological preparation to use the new instructional materials.

The importance of what Klein (1978) called the "stuff" of learning should not be underestimated. The new learning materials certainly can be used by the novice teacher to "direct" the instructional program, but that is not its intent. While each set of

Computers Can Be Used to Motivate Skill Instruction.

materials is typically designed to accomplish specific objectives, it is the teacher's responsibility to adapt the materials for use with specific girls and boys.

Educational technology and the new instructional materials offer teachers and students exciting and motivating means for involvement. For example, a remedial reading project that used programmed skill instruction on a computer for upper-grade students demonstrated that students became more involved and enthusiastic about learning and practicing skills using the computer than they did when using a paper-and-pencil approach (Hertzog, 1982). Learning how and deciding when to use technology, programmed instruction, audio or video cassettes, and other new materials is a professional challenge. Many teachers find it advantageous to take a course in educational technology to prepare for or update teaching skills.

Programmed Instruction. It is necessary to use programmed instruction judiciously. Properly used, it is an effective teaching tool, but it requires careful selection, adherence to directions and intent, and advance preparation. It can be advantageous because the sequential organization facilitates the assessment of skill competence. Programs can be skipped for advanced learners or used sequentially for mastery with the slow learner.

Video Instruction. Both commercial television programs and school district programs are available in many classrooms. The National Information Center for Educational Media (NICEM) at the University of Southern California provides teachers with catalog listings of prepared materials available on videotape. The video cassette can also be used by students to produce programs. In Newhall, California, several fourth-grade teachers had their students research routes to California during the gold rush days. Each class dramatized the travails of a group of miners. Using a Sony Porta-pack unit, each class produced a portion of its own television show demonstrating the route to California. The show was then combined and edited by the students and utilized for enjoyment as well as instruction in the school district.

Filmstrips and Slides. Students can also create their own filmstrips and slide shows. Filmstrip kits are reasonable in cost and allow students to draw the pictures and write a script to go along with them. Language arts skills as well as specific subject field content can be integrated in a motivating manner. Projects can be shared with parents for culmination programs or for the school's open house.

Slide shows provide opportunities for students to take pictures and demonstrate their organization skills. Students can write a script to go along with the slides. The script can be prerecorded, sequenced, and timed to coincide with the slide organization. Sometimes students enjoy programming music to accompany the script and slides. Music and mathematics instruction plus subject field integration can be accomplished with this activity.

It is necessary to remember that, as important as instructional materials and educational technology are to the curriculum, they are dependent upon good instruction. Ellis (1981, p. 424) commented that "No set of materials is capable of salvaging poor instruction. The reverse, however, is also true. Good instruction depends on good ideas and materials."

Evaluating Resources for Learning

Since teachers program the use of instructional materials throughout the school day, it is important that they be involved in the evaluation of those

> Learning materials are considered to be the teachers' tools. Should teachers use these tools 90 per cent of the school day? Why

materials. To evaluate instructional materials teachers are confronted with two basic tasks. First, teachers need to find out what is available for use at the price they or the school district can afford to pay. Second, the materials need to be evaluated for appropriateness and quality. Appropriateness has to do with whether the materials "fit" a specific group of students. For example, materials appropriate for fifth-graders achieving at grade level and living in a rural area of Montana may not necessarily be appropriate for fifth-graders working below grade level in New York City. Quality is determined by utilizing sets of criteria that apply to specific school curriculum objectives and priorities. Let us explore these two tasks and see how they can be accomplished.

Mary Hogan and Greg Thomas were assigned the responsibility of setting up the screening and evaluation process for choosing one or more new reading series and social studies textbooks for their school. Together they worked out both the procedural details and the substantive evaluation process.

PROCEDURES

1. Discuss evaluation process with teachers and school advisory group.
2. Develop criteria or use existing criteria developed by others.
3. Identify textbooks to be screened.
4. Set up committees for preliminary screening.
5. Set up committees for substantive evaluation of textbooks.
6. Choose small group to analyze results and make decision.

Both teachers were aware that many of their colleagues considered the choice of textbooks to be both a professional right and a responsibility;

however, parents and community interest groups believed that they should be consulted about the textbooks children used. To resolve this situation, Hogan and Thomas decided to go to the school advisory group. This group represented teachers, administrators, and the community at their school.

Evaluation Process

Community representatives on the school advisory committee affirmed their interest in the textbook selection process and communicated their concern that textbooks depict a multicultural society and be devoid of racism and sexism.

In meeting with the teachers, Hogan and Thomas learned that the school faculty shared the community's concern about the textbooks, and the teachers expressed their willingness to work on joint committees to review the texts.

Hogan and Thomas set up a joint meeting of teachers from different grade levels and members of the school advisory group. They shared the National Council for the Social Studies' *Curriculum Guidelines for Multiethnic Education* (1976) and the *Guide for Multicultural Education Content and Context* (1977) published by the California State Department of Education. Both of these resources were the results of federal funding under the 1974 Ethnic Heritage Studies Program (Title IX of the Elementary and Secondary Education Act).

The teachers also voiced professional concerns that textbooks should be evaluated in terms of their substantive content and the sequential development of skills. After a great deal of discussion about criteria to be used for evaluating the books, the group came to the following conclusions:

1. An initial screening committee would evaluate the textbooks for relevance using the criteria suggested in the NCSS publication and the California State publication
2. The books would be screened to verify that they were appropriate in terms of cost and aesthetic quality.

The group also agreed that textbooks that "passed" the preliminary screening should be forwarded to a group of professional educators to review using the school's curriculum objectives.

Identifying the Textbook

With the process for the evaluation agreed upon, the two teachers set to work to identify reading and social studies textbooks. They utilized the reports published by the Educational Products Information Exchange Institute (EPIE). They studied the *Social Studies Curriculum Materials Data Book* which is published yearly by the Social Science Education Consortium, Inc.

The two print resource materials (EPIE and the Data Book) yielded information about both reading and social studies text series. Once they were able to identify the names and publishers of specific books, they were able to call the publishers and request books for review purposes.

Preliminary Screening

The teachers chose several members of the faculty, and the advisory committee chose several community persons for the preliminary screening committee. This group evaluated the texts by sampling the content, looking at pictures, print, and format. By sampling the content and observing the choice of pictures in the textbooks, the screening committee evaluated:

- the portrayal of minority persons, places, and culture
- the expression of diversity
- content related to minority groups
- stereotyping portrayals
- diverse opinions and values
- interrelationships among groups
- religious bias
- sex bias (pictures, roles, language).

Preliminary screening committee members responded either "yes" or "no" for each item. Each member of the committee was required to write comments about each textbook that was not recommended for a complete review.

Evaluating Reading Textbooks

The faculty members assigned to the final review of the reading textbooks developed criteria statements to use for their evaluation. They identified the following categories and items:

1. Target Audience
   _____ Low Achiever
   _____ Bilingual
   _____ Urban
   _____ Average Achiever
   _____ Bicultural
   _____ Suburban
   _____ High Achiever
   _____ Majority Culture
   _____ Rural
2. Instructional Approach
   _____ Basal
   _____ Phonics
   _____ Language Experience
   _____ Programmed
   _____ Linguistic
   _____ Other
3. Skill Development (The series provides for . . .)
   - structural analysis
   - word recognition
   - phonic analysis
   - literal comprehension
   - critical reading
   - creative reading
   - functional reading
   - vocabulary development (word forms)
4. Program Development (The series fosters . . .)
   - oral language
   - interrelation of the four language arts components
   - positive self-concept
   - critical reading
   - appreciation of diversity
   - variety of literary forms
   - vocabulary development
5. Format (Yes/No)
   - print is clear, readable, and of proper size
   - pictures facilitate understanding and enjoyment
   - layout is interesting
6. Teacher's Manual (The manual provides . . .)
   - goals and objectives
   - explanations of content
   - instructional approach suggestions
   - question format
   - student activity suggestions
   - evaluation suggestions
   - reference suggestions

The reading panel also decided to use a rating scale from 1 to 3 on each item, with 3 reflecting a high score and 1 reflecting a low score.

Evaluation of Social Studies Textbooks

The social studies panel used the same rating scale as the reading panel, but their analysis of the textbooks was based on the following criteria:

1. Target Audience
   _____ Urban
   _____ High Achiever
   _____ Suburban
   _____ Average Achiever
   _____ Rural
   _____ Low Achiever
   _____ Multiethnic Population
   _____ Other: _____
2. Format (Yes/No)
   - organizing questions structure content
   - subheads differentiate major and minor ideas
   - pictures serve to illustrate concepts
   - readability accurately identified

> Should publishers suggest ways to evaluate students' progress? Why?

3. Content/Program (✓)
   - major concepts clearly identified
   - examples of concepts clear and understandable
   - social science disciplines interrelated
   - suggested student activities facilitate understanding of concepts
   - suggested student activities provide for individual differences
   - content fosters understanding of others
   - content fosters positive self-concept
   - content fosters democratic ideals and values
   - content examines experiences of ethnic group people
   - content includes social problems of ethnic groups

4. Skills (✓)
   Selected content helps students develop skills:
   - to observe and to make categories
   - to use maps, charts, tables, and graphs
   - to use reference materials
   - to respond to questions at varied levels of thinking
   - to find and process information
   - to examine value conflicts
   - to make value judgments
   - to make decisions
   - to differentiate among facts, interpretations, and opinions
   - to make inferences

Should students' textbooks suggest different types of activities? Why?

5. Teacher's Manual (The manual provides . . .)
   - goals and objectives
   - explanation of conceptual approach
   - instructional strategy suggestions
   - suggestions for levels of questions
   - suggestions for student activities for varied interests and abilities
   - performance evaluation suggestions
   - material, media, multireference suggestions

Effective Utilization of Resources for Learning

Guidelines for Selecting Learning Materials

Teachers exercise their responsibility to make the curriculum work by utilizing appropriate learning materials. It is important to recognize the interrelationship among the curriculum components. Figure 4.2 (Chapter 4) exhibited the relationship of instruction to educational goals. To accomplish the instructional goal, learning activities are selected; learning materials are chosen to correspond to the activity and the learning situation.

Learning Materials Should Be Purposeful. Materials should be selected on the basis of the purpose to be accomplished. Will the materials help to achieve the objective of the lesson? How will conceptual understanding or skills be developed or strengthened using the learning materials? How will diverse interests, abilities, attitudes, and appreciations be provided for by using the learning materials? These are the questions that teachers must ask before selecting instructional aids.

Learning Materials Should Be Concrete Whenever Possible. The elementary student learns best when experiences are real and concrete. When direct and real experiences cannot be provided, audiovisual materials should be utilized to expand the student's understandings and skills. Learning resources can be used to expand the student's world beyond the classroom.

Learning Materials Should Be Challenging. The world outside the classroom is often more motivating for students than the world within the classroom. Educational technology provides a means for teachers to "turn students on," but the materials must be appropriate to the maturity of the students. The materials should stimulate thinking by helping students to focus on important ideas, problems, or questions.

Diverse Learning Materials Should Be Selected. Eating oatmeal seven days a week for breakfast would be boring. Different types of materials should be selected to appeal to varied interests and varied learning modalities. Materials should be attractive and utilized to enhance the classroom environment.

The Purpose and Use of the Materials Should Be Understood by the Students. Students' readiness for the materials should be considered. In choosing films, television programs, or reference materials, it is important that students have the necessary knowledge and skills to utilize the experience productively. Students should understand why they are asked to view a program or use maps, globes, or kits. In using models, kits, or other contrived experiences, it is important to ensure that students know how to use the materials appropriately.

Learning Materials Should Be Carefully Prepared and Evaluated. The need for learning materials should be anticipated prior to the lesson and selected before the lesson is commenced. After use, materials should be evaluated in terms of the suggested guidelines. For example, did the materials enhance the lesson? Were students motivated? Did students understand how to use the materials?

Improving the Use of Learning Materials

Realia, Kits

Real objects, models, or specimens provide concrete experiences for students to utilize during instruction. When these real things are available, they should be used to demonstrate concepts or enhance students' experiences. They should be used in conjunction with reading materials or other learning experiences such as field trips or pictures. When possible, the realia should be in its natural setting.

Examples: Using a prism to separate colors in sunlight will be more valuable than reading about the sun's rays. Seeing and touching a powder horn made in Colonial times will be more meaningful than hearing about it or seeing a picture of it. Making a telegraph will increase learning about magnetism and electricity and may be more important in building concepts than if students listen to a lecture. Making a telegraph is also more valuable for students' understanding of concepts than if students were to see one made by someone else.

Demonstrations, Exhibits

The reason *making* the telegraph is more valuable than seeing one has to do with the nature of personal involvement. Making the telegraph requires that students understand the purpose of the telegraph and that they make plans for reproducing one. This means that students will be asking questions, clarifying, and problem solving instead of being passive learners. But sometimes it is not possible for students to be totally involved in a project. When this situation occurs, a demonstration or an exhibit of the desired concepts may be appropriate. To alleviate the shortcomings of a demonstration, the following plans should be considered:

- Be certain that students understand the purpose of the demonstration or exhibit.
- Plan each step of the demonstration so that it is sequenced in a logical manner.
- Keep the demonstration simple and uncluttered; avoid too many purposes and ideas.
- Motivate the demonstration and ask questions periodically to ensure that students are grasping the ideas and not losing interest.
- Be sure that all students can see and hear.
- Keep the demonstration short to avoid the "wiggles."
- Foster students' questions and students' clarifications.
- Plan evaluative questions and follow-up activities to reinforce the demonstrated concepts.

Films and Sound Filmstrips

Sometimes these aids are used in the same way that a babysitter is used—to hold the fort while the adult takes a breather! When this occurs in the classroom, however, teachers are communicating to students that the films are unimportant and not to be taken seriously. These audiovisual materials are too important to be used in a careless manner.

Effective use requires that teachers preview materials and select them because they are pertinent to what is being studied. They should be used in many of the same ways that a textbook is used:

- Preview films and record concepts and vocabulary that may be difficult for the students. Introduce the concepts and new vocabulary prior to the viewing and listening experience.

- Be aware of any ideas or events that may cause a value conflict for the students. Plan to discuss these ideas or events after the experience.
- Note discrepancies related to historical time periods. If the film is particularly old but still useful, prepare students for what they are to view; help them to be good observers—not silly watchers.
- Introduce the film; motivate students to observe specifics; set the stage for viewing.
- Evaluate the film utilizing the concepts presented and the vocabulary. Discuss significant behavior viewed in the film. Remember to discuss what was "fun" or especially enjoyable about the film.

Keep in mind that films do not always have to be viewed from start to end without stopping. Sometimes a film can be used most advantageously by turning it off at a propitious moment to discuss and project what might happen or what has already occurred. Films can also be used without sound to see if students can infer from actions what is happening. Another advantage to films is that they can be reversed to go back to an important concept and study it again. The most important point about films and sound resources is that the teacher should be in control of the experience and utilize it fully as a learning resource.

Videotapes, Radio, Television, Recordings

Once again it is important to select carefully only those experiences that are relevant to the students. These resources are particularly motivating because it is possible to use them at the precise moment when something is happening outside the classroom that is appropriate for reinforcing a particular lesson goal. They can also be used by prerecording important events and utilizing them at the "teachable moment." Suggestions for use:

- Introduce key ideas; prepare students for viewing/listening.
- When possible, use in conjunction with the teaching of note taking. Introduce note-taking categories and prepare students with questions about the episode.
- Utilize follow-up activities to reinforce or evaluate the session. If students have taken notes, provide them with feedback and an opportunity to share their notes.
- Evaluate the session just as you would evaluate other experiences. Note students' development of critical listening and viewing skills.

Pictures

Although pictures are less motivating than films and realia, they are utilized more frequently than any other resource. It is often said that one picture is "worth a thousand words"; perhaps so, but pictures can be misunderstood or misinterpreted by children unless they are taught to "read" their meanings. A painting or a photograph reflects the artist's view of the world, and students will have a perception different than the artist. Students need to learn how to study an art print or enjoy an artistic creation. Pictures cannot be thrust upon them, any more than can films or recordings.

Pictures can be used to motivate a study or to introduce key ideas. The trick is to get students to focus on the picture and help them observe, then to make inferences or interpretations based on the picture. Let us suppose that some sixth-grade students are using the textbook *Idea and Action in World Cultures*, and they are observing the photographs of Samoan girls and Samoan men and boys utilizing Samoan skills (pp. 274–275). The teacher could proceed in the following way:

1. What do we see in these pictures? (People, food, tools, huts, things that grow.)
2. Describe the things you see. (Have the students systematically describe the people—girls, boys, men—and their clothing, tools, and the like.)
3. Describe what the girls are doing. Continue with boys and men. (The older girls are

combing the hair of the younger girls. The men are cutting and preparing what looks like food; the boys are watching.)

4. What ideas and values are the Samoan girls learning? Samoan boys? (To help one another; to learn how to perform certain skills . . .)
5. Do *we* learn from one another? How? What are some examples?
6. In what ways is it advantageous for older children to teach younger children? In what ways is it a disadvantage?

Recall that the questions proceeded through specific thinking stages:

1. The students were asked to *collect data* by observing the content of the pictures.
2. The students *sorted* through the data, describing each item specifically. This could have been accompanied with the teacher working at the chalkboard and helping students *classify* the items: people, behavior, tools, clothing.
3. Students *generalized and made inferences* from the data. Here the students were asked to study the behavior of the people and decide what the younger girls were learning from the older girls and what the boys were learning from the men.
4. Finally the students were asked to *predict* the advantages and disadvantages of learning from older children and from others.

Sandler (1980) commented that students who are poor readers may "read" pictures better than their more advantaged classmates.

In learning to read pictures, students should think about what kind of picture it is—photo, map, advertisement—and why it was selected by the author, the teacher, or the photographer. In using social studies textbooks, students should think about why the author of the textbook chose certain pictures *and* did not personally take the pictures for the textbook. This train of thought should lead to a discussion of author bias and photographer or artist bias. Students can be led to think about what might be missing from the picture or why this particular scene was selected.

Pictures should be used to provide information about basic human activities as well as feelings, human relations, and problem situations. When students give reports, they can be encouraged to select appropriate pictures to accompany their oral and written presentations. When pictures are used on bulletin boards for creative simulation and for research, they should be selected carefully. Suggestions for use:

- Select pictures to convey specific ideas. Avoid distorted and ambiguous pictures or pictures that present misconceptions unless that is the focus of the lesson. Choose clear and vivid pictures.
- Select groups of pictures to demonstrate contrast or continuity.
- Arrange pictures artistically; avoid cluttering the classroom.
- If pictures are to be used on the bulletin board, utilize appropriate questions or captions with them.
- Mount pictures (on bulletin boards) so that the background does not detract from the picture or cause the viewer to focus on the mounting instead of the picture.
- Utilize pictures for discussion purposes either with the whole class or with small groups of students.
- If pictures are to be used as a research resource, classify them by topics or problems and mount them so that students can use them productively.
- Constantly update your picture file collection. Utilize governmental sources, friends, commercial publications, travel agencies, business corporations, embassies, and chambers of commerce.

RESEARCH FINDINGS

Carey, Hannafin, and Albright (1981) investigated the effects of pictorial and verbal stimuli which would generalize across different types of media and learning tasks. After ability blocking, third-graders involved in the study received picture and/or word presentations of a story. The students' concrete and abstract recall was measured. Results indicated that the children learned as much from the pictorial presentations as they did from the verbal presentations. The investigators suggested that media producers could improve the accuracy of perception by supplementing abstract content with pictures and concrete content with words.

Textbooks and Other Print Materials

Print materials are used for a variety of purposes in the classroom. During reading instruction, the textbook guides skill and vocabulary development. Sometimes printed materials are used to identify issues, topics, or problems for study. In addition, textbooks are used to confirm or contradict hypotheses after a discussion or during research. Print materials may be used to obtain information or as a source for conflicting points of view, for meanings, for data, and (heaven forbid!) for enjoyment. This list is not conclusive.

In some classrooms the textbook is used as the dominant tool and may in fact be more important than the teacher because it is used in a lockstep manner to teach the subject. But in most classrooms today printed materials are used judiciously as a resource tool to accompany other resources and used with the teaching program (instead of being the teaching program). School district and teacher philosophy can often be interpreted from the way in which textbooks are used in the classroom. In some schools and classrooms there is an absence of textbooks—or at least up-to-date textbooks. In other classrooms there are too many books and not enough other resources.

To utilize the textbook or other printed materials effectively, the following practices are suggested:

- Preview the material the students are to read. Introduce new vocabulary; help students understand abstract concepts by providing time to "act out" the concepts or to generate examples.
- Give students guiding questions to program their reading. Help them to structure what they need to read. Provide a purpose for reading and be sure that students understand the purpose.
- Verify that students have the necessary skills to read the material. If students are to read graphs, make sure they understand how to do so. Teach the necessary skills at the time of need. Verify that students know how to use the glossary, indexes, and appendixes; provide immediate practice.
- Teach students how to read for different purposes and explain how different material requires different skills and speeds of reading. Teach skimming and scanning skills.
- Evaluate reading and study skills by asking students questions to verify that they can recall details and sequences of events, can comprehend meanings, can generalize, and can make inferences based on the material.

Utilize a variety of printed materials, particularly for students who have reading problems. Newspapers, magazines, and cartoons provide a wealth of material for students to use. Prod poor readers to bring in or draw cartoons and write their own scripts. In utilizing printed materials, suggest to poor readers that they develop questions about the material based on the pictures.

Too often, social studies and science books tend to be out of date. Teachers need to practice a number of techniques to update their written sources of information for students. Textbooks can be supplemented with visuals: pictures, cartoons, charts, graphs. These materials are available from census data, newspapers, magazines, other governmental sources.

Out-of-date material can also be used as springboard lessons. For example, if a reading or social studies book included the price of food and clothing twenty years ago, it would be interesting to have students compare those prices with recent prices for those items. The students might even make timelines based on the change in prices for key items. Nutrition and health concerns change almost daily; textbooks are inevitably out of date, but this fact could be a fine stimulus to a study about changing health practices. Stereotyped information and pictures, particularly about sex roles for women and men, can be compared to up-to-date roles in the community.

When textbooks are misused, it is usually because they are allowed to determine the scope and sequence of study. This is the teacher's fault—not the fault of the author or the publisher. Modern textbooks attempt to meet varied needs for enrichment, diagnostic material, and activities. It is up to the teacher to select books to correspond to needs and to use them wisely.

The Classroom Teacher as Resource Developer

Quite frequently teachers discover that the learning materials they make themselves are more popular with the students and achieve better results than commercially produced materials. This happens for several reasons:

1. You know your objectives better than a publisher, and your materials are created to meet specific instructional purposes.
2. You know your students and their interests and ability levels, and so the materials "fit."
3. Your students appreciate your time, effort, and interest and respond accordingly.

Instructional Decisions

Before developing learning materials for the classroom, there are several decisions to make. These are:

1. What do you need to teach? (concepts, skills, attitudes, values)
2. How much time is available?
3. How do you want to organize students for learning? (reading groups, heterogeneous groups, individualized, whole class)
4. What teaching strategy do you want to use? (reading, artifact kits, case study, role-playing, computer, learning centers)

Once these decisions are made, the teacher should develop the materials, duplicate them for use, and go ahead and try them! The advantage to classroom-built learning materials is that it is easy to revise them.

The classroom teacher is responsible for the development of a variety of learning materials in almost all of the subject fields. While basal reading textbooks and mathematics textbooks are usually adequate for students' use, it is rare for workbooks to be appropriate for all students. As a consequence, most teachers create their own reinforcement activities. In addition, skill games for reading and mathematics are developed to correspond to the needs of specific students. Resource materials are also necessary in language, science, health, and social studies. In these fields it is unusual for commercially prepared learning materials to be in adequate supply.

Resource Information for Students' Research

Most elementary classrooms have a wide range of ability levels which necessitates reading materials to accommodate individual differences. For many school districts it is financially impossible to provide adequate text materials. Writing resource information for students at several reading levels is a professional challenge. However, the classroom teacher can accomplish the task more skilfully than a publisher because the teacher knows precisely what vocabulary students can read. The following guidelines are suggested to facilitate the writing of resource information:

- Identify the concept you want to communicate and write it as simply as possible.
- Use the students' reading vocabulary.
- Provide an example of the concept.
- When preparing material for several reading levels, provide more complex information for more accomplished readers.
- To ensure that each reading level will have something unique to contribute to a discussion, provide something unusual in each selection.

Designing Learning Centers

Examples of learning centers were provided in Section II of this textbook, and although it has been suggested that the teacher attempt to design several centers, guidelines for their development have not been supplied. If you review the centers in Section II, you will note how similar their design is to a lesson plan for teaching. Each center has an objective; this is why it was designed, and the objective states what students are supposed to achieve. Each center lists the materials needed for the activity at the center. The means for evaluation either by teacher, students, or teacher and students together is stated. The procedures were written to tell you, the reader, how to proceed to develop a similar learning center. However, since you are to design your own learning centers, the steps will be somewhat different because you are not concerned with telling others "how to" build a center. The following steps are suggested to design a learning center:

- Identify the objective of the center.
- Identify the activity to accomplish the objective.
- List the materials that will be needed.
- Decide how the activity will be evaluated.

Hints for Designing and Using Learning Centers

A center can be designed to meet the needs of all of the students in the classroom or just those with special needs. If the center is to accommodate all of the students, then it is important to have *multilevel activities* to accomplish the objective. Also, since students have different learning styles, it is advantageous to accumulate *multimodality materials*.

A system for *accountability* involving record keeping by students will allow you to monitor student progress in an efficient manner. You will need to know who has used the center, who needs to use the center, and whether or not the students accomplished the objective of the center.

It is important to *estimate how long it will take* students to complete learning center tasks. If one center takes more time than another, or if other students will be waiting to use the center, adjustments need to be anticipated and communicated to students.

There are a number of *management considerations* that facilitate center design and use. These are briefly discussed.

- Locate centers in areas of the classroom where the traffic patterns will not be impeded.
- Display center materials to motivate the center's use.
- Anticipate material needs at the center, including receptacles for waste materials.
- Name or number the centers so that you can talk about them with students without misunderstanding.
- Explain the purpose of each center with the students *before* sending them to the center for work.
- Develop a time schedule for the use of each center and communicate the schedule to the students.
- Monitor students' work at the center to verify that students' work techniques are appropriate.
- Develop a system whereby students can obtain assistance or communicate the need for assistance while working at the center.

- Provide differentiated tasks at the center to accommodate the low and high achiever.
- Communicate to students where to place completed work.
- Provide for a cleanup system with students so that the center is ready for others to use.

Simulation and Board Games

In recent years there have been increased interest and emphasis on simulations and gaming. The reader is reminded to review the guidelines in Chapter 15 for designing simulations and board games. Other chapters of the text provided examples of inquiry strategies, teaching units, and a case study. Each was provided to introduce the reader to a specific technique and to demonstrate the development process for designing instructional strategy.

Evaluation and Use of Instructional Materials

Since teachers use learning materials for instructional purposes, it is extremely important that teachers be involved in choosing materials and in developing guidelines for the effective use of those materials. Criteria for evaluating textbooks were suggested in this chapter along with sets of guidelines for the effective use of many learning materials. The criteria were purposefully written for very general use and should be considered as a guide to writing more specific criteria in each subject field. In addition, it is important to develop criteria for the evaluation of materials other than textbooks. Sources of information on instructional materials are listed at the end of this chapter to facilitate the process of identifying appropriate learning materials.

Chapter Summary

The importance of instructional materials should not be underestimated. Teachers have become more sophisticated in their use of all kinds of media. Although the textbook takes precedence, teachers use many types of media and instructional technology. This chapter provided an example of procedures that can be used for identifying instructional materials; involving teachers, administrators, and community; and evaluating textbooks. Guidelines for the effective use of learning materials were suggested along with recommendations that teachers develop both their own criteria for evaluation and guidelines for effective use. Suggestions were extended for writing resource information for students and for designing learning centers.

Sources of Information for Identifying Learning Materials

ALERT, Sourcebook of Elementary Curricula: Programs and Projects. Far West Regional Laboratory for Educational Research and Development, San Francisco, CA, 1972. Order from the Superintendent of Documents, U.S. Government Printing Office, Washington, D.C. 20402.

EPIEgram, The Educational Consumers Newsletter. Educational Products Information Exchange Institute, 475 Riverside Drive, New York, NY 10027.

Gaming: An Annotated Catalogue of Law-Related Games and Simulations. Special Committee on Youth Education for Citizenship, American Bar Association, 1155 East 60th St., Chicago, IL 60637.

Materials and Human Resources for Teaching Ethnic Studies: An Annotated Bibliography. Social Science Education Consortium, Boulder, CO 80302.

NASAGA c/o COMEX. North American Simulation and Gaming Association, University of Southern California, 3601 South Flower St., Los Angeles, CA 90007.

NICEM Catalog. National Information Center for Educational Media, University of Southern California, University Park, Los Angeles, CA 90007.

Social Studies Curriculum Materials Data Book. Social Science Education Consortium, Inc., Boulder, CO 80302.

Values Education Sourcebook. Douglas P. Superka, Christine Ahrens, and Judith E. Hedstorm with Luther J. Ford and Patricia L. Johnson. Social Science Education Consortium, Boulder, CO 80302.

Selected United States Government Publications. Superintendent of Documents, Government Printing Office, Washington, D.C. 20402. (Ask to be put on their mailing list).

Other Sources of Information

Sources of Free and Inexpensive Teaching Aids. Bruce Miller, Box 368, Riverside, CA 92502.
Instructional Media Index. McGraw-Hill Book Company, New York, NY 10022.
Using Free Materials in the Classroom. Association for Supervision and Curriculum Development, National Education Association, 1201 16th St. N.W., Washington, D.C. 20002.

Commercial Publishing Sources

(Write for free catalogues)

Addison-Wesley Publishing Co., Inc., 2725 Sand Hill Rd., Reading, MA 01867.
Allyn & Bacon, Inc., 470 Atlantic Avenue, Boston, MA 02210.
American Book Company, 300 Pike Street, Cincinnati, OH 45202.
Denoyer-Geppert, 5235 Ranenswood Ave., Chicago, IL 60640.
Fideler Company, 31 Ottawa Ave., N.S., Grand Rapids, MI 49502.
Follett Educational Corp., 1010 W. Washington Blvd., Chicago, IL 60607.
Ginn and Company, 19 Spring St., Lexington, MA 02173.
Hammond, Incorporated, Maplewood, NJ 07040.
Harcourt Brace Jovanovich, Inc., 757 Third Ave., New York, NY 10017.
Harper & Row, Publishers, 10 53rd St., New York, NY 10022.
Houghton Mifflin Company, 2 Park Street, Boston, MA 02107.
Holt, Rinehart and Winston, 383 Madison Ave., New York, NY 10017.
Macmillan Publishing Company, 866 Third Ave., New York, NY 10022.
Prentice-Hall, Inc., Englewood Cliffs, NJ 07632.
Rand McNally & Company, Box 7600, Chicago, IL 60680.
Scholastic Publications, 50 West 44th St., New York, NY 10036.
Science Research Associates Inc., 259 East Erie St., Chicago, IL 00611.
Scott, Foresman and Company, Glenview, IL 60025.
Silver Burdett Company, Box 362, Morristown, NJ 07960.
Social Studies School Services, 10000 Culver Blvd., Culver City, CA 90230.

Classroom Applications Exercises

1. Every teacher at your school has two hundred dollars to buy science and social studies teaching materials. This money is not to be spent on students' textbooks. What are some things that you would buy?
2. Write to a variety of governmental agencies and private companies to obtain free teaching materials. Utilize source information in this chapter. Share your discoveries with others.
3. Evaluate a series of textbooks and decide whether a specific ethnic group's heritage was reported in terms of the group's problems, influence, and contributions. Use both pictures and narrative.
4. Evaluate only the picture material in reading, social studies, and health textbooks and determine whether ethnic minorities are portrayed in the pictures, with or without supplemental discussion.
5. Use the steps provided in this chapter to design learning centers in several different subject fields.

Suggested Readings for Extending Study

Banks, James A. Evaluating and Selecting Ethnic Studies Materials. *Educational Leadership,* **31** (April 1974), 593096.
Built Environment. American Institute of Architects Environmental Education Committee, U.S.A.
Cruickshank, Donald R. *A First Book of Games and Simulations*. New York: Wadsworth Publishing Co., Inc., 1977.
Curriculum Guidelines for Multiethnic Education. Washington, D.C.: National Council for the Social Studies, 1976.
Gaffney, Maureen and Gerry Bond Laybourne. *What To Do When the Lights Go On: A Comprehensive Guide to 16mm Films and Related Activities for Children*. Phoenix, Ariz.: Oryx Press, 1981.
Grambs, Jean Dresden. *Intergroup Education Methods and Materials*. Englewood Cliffs, N.J.: Prentice-Hall, Inc., 1968.
Guide for Multicultural Education Content and Context. Sacramento: California State Department of Education, 1977.
Klein, M. Frances. *About Learning Materials*. Washington, D.C.: Association for Supervision and Curriculum Development, 1978.

Lemlech, Johanna K. *Classroom Management*. New York: Harper & Row, Publishers, 1979. Chapter 6.

Patton, William E., ed. *Improving the Use of Social Studies Textbooks*. Bulletin 63. Washington, D.C.: National Council for the Social Studies, 1980.

Piechowiak, Ann B., and Myra B. Cook. *Complete Guide to the Elementary Learning Center*. Englewood Cliffs, N.J.: Prentice-Hall, Inc., 1980.

Simms, Richard L., and Gloria Contreras. *Racism and Sexism: Responding to the Challenge*. Bulletin 61. Washington, D.C.: National Council for the Social Studies, 1980.

Waynant, Louise F., and Robert M. Wilson. *Learning Centers: A Guide for Effective Use*. Paoli, Pa.: The Instructo Corp., 1974.

Youngers, John C., and John F. Aceti. *Simulation Games and Activities for Social Studies*. Dansville, New York: The Instructor Publications, Inc., 1969.

Chapter **17**

Strategies for Evaluating and Communicating Learning Progress

After you have completed the study of this chapter, you should be able to accomplish the following:

1. **Define formative and summative evaluation.**
2. **Identify what a teacher must do to evaluate students' learning progress.**
3. **Discuss the meaning of valid test items.**
4. **Identify problems related to testing young children.**
5. **List the types of tests and the purpose of each.**
6. **Write an example of a test question for an essay examination.**
7. **Write several multichoice test items.**
8. **Develop a checklist to evaluate skills, behaviors, or concepts.**
9. **Explain the use of a social matrix or sociogram.**
10. **Observe a student in an elementary classroom and prepare an anecdotal record.**
11. **Discuss teachers' professional responsibility to communicate learning progress to students and parents.**
12. **Identify and explain techniques for communicating progress.**

Dear Mr. Thomas:

Yesterday my son William told me he was getting a "C" in science. William's father works for the Jet Propulsion Lab; he specializes in astrothermodynamics. Mr. Chan spends a great deal of time with William teaching him important scientific facts. Since it is obvious that William takes after his father, we know that he is gifted in science. My husband and I would like you to explain how it's possible for a gifted science student like William to receive a "C". Please call us and set an appointment for a conference.

Sincerely yours,
Mrs. Theodore Chan

Dear Mrs. Chan:

I will be pleased to meet with you and Mr. Chan regarding William's progress this semester. I would like to take the opportunity to share his learning progress in several subject fields during the conference. Will Thursday, May 28th, at 3:30 P.M., be satisfactory?

Yours sincerely,
Greg Thomas

Mrs. Chan does not sound irate, but the tone of her letter certainly indicates that she is displeased with William's grade in science. Greg Thomas will need to explain

- that scientific giftedness probably is not hereditary (!)
- how students are graded in his class
- how teachers find out what students have learned
- how William is progressing in other subject fields.

About Evaluation

Before Greg Thomas has his conference with the Chans, he may want to think about the evaluation process so that he is prepared to answer questions about how he arrives at specific grades for students. Thomas uses evaluation to improve learning, to improve teaching, and to provide feedback for curriculum design. Evaluation is a continuous, cooperative, and comprehensive process. Students are often evaluated before teaching a unit of study or a cluster of skills in order to *diagnose* individual and group needs. During teaching, evaluative measures are used to determine how well students and teacher are proceeding toward instructional goals. This is called *formative* evaluation. Evaluation at the conclusion of an instructional unit is called *summative* evaluation, and Thomas uses it to assess overall performance.

To evaluate students' learning progress, it is necessary to (1) identify what students are expected to learn and (2) measure how well students perform what is expected. This means that the teacher knows the purpose of instruction and evaluates to find out if the purpose was accomplished.

When teachers write behavioral objectives for instruction, they are translating teaching purpose into a standard for performance.

Students will compare and contrast the life-style of people living in Arctic areas with that of people living in temperate zones.

During instruction, the learning activity should be designed to accomplish the objective. For example, perhaps students will view a film that depicts both climatic regions. After the film the students will discuss similarities and differences in life-style related to the social and physical environment. Ultimately these students could be expected to respond to a test question which asks them to identify several ways in which the life-style of people living in an arctic area differs from the life-style of people living in a temperate zone.

In designing test items, teachers must be careful to write *valid* items. This means that the test question must be a representative measure of what was actually taught. If the students' learning activity had been an inquiry activity in which they observed, researched, and discussed the ways in which the physical and social environment affects people, their evaluative activity should also be inquiry oriented. It is important that objectives, learning experiences, and evaluative activity match. One cannot expect students to learn through an inquiry strategy and perform in an objective manner. Both teaching strategy and evaluation must correspond.

Testing Problems

Teachers frequently have a number of concerns about testing elementary students. In the academic subject fields, when students do poorly on a test, it is difficult to know whether their poor performance is a consequence of not knowing the subject matter or not being able to read the test. Teachers need to exercise care that they are not testing reading skills when they want to evaluate academic content.

Another problem encountered by teachers occurs when young students appear to be "sick" during a test. These students may be afflicted with what school nurses frequently call "school stomach." It is a response to the pressure that testing exerts on students and sometimes results in a fear of peer competition, and in extreme circumstances students have been known to fear school attendance.

A third related problem has to do with students' inexperience in test taking. Unaccustomed to performing when required to do so, some students do poorly on a test just because they lack experience or do not recognize the importance of personal effort during the testing situation.

Formal paper-and-pencil tests place still another constraint on teachers. Since students' ability to write involved responses is limited, most elementary tests need to be objective. Although essay examinations can be designed so that they are open-ended and more appropriate for elementary students, the students' lack of verbal facilities limits their use.

> If you need to diagnose whether or not students can demonstrate specific skills or knowledge, what type of evaluation should you use?

Types of Tests

Achievement Tests. Achievement tests are used to find out what students have learned and what they need to learn. Many school systems want to use *standardized* achievement tests so that they can compare how well their students do as compared with the performance of other students across the nation. Standardized achievement tests are *norm-referenced.* This means that you are able to compare the performance of students in California with that of students in Maine. Suppose William in Greg Thomas' classroom got 75 on a science achievement test. Greg Thomas could compare William's performance as a fifth grader with other fifth graders elsewhere.

Norm-referenced evaluation is always used to compare the results with an established norm. However, sometimes norm-referenced evaluation is deceiving. In subject fields such as social studies or science, the test is dependent upon the student's reading skills; thus conceptual attainment may not be measured. If the established norms do not represent minority populations—as many do not—then the test may be related to sociocultural factors and not fair to or indicative of the ability of a minority student. Another problem with standardized achievement tests is that they tend to measure low-level objectives because these objectives are easier to prepare on a test instrument.

Criterion-Referenced Evaluation. It is often desirable to know how well a student can perform a specific skill or deal with specific concepts. When teachers need this information, they test the student focusing on individual performance of a designated task or a specific behavior. The criterion for performance is the desired behavior (or task). Criterion-referenced evaluation is used for diagnostic purposes and, as such, is appropriate for use prior to instruction, during instruction (formative evaluation), or at the conclusion of instruction (summative evaluation). If the criterion for performance is used to determine whether or not students should be taught the next successive skill, then it can be said that students do not proceed until they have "mastered" a specific task. This is characteristic of *mastery learning*.

Teacher-Made Tests. The vast majority of tests given in classrooms are pencil-and-paper examinations designed by teachers to meet specific instructional purposes. As mentioned earlier, the teacher's main task in developing test items is to make sure that each item is valid. Valid test questions correspond with what has been taught and the way in which it was taught. Teachers must also exercise care that questions are clearly stated. If students do not understand the question or if there are several interpretations of the question, then clarity of purpose has not been achieved. Test items must be appropriate for the students taking the test. Sometimes good test questions are not appropriate to the age group or sensible in terms of what the responder must do. For example, if you asked students to name the presidents of the United States in order of their presidency, this would be an inappropriate question because the objective is inappropriate.

Essay and Objective Tests. Typically teachers write two types of tests: essay and objective tests. There are advantages and disadvantages of each. First, consider the essay examination. Essay tests are easier to write because they take less time, *but* they take more time to read; therefore, the teacher must decide whether to take the time to write the exam or take the time to read it. Essay examinations allow students to respond in depth, while the objective examination tends to be comprehensive. The essay examination is more difficult to grade because the teacher must decide on criteria to evaluate the examinations. Essay responses tend to be open-ended with each response differing; this is the reason essay responses are considered subjective. Rubin (1980, p. 446) suggests the use of essay examination under the following circumstances:

- The class is small and the test will not be reused.
- Written expression is to be encouraged.
- Attitudes are to be explored.
- The teacher is more adept as a critical reader than as a writer of objective test items.
- The teacher has more time to read the exam than to write it.

An essay examination requires that the student spend time planning what to write and thinking about ways to express the response. The planning and the writing time use up the bulk of the test time during an essay exam. The objective test requires that the student spend time reading and thinking. Ellis (1981, p. 145) made the following suggestions for writing essay examinations for students:

1. Focus on the main idea rather than specifics.
2. Elicit higher-level thinking from students.
3. Try to make questions clear and unambiguous.

Examples:

1. Make a list of safety rules to be used when experimenting with chemicals. Explain why each rule is important.

Discussion:

This question is specific in delineating what kind of rules students are to write. It is open-ended in that it does not tell students how many to write; the only constraint is that the rules be important. The question should let the teacher assess how much students know about chemicals because, if the rules are inappropriate, the teacher will be able to judge learning.

2. Identify the two emotions described in Robert Frost's poem "Fire and Ice." Which emotion does he consider more significant? Do you agree with Frost? Why or why not?

Discussion:

The question is specific in directing students' thinking to the purpose of the poem. Students' comprehension can be quickly assessed. By allowing students to respond with a personal opinion, the teacher has added the open-ended dimension.

True-False Tests. These tests are easy to grade, and it is possible to include many questions on a test thereby increasing the comprehensiveness of the examination. Since many elementary students lack the ability to write essay responses, an objective test will give these students the opportunity to demonstrate their understanding of what was taught. Disadvantages associated with the objective test relate to the tendency to write low-level questions and to the fact that the test may not match the teaching strategy, if inquiry or problem solving were used.

Example: Rocks are moved from place to place by water and ice.

Discussion:

This is a good question because it is clear rather than ambiguous; it expresses only one idea; the question is totally true. (It is not half true and half false.)

Similar to the true-false test, "yes-no" statements are ideal for lower-grade students. Examples follow:

Circle the right answer.

- Members of the family depend on each other.
  Yes No
- In some families fathers work at home and mothers work away from home.
  Yes No
- Boys and girls should always perform different types of jobs in the family.
  Yes No
- Some families depend on children to work.
  Yes No

Multiple Choice Tests. These are difficult to write because the choices must be reasonable and similarly written. Examples follow:

Choose the best answer:

(Primary)

1. If you were ill, who would you talk to?
   (a) Someone who had the same illness.
   (b) A friend who understands health problems.
   (c) A doctor in the community.

(Middle/Upper Grades)

2. Division of labor means
   (a) Each person performs as many jobs as is possible.
   (b) Each person performs a specific task to produce a specific commodity.
   (c) Each person performs a job as a skilled or nonskilled laborer.

(Middle Grades)

3. Which of these should you consult to find out how to make enchiladas?
   (a) A recipe written by someone who speaks Spanish.
   (b) A recipe written by a nutrition specialist.
   (c) A recipe written by someone who has lived in Mexico.
   (d) A recipe written by the author of a Mexican cookbook.

(Middle Grades)

4. Reading books is
   (a) A lot of fun.
   (b) Sometimes interesting.
   (c) Sometimes dull.
   (d) Very dull

Please note that these four questions would never appear on the same test together! Question four could be used, along with additional questions, to diagnose students' interest in school and school-related tasks.

Informal Strategies for Evaluating Growth

Checklists and Rating Scales. These informal strategies can be used by students or teachers for evaluating skills, specific behaviors, interests, and concepts. The checklist or rating scale utilizes descriptive statements such as "Listens attentively to story," or "Recognizes and uses antonyms," or "Seeks appropriate assistance or guidance." The evaluator checks or rates the item, either numerically or descriptively. By utilizing the checklist at regular intervals throughout the semester, teacher and students have a record of learning progress. The following exhibits will provide examples of different types of checklists or rating systems. The statements included are not necessarily more appropriate for evaluation than other descriptive lists; they are intended for illustration purposes.

Examples of Skills Checklists

Let us suppose that Mary Hogan wants to create a checklist to verify that her second graders are learning the enabling skills for sentence processing. Table 17.1 lists the items of concern.

TABLE 17.1. Sentence Processing.

Skills	Students' Names			
	Gene	Betty	Sam	Mabel
Demonstrates understanding of word order	+	✓	✓	✓
Identifies a simple sentence	+	✓	✓	✓
Uses modifiers to expand a simple sentence	+	✓	✓	✓
Uses transformations to manipulate sentences	✓	✓	−	✓
Unscrambles simple sentences	+	+	✓	✓
Retells a story in sequence	+	+	+	✓−

Code: + ✓ −

Greg Thomas was concerned about his students' dictionary and reference skills. He decided to construct a checklist to verify students' progress (Table 17.2).

There are literally hundreds of items that could be included on a critical thinking checklist. These skill items would relate to reading as well as thinking. The checklist in Table 17.3 is illustrative of typical items considered to be critical thinking. The reader should also review Table 9.3 in Chapter 9.

Table 17.3 could be used diagnostically to determine group teaching needs. For example, it would be possible to sum the scores of the children on each skill. Those skills in which most of the class had low scores would identify areas to teach. Assume that in a class of thirty children, the total group score for "Uses chronology" was 58; obviously, the class needs help using this skill.

When using an individualized reading approach, individual student records are extremely important to identify the mastery of reading skills. As the

TABLE 17.2. Dictionary and Reference Skills.

Skills	Students' Names			
	William	Everett	Tina	Jen
Alphabetizes letters and words by first letter	+			
second letter	+			
third letter	✓			
Uses guide words to locate information	✓			
Uses dictionary keys	✓			
Demonstrates use of phonemic respellings	+			
Uses and interprets diacritical markings	+			
Selects appropriate meaning of a word	✓			
Uses stressed and unstressed syllables	✓			
Uses table of contents	✓			
Uses index	✓			
Locates, identifies, and uses reference sources	✓			

Code: + ✓ −

TABLE 17.3. Critical Thinking.

Skills	Students' Names	Total
Identifies ideas from different resources		
Classifies information by fact and opinion		
Sequences ideas/events		
Uses chronology		
Defines concepts		
Locates relevant data		
Uses evidence to state generalizations		
Applies generalizations to new situations		
Makes inferences based on data		
Identifies cause and effect relationships		
Judges reliability of information		
Makes judgment based on consequences		

Code: 1 = poor, 3 = average, 5 = superior

> If you were a third grade teacher . . .
>
> Design a checklist to evaluate composition skills.
>
> Decide on a coding system. The following are commonly used on checklists:
>
> - Faces (happy, passive, sad)
> - Sharps and Flats
> - Number system
> - Reaction, Responses:
>   frequently, sometimes, rarely
>   often, seldom
>   excellent, good, satisfactory, poor
>   always, usually, seldom, never
>   understand, understand slightly, do not understand

teacher confers with the child about his/her reading performance, the teacher may want to make note of the following comprehension skills (Table 17.4).

The mastery of skill items is often more important than "how well" the skill is performed. For example, at the fifth-grade level it is important to find out how many students can read and interpret different types of maps. Either students can do it or they cannot; thus it is the mastery of the skill that the teacher is concerned about. Table 17.5 provides an example, using map reading for an illustration.

A kindergarten teacher was concerned about the performance of locomotor movements. In order to keep track of the students, the teacher used a record and recorded either "yes" or "no" beside the movement. It is very important to remember to

TABLE 17.4. Comprehension—Individualized Reading Program.

Skills	Students' Names
Identifies main idea	
Identifies cause and effect	
Explains emotional reactions	
Predicts story outcome	
Uses pictures/written material to make inferences	
Identifies fact, make-believe, opinion	
Distinguishes between relevant and irrelevant information	
Discusses story in personal terms	

Code: Awareness = A; Mastery = M

TABLE 17.5. Map Reading.

Reads and Interprets the Following Maps:	Students' Names
1. Climate	
2. Demographic	
3. Historical	
4. Physical	
5. Political	
6. Product	
7. Relief	
8. Transportation	
9. Vegetation	

Code: Awareness = A; Mastery = M

date the records so that progress can be verified (Table 17.6).

This same teacher notes that many of the students had difficulty remembering the songs that were taught. Ultimately the teacher decided to record information about each student and the student's singing skills. Table 17.7 is a checklist that the teacher used.

TABLE 17.6. Demonstrates Locomotor Movements.

Movements	Students' Names
1. Walk	
2. Run	
3. Jump	
4. Skip	
5. Hop	
6. Gallop	

Code: "yes" or "no"

TABLE 17.7. Singing.

Skill	Students' Names
Sings rhythmic patterns	
Sings short song	
Sings songs with syncopated rhythm	
Sings in minor mode	
Sings songs changing meters	
Sings with variety of tone qualities	
Sings expressively	

Code: Accurately/Appropriately = A
Inaccurately/Inappropriately = I

Knowledge components can also be identified on a checklist for recording students' progress. Tables 17.8 and 17.9 identify illustrative art and music concepts.

To Improve Teaching

Gathering evidence to improve both teaching and learning, teachers find that class discussions need to be evaluated for participation, interaction, listening, relevance, and synthesis. The checklist in Table 17.10 can be used at the conclusion of (or during) a whole class discussion.

TABLE 17.8. Art Heritage Concepts.

Concepts	Students' Names
Identifies several American painters, sculptors, and architects	
Relates the purposes of art to different historical time periods	
Recognizes similarities and differences among art objects	
Uses art resource materials to obtain information	
Discusses field trips to galleries, museums	
Identifies the various uses of art	
Identifies career options for artists	

Code: 1 = poor; 3 = average; 5 = superior

TABLE 17.9. Music Concepts.

Concepts	Students' Names
Identifies: staff notation	
scale patterns	
rhythmic notation	
math relationship	
familiar song from notation	
chord pattern	
sharps and flats	
natural symbol	
names of tones	
repeat signs	

Code: 1 = poor; 3 = average; 5 = superior

In this situation the teacher decided to tape-record the discussion session and play it back for the students. The students then critiqued their own discussion and realized that one of their main problems was that they did not listen to the contributions of other speakers. As a consequence, there

TABLE 17.10. Whole Class Discussion Skills.

How many . . . ?
1. Participate
2. Utilize facts
3. Utilize relevant ideas
4. Listen to others
5. Use evidence to present ideas
6. Use ideas of others to present own information
7. Challenge ideas of others
8. Refute ideas using evidence
9. State main point in summation

Code: few; many

TABLE 17.11. Formative Evaluation of Small Group Process Skills.

	good/poor
1. Our planning/discussion was . . .	
2. We made the following agreements/ plans . . .	
3. We accomplished . . .	
4. Our plans were spoiled by . . .	
5. We need to . . .	
6. We anticipate the following material needs . . .	
7. We need assistance to . . .	
8. We do not need assistance because . . .	

was unnecessary repetition. With the teacher's help they came to realize that they needed to prepare for a discussion with notes and evidence so that they could challenge each other's facts. They decided to take turns at the end of a discussion to practice making summative statements.

To improve small group work students can be asked to evaluate their work sessions together. The open-style checklist (Table 17.11) suggests that students write in their comments.

> A parent questions a report card grade you have given in social studies. How will you prove that it was justified?

Table 17.12. Small Group Planning Form.

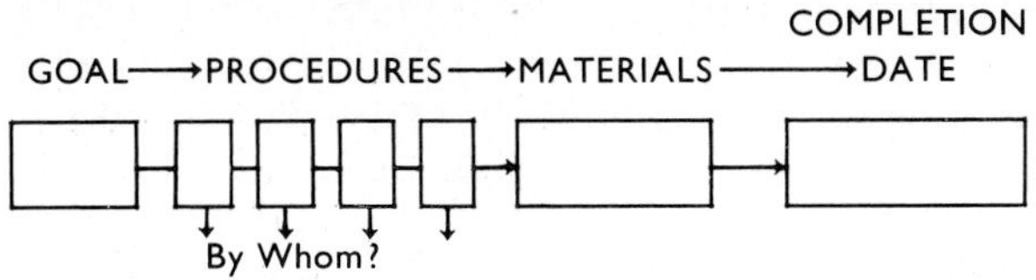

Sometimes a *planning form* such as the one in Table 17.12 will facilitate group work.

When students participate in group work or simulations and gaming, their social participation skills should be evaluated. *The following checklist* would be appropriate after use of the simulation "School Council" (Chapter 15).

TABLE 17.13. Social Participation Skills.[1]

1. Participates and cooperates with others
2. Observes and shares observation
3. Listens to others
4. Expresses own viewpoint
5. Plans with others
6. Assists others
7. Accepts personal responsibility
8. Carries out group tasks, plans, and actions
9. Shares efforts
10. Concludes tasks
11. Identifies agreements or disagreements
12. Interprets agreements or disagreements
13. Facilitates cooperation
14. Bargains and negotiates

1 *Source:* J. K. Lemlech, *Classroom Management* (Harper, 1979), p. 79.

Self-Evaluation

Just as good teachers evaluate themselves, students should be encouraged to appraise the development of work skills, social skills, and academic skills. Self-actualization is dependent upon accurate self-appraisal, but a great deal of care needs to be exercised by teachers to guide students in their self-evaluation because sometimes students are extremely hard on themselves. Students should be taught that some skill development is individualistic and dependent upon growth characteristics; however, social skills and work study skills may be dependent upon personal effort.

Student Accountability. Students can be held accountable for their performance when: (1) they know *what* their assignment is, (2) they know *how* to accomplish it, and (3) they have the necessary work materials. Classroom problems typically result when students are unclear about the purpose of the assignment, or how to use the resources, or when the assignment is due. A number of records can be designed to help students keep track of their responsibilities and to self-evaluate in terms of "How am I doing?" Suggestions follow in Tables 17.14, 17.15, and 17.16.

After group work or learning center participation, the following "I Learned" record is useful.

TABLE 17.14. Student Contract.

Today is ______________	Name: ______________
I will do this:	I accomplished this:
1.	
2.	
3.	
4.	

TABLE 17.15. I Learned . . .

Name: ______________

1. I learned . . .
2. I am excited about . . .
3. I am disinterested in . . .
4. I feel good about . . .
5. I was surprised . . .

TABLE 17.16. Work-Study Skills—Self-Evaluation.

Did I . . .	Yes	No
1. Plan my work?		
2. Understand my assignment?		
3. Begin to work immediately?		
4. Need help?		
5. Help others?		
6. Enjoy my task?		
7. Work quietly?		
8. Feel satisfied with what I accomplished?		
9. Complete my assignment?		
10. Clean up?		

To evaluate work habits Table 17.16 can be used with a "yes-no" response or can be made open-ended so that students write in their responses.

When there are many work-groups in the classroom, it is often difficult for both students and teacher to remember who is to work where—and when. Different types of assignment charts can be devised to keep students on target. The following are illustrative (Tables 17.17 and 17.18).

TABLE 17.17. Work Assignments (Centers and Groups).

Centers	M	T	W	T	F
Science	Green				
Music		Green			
Research			Green		
Media				Green	
Skill					Green

TABLE 17.18. Work Assignments—Pocket Chart.

	WORK PERIODS		
	I	II	III
Library Media Art			

Students' names would be on cards and placed in the pocket chart for the appropriate center and work period.

Sometimes teachers use sign-in sheets at each center. In that way the teacher can verify who worked at the center at a given time and day. In addition, there should be one box for finished work and another one for unfinished work available at each work center.

Obtaining Information About the Classroom Environment

Finding out how students feel about others in the classroom, about their relationships with others, and about their studies provides the teacher with information that assists in planning learning experiences. Frequent assessment of the learning environment communicates to students that a teacher cares how students feel and has respect for them.

For very young children it is also possible to obtain an accurate measure of their feelings by asking them a question and having them respond by checking the appropriate facial expression. Use five faces with the face on the far left reflecting a positively happy, smiling person. The face on the extreme right would reflect a negative, unhappy person, and the faces in between would be at varying stages of emotional reaction from positive to negative.

Students with a positive self-concept typically have several friendships in the classroom and enjoy their classroom and school work. Good academic work appears to be related to a healthy mental attitude about the self and one's relationship to others.

TABLE 17.19. Learning Activity Evaluation.

(Mathematics)
I really learned a lot today. ______
I learned a little bit today. ______
I did not learn much today. ______
This happened because ____________________

TABLE 17.20. Learning Activity Evaluation.

(Mathematics)
I really needed help today. ______
I needed a little bit of help today. ______
I did not need help today. ______
This happened because ____________________

TABLE 17.21. Class Activities.

Class activities were . . .
______ 1. very interesting today.
______ 2. a little bit interesting today.
______ 3. not interesting today

When teachers can help students relate to several others in the classroom, the school situation is perceived more favorably. For this reason it is valuable to measure social relations in the classroom. Simple questionnaires can be devised to obtain the information. With very young children, it is possible to interview each child and obtain the information orally. Another system is to provide each child with a list of classmates. Each class member will have a number in front of his/her name, and in responding to the questions the respondent can refer to the classmate's number rather than write the whole name. The following types of questions can be used to generate information about social relationships:

- Which students in this class are always willing to help others?
  1.
  2.
  3.

There is no magic number of suggested names that students should write, but three seems to be indicative of students' feelings about others.

- Which students in this class do you like to work with most often?
  1.
  2.
  3.

When students are responding to these questions, it is important to assure them that there are no right or wrong answers.

- Which students in this class do you *not* want to work with?
  1.
  2.
  3.
- Who can always be counted on to help in class?
  1.
  2.
  3.
- Who always gets their work done?
  1.
  2.
  3.

It is natural for students to have negative feelings about some of their classmates, and it certainly is valuable for the teacher to know which students cannot work together; however, good judgment is advised before using too many questions that ask for negative judgments about peers. Information derived from questions (Which student do you like to work with? or Who would you most like to sit next to?) can be used to develop a matrix or sociogram of social relationships. Armed with this information, teachers can try to improve relationships among students by helping the isolates and rejected students develop patterns of behavior that can be respected by peers.

Developing a Social Matrix. Let us pretend that in a classroom of 25 students the teacher asked the question, 'Which students do you like to work with?' The matrix would be constructed in the following way:

- Each student has a number from 1 to 25.
- The top of the matrix is numbered and the side of the matrix is numbered.
- Each time a student is named positively the student receives *a* + in the square *under* his/her number *in the row* of the person doing the choosing. The left column indicates the 'choosers,' and the top row indicates the 'chosen.'

Analysis of the data reveals that students numbered 4 and 24 are isolates and student number 19 was chosen by only one person. However, there are several mutual choices in the class: Students 1 & 3, 6 & 7, 5 & 10, 6 & 13, 20 & 2. These students appear to have mutual good feelings about each other. The matrix also reveals that students choose widely among their classmates. Although students 1 and 5 are fairly popular, there are really few students who are totally unpopular. In some classrooms you will find several 'stars' and many students who are not recognized at all by others. In this classroom that does not appear to be the case. The teacher should be able to use the established friendship choices to help students 19, 4, and 24.

TABLE 17.22. Matrix Social Relations.

'Choosers' / "Chosen"	1	2	3	4	5	6	7	8	9	10	11	12	13	14	15	16	17	18	19	20	21	22	23	24	25
1			+				+				+														
2															+					+					+
3	+								+			+													
4		+				+													+						
5										+					+						+				
6					+		+						+												
7						+							+				+								
8					+											+		+							
9			+									+									+				
10					+																	+			+
11		+														+						+			
12	+																+						+		
13					+				+			+													
14														+						+			+		
15	+		+		+																				
16	+									+				+											
17							+											+							
18	+				+						+														
19																				+	+				+
20		+					+	+																	
21						+		+		+															
22					+																+				+
23	+				+	+																			
24		+				+							+												
25																					+	+	+		
Total	6	4	3	0	8	5	4	2	2	3	2	3	3	2	2	2	2	2	1	3	5	3	3	0	4

Note that this matrix does not reflect differences among first, second, and third choices; however, a matrix could be designed to do so.

A *sociogram* is another way to organize data to detect social relationships. When making a sociogram it is often interesting to depict boys and girls in different ways so that one can see instantly whether there is a split between the boys and girls or in the structure of the interaction. Figure 17.1 exhibits a sociogram for a small group of 15 students.

The sociogram is dramatic because it represents pictorially the social relations or social distances in the classroom. It is easy to see that Bill is popular with both boys and girls. Fara, Evelyn, and Dick are isolates. The sociogram is usually used to designate one or two choices, whereas the matrix can represent as many as desired. Colored ink or different types of lines can be used in the sociogram to differentiate between the choices.

In evaluating the relationships in the classroom, it may be worthwhile to determine whether choices would be different if the questions were phrased to make students differentiate between "work" partners and "friendship" partners. Would students choose the same individuals to work with as they would to play with? Or they might also be asked, "Who would you most want to be tutored by?"

Sociometric devices should be used periodically to determine whether there are changes in students' attitudes and values about others in the classroom. Information is incomplete if the teacher does not follow up several weeks or months later to determine whether changes have occurred.

Figure 17.1. Sociogram.

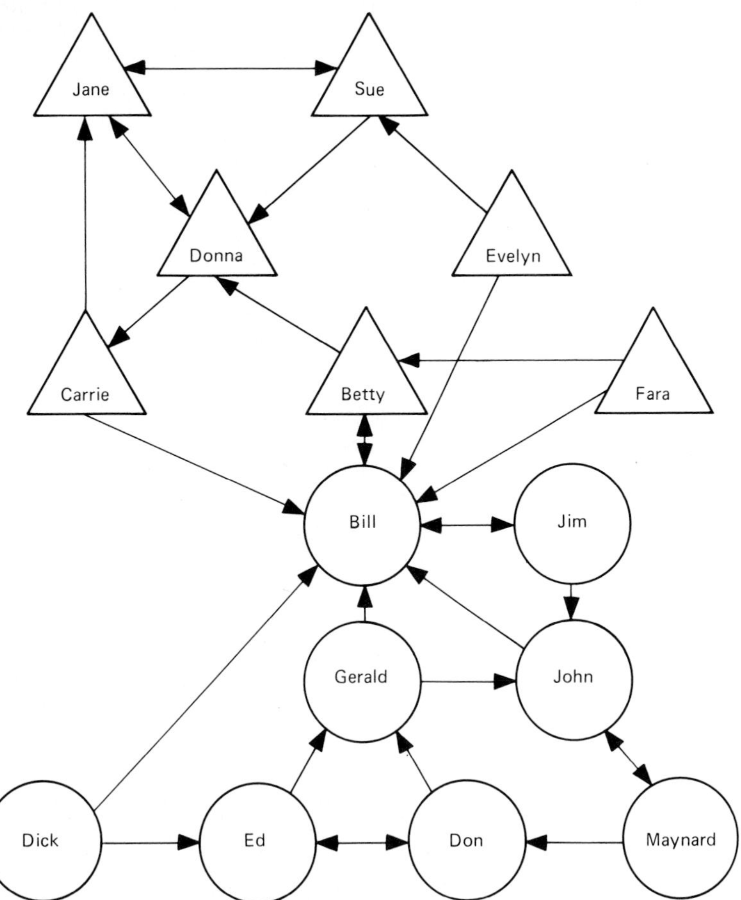

Anecdotal Records

The anecdotal record is an informal technique used to study specific behavior exhibited by a student when that behavior appears to be discrepant or problem causing. The anecdote describes the specific event and behavior as objectively as possible. If the anecdote is to contain an interpretation or evaluation by the observer, it is separated from the description. The purpose of the anecdote is to preserve information about the discrepant behavior so that it can be analyzed by the teacher, parent, or another professional. Sometimes the anecdote will also contain the observer's suggestions or prescription for "treatment." The following example demonstrates the technique (Table 17.23).

Teacher Observation

The anecdotal record is dependent upon the teacher's observation skills. Any interpretation of an observation record must be based on the observed facts. General observations of students' work skills or of teachers performing instructional techniques should be purpose oriented. The observer should be looking for specific behaviors and

TABLE 17.23. Anecdotal Record. Shirley Barry.

	Observation (What happened?)	Interpretation (Why did it happen?)	Prescription (Planned action!)
Mon. Mar. 10	Complained of a headache during math; did not finish work; was excused to see nurse.		
Tues. Mar. 11	Same time; same complaint; same effect.	Hm-m-m-m. I will talk to nurse.	
Tues. 3 P.M.	No temperature; vivacious; fine after rest (Nurse's report).		Conference with student.
Wed. Mar. 12	Same time; same complaint plus stomachache. (Suggested she rest in classroom.)	Must be having problems with math; no apparent interaction problems with peers.	Conference: Helped her with math, *but* she did *not* need the assistance.
Thur. Mar. 13	Same problem; different time!	Nothing to do with math. Home problems?	Call mother. Set up conference.
Fri. Mar. 14	Conference: Mother revealed that parents are separating. Shirley needs counseling. Mother recognizes problem and says that she will alert father to Shirley's security needs. (Hope that next week will be better!)		

have criteria to use in order to recognize the behavior. A review of the checklists in this chapter will reveal that each was designed to gather data about specific behaviors, skills, or attitudes. Teacher observation is a valid evaluative technique for both formative and summative purposes.

Conclusion

Teachers should use a variety of techniques to obtain information about students' learning progress. Effective planning and instruction are dependent upon meaningful evaluation. Thus far in this chapter a variety of techniques, both formal and informal, have been presented. Evaluative means are to some extent dependent upon students' ages and capabilities as well as the interest and philosophy of the teacher. It is up to the classroom teacher to choose evaluative measures that fit teaching style and students' needs.

Techniques for Communicating Change

Feedback and Change

Feedback, according to Warren (1977), is necessary for the improvement of performance. Warren relates a personal example of his own skiing experience in which he found that his improvement was dependent upon information from his instructor concerning what he was doing wrong and suggestions for improving his skiing performance. Feedback generally serves two purposes: to provide a cue about the task to be performed and to provide motivation. The cue guides the learner to make corrective adjustments in performance or procedures. Motivation affects the student's interest or desire to continue or discontinue effort and may be dependent upon pride, self-esteem, shame, or anxiety (Keislar, 1977).

In a critical review of research on evaluation and motivation, Sears (1977) cautioned that there is much we do not know about the role of motivation on young learners or low-ability students and that not enough attention has been given to the effect of self-evaluation. Obviously, students perceive and are affected by evaluation in different ways; some students are motivated by challenge, others need an instructional program that guarantees success. Teachers need to understand their students' responses to success and failure, and perhaps their own motivational patterns as well. Teachers who are discouraged by students' failure will react differently than teachers who perceive failure as a challenge to improve performance.

The communication of learning progress is an extremely important and difficult professional responsibility. Teachers perform this task in as many different ways as they do that of obtaining information about achievement. Block (1977) advised teachers to sequence teaching strategies to gradually increase levels of success. Dweck (1977) suggested that teachers try to change students' causal beliefs so that they understand that success is achieved because of effort. For some students, programs that guarantee success do not provide the appropriate challenge; for these students Maehr and Sjogren (1971) suggested independent study so that personal effort was perceived. Keislar (1977, p. 60) warned that misunderstandings were likely between parent and teacher, "if teachers attribute student success to their good teaching and student failure to the student's lack of effort or ability, while the parent assumes just the opposite."

The Interview or Teacher-Student Conference

Teacher-student conferences or interviews should be carefully planned to accomplish specific purposes. The conference can be used to gather information about the student's progress and to communicate information to the student concerning achievement. During the interview, the teacher should be assessing the student's performance in terms of the child's own ability and personal growth and in terms of a criterion considered appropriate for the student. The child's accomplishments as compared to those of others may also be assessed. The teacher needs to exercise judgment concerning what is to be communicated to the student. The long-range effects of positive versus negative criticism need to be considered.

The conference provides an opportunity to help the student self-evaluate. A checklist may be used at this time. Donoghue (1979) recommended the conference period to help students evaluate their written compositions. During the conference, the teacher can help the student edit his/her own work. It is also possible to determine whether the child expressed him/herself clearly in writing by listening to the child describe his/her thoughts. The conference provides a marvelous opportunity for a one-on-one discussion. All subject fields can benefit from the conference as a means to communicate behavioral change and provide appropriate feedback to the student.

Diaries and Logs

Students can be asked to keep a diary or a log of their personal activities, accomplishments, tasks, and behavior. The written record can then be examined in terms of accomplishments and goals. The diary or log makes a fine accountability measure to facilitate self-evaluation. The diary or log can be shared with others if the student desires it, or it can be used in the teacher-student conference. Primary children can dictate their logs and illustrate their activities.

Graphic Techniques

Another way to encourage students to self-evaluate their progress is to teach them how to graph their accomplishments using a bar graph or the broken line graph. These records are particularly appropriate to help students keep track of their spelling achievement, math achievement, completed homework assignments, or decreasing frequency of teacher admonishments. Once again, these graphic techniques can be discussed during the teacher-student conference and/or shared with parents.

Figure 17.2. Shirley Barry's Math Text Scores

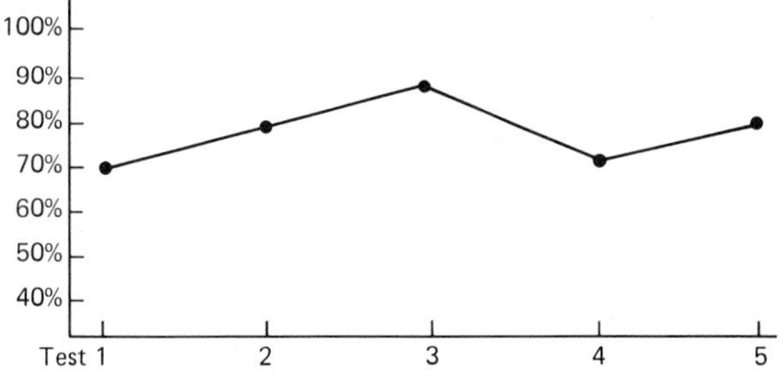

Figure 17.3. Teacher "Reminders" (Shirley Barry)

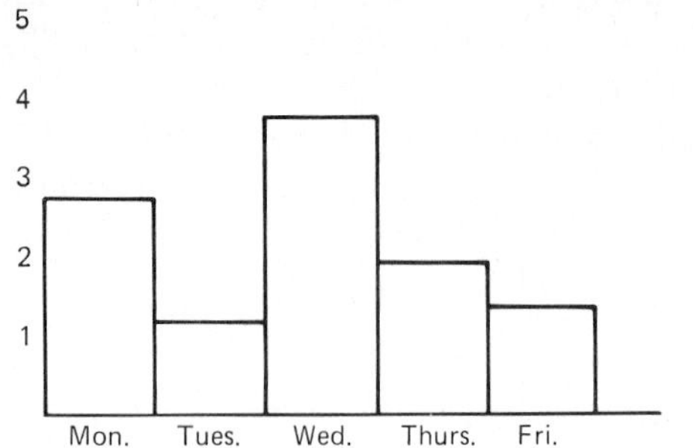

Grading

Grading establishes labels for specific categories (A, B, C, D, F); each category has specific characteristics. In determining grades, the teacher must decide whether the student fits the characteristics of a particular category. If "C" is the "average" or "satisfactory" category, then the teacher must decide on the criteria to be considered average or satisfactory in each subject or skill being graded. While feedback provides information for the student to use to improve performance, grading actually provides no information that is useful. Knowing that you received a "C" in science does not tell you *how* to improve your performance. Dependent upon the criteria that were used, or the group to whom you are being compared, the grade only tells you that the teacher considers you "satisfactory."

A typical problem during grading has to do with the composition of the class population. Suppose that Greg Thomas believes that school grades should reflect the normal bell curve, but perhaps Thomas' fifth graders happen to be unusually bright. Their math tests reflect a narrow range of scores from 85 to 100. Using the normal curve would mean that a student with a score of 85 could conceivably receive a "D" or "F" on the math test. If, on the other hand, the class composition was primarily of low-ability students, then a score of 85 might be an "A," if the range turned out to be 60–85. Thus, it is important to remember that the normal curve should not be applied to grade abnormal groups.

Despite the fact that teachers try to be objective about grading, there are many subjective elements. Teachers usually tell students that homework assignments, class participation, neatness of work, and effort are all considered when assigning a grade. But these elements allow for a great deal of subjectivity and students and parents are well aware of the selective nature of some of the evidence. Grading can never be totally fair; as a consequence, many schools prefer parent-teacher conferences or the use of descriptive, criterion-referenced evaluation instead of the traditional report card. When criterion-referenced evaluation is used, parents receive a list of competencies with information about how their child is performing relative to the list of specific skills or competencies. For example, in the sixth grade there may be a list of 20 reading skills that have been identified as essential by the school or school district. Perhaps 15 of the 20 skills have been verified in terms of the child's progress; however, the other five skills are still beyond the competence of the student. In this way the parents know precisely what skills the child is capable of performing.

Parent-Teacher Conferences

The conference is a time to gather information and to share information. This means that teacher and parent are talking *with* (not *at*) each other and listening to each other. As the teacher attempts to establish rapport with the parent at the beginning of the conference, it is important to let the parent know that you, too, are the child's advocate. (Remember that the parent *ought* to be the child's advocate.) Sometimes parents have preconceived ideas about the conference based on their own childhood memories. For this reason, it is a good idea to be sure that the parent is at ease before focusing on the purpose for the conference.

Guidelines for Parent Conferences

Whether the conference represents a planned or an unplanned happening, it is important to remember that conferences involve the expression of personal feelings, ideas, and judgments. It is as essential for the teacher to listen as it is for the parent. Basic conference components are the same whether the conference has been planned or is unplanned. Suggested guidelines for conferences are as follows:

1. Greet parent(s) and establish rapport through a sharing of interest. Try to put the parent at ease. Sit next to or across from each other. Do not put the teacher's desk between you.
2. Establish the purpose for the conference. If you requested the conference, tell the parent about the problem or the reason for the request. If the parent requested the conference, ask the parent to "tell me about your concern." (If the conference was called to solve a behavior problem, focus on the problem but be sure to avoid judgmental comments, such as "Cecil is a weasel! or Howard is a coward!") Remember, you are an advocate *for* the child!
3. Bring evidence of the student's work to the conference and share the data with the parent. Interpret test scores and progress for the parent. Remember that you are the expert.
4. Answer parent's questions; listen to parent's observations.
5. Discuss your instructional approach. Discuss ways to help the student and discuss anticipated progress.
6. Ask for parental suggestions; remember that the parent knows the child better than you do.
7. Establish joint goals for the future. Set a time for a follow-up conference, if necessary.
8. Summarize the conference:
   (a) Ask parent, "Do you have any questions you want to ask?"
   (b) State your concept of the conference's accomplishments.
      - "We have both agreed that we are concerned about Jed's progress in math."
      - "I intend to . . ."
      - "It is my understanding that you and Mr. E. will monitor Jed's homework . . ."
      - "Our plan is to . . ."
      - "We will keep in touch about . . ."
9. Thank the parent for attending.

Data for the Conference. It is extremely important to prepare evidence of the child's work for the parent to examine. When Greg Thomas has a conference with the Chans, he will need to show them their son's work accomplishments. The following evidence can be assembled for the conference.

1. Results of daily activities: work papers (follow-up materials in reading and math); independent projects, work accomplished at learning centers; social studies, science, art projects.
2. Checklists of skills and social participation. (Greg Thomas will want to show the Chans the Critical Thinking, Inquiry Skills Checklist.)
3. Observational data by teacher or others. This might include an anecdotal record.
4. Test results from both teacher-made tests and achievement tests.
5. Data generated by the student in the form of self-evaluative evidence.

Post-Conference. After the conference, record information about agreements and decisions. Note any follow-up plans. If there is a need for other professional assistance, arrange for the appropriate personnel to consult on the case. Record the data and make note of the evidence that was shared with the parent(s). It is very important to assess accomplishments derived through the conference and to carry out professional commitments.

Chapter Summary

Evaluation is an important factor in learning. To improve the learning process it should be continuous and related to ongoing purposes and long-range goals. Evaluative data can be attained in a variety of forms including work samples, observation and interviews, checklists and rating scales, tests, and projects. Whenever possible, evaluation should be performed by the learner with the teacher acting as guide.

The prime purpose of evaluation is feedback. Feedback is necessary to improve performance. Grades and test scores provide no feedback and can lead to a misinterpretation of the purpose of evaluation. Teacher-student conferences provide a means to share mutual goals, provide information, explore thinking, and teach self-evaluation. The parent-teacher conference provides a means for two-way communication; its success is dependent upon anticipatory planning utilizing evaluative data and the establishment of rapport. Obtaining evaluative data and communicating evaluative judgments are major professional responsibilities.

Classroom Application Exercises

1. Make a list of activities that demonstrate integration of subject fields and could be exhibited to show "how much" students have learned.
2. Develop an objective test using science concepts. Choose any grade level.
3. Choose a specific skill and design a criterion-referenced test to find out if students can perform the skill.
4. Formative evaluation means that a teacher checks on how things are progressing during an instructional episode. What are some ways that you can find out if students are learning what you want them to learn?
5. Use Table 17.15, "I learned . . ." and write comments about what you have learned about evaluation from this chapter.
6. Summative evaluation occurs at the end of instruction. What are some ways to determine what students have learned at the end of an instructional period? Why are summative evaluation and grading closely related?

Suggested Readings for Extending Study

Ebel, Robert. *Measuring Educational Achievement*. Englewood Cliffs, N.J.: Prentice-Hall, Inc., 1965.

Eisner, Elliot W. The Role of the Arts in Cognition and Curriculum. *Phi Delta Kappa*, **63** (September 1981): 1, 48–52.

Gronlung, Norman E. *Measurement and Evaluation in Teaching*. Fourth Edition. New York: Macmillan Publishing Company, 1981.

Keislar, Evan R., guest ed. "Evaluation and Student Motivation." *UCLA Educator*, **19** (Winter 1977): 2.

Miller, William C. "Unobtrusive Measures Can Help in Assessing Growth." *Educational Leadership*, **35** (January 1978): 4, 264–269.

Wick, John. *Educational Measuremennt: Where Are We Going and How Will We Know when We Get There?* Columbus, Ohio: Charles E. Merrill Publishing Company, 1973.

PART **FOUR**

PROFESSIONAL GROWTH

You are a professional, and you are goal oriented; your behavior is guided both by an understanding of your professional commitment and by your personal needs as a growing, self-actualizing person. You are aware that the future of our society depends upon you and other teachers acting responsibly, intelligently, and sensitively to achieve a better tomorrow.

Chapter **18**

Continuing Education—a Personal Responsibility

After you have completed the study of this chapter, you should be able to accomplish the following:

1. **Identify the purposes of staff development programs.**
2. **Suggest ways to utilize the assistance of other adults in the classroom.**
3. **Select personal instructional improvement goals and prioritize them; utilize the list of goals in this chapter.**
4. **Develop a self-evaluative checklist to use in your own classroom or during student teaching.**
5. **Identify one or more professional associations of personal interest.**

In the school where Mary Hogan and Greg Thomas teach, the faculty is divided into teaching teams. Each team specializes in a specific subject field. Thomas is a member of the social studies team, while Hogan works with the language arts team. Each team is composed of teachers at different grade levels. The purpose of the team approach is to offer collegial assistance to other teachers by sharing ideas and techniques that pertain to the teaching of the field of specialization.

Mary Hogan and her team members are responsible for planning a staff development program in the language arts. Their plan has several stages:

STAGE I

- Interested teachers submit personal proposals for improvement.
- Teachers identify schoolwide areas for improvement.
- Language Arts team screens proposals to determine common needs for a staff development program.

STAGE II

- Teachers meet together with team and principal and a language arts consultant to discuss needs and proposed staff development program.
- Consultant and other specialists present theory and research to teachers and principal.
- Released time is utilized by having the language arts team, along with other teachers, "double up" so that those involved in the staff development program can observe some planned demonstrations.
- Meetings are arranged with consultant to discuss the demonstrations, which will be performed by experienced teachers modeling the techniques.

STAGE III

- Teachers share ideas and techniques at a weekly meeting.
- Teachers arrange to practice new techniques with a partner observing.
- Partner groups provide feedback.

STAGE IV

- Teachers utilize new techniques in daily planning.
- Consultant and principal provide feedback.
- Teachers evaluate successes and failures.

School Improvement through Staff Development: What Works?

In recent years there have been a number of professional development studies to determine effective techniques for staff development. The plan utilized by Mary Hogan and her colleagues incorporated many of the components of successful inservice systems. Joyce and Showers (1980) identified two purposes of staff development programs:

- To improve teaching skills
- To master new approaches

The improvement of skills typically focuses on asking more insightful questions, facilitating student involvement, management and organizational techniques, and understanding subject matter.

Mastering new approaches is more difficult. In this type of staff development program the emphasis is on increasing the instructional repertoire of teaching strategies, learning about new techniques and research, and developing new or alternative curriculum.

Components of Staff Development Programs. Joyce and Showers (1980, p. 380) found that most in-service programs consisted of five basic components:

1. Theory, rationale, or description of the skill or strategy;
2. Planned demonstrations or modeling of the desired skill or strategy;
3. Practice of the skill or strategy by teachers in own classrooms or in a simulated environment;
4. Feedback about performance;
5. Coaching for application to apply the skill or strategy in the teacher's own classroom.

In evaluating the effectiveness of the five components, Joyce and Showers noted that the presentation of the theory or rationale of the skill or strategy was important to raise the level of awareness about the need for acquisition of the technique. However, theory by itself will not change classroom performance. The first component needs to be used in conjunction with the other components. The second component (demonstrations/modeling) can be used by some teachers to gain insight in order to refine teaching performance, but most teachers need the third component (practice) in order to successfully implement a new way of teaching. Feedback about performance during the practice period is extremely important because when implementing a new technique it is possible to practice the strategy incorrectly; without feedback about performance, incorrect procedures may become habitual. The last component is necessary for some teachers to find ways to apply the new technique in curriculum planning. Coaching can be provided most successfully by colleagues who are experienced with the application of the skill.

Successful Staff Development Programs. Research on staff development programs indicates that effective programs

- focus on the improvement of specific skills
- emphasize demonstrations and opportunities for practicing new skills and receiving feedback
- relate to the personal on-the-job needs of each participant
- continue throughout the entire school year
- meet more often at the local school than elsewhere
- include opportunities to observe teachers who have mastered the desired skill
- include principals as participating members of the staff development program (*Educational Leadership*, 1980, p. 184).

Improving Schools through Staff Development. Good teaching is contagious. Successful teachers attract other teachers who want to learn new ideas and techniques. Schoolwide improvement occurs simultaneously as teachers improve.

RESEARCH FINDINGS

Bethel (1982) found that 73 per cent of elementary teachers involved in a study of in-service needs in central Texas desired to learn more about science concepts. Responses to the needs assessment indicated that only 2 per cent of the school day was used for science teaching, and in nearly 60 per cent of the classrooms, science was not taught.

Improvement of teaching performance happens slowly and developmentally. Most teachers are motivated to improve their instructional performance because they care about the students they teach. Research indicates that paying teachers to participate in staff development programs is not as effective as appealing to teachers' natural motivation to improve abilities and become better at what they do.

Improvement at the school level is dependent upon individual teachers. Concerned teachers must be involved in the planning of the improvement process. For schools to improve, teachers must meet together, be aware of the scope of the problem, and be committed to improvement. Teachers are professional experts and must make the decisions about the change process. The Rand Change Agent study indicated that principals needed to be a part of the staff development program and visibly demonstrate knowledge and support of the program.

Lieberman and Miller synthesized the research on improving schools and found:

- Schools, like individuals, adapt to improvements developmentally.
- Schools in which programmatic or schoolwide concerns are linked to individual teacher concerns have the greatest possibility for positive change.
- Schools must provide the necessary conditions for improvement; these conditions are motivated primarily by the principal (Lieberman & Miller, 1981, p. 583).

Network Approach. The League of Cooperating Schools (Bentzen, 1974; Goodlad, 1975) functioned as an educational network. For five years (1966–1971) 18 schools in the Los Angeles area worked together in a loose and informal association. Educators met together and discussed mutual curricular and organizational problems and provided each other with innovative ideas. Some members of the group were active participants; others took part when they felt like it. The network served as an alternative resource group to the members to provide information, support, and feedback apart from typical school district group meetings. Two key features of the network approach are the ideas of *linkage* and *developmentalism*. Linkage refers to the organizational arrangement of members who may or may not be members of the same system or organization, but who meet together and bring information to one another. Developmentalism relates to the step-by-step, gradual approach to change. Developmentalism is accepted by the group members as a structural means to begin with the here-and-now problems and levels of development and recognize the potential for change.

IF YOU WERE THE TEACHER . . .

While walking by the classroom next door, you were surprised to see many children wandering aimlessly around the classroom. The teacher, who was working with a small group of students, paid no attention. The classroom was noisy, and you wondered how the teacher could stand it. If the teacher were to ask for help, what would you suggest?

Successful Staff Development Models

Partnership Model: University and School District. The university–school district partnership model offers teachers another approach to continuing education. Hanes et al. (1982) described the success of the model that links the Ann Arbor, Michigan, school district with Eastern Michigan

University, Ypsilanti. Committed teachers participate by submitting personal proposals for improvement to the school distrct. Working with their building principals, the teachers also identify a schoolwide problem as an area of focus. Program participants are selected by a committee of teachers, administrators, and school board members. The participants meet together to plan the staff development program by identifying their professional needs.

During the summer the university offers a two-week seminar for the teachers and their principals. The seminar focuses on the identified problems and perceived instructional needs and on curriculum planning. During the seminar the teacher and principals design instructional sequences and submit curriculum plans.

In the fall, the plans are implemented and teachers practice new skills and techniques. Reinforcement and feedback are provided by the principals, district staff leaders, and university specialists. Successful curriculum plans are disseminated throughout the school district for others to use.

Teacher Centers. Teacher centers were first created in England and Wales. In the United States, the centers were first funded in 1978. Their purpose was to give teachers control over their own professional development. Although most centers have university faculty involvement, they were created to move continuing professional education away from the college campus.

Every teacher center has a policy board made up of a majority of teachers, administrators, and university faculty members. The policy board along with the center's director supervises the center.

Teacher centers have the potential to provide innovative professional activities for continuing education. Each center is different and provides different services and activities for teachers. Some centers focus on traditional in-service approaches while others are resource centers and offer mini-courses and workshops on alternative approaches to curriculum areas.

In the future, teacher centers may be staffed by teacher specialists in each curriculum area. These teachers may be released for a set period of time or as part-time specialists by their school district. Teachers will be able to visit the center to obtain new curriculum ideas or resource materials. As presently established, the center is responsible for attracting teachers, identifying teacher needs, and providing professional service to teachers.

The Extended-year Program. The Extended-Year Program was initiated in 1980 in suburban Chicago and involves 25 per cent of the school district's teachers and 100 per cent of the district's administrators. For 15 to 18 consecutive days at the end of the school year, the teachers and administrators participate in in-service education. Teachers are motivated to participate voluntarily by the high-quality program and a daily stipend which is equivalent to each teacher's daily teaching salary.

The school district's board of education is financially committed to the program and allocates more than 1 per cent of the educational fund to the in-service program. Programs are carefully evaluated and planned to be relevant to teachers' needs. The program focuses on three topics: interpersonal relationships, teacher strategies, and specific content areas of the curriculum.

Program participants are encouraged to identify both specific needs and anticipated achievements. Interactive communication styles and collegial decision making are taught. Activities encourage risk taking and help participants face criticism and rejection. The program assists participants in accepting personal responsibility for decisions and teaches them to analyze their teaching skills and practices. When participants develop self-confidence with other group members, they are encouraged to record sample lessons on videotape.

Working independently and in small groups, the teachers apply what they have learned about interpersonal relationships and teaching strategies to specific content areas. Music and physical education teachers develop lessons to correlate with language arts objectives. Other teachers work on questioning strategies for reading or social studies programs. Participants choose their area of interest to apply what they learned.

Program developers attribute success to the careful planning and balance of content and process, mental and physical activity, and acquiring and sharing of knowledge and skills (Conran & Chase, 1982).

RESEARCH FINDINGS

What do teachers value in in-service education? Holly (1982, p. 418) found that teachers "value self-chosen, informal, participatory activities. They particularly preferred activities that allowed them to work with other teachers, from whom they often felt isolated. Teachers described their colleagues as valuable sources of practical ideas and information, helpful advisors on professional problems, the most useful evaluators of teaching skills, and understanding allies."

Team Teaching: Contribution to Professionalism

Team teaching is a way of combining the instructional efforts of two or more teachers in order to use their abilities to best advantage. Teacher aides or assistants may also be included in the teaming arrangement. Teaming can be particularly advantageous at the elementary level because of the diversity of subjects that are taught. For example, if several fourth-grade teachers at a school teamed, each might be a "team leader" for a different subject of the curriculum. The team leader would accept greater responsibility for planning and teaching in the area of his/her expertise. The other members of the team would serve as assistants during instruction and would help with reinforcement.

Group planning time is extremely important when working in a team situation. Members of the team need to share plans and objectives and receive feedback about whether a lesson accomplished its purpose. Team teaching provides a system whereby new and inexperienced teachers can learn teaching methodologies from more experienced colleagues and receive feedback about their own teaching performance.

Implementation of teaming is different in each situation. In some schools an experienced teacher is called the "lead" teacher and is responsible for most of the planning. However, the professional reason for teaming should be to refine instructional techniques and provide students with instruction from teachers who are motivated and superior in each subject field. Teaming provides a built-in system for staff development.

Nongraded Classrooms. Since teachers pool their respective classes in team teaching, this organizational system allows students to be grouped by need rather than by grade. Students move from one group to another depending upon the subject and the student's ability. Nongraded teaching teams from primary, middle grades, or upper grades are popular in many elementary schools.

Working with Other Adults in the Classroom

As we approach the year 2000, educational systems and the teacher's role will change. Many of the factors and events causing these changes were discussed in Chapter 1. The educational program is broader and more versatile than programs designed in past years. Today, in many classrooms the teacher is responsible for providing leadership and guidance to other adults working in the classroom. Auxiliary personnel in the classroom may be parent volunteers, paid adults (aides), or teacher assistants (paraprofessionals) who are enrolled in preparatory teacher education courses. The reader may want to review the discussion about assuming professional responsibilities in Chapter 4.

The elementary teacher frequently finds that s/he is responsible for leading a diverse teaching team composed of volunteers, aides, cross-age tutors, and special consultants. In this new managerial and leadership role, teachers need to anticipate meaningful non-teaching tasks for the auxiliary personnel. These tasks need to be assigned, explained, guided, and evaluated.

Planning time needs to be arranged with the classroom team, and teachers must be sure that everyone understands the classroom program and desired room standards. Emergency procedures and duties should be communicated. Preparation should be made to keep the auxiliary personnel meaningfully involved; this may mean that an ongoing system needs to be devised so that classroom team members always know "what to do next."

Frequently the classroom aide or volunteer is older than the teacher; however, it is the teacher who has the professional expertise. Leadership should be demonstrated by defining and guiding what needs to be accomplished in the classroom. Interpersonal relations should be warm, friendly, but appropriately professional. This means that the teacher when working with other adults in the classroom

- encourages the exchange of ideas
- accepts feedback
- asks questions to clarify own and others' understanding
- acts respectfully and encourages trust and respect
- provides both positive and negative feedback
- assigns meaningful tasks without "overloading" the aide
- speaks simply and clearly without use of professional jargon
- exercises care to protect students' confidential records and to withhold personal information about students.

In accepting the assistance of auxiliary personnel in the classroom, the teacher needs to keep in mind that the purpose of other adults' helping in the classroom is to individualize instruction. Sometimes in the assignment of work tasks, this is forgotten and aides are given busywork and clean-up chores exclusively. Although these work tasks may be helpful, the idea of teacher aides is to free the teacher to spend more time with students and provide additional tutoring time for students.

If aides are to tutor students, they will need to understand the nature of the child's learning problem (if there is one) and appropriate methodological techniques for assisting. This means that the classroom teacher is responsible for staff development with the classroom aides to ensure that tutoring tasks are performed correctly. The teacher may want to suggest to the aide observation, interschool and interclass visits, and special classes designed for paraprofessionals to develop the skills necessary for classroom assistance. The teacher should be constantly alert to opportunities to provide appropriate continuing education for the assistants.

Figure 18.1 provides an example of an assignment sheet prepared by a first-grade classroom teacher for the aide. This teacher duplicated the blank assignment sheet and then filled it in each day with the assigned tasks. The teacher will have to verify that the aide understands the tutoring tasks. Also note that the teacher performs the diagnosis and makes the decisions about what kind of help the student should receive.

Accepting Personal Responsibility

Are teachers good learners? Studies of the efficacy of inservice models reveal that teachers are good learners and can improve their teaching skills and repertoire of instructional strategies. However, as with other adult learners, certain conditions are necessary for growth and change. The studies indicate:

1. Adults are motivated to learn when needs and interests are used as starting points.

Figure 18.1. Assignment Worksheet for Auxiliary Personnel.

Name: Date:

Work Assignments

1. Prepare paper and paints for art center.
2. Duplicate math worksheets.
3. During reading: *Tutor*
   - Billy and Dawn: Beginning consonant sounds (b,p,d,m)
   - Erick: Words with short vowel sound (a,e,i,o,u)
4. Supervise clean-up of art center.
5. During math, *Tutor*:
   - Jay and Shelly: Compare and classify objects by size and shape
   - Maria and Tom: Identify geometric shapes
   - Jennie: Identify events in sequence
6. During Writing: *Tutor*:
   - Alphonse: Identify alphabet letters
7. During physical education: Supervise Jerry's team on the apparatus
8. Check science kits to prepare for magnet experiment.

2. Adults are pragmatic learners, and studies should begin with life-centered situations.
3. Personal experiences of adults should be analyzed.
4. Adults should be given opportunities to direct their own learning and to engage in a process of mutual inquiry.
5. Learning situations should be arranged so that differences in learning style, time, place, and pace of learning are considered (Bents & Howey, 1981, p. 33).

Set Personal Goals. To improve personal performance, it is important to set goals that focus on your behavior rather than on students' behavior or on the improvement of the school's educational program. McGreal (1980, p. 418) listed a number of goals which most teachers would recognize as being important to instructional improvement:

- Increase the use of instructional objectives as a basis for teaching strategies
- Increase verbal interaction of students
- Increase teacher-student contacts and the use of students' ideas in lecture/discussion settings
- Increase teacher enthusiasm while teaching, through voice and nonverbal expressions
- Ask questions at varied levels
- Use more student-centered teaching techniques
- Present concepts clearly utilizing structuring comments
- Increase the use of direct instruction in basic skills teaching
- Demonstrate the relationships among method, content, and students

To *this* list, the author would add the following goals:

- Differentiate instruction based on students' needs, interests, and learning styles
- Improve organizational skills to decrease non-teaching time
- Integrate subject fields to unify learning
- Utilize academic fields to teach reading comprehension skills
- Utilize developmental skill sequences to diagnose skill needs
- Increase teacher feedback to students during direct instruction
- Increase flexible grouping of students throughout the school day
- Increase output activities for students
- Increase professional reading
- Apply research findings in the classroom.

IF YOU WERE THE TEACHER . . .

Although you are a beginning teacher, you are considered an expert in science because you majored in physical sciences. You have noticed that most of the teachers in your school teach science "by the book." If you were to design an in-service class for your colleagues, what would you emphasize?

Analyze Your Own Performance. It is possible to analyze your own performance to verify what it is you need to improve. Using a tape recorder in the classroom, small episodes of instruction can be recorded for later analysis. Before listening to the episode, decide on the purpose of your evaluation.

- Do you want to listen to the questions you asked?
- Are you listening for the number of responses and degree of interaction?
- Are you concerned about management skills?
- Is it enthusiasm or clarity of instructions that interest you?

Do not attempt to critique everything. Focus on one or two elements of your teaching style and develop a checklist that will enable you to listen in a purposeful manner.

Another way to help you analyze your performance is to invite a trusted colleague to observe. You and your colleague should develop an observation chart to enable your friend to observe specific elements of instruction.

It is also possible to develop a checklist for older boys and girls to use to give you feedback about teaching. You should design this checklist and be certain the students understand what it is they are to evaluate. It is a good idea to let them know that you are always striving to improve your teaching techniques, and that you value their assistance.

Ask the right questions. Sometimes the areas of performance that need to be improved cannot be detected easily using a tape recorder or feedback from others. For example, suppose that you suspect that you are wasting too much teaching time with organizational matters and with classroom management. If this is the case, you may want to develop a list of questions to ask yourself to determine how likely is it that essential teaching time is not being used productively. Miller (1980, p. 164) suggested the following questions about the use of concrete time:

- How much time is spent in academic subject areas?
- How much time is spent in other activities?
- How much time is spent in transitions?
- How much time is spent in maintenance?
- How much time is spent in diagnosing students' needs?
- How much time is spent in feedback activities?

Design a Self-help Program. After analyzing your performance, decide on your goal and arrange a time line to accomplish your objectives. Consider what you have learned about "successful" staff development programs and, using that information, model your personal program. For example, to increase your awareness and knowledge about your goal you could decide to:

- Read professional literature
- Attend a professional class
- Talk to a knowledgeable expert

Your next task may be to find another teacher who is "expert" in the technique you want to master. Ask your colleague if you may visit his/her classroom during a particular session so that you will have an appropriate model. You may need to share your goal and your plan with your principal so that provisions can be made to allow you to visit other teachers.

Figure 18.2. Self-evaluative Checklist.

Develop your own self-evaluative checklists similar to this one.

	Yes	No
I plan my lessons before presenting them.	___	___
I choose instructional materials that are relevant and appropriate for my students.	___	___
My directions are clear and concise.	___	___
My follow-up materials reinforce my lessons. (They are not busywork).	___	___
I self-edit my handouts to see that they are grammatical and legible.		
I pace my lessons to keep students interested.	___	___
I encourage students to participate.	___	___
I try to talk to each student individually.	___	___
I listen when students want to talk to me.	___	___

Your third task is to develop a plan for practicing the skill. You will probably have to arrange to have someone observe your performance so that you can receive feedback.

Finally, after appropriate practice and feedback, work out a system whereby you utilize the technique consistently in your teaching. Once again, you may want the assistance of a colleague to help you plan instruction utilizing the new skill.

IF YOU WERE THE TEACHER . . .

The third-grade teacher in Room 14 teaches reading from 8:30 to 11:30 AM. The third-grade teacher in Room 16 teaches reading from 8:30 to 9:45 AM. Although the classes in your school are heterogeneously arranged, the students in Room 16 achieved higher scores on their standardized reading test. What are some reasons why this might happen? If you were the teacher in Room 14, what would you do?

Professional Associations Contribute to Professional Development

Elementary teachers have a wide range of professional group choices available to them for membership. There are professional associations related to almost every subject field. The following organizations provide services to elementary teachers:

- International Reading Association
- National Council for the Social Studies
- National Council of Teachers of Mathematics
- National Science Teachers Association

Some elementary teachers also enjoy membership in the following groups:

- National Music Educators Association
- National Art Education Association
- American Association for Health, Physical Education and Recreation
- National Association for Bilingual Education

Professional development is enhanced by membership in these national groups. Each of the associations offers members periodic journals, newsletters, bulletins, and research information. In addition, they typically hold a national conference that meets over a long weekend. The conference location shifts each year to both vary the local perspective and shift the length of travel time. At these conferences teachers take part in committee work, workshops, and discussion groups. Each association arranges to bring in noted scholars in the subject field who report on noteworthy curriculum development, research, and socially significant issues. Frequently the association, in cooperation with a local university, manages compressed classes for teachers interested in unit credit. Publishers' exhibits at these conferences provide teachers with the opportunity to view and critique the latest instructional materials and media related to the subject field.

In recent years the professional associations have assumed the responsibility of providing their members with continuing education. The conference enhances professional life and provides teachers with an enjoyable way to engage in dialogue with other professionals.

Two other national groups need to be recognized for their contribution to the professional advancement of teachers. The National Education Association (NEA) and the American Federation of Teachers (AFT) both provide members with ethical, legal, and political leadership and services. NEA serves members who primarily live in suburban and rural areas, whereas the AFT members typically live in the large urban areas. NEA publishes *Today's Education* and the *NEA Reporter*. AFT publishes *Changing Education* and the *American Teacher*. Both groups furnish members, through their journals and newsletters, with congressional and political information important for the profession, as well as curriculum and instruction articles.

Local and State Associations. Many of the national professional associations have local and state chapters. These smaller groups often have their own newsletter or journal and regional conferences. The local meetings focus on classroom and community problems and function as a collegial support system. Committee and task force participation is encouraged by these groups. Frequently state legislative information or problems are handled by these state associations, and state departments of education will turn to the local chapters for assistance and for information about educational problems and priorities.

Research and the Classroom Teacher

Professional development also occurs by reading research findings and applying them in the classroom. The Institute for Research on Teaching tried a "consumer validation" approach with teachers in order to improve understanding of the time-on-task research (discussed in Part I of this text). After conducting seminars to present the findings, they encouraged teachers to keep records of the ways in which they used the findings. Then at follow-up meetings the teachers shared with each other lists of ways in which the research worked (*ASCD Update*, March, 1982).

How could you help other teachers see the value of research on teaching?

Action Research. The purpose of action research is to improve school practices. This type of research is focused on the application of research to specific educational problems in the classroom. Typically, teachers along with a research specialist are involved in the study. Action research is aimed at helping teachers develop (a) objectivity, (b) research process skills, (c) the ability to work harmoniously with others, and (d) professional spirit (Best, 1981, p. 22).

The Far West Laboratory has been testing the Interactive Research and Development on Teaching approach (Tikunoff et al., 1980) utilizing action research. The research team is composed of teachers, a researcher, and a developer-trainer. The team identifies a contemporary classroom problem and checks to see if the problem is "universal." If it is, the team gathers evidence in the classroom setting and uses the evidence as an intervention strategy. The selected problems arise from practical needs of teachers. After the data are analyzed, teachers apply the intervention strategy and provide professional assistance to colleagues. The strength of the team is probably related to the fact that the composition of the team encourages objectivity.

Professional Certification and the Beginning Teacher

States differ in professional certification requirements. It is the responsibility of the individual to be familiar with those requirements. If you intend to move out of state, then it is important to find out whether there is reciprocity between the state where you were certificated and the state in which you want to live. Approximately 35 states have reciprocity agreements. Continuing education requirements appear to be a new trend in professional certification, and teachers should be alert to the rules governing renewal of teaching certificates.

Personal Development through Extracurricular Activities

It is as important to grow as a mature and cultured adult as it is to develop as a professional person. It is commonly recognized that "all work and no play" can truly make one a very dull person. The all-work syndrome also contributes to the phenomenon known as teacher burnout, discussed in Chapter 1. Outside interests, activities, and friendships distinct from professional associations and activities help the professional person achieve balance.

Teachers join drama groups, political party groups, book clubs, and recreational organizations in order to get away from school and gain a different perspective about community life. Significant involvement in community affairs and in the cultural life of the community help teachers develop vital intellectual, social, and emotional capacities. Continuing education encompasses all aspects of human development. Adult growth is dependent upon positive relationships with others as well as interaction with one's life work.

Chapter Summary

In this chapter professional growth was outlined in the context of both school improvement and personal growth activities. Several successful staff development programs were described. Self-evaluation and a personal continuing education program were suggested. Professional associations were listed and advocated for collegial interaction and support. Involvement in the application of research was cited as a strategy for professional development. Adult growth through significant interaction with others and involvement in socio-civic affairs are considered vital to emotional fulfillment and social and intellectual development.

Classroom Application Exercises

1. You have recently read the research findings related to academic learning time. How would you apply this research in your classroom?
2. Why is it important for beginning teachers to join professional associations?
3. Identify some instructional areas for improvement. What are some activities that will help you improve your performance?
4. How would you encourage professionalism and continuing education?
5. Using the information about successful staff development programs in this chapter, suggest some questions to evaluate a staff development workshop.
6. Name one or more books on the current best seller list.
7. List the cultural events you have attended in the last month. (Delete movies from your list.)

Suggested Readings for Extending Study

Best Sellers – Fiction and Nonfiction
Classics
Daily Newspapers
Current News Journals
Professional Journals

May You Be Influential and Forward-Seeking in Your Professional Life. Good Luck.

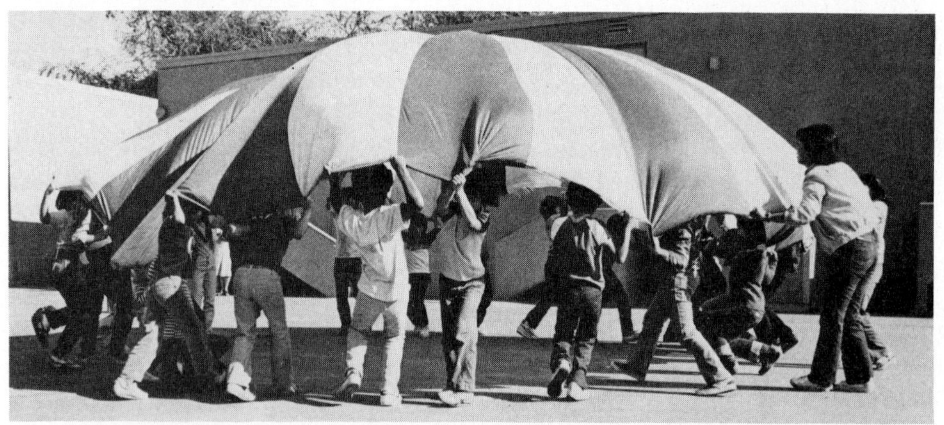

BIBLIOGRAPHY

Anderson, C. J., and L. F. Anderson. "Global Education in Elementary Schools: An Overview." In *Social Studies and the Elementary Teacher: Promises and Practices*, Bulletin #53, edited by W. W. Joyce and Frank L. Ryan, pp. 135–140. Washington, D.C.: National Council Social Studies, 1977.

Anderson, L. M., C. M. Evertson, and J. E. Brophy. "The First Grade Reading Group Study: Technical Report of Experimental Effects and Process-Outcome Relationships." *R & D Report* no. 4071, vol. I. Austin, Texas: Research and Development Center for Teacher Education, University of Texas at Austin, 1978.

Anderson, R. C., and W. B. Biddle. "On Asking People Questions about What They Are Reading." In *The Psychology of Learning and Motivation: Advances in Research and Theory*, vol. 9, edited by G. H. Bower. New York: Academic Press, Inc. 1975.

Andrews, Jerry W., C. Robert Blackmon, and James A. Mackey. "Preservice Performance and the National Teacher Exams." *Phi Delta Kappan* **61** (January 1980): 358–359.

Anyon, Jean. "Elementary Social Studies Textbooks and Legitimating Knowledge." *Theory and Research in Social Education* **6** (September 1978): 40–55.

Applebee, Arthur N. "Writing." In *Developing Basic Skills Programs in Secondary Schools*, edited by Daisy G. Wallace, pp. 59–70. Alexandria, Va.: Association for Supervision and Curriculum Development, 1981.

Arbuthnot, Jack Braeden, and David Faust. *Teaching Moral Reasoning: Theory and Practice*. New York: Harper & Row Publishers, 1981.

Arlin, M. "Teacher Transition Can Disrupt Time Flow in Classrooms." *American Education Research Journal* **16** (1979): 42–56.

Armbruster, Bonnie B., and Thomas H. Anderson. "Research Synthesis on Study Skills." *Educational Leadership* **39** (November 1981): 154–156.

Association for Supervision and Curriculum Development. "Synthesis of Research on Staff Development." *Educational Leadership* **38** (November 1980): 182–185.

Association for Supervision and Curriculum Development. *ASCD Update* **24** (March 1982).

Austin, Mary C., and Coleman Morrison. *The First R: The Harvard Report on Reading in the Elementary Schools*. New York: Macmillan Publishing Company, 1963.

Ausubel, D. P., and F. G. Robinson. *School Learning*. New York: Holt, Rinehart and Winston, 1969.

Barnett, Carol B. "Sexism in the Curriculum: A Study of Discrimination." In *Curriculum Handbook*: The Disciplines, Current Movements, and Instructional Methodology. Edited by Louis J. Rubin. Boston: Allyn & Bacon, Inc., 1977.

Barr, Robert D. "Alternatives for the Eighties: A Second Decade of Development." *Phi Delta Kappan* **62**(8) (April 1981): 570–573.

Barr, Robert E., James L. Barth, and S. Samuel Shermis. "Defining the Social Studies." *National Council Social Studies Bulletin* **51** (1977).

Barrows, T. S., and A. Jungleblut. "Children's Attitudes Toward and Perceptions of Other Nations and Other Peoples." Paper presented at the American Education Research Association meeting, San Francisco, Calif., April 1976.

Battle, E., and J. Rotter. "Children's Feelings of Personal Control As Related to Social Class and Ethnic Group." *Journal of Personality* **31** (1963): 482–490.

Bayles, E. *Democratic Educational Theory*. New York: Harper & Row, Publishers, 1960.

Beane, James A., Richard P. Lipka, and Joan W. Ludewig. "Interpreting the Research on Self-Concept." *Educational Leadership* **38** (October 1980): 84–89.

Benjamin, Harold. *The Saber-Tooth Curriculum*. New York: McGraw-Hill Book Company, 1939.

Bents, R. H., and K. R. Howey. "Staff Development—Change in the Individual." In *Staff Development/Organization Development*, by Association of Supervision and Curriculum Development, pp. 11–36. Alexandria, Virginia, 1981.

Bentzen, M. *Changing Schools: The Magic Feather Principle*. New York: McGraw-Hill Book Company, 1974.

Best, J. W. *Research in Education*. 4th ed. Englewood Cliffs, N.J.: Prentice-Hall, Inc., 1981.

Bethel, Lowell J. "Tailoring Inservice Training in Science to Elementary Teachers' Needs." *Phi Delta Kappan* **63** (February 1982): 416.

Blatt, M., and L. Kohlberg. "The Effects of Classroom Moral Discussion upon Children's Level of Moral Judgment." *Journal of Moral Education* **4** (1974): 129–161.

Block, James H. "Motivation, Evaluation, and Mastery Learning." *UCLA Educator* **19** (Winter 1977): 31–36.

Block, James H. "Success Rate." In *Time To Learn*, edited by Carolyn Denham and Ann Lieberman, pp. 95–106. Washington, D.C.: California Commission for Teacher Preparation and Licensing and National Institute of Education, 1980.

Bloom, Benjamin S. "The New Direction in Education Research: Alterable Variables." *Phi Delta Kappan* **61** (1980): 382–385.

Bloom, Benjamin S. *Stability and Change in Human Characteristics*. New York: John Wiley & Sons, Inc., 1964.

Bloom, Benjamin S., ed. *Taxonomy of Educational Objectives: Handbook I: Cognitive Domain*. New York: David McKay Co., Inc., 1956.

Bloom, Robert B. "Teachers and Students in Conflict: The CREED Approach." *Phi Delta Kappan* **61** (May 1980): 624–626.

Blough, G. O., and J. Schwartz. *Elementary School Science and How to Teach It*. 6th ed. New York: Holt, Rinehart and Winston, 1979.

Blumenberg, Eleanor. "Responses to Racism: How Far Have We Come?" In *Racism and Sexism: Responding to the Challenge*, NCSS Bulletin 61, edited by Richard L. Simms and Gloria Contreras, pp. 23–44. Washington, D.C.: National Council Social Studies, 1979.

Boyle, David, and Robert L. Lathrop. "The IMPACT Experience: An Evaluation." *Music Educators Journal* **59** (January 1973): 42–47.

Bremer, John, and Michael VonMoschzisker. *The School* Without *Walls*. New York: Holt, Rinehart and Winston, 1971.

Brooks, Martin, Esther Fusco, and Jacqueline Grennon. "Cognitive Levels Matching." *Educational Leadership* **40** (May 1983) 4–8.

Brophy, J. E., and C. M. Evertson. *Learning From Teaching, A Developmental Perspective*. Boston: Allyn & Bacon, Inc., 1976.

Bruner, J. "The Act of Discovery." In *Readings in Contemporary Psychology in Education*, edited by C. E. Meyers and R. G. McIntyre. New York: Selected Academic Readings, 1966.

Bucher, Charles A. *Foundations of Physical Education*. 7th ed. St. Louis: The C. V. Mosby Company, 1975.

Bundy, Robert F. "Accountability Is Self-Defeating." In *Taking Sides: Clashing Views on Controversial Educational Issues*, edited by James W. Noll. Guilford, Conn.: Dushkin Publishing Co., Inc., 1980.

Bussis, A. M. "Burn It At the Casket: Research, Reading Instruction, and Children's Learning of the First R." *Phi Delta Kappan* **64** (December 1982): 237–241.

California State Department of Education. *Art Education Framework for California Public Schools K–12*. Sacramento, Calif.: California State Department of Education, 1971.

California State Department of Education. *Music Framework for California Public Schools, K–12*. Sacramento, Calif.: California State Department of Education, 1971.

California State Department of Education. *Physical Education Framework for California Public Schools, K–12*. Sacramento, Calif.: California State Department of Education, 1973.

California State Department of Education. *History-Social Science Framework for California Public Schools*. Sacramento, Calif.: California State Department of Education, 1981.

Cardinell, Charles F. "Teacher Burnout: An Analysis." *Action In Teacher Education* **2** (Fall 1980): 9–15.

Carey, James O., Michael Hannafin, and Michael Albright. "Effects of Different Media Presentations and Messages on Children's Learning of Information." Presentation at American Educational Research Association Annual Meeting, Los Angeles, 1981.

Carney, Loretta J. "Responses to Sexism: Two Steps Forward and One Back?" In *Racism and Sexism: Responding to the Challenge*, NCSS Bulletin 61, edited by Richard L. Simms and Gloria Contreras, pp. 45–64. Washington, D.C.: National Council Social Studies, 1980.

Carroll, John B. "Psycholinguistics and the Study and Teaching of Reading." In *Aspects of Reading Instruction*, edited by Susanna Pflaum-Connor, pp. 11–43. Berkeley: McCutchan Publishing Corporation, 1978.

Carroll, Lewis. *Alice in Wonderland*. Philadelphia: John C. Winston Co., 1957.

Case, Barbara J. "Lasting Alternatives: A Lesson in Survival." *Phi Delta Kappan* **62** (April 1981): 554–557.

"Cash-Laden Foreign Interests Make U.S. Energy Firms Takeover Targets." *Los Angeles Times*, July 7, 1981.

Central Eastern Regional Educational Laboratory. *CEMERL*. St. Louis, Mo., 1971.

Chapin, J., and R. Gross. *Teaching Social Studies Skills*. Boston: Little, Brown and Company, 1973.

Chomsky, Carol. "Language Development after Age Six." In *Language and the Language Arts*, edited by Johanna S. DeStefano and Sharon E. Fox, pp. 59–62. Boston: Little, Brown and Company, 1974.

"Citizenship Development Program." *Quarterly Report*,

Mershon Center, Ohio State University, **2** (Winter 1977).

Clark, Richard E. "Is Achievement Enjoyable?" Paper presented at the American Educational Research Association national convention, Los Angeles, April 1981.

Cobb, Russell L. "Perspective Ability and Map Conceptualization in Elementary School Children." *Journal of Social Studies Research*, University of Georgia, **1** (Winter 1977): 10–19.

Cohen, Elaine G. "Constructing A Multiability Curriculum." Tape Recording 612-20226. Alexandria, Va.: Association of Supervision and Curriculum Development, 1981.

Cohen, Elizabeth P., and R. S. Gainer. *Art: Another Language for Learning*. New York: Citation Press, 1976.

Coleman, J. S. *Equality of Educational Opportunity*. Washington, D.C.: U.S. Department of Health, Education and Welfare, Office of Education, Government Printing Office, 1966.

Coles, Robert. "The South Goes North." In *Children of Crises*, vol. III. Boston: Little, Brown and Company, 1967.

Combs, Arthur W. "What the Future Demands of Education." *Phi Delta Kappan* **62** (January 1981): 369–372.

"The Computer Moves In." *Time Magazine*, January 3, 1983, pp. 12–24.

Copeland, R. W. *Mathematics and the Elementary Teacher*. 4th ed. New York: Macmillan Publishing Company, 1982.

Conran, Patricia C., and Aurora Chase. "The Extended-Year Program in Suburban Chicago: A Different Approach to Inservice Training." *Phi Delta Kappan* **63** (February 1982): 398–399.

Cooper, L., D. W. Johnson, R. Johnson, and F. Wilderson. "Effects of Cooperative, Competitive, and Individualistic Experiences on Interpersonal Attraction Among Heterogeneous Peers." *Journal of Social Psychology* **111** (1980): 243–252.

Culbertson, F. M. "Modification of an Emotionally Held Attitude Through Role-Playing." *Journal of Abnormal Social Psychology* **54** (1957): 230–233.

Danoff, Malcolm N. *Evaluation of the Impact of ESEA Title VII Spanish/English Bilingual Education Program: Overview of Study and Findings*. Palo Alto: American Institutes for Research, 1978.

Davis, R. B. "Response." In *Mathematics Education Research: Implications for the 80's*, edited by E. Fennema, pp. 149–153. Reston, Va.: Association for Supervision and Curriculum Development, 1981.

"Day 11—Is Society Unraveling? British Riots Pose a Grim Question." *Los Angeles Times*, July 13, 1981.

Denham, Carolyn, and Ann Lieberman, eds. *Time To Learn*. Washington, D.C.: National Institute of Education, U.S. Department of Education, 1980.

DeRose, J. V., J. David Lockard, and L. G. Paldy. "The Teacher is the Key: A Report on Three NSF Studies." In *What Are the Needs in Precollege Science, Mathematics, and Social Science Education: Views From the Field*, pp. 43–52. Washington, D.C.: National Science Foundation, Office of Program Integration, Directorate for Science Education, SE 80–9.

DeStefano, Johanna S., and Sharon E. Fox. *Language and the Language Arts*. Boston: Little, Brown and Company, 1974.

DeVault, M. Vere. "Computers." In *Mathematics Education Research: Implications for the 80's*, edited by E. Fennema, pp. 139–148. Reston, Va.: Association for Supervision and Curriculum Development, 1981.

deVries, Hubert A. *Physiology of Exercise for Physical Education and Athletics*. Dubuque, Iowa: Wm. C. Brown Co., 1966.

Dewey, John. *How We Think*. Boston: D. C. Heath & Company, 1933.

"Do Noisy Schools Make a Difference in Student Achievement?" *ASCD Update*, Association for Supervision and Curriculum Development, **24** (November 1982): 7.

"Do Students Learn from Seatwork?" *Communication Quarterly*, The Institute for Research on Teaching, Michigan State University, **5** (Summer 1982): 2.

Donoghue, Mildred R. *The Child and the English Language Arts*. Dubuque, Iowa: Wm. C. Brown Co., 1979.

Dunfee, Maxine, and Helen Sagal. *Social Studies Through Problem Solving, a Challenge to Elementary School Teachers*. New York: Holt, Rinehart & Winston, Inc., 1966.

Dunkin, M., and B. Biddle. *The Study of Teaching*. New York: Holt, Rinehart and Winston, 1974.

Dunn, Rita, and Kenneth Dunn. *Practical Approaches to Individualizing Instruction*. West Nyack, N.Y.: Parker Publishing Co., 1972.

Dunn, Rita, and Kenneth Dunn. *Teaching Students Through Their Individual Learning Styles: A Practical Approach*. Reston, Va.: Reston Publishing Co., Inc., 1978.

Dweck, Carol S. "Learned Helplessness and Negative Evaluation." *UCLA Educator* **19** (Winter 1977): 44–49.

Edelfelt, Roy A. "Critical Issues in Developing Teacher

Centers." *Phi Delta Kappan* **63** (February 1982): 390–393.

Educational Policies Commission of National Education Association. *Education for All American Youth.* Washington, D.C.: 1944.

Educational Policies Commission of National Education Association. *Purpose of Education in American Democracy.* Washington, D.C.: 1938.

Eisner, Elliot. "Mind as Cultural Achievement." *Educational Leadership* 38 (March 1981) 466–471.

Elkin, Frederick. *The Child and Society: The Process of Socialization.* New York: Random House, Inc., 1968.

Ellis, A. K., and A. D. Glenn. "Effects of Real and Continued Problem-Solving on Economic Learning." *The Journal of Economic Education* **8** (Spring 1977): 216–222.

Ellis, Arthur K. *Teaching and Learning Elementary Social Studies.* 2nd ed. Boston: Allyn and Bacon, Inc., 1981.

Emmer, Edmund T., and Carolyn M. Evertson. "Synthesis of Research on Classroom Management." *Educational Leadership* **38** (January 1981): 342–347.

English, Raymond. "Ten Discoveries About Basic Learning." *Social Education,* **41** (February 1977): 106.

Esposito, James P. "School Climate Affects Teacher Absenteeism." *Phi Delta Kappan* **62** (February 1981): 458.

Evertson, C. M., and C. M. Anderson. "Beginning School." *Educational Horizons* **57** (1979): 164–168.

Fennema, E. "The Sex Factor." In *Mathematics Education Research: Implications for the 80's,* edited by E. Fennema, pp. 92-104. Alexandria, Va.: Association for Supervision and Curriculum Development, 1981.

Fineberg, Carol. "Arts in Education–Beyond Rhetoric." *Educational Leadership* **37** (April 1980): 583–587.

Fisher, Charles W., David C. Berliner, Nikola N. Filby, Richard Marhave, Leonard S. Cohen, and Marilyn M. Dishaw. "Teacher Behaviors, Academic Learning Time, and Student Activities: An Overview." In *Time To Learn,* pp. 7–32. Edited by Carolyn Denham and Ann Lieberman. Washington, D.C.: Commission for Teacher Preparation and Licencing, 1980.

Fisher, W. W. *Geo-cepts.* Chicago: Denoyer-Geppert, 1977.

Flavell, John J. *The Developmental Psychology of Jean Piaget.* Princeton, N.J.: Van Nostrand Reinhold Company, 1963.

Florida Department of Education. *The Florida Catalog of Art Objectives.* Tallahasee, Fla.: Department of Education, 1974.

"Florida Puts Student Basic Skills to Test." *Los Angeles Times,* May 12, 1978.

"Foreign Firms Build More Houses in U.S., Upset Some Americans." *Wall Street Journal,* July 7, 1981.

Friedman, H., and P. Friedman. "Frequency and Types of Teacher Reinforcement Given to Lower- and Middle-class Students." Paper presented at American Educational Research Association, 1973.

Galbraith, R. E., and T. M. Jones. "Teaching Strategies for Moral Dilemmas." *Social Education,* **39** (January 1975): 16–22.

Gallagher, Arlene F. "Premises for Law." In *Social Studies and the Elementary Teacher: Promises and Practices,* NCSS Bulletin 53, edited by W. W. Joyce and Frank C. Ryan, pp. 106–111. Washington, D.C.: National Council Social Studies, 1977.

Gallahue, D. L., P. H. Werner, and G. Luedke. *A Conceptual Approach to Moving and Learning.* New York: John Wiley & Sons, Inc., 1975.

Gallup, G. "The 12th Annual Gallup Poll of the Public's Attitudes Toward the Public Schools." *Phi Delta Kappan* **62** (September 1980): 33–46.

Gallup, G. "The 13th Annual Gallup Poll of the Public's Attitudes Toward the Public Schools." *Phi Delta Kappan* **63** (September 1981): 33–47.

Gega, P. C. *Science in Elementary Education.* 3d ed. New York: John Wiley & Sons, Inc., 1977.

Gilliam, Thomas. "Fitness Through Youth Sports: Myth or Reality?" *Journal of Physical Education and Recreation* **49** (March 1978): 41–42.

Gilliom, M. Eugene. *Practical Methods for Social Studies.* Belmont, Calif.: Wadsworth Publishing Co., Inc., 1977.

Glenn, A. D., and A. K. Ellis. "Direct and Indirect Methods of Teaching Problem Solving to Elementary School Children." *Social Education* **46** (February 1982): 134–136.

Glick, Harriet M., and Marsha Schubert. "Mainstreaming: An Unmandated Challenge." *Educational Leadership* **38** (January 1981): 326–329.

Good, T. L., and D. A. Grouws. "Process-Product Research." In *Mathematics Education Research: Implications for the 80's,* edited by E. Fennema, pp. 82–91. Alexandria, Va.: Association for Supervision and Curriculum Development, 1981.

Goodall, Robert, and Les Brown. "Understanding Teacher Stress." *Action in Teacher Education* **2** (Fall 1980): 17–22.

Goodlad, John I. *Dynamics of Educational Change: Toward Responsive Schools.* New York: McGraw-Hill Book Company, 1975.

Goodlad, John I. "Personalized Education is Possible." In *Taking Sides: Clashing Views on Controversial Educational Issues*, edited by James W. Noll, pp. 279; 288–292. Guilford, Conn.: Dushkin Publishing Co., Inc., 1980.

Goodman, Kenneth S. "Reading: A Psycholinguistic Guessing Game." In *Theoretical Models and Processes of Reading*, 2nd ed., edited by Harry Singer and Robert B. Ruddell. Newark, Del.: International Reading Association, 1976.

Gordon, Alice. *Games for Growth*. Palo Alto, CA: Science Research Associates, 1970.

Graves, Donald H. "An Examination of the Writing Processes of Seven-Year-Old Children." *Research in the Teaching of English* (Winter 1975): 235.

Greene, David M., and Alan H. Jones. "Professional Standards, Problems, and Needs." Sacramento, Calif.: Commission for Teacher Preparation and Licensing, May 27, 1981. Unpublished position paper.

Greer, W. Dwaine. "Curriculum in the Visual Arts." In *Curriculum Handbook: The Disciplines, Current Movements, and Instructional Methodology*, edited by Louis Rubin, pp. 196–203. Boston: Allyn & Bacon, Inc., 1977.

Grover, George A. "New York State's New Regulations Governing Physical Education." *Journal of Health, Physical Education, and Recreation* **46** (September 1975).

Hall, Edward T. "Listening Behavior—Some Cultural Differences," from *Language and the Language Arts*, ed. Johanna S. DeStefano and Sharon E. Fox. Boston: Little, Brown, 1974.

Hall, J. Tillman, Nancy H. Sweeny, and Jody Hall Esser. *Physical Education in the Elementary Schools*. Santa Monica, Calif.: Goodyear Publishing Co., Inc., 1980.

Hanes, M. L., E. G. Wangberg, and P. Yoder. "University/School District Partnership in Professional Development: A Model." *Phi Delta Kappan* **63** (February 1982): 388–389.

Hanna, Paul. "Design for a Social Studies Program." In *Department Elementary School Principals*, pp. 28–46. Washington, D.C.: National Education Association, Department of Elemantary School Principals, 1965.

Hanna, Paul R. "Revising the Social Studies: What Is Needed?" *Social Education* **27** (April 1963): 190–196.

Harris, N. E. "A Study of Certain Critical Thinking Skills Among Fifth Graders in the Area of Propaganda in Advertising." Unpublished doctoral dissertation, Boston University School of Education, Boston, Mass., 1975.

Helgeson, S. L., P. E. Blosser, and R. W. Howe. *The Status of Precollege Science, Mathematics, and Social Science Education: 1955–1975*. Vol. I. Washington, D.C.: Science Education National Science Foundation Report SE 78-73, U.S. Government Printing Office, 1977.

Hertzog, Hillary S. "The Effect of Computer Assisted Instruction in Reading on Fourth and Fifth Grade Disabled Readers." Unpublished master's thesis, University of Southern California, 1982.

Hiebert, J. "Children's Thinking." In *Mathematics Education Research: Implications for the 80's*, edited by E. Fennema, pp. 41–61. Alexandria, Va.: Association for Supervision and Curriculum Development, 1981.

Hofferth, Sandra L. "Day Care in the Next Decade: 1980–1990." *Journal of Marriage and the Family* **41** (August 1979): 649–656.

Holbrook, Leona. *Current Status of Physical Education, Sport, and Active Recreation:* Documentary statement. Washington, D.C.: American Alliance for Health, Physical Education, Recreation, and Dance, International Council on Health, Physical Education, and Recreation, 1977. ERIC Document Reproduction Service, ED 180–998.

Holly, Mary L. "Teachers' Views on Inservice Training." *Phi Delta Kappan* **63** (February 1982): 417–418.

Horwitz, R. A. 'Psychological Effects of the Open Classroom." *Review of Educational Research* **49** (1979): 71–85.

Hullfish, G. H., and P. G. Smith. *Reflective Thinking: The Method of Education*. New York: Dodd, Mead & Company, 1961.

Hunsicker, Paul, and Guy Reiff. *AAHER Youth Fitness Test Manual*. Washington, D.C.: American Alliance for Health, Physical Education, and Recreation, 1975.

Hunt, David E. *From Psychology Theory to Educational Practice: Implementation of a Matching Model*. ERIC Document Reproduction Service ED 068-438. Washington, D.C.: Educational Research Information Center, U.S. Office of Education, April 1968.

Hunt, Kellogg W. *Grammatical Structures Written at Three Grade Levels*, Research Report No. 3. Urbana, Ill.: National Council of Teachers of English, 1965.

Hyman, R. T. *Strategic Questioning*. Englewood Cliffs, N.J.: Prentice-Hall, Inc., 1979.

Instructional Planning Division. *Elementary School Curriculum: A Balanced Program*. Los Angeles: Los Angeles Unified School District, 1979.

Iverson, Barbara K. "Play, Creativity, and Schools Today." *Educational Leadership*, **63** (June 1982): 693–694.

Janis, I. L., and B. T. King. "The Influence of Role-

Playing on Opinion Change." *Journal of Abnormal Social Psychology*. **49** (1954): 211–218.

Jarolimek, John. "The Basics in Social Studies: Implication for the Preparation of Teachers." In *Competency Based Teacher Education: Professionalizing Social Studies Teaching*, Bulletin #65, edited by Dell Felder, pp. 17–36. Washington, D.C.: National Council of Social Studies, 1978.

Jarolimek, John, and D. C. Foster. *Teaching and Learning in the Elementary School*. 2d ed. New York: Macmillan Publishing Company, 1981.

Jencks, Christopher, et al. *Inequality, A reassessment of the Effect of Family and Schooling in America*. New York: Basic Books, Inc., Publishers, 1972.

Johnson, D. W., and R. T. Johnson. "Cooperative Learning, Powerful Sciencing." *Science and Children* **17** (November/December 1979): 26–27.

Johnson, R. E. "The Relationship Between Social Studies and Reading." *Social Studies Review* **13** (Fall 1973): 24–29.

Joyce, B. *New Strategies for Social Education*. Chicago: Science Research Associates, Inc., 1973.

Joyce, B., and B. Showers. "Improving Inservice Training: The Messages of Research." *Educational Leadership* **37** (February 1980): 379–385.

Joyce, B., and M. Weil. *Models of Teaching*. 2nd ed. Englewood Cliffs, N.J.: Prentice-Hall, Inc., 1980.

Kamii, C. "Encouraging Thinking in Mathematics." *Phi Delta Kappan* **64** (December 1982): 247–251.

Keislar, Evan R. "The Teacher As Internal Evaluator of Student Performance." *UCLA Educator* **19** (Winter 1977): 57–62.

Kennedy, D. K., and P. Weener. "Visual and Auditory Training with Cloze Procedure to Improve Reading and Listening Comprehension." *Reading Research Quarterly* **8** (Summer 1973): 524–541.

Kepler, Karen B. "BTES: Implication for Preservice Education of Teachers." In *Time To Learn*, edited by Carolyn Denham and Ann Lieberman, pp. 139–158. Washington, D.C.: Commission for Teacher Preparation and Licensing, 1980.

King, Nancy. *Giving Form to Feeling*. New York: Drama Book Specialists, 1975.

Klein, M. Frances. *About Learning Material*. Washington, D.C.: Association for Supervision and Curriculum Development, 1978.

Kohlberg, Lawrence. "Moral Stages and Moralization: The Cognitive-Developmental Approach." In *Moral Development and Behavior: Theory, Research, and Social Issues*. Edited by Thomas Lickona. New York: Holt, Rinehart & Winston, 1976.

Kolb, David D. *Learning Style Inventory Technical Manual*. Boston: McBer & Co., 1978.

Kossack, Sharon W., and Woods, Sandra L. "Teacher Burnout: Diagnosis, Prevention, Remediation." *Action In Teacher Education* **2** (Fall 1980): 29–35.

Kounin, Jacob S. *Discipline and Group Management in Classrooms*. New York: Holt, Rinehart and Winston, 1970.

Kounin, Jacob S., and P. H. Doyle. "Degree of Continuity of a Lesson's Signal System and the Task Involvement of Children." *Journal of Educational Psychology* **67** (1975): 159–164.

Kounin, Jacob S., and Lawrence W. Sherman. "School Environments as Behavior Settings." *Theory Into Practice* **18** (June 1979): 145–151.

Kozol, J. *Children of the Revolution: A Yankee Teacher in the Cuban Schools*. New York: Delacorte Press, 1978.

Krathwohl, D. R., B. S. Bloom, and B. B. Masia. *Taxonomy of Educational Objectives. Handbook II: Affective Domain*. New York: David McKay Co., Inc., 1964.

Kraus, Hans. *The Cause, Prevention, and Treatment of Backache, Stress, and Tension*. New York: Pocket Books, 1969.

Kuntzleman, Charles T., and Beth Kuntzleman. *Fitness with Fun*. (National Board of YMCA.) Spring Arbor, Michigan: Arbor Press, 1978.

Labov, William. "The Logic of Nonstandard English." In *Language and the Language Arts*, edited by Johanna S. DeStefano and Sharon E. Fox, pp. 134–147. Boston: Little, Brown and Company, 1974.

Lamb, Charles E. "Application of Piaget's Theory to Mathematics Education." In *Piagetian Theory and the Helping Professions*, pp. 191–199. Los Angeles: University of Southern California, 1977.

Land, Lois R., and Mary A. Vaughan. *Music in Today's Classroom: Creating, Listening, Performing*. 2d ed. New York: Harcourt Brace Jovanovich, Inc., 1978.

"Learning to Survive in the Classroom." *The American Teacher* **65** (February 1981): 6–7.

Lemlech, Johanna K. *Classroom Management*. New York: Harper & Row, Publishers, 1979.

Lemlech, Johanna K. "Social Participation Skills in Elementary Classrooms." *Social Studies Review* **16** (Fall 1976): 43–50.

Lemlech, Johanna K., and Merle B. Marks. *The American Teacher: 1776–1976*. Bloomington, Indiana: Phi Delta Kappa Educational Foundation, 1976.

Lemlech, Johanna K., and Sue Wood. "Evaluation of the Mid-Valley YMCA Feelin' Good Program, Grades 2–4." Unpublished.

Lesser, G., G. Fiefer, and D. Clark. "Mental Abilities of Children in Different Social and Cultural Groups." *Monograph of the Society for Research in Child Development*, Report No. CRP-1635, 1964.

Lessinger, Leon N. "Accountability Insures Improvement." In *Taking Sides: Clashing Views on Controversial Educational Issues*, edited by James W. Noll, pp. 151–172. Guilford, Conn.: Dushkin Publishing, Inc., 1980.

Lewis, J., and I. C. Potter. *The Teaching of Science in the Elementary School*. 2d ed. Englewood Cliffs, N.J.: Prentice-Hall, Inc., 1970.

Lieberman, Ann, and L. Miller. "Synthesis of Research on Improving Schools." *Educational Leadership* **38** (April 1981): 583–586.

Lieberman, Myron. "Against the Grain." *Phi Delta Kappan* **61** (May 1980): 635–637.

Lippitt, Ronald, Robert Fox, and Lucille Schaible. *The Teacher's Role in Social Science Investigation*. Chicago: Science Research Associates, Inc., 1969.

Little, Timothy. "A Simulation to Launch a Study of Law and Consumerism." *Social Education* **39** (March 1975): 159–162.

Lockhead, Jack. "Research Synthesis on Problem Solving." *Educational Leadership* **39** (October 1981): 68–70.

Long, Sandra M. "The 1980 Census: Implications for Education." *Phi Delta Kappan* **62** (May 1981): 619.

Los Angeles Unified School District. *Elementary School Curriculum, A Balanced Program*, publication no. X-107. Los Angeles: Los Angeles Unified School District, 1979.

Los Angeles Unified School District. *Performing Arts*. Los Angeles, Calif.: The Author, 1980.

Lotto, Linda S. "What Research Says about Beginning Reading." In *Classroom-Relevant Research in the Language Arts*, edited by Harold G. Shane and James Walden, pp. 61–72. Washington, D.C.: Association for Supervision and Curriculum Development, 1978.

Lowenfield, Viktor. *Creative and Mental Growth*. New York: Macmillan Publishing Company, 1947.

McAdam, R. E., and Carleen Dodson. *Concepts and Practices in Elementary Activity Programs*. Springfield, Ill.: Charles C. Thomas, Publisher, 1981.

McGreal, T. L. "Helping Teachers Set Goals." *Educational Leadership* **37** (February 1980): 414–419.

McKinney, James D. "Problem Solving Strategies in Reflective and Impulsive Children." *Journal of Educational Psychology* **67** (December 1975): 807–820.

McNeil, J. D., L. Donant, and M. C. Alkin. *How to Teach Reading Successfully*. Boston: Little, Brown and Company, 1980.

MacNaughton, D. E. "The Relationship Between Critical Thinking and Selected Variables." Unpublished doctoral dissertation, University of Calgary, Alberta, Canada, 1976.

Madden, N. A., and R. E. Slavin. "Cooperative Learning and Social Acceptance of Mainstreamed Academically Handicapped Students." Paper presented at the Annual Convention of American Psychology Association, Montreal, Canada, 1980.

Maehr, M. L., and D. D. Sjogren. "Atkinson's Theory of Achievement Motivation: First Step Toward a Theory of Academic Motivation?" *Review of Educational Research* **41** (1971): 143–161.

Marcus, M. "The Cinquain as a Diagnostic and Instructional Technique." *Elementary English* **41** (April 1974): 561–566.

Massialas, B. G., and B. Cox. *Inquiry in Social Studies*. New York: McGraw-Hill Book Company, 1966.

Mathematics Framework and the 1980 Addendum for California Public Schools. Sacramento, Calif.: California State Department of Education, 1982.

Mehlinger, Howard D. Foreword. In *Building Rationales for Citizenship Education*, Bulletin No. 52, edited by James P. Shaver, p. iii. Washington, D.C.: National Council on Social Studies, 1977.

Mercer, Jane. "Sociocultural Factors in Labeling Mental Retardates." *Peabody Journal of Education* **48** (April 1971): 19.

Michaelis, John, Ruth H. Grossman, and Lloyd F. Scott. *New Dimension for Elementary Curriculum and Instruction*. New York: McGraw-Hill Book Company, 1975.

Michigan Department of Education. *Minimal Performance Objectives for Art Education in Michigan*. Lansing, Mich.: The Author, 1974.

Miller, Lynn. "BTES: Implications for Staff Development." In *Time To Learn*, edited by Carolyn Denham and Ann Lieberman, pp. 159–172. Washington, D.C.: Commission for Teacher Preparation and Licensing, 1980.

Mitsakos, Charles L. "A Global Education Program Can Make a Difference." *Theory and Research in Social Education* **6** (March 1978): 1–15.

Moffett, James. *A Student-Centered Language Arts Curriculum, Grades K–13: A Handbook for Teachers*. Boston: Houghton Mifflin Company, 1968.

Moffett, James, and Betty Jane Wagner. *Student-Centered Language Arts and Reading, K–13, A Handbook for Teachers*. 2d ed. Boston: Houghton Mifflin Company, 1976.

Morris, Jeanne B. "A survey of Multiethnic Educational

Attitudes and Practices of Early Childhood Teachers." Unpublished doctoral dissertation, University of Illinois, 1979.

Moses, Nelson. "Using Piagetian Principles to Guide Instruction of the Learning Disabled." *Topics in Learning and Learning Disabilities* **1** (April 1981): 11–19.

Newmann, Fred M., and Donald W. Oliver. "Case Study Approaches in Social Studies." *Social Education* **31** (February 1967): 108–113.

Northern, E. F. "The Trend Toward Competency Testing of Teachers." *Phi Delta Kappan* **61** (January 1980): 359.

Nye, R. E., and V. T. Nye. *Essentials of Teaching Elementary School Music*. Englewood Cliffs, N. J.: Prentice-Hall, Inc., 1974.

O'Neill, William F. *Educational Ideologies. Contemporary Expressions of Educational Philosophy*. Santa Monica, Calif.: Goodyear Publishing Co., Inc., 1981.

Ornstein, Allan C., and Daniel V. Levine. *An Introduction to the Foundations of Education*. 2d ed. Boston: Houghton Mifflin Company, 1981.

Ornstein, Allan, and Harry L. Miller. *Looking Into Teaching*. Chicago: Rand McNally, 1980.

Otto, W., R. Rude, and D. L. Spiegel. *How To Teach Reading*. Reading, Mass.: Addison-Wesley Publishing Co., Inc., 1979.

Patton, William E. "Updating the Outdated in Textbooks." In *Improving the Use of Social Studies Textbooks*, Bulletin 63, edited by William E. Patton, pp. 1–8. Washington, D.C.: National Council of Social Studies, 1980.

Peet, Bill. *The Wump World*. Boston: Houghton Mifflin Company, 1970.

Peterson, Penelope L. "Direct Instruction: Effective for What and for Whom?" *Educational Leadership* **37** (October 1979): 46–48.

Peterson, Penelope L., and T. C. Janicki. "Individual Characteristics and Children's Learning in Large-Group and Small-Group Approaches." *Journal of Educational Psychology* **71** (October 1979): 677–687.

Petrie, Thomas A. "Prejudice and the Classroom." In *Prejudice Project*, edited by AntiDefamation League and University of Nebraska at Omaha, pp. 47–50. Omaha: AntiDefamation League and University of Nebraska, 1980.

Piaget, Jean. "How Children Form Mathematical Concepts." In *Mathematics in Elementary Education*, edited by Nicholas J. Vigilante, pp. 135–141. New York: Macmillan Publishing Company, 1969.

Popham, W. James, and Stuart C. Rankin. "Minimum Competency Tests Spur Instructional Improvement." *Phi Delta Kappan*, **62** (May 1981): 637–639.

Postman, Neil, and Charles Weingartner. *Teaching as a Subversive Activity*. New York: Delacorte Press, 1969.

President's Commission on National Goals. *Goals for Americans*. Englewood Cliffs, N.J.: Prentice-Hall, Inc., 1960.

President's Council on Physical Fitness. *Statement of Basic Beliefs*. Washington, D.C.: Bureau of Publications, 1971.

Proceedings, White House Conference on Education. Washington, D.C.: U.S. Government Printing Office, 1955.

Prudden, Bonnie. *How to Keep Your Family Fit and Healthy*. New York: Reader's Digest Press, 1975.

Prudden, Bonnie. *Teenage Fitness*. New York: Harper & Row, Publishers, 1965.

Raebeck, L., and L. Wheeler. *New Approaches to Music in the Elementary School*. 4th ed. Dubuque, Indiana: William C. Brown Company, Publishers, 1980.

Ramsey, Imogene. "Comparison of First Negro Dialect Speakers' Comprehension of Standard English and Negro Dialect." *Elementary English* **49** (May 1972): 688–696.

Ravitch, Diane. "The Meaning of the New Coleman Report." *Phi Delta Kappan* **62** (June 1981): 718–720.

Raywid, Mary Anne. "The First Decade of Public School Alternatives." *Phi Delta Kappan* **62** (April 1981): 551–554.

Reading Framework for California Public Schools, Kindergarten Through Grade Twelve. Sacramento: California State Department of Education, 1980.

Renzulli, Joseph, and Linda H. Smith. *Learning Styles Inventory: A Measure of Student Preference for Instructional Techniques*. Mansfield Center, Conn.: Creative Learning Press, Inc., 1978.

Richardson, P. A., R. S. Weinberg, L. Bruya, William Baun, A. Jackson, I. Caton, and Loma Bruya. "Physical and Psychological Characteristics of Young Children in Sports: A Descriptive Profile." *The Physical Educator* **37** (December 1980): 187–191.

Rist, R. "Student Social Class and Teacher Expectations: The Self Fulfilling Prophecy in Ghetto Education." *Harvard Educational Review* **40** (1970): 411–451.

Robiner, Linda G. "Education for Aesthetic Awareness: A Powerful Process." *Phi Delta Kappan* **61** (April 1980): 547–548.

Robinson, F. P. *Effective Study*. New York: Harper & Row, Publishers, 1946.

Rosenshine, Barak V. "Classroom Instruction." In *The Psychology of Teaching Methods, NSSE 75th Yearbook*. Chicago: University of Chicago Press, 1976.

Rosenshine, Barak V. "Content, Time, and Direct Instruction." In *Research on Teaching: Concepts, Findings, and Implications*, edited by P. L. Peterson and H. J. Walberg. Berkeley, Calif.: McCutchan, 1979.

Rotter, J. "Generalized Expectancies for Internal Versus External Control of Reinforcement." *Psychological Monographs* **80** (1966): 609.

Rowe, M. B. "Science, Silence, and Sanctions." *Science and Children* **6** (1969): 11–13.

Rowe, M. B. "Wait-Time and Rewards as Instructional Variables, Their Influence on Language, Logic, and Fate Control: Part One. Wait-Time." *Journal of Research in Science Teaching* **11** (1974): 81–94.

Rubin, Dorothy. *Teaching Elementary Language Arts*. 2nd ed. New York: Holt, Rinehart and Winston, 1980.

Salerno, Joan. "The Best Laid Plans." In *Vistas*, pp. 2–4. Los Angeles, Calif.: Loyola Marymount University, Spring 1981.

Samuels, S. Jay. "Diagnosing Reading Problems." *Topics in Learning and Learning Disabilities* **2** (January 1983): 1–11.

Samuels, S. Jay. "The Effect of Letter-Name Knowledge on Learning to Read." *American Educational Research Journal* **9** (Winter 1972): 65–74.

Sandler, Martin W. "How to Read Pictures." In *Improving the Use of Social Studies Textbooks*, Bulletin 63, edited by W. E. Patton, pp. 27–34. Washington, D.C.: National Council on Social Studies, 1980.

Sawyer, Diane J., and Sally Lipa. "The Route to Reading: A Perspective." *Topics in Language Disorders* **1** (March 1981): 43–60.

Sayegh, Alia. "Ingredients for Successful Arts Programs." *Educational Leadership* **38** (April 1981): 581, 588.

Schrag, Peter. "End of the Impossible Dream." *Saturday Review*, September 19, 1970.

Schwartz, S. K. "Preschoolers and Politics." In *New Directions in Political Socialization*, edited by D. C. Schwartz and S. K. Schwartz, pp. 229–253. New York: The Free Press, 1975.

Sears, Pauline S. "Evaluation and Motivation: A Critical Review." *UCLA Educator* **19** (Winter 1977): 26–30.

Sedlacek, William E., and Glenwood C. Brooks. *Racism in American Education: A Model for Change*. Chicago: Nelson-Hall, 1976.

Seefeldt, Vern, and John Howbenstricker. "Competitive Athletics for Children—The Michigan Study." *Journal of Physical Education and Recreation* **49** (March 1978): 38–41.

Seeley, David S. "Reducing the Confrontation Over Teacher Accountability." *Phi Delta Kappan* **61**(4) (December 1979): 248–251.

Selman, Robert L., and Marcus Lieberman. "Moral Education in the Primary Grades: An Evaluation of a Developmental Curriculum." *Journal of Educational Psychology* **67** (October 1975): 712–716.

Selye, Hans. *Stress Without Distress*. Philadelphia: J. B. Lippincott Co., 1974.

Shane, Harold G. 'A Curriculum for the New Century." *Phi Delta Kappan* **62** (January 1981): 351–355.

Shane, Harold G. "Education for a New Millenium." Tape recording 612-20246. Alexandria, Va.: Association Supervision Curriculum Development, 225 N. Washington St., 1981.

Shane, Harold G., and M. Bernardine Tabler. "Probable Developments in the Social Sciences and Their Consequences for Educational Content: 1980–2000." Paper presented at UNESCO Symposium, New York, 1979.

Shane, Harold G., and James Walden, eds. *Classroom-Relevant Research in the Language Arts*. Washington, D.C.: Association Supervision Curriculum Development, 1978.

Shaftel, George, and Fannie Shaftel. *Role-Playing for Social Values*. Englewood Cliffs, N.J.: Prentice-Hall, Inc., 1967.

Sharma, Mahesh J. C. "Using Word Problems to Aid Language and Reading Comprehension." *Topics in Learning and Learning Disabilities* **1** (1981): 152–160.

Sherrill, Claudine. *Adapted Physical Education and Recreation*. Dubuque, Iowa: William C. Brown Company, Publishers, 1977.

Sigel, Irving E. "The Piagetian System and the World of Education." In *Studies in Cognitive Development*. Edited by David Elkins and John Flavell. New York: Oxford University Press, 1969.

Silverman, Rita, Naomi Zigmond, Judith Zimmerman, and Ada Vallecorsa. "Improving Written Expression in Learning Disabled Students." *Topics in Language Disorders* **1** (March 1981): 91–99.

Sinatra, Richard. "Brain Research Sheds Light on Language Learning." *Educational Leadership* **40** (May 1983): 9–12.

Singer, H. "Active Comprehension: From Answering to Asking Questions." *The Reading Teacher* **31** (1978): 901–908.

Slavin, Robert E. "Synthesis of Research on Cooperative Learning." *Educational Leadership* **38** (May 1981): 655–660.

Smith, F. *Understanding Reading*. 2nd ed. New York: Holt, Rinehart and Winston, 1978.

Smith, Gerald R., Thomas B. Gregory, and Richard C. Pugh. "Meeting Student Needs: Evidence for the

Superiority of Alternative Schools." *Phi Delta Kappan* **62** (April 1981): 561–564.

Smith, Herbert A. "A Report on the Implications for the Science Community of Three NSF-Supported Studies of the State of Precollege Science Education." In *What Are the Needs in Precollege Science, Mathematics, and Social Science Education? Views From the Field*, pp. 55–78. Washington, D.C.: National Science Foundation, Office of Program Integration, Directorate for Science Education, SE 80-9, 1980.

Smith, N. B. "The Many Faces of Reading Comprehension." *Reading Teacher* 1969: 249–259.

Smith, Vernon, Robert Barr, and Daniel Burke. *Alternatives in Education.* Bloomington, Indiana: Phi Delta Kappa, 1976.

Soar, R. S. Final Report, Follow Through Classroom Process Measurement and Pupil Growth (1970–1971). Gainesville: Institute for the Development of Human Resources, University of Florida, 1973.

Southwest Regional Laboratory for Education, Research, and Development. *Comprehensive Arts Program.* Los Angeles, Calif.: 1981.

Stake, R. E., and J. Easley. "Case Studies in Science Education." *National Science Foundation Report* SE 78–74. 2 vols. Washington, D.C.: U.S. Government Printing Office, 1978.

Stallings, Jane A. "How Instructional Processes Relate to Child Outcomes in a National Study of Follow Through." *Journal of Teacher Education* **37** (Spring 1976): 43–47.

Stallings, Jane A., and D. Kaskowitz. *Follow-Through Observation Evaluation.* Menlo Park, Calif.: Stanford Research Institute, 1974.

Stanley, J. C. and H. J. Klausmeier. "Opinion Constancy After Formal Role-Playing." *Journal of Social Psychology* **46** (1957): 11–18.

Stevens, Robert, and Barak Rosenshine. "Advances in Research on Teaching." *Exceptional Education Quarterly* **2** (May 1981): 1–9.

Suchman, J. R. *Developing Inquiry*. Chicago: Science Research Associates Inc., 1966.

Suydam, M. N. *State-of-the-Art Review on Calculators: Their Use in Education.* Columbus, Ohio: Calculator Information Center, Ohio State University, 1978.

Taba, Hilda. "Implementing Thinking as an Objective in Social Studies." In *Effective Thinking in the Social Studies*, edited by J. Fair and F. Shaftel, pp. 25–50. Washington, D.C.: National Council for the Social Studies, 1967.

Taba, Hilda. *Teacher's Handbook for Elementary Social Studies.* Palo Alto, Calif.: Addison-Wesley Publishing Co., Inc., 1967.

Tikunoff, William J., David C. Berliner, and Ray C. Rist. *An Ethnographic Study of the Forty Classrooms of the Beginning Teacher Evaluation Study Known Sample.* Technical Report No. 75-10-5. San Francisco: Far West Laboratory for Educational Research and Development, 1975.

Tikunoff, William J., B. Ward, and G. Griffin. *Interactive Research and Development on Teaching: Final Report.* San Francisco: Far West Laboratory for Educational Research and Development, 1980.

Toffler, Alvin. *Future Shock.* New York: Random House, Inc., 1970.

Toffler, Alvin. *The Third Wave.* New York: William Morrow & Co., Inc., 1980.

Trecker, Janice Law. "Women in U.S. History Textbooks." *Social Education* **35** (March 1971): 249–260.

Troike, Rudolph C. *Research Evidence for the Effectiveness of Bilingual Education.* Arlington, Va.: Center for Applied Linguistics and National Clearinghouse for Bilingual Education, 1978.

Tyler, Ralph W. *Basic Principles of Curriculum and Instruction.* Chicago: University of Chicago Press, 1949.

Ulrich, C. "She Can Play As Good As Any Boy." *Phi Delta Kappan* **55** (1973): 113–117.

United States Congress. *Education Amendments, PL 93-380.* Washington, D.C.: Government Printing Office, 1974.

Van Til, William. "One Way of Looking at It." *Phi Delta Kappan* **59** (April 1978): 556–557.

Veatch, Jeanette. *Individualizing Your Reading Program.* New York: G. P. Putnam's Sons, 1959.

Warren, Jonathan R. "Evaluation, Motivation, and Grading." *UCLA Educator* **19** (Winter 1977): 22–25.

Weaver, J. F. "Calculators." In *Mathematics Education Research: Implications for the 80's*, edited by E. Fennema, pp. 154-168. Alexandria, Va.: Association for Supervision and Curriculum Development, 1981.

Webb, Rodman B. *Schooling and Society.* New York: Macmillan Publishing Company, 1981.

Weiner, Bernard, ed. *Cognitive Views of Human Motivation.* New York: Academic Press, Inc., 1974.

Weiss, I. R. "Report of the 1977 National Survey of Science, Mathematics, and Social Studies Education." *National Science Foundation Report* SE 78–72. Washington, D.C.: Government Printing Office, 1978.

Werner, Peter H. *A Movement Approach to Games for Children.* St. Louis: The C. V. Mosby Company, 1979.

Wesley, Edgar B., and Stanley P. Wronski. *Teaching Social Studies in High Schools.* Boston: D. C. Heath & Company, 1958.

Whimbey, Arthur. "Students Can Learn To Be Better Problem Solvers." *Educational Leadership* **37** (April 1980): 560–565.

Wilkinson, Andrew. "Oracy in English Teaching." In *Language and the Language Arts*, edited by Johanna S. DeStefano and Sharon E. Fox, p. 64. Boston: Little, Brown and Company, 1974.

Wilson, Robert M., M. Hall. *Reading and the Elementary School Child*. New York: Van Nostrand Reinhold Company, 1972.

Wright, Joyce E. "The Role and Status of Elementary Arts Programs." In *A Study of Schooling*, Technical Report No. 21. Los Angeles, Calif.: University of California at Los Angeles, 1980.

Wright, R. J., and J. P. Ducette. "Locus of Control and Academic Achievement in Traditional and Nontraditional Educational Settings." ERIC Document Reproduction Services ED 123–203.

Yando, Regina M., and Jerome Kagan. "The Effect of Teacher Tempo on the Child." *Child Development* **39** (1968): 27.

Young, Tim. "Teacher Stress: One School District's Approach." *Action In Teacher Education* **2** (Fall 1980): 37–40.

APPENDIX

Illustrative Unit: Water

General Information

To illustrate the concept of integration of subject fields, the unit "Water" was designed for grades 4–6. The "key questions" column of the unit expresses the focus of the unit. There are many additional questions that could or should be asked. Similarly, the learning experience column is just a skeleton of appropriate experiences to facilitate the major understandings of the unit. As an example, the suggested activity of reading and discussing nutritional needs using health and science books could be extended by using a film, making charts of major food groups, or performing additional experiments.

The purpose of the column entitled "integration" is to call attention to the subject fields in addition to social studies that should be integrated into the unit at the precise moment in order to broaden the students' perspective or take advantage of prior experiences.

Whenever students are asked to do research or to discuss or use maps, charts, or tables, reading and writing or speaking and listening are involved; therefore, language arts has been designated. Also, it should be remembered that whatever students are required to read in order to gain information, the material should be previewed by the teacher to determine whether the concepts and ideas in the selection will need to be introduced and explained prior to the reading assignment.

The resource column is a suggested list of appropriate materials for this unit. There would be a wide variety of materials at most schools that would facilitate the teaching of this unit.

Bulletin Board Displays

A map of the Southwestern states and topographic maps of the United States could be displayed on the bulletin board. Weather maps and trend information could be used on the bulletin board to provide information. Health information and poetry or the lyrics to "Mayim" would enhance the classroom environment.

Learning Centers/Demonstrations

Additional science experiments other than those already suggested in the unit could be used for student experimentation in a learning center. Both water pressure and buoyancy would be appropriate for students to study at centers. Appropriate activities can be found in Victor (1980) or other science textbooks.

WATER UNIT—GRADES 4–6

Social Science Concepts: needs and wants; culture, environment; survival; adaptation; rights and responsibilities

Objectives:

1. After participating in small group research, students will compare cultural adaptation of different groups in particular environments.
2. After reading about the early Mexican settlers, students will identify water and land laws initiated by the Mexican settlers in the southwest United States.
3. After reading, experimenting, and discussing concepts related to the water cycle, students will draw and explain the water cycle.
4. After reading, experimenting and discussing, students will explain concepts such as water pressure, buoyancy, volume, evaporation, irrigation, riparian rights, needs, environment.
5. Using graphs and resource maps, students will infer relationships between present needs and usage of water and future needs and usage.

[continued on page 399]

Key Questions	Learning Experiences	Integration	Resources
In what ways have you used water today? What are some other uses of water?	*Discuss:* Students list ways (*Categorize and label* uses: health and nutrition, recreation, industry, transportation, agriculture.)	Language Arts	
	Observe: Film—"Water." *Discuss* film.		USDA film
Why is water important?	*Discuss:* Review prior discussion of needs and wants.	Health/Science	Health/Science textbooks
	Read and Discuss: Nutritional needs		
	Observe and Compare: Pictures of desert and irrigated lands; watered and unwatered plants.		*Environments* Children's textbook
What do you think this plant needs? How can we find out if water is important to this plant?	Using several wilted plants, students *experiment* (in small groups).	Science	
	Observe and record changes in looks and growth of plant.		
	Share results of experiment.		
(Do roots absorb water? How do plants carry water?)	*Perform experiments* in small groups.	Science	
	Evaluate experiments. (Discuss)		
Why do the Israelis have a song entitled "water?" ("Mayim")	*Read and discuss* lyrics of "Mayim."	Music/Literature	*Family of Man* "Kibbutz Family" *Exploring Music*
	Sing songs/*write* poetry or story about water.		
	Listen to a story about human needs for water.		
	Make up sounds to describe a storm. Sing the song "Rainy Day."		
How did the American Indians plea for rain?	*Perform* Indian Dance Steps using rhythm instruments.	Physical Education Music	
Where do we get water from?	*Identify* bodies of water: oceans, Great Lakes, Rivers: Mississippi, Ohio, Missouri, Columbia, Delaware, Colorado, Snake.	Language Arts	Physical maps of U.S. and Canada Water resource maps
What are the sources for Los Angeles?	*Discuss* other sources of water (underground).	Science	Annual rainfall charts
Where do rivers and lakes begin?	*Read, Experiment and discuss* water pressure, buoyancy, salinity, evaporation, temperature, volume.	Sci. Math	*Environments* *World Book*
	Observe a demonstration of the water cycle. (The teacher uses hot water from a teakettle with the vapors condensing on a container that holds ice and water.)		

[continued on page 398]

Key Questions	Learning Experiences	Integration	Resources
Will future needs for water be greater than in the past? Why?	*Draw* the Water Cycle: trace water from the clouds to the rivers.	Science	*Science Far and Near*
	Examine water resource maps and annual rainfall chart, *infer* relationships between supply and demand. *Compare* current needs with past.	Science Math	Weather Dept. speaker
	Make weather charts and maps. *Infer* relationships of past, present, future.		
Who does water belong to? (Why do we have rules?) (Why are water laws important?)	*Read and Role-play* the water hole fights.		*Story of the Mexican American.*
	Small Group Research: Why did every community have an acequiero? What other laws regulated water?	Language Arts Reading	Teacher-prepared information
	Teacher-directed lesson on note taking techniques.		
How did English laws differ from Mexican laws?	*Research and discuss:* land and water monopoly.		
In what ways were the needs of settlers in the SW U.S. different from the needs of settlers on the East coast?	Explain latin word derivations: ripa = river bank.	Language Arts Spelling	See above
	Role-play conflict situation involving riparian proprietors monopolizing, diverting, or contaminating water.		
How did land laws affect life in the SW?			
(How were riparian rights used unscrupulously?)			
How do different cultural groups survive (adapt) in particular environments?	*Review* basic needs of all people.	Health/Science	
	Small Group Research: Mexicans (Spanish) in SW U.S.; Life in Israel (compare to Calif.); Kalahari Bushpeople of Africa.	*(Choose specific groups on the basis of resources available.)	Social studies texts
	Write group reports.		
How does water influence our way of life? Why are water resources a public concern?	*Present* student group reports.	Language Arts	
	Discuss; Compare cultural group adaptation.		
How do people farm in dry regions?	Introduce and *define* vocabulary: irrigation, aqueduct, drought.	Language Arts Spelling	*Where on Earth? Environments Concepts and Values* (4)
How do people practice irrigation?	*Teacher-directed lesson:* Irrigation practices, erosion problems.		

Key Questions	Learning Experiences	Integration	Resources
How do people maintain a watershed?	Students *construct* overshot water wheel, irrigation system in a sandbox; demonstrate erosion, watershed. (Observe watershed areas of schoolyard.)	Industrial Arts Math	Apple boxes Dowling Sand
	Compare rainfall statistics. Use math equivalents.	Math	Pamphlets: "The Natural Water Cycle"
How is water made pure? (What happens if it is not?)	*Field Trip:* Water treatment plant, reservoir, sewage disposal plant *Experiment & Discuss.*	Health/Science	"Watersheds" Newspapers
How can we prevent water pollution? How can we conserve water?	*Small Group Investigation* into: Water treatment to enable reuse of water; development of additional ground water use; ground storage; suppression of evaporation; desalination. Individual *story writing* or *charts. Synthesizing* pollution and conservation issues. *Evaluative discussion.*	Language Arts Science	Speakers Pamphlets Teacher info.

6. Upon completion of the unit, students will write stories or develop an appropriate chart synthesizing means to prevent pollution and conserve water.

Skills:

1. Acquire information through reading, listening to others, field trip, experiments
2. Compile and organize information
3. Interpret information: using maps, graphs, globes, charts, tables, pictures
4. Communicate orally and in writing
5. Make inferences using data from experiments and acquired information
6. Predict on the basis of data from experiments and other sources
7. Evaluate data
8. Cooperate in group work
9. Respect others' viewpoints and participation
10. Recognize differences in opinion
11. Accept responsibility

RESOURCES

Students

Acuna, R. *The Story of the Mexican Americans.* American Book Company.

Concepts and Values, Book 4. Harcourt Brace Jovanovich, Inc.

Environments, Level D. American Book Company.

Where on Earth, Level 4. Rand McNally.

Exploring Music, Level 2. Holt, Rinehart and Winston.

Science Far and Near, Level 4. D. C. Heath & Company.

Teachers

McWilliams, Carey, *California: the Great Exception.* Santa Barbara: Peregrine Smith, Inc., 1979.

The Third Wave, Conservation Yearbook No. 3. U.S. Dept. of Interior.

People and Their Environment, Teacher's Curriculum Guide to Conservation Education. Fergusen Publishing Co.

Victor, Edward. *Science For The Elementary School.* 4th ed. New York: Macmillan Publishing Company, 1980.

Pamphlets

"The Natural Water Cycle." U.S. Forestry Service.

"Watersheds." U.S. Forestry Service.

"Water—and the Land." U.S. Health, Education, and Welfare.

"What's Happening to Our Waters?" U.S. Health, Education, and Welfare.

"What Can We Do for Clean Water?" U.S. Health, Education, and Welfare.

Films

Water for Farm and City. U.S. Department of Agriculture.

Water. U.S. Department of Agriculture.

Mayim, Mayim (Water, Water)
with joy shall you draw water out
of the wells of salvation
Water, water, water, water!
Hey! Water with joy!
Water, water, water, water
water, water with joy!*

* From: *Family of Man.* "Kibbutz Family," Selective Educational Equipment, 1972.

AUTHOR INDEX

To facilitate use of the author index some of the page numbers have been followed by a letter to provide the following information: page number only = author's name appears in text; page number followed by *rn* = author's name appears in a research box note; page number followed by *n* = author's name appears in footnote; page number followed by *s* = author's name appears in the Suggested Readings at the end of the chapter.

SUBJECT INDEX